INSIDERS' GUIDE® TO

SANTA BARBARA

INCLUDING CHANNEL ISLANDS NATIONAL PARK

FOURTH EDITION

**KAREN HASTINGS
AND NANCY A. SHOBE**

INSIDERS'GUIDE®

GUILFORD, CONNECTICUT
AN IMPRINT OF THE GLOBE PEQUOT PRESS

The prices and rates in this guidebook were confirmed at press time. We recommend, however, that you call establishments before traveling to obtain current information.

To buy books in quantity for corporate use or incentives, call **(800) 962–0973** or e-mail **premiums@GlobePequot.com.**

INSIDERS' GUIDE®

Text design by Nancy Freeborn
Maps by XNR Productions, Inc. © Morris Book Publishing, LLC

ISSN: 1536-8580
ISBN: 978-0-7627-4555-5

Printed in the United States of America
10 9 8 7 6 5 4 3 2 1

CONTENTS

CONTENTS

Directory of Maps

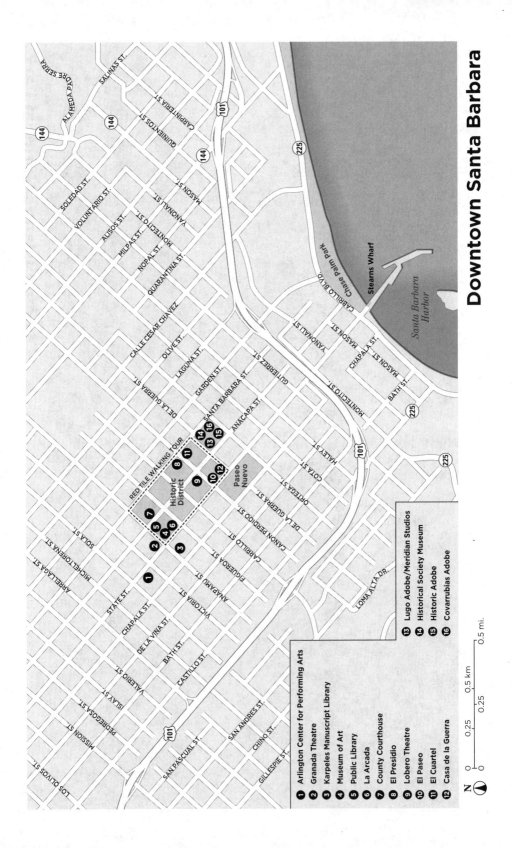

Downtown Santa Barbara

1. Arlington Center for Performing Arts
2. Granada Theatre
3. Karpeles Manuscript Library
4. Museum of Art
5. Public Library
6. La Arcada
7. County Courthouse
8. El Presidio
9. Lobero Theatre
10. El Paseo
11. El Cuartel
12. Casa de la Guerra
13. Lugo Adobe/Meridian Studios
14. Historical Society Museum
15. Historic Adobe
16. Covarrubias Adobe

N

0   0.25   0.5 km
0   0.25   0.5 mi.

Santa Barbara Harbor

Stearns Wharf

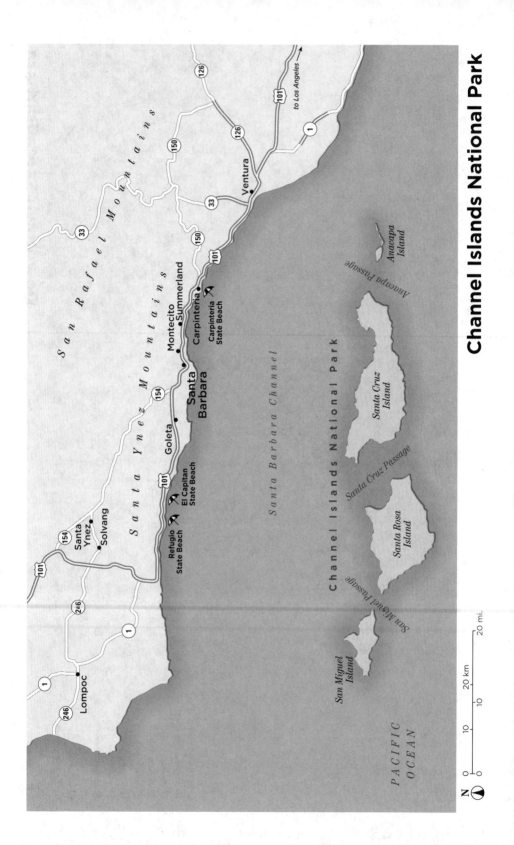

Channel Islands National Park

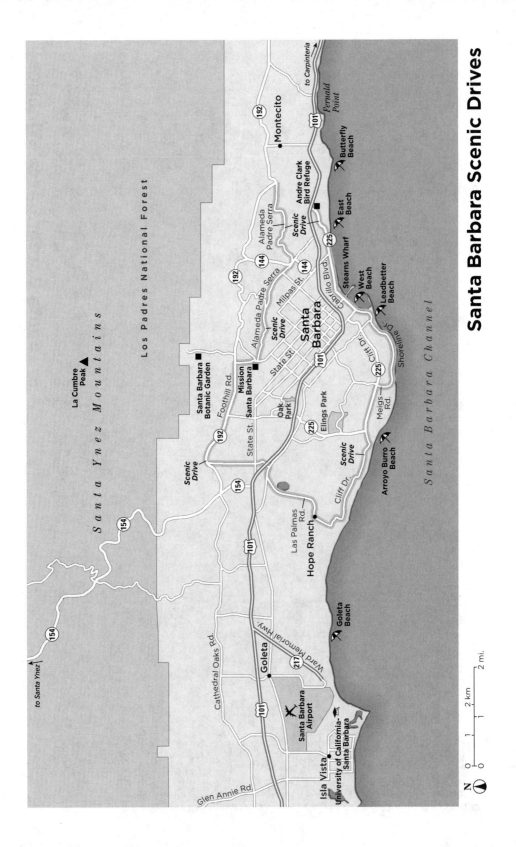

Santa Barbara Scenic Drives

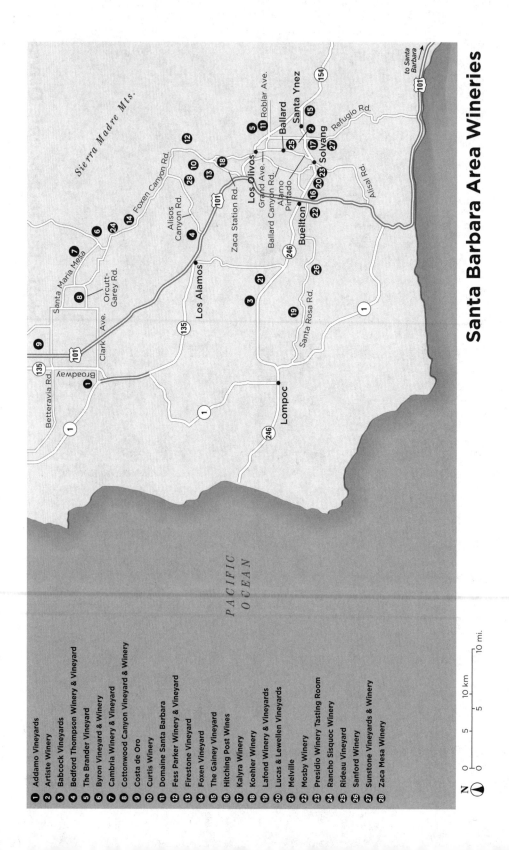

Santa Barbara Area Wineries

1. Addamo Vineyards
2. Artiste Winery
3. Babcock Vineyards
4. Bedford Thompson Winery & Vineyard
5. The Brander Vineyard
6. Byron Vineyard & Winery
7. Cambria Winery & Vineyard
8. Cottonwood Canyon Vineyard & Winery
9. Costa de Oro
10. Curtis Winery
11. Domaine Santa Barbara
12. Fess Parker Winery & Vineyard
13. Firestone Vineyard
14. Foxen Vineyard
15. The Gainey Vineyard
16. Hitching Post Wines
17. Kalyra Winery
18. Koehler Winery
19. Lafond Winery & Vineyards
20. Lucas & Lewellen Vineyards
21. Melville
22. Mosby Winery
23. Presidio Winery Tasting Room
24. Rancho Sisquoc Winery
25. Rideau Vineyard
26. Sanford Winery
27. Sunstone Vineyards & Winery
28. Zaca Mesa Winery

PREFACE

Say "Santa Barbara," and what springs to mind? Is it beaches, blondes, and balmy weather?

Visit Santa Barbara, and no doubt you will see those idyllic palm-lined beaches where bronzed bodies spike volleyballs and jog along the shore without breaking a sweat. You'll see Spanish Revival architecture—bubbling fountains, cream-colored stucco, and red-tiled roofs. You may even spot a celebrity or two. In fact, on the surface, Santa Barbara is alluringly seductive and glamorous. But read this book, get to know the town more intimately, and you will learn that Santa Barbara's beauty is more than "skin deep."

Despite all the images of glittering materialism and the extremely high cost of living, Santa Barbara is actually quite conservative and unpretentious. Shunning the conspicuous consumption of big city life, the town prefers instead to bask in its wealth of natural beauty.

Few spots on earth are blessed with such a stunning mix of natural assets—broad, sunny beaches, rugged coastal peaks, golden valleys, giant kelp forests, and windswept islands. Cruise the sparkling waters, and you might spot seals, dolphins, and migrating whales. Hike the canyons, and you'll feel as though civilization is a million miles away.

Beneath this wildly beautiful visage, Santa Barbara's culture and history run deep. It may have the soul of a small beach town, but it exudes all the sophistication of a world-class city. Opera, theater, ballet, art galleries, museums, and gourmet restaurants abound, and Santa Barbara's renowned educational resources attract students from around the world.

Santa Barbara is rich in history, a history that began with the Chumash Indians and Spanish settlers. Catch its history in the style of architecture, in the taste of locally grown food, or while driving along streets named for its ancestors.

As culturally diverse and pristine as Santa Barbara is, Santa Barbarans love to party. No matter what time of year you visit, you're sure to find something fun to attend—whether it's the "Old Spanish Days" celebration each August ("Fiesta" to the locals), the colorful floats of the eclectic Summer Solstice Parade, or the annual Santa Barbara Film Festival.

And then there's us—the people who live here. Many of us traveled here for vacation and vowed to return—permanently. Others were lucky enough to be born here. We are artists and authors, students and professors, builders and gardeners, engineers and entrepreneurs. And yes, there are even celebrities and film folk among us. Though we come from diverse backgrounds, we all choose to live in Santa Barbara for the same reason— we simply cannot find the same quality of life anywhere else.

We especially love our nearly year-round Santa Barbara sunshine that allows us to be constantly outdoors. In fact, as you explore our little piece of paradise, we'll be right beside you—hiking the wilderness trails, kayaking, cycling, surfing, fishing, and sailing. Rain is a cherished treat for us. Most of us don't even own an umbrella, and we actually look forward to the few weeks of the year when we can bundle up in sweaters.

Thanks to all this sunny weather and clean air, we're a fairly casual and friendly bunch of people. So don't be surprised if we strike up a conversation or wave you ahead of us in traffic.

We invite you to get acquainted. If you're visiting, use this book to find the best of Santa Barbara. If you're moving here, congratulations.

To ease your transition into Santa Barbara life, we've included detailed information on education and child care, newspaper and television options, health care, and retirement opportunities. Don't let Santa Barbara's high cost of living scare you away. Bargains abound here, and we'll show you where to find them.

For whatever reason you've turned to the *Insiders' Guide,* we hope this book serves as a trusty companion. Take it with you on your adventures. As you flip the pages, you'll get to know the real Santa Barbara and the people who live here—our quirks, fancies, pet peeves, and charms. You'll discover we're much more down-to-earth than you may have imagined. So relax, "kick back," and "Viva la Fiesta!"

ACKNOWLEDGMENTS

I love thank-you notes—fresh, crisp cards inked with cursive. Although this thank-you is less personal in nature, it is by no means less heartfelt.

Countless people helped me rediscover Santa Barbara during the time I worked on this book. There were the many store owners and restaurateurs, friendly innkeepers and business leaders who generously volunteered information. Rod Lathim, the king of the Santa Barbara arts scene, added his expert tips. Shannon Turner Brooks of the Santa Barbara Conference & Visitors Bureau shared her profound Insiders' knowledge. Bill Macfadyen e-mailed his Rolodex of contact numbers, and Susan Shapiro contributed her keen photographic works. To all of you, thank you.

Karen Hastings, author of the second and third editions, entrusted me with the fourth edition when she and her family were successfully lured back to her homeland, Australia. Karen, thanks for passing the baton to me.

There are two people without whom I never could have completed this work. They good-naturedly joined me on excursions around town and shared their brutally honest opinions. To my partner, Ludwig Keller, who sees what I don't see, says what I often can't say, and intuits in a way in which I am constantly amazed: Thank you for your constant support and inspiration and for your willingness to test-drive Santa Barbara with me. To my daughter, Allison Stelyn, who inspired me with her artistically composed photos, indulged me in my last-minute "stop the car" detours, and provided unfailing humor during this endeavor: This adventure wouldn't have been the same without you. I cherish you and our life journey together. Thank you.

For a lover of people and lover of land, Santa Barbara has an undeniable allure. Thank you to my dedicated parents, Barbara and Richard Shobe, for teaching me the art of loving both.

I would be remiss if I didn't add in one final thank-you—to the city of Santa Barbara. For 17 years, you have been my daughter's and my home. Whether it's lounging by the ocean, hiking in the mountains, or awakening each morning to the trilling of the birds, we revel in your beauty. Thank you, Santa Barbara.

HOW TO USE THIS BOOK ?

Whether you're lounging on the beach, hiking the mountains, cruising the ocean, or sightseeing in town, carry this book with you. It's meant to help you discover the best Santa Barbara has to offer, from entertainment and recreation to attractions, lodging, and more. We've arranged the book in straightforward, stand-alone chapters to give you quick and easy access to specific information. You can read the chapters in any order.

As you're planning your trip, you'll probably want to consult the Hotels and Motels, Bed-and-Breakfast Inns, and Vacation Rentals chapters. If you've just arrived and want to head straight for the sand, flip to the Beaches and Watersports chapter to decide which beach you'll visit first. When you're craving some mouthwatering Santa Barbara cuisine, turn to the Restaurants chapter for an overview of your options. If you're moving here, peruse the Relocation chapter as soon as possible.

We've spiced up every chapter with handy Insiders' tips (represented by an ⓘ) and illuminating Close-ups on noteworthy people and places. We highly recommend that you read the Area Overview, Getting Here, Getting Around, and History chapters before embarking on your explorations.

The History chapter will shed light on Santa Barbara's unusual architecture and location names. The Area Overview chapter will help you understand who we are and what makes us tick. Armed with this information, you'll get a lot more out of what you see and do.

The Getting Here, Getting Around chapter explains the layout of the city. Read this and you'll be less likely to get lost, which is easy to do when you're navigating our many one-way,

dead-end streets, and traffic "roundabouts" for the first time. In the Attractions chapter, you'll find a list of our favorite things to see and do. We've also added some suggested itineraries at the end of the chapter to help you decide.

Worried about all those fires, earthquakes, and floods you've read about in the news? The Living with Mother Nature chapter can ease your mind. We'll tell you how locals live in tandem with nature's unusual gifts and whims, including El Niño patterns, Santa Ana winds, and earthquakes.

Traveling with your dog? To save you the hassle of calling around to find out whether Fido is welcome, we've noted pet-friendly places in the Hotels and Motels chapter.

The region covered in this book stretches along U.S. Highway 101 from Gaviota in the west to Carpinteria in the east. We've included a section on Channel Islands National Park and a chapter on the wineries in the North County, on the other side of the Santa Ynez Mountains. We also feature Cachuma Lake, a recreation area about 35 miles north of Santa Barbara.

Where appropriate, the chapters in this book are divided into geographic sections based on this west-east orientation. First, we cover Santa Barbara (the main city). Then we explore Goleta at the western end (including the beaches and rural areas between Gaviota and Goleta), followed by the towns east of Santa Barbara: Montecito, Summerland, and Carpinteria.

Most of the restaurants we've listed are in the city of Santa Barbara, and because it takes no more than 15 or 20 minutes to drive from Santa Barbara to Goleta, Montecito, or Carpinteria, we've disregarded geographic orientation in the Restaurants chapter; instead, it's arranged by cuisine type.

We've tried to make this guide so informative that you'll soon feel like an Insider, too. Stash it in your beach bag, backpack, or car. Mark it up, shake out the sand, and dogear the pages you turn to the most. Please write and tell us about your favorite discoveries or haunts, and be sure to let us know about any fantastic places we somehow overlooked. We also want to know when something doesn't match our description.

Write to us at *Insiders' Guides,* The Globe Pequot Press, P.O. Box 480, Guilford, Connecticut 06437-0480. You can also contact us at the Insiders' Guide Web site: www.Insiders Guides.com.

Welcome to Santa Barbara. Have a fantastic stay!

AREA OVERVIEW

Santa Barbara has been nicknamed the American Riviera®, the last unspoiled city in a Mediterranean climate, and even paradise itself. It's not hard to see why. Cruise our broad palm-lined drives and you'll see only blue skies, no skyscrapers to mar the mountain views. Wend your way through beautifully groomed parks and gardens that adorn almost every neighborhood. Skim across the ocean to the wind-whipped Channel Islands and you'll discover an untamed dimension of pure wilderness to explore. Secluded coves and sea caves lace the shores, and an amazing diversity of wildlife still thrives on these rocky isles and in their surrounding waters. Cradled between these rugged islands and towering coastal peaks, Santa Barbara has a nearly perfect climate. For most of the year, it's so bright and brilliant and sunny here, it's hard not to just stop and revel in the beauty of it all.

In addition to all these natural riches, Santa Barbara shares its intriguing past with the world in ways that capture the heart and the imagination. Its hallmark Spanish-Moorish architecture is everywhere, from the facade of Mission Santa Barbara, known as the "queen" of the California missions for its exceptional beauty, to the stunning Santa Barbara Courthouse. Stroll the streets of Santa Barbara, and you'll discover that even contemporary buildings sport red-tile roofs, hand-painted tiles, open courtyards, and arched facades, a testament to a Spanish heritage that is widely celebrated today. Many streets bear the names of Chumash Indian chiefs, Spanish conquistadores, influential early residents, and even historical events. (See the Getting Here, Getting Around chapter for background information on many of Santa Barbara's unusual street names.)

If Santa Barbara was for a time a well-kept secret, its days of anonymity are over. During the Reagan years, the president often visited his western retreat in the mountains above the city, and the press followed in droves. Hanging out in local hotels and restaurants (the Palace Grill was reportedly a White House press corps favorite) and reporting from scenic seaside overlooks, the media showcased the city incessantly. When the queen of England visited the Reagan ranch in 1983, the international press moved in and splashed images of Santa Barbara across newspapers and television screens around the world. And in 2004, the nation watched as Santa Barbara became Reagan's final resting spot. Adding to the mystique, the popular soap opera *Santa Barbara* solidified the city's image as a playground for the rich and famous and attracted hordes of foreign tourists to our sunny shores.

Santa Barbarans are known to be exceptionally friendly and are practitioners of the laid-back California lifestyle. Beyond barring patrons without shirts or shoes, most shops and restaurants expect a casually dressed clientele, and shorts or jeans worn with sandals or athletic shoes are the norm. Even the working professionals dress casually, except in a few formal offices (mostly law firms). But, when it comes to nonprofit gala events, which comprise most of the socializing in town, be

i For a free copy of *Santa Barbara—A Visitors Guide to the American Riviera®*, with comprehensive information on accommodations, attractions, and events, call the Santa Barbara Conference & Visitors Bureau at (805) 966–9222 or (800) 676–1266, or visit www.santabarbara ca.com to send an e-mail request.

prepared to don only the finest in evening attire.

Grabbing a bagel and a cup of coffee and plopping down with a newspaper at an outdoor cafe is a popular local pastime, as are running, biking, and strolling along the waterfront. Extremely health-conscious Santa Barbarans often pick up organic produce at one of several local farmers' markets, patronize the area's health food stores, or stop by for a fresh fruit smoothie (wheat grass, ginseng, and protein powder are some of the available add-ins) to drink on the way to the gym. By California law, smoking is not allowed in any public building, restaurant, or bar, an ordinance that suits most Santa Barbara residents just fine.

Santa Barbara is also big on culture. In addition to its excellent art museum, the city has dozens of galleries exhibiting the work of local and nationally known artists. The city also has its own symphony orchestra, ballet troupe, opera, chamber orchestra, and several theater companies, all of which present a full lineup of outstanding performances. In addition, the University of California at Santa Barbara Arts & Lectures program brings a world-class assortment of music, dance, theater, and lectures to local residents.

Fiercely protective of our beautiful home, we Santa Barbarans work hard to preserve the qualities that make our region so special, and many issues are close to our hearts. Mention development, affordable housing, or offshore oil drilling, and be prepared for a lively discussion. You'll learn more about some of these issues as you flip through the pages of this book and chat with the locals when you visit.

NATURE IS MOSTLY KIND

Overall, Santa Barbara enjoys very pleasant weather. Temperatures are generally balmy along the coast for most of the year, with monthly averages between 65 and 75

i Santa Barbara averages 300 days of sunshine a year. No wonder why we love it here!

degrees Fahrenheit (approximately 18° to 24° Celsius). Inland, temperatures can be quite a bit higher during the day (especially in summer) and much cooler at night. To cope with changing weather conditions, most Santa Barbarans have mastered the art of layering when dressing, wearing a sweater or jacket over a long-sleeved shirt over a still lighter shirt in case the day warms up.

About 18 inches (46 centimeters) of rainfall is normal for the year, with most of it falling between December and March. Fog is often a factor in spring and early summer, when it can hang over the coastline until late morning or early afternoon. In most cases, it's a high fog that only blocks out the sun, but the thick, drippy, wet, turn-on-your-windshield-wipers kind also occurs at various times of the year. On the other hand, in late summer and fall, mild and sunny conditions occasionally give way to temperatures in the 90s or 100s (30s or 40s Celsius), especially if hot Santa Ana (or "sundowner") winds blow in from the north. (See Living with Mother Nature for more information on Santa Ana winds.) When temperatures rise, both literally and figuratively, some overheated residents look to the sea and pray for the cooler, formerly unwelcome fog banks to return.

We tend to discount natural disasters, probably because they happen so seldom (or at least a lot less often than all the good stuff in Santa Barbara). Californians often joke about earthquakes and brush fires, but Insiders know that ignoring the potential for either is foolish. Find out all you can about being prepared for an emergency, then do something about it. Simply knowing what to do during an earthquake, having a map in case of an evacuation, or keeping shoes and flashlight next to your bed will help keep you safe if and when a disaster strikes.

DIVERSITY IS OUR MIDDLE NAME

The population of the city of Santa Barbara is just over 90,000, roughly a quarter of the total population of greater Santa Barbara County. Several unincorporated areas lie outside the city boundaries, including parts of Goleta to the west; Montecito to the east, with about 10,000 residents; and Hope Ranch east of Goleta, a relatively small community tucked between the city of Santa Barbara and the sea.

With a population almost as large as Santa Barbara's, Goleta has been debating for decades whether to become an incorporated city or be annexed to Santa Barbara. In November 2001, voters finally approved a proposal to incorporate parts of Goleta, creating the South County's second-largest city (population 29,182) behind Santa Barbara. The new city government took effect on February 1, 2002 (see the Relocation chapter for details). Montecito and Hope Ranch are the most expensive areas of Santa Barbara, with sprawling estates and ranch homes rimmed by gates and security fences. East of Montecito is the funky hillside community of Summerland (famous for its antiques stores) and Carpinteria, a friendly, family-oriented beach community where agriculture thrives.

The large Latino population currently accounts for a sizable 35 percent of Santa Barbara County. Some Latino families trace their roots to the city's original Spanish and Mexican occupants, and a strong sense of tradition permeates the city. Spanish dance studios are full of young women hoping to one day lead the Old Spanish Days parade as the "Spirit of Fiesta" in honor of their heritage. (See the Annual Events chapter for more information on Fiesta.) Because of this large Hispanic contingent, many government and agency officials are bilingual in English and Spanish.

Santa Barbara has a diverse mix of industries—human services, the retail trade, tourism, government, and agriculture—

employ the most workers locally. The University of California at Santa Barbara is a major local employer, as are several high-tech and software firms, school districts, and major health care facilities. The heart of Santa Barbara's agricultural activity is the "North County," between 45 and 100 miles (70 and 160 kilometers) up the coast from the city of Santa Barbara. Broccoli, wine grapes, olives, lemons, flowers, strawberries, avocados, and the famous Central Coast pinquito bean are all part of the local agricultural scene, and many of these crops are celebrated in annual festivals such as Lompoc's Flower Festival (June), Goleta's California Lemon Festival (October), and the California Avocado Festival, held in the city of Carpinteria each fall.

All things considered, Santa Barbara has a lot going for it, but the city has no plans to rest on its laurels. The community continually strives to preserve and enhance the qualities that make Santa Barbara such a desirable place to live and visit. Currently, the city is tackling issues ranging from traffic congestion to affordable housing. Maintaining the city's natural beauty is a top priority, and you can bet Santa Barbarans are involved in every decision as they continue to fight for the environmental integrity of their beloved city.

JUST A FEW CAVEATS

Santa Barbara would indeed seem to have it all: glorious weather, friendly people, beautiful ocean vistas, a healthy lifestyle, an impressive offering of cultural arts, and a collective consciousness dedicated to preserving it all for generations to come. Despite its shiny image, however, we feel obliged to let you know that

i In Spanish, Montecito means "little mountain." Goleta means "schooner," and Carpinteria was named after the Spanish word for "carpenter's shop," because the Chumash Indians used to build their canoes (*tomols*) there on the beach.

Santa Barbara Resources

Santa Barbara Conference & Visitors
Bureau and Film Commission
1601 Anacapa Street
Santa Barbara, CA 93101
(805) 966-9222, (800) 676-1266
www.santabarbaraca.com
www.filmsantabarbara.com

Santa Barbara Region Chamber of
Commerce
924 Anacapa Street, Suite 1
Santa Barbara, CA 93101
(805) 965-3023
www.sbchamber.org

the city probably falls a few notches short (but just a few) of being paradise. So, in the interest of full disclosure, here are a few things to watch out for.

In a time when travelers sometimes become victims, Santa Barbara is proud of its low crime rate. Serious crimes are rare, but some gang violence is beginning to appear on our streets. Let common sense be your guide. Despite the appeal of a late-night solitary stroll on the beach, unescorted women need to consider safety first. Also, local police recommend you lock your car and stow valuables out of sight, especially when parking your car at a trailhead.

It's so easy to be seduced by our gorgeous beaches. Standing at the foot of Stearns Wharf and looking back at the mountains as the sun sets provides one of the most spectacular views in California. Residents and tourists alike look to the beaches for solace and beauty, and most times the beaches deliver. However, bacteria contamination, especially after heavy rains, has become a concern. An Ocean Water Quality Hotline has been set up by Santa Barbara County Environmental Health Services (805-681-4949; www.sbcphd.org/ehs/ocean.htm). Although your day at the beach is not likely to be ruined

by such pollution, it's wise to check the charts and watch for signs that indicate beach closure.

Tar is an all-too-familiar fact of life for Santa Barbara beachgoers. Locals often differ about whether beach tar comes from natural seepage on the ocean floor or is somehow caused by oil drilling in the Santa Barbara Channel, but the reality is that nearly every visit to the shoreline calls for tar removal.

Water, Water—Almost Everywhere

Santa Barbara doesn't really discuss its "water problem" these days because it seems as if it's been solved. The truth is, though, that rainfall varies from year to year, and long-term droughts are often followed by exceptionally rainy seasons. After a series of drought years that left local reservoirs close to empty, citizens succumbed to the temptation of buying into California's state water system. Currently, Santa Barbarans receive their water supply from Lake Cachuma and the Gibraltar Reservoir, the State Water Project, and recycled water. Droughts in Santa Barbara prompted city officials to build a $34 million seawater desalination plant in 1991–1992. Because of rainfall, the plant is not operating (something some locals find amusing) but city officials consider it money well spent if there is another severe drought or catastrophic event.

Unreal Estate

To put it succinctly, all real estate in Santa Barbara is expensive. A three-bedroom, 30-year-old tract home can run around $1 million, and you can easily pay $2,600 or more a month to rent a two-bedroom, two-bath unfurnished house, or $1,200 for a studio apartment. Although the median home price of above $1 million has been reported to have dropped,

i Are your feet dappled with bits of tar after your walk on the beach? A little baby oil on a paper towel is all you need to remove the beach tar.

locals are shaking their heads wondering where the 20 percent devaluation has hit. We haven't seen it. Sure, it's expensive to live in Santa Barbara. But would so many people be looking for homes here if they were just putting out big bucks for wood and stucco? We doubt it. Insiders know that when you buy a house here, the price includes the beach, the sunsets, the nonprofit social scene, the balmy weather, the palm trees, and many more delightful things you'll soon discover.

There is a downside to this unquenchable demand. As property prices skyrocketed, the lack of affordable housing reached crisis proportions, perhaps the worst in the state if not the nation. Unforgiving mortgages and rents have forced low-income workers out of the region. To solve the problem, the county has several high-density housing projects on the drawing board. But, while everyone agrees

> **i** Conservation is a way of life in Santa Barbara. Efforts by Insiders to conserve water has reduced the per capita water demand by 25 percent since 1988.

that something needs to be done, most residents don't want the increased development in their own backyard. Which brings us to the local political scene.

To Grow or Not to Grow?

For years, "pro-growthers" and "slow-growthers" have been at war in Santa Barbara, making every local election a down-and-dirty quest for power. Nearly every campaign addresses the issues of growth versus quality of life, progress versus stagnation, and developers' rights versus preservation. Most of these political battles are the focus of races

Santa Barbara Vital Statistics

Santa Barbara's nickname: The American Riviera®

Population: Santa Barbara City: 92,325; Carpinteria: 15,194; Goleta (City): 29,182; Goleta (unincorporated): 55,200; Santa Barbara County: 399,347

Average temperatures:
January high/low: 65°/42°F, 18°/6°C
July high/low: 76°/56°F, 24°/13°C

Average annual rainfall: 18 inches (46 cm)

Major universities and colleges: University of California at Santa Barbara, Santa Barbara City College, Antioch University, Brooks Institute of Photography, Fielding Graduate Institute, Music Academy of the West, Santa Barbara College of Law, Santa Barbara College of Oriental Medicine, Southern California Institute of Law, Westmont College

Driving laws: Passengers and drivers must wear seat belts at all times. Children must be properly secured in a child seat that meets federal safety standards until they are at least six years old or weigh 60 pounds. A child who weighs more than 40 pounds and is riding in a car without combination lap and shoulder belts in the back seat may wear just a lap belt.

Alcohol laws: See the Nightlife chapter

Daily newspaper: *Santa Barbara News-Press*

Sales tax: 7.75 percent

Room tax: 12 percent (10 percent county, 2 percent Creeks Fund)

Average household income: $66,844

An aerial view of Santa Barbara. NIK WHEELER/SANTA BARBARA CONFERENCE & VISITORS BUREAU

for mayoral or city council seats in Santa Barbara, and races for the Board of Supervisors, which administers the affairs of Santa Barbara County. When the balance of slow-growthers and pro-growthers in a local governing body is at stake, you're guaranteed both a heated battle and a close election, and Insiders know that every vote counts when the future of the city or county is on the line. With adamant advocates on both sides of almost any local issue, the political sparks are always flying.

Pushing the Comfort Zone

Santa Barbara is only 90 miles (145 kilometers) north of Los Angeles but a world away in attitude. Life is slower here. Development is carefully controlled, and a laid-back approach is the order of the day. But locals are very much aware that the Big City is knocking at our back door. For some residents, the ever-expanding megalopolis of L.A. is getting too close for comfort, but others enjoy the proximity for the cultural and recreational events. A trip to Disneyland, attending a big-league athletic event, or a museum opening is easily doable in a day, but after such an excursion,

i For up-to-date economic forecasts, log on to the University of California at Santa Barbara's Economic Forecast Project Web site at www.ucsb-efp.com.

i The shoreline juts sharply to the west just north of Ventura County, and all of southern Santa Barbara County's beaches are south-facing. Hence the name "South Coast," which is often used when referring to the South County.

Santa Barbarans inevitably rush home and swear they wouldn't be caught dead suffering the indignities of L.A. gridlock on a daily basis.

The reality is, though, that you sometimes feel like you're in L.A. sitting in bottlenecks on Highway 101 in Santa Barbara. Plans are being considered to widen the freeway, but many locals are nervous. The thought of Santa Barbara becoming "another L.A." is unsettling, and residents cast anxious glances southward as a hazy cloud of smog continues its almost imperceptible crawl up the coast.

Despite our traffic woes, we still like to think of Santa Barbara as a pristine enclave—a sanctuary from the stress of the Big City. Of course, Santa Barbara isn't perfect. What place is? But as long as the jobs, the housing, and the water hold out and Mother Nature behaves herself, we'll continue to adore our beloved city and be forever grateful that we are perched on one of the most favored plots of land on the planet.

GETTING HERE, GETTING AROUND

Before the 1870s, getting to and from Santa Barbara was pretty much limited to travel by stagecoach. The bulky vehicles lurched over San Marcos Pass or traveled south to Ventura, veering out onto the beach at low tide when they reached Rincon Point on their southward run. This was not the most comfortable way to travel, of course, nor the safest, as stages were held up on a regular basis, especially as they traversed bandit-ridden San Marcos Pass. After Stearns Wharf was completed in 1872, steamships had access to the city, and—with a little help from the adoring press—Santa Barbara began its transformation from a small town to a busy city with a lively tourist trade.

It was soon clear that a way was needed to accommodate all the visitors who were making their way from the wharf to the popular Arlington Hotel on State Street (see the introduction to the Hotels and Motels chapter for the history of the Arlington). So, in 1875, the Santa Barbara Street Railroad Company began operating mule-drawn railway cars that each held 12 passengers and followed a narrow-gauge track that ran from the beach to the hotel. The completion of the Southern Pacific Railroad's link with Los Angeles in 1887 marked another transportation milestone for Santa Barbara. In the early 1900s, luxury rail-cars transported magnates like the Rockefellers, Vanderbilts, and Du Ponts west to Santa Barbara, along with artists, poets, and

authors. The resulting influx of visitors necessitated expansion of the street railway, which added two new lines and an additional 4 miles of track, including passing tracks that allowed more than one car to travel on State Street at once.

The street railway lasted in Santa Barbara until the 1890s, when a more modern mode of transportation, the electric trolley, began providing a convenient and inexpensive means of getting to and from just about anywhere in the city. The trolley era came to a close more than three decades later, when passenger automobiles became an attractive alternative form of transportation and began to compete for space on local streets. By 1929, it is estimated that 10,000 autos were buzzing around the city, and from then on, Santa Barbara was hooked on cars, an infatuation that continues today. Not long after the advent of automobiles, Santa Barbarans were able to take to the skies at the Santa Barbara Municipal Airport, which evolved from a small flight school near the corner of Hollister and Fairview Avenues in Goleta. The first commercial flight (via Pacific Seaboard Airlines), Los Angeles–bound, was made on August 1, 1931.

Today, of course, Santa Barbara has all the transportation options needed to get you here from almost anywhere. You'll also be pleased to know downtown Santa Barbara is easily walkable. Most of the shops and historic attractions lie in a compact area a short stroll from each other. (See the Red Tile Walking Tour Close-up in the Attractions chapter for a self-guided tour of Santa Barbara landmarks.) Still, getting (and parking) around Santa Barbara proper can be tricky for a number of reasons, so we've included information to help you find your way around town, as well as ideas on how to get in or out of town.

i Insiders know that gasoline is more expensive in Santa Barbara than just about anywhere else. When traveling to Los Angeles, they leave Santa Barbara with half a tank, then fill 'er up in Los Angeles, returning with half a tank of bargain fuel.

HIGHWAYS AND BYWAYS

U.S. Highway 101 is the West Coast's major north-south freeway and the "main drag" through Santa Barbara. You can take U.S. 101 south to the Mexican border or north to the Canadian border, and because it literally bisects Santa Barbara, it's within a few minutes' drive of anywhere in the city. If you're taking the freeway south, be aware that it narrows from six lanes to four in Montecito, which creates a huge backup on holidays and weekends. In fact, now it seems you can get stuck in traffic at any time of the day in both directions—especially in the summer when hordes of holidaymakers travel along this major West Coast corridor. If you have a choice, try to travel during off-peak times of the day, and you should avoid the bottlenecks. A proposal to widen the freeway to six lanes has been met with scorn by many local residents, who don't want any more pieces of paradise bulldozed to accommodate what they perceive as a glut of weekending Los Angeles drivers. Most people agree, though, that something needs to be done. As of now, the community is hotly debating the issue while commuters continue to grit their teeth in gridlock.

California Highway 154 (San Marcos Pass), which connects Santa Barbara's South County with Solvang, Cachuma Lake, the wine country, and the rest of the North County, is a mixed blessing. You can get to the same places by taking U.S. 101, but it takes about 15 minutes longer than zipping over the pass. Unfortunately, zipping is what people have a tendency to do on this winding narrow road, which has no center divider and very few traf-

i Choose your time carefully to travel U.S. 101. Northbound from Ventura to Santa Barbara is bumper-to-bumper from 7:00 to 9:00 a.m. Southbound from Santa Barbara to Ventura is gridlocked from 4:00 to 6:00 p.m. Vacationers know that heading south on Sunday afternoon or early evening is no picnic either.

fic lights. Combine a few impatient, speeding, or intoxicated drivers with darkness, high winds, fog, or other weather problems, and you have the potential for a serious accident.

This can be an extremely dangerous stretch of roadway, so if you take the pass, drive defensively, get over into one of the right lanes if traffic is stacking up behind you, and pass with extreme caution. In inclement weather, the pass is subject to rock or mudslides, which often close the road for hours or even days and add another element of danger.

In short, if you're going to drive the pass (and yes, Santa Barbarans do it all the time), be careful.

California Highway 217 is a short stretch of highway that links northbound U.S. 101 with the University of California at Santa Barbara (UCSB), the Santa Barbara Airport, and the rest of Goleta. The exit is just past the northbound Patterson Avenue off-ramp for U.S. 101, and from HIghway 217 you can reach the airport and Goleta Beach Park by taking the Sandspit Road exit. Downtown Goleta is off the Highway 217 Hollister exit. The highway ends at the entrance to the UCSB campus.

IN SANTA BARBARA

"Blame It All On Captain Haley," wrote Barney Brantingham, a local newspaper columnist and author, referring to Santa Barbara city streets. And, indeed, it seems that Captain Haley has to shoulder most of the blame, even though he died decades ago and isn't around to hear the modern-day commentary on his 1851 survey. Salisbury Haley was a sea captain, after all, who just happened to be in port when the city was taking bids for the laying out of Santa Barbara's streets. Figuring he could make a quick $2,000 (which turned out to be the lowest bid), Haley became a landlubber just long enough to do the job, which looked good enough on paper to city planners. Problem was, Haley's survey chain had broken and been repaired with rawhide

Close-up

Car-free and Carefree

Tired of parking hassles and exorbitant gas prices? Below are a few local organizations that will help you explore Santa Barbara car-free.

• For an overview of alternative travel options, check out Santa Barbara Car Free (www.santabarbaracarfree.org). Led by the Santa Barbara Air Pollution Control District, this cooperative venture helps visitors and residents find ways to travel around Santa Barbara without their cars.

• Traffic Solutions (805-963-SAVE; www.trafficsolutions.info), a division of the Santa Barbara County Association of Governments, publishes commuter carpool match lists and vanpool vacancies, as well as an excellent bike route map.

• Santa Barbara Metropolitan Transit District (MTD; www.sbmtd.gov) operates local buses and electric shuttles. To plan your trip, call (805) 683-3702 and speak to a transit adviser. Bus passes may be purchased online at www.sbmtd.gov, and schedules may be downloaded to your PDA.

• Santa Barbara Trolley Company (805-965-0353; www.sbtrolley.com) operates narrated trolley tours of Santa Barbara attractions, running from Stearns Wharf to the Santa Barbara Mission. Save dollars when you purchase tickets online.

thongs that shrank and expanded, depending on the weather. So by the time he was finished, everything was off by just a little—and sometimes by a lot. Later surveys showed that none of the city blocks Haley surveyed were the same size, with some being as much as 14 feet over the proposed size of 450 square feet. Haley, of course, had long since gone back out to sea.

Today, the streets are still crooked, city blocks are all different sizes, and there are enough one-way streets crisscrossing downtown to practically ensure that taking the most direct route to anywhere will still require going a block or two out of your way. Add the perennial road construction, potholes, cracks, torn-up streets, wooden barriers, and

detours, and you have a typical day's drive in Santa Barbara.

It won't take you long to notice (whether you read the map or not) that Santa Barbara street names are both confusing and difficult to pronounce. (See the Close-up in this chapter for an Insiders' look at the origins of the city's street names.) Then there is our unique geographical orientation. Many Insiders have lived here for years and still can't point out which way is north. As one of the few stretches of Pacific coastline between Alaska and the South Pole that has mountains running east-west, Santa Barbara also has south-facing beaches. To everyone who knows that the Pacific Ocean is always to the west in California (and almost everyone does know that, don't they?), this state of affairs causes no end of confusion. Whether Salisbury Haley gave much thought to compass directions is debatable, but he chose to lay out the city's streets running diagonally from southeast to northwest and from southwest to northeast. In the middle is State Street, the main downtown business thoroughfare; once you've found your way there, you have a good point of reference for exploring the rest of the city.

Our best advice? Study your map before you go exploring, or—if all else fails—ask someone. We Santa Barbarans are unbelievably friendly and helpful.

Clean Commuting

As the cost of buying a home in Santa Barbara skyrocketed, so did the number of workers commuting from lower cost areas of the county. In other words, traffic congestion is getting worse. Thankfully, county officials are trying to do something about the problem. Traffic Solutions (805-963-SAVE; www.traffic solutions.info), a division of the Santa Barbara County Association of Governments, tries to help commuters find alternatives to single-passenger car trips that clog the roads and pollute the air. Whether you're driving, walking, biking, or taking public transportation to work, Traffic Solutions wants to help you find the most efficient way to do it. The organization has a database of more than 800 commuters interested in carpooling, and you can be matched with someone going your way. It also dispenses information on bus routes and schedules, walking, and even telecommuting. There's even a detailed bike route map online (www.trafficsolutions.info/bikemap.htm).

An option for out-of-county commuters is Clean Air Express (805-963-SAVE; www.clean airexpress.com). This fleet of buses runs on clean-burning natural gas and provides commuter service between Santa Maria and Lompoc south to Santa Barbara. Cost for travel is $135 a month, a wonderful savings given the high price of gas today.

Parking

Compared to big cities, parking in Santa Barbara is reasonably stress-free. However, you may find it a challenge on busy summer weekends and holidays—especially during festivals and events. If you're headed downtown, you'll find 12 public parking lots near State Street between Victoria and Haley Streets with easy access from Chapala or Anacapa Streets. Both streets run parallel on either side of State Street. But beware: Anacapa Street is one-way, as is the section of Chapala Street north of Carrillo Street, so you may have to double back a few blocks to reach your destination. Public parking facilities are open 24 hours a day, 7 days a week, and parking is free for the first 75 minutes. For every hour or part of an hour thereafter, you'll pay $1.50, which accrues until you leave. To see a map of downtown parking lots, visit www.santabarbara downtown.com.

When public lots are full, you may be forced to park on a side street, as no parking is permitted on State Street in the downtown district. This can be difficult. Nearly all downtown streets have only 75- or 15-minute parking zones (except Sundays), and vigilant parking authorities regularly patrol the streets writing tickets for infractions. So if you do park in one of these zones, make sure you move your car before the time is up. To be on the safe side, we suggest you allow 10 minutes for parking your car and walking to your destination—perhaps a little longer during peak holiday periods. That way, if you nab a spot quickly, you can take your time and do a little window shopping along the way.

Take the Bus

If all this talk about traffic and parking has you feeling nervous about driving downtown, you have several other options to get you there and get you around. The Santa Barbara Metropolitan Transit District (805-683-3702; www.sbmtd.gov) provides bus service throughout the greater Santa Barbara area, from Carpinteria to Ellwood. There are also electric shuttles such as the Downtown-Waterfront

Shuttle (fare: 25 cents), the Seaside Shuttle in Carpinteria (fare: 25 cents), and the seasonal Wharf Woody, which runs along Stearns Wharf. You can pick up a schedule at the main transit center (1020 Chapala Street, Santa Barbara), on MTD buses, or at visitor centers and most waterfront hotels. For help planning your route, call (805) 683-3702 and speak to a transit adviser. If you're already out and about, look for the bus stops with the yellow-and-black MTD signs every few blocks along the route. Exact change is required for all passengers. The standard one-way fare is $1.25; seniors 62 and older and disabled persons pay 60 cents, and the Downtown-Waterfront Shuttle, which runs up and down State Street, costs just 25 cents. Blind passengers with an MTD ID card (ask your driver) and children no taller than 45 inches (with shoes on) accompanied by an adult ride free. Note that 30-day discounted passes are $41 for adults, $32 for youth K–12, and $18 for seniors 62 and over, offer a great savings for frequent travelers.

Bike and Bus

If you'd like to take the bus and then bike your way around town, consider the Bike & Bus program, which allows you to stow your bike on a special rack on the bus, then disembark and ride away. Taking your bike incurs no extra charge, but Bike & Bus options are available only on certain lines. To find out which lines apply, call (805) 683-3702, visit MTD's Web site, or pick up a *Routes & Schedules Guide* available at the main transit center (1020 Chapala Street, Santa Barbara), on MTD buses, or at visitor centers and most waterfront hotels.

Downtown-Waterfront Shuttle

An extremely popular way to get around is the Downtown-Waterfront Shuttle, also operated by the MTD. Making use of this service, you can shop State Street, tour the waterfront, then take the kids over to the zoo, all without the hassle of negotiating traffic jams or parking lots. The little electric shuttles with the blue-and-black sailboat symbol are a familiar

sight on State Street. Just hop aboard! The Downtown Shuttle runs daily from State Street at Sola Street to Stearns Wharf and back again, with service every 10 minutes between 10:15 a.m. and 6:00 p.m., depending on the time of year. Fare is 25 cents one way. Children under five ride free. You can get on or off at any stop along the way (the shuttle stops on every block). Transfers to the Waterfront Shuttle are complimentary, but you need to ask your driver for a shuttle transfer when you first board. The Waterfront Shuttle runs daily from 10:00 a.m. to 5:45 p.m. along Cabrillo Boulevard from the Santa Barbara Zoo to the harbor every 30 minutes. There is nonstop service between the zoo and the Arlington Theatre every 30 minutes from 7:30 to 10:00 a.m. Monday to Friday, 8:00 to 10:00 a.m. Saturday, and 9:00 to 10:00 a.m. Sunday.

To the Valley

Insiders are thrilled to have this new option for commuting. Running between Solvang and Buellton and Goleta and Santa Barbara, the Valley Express (www.sbmtd.gov/MTDproject/mtdnewsite/navbarpages/valleyexpress.htm) gives commuters and visitors a way to make the trek without having to transverse San Marcos Pass or navigate the freeway. For only $4 for a one-way pass or $120 for an unlimited 30-day pass, this economical ride lets passengers luxuriate in a good book or stare idly out the window. No discounted fares are offered for seniors, students, or the disabled.

In Carpenteria

Climb aboard the electric Seaside Shuttle and you can cruise in ecofriendly style between Carpinteria's downtown shopping district, residential areas, and the beach. The shuttle also

i Looking for a quick trip from the waterfront to downtown? For 25 cents, you can't beat the Downtown-Waterfront Shuttle. TotalSantaBarbara.com has an excellent map of the shuttle's route at www.totalsantabarbara.com/dws.shtml.

connects with MTD's other lines for trips to downtown Santa Barbara, but make sure you ask your driver for a transfer when you pay. It's 25 cents for a one-way ride; children no taller than 45 inches (with shoes) are free. The shuttle operates every 30 minutes Monday through Friday from 6:00 a.m. to 7:00 p.m. and Saturday and Sunday from 8:00 a.m. or 9:00 a.m. to 6:00 p.m. or 7:00 p.m., depending on the season. Call (805) 683-3702 or click on "Seaside Shuttle" on www.sbmtd.gov for more information.

For Disabled Passengers

The nonprofit Easy Lift Transportation (805-681-1181; www.easylift.org) provides curb-to-curb, wheelchair-accessible transportation for passengers with disabilities and covers southern Santa Barbara County. The service runs Monday through Friday from 5:25 a.m. to midnight, Saturday from 6:00 a.m. to 11:20 p.m., and Sunday from 6:20 a.m. to 10:00 p.m. The fare is $2 a ride. Reservations are essential and can be made up to two weeks in advance.

Taxis

There's a joke in Santa Barbara that all you need to do is think of a color, and you have the name of a taxi service. The cost for a trip from the airport to downtown Santa Barbara will run you around $30. Call the Rose Cab Company (805-564-2600), Gold Cab (805-685-9797), Yellow Cab Company (805-965-5111), A-1 Yellow Cab (805-964-1111) or Blue Dolphin Cab (805-966-6161).

Limousine Service

Since there are plenty of celebrities (and plenty of celebrity wanna-bes) in Santa Barbara, the city has more limo companies than you might expect. Most provide everything from sedans to super-stretch limos, so if you have something special in mind, be sure to ask (being aware, of course, that the fancier you get, the more it will cost). In general, limo transportation from the airport to downtown runs around $150 to $200, including tax and gratuity. Choose a company from the following list, and ride in style.

American International Transportation Services
(805) 643-5466, (888) 334-5466
www.aitslimo.com

Executive Limousine Service
(805) 969-5525, (800) 247-6980
www.goexeclimo.com

Limousine Link
(805) 564-4660, (888) 399-5466
www.santabarbaralimousinelink.com

Rockstar Taxi & Limousine Inc.
(805) 451-9999, (877) 418-7267
www.rockstarsb.com

Spencer's Limousine & Tours
(805) 884-9700
www.spencerslimo.com

Zeus Transportation LLC
(805) 571-1400
www.zeuslimo.com

Rental Cars

You can find most major rental car companies in the Santa Barbara area. Currently, Budget, Enterprise, Hertz, and National have counters at the airport, located in a building just south of the terminal. Avis and Thrifty have off-site locations. Courtesy phones are located in the terminal. Not all companies provide pickup service, so you may need to hoof it a short distance to get to your car or take other airport transportation to the rental office if it's located downtown. Be sure to ask what the company policy is if you need pickup service either from the airport or from a downtown location.

Avis Rent-a-Car
(805) 965-1079, downtown Santa Barbara; (805) 964-4848, airport; (800) 331-1212
www.avis.com

Street Names

In addition to the tricky geographical orientation of Santa Barbara, visitors are often struck—and sometimes confused—by the city's downtown street names. Spanish military men, Chumash chiefs, and early settlers are all memorialized on city street signs, a fact that may leave you wondering whatever happened to Main Street, Maple Lane, and other classic American street names. (Well, we do have State Street.) Although we may not be able to walk you through all of the pronunciations (you can ask locals, but even they sometimes disagree), we can at least fill you in on the origins of the likes of Micheltorena, Salsipuedes, and Alameda Padre Serra. So read on for a crash course. (You can read more about many of these historical figures in the History chapter, or stop by the Santa Barbara Historical Society library, 136 East De la Guerra Street, and do some research of your own.)

Alameda Padre Serra
Called simply APS by Insiders, this winding road just above Mission Santa Barbara leads to the city's Riviera. It was named in honor of Father Junipero Serra, the Franciscan friar who founded the mission.

Anacapa Street
Anacapa comes from the Chumash word meaning "ever-changing" or "mirage." The natives noticed that, depending on the weather conditions, Anacapa Island, which is actually made up of three small islets, could also appear as one large mesa or, when the island was reflected in a mirage, a body of land much bigger than its actual size. Anacapa Street points in the direction of Anacapa Island.

Anapamu Street
Anapamu was a Chumash chief.

Arrellaga Street
José Joaquin de Arillaga was governor of California from 1792 to 1794, and this street was named for him, although the street name is a misspelling of the governor's name.

Brinkerhoff Avenue
This avenue is named for Samuel Bevier Brinkerhoff, the city's first medical doctor.

Canon Perdido Street
Literally "Lost Cannon Street," this downtown thoroughfare's name marks a famous local incident that happened in 1848. Four boys stole a cannon from the beach as a practical joke, but local military leaders were convinced that someone was trying to stockpile weapons for a rebellion against the American occupation forces. The military governor of California, Richard Mason, decided that if the cannon wasn't promptly returned, the people of Santa

Barbara would have to pay a $500 fine (a pretty hefty fee in those days). Local residents were forced to cough up the money, and the cannon didn't make another appearance until 1859, when it was found mired in Mission Creek.

Cabrillo Boulevard
This waterfront boulevard is named for Juan Rodriguez Cabrillo, the Portuguese explorer who sailed into the Santa Barbara Channel in 1542, becoming the first European to see the Santa Barbara coastline.

Carrillo Street
The name of this street reflects the role of the Carrillo family in Santa Barbara's history. Jose Raimundo Carrillo served as captain of the Presidio, and his son, Carlos Antonio de Jesús Carrillo, born at the Presidio, was appointed governor of California in 1837. The appointment was rescinded shortly thereafter, but he remained active in public life in Santa Barbara until his death in 1852.

Castillo Street
The name means "castle," and the street ends at a hill where a Spanish fortress once stood.

De la Guerra Street
The name literally means "of the war," but in this case it honors the family of Jose Antonio Julian de la Guerra y Noriega (better known simply as Jose de la Guerra), who became commandant of the Presidio in 1815, serving until 1842. His family's large adobe home was constructed facing what is now De la Guerra Plaza.

Figueroa Street
Jose Figueroa was a popular Mexican governor in early California.

Gutierrez Street
Benigno Gutierrez was a Chilean who came to California in 1849 to make his fortune in the gold fields. After amassing a substantial sum of money, he came to Santa Barbara in 1854 and became the city's first pharmacist.

Haley Street
This street is named for Salisbury Haley, a steamship captain who came to Santa Barbara in 1851 and, with questionable surveying skills, laid out the streets.

Indio Muerto Street
The translation is literally "dead Indian"—Captain Haley found one here as he was doing his survey.

Los Olivos Street
"The Olives" Street once bisected the Mission's olive grove.

Micheltorena Street
Mexican governor Manuel Micheltorena became governor of California in 1842 after Mexico overthrew the Spaniards.

Milpas Street
Milpas comes from a native word meaning "ground sown to grain," and the word *milpo,* an Americanized Spanish word, means "cornfield." The street is named for the farmland overseen by the natives and padres from Mission Santa Barbara.

Ortega Street
Lieutenant Jose Francisco de Ortega was chosen in 1782 to be the builder and first commandant of the Presidio.

Pedregosa Street
The name is from the Spanish word meaning "stony"; this street was bisected by a stony creek.

Salsipuedes Street
In Spanish, *salsipuedes* means "leave if you can," a concept that residents continue to take literally when winter rains turn the area into a swamp.

Sola Street
Pablo de Sola was the last Spanish governor in California.

Valerio Street
Valerio was an infamous Native American robber who lived in a cave in the Santa Ynez Mountains and made forays into the city to steal from local residents.

Yanonali Street
This name is a variation on Yanonalit, who was the Chumash chief when the Spanish arrived to establish the Presidio in 1769. After he was converted to Christianity, Pedro became his Christian name.

Budget Car & Truck Rental
downtown and airport
(800) 527-0700
www.budget.com

Enterprise Rent-a-Car
(805) 966-3097, downtown Santa
Barbara; (805) 683-0067, Goleta;
(800) RENT-A-CAR, (800) 736-8222
www.enterprise.com

Hertz Rent-a-Car
(805) 967-0411, airport; (800) 654-3131
www.hertz.com

National Car Rental
(805) 967-1202, airport;
(800) CAR-RENT, (800) 227-7368
www.nationalcar.com

Thrifty Car Rental
(805) 681-1222, airport; (800) 367-2277
www.thrifty.com

U-Save Auto Rental
(805) 963-3499, downtown Santa
Barbara; (805) 964-5436, Goleta
www.usavesantabarbara.com

i Honking your horn while driving is simply not done in Santa Barbara. According to state Motor Vehicle Code, it's illegal to blast your horn out of anger.

THE SANTA BARBARA AIRPORT

Quaint and *charming* would be the words we'd use to describe the Spanish-style Santa Barbara Airport complex, which lies about 8 miles (13 kilometers) west of downtown. You, on the other hand, might think of something a bit more disparaging, especially if you're used to big-city technology and efficiency. But Santa Barbarans love their open-air airport, and most visitors think its beautiful architecture and colorful Mission gardens are fitting for the gateway to a town so steeped in Spanish history. In February 2007, the city's Architectural Board of Review and Planning Commission provided concept approval to a $60 million redesign called the Santa Barbara Airport Terminal Project. The project aims to increase the size, accessibility, and traffic at the airport while preserving "the Santa Barbara feel." If all goes well, construction is expected to be completed in 2010 or 2011.

Like all the nation's airports, Santa Barbara Airport has tightened security since 9/11.

Expect frequent baggage checks and passenger screenings, and make sure you keep your boarding passes and identification handy. The airport is often crowded, but in a friendly sort of way. There are no snug walkways out to your plane, so you have to cross the tarmac and go up the ramp. This means you'll need an umbrella if it's raining. Special assistance is available if you can't climb the steps.

Keep in mind that air service is limited and generally requires a nonstop connecting flight to Los Angeles, San Francisco, San Jose, Las Vegas, Seattle, Denver, Salt Lake City, Dallas/Ft. Worth, Portland, or Phoenix in order to board an international flight or even one that goes to the eastern half of the country. But if everything goes according to plan, you can enjoy a one-stop journey to around 200 destinations from our little airport and save the time of a two-hour trek to Los Angeles International Airport.

Currently, the airport has nearly 90 daily commercial flights. Major airlines servicing Santa Barbara include Alaska Air (800-252-7522; www.alaskaair.com), American Eagle (800-433-7300; www.aa.com), Express Jet (888-958-9538; www.xjet.com), Delta Connection (800-325-8224; www.delta.com), Horizon Air (800-547-9308; www.horizonair.com), United Express (800-241-6522; www.ual.com) with air service by SkyWest Airlines and Air Wisconsin, and U.S. Airways (800-428-4322; www.USAirways.com). Express Jet specifically serves commuters from Santa Barbara to Sacramento or San Diego. But remember, the travel industry is volatile, and airline affiliations and services change from time to time. Santa Barbara's runway is relatively short, so air travel in or out of the city is almost always by regional jets. Most of the local airlines are linked to major airlines, so you can easily make connections, and you can even get a boarding pass and seating assignment for a longer trip as you board in Santa Barbara, saving time later.

Information on airlines serving the Santa Barbara area, the types of planes they fly, and their worldwide connections, as well as parking instructions and rates, are available from the Airport Information Line, (805) 683-4011. Better still, visit the Santa Barbara Airport Web site at www.flysba.com.

Airport Parking

The good thing about the short-term parking lot at the Santa Barbara Airport is that it is right across from the terminal. You can whiz into the lot five minutes before Grandma's plane arrives and be at the gate in time to see her disembark. At peak travel seasons, however, part of the short-term lot (805-967-2745) may be used for long-term parking if the long-term lot (805-967-4566) is full, which means you may drive around a while before finding a spot.

This doesn't help you if you're picking up passengers, however, and you may find your best bet is a quick stop in front of the terminal. If you do choose that option, don't leave your car unattended at the curb. If you plan to park in the short-term parking lot, located to your left as you enter the airport, you'll pay $1 for up to 15 minutes, $2 for 16 to 60 minutes, and $1 for each additional hour, with a maximum $16 daily fee.

The entrance to the long-term parking lot is farther east than the main airport entrance, which puts you farther away from the terminal, but it's still not much of a walk for the physically fit. Senior citizens, however, may find the trek a bit of a hardship, so you may want to drop them (and any heavy bags) off at the terminal before parking. Rates for long-term parking are $2 for the first hour, $1 for each additional hour (with an $8 daily maximum), and $48 a week. As noted above, if the long-term lot is full, it may encroach on the short-term lot, and on the rare occasions that this occurs (usually only at Christmas), a temporary parking lot, Long Term Lot 2, is opened off Hollister Avenue near Fairview Avenue. A free airport shuttle will take you from there to the terminal, but you should arrive two hours before your flight to allow enough time for parking and checking in. The overflow parking rate is $8 a day and $48 a week. Note that all the parking rates are raised periodically, and all airport parking lots accept cash and major credit cards.

Leaving the Airport

To head to downtown Santa Barbara from the airport, turn right as you exit the parking lot and follow Sandspit Road past Goleta Beach Park, merging onto Highway 217. Stay in the left lanes, which merge with southbound U.S. 101 at Patterson Avenue, and continue until you see the signs for downtown Santa Barbara. If you're staying in Goleta or headed farther north, exit the airport to your left and follow Fairview Avenue to Hollister Avenue or Calle Real, two major thoroughfares in downtown Goleta. If UCSB is your destination, it borders airport property on the west, so you're not far away. To get there, turn right out of the airport parking lot and take a quick left as the signs direct (if you go past Goleta Beach Park, you've gone too far). This will link you to the last stretch of Highway 217 and take you to the entrance of the university.

i If you're heading northbound to Santa Barbara on U.S. 101, read the signs carefully. Cabrillo Boulevard, Carrillo Street, and Castillo Street are all U.S. 101 exits in close succession. Cabrillo (Cabr-EE-o) Boulevard runs along the Santa Barbara waterfront, Carrillo (pronounced Ca-REE-o) Street is one of the main downtown exits, and Castillo (Cas-TEE-o) Street will take you to Bath Street and the Santa Barbara Harbor.

Airport Shuttle Service

SuperRide Shuttle & Tours
P.O. Box 80431, Goleta 93118
(805) 683-9636, (800) 977-1123
www.SuperRide.net
SuperRide provides on-demand, door-to-door shuttle service between the Santa Barbara Airport and the greater Santa Barbara area 24 hours a day. Reservations should be made 24 hours in advance; the fares vary. A courtesy phone is located in the baggage claim area.

Shuttle Service to LAX

Central Coast Shuttle Services, Inc.
Santa Maria Public Airport
3249 Terminal Drive, Suite 102, Santa Maria
(805) 928-1977, (800) 470-8818
www.centralcoastshuttle.com
Although most of their shuttles originate in Santa Maria or Buellton, Central Coast Shuttle Services also offers Flag Stop Services from Santa Barbara Airport or Santa Barbara to Los Angeles International Airport (LAX). Services depart from Santa Barbara Airport from 5:15 a.m. to 6:45 p.m. and return from LAX anywhere from 11:15 a.m. to 12:15 a.m. Reservations may be made online.

Road Runner Shuttle and Limousine Service
240 South Glenn Drive, Camarillo
(800) 247-7919
www.rrshuttle.com
One of our favorite ways to hitch a private ride to Los Angeles, this courteous and reliable door-to-door service offers van transportation or private car. The van transportation takes significantly longer to arrive at LAX due to its many stops, so if you can afford it, splurge on the private town car service. Or, if price is really no object, then shoot for the stretch H2 Hummer that will have heads turning all the way to Los Angeles. Road Runner also has a host of other excursions that will tickle your fancy. Visit their Web site for fares and reservations.

Santa Barbara Airbus
5755 Thornwood Drive, Goleta
(805) 964-7759, (800) 423-1618
www.sbairbus.com
Santa Barbara Airbus is a friendly local company that aims to save Santa Barbara travelers the hassles of driving to and departing from LAX. It currently schedules seven daily round trips to LAX in comfortable buses originating at the company's Goleta office and stopping for pickups in Santa Barbara (at the Hotel Mar Monte, 1111 East Cabrillo Boulevard)) and Carpinteria (outside the International House of Pancakes at 1114 Casitas Pass Road). Trips to and from LAX generally take two to two-and-a-half hours, depending on traffic. It seems that almost everyone in Santa Barbara has taken the Airbus at one time or another. The service is very reliable, and it's generally cheaper than connecting with LAX via a commuter flight. It's a pleasant drive, and what could be better than being dropped off in front of your LAX terminal? The fare to LAX for one person (if you make a reservation at least 24 hours ahead) is $42 one-way and $80 round-trip. You can show up without a reservation and hope there's room for you, but the fare goes up to $46 one-way and $86 round-trip. Discounts apply if two or more passengers travel together. Baggage is limited to two bags, plus a small carry-on, and an excess-baggage charge is levied if you exceed the limit or if you transport unusual items such as bicycles, surfboards, or large boxes or trunks. Wheelchair-accessible vehicles require reservations 48 hours in advance.

The company also arranges Day Trip Adventures to Los Angeles and Palm Springs destinations.

i The first road to be closed due to inclement weather is almost always California Highway 154, so call CalTrans for highway conditions, (800) 427-7623, before setting out.

RAIL

Amtrak
209 State Street, Santa Barbara
(800) USA-RAIL
www.amtrak.com
Pulling into our Spanish-style railway station in the heart of downtown is a great way to arrive in Santa Barbara. The Santa Barbara station is fully staffed with ticketing, checked baggage, and package express service available. Long-term parking is available in a lot operated by the City of Santa Barbara. Separate, unstaffed, no-frills boarding platforms are in Carpinteria, at 475 Linden Avenue, and

Amtrak travels north along the shoreline. NANCY SHOBE

in Goleta, at 25 South La Patera Lane between U.S. 101 and Hollister Avenue, but most passengers board at State Street.

Santa Barbara is served daily by Coast Starlight trains, which run between Seattle and Los Angeles, and the Pacific Surfliner, which offers round trips daily between here and San Diego. The Pacific Surfliner is a must-do to San Diego. We recommend upgrading to business class; it's worth the extra bucks for a quieter cabin and more luxurious seating. Electrical plugs allow you to work on your computer during the three-and-a-half-hour trip, and the munchies passed (part of your ticket price) more than satiate the appetite. We make a spring annual day trip north to San Luis Obispo, where we can view the wildflowers dotting the fields, then disembark in San Luis for a brewski and some serious window shopping.

LONG-DISTANCE BUS SERVICE

Greyhound Lines Inc.
34 West Camillo Street at Chapala, Santa Barbara
(805) 965-7551, (800) 231-2222
www.greyhound.com
Greyhound bus services will connect you to almost anywhere in the continental United States. Service is offered to Los Angeles and San Francisco. Information on all Greyhound routes and fares is available at the terminal, by calling the toll-free number above, or accessing their Web site.

HISTORY

Let's say you've just arrived in beautiful Santa Barbara for a week's vacation. You can't wait to get to the beach, you've been looking forward to sampling some local wines, and you plan to take in a concert or two. You couldn't care less about the history of Santa Barbara—you generally find history tedious and boring—and you'd just as soon skip the historical sights and get on with the good stuff.

Well, guess what? You don't have to go looking for history in Santa Barbara. It's right there every time you turn around.

Santa Barbara's roots are deep, and their evidence is everywhere: in the architecture, the street names, the celebrations, the shopping malls, the public parks and monuments, and the food. Pretty soon you'll be so intrigued by everything around you that you'll be begging to learn more. Really.

IN THE BEGINNING

Long before the celebrities and tourists hit the Santa Barbara beaches, the virgin stretches of sand and sea were home to the Chumash Indians, a gentle people who called their home "the land of the gods—the place where man was born."

Remains of Chumash villages have been found on both the mainland (the center of the Chumash capital city of Syukhtun was located on the present-day intersection of Cabrillo Boulevard and Chapala Street) and on the islands more than 20 miles (32 kilometers) offshore (now called San Miguel, Santa Rosa, Santa Cruz, Anacapa, and Santa Barbara or, collectively, the northern Channel Islands).

Ten thousand years ago, finely crafted 20-foot boats handcrafted from driftwood and fallen Northern Californian redwood trunks, sealed with the abundant local tar, carried the Chumash back and forth across the Santa Barbara Channel as they brought their wares to market at Syukhtun or gathered to celebrate with dance, music, storytelling, and sacred ceremonies. The Chumash lived off the land and sea and developed a complex language, economy, and system of trade and taxation. When the Portuguese explorer Juan Rodriguez Cabrillo sailed to the Channel Islands in the fall of 1542, the Chumash paddled their massive canoes out to meet his two small ships, never realizing that his visit heralded changes that would eventually decimate their lives and culture.

SANTA BARBARA, PROTECT US!

Many seafaring explorers followed Cabrillo (who is reportedly buried somewhere on San Miguel Island), including Sir Francis Drake. On December 3, 1602, the eve of the feast day of Saint Barbara, patron saint of mariners, Sebastian Vizcaino's ship was in the channel when a violent storm erupted.

Fearing that he and his entire expedition were about to be swept to a watery grave, Vizcaino called upon the ship's friar to appeal to the saint, who was credited thereafter with sparing their lives.

In gratitude, the friar christened the channel Santa Barbara. None of the expedition disembarked, and it would be another 167 years before the land on either side of the channel was claimed for Spain.

> **i** Santa Ynez Valley's Chumash Casino Resort is the major employer in Santa Ynez Valley—it provides jobs for over 1,500 residents in Santa Barbara County.

The last speaker of the Chumash language died in 1965.

THE ROYAL PRESIDIO

On August 14, 1769, José Francisco de Ortega, a scout for the land expedition of Captain Gaspár de Portol, became the first non-Chumash of record to set foot in this area. The expedition, under the commission of King Carlos III of Spain, was sent with Father Junipero Serra to establish a series of both military and religious strongholds along the California coast in hopes of putting the entire region under the control of the Spanish crown.

Thirteen years later, Lieutenant Ortega brought a band of settlers and soldiers back with him and selected a spot for a fort approximately 1 mile (1.6 kilometers) inland from the south-facing shore. The last military outpost of the Spanish Empire in the New World thus originated on what is now the corner of Canon Perdido and Santa Barbara Streets. Father Serra celebrated a mass, and the fort was christened El Presidio Real de Santa Barbara (The Royal Fort of Saint Barbara).

MISSION SANTA BARBARA

By the late 1780s, several more structures had been added to the Presidio, including high walls with locked gates to surround it. Security had been one of the highest priorities of the Spanish, and with the settlement now enclosed and guarded, they were ready to turn their attention to building a mission for Father Serra. Unfortunately, the good father, knowing that construction of the mission would not begin until after the Presidio was completed, had already gone north to Monterey, where he died. His successor, Padre Fermín Francisco de Lasuen, raised and blessed the cross at Mission Santa Barbara on December 4, 1786. In addition to the dawning of organized religious life in Santa Barbara, the day's ceremonies marked the beginning of the end of the Chumash culture.

It was the Chumash who had provided most of the labor for the building of the mission. The first structures were made of logs and mud, and the mission itself looked nothing like it does today. A small chapel, a kitchen, a granary, and separate quarters for the padres and the servants, arranged in a quadrangle, made up the early mission complex. Amid these humble surroundings, more than half of the Chumash population—including their chief, Yanonalit—eventually embraced Christianity, taking up residence nearby in a village that grew to include more than 250 adobe houses by the year 1800. Although the Chumash learned agriculture, animal husbandry, and other skills, the arrival of the Europeans took a terrible toll. Between 1787 and 1841, more than 4,000 natives died, most from European diseases. By 1812, however, the faithful Chumash had been instrumental in building two more churches on the mission site, including one adobe structure with six side chapels.

EARTHQUAKE!

On December 12, 1812, a major earthquake wreaked havoc on the mission and surrounding areas. Following the initial shock, which caused most roofs to collapse, a series of tidal waves thundered as far inland as the Presidio, crushing and scattering what was left of the buildings. The Chumash were terrified, and many fled the area, never to return.

In the ensuing weeks, aftershocks caused even more devastation, mud bubbled up from the ground, landslides buried many foothill canyons, and it seemed as though life would never be the same at Mission Santa Barbara. As the earth began to quiet, however, the rebuilding process began. In 1815 the remaining Chumash, aided by soldiers and local artisans, started reconstructing the mission church using pink sandstone blocks and limestone mortar.

The new building, reportedly inspired by a drawing of a temple by Roman architect M. Vitruvius Polion from the first century B.C., had a single bell tower that was hung with six bells brought from Peru. On September 10, 1820, eight years after the disastrous quake, a formal dedication followed by a three-day fiesta celebrated its completion. A second tower was added just over 10 years later.

THE REBELLION

After the reconstruction of the mission, the Chumash began to sorely resent their role as servants and builders. No longer free to roam the land they loved, they were sick, tired, and hungry, and they were often beaten for being lazy or disobedient.

The Mexicans, who took over the local government after the Mexican Revolution in 1822, were no kinder to the local tribes than the Spanish had been, and in early 1824 the Santa Barbara Chumash joined forces with Chumash at the La Purísima, Ventura, and Santa Ines missions to overthrow their oppressors.

After the severe beating of a young Chumash in February 1824 at Santa Ines, tribesmen seized the mission and set fire to it. Demonstrations of support were staged at the three other missions, but the rebels were ultimately forced to flee when the military was called in to stop the revolt. After seeking refuge for a time with the Tulare tribe in the interior valley, the Chumash returned to Santa Barbara when the regional governor issued a guarantee of amnesty.

THE MEXICAN PERIOD

Not long after Santa Barbara came under the political control of independent Mexico, foreign trade laws enforced under Spanish rule were abolished, and the city began to trade tallow and hides with the New England states, drawing Yankee traders such as William Goodwin Dana and his ship *Waverly* to the Santa Barbara area. (It was William Dana's cousin, Richard Henry Dana, who wrote *Two Years Before the Mast,* describing the latter's voyages to the area.)

> **i** El Cuartel or "Soldiers Quarters," built in 1782 and preserved in the El Presidio de Santa Barbara State Historic Park downtown, is the oldest residence in Santa Barbara and the second-oldest in California. It is located next door to the U.S. Post Office on East Canon Perdido Street.

The traders' visits were often filled with a whirlwind of social events arranged by hospitable Santa Barbara residents, including wealthy landowning Spanish dons and doñas whose families had stayed on after the Mexican Revolution.

On more than one occasion, dashing young sea captains fell in love with dark-eyed Santa Barbara señoritas and converted to the Catholic faith in order to marry them. William Dana himself fell for the charms of Josefa Carrillo, daughter of Carlos Antonio de Jesús Carrillo (better known as Don Carlos Carrillo), whose four sisters also married Americans.

Soon, it seemed everyone had heard of Santa Barbara, and its economic importance began to draw the attention of the U.S. government. During the Mexican War, in the late summer of 1846, a contingent of U.S. marines led by Commodore Robert Field Stockton came ashore and raised the American flag over the Presidio. By Christmas Day, attempts by the Mexicans to regain control of the city had been put down by Captain John Fremont, and Santa Barbara belonged to the Americans.

The Californios (Hispanic residents who lived in Santa Barbara before it was captured by the United States) were furious about the takeover. As Americans continued to pour into Santa Barbara, Californios began to lose both their rights and their property; land was sold to the newcomers for 25 cents for an acre of farmland and $1 for a city lot.

Frustrated and angry, the Californios began to strike out at the Yankees by robbing and plundering them at every turn, but their efforts were futile. A drought in 1863–1864

Santa Barbara's Pearl

She was not a Santa Barbara native, never held a local office, and rarely dabbled in politics, but when it came to preserving, cleaning up, and beautifying Santa Barbara, Pearl Chase was a champion par excellence. She has been called tireless, persuasive, and selfless as well as bossy, arrogant, and curt, but no one disputes her lasting contribution to the city. At the time of her death in 1979 at the age of 90, Chase had received countless honorary degrees and national awards, was written up in a *Reader's Digest* article that dubbed her "Santa Barbara's Pearl," was voted the city's first Woman of the Year, and had done, according to one local writer, "more to beautify her adopted hometown of Santa Barbara than any other individual."

Born in Boston in 1888, Pearl Chase moved to Santa Barbara with her family when she was 12 years old. It wasn't until 1906, however, when she stepped off the train at Victoria Street Station with a degree from the University of California at Berkeley firmly in hand, that her commitment to civic activism was born. "I was," she said, "ashamed of the dirt and dust and ugly buildings and resolved then and there to devote my life to making Santa Barbara beautiful." And devote her life she did. Her resolve to dedicate herself to the public good got in the way of marriage and motherhood, but Chase had plenty to keep her busy during 70 years of public life. She had a magnificent vision of Santa Barbara's possibilities as a Mediterranean paradise or a "New Spain" and ferociously set about making her dream become a reality. She had little tolerance for laziness or excuses and handily took on anyone who got in her way.

Chase was instrumental in ridding the city of one of its worst eyesores, the local slaughterhouse, which she felt was both ugly and filthy. Then she started on the local dairies, which became veritable showplaces of sanitation and efficiency under her influence. She later took on the Southern Pacific Railroad, convincing corporate officials that the unsightly roundhouse on East Beach Boulevard should be rebuilt to resemble a Spanish bullring. It was done. She took up the cause of the poor, pushing for a new county hospital, collecting food and toys for underprivileged children at Christmas, and securing low-income housing in the city. Her dedication to the needs of Native Americans as vice president of the Santa Barbara Indian Defense Association for 14 years earned her the title of honorary Navajo Indian chief. In 1920 she helped form the Community Arts Association and placed herself on the Plans and Planting Committee, which heavily influenced almost all development within Santa Barbara at the time.

Despite her string of successes, however, that unpleasant hodgepodge of ugly commercial buildings downtown was a growing problem that even the formidable Pearl Chase seemed unable to remedy. Enter Mother Nature. On June 29, 1925, a magnitude 6.8 earthquake shook the Santa Barbara area, collapsing many of the downtown buildings that Chase and her committee found so objectionable. It was a golden opportunity. Almost immediately, the Plans and Planting Committee joined with the newly appointed Architectural Board of Review, and the "Santa Barbara look" was born. All reconstruction of buildings destroyed by the quake, as well as all new construction, was to conform to strict architectural standards. A Spanish-Mediterranean theme was to prevail, with red-tile roofs, arched facades, central courtyards, and muted plaster exteriors.

In 1927 Chase became chairwoman of the Plans and Planting Committee, a position she held until her retirement in the 1970s. She fervently pushed her agenda, advocating that no building in the city be taller than four stories and urging the banning of billboards along local highways. She convinced several major oil companies to construct their local gas stations in the Spanish style and took Standard Oil to task for plans to chop down a huge Moreton Bay fig tree at U.S. Highway 101 and Chapala Street, making the tree a public landmark in the process. In her spare time, Chase established the California Conservation Council, was a board member of the Save the Redwoods League, and continued to fight for the rights of the poor. In 1952 the *Los Angeles Times* named her its Woman of the Year, and in 1956 Santa Barbara bestowed the same honor. In 1963 Chase organized the influential Santa Barbara Trust for Historic Preservation, which remains dedicated to the preservation of historic buildings and sites in Santa Barbara County. Once a year in mid-November, a luncheon is held in Chase's honor, and the trust presents its annual Pearl Chase Award to a community activist who has dedicated his or her life to preserving and beautifying the city that Chase so loved.

The staggering impact that Pearl Chase had on the development of the city of Santa Barbara is in evidence everywhere today. Without any political authority whatsoever, Chase used pluck and determination (and her telephone) to fight for her causes. It is said that she knew just about everyone in town and prided herself on being a "burr under the saddle" of her opponents, many of whom gave in to her demands simply to end the tireless badgering. After her death, the hundreds of photographs and papers dealing with Chase's public life and service were donated to the Special Collections Library at the University of California at Santa Barbara, which now bestows a scholarship in her name. Several plaques around town call grateful attention to her achievements, and Chase Palm Park, along the local waterfront, is named in her honor. Although many historians have paid her homage, and young scholars continue to learn of her influence on the Santa Barbara of today, one question looms unanswered: Could Pearl Chase possibly have had anything to do with that fortuitous 1925 earthquake? Those who knew her don't doubt it for a second.

was the final economic blow to most of the remaining Californios, and many were forced to move to the poorer sections of town.

Soon after, displaced Chinese laborers from the California gold country moved into the city and often into the abandoned homes of the Californios. Shops, laundries, and gambling houses sprang up along Canon Perdido Street between State and Santa Barbara Streets. In response to some of the illegal activities of the Chinese, a law was eventually passed forbidding them to own land and thus forcing most of them to move to the outskirts of town. The social and economic future of Santa Barbara now rested squarely on the shoulders of the Americans, who by the late 1800s wielded most of the power and controlled nearly all of the land and the money.

THE AMERICAN PERIOD

Full "Americanization," which included the adoption of English as the official language, slowly began to change Santa Barbara's character. By 1870 it was a growing American city with its own newspaper, boarding school, wharf, and expanding number of tourist attractions. Articles in major publications, including some New York City newspapers, praised the city's climate, hot springs, and other amenities, and before long tourists were coming in droves to stay at an increasing number of new hotels and boardinghouses.

Stearns Wharf was completed in 1872 at a cost of $40,000, making Santa Barbara accessible by sea, and the Lobero Theatre, also completed in 1872, offered a new venue for the cultural arts. When the Southern Pacific Railroad connected Santa Barbara with Los Angeles in 1887 (the same year that State Street installed electric lights), the city became a full-blown tourist destination, hosting such luminaries as John D. Rockefeller Sr., Andrew Carnegie, the Vanderbilts, and the Du Ponts.

By the turn of the century, Santa Barbara was booming. In 1910 Santa Barbara became

i California's first female lighthouse keeper, Julia Williams, "wo"-manned Santa Barbara's lighthouse for over 40 years. The "Lighthouse Lady" assumed her position in 1865 after her husband quit the job. Julia faithfully beacon-tended while also raising their six children. As if that wasn't enough, she oversaw lighthouse improvements and the sinking of a 50-foot well and copiously documented oil usage, hours burned, and weather conditions.

the "Film Capital of the World" when the American Film Company opened its Flying A Studio on the northwest corner of State and Mission Streets. The rugged backdrop of San Marcos Pass was often used for filming Westerns, and local beaches served as stand-ins for exotic island shores. Movie stars often sought respite in luxurious beachside hotels or relaxed in one of several local mineral springs.

With the continued Americanization of the city, Santa Barbara's Spanish architecture began to be eclipsed by more "modern" buildings, resulting in a sort of hodgepodge look in the downtown area. Although many found this trend disturbing, no one was sure what to do about it. On June 29, 1925, a solution emerged in the form of a major earthquake that destroyed most of the downtown buildings, opening the way for reconstruction in what was to become the classic Santa Barbara style (see the Close-up in this chapter on Pearl Chase). During the 1930s, Santa Barbara's population continued to grow, and it remained a popular getaway for the rich and famous. Posh hotels such as Charlie Chaplin's Montecito Inn and Ronald Colman's San Ysidro Ranch catered to an upscale clientele.

Times were leaner during the Great Depression, and because the city was perched on the Pacific shoreline, there were many anxious moments during the war years that followed. In February 1942 a Japanese submarine fired on a beach approximately 10 miles (16 kilometers) west of the city, marking the first enemy shelling of the American mainland since 1812. Little damage was done, but tensions grew and coastal property values fell as a result of the incident. After World War II, Santa Barbara enjoyed the economic boom experienced by the rest of the country. The University of California at Santa Barbara campus accommodated young soldiers seeking an education on the GI Bill, and local government officials scrambled to secure enough water to meet the needs of the growing population. Bradbury Dam was completed in 1953, Cachuma Lake spilled over five years later, and the city's water problems seemed to be solved.

City boundaries expanded between 1960 and 1970, and Santa Barbara's population grew from 19,000 to more than 60,000. Research and development companies employed more than 160,000 workers by 1974, as families came to Santa Barbara from all over the country, drawn by the healthy economy and alluring lifestyle. The booming tourist economy was almost dealt a death blow in 1969 when a Union Oil platform 5 miles off the Santa Barbara coast blew out, sending thick waves of black crude oil onto local beaches. Tourism, as well as sea creatures and birds, took an extremely hard knock until the mess was cleaned up, and local environmentalists were livid, vowing to protect their beaches in the future. Since then, the activities of oil companies, who own drilling and tankering rights in the Santa Barbara Channel, have been under constant scrutiny.

Wildfires have also plagued Santa Barbara, the most recent being the 1990 fire that killed one person and destroyed hundreds of homes and several businesses. Started by an arsonist, the blaze roared from the top of San Marcos Pass to the outskirts of Hope Ranch, driven by hot down-canyon winds. The threat of a brush fire is ever present in Santa Barbara, especially during drought years, when the canyons are overgrown with tinder-dry

The front of the courthouse. GREG PETERSON/SANTA BARBARA CONFERENCE & VISITORS BUREAU

Going Green in Santa Barbara

Santa Barbara is a "green machine." Nature dapples the city with earthy hues of green. Farmers' markets are filled with locally grown greens. As for the residents, well, many of them have plenty of "green." But did you know that Santa Barbara is also heralded as the birthplace of the "Green" movement?

In 1969 a major oil spill off the coast of Santa Barbara caused several grassroots organizations, including Get Oil Out (GOO), to join to protect the environment from future oil spills. The late Senator Gaylord Nelson (D–Wisconsin) visited Santa Barbara during the spill and was so dismayed by the damage that he quickly conceived and promoted the idea of Earth Day as an educational solution to avoid future spills.

Santa Barbarans glommed onto the idea by creating a citywide celebration of Earth Day (www.SBEarthDay.org) every April. The nonprofit Community Environmental Council and University of California at Santa Barbara's Bren School for Environmental Science and Management host the event at the Santa Barbara Courthouse Sunken Gardens. The Green Car Show and Advanced Transportation Marketplace, one of its unique highlights, showcases a myriad of vehicles demonstrating electric, fuel cell, biodiesel, hybrid, and compressed natural gas technology. Experts discuss and demonstrate the hybrid and advanced fuel options. It's no wonder why renting a hybrid to tool around town is always an option. Some Insiders are making their own environmental stand by getting rid of their SUVs and driving fuel-efficient cars.

In the early 1990s, a slew of Santa Barbara agencies gathered together to create the Green Award Consortium. This consortium works to recognize and promote local businesses that are focusing on protecting the environment (www.greendifference.org). It also seeks to teach citizens how to lessen our impact on the environment through water conservation, organic pest control, and green building construction, to name a few.

City TV (Channel 18) recently stepped up and stepped in with a hilarious local show called the *Garden Wise Guys* (www.citytv18.com) that airs Sundays at 9:00 p.m. Two renowned landscape architects, Owen Dell of County Landscape & Design, and Billy Goodnick of the City of Santa Barbara Parks and Recreation Department, offer a trove of landscaping ideas and water-sustainability information through a 30-minute on-air schtick. They confess to their Three Stooges–like ways, but some say their routine is more Seinfeldean in nature. Either way, who would have ever thought there was a lighthearted side to conservation and sustainability?

Santa Barbara aims to be environmental right to its core, but in a tamer and less granola-crunch way than some of our neighboring cities to the north. With a panorama as breathtaking and pristine as Santa Barbara's, it makes sense why Insiders are constantly trying to protect it.

brush. (See the Living with Mother Nature chapter.) Fire was also a factor in November 1998 when one of the city's most popular tourist attractions—Stearns Wharf—was hit by a $12 million blaze that destroyed 20 percent of the pier. Broadcast throughout the country, scenes of the spectacular blaze (as well as early reports that the wharf had been completely destroyed) led some to exclaim that Santa Barbara would never be the same. "Nonsense!" exclaimed city officials, who promptly plopped down a 70-foot Christmas tree on what was left of the rubble. With the burned-out section roped off, the pier reopened to the public a few days after the fire, and repairs on the rest of the pier have now restored the landmark to its former glory.

Given that Santa Barbara's past is fraught with political skirmishes, water woes, environmental disasters, and economic downturns, the city has done well to maintain its reputation as a modern-day paradise. No matter how turbulent, every era of history has in some way left its mark, and the Chumash, Franciscan friars, Spanish dons, Mexican landowners, and irrepressible Yankee traders

i On June 29, 1925, a magnitude 6.8 earthquake destroyed many of Santa Barbara's downtown buildings. After the quake, Pearl Chase and the Plans and Planting Committee joined with the Architectural Board of Review and recommended all new buildings be constructed in the Spanish-Mediterranean style, creating Santa Barbara's famous skyline of red-tiled roofs you see today.

have all added something to the flavor of Santa Barbara. If you've any doubt, spend a few hours enjoying the festivities at the Old Spanish Days celebration, held each August (see the Annual Events chapter). On any given evening, you can watch Chumash dancers, see a living representation of Saint Barbara (a local woman is chosen to dress in costume and represent the saint), dance the fandango (complete with castanets), eat tacos washed down with tequila, and stop for a cappuccino on the way home. In no time at all, you'll be shouting "Viva la Fiesta!" right along with the natives.

HOTELS AND MOTELS

Santa Barbara has been known for its gracious hotels for more than a century. Word spread quickly about the region's natural assets, and Santa Barbara earned a reputation as a popular health resort. But in the early days, visitors didn't come for the sand, sea, and surf.

Santa Barbara's main draw in the late 19th century was its gentle climate. People came to "take the cure" in the local hot springs and reap the health benefits of the warm, dry air. In fact, many of the area's first hotels stood inland away from the damp sea breezes. In 1871 a wealthy Boston banker built The Lincoln House, one of the region's first guesthouses, near the center of town. According to an 1873 advertisement in the *Santa Barbara Gazette,* the hotel was situated "on high ground and in a very desirable location especially for those seeking health." The New England Italianate-style hotel welcomed its affluent guests with 10 bedrooms, three bathrooms, quoits, croquet, and an adjacent stable for their horses and buggies. Today that structure is part of The Upham Hotel, still a popular lodging choice in Santa Barbara.

The most famous of Santa Barbara's grand hotels, the Arlington Hotel on State Street, was also built inland four years after The Lincoln House. A magnificent three-story structure with 90 luxurious rooms, the Arlington was famous throughout the country as a retreat for discriminating travelers. Presidents, kings, celebrities, and America's social elite graced the guest list, and the hotel continued to draw the rich and famous for more than 30 years until it burned to the ground in 1909.

In 1902 yet another grand hotel, The Potter, played host to wealthy travelers of the day. The Potter was one of the first hotels built by the waterfront, near West Beach, where most of the tourist action is centered today. Unfortunately, an arsonist destroyed the 600-room luxury resort in 1921, but in the hotel's heyday, guests forked out $3 to $4 a night to stay there and romp at the posh country club with its racetrack, polo grounds, and golf course.

Today Santa Barbara is as popular as ever, and the hotel industry is thriving. Some of the world's most exclusive hotels can be found here. Beanie Babies toys mogul Ty Warner, named on the *Forbes 400* Richest Americans list, recently purchased and refurbished Montecito's San Ysidro Ranch and the Five Diamond Four Seasons Resort The Biltmore Santa Barbara. Lavish renovations turned these well-known first-class hotels into luxurious resort destinations. In addition to these well-appointed Montecito hotels is the much talked about $200 million Bacara Resort & Spa that sits on 72 acres in west Goleta. Since its debut in 2000, this glamorous Mediterranean-style resort has lured a stream of A-list celebrities and played host to high-profile weddings and events.

For those with more frugal pockets, don't be put off by the seemingly outrageous lineup of well-heeled resorts. Santa Barbara also has a myriad of very affordable accommodations—everything from cozy inns and historic hotels to family-friendly waterfront resorts.

Many Santa Barbara hotels have fascinating guest lists, so we've included some interesting tidbits and even dropped a few names where appropriate. Older hotels are anxious to share their history with guests, and you can often find pamphlets or books in the lobby, so make sure you take the time to read them. (Who knows, Jacqueline Kennedy may have stayed in your cottage.)

Given Santa Barbara's reputation as a

sanctuary for the rich and famous, you might be concerned about our city's high prices. Can you afford a vacation in paradise? Sure, we have a selection of luxury resorts, the kind you always read about in glossy travel magazines, but you can find some moderately priced lodging options here, too. In this chapter we'll tell you all about them.

If you want a bare-bones kind of lodging option, you'll find an assortment of area Motel 6 (www.motel6.com) accommodations: (805) 564-1392 or (805) 687-5400 in Santa Barbara; (805) 964-3596 in Goleta; (805) 684-6921 or (805) 684-8602 in Carpinteria; or call (800) 4-MOTEL-6 for toll-free reservations. There's also a Super 8 Motel (www.super8.com) in Goleta; call (805) 967-5591 or (800) 800-8000. There's also the Days Inn Santa Barbara (www.daysinn.com) across from the beach; call (805) 963-9772 or (800) 329-7466.

Bear in mind that you can score discounts on even the priciest accommodations during the off-season (generally November through March, although many local hotels consider the Christmas holidays peak season), and several managers we talked to said they would often let rooms go for a song if they're available midweek at low season, so don't be afraid to haggle.

Before you pick up the phone, here are a few more facts that will help you make your decision. A 12 percent occupancy tax is added to all hotel room rates in the greater Santa Barbara area, so figure the extra into your total cost. Also, some hotels have a two-night minimum on weekends—especially during the high season. Most hotels and motels listed here offer discounts (AAA, corporate, AARP, etc.), cable television with at least one premium channel (HBO, Showtime, etc.), and free wireless service. They all accept major credit cards, but only a few accept pets. We've noted the pet-friendly spots.

Many hotels and motels offer a complimentary continental breakfast. Although the specifics may vary from place to place, this usually means pastries, muffins or bagels, fresh fruit, and coffee, tea, milk, or juice. Generally, this fare is available for a limited time each morning, so check the hours and realize that if you're a late sleeper, you may have to eat breakfast elsewhere.

All hotels are required by the Americans with Disabilities Act to provide fully accessible rooms (including bathrooms), so every lodging place we list has at least one. In addition, there may be several partially accessible rooms on lower floors, so if you are in need of any special facilities, make your needs known when you reserve your room.

Where we use the terms "full" or "fully stocked" kitchen, we mean a kitchen with everything you need to cook and serve a meal and clean up afterward. A stove or stovetop, refrigerator, microwave, coffeemaker, and pots, pans, dishes, and silverware will be on hand, and you'll have a sink to wash dishes in and towels to dry everything. If you have any question about kitchen facilities, ask.

One more thing: Many hotels offer privileges at local health clubs and golf courses. In some cases, this means you get to use the facilities for free or at a discounted price, but in others, it means you get access but have to pay regular prices (this is especially true for privileges at private golf courses). Finally, Santa Barbara has some of the highest hotel occupancy rates in Southern California, so if you're planning to visit at a busy time of year (long weekends, summer, and Christmas), try to book your hotel well in advance.

Price Code

These prices are based on a one-night, double-occupancy stay in the high season and do not include taxes and fees for added services. Bear in mind that these are averages, so some rooms may be quite a bit more expensive. And, of course, fancy suites or cottages can run you into the several hundreds or thousands at the finest resorts.

$ . . . . $120 to $150
$$ . . . . $151 to $190
$$$ . . . . $191 to $250
$$$$ . . . . $251 and more

ℹ️ Many Santa Barbara hotels offer Internet specials on their Web sites. Check before you book.

SANTA BARBARA

By the Beach

Best Western Beachside Inn $$–$$$
336 West Cabrillo Boulevard, Santa Barbara
(805) 965-6556, (800) 932-6556
www.beachsideinn.com

This dog-friendly hotel is right at the edge of the action, located directly across from the waterfront and beach. The recently remodeled comfortable hotel offers 60 guest rooms, several with ocean-view balconies. A continental breakfast is served every morning—an enticing array of cereals, juices, fruit, and pastries. Tired of washing the sand from your feet? Cool off with a refreshing dip in the sizable pool. For those reveling in Fiesta, this hotel gives you a great view of the parade and involves you right in the action. Dogs are priced at an extra $20 per night. Wireless service is free.

Brisas Del Mar, Inn at the Beach $$
223 Castillo Street, Santa Barbara
(805) 966-2219, (800) 468-1988
www.sbhotels.com

Emerging from a $1.5 million renovation in 2003, Brisas Del Mar offers a comfortable and affordable alternative to the oceanfront Cabrillo Boulevard hotels. Although Castillo Street is busy with beach traffic during the day, it mellows at night, and most rooms are set back from the street. West Beach and the harbor are just 2 blocks away, and you can walk to restaurants and Stearns Wharf.

Your accommodation choices range from French country–style standard rooms with a king-size or two queen-size beds to the newly refurbished Mediterranean-style family suites for up to six guests with full-size kitchens, marble inlay counters, and fireplaces. Every room comes with a refrigerator, coffeemaker, hair dryer, and TV, and all are nonsmoking.

Outdoors, you can splash around in the heated pool, soak in the Jacuzzi, and lounge on the scenic sundecks overlooking the dolphin fountain. Fitness buffs will appreciate the new exercise room. Rates here include a complimentary continental breakfast, evening wine and cheese, and bedtime milk and fresh-baked cookies. Parking is free, and guests can use the coin-operated laundry on-site. If you're planning on staying a while, ask about weekly and monthly rates.

Cabrillo Inn at the Beach $–$$
931 East Cabrillo Boulevard, Santa Barbara
(805) 966-1641, (800) 648-6708
www.cabrillo-inn.com

This modest, nonsmoking, family-run motel is not exactly deluxe, but it offers a relaxed atmosphere, sparkling clean rooms, and great oceanfront value. It's just a stone's throw from East Beach and the Cabrillo Bathhouse and about a mile from downtown. Second-floor rooms have the best views of the ocean and islands, and some rooms have private balconies. Each of the 39 rooms has a king-size or two queen-size beds, an in-room refrigerator, and a phone (local and credit card calls are free).

You might find it hard to choose between the white sands across the street and the motel's two pools with two second-floor sundecks. Every morning you can head down to the ocean-view lounge for a complimentary continental breakfast and the morning paper.

Cabrillo Inn also has two Spanish-Mediterranean vacation cottages adjacent to the hotel that rent by the week or for the month. Each 1,600-square-foot unit has two bedrooms, two bathrooms, a large living room with a gas fireplace and sofa bed, a large, fully equipped kitchen with a dishwasher and microwave, direct-dial telephones with a private number and answering machine, laundry facilities, a DVD player, and daily maid service. Cottage guests also have access to a patio and barbecue and can use the inn's amenities.

Casa Del Mar $$
18 Bath Street, Santa Barbara
(805) 963-4418, (800) 433-3097
www.casadelmar.com

For those seeking a little more serenity, come to Casa Del Mar—a charming Mediterranean-style "house by the sea." It's a cross between a bed-and-breakfast inn and a small hotel, with very friendly service and a helpful staff. Although you won't see the ocean from your room, the inn lies in a quiet neighborhood a one-minute walk from West Beach. Some of the 21 rooms and suites have full kitchens, and 12 have mini-kitchens (a refrigerator and microwave), so this is a good choice for vacationing families, business travelers, and anyone who likes to prepare a few simple meals at "home." You can relax in the whirlpool spa or sit on the courtyard sundeck amid the colorful geranium gardens. Guests also score a discount at Spa de Menicucci at nearby Fess Parker's DoubleTree Resort. All rooms have king- or queen-size beds and private baths, and some have a gas fireplace. Thoughtful touches include fresh flowers from the local farmers' market, hair dryers, coffeemakers, and irons in every room.

Every morning guests enjoy a generous breakfast buffet in the lounge. In the evening you can mix with other guests over wine and cheese. Business travelers appreciate the desk and telephone in every room and the fax service in the inn's office. All rooms at Casa Del Mar are nonsmoking, and golf packages are available. Dogs and cats are welcome at an extra charge of $15 per night per pet, but they must never be left unattended. Note that Casa Del Mar offers special discounts on their Web site at certain times of the year.

Colonial Beach Inn $$-$$$
206 Castillo Street, Santa Barbara
(805) 963-4317, (800) 649-2669
www.sbhotels.com

Another in the group of hotels owned by SB Hotels, the Colonial Beach Inn is located directly across the street from the Brisas Del Mar, Inn at the Beach. Unlike the others, this

i Time to attend to Rover's need for a daily walk? Head over to the dog-friendly Douglas Family Preserve, Chase Palm Park, Shoreline Park, or Oak Park for a trek along waterfront stretches or over untamed land. Just be sure to pick up any little messes Rover may leave behind. (Some parks provide plastic bags.) Santa Barbarans are very insistent on keeping their environs pristine.

hotel exudes a Southern country charm reminiscent of magnolia trees and genteel hospitality. Its 23 nonsmoking rooms, featuring quilts, floral decorations, and cherry furnishings, allow you to unwind in true Southern style. If the beach wasn't so alluring and only 2 blocks away, you might never leave your room. Even though it is the smallest of the SB Hotel group, the inn's effusive staff was quick to point out that the Colonial Beach has the largest pool. Continental breakfast, afternoon wine and cheese, and evening milk accompanied by freshly baked cookies are all served in the sunroom. Have some questions about Santa Barbara? Just ask the lobby receptionist, who is a veritable warehouse of knowledge.

Fess Parker's DoubleTree Resort $$$$
633 East Cabrillo Boulevard, Santa Barbara
(805) 564-4333, (800) 879-2929 (outside 805 area code)
www.fpdtr.com

You can't miss this sprawling white stucco and red-roofed resort as you drive along the Santa Barbara waterfront. It's one of the city's largest and most eye-catching hotels, with 337 rooms and 23 deluxe suites, all set on 24 beautifully landscaped oceanfront acres about a 1/2 mile (0.8 kilometer) east of Stearns Wharf. With its expansive meeting and banquet facilities, the resort draws large numbers of conferees, but it's also popular with tourists. Even if you don't stay here, you can stroll, picnic, and people-watch in the grassy

i Visiting Santa Barbara with Fido and need information on pet-friendly services? Go to www.allforanimals.com and click on the "Santa Barbara Animal Directory" link. You'll find listings for doggie day care, emergency hospitals, groomers, and specialty stores.

expanse that fronts the hotel (it's a city park, though you won't see too many signs announcing this fact).

"Extra oversize" is the best way to describe the guest rooms at the Double-Tree—each averages 425 to 450 square feet and holds either a king-size or two queen-size beds with feather pillows. Dressed in ocean-inspired colors, each room has a patio or balcony, bathroom with a double vanity, minibar, sitting area, work desk, iron and ironing board, and coffeemaker. Make sure you request a room close to reception if you have difficulty walking around.

In many ways, this resort resembles a health spa: You can play tennis on the lighted courts, swim some laps in the pool, hit a few balls on the putting green, work out in the fully equipped health center, or indulge in some relaxing treatments at Spa de Menicucci. Many guests rent bikes or in-line skates (for a fee) and cruise along the beachfront bike path across the street. You don't have to go far to replenish yourself after burning up all those calories. The two restaurants on the premises—Cafe Los Arcos and Rodney's Steakhouse (see the Restaurants chapter)—serve excellent food. If you're starving at 2:00 a.m., you can call upon the 24-hour room service to sate your hunger pangs. Believe it or not, this is a pet-friendly resort. All you need to do is sign a Pet Policy and make a one-time $40 nonrefundable deposit.

Franciscan Inn $–$$
109 Bath Street, Santa Barbara
(805) 963-8845
www.franciscaninn.com
If you're looking for an affordable Spanish-Mediterranean hideaway a few blocks from

the beach, we highly recommend this friendly family-owned inn. It's in a quiet residential area, and you can easily stroll to West Beach, the Santa Barbara Harbor, Stearns Wharf, State Street, and many shops and restaurants from here. The hotel's moderate size enables the owners to maintain a tranquil, family-style atmosphere and a high level of personalized service. Many guests return year after year and rave about the Franciscan's dedicated staff, some of whom have worked here for a decade or longer.

Brightened with homey floral touches, the 53 rooms and suites were designed to meet a variety of budgets. Choices range from a cozy room with a single bed to spacious suites with a living room, wet bar, and fireplace. Many rooms feature comfortable sitting areas, and nearly all the suites provide fully stocked kitchenettes (one comes with a full kitchen). All rooms and suites include direct-dial telephones with free local calls, hair dryers, coffeemakers, big TVs, and DVD players, and guests can use the free video library and reading library. Outdoors you can swim in the spacious pool or soak in the private spa tucked away in a secluded garden setting.

The Franciscan attracts many business travelers and extended-stay visitors and has free wireless Internet service. Ask about their weekly rates if you plan on staying a while. Other extras at the Franciscan include complimentary continental breakfast, an afternoon tea-and-cookie hour, self-service laundry facilities, and valet service for dry cleaning.

Harbor View Inn $$$$
28 West Cabrillo Boulevard, Santa Barbara
(805) 963-0780, (800) 755-0222
www.harborviewinnsb.com
Luxurious yet casual, this Four-Diamond family-friendly Spanish-Mediterranean resort ranks among our favorite beachside hotels. It enjoys a prime waterfront location, overlooking Stearns Wharf and West Beach, just a half-block west of State Street (you can't get much closer to the tourist action). Originally built in

1985, the inn has undergone extensive makeovers and now includes luxury rooms and suites (most with ocean views), a gift shop, and business center. Under the same ownership, the adjacent Eladio's Restaurant & Bar serves high-quality California cuisine with the same delicious ocean views as the hotel.

Offering either ocean or mountain views, the 102 spacious, air-conditioned guest rooms and 13 luxury suites are tastefully decorated with specially designed fabrics, upholstery, tile, and artwork.

Many rooms feature oversize marble baths, sunken tubs, cathedral ceilings, wet bars, sliding louvered shutters, and garden patios or balconies. Other touches include air-conditioning, refrigerators, coffeemakers, safes, robes, TVs, free wireless Internet access, and an iron and ironing board in every room.

Outdoors, you can soak up the sun across the street at the beach or on the second-floor sundeck, then unwind in the large, glass-enclosed pool (young children can splash about in their own separate wading pool). Health buffs can work out in the tiny fitness center, and at day's end you can stroll in the gardens and stargaze while relaxing in the outdoor Jacuzzi. Room service runs from 6:30 a.m. to 9:30 p.m. The lobby is always open and staffed by friendly professionals who really do go the extra mile to make your stay enjoyable. The entire complex is nonsmoking.

Hotel Mar Monte $$$–$$$$
1111 Cabrillo Boulevard, Santa Barbara
(805) 963-0744, (800) 643-1994
www.hotelmarmonte.com

Formerly the Radisson Hotel, this sprawling Mediterranean-style oceanfront property is ideal for family vacations and relaxing getaways. East Beach, the Cabrillo Bathhouse, and a beachfront playground are just across the boulevard, and the zoo is 1/2 block away. To reach Stearns Wharf and State Street (about a mile down the road), hop on the electric shuttle that stops right in front of the hotel.

The hotel takes up an entire city block,

and the rooms are spread out in four buildings, so be sure to request accommodations close to the facilities if you have mobility problems. Hotel Mar Monte offers 173 guest rooms, most with panoramic ocean or mountain views and either one king-size or two queen-size beds. Each room has a Serta Master Series Sleeper mattress, cozy down comforter, plush robes, a coffeemaker, a hair dryer, robes, and an iron and ironing board. Built in 1931 to take advantage of the ocean views, Hotel Mar Monte has been remodeled to take advantage of the old world charm in a new world way. You and the kids can splash in the heated outdoor pool and gaze at the ocean at the same time, or sink into the new Jacuzzi for a relaxing soak. When you feel like working out, just head for the hotel fitness center.

If you don't feel like venturing far away for meals, you can dine at the oceanview Bistro Eleven Eleven, "where the food gets dressed up, but you don't have to." The restaurant serves breakfast, lunch, and dinner, and the lounge offers live entertainment on weekends. Parking is complimentary.

Inn by the Harbor $–$$
433 West Montecito Street, Santa Barbara
(805) 963-7851, (800) 626-1986
www.sbhotels.com

Inn by the Harbor sits right next to the Brisas Del Mar, Inn at the Beach—they both belong to the same hotel family. However, the no-frills Inn by the Harbor is a little less expensive than its sister property. In 1999 the hotel was completely revamped. You enter the parking lot from a busy street, but most rooms are set back away from the street noise. From here you can walk 3 blocks to West Beach and the marina, then just a few more blocks to Stearns Wharf and State Street.

The inn offers 42 rooms, all nonsmoking and decorated in Spanish country decor, plus complimentary continental breakfast every morning. Room choices range from standard rooms with king- or queen-size beds to family suites with kitchens. One of the motel's best features is a peaceful, enclosed tropical courtyard pool area, where you can sit and soak up some rays.

West Beach Inn at the Harbor $$
306 West Cabrillo Boulevard, Santa Barbara
(805) 963-4277, (800) 716-6199
www.westbeachinn.com

The three-story, Mediterranean-style West Beach Inn is fresh, cheery, and more affordable than most oceanfront accommodations. It's right across the street from the harbor and near West Beach. Each of the 44 sparkling rooms has a refrigerator, coffeemaker, complimentary high-speed wireless Internet access, hair dryer, iron and ironing board, bathrobes, and air-conditioning. Many rooms also have views of the yachts bobbing in the harbor. Choose a one-bedroom suite if you'd like a kitchen. During the winter months, you might prefer a two-bedroom suite with a fireplace. The pool and spa overlook the ocean, so you can easily check out what's happening across the way. The inn serves a complimentary continental breakfast every morning and wine and cheese every afternoon.

Long-term visitors or large families may be interested in the 2,000-square-foot suite. It sleeps up to 8 and features three bedrooms, a kitchen and dining room, and five plasma TVs.

In Town

Best Western Encina Lodge and Suites $$
2220 Bath Street, Santa Barbara
(805) 682-7277, (800) 526-2282
www.sbhotels.com

We really like this well-managed hotel, which lies about 2 miles (3.2 kilometers) inland and 1 mile (1.6 kilometers) from downtown. It's cheerful and well maintained, and the property was updated with a $3 million face-lift in 2002, so it still feels fresh and new. Tucked into a residential neighborhood about 1/2 block from Santa Barbara Cottage Hospital and the renowned Sansum–Santa Barbara

Medical Foundation Clinic (see the Health Care and Wellness chapter), the property caters to older guests, many of whom are visiting local clinics or providing support to hospitalized friends or family.

The range of accommodations is exhaustive, with seven buildings housing regular guest rooms, apartments (some with two bedrooms and/or full-size kitchens), town houses, pool suites, and efficiency units with kitchenettes. All rooms are decorated in a country style, with many pleasing decorative touches.

Most of the 121 units have a hair dryer, refrigerator, iron and ironing board, and coffeemaker, and there is a wall safe in every room. The staff puts hard candy, apples, oranges, and packaged cookies in each room every day, which is another of those small touches that make you feel at home.

A large pool, whirlpool, massage facility, beauty shop, and aviary are located on the grounds. A Capella Restaurant will have you singing in glee over its eggs Benedict, crab Louie, or comforting potpie.

In addition to the standard discounts, Encina Lodge offers discounts for anyone going to a Santa Barbara medical facility and will provide free transportation to doctors' appointments in the area as well as to the Santa Barbara Airport or the train station.

Best Western Pepper Tree Inn $$
3850 State Street, Santa Barbara
(805) 687-5511, (800) 338-0030
www.sbhotels.com

Dotted with palms on Santa Barbara's busy State Street, this well-maintained Spanish-Mediterranean mini-resort is similar in many ways to its sister, the Best Western Encina Lodge. Friendly staff, comfortable rooms,

> **i** For quick reservations for Santa Barbara–area hotels, call Coastal Escapes Reservations Services at (800) 292-2222 (www.coastalescapes.com) or Santa Barbara Hot Spots at (800) 793-7666 (www.hotspotsusa.com).

attractive grounds, and reasonable rates make this a popular choice with budget-conscious travelers. The inn is set on five beautifully landscaped acres in the Upper State Street shopping district, across the street from La Cumbre Plaza Mall. You'll need a car if you want to head downtown to the heart of the tourist action. Each of the 150 individually decorated guest rooms has a private patio or balcony overlooking garden courtyards. Most of the rooms are dressed in floral fabrics and have air-conditioning, coffeemakers, refrigerators, free high-speed wireless Internet service, and thoughtful touches, such as fresh fruit and cookies. Extra amenities include two large tiled pools and whirlpools, an exercise room, a sauna, a massage room, hair salons, valet laundry service, and a gift shop.

The Treehouse Restaurant and Lounge serves breakfast, lunch, and dinner in a casual atmosphere and will also deliver to your room or poolside.

When you need a ride to or from the airport or train station, just make arrangements with the staff for complimentary transportation.

El Encanto Hotel and Garden Villas $$$$
1900 Lasuen Road, Santa Barbara
(805) 568-1357, (800) 346-7039
www.orient-express.com
Temporarily closed, fall 2008 marks the completion and reopening of the multimillion-dollar renovated historic crown jewel of Santa Barbara's picturesque Riviera, the El Encanto. The El Encanto (which means "the enchanted" in Spanish) became a hotel in 1918. This venerable hideaway was designated a charter member of Historic Hotels of America in 1990. The restoration of the 91 guest rooms and suites marks the appearance of the first Orient Express Hotel on the West Coast. The elegantly tiered dining terrace, once an Insiders' favorite, will be enhanced, and a spa with six treatment rooms, a grotto mineral pool, a eucalyptus steam room, and an outdoor terrace will be added. Insiders can only imagine

what else this plush remodel will have to offer. Rumor has it that there will be a zero-edge swimming pool, tennis courts, herb garden, and reading and strolling gardens. The luxurious cottages and upscale rooms will most assuredly continue to draw celebrities and business leaders.

El Prado Inn $
1601 State Street, Santa Barbara
(805) 966-0807, (800) 669-8979
www.elpradoinn.com
Family-owned and -operated, El Prado is not one of those splashy Santa Barbara accommodations, but rather a cozy and reasonably priced little motor inn on busy State Street offering value for your money and personalized service. The lobby is homey and welcoming to new arrivals. Guests can enjoy the daily paper while sipping a cup of tea or coffee in the lobby.

The inn has well-kept rooms with queen- or king-size beds and suites with refrigerators, microwaves, sitting areas, and patios. Free continental breakfast is provided, and meeting space is available. A heated pool and patio are about the only other amenities, but a coin-operated laundry and a market are right across the street, and you can walk to many of the area's attractions in just minutes.

Holiday Inn Express—Hotel Virginia $$
17 West Haley Street, Santa Barbara
(805) 963-9757, (800) 549-1700
www.hotelvirginia.com
One of downtown Santa Barbara's boutique hotels is the 1925 Hotel Virginia, which is currently listed on the National Registry of Historic Places. It opened in January 1999 after undergoing a $5 million renovation and now combines the historic Spanish Colonial elements of the building with an Art Deco–style interior, including a mosaic fountain in the lobby and replicas of Malibu and Catalina tilework throughout. A second renovation was completed in 2005. This is a great spot to stay if you're in town for business or want easy access to the shops, restaurants, and

i Want to stay at the beach but afraid you can't afford the prices? Even a block away from the ocean, rooms are cheaper.

businesses downtown. You won't find a pool on-site, but the hotel is only 4 blocks from the beach. The 61 guest rooms are decorated in classic California Spanish Revival style and feature advanced phone systems with data-ports, hair dryers, and ironing boards with irons. Upstairs rooms are the best picks. Guests also receive a complimentary conti-nental breakfast and can park their cars in a private lot for a fee—a big bonus in the down-town area. It's a nonsmoking hotel. Reserva-tions for bachelor and bachelorette parties are not accepted.

Hotel Andalucia $$$$
31 West Carrillo Street, Santa Barbara
(805) 884-0300, (877) 468-3515
www.andaluciasb.com
Want to be in the heart of the action while still steeping yourself in luxury? If so, the Hotel Andalucia should be your pick. Once a retirement home called The Carrillo Hotel, this magically transformed boutique property has attracted quite a star-studded list of celebrities, such as Annette Bening, David Duchovny, and Martin Landau. Elegance drips from the 77 guest rooms and 20 suites finely appointed with embroidered linens, mosaic bath tiles, and window textiles by a renowned Santa Barbara firm. Televisions with DVDs and CD players, wireless Internet service access, minibar, coffeemaker, and robes are also part of the package. The 31 West, its restaurant, is strangely part of the hotel lobby. The cuisine is truly a diner's treat, but the ambience is somewhat discon-certing—guests are wheeling in their bag-gage and checking in while you are dining. El Cielo, the rooftop outdoor terrace and pool, is a must-do for a late-night drink. Enjoying the 360-degree view of Santa Barbara and its red-tiled roofs while under the canopy of a

brilliant nighttime sky makes for an evening you won't soon forget.

Hotel Santa Barbara $$–$$$
533 State Street, Santa Barbara
(805) 957-9300, (800) 549-9869
www.hotelsantabarbara.com
Before Hotel Santa Barbara opened in mid-1997 after a $4 million renovation to the 100-year-old building, there wasn't one hotel on lower State Street that we would have included on our "best and brightest" list. This hotel changed all that in a big way, providing well-appointed lodging in the heart of down-town's social scene.

Although the hotel is on bustling State Street, the indoor corridors make it quiet and secluded. It's near downtown shops and restaurants and within 5 blocks of Stearns Wharf and the waterfront. Seventy-five air-conditioned rooms and nine suites are appointed with queen- or king-size beds, with pullout sofas in the suites. All rooms are non-smoking and have coffeemakers, hair dryers, and bottled water. Guests may request refrig-erators. A complimentary continental break-fast is served to guests each morning, and coffee is available in the lobby throughout the day. Two conference rooms are also available. If the view is important to you, ask for one of only four rooms that overlook State Street and the mountains, subject to occupancy.

As we see it, the only drawback to Hotel Santa Barbara is its tricky parking situation. There is one pullout space in front of the hotel for loading or unloading, but the main parking lot is located behind the hotel with valet park-ing access in an extremely narrow driveway on Cota Street.

Inn of the Spanish Garden $$$$
915 Garden Street, Santa Barbara
(805) 564-4700, (866) 564-4700
www.SpanishGardenInn.com
Deep in Santa Barbara's oldest neighborhood amid a mix of low-rise businesses and resi-dences, this intimate Spanish-Mediterranean boutique hotel has received rave reviews

since it opened in 2001. Highlighted as "Inn of the Month" in *Travel & Leisure* magazine, the inn lies only a few blocks from downtown, so you can easily stroll to restaurants, shops, theaters, and businesses. Leisure guests and business travelers love the personalized service, plush rooms, and classy touches at this stylish inn, where modern technology mixes well with old world charm. All of the 23 spacious guest rooms and suites are air conditioned and come with luxuriously comfortable king- or queen-size beds with Frette linen, DSL lines for high-speed Internet access, French press coffeemakers, thick robes, hair dryers, TVs, DVD players, and ceiling fans. The rooms also feature Spanish-style tiling, high ceilings, fireplaces, secluded garden patios or balconies, private baths (with oversized soaking tubs in most), and deluxe toiletries. All are nonsmoking. In your free time, you can paddle in the lap pool, work out in the fitness room, or snuggle around the outdoor fire pit on cool nights. Guests love the gourmet continental breakfast and evening wine hour included in the rates, and the inn offers free underground parking and an intimate boardroom for business meetings.

i During Fiesta in early August, it's nearly impossible to find lodging in Santa Barbara. Make your reservations well ahead of time. For more affordable rates, try booking a room in Carpinteria or other areas outside the city.

The Upham Hotel $$$
1404 De la Vina Street, Santa Barbara
(805) 962-0058, (800) 727-0876
www.uphamhotel.com

At the stately Upham Hotel, established in 1871, you can experience a bit of Santa Barbara history and enjoy easy access to the arts and culture district. This elegant city landmark is the oldest continuously operating hostelry in Southern California. The Victorian hotel and garden cottages occupy a corner of De la Vina and Sola Streets, just 2 blocks from State Street and within walking distance of the Arlington Theatre, the Museum of Art, restaurants, and shops.

The Upham was built by Boston banker Amasa Lincoln (a distant cousin of Abraham Lincoln) in 1871. The Lincoln House (its original name) was an elegant, New England–style boardinghouse made of redwood timbers. Since it was built before mule-powered streetcars and the railroad came to town, the first guests arrived on foot or by horse or steamship. A subsequent owner, Cyrus Upham, changed the name to Hotel Upham in 1898.

Today the Upham continues its tradition of warm hospitality. The hotel features a cozy lounge with a large fireplace and comfy sofas, and guests love the tranquil gardens. The atmosphere is very much bed-and-breakfast–style—in fact, the Upham frequently appears in bed-and-breakfast listings.

Fifty guest rooms and suites are available in the original main building, three Garden Cottage buildings, the Lincoln Building, the Carriage House, and the Jacaranda and Hibiscus buildings. Each unit is individually decorated and filled with antiques and period furnishings. Fresh flowers add a homey touch.

All rooms have a private bath, direct-dial phone, and cozy comforters; VCRs and fax machines are available on request. Units in the Garden Cottages feature porches or secluded patios; several have gas fireplaces. For the ultimate splurge, book the master suite with a Jacuzzi tub, fireplace, wet bar, and private yard, where you can nap peacefully in the hammock.

Rates include a continental breakfast buffet (nutbreads and pastries, muffins, rolls, juices, cereals, fruits) and afternoon wine and cheese. Oreos and milk await you in the lounge every evening, and coffee, tea, and fruit are always set out. The popular Louie's Restaurant adjoins the main lobby. Louie's offers innovative lunch and dinner menus featuring fresh seafood, pasta, and California cuisine crafted by a head chef who's been with

Louie's for over 20 years. You can dine on the wide, wooden veranda year-round. (See the Restaurants chapter for details.)

GOLETA

Bacara Resort & Spa $$$$
8301 Hollister Avenue, Goleta
(805) 968-0100, (877) 422-4245
www.bacararesort.com

Set on 78 palm-studded beachfront acres, 13 miles (21 kilometes) north of Santa Barbara, the exclusive Spanish Colonial–style Bacara (pronounced Ba-CAR-ah) Resort & Spa opened its doors in September 2000 after 18 years of red tape and revisions. Since its debut, the resort has drawn mixed reviews for its service, but this plush property continues to welcome a star-spangled list of celebrities, including actress Debra Messing, and was the setting for Oprah WInfrey's famed Legends Ball.

Bacara promises "The Good Life," and with its 311 luxury guest rooms, 49 suites, three gourmet restaurants, sprawling pools, impressive recreational facilities, grand ballroom, and multilevel spa, it seems poised to deliver. This ambitious venture is the company's first foray into the hospitality business, and it's certainly spared no expense. Wander the light, airy interior and you will see hand-woven rugs imported from India, rich mahogany accents, and corridors full of commissioned art. Bacara's fine dining restaurant, Miró, uses fresh produce from the resort's 1,000-acre ranch (see the Restaurant chapter). The Spa Café overlooking one of the pools serves up healthy fare, and The Bistro offers ocean views from both indoors and its alfresco seaside terrace. The landscaping is tropical meets the Mediterranean, with plenty of palms, bougainvillea, lush courtyards, and gushing fountains. In your spare time, you can pamper yourself in the opulent spa, relax on the beach, jog along the seaside running track, go horseback riding, play tennis on the Har-Tru courts, or hit a few rounds at the celebrated Sandpiper Golf Course next door. High-tech meeting facilities cater to everything from intimate cocktail soirees to large-scale conventions. The stylish guest rooms feature raised king-size or twin beds with Frette linens, warm-toned Spanish tiling, mahogany furnishings, video entertainment systems, high-speed Internet access, robes, Kiehl's toiletries, and fresh flowers. All have private balconies or patios with ocean, mountain, or garden views. Half are warmed by gas log fireplaces, and some of the suites boast romantic candlelit Jacuzzi tubs. Bacara strives to evoke the beauty and glamour of a bygone era, but to stay here you'll have to pay a pretty price. Pooches are welcome, too (though the hotel doesn't advertise the fact); just be prepared to fork out an additional $150 nonrefundable one-time fee.

Best Western South Coast Inn $$
5620 Calle Real, Goleta
(805) 967-3200, (800) 350-3614
www.bwsci.com

This spiffy little Three Diamond inn lies only 2 miles (3.2 kilometers) from Santa Barbara Airport and UCSB. It's a great choice if you're visiting the university or holding a small meeting or conference. Accommodations include 121 well-appointed guest rooms with queen- or king-size beds. Each room is equipped with air-conditioning, a refrigerator, a coffeemaker, a microwave, a minifridge, a hair dryer, and cable TV. Business travelers appreciate the voice mail, free local calls, and high-speed Internet access in each room, and complimentary continental breakfast is served in the lobby.

For recreation, you can splash about in the heated pool and whirlpool, relax on lounge chairs around the sundeck, or play a few rounds of table tennis on the patio. Rose and topiary gardens and a bubbling fountain add a touch of elegance to the grounds. A great deal here is the free shuttle that whisks guests to UCSB campus and the airport. Guests also have free admission to the Goleta Valley Athletic Club.

Extended Stay America $
4870 Calle Real, Santa Barbara
(805) 692-1882, (800) EXTSTAY
www.extstay.com

Geared to the business traveler who plans to stay for a week or more, this good-value hotel lies near the western edge of Goleta just off U.S. Highway 101, about 10 minutes from downtown Santa Barbara. The hotel includes 104 rooms, most with queen-size beds, a kitchenette (with full-size refrigerator, electric stovetop, and dishes for two), desk, dataport phones, and voice mail. There are also two suites, each with a separate sitting area and king-size bed, but they're usually booked up.

You won't find a lot of frills here—no pool, Jacuzzi, or food service (but then, you'll be cooking in your room, remember?). The hotel's rates are flexible, but two people can stay for around $650 a week during high season in Santa Barbara.

Everything's fresh and clean here. You have freeway access right out the front door, and there are enough restaurants and grocery stores nearby to meet your needs (a coin laundry is on the premises). We think this is a great bet for the business traveler or for anybody relocating to the area and needing transitional accommodations. Reservations are accepted no sooner than 90 days in advance.

Holiday Inn $$
5650 Calle Real, Goleta
(805) 964-6241, (888) HOLIDAY
www.holiday-inn.com

This property offers the standard Holiday Inn ambience and amenities and represents a moderately priced lodging option in the Goleta Valley. In addition to 4,500 square feet of meeting space, there are 160 guest rooms, most with one king-size bed or two double beds. Four executive rooms have a king-size bed, pullout sofa, and wet bar. All rooms have coffee-makers and computer dataports, and refrigerators can be supplied on request for a small charge.

The grounds are nicely manicured and well kept, and you can loll around a large pool area, which has lots of lounge chairs for sunning. If you feel like a real workout, take advantage of a complimentary pass to the nearby Goleta Valley Athletic Club. If you're feeling hungry, you can enjoy breakfast and dinner at Remington's, the on-site restaurant, or you can go across the street to Carrow's or visit one of several restaurants and fast-food establishments within walking distance on Calle Real. This hotel attracts corporate travelers as well as families looking for familiar Holiday Inn amenities.

Pacifica Suites $$
5490 Hollister Avenue, Goleta
(805) 683-6722, (800) 338-6722
www.pacificasuites.com

Currently the only all-suites hotel in the Santa Barbara area, this charming property takes the restored 1880 Joseph Sexton house as its centerpiece. To design the house, Joseph Sexton, a successful Goleta nurseryman, enlisted the services of local architect Peter J. Barber, who also designed the first Arlington Hotel and the historic Upham Hotel.

After the Sextons died, the house had a number of owners but then fell into disrepair until the Invest West Financial Corporation acquired it in 1984. Before the complex was developed into a lodging property, the original home and grounds were completely restored, including the replacement of many of the large trees that had been lost over the years.

Today, the towering trees and expansive lawn create a parklike setting, and the old Sexton House is available for business or social functions. The plush sitting area just off the lobby has a fireplace and bar and is used for social functions or for guests to sit back and relax. The design of the rest of the complex echoes that of the Sexton House, with the same elegant architectural style and muted colors.

The hotel has 87 suites, each with a king-size bed or two double beds, a pullout sofa, a refrigerator, a microwave, a coffeemaker, an AM/FM cassette player, and complimentary high-speed Internet access. A full, cooked-to-order complimentary breakfast is served to guests in the breakfast room or on the outside terrace. Wine tastings are held 5:00 to 7:00 p.m. every day.

There is a pool and Jacuzzi, and guests also receive a $5 per day gym pass to Spectrum Gym. The property is located adjacent to California Highway 217, so there is some traffic noise, which is loudest on the west side of the complex. Pets are welcome in the designated smoking rooms for an extra fee of $10 a night.

Ramada Limited $$
4770 Calle Real, Santa Barbara
(805) 964-3511, (800) 654-1965
www.sbramada.com

Known locally as the Cathedral Oaks Lodge until it was acquired by Ramada, this motel has 126 rooms and three suites. Accommodations here are standard, but the courtyard in the middle of the complex features a lovely lagoon with waterfalls, a footbridge, water lilies, and a small population of resident ducks. Quiet walkways lead you through the surrounding gardens under swaying palms, a welcome respite for a hotel on a busy main street.

The rooms face indoor corridors and open onto patios or balconies that look out on either the courtyard or the parking lot (if you'd rather see the lagoon, you'll pay more for the privilege). All are air conditioned, and each comes with a coffeemaker, iron and ironing board, desk, and two phones with voice mail. Local calls are free. Upstairs rooms have higher ceilings, and there's a modest amount of meeting space on-site. A complimentary continental breakfast is served every morning. In your spare time, you can swim in the heated pool or relax in the hot tub.

The Ramada is near the eastern boundary

> **i** Hotels in Goleta are closer to the Santa Barbara Airport and the University of California at Santa Barbara than lodgings in the city of Santa Barbara.

of Goleta, about 10 miles (16 kilometers) from downtown Santa Barbara. You are not particularly close to any tourist attractions here, but the motel is moderately priced, and it's only a 10-minute drive to Santa Barbara's waterfront and other attractions.

MONTECITO

Coast Village Inn $$
1188 Coast Village Road, Montecito
(805) 969-3266, (800) 257-5131
www.coastvillageinn.com

Modest by Montecito standards, this little motel is cheerful, well kept, and near the exclusive boutiques and restaurants that line Coast Village Road (the local farmers' market is held across the street on Friday). The property was opened in the 1930s but has been upgraded on a regular basis. In 2003 the entire property was refurbished and the guest rooms were refreshed with new carpet, fabrics, and linens. (You may want to avoid the back rooms, which open onto the parking lot.)

The 28 nonsmoking rooms and suites are decorated with country pine furniture. Typical features include ceiling fans, cable TVs, phones with voice mail, and wireless high-speed Internet access. You won't find many amenities at this quiet little spot, but guests can enjoy the inn's newly revamped heated pool, free parking, complimentary use of bicycle cruisers, and complimentary breakfast at Peabody's next door. The entire inn is nonsmoking.

Four Seasons Resort The Biltmore Santa Barbara $$$$
1260 Channel Drive, Montecito
(805) 969-2261, (800) 332-3442
www.fourseasons.com

This newly minted, Five Diamond hotel just completed a six-year, $250 million renovation funded by Ty Warner Hotels & Resorts. The 207 guest accommodations, including 12 one-story cottages, are situated on 20 acres of some of the world's most exclusive turf. Even with a train running through the back of the property, this is a place of elegance and romance where the well-heeled love to stay.

Originally built in 1927 as a private mansion by renowned architect Reginald Johnson, this Mediterranean-style complex offers only the finest in hotel amenities. Down pillows (hypoallergenic ones are available), plush terry robes, CDs and DVD players, refrigerated bars, and twice daily housekeeping services are just a few of the luxuries this property has to offer.

Situated directly across from Montecito's stunning Butterfly Beach, the property offers easy beach access. Fitness facilities and 10,000 square feet of spa services are on-site. Basking by the pool, playing tennis, sharpening your putting skills on the practice greens, and exploring the scenic routes on complimentary bicycles are some of the other options. Windsurfing, horseback riding, sailing, and parasailing are all within no more than 20 minutes' reach. No wonder celebrities and business moguls flock to The Biltmore (as Insiders know it).

Two on-site restaurants make The Biltmore experience complete. Bella Vista is a sophisticated restaurant where the natural elements of fire and water meet rich mahogany and elegant marble. It's known for Martin Frost's eclectically delicious California wine-country cuisine. The Ty Lounge, with its mesmerizing ocean view and fireplace, offers a splendid location for an evening nightcap.

Traveling with children can be a task, but not so at The Biltmore. If you provide the names and ages of your children when you make your reservation, your kids will each receive a welcome amenity, child-size bathrobe, and complimentary baby or child toiletries. There's a special children's menu at Bella Vista, and babysitting services can be arranged 24 hours prior to your need.

Montecito Inn $$$–$$$$
1295 Coast Village Road, Montecito
(805) 969-7854, (800) 843-2017
www.montecitoinn.com
The minute you drive up to the Montecito Inn,

you know it's a different kind of small hotel. For one thing, you'll see Charlie Chaplin's face on the sign out front—a theme the hotel carries throughout, with statues of Chaplin in the lobby, his figure etched on the door of the meeting and banquet room, and authentic art posters hanging in the public areas.

Chaplin was one of the original investors in the hotel, which opened in 1928 and drew the rich and famous of the day, including Lon Chaney Sr., Carole Lombard, Wallace Beery, and Norma Shearer, to name a few.

Since its Hollywood heyday, the hotel has enjoyed some refreshing face-lifts. In 2003 management treated the rooms to a major Mediterranean makeover, and they now exude old world elegance with fresh carpet, paint, fabrics, new furnishings, and historic photographic prints of Santa Barbara on the walls. Ceiling fans cool the 52 standard rooms, and all include refrigerators, hair dryers, large TVs, DVDs, high-speed Internet access, and petite bathrooms. Nine luxury rooms come with a diversity of things such as air-conditioning, separate liviing rooms, fireplaces, and soundproofing.

In your free time, you can tour upscale Montecito on the complimentary bikes, tone up in the workout room, or relax in the small pool, sauna, and Jacuzzi (although their proximity to the freeway makes the area a bit noisy). If you're feeling nostalgic, you can pick a flick from the complete library of Charlie Chaplin films. Each morning, the staff lay out a complimentary continental breakfast in the lobby for you to enjoy in the sunny Montecito Cafe, by the pool, or in the privacy of your room.

This charming little inn is truly unique for Santa Barbara, with a personalized, European feel. A two-night minimum stay is required for Saturday arrivals.

San Ysidro Ranch $$$$
900 San Ysidro Lane, Montecito
(805) 565-1700, (800) 368-6788 (from outside the 805 area code)
www.sanysidroranch.com

Set far from the touristy beachfront in the Montecito foothills, the 540-acre San Ysidro Ranch has been cloistering the rich and famous of the world for more than a century. The first cottages were built on the property in the 1890s, and guests began arriving in January 1893.

In the 1930s, actor Ronald Colman bought the property, and soon the likes of Gloria Swanson, Merle Oberon, David Niven, Fred Astaire, Groucho Marx, Lucille Ball, and other Hollywood luminaries were on the guest list. John Huston finished the script for *The African Queen* while ensconced in a ranch cottage, and Vivien Leigh and Lawrence Olivier were married in the Wedding Garden at the stroke of midnight.

A $120 million renovation of the San Ysidro Ranch was recently completed. Forty individual cottages were designed in true bungalow style, most with king-size beds, fine linens, fireplaces, and private patios. Hot tubs sunken into outdoor decks, rain showers, radiant floor heat, hand-cut stone decks, and a multitude of exquisite antiques accentuate the decor.

To woo a special someone, try out the Kennedy Cottage. Sleep where Jackie and John placed their honeymooning heads. This cottage continues to exude romance today with its newly refurbished twin master suites, each hosting a king bed, fireplace, private bathroom, and ocean-view deck. The Warner Cottage is a charming country European single-level home featuring two master bedrooms, two and a half baths, three wood-burning fireplaces, a living room and dining area, and a full kitchen. A private fenced yard has a heated pool, hot tub, and gas grill. What more could a couple in love really need?

If you haven't experienced San Ysidro Ranch, there's nothing like it. You won't want to leave the property or even your room. If you do decide to venture out, there's so much to enjoy—hiking along the 17 miles (27 kilo-meters) of trails in the Santa Ynez Mountains, sipping robust reds in Santa Ynez's abundant wine country, biking, golfing, or indulging in a spa treatment.

Gwyneth Paltrow and Coldplay's Chris Martin hid out at the Ranch for their private wedding, and Julia Roberts and Danny Moder followed in the Kennedys' steps by making the Ranch their honeymoon choice. J-Lo and Marc Anthony paid a visit just after their wedding. It seems like romance is always abloom at this luxurious, first-class resort.

Locals have been enjoying The Stone-house, San Ysidro Ranch's exquisite restaurant, for years. Located in a 19th-century citrus packing house, this hideaway provides the ideal lunch spot. Recommended is the outdoor terrace, but if you can't get that, then cozy up to the indoor fireplace.

This is not a hotel for the faint of heart. The average price can set you back, but if you're in the mood for the finest or just trying to avoid the paparazzi, then San Ysidro Ranch should be your choice. By the way, pets are welcome for $100 a stay.

CARPINTERIA

Best Western Carpinteria Inn $
4558 Carpinteria Avenue, Carpinteria
(805) 684-0473, (800) 780-7234
www.bestwestern.com/carpinteriainn
Rimmed by colorful geraniums, this attractive Spanish-style hotel is a great choice for families, business travelers, and anyone who wants a comfortable yet affordable place to stay in the South County. It's just 3 blocks from downtown Carpinteria's main street, and you can walk to Carpinteria Beach. When you want to visit downtown Santa Barbara, just hop in your car and drive 9 miles (14 1/2 kilometers) up the freeway.

The 144 nonsmoking air-conditioned guest rooms and suites are equipped with refrigerators, hair dryers, safes, irons and ironing boards, coffeemakers, cable TVs, and high-speed Internet access. Amid the red-tile roofs of the inn's main buildings, you'll find a lovely courtyard with a swimming pool, Jacuzzi, fountains, and a koi pond, and you can keep fit in the inn's small workout room. When you're hungry, you can feast at the hotel's Sunset Grille Restaurant and quench your thirst at the full bar.

BED-AND-BREAKFAST INNS

Staying at an intimate bed-and-breakfast gives you a great opportunity to experience Santa Barbara's rich history and character. You can also mix with other guests and enjoy a more personalized level of service than most large hotels can offer. The area's first official bed-and-breakfast, The Old Yacht Club Inn, opened in 1980. A number of regional inns have since joined the ranks.

Each bed-and-breakfast listed here exudes its own personality and offers a range of services for visitors seeking a quiet respite from daily life. Most are beautifully restored, turn-of-the-20th-century Victorian or California Craftsman homes filled with antiques and memorabilia.

The majority are located in historic residential areas close to mid-State Street, where you can escape from city noises but easily walk to restaurants, theaters, and shops. Several offer a peaceful refuge near the beach, while a few cater to those who prefer off-the-beaten-track hideaways.

Santa Barbara bed-and-breakfasts have much in common. You can expect gracious innkeepers to extend a warm welcome upon your arrival and provide excellent hospitality throughout your stay. Each inn serves either a full gourmet or a generous continental breakfast and has an afternoon or evening social hour, usually with wine and cheese and crackers or other appetizers. (If something more elaborate or unusual is provided, we've noted it in the description.) Most also set out port or sherry, homemade cookies, or a snack in the evenings. Vegetarian or other special diets can usually be accommodated with advance notice.

Santa Barbara's high season typically starts in March and lasts through October. You should make your reservations as far in advance as possible, especially if you plan to visit on a weekend or holiday or in the summer months. Many of the inns are fully booked two or three months in advance. Also, the earlier you call, the better your chances of reserving the room of your choice.

When you call to make your reservation, be sure to inquire about the inn's minimum-stay and cancellation policies. Most require a two-night minimum stay on weekends and at least a week's advance notice if you cancel.

All inns listed here accept most major credit cards. Quoted rates are usually based on double occupancy. Additional guests pay anywhere from $15 to $40 per night. Although a few inns have daybeds or roll-aways, most do not. If you have more than two people in your party, your best bet is to book a suite, if you can get one. Most establishments adhere to strict maximum capacity codes, so you should definitely inquire about these rules and other details before making your reservation. Children are welcome at all Santa Barbara bed-and-breakfast inns—it's the law. However, most innkeepers allow children only in certain rooms and discourage their presence at busy times when other guests may be honeymooning or escaping from their own kids. If you plan to bring the kids along, call ahead and discuss your options with the innkeeper.

Most bed-and-breakfast buildings were constructed many years ago, so they often have narrow stairs, walkways, and baths that may present problems for the physically challenged. If you have accessibility concerns, call

i Many bed-and-breakfasts offer special packages as well as reduced rates on weekdays and/or in the low season (usually November through February). Be sure to inquire about possible deals when you make reservations.

ahead and discuss your particular needs and the building's layout with the innkeeper. Some buildings have one or two rooms that have worked out well for guests in wheelchairs or those who have trouble negotiating flights of stairs.

Smoking is absolutely forbidden at all the bed-and-breakfasts listed here. If you're a smoker, you can usually light up outside in the garden or patio, but only if other nonsmoking guests aren't out there sharing your smoke. Some bed-and-breakfasts even enforce stiff fines on guests caught smoking in their rooms. So, however strong your urge to smoke, don't tempt fate by lighting up indoors.

Sorry, pets—Santa Barbara's gracious bed-and-breakfast hospitality doesn't extend to you. None of the inns we've listed here allow animals of any kind. Try the establishments listed in the Hotels and Motels and Vacation Rentals chapters.

Price Code

The pricing key indicates the average cost of double-occupancy accommodations on weekends during the high season (March through October) and does not include tax and fees for added services.

$	$135 to $170
$$	$171 to $210
$$$	$211 to $260
$$$$	$261 and more

SANTA BARBARA BEACH AREA

The Old Yacht Club Inn $–$$
431 Corona del Mar Drive, Santa Barbara
(805) 962-1277, (800) 549-1676 in California, (800) 676-1676 outside California
www.oldyachtclubinn.com
If you're longing for a convivial bed-and-breakfast experience, along with easy access to the beach, this friendly inn will fulfill your wishes. Built as a private family home on East

Beach in 1912, the Craftsman-style building served as the Santa Barbara Yacht Club's temporary headquarters for several years during the Roaring 20s after the first clubhouse washed out to sea in a freak storm.

In 1928 the building was moved just a block inland to its current location tucked behind two olive trees on a peaceful residential street. In 1980 four schoolteachers purchased and meticulously restored the home, then opened it as Santa Barbara's first bed-and-breakfast inn. Two of the teachers, Nancy Donaldson and Sandy Hunt, remained as the innkeepers/owners for years before selling the inn to a local couple, Eilene Bruce and Vince Pettit, in 2000. The new owners continue the inn's tradition of warm hospitality and fantastic food. Breakfasts alternate between mouthwatering egg dishes, such as egg soufflé, and bread dishes, such as cinnamon swirl French toast.

The inn offers 14 rooms, including three suites, in the cozy main building and the adjacent Spanish-style Hitchcock House, built in 1926. All rooms have telephones and private baths, and the rooms in the Hitchcock House are equipped with cable TV. Both houses are filled with classic European and Early American antiques, Oriental rugs, historic photos, and memorabilia.

One of the inn's largest rooms is the spacious Santa Rosa Suite. It has a separate sitting room, a king-size four-poster bed, and a large bath with whirlpool tub. Other popular rooms include the Captain's Corner, which features a private "aft" deck, and the Castellamare Room, with a balcony and whirlpool tub. The new three-bedroom Beach House Suite is perfect for families with its private entrance, porch, and large master bedroom with a king-size four-poster bed. Big sellers at The Old Yacht Club Inn include gourmet baskets filled with local wines, imported cheeses, and crackers ($60 to $100) and custom flower arrangements ($35 to $65).

Since it takes only a minute to saunter over to East Beach, you should definitely take advantage of the inn's beach towels and chairs (available free of charge) and relax by the sea. You can also hop on one of the inn's bicycles (also available free of charge) and tool around the waterfront. A two-night minimum stay is required on weekends if a Saturday is included. Special business and midweek rates are available from October to May. A three-night stay is necessary with weekend bookings in July and August.

Villa Rosa $$–$$$
15 Chapala Street, Santa Barbara
(805) 966-0851
www.villarosainnsb.com

Although this cozy residence looks and feels like a small hotel, it has many characteristics of a typical bed-and-breakfast: a historic structure (built in 1931 in Spanish Revival style), personalized service, a satisfying continental breakfast, and the *Los Angeles Times* delivered to your door every morning. But the best thing about Villa Rosa is its location: It's only 84 steps from West Beach and a hop, skip, and jump from the marina and Stearns Wharf.

The building was remodeled in the early 1980s as a Santa Fe–style bed-and-breakfast. You can choose from 18 rooms with ocean, harbor, garden, or mountain views (but only two have glimpses of the sea). Several deluxe rooms feature fireplaces and/or private gardens, and the upstairs corner rooms are among the brightest units thanks to their extra windows and elevated views. Though the rooms lack televisions, all have tiny private baths (some are especially cramped), telephones, clock radios, bathrobes, hair dryers, and sitting areas.

When you're not exploring the town or sailing the sparkling harbor, you can relax in the cozy lounge, take a dip in the small, solar-heated pool and Jacuzzi, or soak up some sun on the lovely outdoor garden patio. After a night on the town, you can look forward to sipping the complimentary port and sherry that are available in the lounge every evening. Nightly turndown is sweetened with Belgian chocolates. Children are welcome as long as they are at least 14 years old, because the

pool is unfenced. A conference room accommodates 20. The clientele is eclectic but typically includes young couples and groups of friends looking for a more affordable option to the pricier beachside hotels in this area.

SANTA BARBARA

The Cheshire Cat Inn and
Cottages $$–$$$
36 West Valerio Street, Santa Barbara
(805) 569-1610
www.cheshirecat.com

An extremely popular destination for honeymoons and romantic getaways, Cheshire Cat is set amid colorful English gardens in a quiet residential area just 1 block from State Street and a five-minute walk to restaurants, shops, and theaters. Owner Christine Dunstan, an experienced innkeeper from Cheshire, England, has done an incredible job of restoring and remodeling two neighboring Queen Anne Victorian homes (now more than 100 years old), a coachhouse, and three nearby cottages into a sophisticated, romantic retreat. She added modern conveniences and charming personal touches, such as English antiques and Laura Ashley wallpaper and draperies. As a special bonus, the inn offers an enticing array of facials, massages, and spa treatments to soothe the mind and pamper the body. Treatments can be administered in your own room or in the on-site spa rooms.

As you might guess, the inn's theme hails from the English classic *Alice's Adventures in Wonderland*. Most of the sparkling clean 17 rooms are named for characters in the book. For the ultimate romantic retreat, stay in Tweedledum, a luxurious two-room suite with a Jacuzzi, fireplace, sitting room with Oriental rugs, a king-size brass bed, and a wet bar/kitchen. If you don't need a kitchen, try the Queen of Hearts—an equally romantic but smaller room with a Jacuzzi.

Even if you don't have a Jacuzzi room, you can soak in the outdoor spa and enjoy the tranquil gardens. All rooms have private baths, robes, and direct-dial phones; some have TVs, DVD players, and beautiful potted orchids. Breakfast is served daily on Wedgwood china, either outside on the lovely brick patio or in the privacy of your room. On the weekends, you'll be treated to pecan cream cheese–stuffed French toast, poached pears or apples, or a Mexican casserole dish.

In 1997 the inn opened the Woodford, Prestbury, and Mobberly Cottages, named after three villages in Cheshire. Each has two bedrooms (one with a queen-size bed and one with a king-size), a private redwood deck, and a hot tub. Other features include a large living room with TV and VCR, a fireplace, a dining nook, a full bathroom, and a kitchen. The cottages may be rented by the day, week, or month. The Mobberly Cottage has a Spa Therapy Room for one or two people. Treatments are offered between 8:00 a.m. and 8:00 p.m. Monday through Friday or in your room on the weekends. Children are allowed only in the cottages, which can also be rented as one-bedroom suites; tots younger than five stay free. This meticulously maintained inn oozes personality and is a top choice for those who yearn for a historic bed-and-breakfast experience with a delightful English twist and a dash of whimsy.

Secret Garden Inn and Cottages $–$$
1908 Bath Street, Santa Barbara
(805) 687-2300
www.secretgarden.com

The lush gardens of this secluded enclave aren't really secret, but they certainly enhance its peaceful, romantic atmosphere. In 1999 French artist Dominique Hannaux purchased the inn and added her own sense of warm hospitality and European flair. Dominique is a delightful host and loves to cultivate artistic talent. Works by local artists adorn the inn's common rooms, and every few months, Dominique hosts art openings with performances by local musicians. Guests are invited to attend.

Set back off the street in a quiet residential area about 6 blocks from downtown, the Secret Garden includes 11 rooms and suites dispersed among a historic main house (ca. 1905) with 9 rooms in cottages, all with private entrances. Five rooms feature private outdoor hot tubs. Many of the baths have antique clawfoot tubs. Other amenities in certain rooms include fireplaces, private decks, refrigerators, beautiful hardwood floors, Oriental rugs, and European art. Televisions can be added on request. One of the most popular rooms is the bright and sunny Meadow Lark in the main house, which offers great value and comes with an antique queen bed, a beautiful bay window, and a private bath with tub and shower. The Oriole and Hummingbird cottages with hot tubs are also popular, and the Nightingale offers a fireplace. We loved The Garden with its striking French blue decor, honey-colored hardwood floors, skylit queen-size bed, and spacious bath done in white Italian tile.

Breakfast is a buffet of quiche, breads, scones, bagels, and croissants served in the kitchen. Those who prefer to dine in the privacy of their rooms can order room service in advance. Or, when the weather's fine, which is most of the time, you can savor your meal in the gardens, beneath the persimmon and avocado trees. Be prepared to commune with raccoons, possums, and birds.

The tranquility of this inn is hard to beat. None of the rooms have telephones, so you can easily escape the stress and strain of the workaday world. In the evening, you can help yourself to cookies, brownies, and hot cider. Children are welcome. Special midweek winter packages are available. This secluded inn appeals to couples, families, and artistic types who prefer chic European decor to fussy frills and ruffles.

i Celebrating a birthday or anniversary? With advance notice, most bed-and-breakfasts will offer fresh flowers, champagne, or a gift basket in your room. Ask when you book.

Simpson House Inn $$$$

121 East Arrellaga Street, Santa Barbara
(805) 963-7067, (800) 676-1280
www.simpsonhouseinn.com

Just do it; you deserve it. Book a room today. This world-class inn is not just the empress of Santa Barbara bed-and-breakfasts, it's North America's only Five Diamond bed-and-breakfast. When you stay here, you're guaranteed a fabulous, one-of-a-kind experience, well worth every dollar spent.

Scotsman Robert Simpson built this Eastlake Italianate Victorian with a wraparound porch in 1874. In the 1970s the dilapidated but still beautiful estate fell into the hands of several development companies. It faced near-certain demolition until Glyn and Linda Davies purchased it as a family residence for themselves and their two children.

Together, the family totally restored the home to its former elegance, scraping old paint, hunting down antique fixtures, and adding a foundation. They transformed the overgrown grounds into an acre of blissful, immaculate gardens with historic trees and native California plants arranged in a formal English-style setting.

The Davies' painstaking restoration efforts resulted in the City of Santa Barbara declaring the Simpson House and its gardens a Historic Landmark in 1992. It is considered one of the most distinguished homes of its era in Southern California.

When the kids went off to college, the senior Davies decided to convert their historic home into a bed-and-breakfast inn. Located just a few blocks from State Street and the Arlington Center for the Performing Arts, Simpson House Inn's 15 rooms, suites, and cottages are interspersed among several buildings. The original house contains six guest rooms, a formal dining room, and a living room with a fireplace.

The restored 1878 barn features four rooms, each with a king-size bed, sitting area, fireplace, TV and DVD players, stereo, and wet bar. Stroll through the oak tree–dappled garden to The Garden Room, where large French doors open up to a king bed and bath. The three private garden cottages have Jacuzzis, fireplaces, and antique queen-size canopied feather beds. All rooms and suites have private baths, telephones, and CD players. TVs and DVD players are in the rooms or available on request, and guests can enjoy movies from the extensive video library, as well as popcorn made on request.

Sprawling gardens surround all the buildings. You can read, relax, and stroll among mature oaks, magnolias, exotic plants, and manicured lawns, serenaded by the soothing sound of flowing water from seven strategically placed fountains. Sandstone walls and tall hedges promote a sense of privacy and conceal the street from the oasis within.

The full gourmet vegetarian breakfast at the Simpson House is a real treat, with organic California juices, fruits, and house specialties. You can choose to eat in your room or on the veranda or garden patios. In the afternoon you can feast on a lavish Mediterranean hors d'oeuvres buffet featuring local wines.

Why not go for the ultimate indulgences at this luxurious retreat? Pamper your body and soothe your soul by arranging for the inn's European spa services in the privacy of your room. Choose from various types of massages and facials. You can also arrange for a guest pass to a nearby fitness facility.

Since the Simpson House is such a highly rated establishment, you might expect snootiness and snobbery to prevail among the staff and clientele. Not here—the casual atmosphere (jeans and shorts are just fine) and the super-friendly staff will make you feel at ease as soon as you arrive. Children are welcome in certain rooms.

> **i** If you want to avoid crowds, plan your trip to Santa Barbara during the winter months. The weather's still mild, fewer people are on the beach, and the clear winter skies provide fantastic views of the mountains and Channel Islands.

Tiffany Country House $$–$$$

1323 De la Vina Street, Santa Barbara
(805) 963-2283, (800) 999-5672
www.tiffanycountryhouse.com

Honeymoon, wedding, getaway, business—whatever your reason for coming to Santa Barbara, you'll find an intimate getaway at the 100-plus-year-old Tiffany Country House. In late 1999 Vintage Hotels, owners of the Upham (see the Hotels and Motels chapter), purchased this grand Victorian, stripped some of the frills and ruffles, and exposed more of the inn's dark woods, adding to its feel of formal elegance. Perhaps the best feature of this inn is its convenient location just 3 blocks from State Street and the heart of downtown, an easy walk to restaurants, shops, and museums.

The Tiffany's seven rooms all have telephones, TVs, DVD player, and private baths, and all but two come with Jacuzzi tubs. The award for most spacious and comfortable quarters goes to the Penthouse Suite. It occupies the entire third floor and offers a sprawling bedroom with a fireplace, a private terrace, spectacular city, mountain, and ocean views, a refrigerator, a double Jacuzzi tub, and a sitting area and writing nook.

Just got hitched or want to celebrate a special anniversary? Go for the romantic Windsor Suite, which is also warmed by a wood-burning fireplace. The staff delivers a full gourmet breakfast directly to both suites every morning.

If you're staying in one of the less expensive rooms, you'll find your equally delicious breakfast of homemade granola, crepes, quiches, or waffles waiting in the dining room downstairs or out on the deck. Be sure to try some of the freshly baked cookies the cook sets out every evening and to stroll in the beautiful rose garden.

SUMMERLAND

Inn on Summer Hill $$$

2520 Lillie Avenue, Summerland
(805) 969-9998, (800) 845-5566
www.innonsummerhill.com

Built in 1989 in California Craftsman style, the elegant Inn on Summer Hill rests on a hillside just off the freeway near the shores of Summerland. The out-of-town, seaview location makes it a great choice for a small-town romantic retreat. You can easily walk or bike to Summerland beach, while village shops, antiques stores, and restaurants are a short stroll down the road. When you feel like exploring farther afield, hop in your car (the inn has plenty of on-site parking) and drive just 5 to 10 minutes to Montecito and downtown Santa Barbara.

What this inn lacks in history, it makes up for in creature comforts and delicious gourmet cuisine. The inn's skillfully decorated rooms evoke an English country feel, with their king- or queen-size canopy beds, billowy down comforters, country pine antiques, and custom floral fabrics. Choose from upstairs balcony rooms with vaulted pine ceilings or downstairs patio rooms. All have double-paned windows and double-insulated walls to block out noise from the outside world. The rooms are similar in layout and appointments, but each has a unique color scheme. All 15 mini-suites include imported furniture, sitting areas, TV/DVD players, stereo cassette players, hair dryers, tea- and coffeemaking facilities, mini-fridges, phones, fireplaces, and whirlpool tubs. Whichever room you choose, you can take in glorious sunset views across the ocean from your private balcony or patio.

If money's no object, you can't go wrong staying in the Deluxe Suite, the inn's most spacious quarters. It features three ocean-view balconies, two fireplaces, a living room with hardwood floors and a wet bar, a bedroom with a king-size canopy bed, and his-and-her bathrooms with a whirlpool tub in between. Rates for other rooms vary according to location (patio or balcony) and bed size.

Wander out back and you'll find colorful gardens, English country benches, birdhouses, and a pergola with a spa—a great place to soak under the stars. Guests rave about the inn's gourmet food. The sumptuous breakfast, served in the downstairs dining room amid a collection of antique teapots, features such treats as Italian eggs Benedict, frittata, and omelets. Feel like lounging around? For an additional fee, you can order breakfast in bed. In addition to the delicious breakfasts, you can feast on hors d'oeuvres from 3:00 to 5:00 p.m. and end your evening with a complimentary dessert from 8:00 to 9:00 p.m.

The Inn on Summer Hill offers various special packages, some seasonal and a few throughout the year. Check out the Romantic Getaway package with massages for two and breakfast in bed. This inn appeals to anyone seeking the traditional flourishes of the bed-and-breakfast experience with a fresh country feel, outstanding cuisine, and sparkling sea views.

CARPINTERIA

Prufrock's Garden Inn $$$
600 Linden Avenue, Carpinteria
(805) 566-9696
www.prufrocks.com
Owners/innkeepers Jim and Judy Halvorsen converted a 1904 historic family home into this cute little inn, which provides a homey bed-and-breakfast experience in a small-town atmosphere. Prufrock's sits right on one of Carpinteria's main arteries from downtown to the beach, but it's in a quiet section. You can park your car at the side and walk nearly everywhere: to restaurants, a great playground, the "world's safest beach," and the Carpinteria pool. The Amtrak station is a few blocks away, and Santa Barbara proper lies just 12 miles (19 kilometers) north on the freeway.

The entire inn exudes an early California seaside ambience, with hardwood floors, antiques, and soft color schemes. Feast on a full breakfast either in your room, in the lovely garden, or at the family-style dining table. Evenings, you can help yourself to the cookies, cake, fruit, crackers, cheese, iced tea, and lemonade that are left out for guests.

The cozy guest rooms are either in the house or in a jasmine-draped cottage out the back, renovated by the owners in 1998. They range dramatically in size and price, so be sure to specify your needs when you book.

In the main house, the largest room, Garden Hideaway, has French doors that open to a private porch overlooking the colorful garden. Village Charm features a clawfoot tub and a private entry. Cottage Trellis offers a private view of the gardens. All three rooms have private baths, while the more affordable upstairs Ocean Breeze and Mountain View rooms share a full bath. The overpriced cottage rooms are a little more secluded, but they lack air-conditioning and tend to be quite stuffy when it's hot. They have private entrances, Jacuzzi tubs, and concrete patios with porch swings and fireplaces. The Afternoon Delight Suite here is a good choice for families. Fling open the windows and the jasmine-scented breeze wafts through to cool the interior. It's fine to bring children to Prufrock's—three rooms have daybeds. Call to find out about special weekday rates and birthday and anniversary packages. This hospitable little inn is a home-away-from-home for all who stay here.

VACATION RENTALS

To find a vacation home for rent in Santa Barbara, you have to know who to ask, and you have to think ahead—and we mean way ahead. The high price of real estate discourages ownership of investment property, so the demand for seasonal rentals far outpaces supply in this fair city-by-the-beach. If you're planning a summer vacation, you need to start looking (and in some cases, making reservations) at least six months ahead. We've listed here some of the available options, which include rental units in complexes and on hotel grounds and, for those willing to forgo staying in Santa Barbara proper, accommodations in seaside Carpinteria. Few local hotels offer "vacation rentals" as such, but they may offer weekly or monthly rates that represent a savings over the regular room rate, so ask when making reservations.

A few cautions: Always ask exactly what is included in the cost of your rental. Some places charge for the use of towels and other necessities, which will run your bill higher than just the cost of the lodging. Also ask what you're required to bring. When linens are not supplied (at a cost or otherwise), you may have to lug along towels, sheets, and other personal items. Find out what's in the kitchen, whether a VCR is included, and what the parking situation is. Figure security deposits (usually refundable if you leave the rental in the same condition that you found it in) and occupancy taxes into your total cost, and be sure to ask for an immediate confirmation of your reservation after you've paid.

Finally, be aware that there are no truly "beachfront" homes in the city proper. Some may overlook a beach from a bluff or cliff, but you may have to drive 10 or 15 minutes to dig your toes in the sand.

A final thought: Yes, vacation rentals are expensive in Santa Barbara, but think of all that money you'll save by not having to eat out all the time.

RENTAL AGENCIES

In addition to the companies listed below, which specialize in vacation rentals, several other real estate agencies in town handle vacation rentals as part of their services. Check the Relocation chapter for a listing of local real estate firms and inquire about vacation rental opportunities.

Coastal Properties
1086 Coast Village Road, Montecito
(805) 969-1258

5030 Carpinteria Avenue, Carpinteria
(805) 684-8777
www.coastalrealty.com
Coastal Properties is the only vacation rental company in Santa Barbara that is a member of the National Vacation Rental Managers Association—and it has the largest inventory of vacation rentals in the area. It handles upscale owner-occupied Santa Barbara properties that rent for between $750 and $7,500 a week while the owner is absent. Homes come with absolutely everything (including linens), and Coastal Properties can arrange extras, such as maid service and chefs. The vast majority of the homes are nonsmoking, many do not allow pets, and all rentals require a cash payment 60 days in advance of occupancy (no credit cards are accepted except to hold a

i A 12 percent tax on short-term accommodations is automatic everywhere in the city of Santa Barbara (10 percent in Carpinteria), so be sure to figure in the extra amount when assessing your rental costs.

rental temporarily). Rental periods vary from a required three-day minimum (a week on beach properties) to leases of several years, and renters often love the area so much that they end up buying a home. Most of Coastal's summer rental properties are booked three to six months in advance. Winter rental of beach properties can cost as much as 33 percent less than summer rentals.

RENTAL COMPLEXES

Solimar Sands
4700 Sandyland Road, Carpinteria
(805) 684-5613, (800) 684-5613
www.solimarsands.com

Located 1/2 block from the beach in Carpinteria, Solimar Sands includes 30 one-, two-, and three-bedroom, two-bath condos available for weekly (in summer) and monthly rental. The condos include everything you need except sheets and towels, which you are expected to bring. There are no phones in some of the units, but pay phones are available on the grounds. The high season is July and August. High-season prices range from $1,485 weekly for a one-bedroom condo to $2,585 for a three-bedroom, two-bath unit plus 10 percent tax; winter rates range from $913 weekly to $1,694, respectively. Weekly rates do not include utilities. Monthly rates do not include electricity. You'll need to pay a 50 percent deposit to hold the reservation, and the balance is due 30 days prior to arrival. No credit cards are accepted, and minimum rental is seven days.

Sunset Shores
4980 Sandyland Road, Carpinteria
(805) 684-3682, (800) 343-1544
www.carpinteriasunsetshores.com

Sunset Shores is a two-story apartment complex across the street from the "world's safest beach" in Carpinteria, with an on-site heated pool and hot tub. The units include studios and one- and two-bedroom apartments that range in cost from $700 a week for a small studio in winter to $1,900 a week for a two-bedroom in summer. Furnishings and utilities are included, but you must bring your own towels and sheets. A security deposit of $500 is required, and cleaning fees are assessed at $105 per unit. The reservation fee is $35.

Villa Elegante
402 Orilla del Mar, Santa Barbara
(805) 565-4459
www.villaelegante.com

Built in 1997 a block from East Beach in Santa Barbara, family-run Villa Elegante comprises six Mediterranean-style units with spacious two- and three-bedroom suites in duplexes. All the units are nonsmoking and are rented by the week or month. Everything is provided, including linens, and each suite has air-conditioning, a gourmet kitchen, TV, VCR, DVD, stereo, washer and dryer, wood-burning fireplace, high-speed Internet access, and individual parking garage. Upstairs units have balconies and ocean views. Book way ahead, as these units go quickly. Rentals are Saturday to Saturday (some exceptions may apply). Villa Elegante accepts pets in one of the units.

RENTALS AT HOTELS AND INNS

A few hotels and bed-and-breakfast inns rent cottages or villas by the day, week, or month. All of the accommodations listed in this section are included in the Bed-and-Breakfast Inns and Hotels and Motels chapters, where you'll find more information.

Cabrillo Inn at the Beach
931 East Cabrillo Boulevard, Santa Barbara
(805) 966-1641, (800) 648-6708
www.cabrillo-inn.com

Behind the inn, which is across the street

i Looking for a low-cost solution for a vacation rental? Google Craig's List Santa Barbara. Locals list their rentals on this free site. There is also a "House Swap" section for a truly affordable vacation.

from the beach, a Spanish-style complex houses two units available as vacation rentals. Each unit is a 1,600-square-foot, two-bedroom, two-bath upstairs-downstairs duplex that accommodates up to five people. Gas fireplaces and built-in bookcases lend a homey feel, and sunlight streams in through the French casement windows. Each unit has a private phone line with an answering machine, a TV/VCR, and daily maid service. The units also feature a laundry plus full kitchen with a dishwasher and microwave, and you have access to the pool and other amenities available at the inn. Weekly rates range from $2,450 to $3,465, depending on the season. The units are generally booked several months ahead. If you want to stay for longer than a few weeks, ask about the monthly rates.

The Cheshire Cat Inn
36 West Valerio Street, Santa Barbara
(805) 569-1610
www.cheshirecat.com

You'll vacation in style at this charming bed-and-breakfast inn, which has three cottages for rent by the week or month. Two two-bedroom cottages are individually decorated, and each has a private front entrance, a living room with a TV and VCR, private phone lines, gas fireplaces, a dining nook, and a fully stocked kitchen. All have private decks with hot tubs. No more than four people can stay in any cottage at once, but children are welcome. Weekly rates range from $2,000 for a one-bedroom cottage in low season (October through May) to $2,300 a week for a two-bedroom cottage in high season. Call for monthly rates. No pets are allowed.

Hotel Mar Monte
1111 East Cabrillo Boulevard, Santa Barbara
(805) 963-0744, (800) 643-1994
www.hotelmarmonte.com

In addition to its regular guest rooms, the Hotel Mar Monte has five fully furnished apartments that can be rented for a minimum 30-day stay. Four of the units have one bedroom with a king-size bed in addition to a living room area and kitchen. The fifth is a two-bedroom, 1,600-square-foot apartment on the third floor with ocean views and a balcony. Maid service is provided twice a week, and all of the Hotel Mar Monte's amenities (including room service) are available to apartment guests. The apartments rent for between $2,600 and $4,000 a month, and reservations can be made no more than a year ahead. Sometimes units are available on the spur of the moment, but they are often booked far ahead for the summer months and Christmas holidays. Because of the 30-day minimum stay, the local 12 percent bed tax does not apply.

San Ysidro Ranch
900 San Ysidro Lane, Montecito
(805) 969-5046, (800) 368-6788 (from outside 805 area code only)
www.sanysidroranch.com

One of the most exclusive resorts in the Santa Barbara area, San Ysidro Ranch offers a secluded hideaway in several bungalow-style cottages sprinkled amid the oaks and orange blossoms. The largest cottage is the Warner Cottage, a two-bedroom house with three wood-burning fireplaces, two and a half bathrooms, and its own private heated swimming pool. Each cottage has a private patio, hot tub, and wet bar, but no kitchen. Eat at the ranch's posh restaurant, or order room service. You may also use the pool and tennis courts or arrange horseback riding. A flat nightly rate runs from $795 to $3,990, depending on the cottage you choose.

RESTAURANTS

Few cities in the country boast as many restaurants per capita as Santa Barbara. There are more than 500 in the greater Santa Barbara area, and during the busy summer months and holiday seasons, nearly all are filled to capacity with diners from around the world. Our restaurants represent all colors of the culinary spectrum. The mind-boggling array of international cuisine means you can always find the type of meal you're looking for, whether you're hankering for tacos or tournedos.

In recent years Santa Barbara has become a magnet for the haute gourmet, attracting some of the nation's best chefs as well as discerning diners craving the types of meals they read about in *Bon Appetit* and *Gourmet* magazines.

The burgeoning local wine industry has contributed to this restaurant renaissance, and many dining establishments offer pairings of acclaimed local wines with seasonal meals. (For more information on local wines, read the Santa Barbara Wine Country chapter.)

Don't worry if you're not an epicurean—you'll find plenty of restaurants to please your palate as well as your pocketbook. Wholesome fare reigns supreme in health-conscious Santa Barbara, and most menus include vegetarian and low-fat entrees. California cuisine—which features artistic presentations of seafood, grilled meats, seasonal vegetables, and salads made with fresh, locally grown produce—dominates the current restaurant scene. Here in Santa Barbara, chefs create their own versions of California cuisine, often adding local avocados, citrus fruits, and salsas to their concoctions.

Pacific Rim seafood, spices, and sauces are currently in vogue. Ahi tuna, for example, appears in creative variations on many local menus. You can order it as sashimi or a sushi roll, seared, pan-broiled, grilled, or coated with peppercorns or sesame seeds. If your palate seeks adventure, you can take a culinary safari to our many international restaurants, from Mexican and Moroccan to South American and Thai. Restaurants serving traditional American fare—burgers, french fries, pizza, steak, and potatoes—will never go out of style here. Several local restaurants have been serving the same hearty American meals for more than 50 years.

According to our visiting friends and relatives, we locals are spoiled by all these choices, not to mention the convenience. It takes less than 15 minutes to drive to most restaurants—and the hard part is choosing where to eat.

Sometimes we just park in a city lot and walk up and down State Street, Cabrillo Boulevard, or Coast Village Road in Montecito, savoring the aromas of steamed shellfish, grilled seafood, and bubbling stews. Then we let our appetites determine which restaurant we'll enter.

So where will you dine this evening? To help you narrow down your choices, we've compiled an extensive list of our favorite restaurants, organized by the type of food they serve: Asian Fusion, Cajun, California/American, Chinese, French, health food, Indian, Italian, Japanese, Mexican, Moroccan, South American, and Thai.

In this chapter we focus on the dining experience. Several restaurants offer music, dancing, and/or other entertainment in addition to meals, and we've highlighted these in the Nightlife chapter. You can also find more information on hotel restaurants in the Hotels and Motels chapter. Nearly all the restaurants listed here accept reservations as well as credit cards. If not, we've noted it in the description. We recommend that you always call ahead to reserve a table on weekends and holidays and at any time during the busy summer months. The most popular restaurants fill up quickly, and if you don't have a reservation, you might have to wait for an hour or two before you're seated.

Many restaurants have heated outdoor courtyards and patios, so you can dine alfresco, even in the evening and during the winter months. Which brings up two other important issues. The first is smoking. California law prohibits smoking in any restaurant or bar. If you want to light up, you'll have to do so outdoors. Some restaurants have cigar terraces reserved for smokers. We've mentioned these in the individual write-ups.

The second issue is pets. Legally, animals are not allowed in dining areas—inside or out. But if your pooch is leashed and isn't bothering other customers, you may be able to park him near a restaurant patio. To help you out, we've mentioned in the individual write-up if the restaurant offers an alfresco eating area. At least that way, you can sit where you can see your little buddy.

Children's menus are available at many restaurants, and unless we've mentioned otherwise, the eateries listed here are wheelchair accessible. Casual dress is fine at most, and we know only a few that require a coat and tie. If you're going to an expensive restaurant for dinner, however, you probably want to change from your shorts, T-shirts, and flip-flops into somewhat dressier attire. So rev up the car and get started on your savory Santa Barbara safari. And be sure to let us know if you run into any fantastic restaurants we haven't mentioned. Bon appétit!

Price Code

The price key symbol in each restaurant listing represents the average cost for a dinner for two, excluding appetizers, dessert, cocktails, beer or wine, tax, and tip. Keep in mind that many restaurants offer a range of entrees at varying prices. You could, for example, order a $10 pasta dish instead of the $25 lobster. These symbols provide only a general guide so you'll know whether a restaurant is basically inexpensive, upscale, or something in between.

$	Less than $20
$$	$20 to $40
$$$	$41 to $60
$$$$	$61 and more

ASIAN FUSION

Elements   **$$**
129 East Anapamu Street, Santa Barbara
(805) 884-9218
www.elementsrestaurantandbar.com
For lunch, it's the suits that hang out at Elements. Attorneys and CPAs hoof it over from the courthouse or one of the other downtown professional buildings to have a working lunch. This uniquely designed restaurant highlights the elements of nature—air, fire, earth, and water—and exudes a fusion elegance that parallels its mouthwatering cuisine. Try the cinnamon-spiced duck confit risotto or the sesame-encrusted ahi tuna steak. Elements serves up an award-winning list of fine wines and signature martinis that are eagerly sipped by the late-night younger set around the not-big-enough bar. Lunch is served Monday to Saturday, dinner is served every night. Brunch happens every Sunday from 9:00 a.m. to 2:00 p.m. Always packed, reservations are highly recommended.

CAJUN

The Palace Grill   **$$–$$$**
8 East Cota Street, Santa Barbara
(805) 963-5000
www.palacegrill.com
The good times roll in a big way every evening of the week at the Palace, which is consistently named one of the best Cajun restaurants in California. It's been written up in *Gourmet, Bon*

i Don't feel like going out but you're still yearning for tantalizing food? Call Restaurant Connection, Santa Barbara's "Original Restaurant Delivery Service," which picks up at over 35 restaurants and delivers meals right to your door. Call (805) 687-9753, or visit them online at www.restaurant connectionsb.com. Or try the newer Dining Car (805-965-9669; www .dining-car.com).

Appetit, Los Angeles magazine, and many other publications.

The colorful, lively Bourbon Street atmosphere provides a perfect complement to the spicy food. When Ronald Reagan was president and visited his nearby ranch, the Secret Service and press corps reportedly ate regularly at the Palace. We've also heard of people driving for five hours just to eat here. The Palace actually offers a mix of New Orleans, Creole, and pasta dishes, plus steak, fish, and chicken dishes for those who prefer more subtle, less spicy seasonings. All meals are served by a waitstaff that works as a well-oiled team. Fresh seafood, typically redfish, crawfish, and prawns, is flown in direct from New Orleans.

Jazzing up the mouthwatering menu are Cajun crawfish popcorn (one of our favorites), blackened redfish or ahi tuna, Louisiana softshell crabs, gumbos, crawfish crab cakes, and oysters Rockefeller.

Quench your thirst with a pepper martini, or just head for the self-service wine bar. For dessert, save room for the sinful bread pudding soufflé (which you need to order before dinner because it takes a while to prepare) or the Key lime pie made with real Florida Key limes.

The Palace Grill is open for lunch and dinner seven days a week. Dinner reservations are accepted for Sunday through Thursday, but on Friday and Saturday nights they're taken for the first seating only (5:30 p.m.)—after that, it's first come, first served. Without reservations, plan on a wait of an hour or longer during prime dinner hours. The time usually passes quickly, though, while you're chatting with the interesting people in line, watching the magician who entertains on busy nights, and listening to the jazz musicians who often play here.

If you don't want to search for a parking place, take advantage of the Palace's valet parking. Just pull up to the front door (between State and Anacapa Streets) and ask for the service.

CALIFORNIA/AMERICAN

Arts & Letters Cafe $$
7 East Anapamu Street, Santa Barbara
(805) 730-1463
www.sullivangoss.com
Hidden in a walled garden courtyard behind Sullivan Goss Books and Prints (see the Shopping chapter), this evocative Mediterranean-style cafe is a delightful spot for lunch. Sip a glass of wine by the bubbling fountain, and you'll feel as though you're in a romantic European gem. In the summer on Thursday evenings, you can buy tickets for the popular Opera under the Stars prix fixe three-course dinner for $55 and enjoy live classical and Broadway musical performances while you dine in the candlelit courtyard. At other times of the year, the restaurant is only open for lunch and special events.

The menu varies with the seasons and draws from the fresh local bounty. Lunch dishes include delicious hot soups, gourmet salads, such as Riviera seafood, roast chicken, and smoked turkey; panini sandwiches; and a range of entrees, including risotto, roast chicken, and grilled salmon. The cafe has a full bar and is open for lunch seven days a week.

Beach Grill at Padaro/Pizza Mizza $
3765 Santa Claus Lane, Carpinteria
(805) 566-3900
www.beachgrillpadaro.com
Packed with beachgoers in the summer, family-friendly Beach Grill at Padaro/Pizza Mizza,

is ideal for an alfresco meal before or after a day in the sun. The toy-stuffed sandbox and fenced lawn make this a paradise for parents with young kids in tow (see the write-up in the Kidstuff chapter), and the seaside outdoor setting, set off from Santa Claus Lane Beach by a fence, is a hit with everyone. Line up inside to order classic surfside cuisine—burgers, sandwiches, salads, pasta, fish tacos, filet mignon kebabs, and gourmet pizzas are just some of the offerings. Place your order, then pick an Adirondack chair or a picnic table on the lawn and relax with a glass of beer or wine while you wait for your meal. (The kitchen will buzz you on your personal pager when it's ready). Beach Grill at Padaro/Pizza Mizza is open for lunch and dinner daily in the summer. In winter the restaurant serves lunch daily. A special brunch menu is also available on weekends. Live concerts and an outdoor wood-burning pizza oven are in the works for the future—call for details. Tip: Leashed pets are welcome on the street side of the lawn.

Beachside Bar-Cafe $$
5905 Sandspit Road (in Goleta Beach Park), Goleta
(805) 964-7881
This is one of our personal favorites and one of only a few area restaurants that is right on the beach. As you might expect, it draws a large crowd of locals and visitors looking for great seafood with a view. The Beachside boasts a fresh seafood bar with specialties such as bluepoint oysters, ceviche, and steamed mussels and clams. The seafood is wonderful, and you'll find a good selection of pastas and salads as well as chicken and beef dishes.

In the main dining room, large windows look out onto the beach (illuminated at night by floodlights), or you can opt for a table on the spacious patio, where you can smell the sea breeze and soak up the sun (there are umbrellas for shade, heaters for cold days, and a large fireplace that adds a cozy touch).

The restaurant has a lively bar scene (plus beer on tap and a good wine list), which means it can be pretty noisy inside, but everyone's having a good time and loving the food. Live jazz spices up the weekends. The Beachside is open daily for lunch and dinner. On weekends you might wait up to an hour for a table unless you have reservations.

Bella Vista $$$$
1260 Channel Drive, Montecito
(805) 969-2261
www.fourseasons.com/santabarbara
Bella Vista is the formal dining room at the Four Seasons Resort The Biltmore Santa Barbara. It's definitely a special-occasion place where you can spend a small fortune on food and wine, be treated like royalty, and go home feeling that you got your money's worth. The newly renovated space, combined with the California regional cuisine of executive chef Martin Frost, is guaranteed to please. Frost, a veteran of several Four Seasons properties, has a special flair for interesting creations, including maple roast breast of duck, homemade red wine pappardelle, and peppered seared rare ahi tuna.

Bella Vista is open for breakfast, lunch, and dinner daily. Dress up for the occasion (sports coats are recommended for men), and let the valet park your car.

> **i** Santa Barbara's laid-back style means you can dress casually in almost every restaurant in town (but shirts and shoes are always minimum requirements).

Blue Agave $$
20 East Cota Street, Santa Barbara
(805) 899-4694
www.blueagavesb.com
This trendy, two-story restaurant and bar opened in 1995 and quickly became a popular hangout for young professionals, Hollywood celebrities, and chic singles and couples. Blue Agave's popularity has a lot to do with its winning combination of contemporary decor, soft

romantic lighting and seating, creative cuisine, a full bar stocked with dozens of different tequilas, and lively crowds.

The menu is eclectic, including satay kai, tortilla soup, beer-battered goat cheese, steak au poivre, chicken mole, and the can't-get-enough-of Cowboy Plate. Upstairs, you can order a martini, lounge on couches around the fireplace, or head out to the cigar balcony overlooking Cota Street. For parties of four, we think the best dining nooks are the cozy and very private booths on this upper level. Blue Agave is open for dinner daily. Only parties of six or more can make reservations. If your party has fewer than six people, you'll be seated on a first come, first served basis. It's best to show up before 8:00 p.m. if you don't want to wait for a table.

Bouchon $$$
9 West Victoria Street, Santa Barbara
(805) 730-1160
www.bouchon.net

If you can't make it to the wine country for a meal, come to Bouchon instead. The name is French for "wine cork," and owner Mitchell Sjerven opened this very civilized eatery in the summer of 1998 with a desire to conjure a wine-country dining experience in the heart of downtown Santa Barbara. He must be doing something right. Since its launch, Bouchon has earned a place at the table with Santa Barbara's restaurant elite, receiving enthusiastic reviews from *Wine Spectator* and the local press. From the cozy exhibition kitchen, the experienced chef concocts an imaginative menu of regional wine-country cuisine using fresh local produce. Depending on the season, you can feast on such specialties as lime-seared sea scallops, Santa Barbara spiny lobster pie, braised Kurobata pork shank, and the popular bourbon-and-maple glazed duck breast with fava bean, butternut squash, and applewood-smoked bacon succotash. And if that's not enough of a mouthful, Bouchon's wine list will dazzle your palate. Oenophiles can choose from an impressive lineup of more than 50 Central Coast wines by the glass, as

well as bottles from Northern California, the Pacific Northwest, and France. You can sit in the bright and airy dining room or dine alfresco on the covered garden patio fronting Victoria Street. Planning a special party? Reserve the private Cork Room, lined with—you guessed it—cork, and the chef will design a special menu just for you and your guests. Of course, all this doesn't come cheap, but this is a special spot for special occasions. It's open for dinner seven nights a week. Tip: If you want tap water to accompany your meal, make sure you specify, or you may be charged for expensive imported water.

Brophy Bros. $$
On the breakwater at the harbor, Santa Barbara
(805) 966-4418
www.brophybros.com

So who wants to climb a flight of stairs, wedge into a tiny, crowded, and noisy restaurant, and spend the next hour trying to hear yourself talk? Seafood lovers, that's who. Brophy Bros. has been around since 1987 and is well loved by locals for its salty, down-to-earth ambience, fresh, simply served seafood, and spectacular harbor views. It also has the best clam chowder in town. Order up a shrimp cocktail and gaze out the open windows toward Stearns Wharf, or take in some of the local fishing and wharf memorabilia lining the walls.

You'll find a large selection of fresh seasonal fish on the menu, including mahimahi, salmon, and albacore. It's served with mountains of coleslaw and fries and your choice of salad or clam chowder. The clam bar is a favorite hangout, but you can also ask for a table on the small balcony, which is the perfect vantage point for watching the comings and goings in the harbor. If you can't climb the stairs to the main dining room, you can eat at the even smaller, downstairs version (same food) Thursday through Sunday.

Brophy Bros. is a natural magnet for tourists, so you may find it crowded on weekends and during the summer. If you don't want to wait too long for a table, we suggest you turn up early. The restaurant doesn't take reservations, but it will equip you with a pager, so you can stroll around the harbor while you wait. It's open for lunch and dinner seven days a week.

Chad's $$$
625 Chapala Street, Santa Barbara
(805) 568-1876
www.chadsrestaurant.com

If you're looking for a special-occasion meal in a festive (but not raucous) atmosphere, Chad's will more than fit the bill. When you enter the restaurant, you feel as if you're entering someone's home. That's because it's in a renovated Victorian house built in 1876, with rambling porches, a living room with a full bar (that's packed for happy hour) and fireplace, and several dining rooms—some quieter and more romantic than others. Most people dress up a bit to come to Chad's, but the atmosphere is far from stuffy.

Chad's menu features regional American dishes, such as Downtown meat loaf, oysters Rockefeller, blackened or broiled seafood, Montana pork chops, and chicken Brie pasta. Accompanying most dishes are Chad's famous garlic mashed potatoes. Save room for the chocolate Jack Daniel's soufflé. Chad's is open for dinner daily except Sunday. If you're planning to eat at a traditional dinner hour on a weekend, you should make your reservations as early as possible. Chad's is sometimes fully booked several weeks in advance.

Chuck's Waterfront Grill $$$
113 Harbor Way, Santa Barbara
(805) 564-1200
www.waterfrontgrill.net

Craving some fresh-from-the-boat seafood and some dreamy harbor views? Chuck's Waterfront Grill, the fancier downstairs sibling to Endless Summer Bar-Café (see separate entry), is a great choice. You can relax on the raised outdoor terrace, while gazing at the boats bobbing on the harbor, or dine inside and drink in the views. This is a popular spot with tourists, who pop in here for dinner after a stroll along the waterfront. The fish is so fresh it almost flops off your plate. Menu highlights are the marinated grilled New England mussells, prawn cocktail, Waterfront clam chowder, and grilled sea scallops. For those not in a seafood mood, the menu offers thick hand-cut steaks and hearty pasta dishes. Chuck's Waterfront Grill has a full bar, so you can order up a fruity cocktail, sit back, and enjoy the sunset while you wait for your meal. The restaurant serves up lunch and dinner daily and offers Sunset Dinner Specials from 5:00 to 6:30 p.m. Valet parking is available in the lot out back.

Crocodile Restaurant & Bar $$
2819 State Street, Santa Barbara
(805) 687-6444
www.treeinns.com

Upper State Street's Lemon Tree Inn has a great little bistro in the Crocodile Restaurant & Bar. The American fare ranges from club sandwiches to vegetarian dishes and pasta, but seafood and charbroiled steaks are the specialties. You'll also find sophisticated dishes such as rosemary chicken in a lemon cream sauce and filet mignon with portobello mushroom wine sauce, as well as a special menu for the kids. All the breads, pastries, and desserts are baked fresh on the premises. Sit inside or opt for the tropical outdoor patio. The Crocodile is open for breakfast, lunch, and dinner daily. Pop in for the lively happy hour from 4:00 to 6:00 p.m. daily.

Downey's $$$
1305 State Street, Santa Barbara
(805) 966-5006
www.downeyssb.com

Downey's is proof that good things come in small packages. Only 15 tables are tucked into this little dining room, but chef John Downey consistently serves up some of the finest cuisine in the city (just look at all the awards amassed on the wall, and *Zagat's* rates it tops for food in Santa Barbara).

The menu changes often, incorporating the freshest local and seasonal ingredients. Such specialties as Santa Barbara mussels with sweet corn and chile vinaigrette and homemade duck sausage with lentils are favorites. A few heart-smart options are sprinkled throughout the menu as well.

In addition to the fabulous food, Downey's offers a superb wine list, spotlighting local wines, and attentive service. Reserve ahead or you may be disappointed. Downey's serves dinner only Tuesday through Sunday.

Eladio's Restaurant & Bar $$$
1 State Street, Santa Barbara
(805) 963-4466
www.harborviewinnsb.com

In a prime location directly across Cabrillo Boulevard from Stearns Wharf in the heart of the tourist district, Eladio's is under the same ownership as the adjacent Harbor View Inn and draws many guests from that hotel and others nearby. Now exuding a more formal ambience and wearing a bold sea-themed decor with a dramatic frescoed ceiling, the restaurant serves up seasonal menus of high-quality California cuisine prepared with fresh local produce. Sink into the well-cushioned banquettes and enjoy sweeping views of Stearns Wharf, the beachfront bike path, and the mountains while you dine. On warm days, you can also dine alfresco by a fountain in the courtyard. The lunch menu offers elaborate seafood, chicken, and beef dishes as well as gourmet salads and sandwiches. Dinners and desserts are just as delicious, and the menu offers a good selection of wines, ports, and single malt whiskeys. Eladio's has a full bar and is open for breakfast and dinner daily and lunch Monday to Saturday.

El Encanto $$$
1900 Lasuen Road, Santa Barbara
(805) 687-5000
www.elencantohotel.com

El Encanto is currently closed for restoration until fall of 2008, but locals can't wait to have their elegantly tiered restaurant back in action.

Endless Summer Bar-Cafe $$
113 Harbor Way, Santa Barbara
(805) 564-4666
www.endlesssummerbarcafe.net

This surfing-inspired eatery is a bright, casual dining choice overlooking the Santa Barbara harbor. As with its downstairs fine-dining sibling, The Waterfront Grill, the emphasis here is on fresh-caught fish and seafood dishes, but you'll also find a great selection of juicy burgers, sandwiches, soups, and salads. Some claim it has the best clam chowder in town, while others say the sesame–black pepper halibut is divine. Slide into a banquette at a Hawaiian-print table, perch on stools at the full cocktail bar, or dine alfresco on the harbor-view terrace. The restaurant has an elevator for wheelchair access and is open for lunch and dinner daily.

Enterprise Fish Company $$
225 State Street, Santa Barbara
(805) 962-3313
www.enterprisefishco.com

Plop yourself down in a huge warehouse full of fishing memorabilia, laughter, and lively conversation and order up some really fresh seafood. One of Santa Barbara's old-time favorite seafood restaurants, Enterprise has some of the largest selections of fresh fish in town. Choose from the daily chalkboard specials (they change according to the season and which fish are available), which could feature salmon, halibut, snapper, catfish . . . quite literally, any fish. Check out the live Maine lobster special on Monday and Tuesday for $26.95.

Everything is grilled over mesquite and served with your choice of potatoes Romano (a favorite), rice pilaf, fries, vegetables, coleslaw, tossed green salad, or clam chowder. There's also an oyster and seafood bar and a sushi bar, plus a kids' menu. Cocktails and a modest selection of wines and beers

Best Breakfasts

Need some serious sustenance to kick-start your day? Below is a list of some of our favorite breakfast nooks. Turn up in your shorts and flip-flops, refuel with some fresh-brewed java, and chow down on good old-fashioned breakfast grub.

Breakwater Restaurant, 109 Harbor Way, Santa Barbara; (805) 965-1557. Gaze out at bobbing boats over bacon and eggs at this harborside cafe. You can order all the classics here, bask on the sunny deck, then burn some calories strolling along the breakwater.

Cajun Kitchen, 1924 De la Vina Street, Santa Barbara (805) 687-2062; 901 Chapala Street, Santa Barbara, (805) 965-1004; 865 Linden Avenue, Carpinteria, (805) 684-6010; 6831 Hollister Avenue, Goleta, (805) 571-1517, www.cajonkitchensb.com. Spice up your day with some Louisiana hot sausage, blackened catfish, and jambalaya. Cajun Kitchen serves breakfast all day.

East Beach Grill, 1188 East Cabrillo Boulevard, Santa Barbara; (805) 965-8805. Grab a table on the boardwalk, order the multigrain pancakes, and watch the beautiful bodies bronzing on the beach. Get there early, though—tables fill up fast.

Eladio's, 1 State Street, Santa Barbara; (805) 963-4466; www.harbor viewinnsb.com. Part of the Harbor View Inn, Eladio's offers a delicious start to your day while people-watching at this location across from Stearns Wharf.

The Montecito Coffee Shop, 1498 East Valley Road, Montecito; (805) 969-6250. The Montecito Coffee Shop has been providing a simple breakfast menu to residents for over 60 years. This is a true locals' hangout.

Sambo's on the Beach, 216 West Cabrillo Boulevard, Santa Barbara; (805) 965-3269; www.sambosrestaurant.com. This is the original and last-standing Sambo's, founded in 1957. Big stacks of pancakes are made from scratch, and over the years some healthy alternatives have been added, including turkey sausages. Portions are generous, and so are the crowds. Be prepared to wait.

Shoreline Beach Cafe, 801 Shoreline Drive, Santa Barbara; (805) 568-0064. Smack bang on beautiful Leadbetter Beach, this is the only restaurant in Santa Barbara where you can dig your toes in the sand while you dine. Savor the seascape and start your day with a breakfast burrito or Shoreline omelet stuffed with shrimp and salsa fresca.

Summerland Beach Cafe, 2294 Lillie Avenue, Summerland; (805) 969-1019; www.summerlandbeachcafe.com. Sleepyheads can order breakfast all day at this colorful old Victorian house. Pick a table on the sunny porch and feast on omelets, Belgian waffles, and huevos rancheros.

ℹ Would you like to "get fresh" on the American Riveria? Ask for the complimentary 32-page culinary travel planner highlighting Santa Barbara County's culinary attractions, cooking classes, and locally grown produce. Call (800) 676-1266, or log on to www.santabarbarafresh.com, to order yours.

are also available. Enterprise Fish Company is open for lunch and dinner daily. Happy hour is 4:00 to 7:00 and 9:00 to 10:00 p.m. in the bar. Stop in for a bite, then head down to the wharf for an after-dinner stroll.

Epiphany $$$
21 West Victoria Street, Santa Barbara
(805) 564-7100
Epiphany is tucked in a cozy 1800s cottage. Owners Alberto and Michelle Mastrangelo (with actor Kevin Costner as partner) revamped the interior, enlisted a top-rate chef, and launched their sophisticated new eatery in 2001. It's a huge hit, drawing rave reviews for its creative California cuisine with a Mediterranean and Asian twist, but this is not the place to come if you're in a hurry—as the elaborate entrees take time to prepare. Step inside and you'll feel as if you've entered a cozy private home. The interior features an open kitchen, a chic bar buzzing with handsome couples (wear something black), and multiple dining rooms with warm wooden floors and crisply set tables well spaced for privacy. You can also sip cocktails or order from the bar menu by a bubbling fountain in the garden. The food is exquisite. Epiphany's chef conjures up imaginative versions of pan-roasted white fish, paella, rib eye steak, and crab cakes. Those with an adventurous palate will love it here. Epiphany is open for dinner seven nights a week.

FisHouse $$
101 East Cabrillo Boulevard, Santa
Barbara
(805) 966-2112

Thanks to its location on Cabrillo Boulevard, FisHouse is another of those restaurants that's often filled with tourists. It's owned by Tom White of the popular Santa Barbara Shellfish Company on Stearns Wharf, so it's no surprise that the focus here is on fresh local seafood. Wander into the light-filled, fish-themed dining room with its soaring ceilings, white-washed woods, and ocean views, and you'll feel as if you're in Maui. The menu features such briny treats as fresh-shucked oysters (there's an oyster bar here), steamed mussels and clams, crab cakes, clam chowder, cioppino, and bacon-wrapped scallops. When it's available, the lobster is a treat, and the calamari is also good. If you don't like seafood, you'll find plenty to please your palate, including pasta, steak, and chicken. The front patio is a lovely spot to sit on warm summer evenings, and you can cozy up by the crackling fire here on cool nights. FisHouse has a full bar and a strong leaning to local wines. It's open daily for lunch and dinner. Happy hour is Monday through Friday from 5:00 to 7:00 p.m.

Fresco at the Beach $$
Santa Barbara Inn
901 East Cabrillo Boulevard, Santa Barbara
(805) 963-0111
www.santabarbarainn.com
Voted "Best New Restaurant" in 2007 by readers of the *Santa Barbara News-Press*, this is a more upscale restaurant than its sibling, Fresco Cafe, and is located on the top floor of the Santa Barbara Inn. *Upscale* means more than exquisitely prepared cuisine with high prices. It also means a romantic ambience, a heartier meal, and a commanding view of the Pacific. Menu choices include Milanese pork chop, Gorgonzola walnut salad, coq au vin, and pan-seared wild salmon. After a recent celebratory birthday, there was only one complaint —the acoustics are so bad that you can barely hear each other over the din. Lunch is served Monday through Saturday. Dinners are offered daily. There's also a special Sunday brunch.

Fresco Cafe $
3987-B State Street, Santa Barbara
(805) 967-6037
www.frescosb.com

This small cafe has grown in size and stature since its beginnings in 1995. Mark and Jill Brouillard, proprietors, developed a popular system, with food orders placed at the front. Patrons then seat themselves, and the dishes are delivered when they are ready. There's something about this cafe that makes you just want to slide down into your seat and slip into conversation with your friends. Even though the tables are relatively close, the acoustics are so good so you can't hear neighboring tables' conversations. The all-day menu brims with salads, sandwiches, homemade soups, and desserts. Our personal favorite is the warm goat cheese salad and the turkey club triple decker. The success of this restaurant enticed the owners to open up another down at the beach, Fresco at the Beach. Breakfast, lunch, and dinner is served every day except Sunday.

Frog Bar & Grill $$
405 Glen Annie Road (at the Glen Annie Golf Club), Goleta
(805) 968-0664
www.glenanniegolf.com

Overlooking the rolling greens of the Glen Annie Golf Club, the Frog Bar & Grill is a popular spot for lunch. The restaurant also serves a great-value prime rib dinner on Thursday nights. You can fill up on meat, chicken, and fish specials and graze at the all-you-can-eat salad bar for under $15. The dining room has a cozy feel and affords gorgeous views of the coastline. You can also pick a table on the spacious patio, which has a fireplace and heaters for chilly days. The food is upscale and well prepared, and the lunch menu offers everything from sandwiches, crepes, pizza, and salads to seared ahi wraps, Sicilian chicken pizza, and chicken panini. You can order a cocktail from the full bar or choose a bottle from the wine list. The Frog Bar & Grill

serves lunch Monday through Saturday, dinner Thursday, and brunch on Sunday.

The Habit $
628 State Street, Santa Barbara
(805) 892-5400

216 South Milpas Street, Santa Barbara
(805) 962-7472

5735 Hollister Avenue, Goleta
(805) 964-0366
www.habitburger.com

The Habit is true to its name for a loyal flock of locals who come here regularly to get their fix on fresh, juicy charburgers. Just head to the general vicinity of the stores, and the aroma of sizzling beef, chicken, and fish will lead you to the source. In 1976 owner Brent Reichard went from flipping burgers in a Goleta walk-up window to buying the joint with his brother Bruce. Together they introduced the famous charbroiled burger, and the rest, as they say, is history. Today that modest stand has grown to 13 locations across Southern California with casual on-site dining. All the burgers are made to order with only the highest quality ingredients, and the buns are baked fresh on the premises. Local addicts swear by the classic charburger, but you can also order burgers bulging with charbroiled chicken, fresh albacore, pastrami, tri-tip (see the Close-up in this chapter), and even a vegetarian patty. Top off your meal with a creamy shake and a chocolate sundae, and you'll be on a high for the rest of the day. The Habit is open for lunch and dinner daily.

The Harbor Restaurant $$$
210 Stearns Wharf, Santa Barbara
(805) 963-3311
www.stearnswharf.org

Halfway down Stearns Wharf, with ocean views to die for, The Harbor Restaurant can't help but be a touristy kind of place. It's always full of out-of-town visitors looking for fresh seafood and a seaside perch from which to enjoy the busy waterfront scene.

The restaurant's interior is upscale and nautical, but casual dress is perfectly acceptable, and The Harbor Restaurant often draws diners from the busy Stearns Wharf foot traffic.

In addition to seafood, the menu offers steak, prime rib, and chicken, plus pastas, salads, and sandwiches. You'll also find a full bar here and a fair wine list. The Harbor is open for lunch and dinner daily, and breakfast on the weekends.

Harry's Plaza Cafe $$
3313 State Street, #13, Santa Barbara
(805) 687-2800

Opened in 1968, this lively, old-style restaurant has a 30-year tradition of serving down-home American food and very strong drinks. An experienced Santa Barbara restaurateur bought the restaurant in 2001 and has managed to preserve the cafe's unpretentious personality. You can order steak, seafood, pastas, salads, sandwiches, and daily specials. The regulars at Harry's form an eclectic group that transcends all age groups: It's not unusual to see motorcycle riders, construction workers, retirees, and business professionals in business suits seated side by side at the bar. A number of celebrities have popped into Harry's over the years.

You'll find Harry's in Loreto Plaza at the corner of Las Positas Road and State Street. It's open daily for lunch and dinner.

Intermezzo $$
813 Anacapa Street, Santa Barbara
(805) 966-9463
www.winecask.com

A delightful little addition to the Wine Cask (see separate listing), this wine bar offers light, bistro-style dining in a casual and intimate atmosphere. You can sip one of the cafe's interesting coffees or teas while relaxing on the patio, or cuddle on the couch inside near the fireplace and play chess while enjoying a glass of one of the 40 offered wines.

The menu is as casual as the surroundings, with an emphasis on salads, pastas, pizzas, and sandwiches—great for lunch or a late-night stop after the theater. Popular entrees include lamb kibbe, wild mushroom napoleon, truffle fries, and three-cheese plate. All of the desserts are homemade, and the wine list, drawn from the Wine Cask's selection, is one of the best in the city. Intermezzo also offers a martini menu and other mixed drinks from the bar and sells cigars, which you can puff on the front patio.

Intermezzo is open daily for lunch and dinner.

Joe's Cafe $$
536 State Street, Santa Barbara
(805) 966-4638

Joe's is one of the oldest and most famous restaurants in all of Santa Barbara. Joe Ferrario opened the original restaurant at 512 State Street in 1928 during Prohibition, and according to local legend, Joe's was a popular speakeasy.

In the 1980s the restaurant moved just a few doors up from the original Joe's to larger quarters on the corner of Cota and State Streets and continued to draw huge crowds. In 2003 local restaurateur Gene Montesano (owner of Lucky's and Ca Dario plus more) added Joe's to his burgeoning portfolio of Santa Barbara eateries, but regulars are relieved that not much has changed. You'll still find the same friendly staff and unpretentious Italian diner ambience with red-checked tablecloths and a raucous bar serving some of the stiffest drinks in town. Come hungry. The menu lists longtime favorites, like home-style fried chicken, French dip, pot roast, spaghetti, calamari, prime rib, a great club sandwich, and charbroiled steaks using only prime-grade Midwestern beef. Joe's is open daily for lunch and dinner and breakfast Saturday and Sunday.

Left at Albuquerque $$
700 State Street, Santa Barbara
(805) 564-5040
www.leftatalb.com

Even before you start thinking about the Southwestern menu here, you can choose from more than 40 brands of tequila for a before-dinner drink. The restaurant bustles with fellow imbibers, many spilling out onto the patio, making it a friendly, noisy sort of place.

The food is a mix of Anglo, Mexican, and Native American cuisine with a bit of a trendy kick, as exhibited by dishes such as the green monster chicken enchiladas. In addition to the tequilas, Left at Albuquerque has a full bar and microbrewed beers on tap. Happy hour runs from Monday through Friday from 4:00 to 7:00 p.m.

Louie's California Bistro $$
1404 De la Vina Street, Santa Barbara
(805) 963-7003
www.uphamhotel.com

Pamper yourself at Louie's, a sophisticated California-style bistro in the historic Upham Hotel (see the Hotels and Motels chapter for a detailed description of Santa Barbara's oldest hostelry). Louie's is a favorite with the local business lunch crowd, and the intimate, casually elegant atmosphere makes it a perfect place for a birthday lunch or dinner or romantic tête-à-tête. You can dine inside or on the heated wraparound veranda.

The restaurant is best known for gourmet cuisine at prices that won't make a huge dent in your budget. Dishes include Louie's famous Caesar salad with blackened chicken or shrimp, chicken in puff pastry, stuffed Anaheim chili, and quiche. Louie's serves beer and wine only. It's open for lunch Monday through Friday, 11:30 a.m. to 2:00 p.m., and for dinner seven days a week.

Lucky's $$$–$$$$
1279 Coast Village Road, Montecito
(805) 565-7540

This sleek steakhouse in the old Coast Village Grill location is the hip hangout in Montecito for locals, celebrities, and wanna-bes. Owner Gene Montesano (of Lucky jeans fame) and his partners have infused this place with some minimalistic glamour. From the old black-and-white photographs of celebrities adorning the walls to the smartly clad waiters, the valet parking, and the impressive list of champagnes, Lucky's exudes a kind of nouveau nostalgia. It's famous for its juicy steaks aged well and cooked to order—the filet porterhouse and the New York strip steak among them. Side selections include golden onion rings, home fries, and creamed spinach. You'll also find a few enticing seafood options. If you're dining alone, you can perch at the bar and watch your favorite sports game or pick a people-watching spot on the street-side patio. The wine list is excellent, with many French selections and a few big-ticket bottles that are a good indication of the clientele here. Lucky's is open daily for dinner and Saturday and Sunday for lunch. It's not for the miserly, but the beef is worth the bucks.

i For the latest buzz on the Santa Barbara restaurant scene, visit www.diningsantabarbara.com. You can also rate restaurants, read reviews, and chat with fellow foodies.

Miró $$$$
Bacara Resort & Spa
8301 Hollister Avenue, Goleta
(805) 571-4204
www.bacararesort.com

Sitting on a bluff overlooking the Pacific at the ritzy Bacara Resort & Spa, this sophisticated gourmet affair is a high point in Santa Barbara dining, with lofty prices to match. Of the three restaurants at Bacara, Miró is the most formal. The restaurant is named for Joan Miró, the Spanish abstract expressionist, and the dining room displays some of the artist's original bronzes as well as reproductions of his whimsical paintings. Gazing at this evocative collection is a fitting prelude for the artistic California-French cuisine to follow. The chef composes artful presentations that are almost as colorful as Miró's dramatic art using organic vegetables grown at the Bacara ranch as well as fresh local seafood. Some of the favorite menu items are the Atlantic cod a la plancha, grilled veal chop, and breast of duck with Swiss chard.

As soon as you slip into the red leather seats here, experienced staffers will cater seamlessly to your every whim. Obsessing over the wine selection? Enlist the services of the refreshingly unpretentious sommelier. She'll be happy to suggest the perfect pinot from the restaurant's 7,000-bottle cellar. You can also preface your meal with a creative cocktail from Miró's full bar. The restaurant is open for dinner Tuesday through Saturday. Private party areas are available, and reservations are essential (jackets are recommended for men).

Montecito Cafe $$
1295 Coast Village Road, Montecito
(805) 969-3392
www.montecitoinn.com
The Montecito Inn was a famous Hollywood hangout back in the 1920s and '30s (read more in the Hotels and Motels chapter), and some of the light, romantic history is preserved in the charming Montecito Cafe, just off the lobby.

The California cuisine is excellent, and the prices extremely reasonable for such high-quality fare. You'll find imaginative dishes, such as grilled chicken breast with roasted Anaheim chiles, a peppered New York steak, and fettucine with a pesto cream sauce and grilled lamb sausage—all under $16. An excellent list of wines and champagne provides the perfect accompaniment. The Montecito Cafe is open daily for lunch and dinner.

Nordstrom's Cafe $
17 West Canon Perdido Street, Santa Barbara
(805) 564-8770
Mothers and daughters alike love capping off their morning of shopping with a delicious lunch at the third-floor Nordstrom's Cafe. Sit outside on the terrace for a bird's-eye view of the coast and Santa Ynez Mountains.

Although the decor is unimpressive, this is a classic case of not judging a book by its cover. Our perennial favorites are Chinese chicken salad and lime chicken salad.

Nu $$$
1129 State Street, Santa Barbara
(805) 965-1500
www.restaurantnu.com
Nu means "naked" in French, and although you won't find any nudity here, you can count on fresh seasonal ingredients stripped to their essence and combined to create a festival for the palate. Nu wows local critics with its creative California cuisine showing subtle European undertones. No wonder—the owners are former employees of the esteemed Wine Cask (see the write-up later in this chapter), including Executive Chef David Cecchini, who works magic in the kitchen here. Besides the food, one of the best things about this restaurant is the romantic fountain courtyard. Softly lit and framed with potted palms, it's the perfect venue for a special date. You can also sit in the dramatic dining room and gaze out through a wall of giant arched windows or enjoy an aperitif in the elegant multilevel bar and lounge. To give you an idea of the caliber of cuisine, the seasonal menu may list options like Maine lobster with saffron gnocchi or foie gras with soft polenta, sautéed apples, and sauterne reduction. Nu has a full bar, and you can complement your meal with a bottle from the impressive wine list, which includes half bottles, wines by the glass, and a good selection of champagnes and ports. Complete the experience with a decadent dessert and imported cheeses. After all, this is the kind of place where you'll love to linger. Nu is open for lunch Monday through Friday and serves dinner nightly. Casual elegance is the tone here, and reservations are recommended.

The Nugget $
2318 Lillie Avenue, Summerland
(805) 969-6135
This saloon-style restaurant with an Old West theme seems a bit out of place amid Summer-

land's colorful Victorian cottages, but it's been a steadfast local favorite for more than 50 years. The Nugget recently changed ownership and has been reprieved of its "everything fried" menu, thank goodness. The salmon salad, pork chops, and T-bone steaks are reputedly "to die for." It's open for lunch and dinner daily.

Opal Bar and Restaurant $$
1325 State Street, Santa Barbara
(805) 966–9676
www.opalrestaurantandbar.com

The casual and cozy bistro-style dining room at Opal Bar and Restaurant is always bubbling with the chatter of happy diners, and if you like a wide selection of innovative international dishes, you'll love it here too. The menu is "California eclectic" with influences from around the world, and the daily specials add even more diversity. Favorite dishes are the bouillabaise of fresh tiger prawns, sea scallops and fresh shucked oysters, and the gourmet pizzas cooked in a wood-burning oven. Be sure to leave room for one of the incredible desserts. A popular pick is the Like Water for Chocolate Surprise, a decadent mix of white and milk chocolate mousse.

More than 300 bottles from around the world grace the award-winning wine list, plus you'll find a good variety of unusual beers and spirits, and you can top off your meal with a frothy cappuccino.

Opal is open for lunch Monday through Saturday and for dinner nightly.

The Palms $
701 Linden Avenue, Carpinteria
(805) 684-3811
www.thepalmsrestaurant.com

This popular, informal Carpinteria hangout has been family-owned and -operated for some 40 years. Barbecue your own steak on the grill if you wish, or ask the chef to do it for you. You can also order fresh seafood and serve yourself from the salad bar. Park yourself by one of the two fireplaces, order a beer, and chat with the locals.

The Palms offers a full slate of traditional American food, including burgers, steaks, and fresh seafood. It's open for dinner seven evenings a week and has a cocktail lounge with live music Thursday through Saturday.

Paradise Cafe $$
702 Anacapa Street, Santa Barbara
(805) 962-4416
www.paradisecafe.com

Many a local resident and visitor have wined and dined at this casual, quintessential Santa Barbara restaurant since 1983. It occupies a converted house on the corner of Anacapa and Ortega Streets, just a block from State Street.

The Paradise is best known for its tasty meats and burgers, but it also serves a pleasantly spicy black bean soup. You can order from an extensive list of Santa Barbara County wines, including its own Paradise Chardonnay, made by the Qupé winery. When the weather's warm, most people prefer to eat outside amid the tropical flowers. The separate bar area draws a hip singles crowd.

The Paradise Cafe is open for lunch and dinner daily and also for breakfast on Sunday.

Rocks Restaurant and Lounge $$$
801 State Street, Santa Barbara
(805) 884-1190

This contemporary, slightly upscale restaurant and bar is one of downtown's most popular nightspots. It's actually two bars—one upstairs and one downstairs—and you can dine on either level. We like to sit on the balcony overlooking State Street so we can people-watch—especially on a Saturday night.

The menu at Rocks features California cuisine with Pacific Rim accents and lots of fish in every way, shape, and form. You can choose from a variety of pastas, pizzas, salads, and meat dishes. Order one of Rocks' famous martinis while you wait for your meal to arrive, then sit back and enjoy the scene. Rocks is open for lunch and dinner daily.

Rodney's Steakhouse $$$
Fess Parker's DoubleTree Resort
633 East Cabrillo Boulevard, Santa
Barbara
(805) 884-8581
www.rodneyssteakhouse.com

Rodney's was one of Santa Barbara's first upscale steak houses, and many locals say it has the best beef in town. *Zagat's* even recognized it with scores of 27 for its food. With its contemporary beach-inspired blue-and-gold decor, it's also a little more sophisticated than your average steak spot. Pining for a juicy porterhouse, grilled prime rib, or a thick slab of filet mignon? At Rodney's, you order the cut. The USDA prime-grade beef is aged 21 to 28 days and presented before preparation. Then it returns to you cooked to order and smothered in the mouthwatering sauce of your choice—either béarnaise, green peppercorn, bordelaise, or maitre d' lemon-parsley butter. Not everyone's a meat lover. For those who prefer seafood, the menu offers some appealing alternatives, such as the baked Maine lobster plucked straight from the tank. If you have any room left, you can top off your evening with a vanilla bean soufflé or some refreshing sorbet. The full-service cocktail bar specializes in martinis, and the wine list spotlights Californian and Santa Barbara County vintages (including some by Fess). Rodney's serves dinner Tuesday through Saturday. Reservations are recommended.

Roy $$
7 West Carrillo Street, Santa Barbara
(805) 966-5636

If you just wandered by Roy, tucked amid shops on Carrillo Street downtown, you'd never think this unpretentious restaurant and bar serves some of the most delicious and best-value food in Santa Barbara. The owner and chef, Roy Gandy, has been surprising locals and visitors for more than 15 years with his creative concoctions made with fresh organic produce from local farmers' markets.

Open until midnight, Roy is also a favorite late-night dining spot. Bold, modern art leaps off the walls in the funky midnight-blue dining room, where you can slide into a banquette and order one of the best-value prix fixe dinners in town. Entrees come with warm homemade bread, soup, and a tasty salad of mixed greens topped with the house dressing. The desserts are wonderful, too. Add a great list of wines and ales, a funky bar, and you've got yourself a fabulous night out at a bargain price. Roy is open until midnight for dinner seven nights a week.

i Got the late-night munchies? Roy is consistently voted best spot for late-night dining in local newspaper polls. It's open until midnight daily. If you've had a big night bar-hopping and the clock's struck 12, head to the downtown Carrows Restaurant at 210 West Carrillo. It's open 24 hours.

Sage and Onion $$$
34 East Ortega Street, Santa Barbara
(805) 963-1012
www.sageandonion.com

If you want to splurge on some of the best food in Santa Barbara, this is the place to come. This upscale fine dining spot opened in 1999 and has since garnered a string of rave reviews. The man behind the magic here is British owner/chef Steven Giles. Trained in the classic French style, Chef Steven makes cooking an art. He describes the seasonal menu as European/American cuisine with an "English twist." The dining room is cozy and contemporary—it feels like dining at a friend's house. You can also eat alfresco on the intimate street-side patio or, if you're dining alone, perch at the sleek wood bar. When you arrive, a single sage leaf on your fresh linen napkin sets the tone for an evening of simple elegance, crisp service, and exquisite cuisine. The menu changes with the seasons. The spring menu features such enticing creations as the free-range chicken breast with apricot pork stuffing and Peking duck. The extensive wine list spotlights California wines, and desserts such as the liquid center lava chocolate cake and steamed maple sponge pudding are delicious—make sure you leave room. Sage and Onion serves beer and wine and is open for dinner daily. Walk-ins are welcome, but reservations are recommended.

Santa Barbara Brewing Company $$
510 State Street, Santa Barbara
(805) 730-1040
www.sbbrewco.com

Primarily known for its great selection of microbrewed beers (including Santa Barbara Blonde, Rincon Red, and Pacific Pale Ale), the Santa Barbara Brewing Company is a convivial place to hang out and enjoy some great food as well. Burgers, pizza, pasta, steak, and seafood are on the bill of fare (everyone loves the garlic rosemary fries), and there's a kids' menu with fish and chips, grilled cheese sandwiches, and other child-friendly foods. In addition to a wide choice of beers and ales, there's a full wine list. The Brewing Company is open for lunch and dinner daily and features a happy hour Monday through Friday from 3:00 to 6:00 p.m.

Shoreline Beach Cafe $$
801 Shoreline Drive, Santa Barbara
(805) 568-0064

Shoreline Beach Cafe lets you dine with your toes in the sand of Leadbetter Beach. Show up in your bathing suit or casual clothes and sit beneath colorful umbrellas on the deck, glass-enclosed patio with heaters, or right on the beach. The kids can play in the sand while you eat.

The cafe is owned and operated by the same folks who run the popular Paradise Cafe downtown. Fill up on the famous half-pound Shoreline Burger, grilled shark burrito, tuna taco, or a bucket of steamed mussels and clams. You can also choose from various salads.

Shoreline Beach Cafe is open for breakfast, lunch, and dinner daily.

Stella Mare's $$–$$$
50 Los Patos Way, Montecito
(805) 969-6705
www.stellamares.com

Stella Mare's scores top points for its evocative French country ambience and fresh seasonal wine country cuisine cooked on a wood-burning grill. This upscale bistro-style restaurant and bar in a historic (1872) Victorian house overlooks the tranquil Andree Clark Bird Refuge and is a popular venue for special events—many bridal showers and wedding receptions take place here.

You can choose a seat in the gorgeous dining room, on the vine-draped patio, or in the stunning solarium, which floods with sunlight during the day and flickers with candlelight in the evening. People rave about the braised lamb shanks, grilled pork tenderloin, and fresh local fish, as well as the homemade pastas and desserts. After dinner, you can sink into one of the overstuffed shabby chic lounges by the fire and sip a coffee.

Stella Mare's offers live jazz on Wednesday nights. The restaurant is open for lunch and dinner Tuesday through Sunday and serves an excellent brunch on Saturday and Sunday.

Stonehouse Restaurant $$$$
900 San Ysidro Lane, Montecito
(805) 969-4100
www.sanysidroranch.com

The rustic look of the small stone house (formerly a citrus packing house) nestled on the grounds of the San Ysidro Ranch (see the Hotels and Motels chapter) belies its refined interior. Crisp table settings, Persian rugs, antiques, and original art infuse a sense of easy elegance into the dining room, and the food is every bit as impeccable as the decor.

Chef John Trotta cooks up a storm in the kitchen, combining fresh organic ranch-grown herbs, fruit, and vegetables with flavorful

Close-up

Tri-what?

If you're a newcomer to Santa Barbara, you've probably never heard of tri-tip, but you soon will, because everyone in Santa Barbara knows about tri-tip and has eaten it at family barbecues, school picnics, and political fund-raisers.

This unique cut of beef was born in Santa Barbara County, and as far as we know, until very recently no one else in any other part of the country had heard of it or known what to do with it. So if you're new to Santa Barbara, here's the scoop: A cow is a cow is a cow, of course, but tri-tip supposedly came to be in a now-defunct Safeway grocery store in Santa Maria way back in the 1950s. (We can't be absolutely sure of its origins, of course. Santa Marians have been eating good barbecue for about a century.)

Anyway, as the story goes, a butcher who was cutting beef loins into sections of top block sirloin and filet mignon set aside the triangular-shaped tip of the sirloin (as usual) to be cut into stew meat or ground up into hamburger. That fateful day, however, there was no need for more stew meat or hamburger, so the meat market manager, seeing that the triangular tip was going to be wasted, seasoned it with salt, pepper, and garlic salt and put it on the rotisserie. Much to the surprise of the butchers, after the meat had cooked for an hour or so, it came off the rotisserie succulent, tender, and delicious.

Of course, stew meat is usually tough, but it seemed that the newly christened "tri-tip," when left in one piece and seasoned and cooked, was a different animal (so to speak). Tri-tip was born!

Tri-tip was a whole lot less expensive than those other fancy cuts, a fact that was bound to pique some interest. It wasn't long before the Safeway meat manager opened his own meat market, and tri-tip became his baby. He let people sample it, promoted it, and even showed customers how to cook it.

seasonings and adding influences from around the world.

Desserts are as appealing as the entrees, and the wine list shines. The Stonehouse has received many culinary awards over the years, including a *Wine Spectator* Award of Excellence, the James Beard Foundation 10th Anniversary Award, and a Distinguished Restaurants of America Award. This is also one of the most expensive restaurants in Santa Barbara, so be prepared when the tab arrives.

The Stonehouse is open for dinner daily. This is one of the few places in town where you really should dress for dinner. More

casual is the Plow and Angel Bistro downstairs.

The Tee-off Restaurant and Lounge $$
3627 State Street, Santa Barbara
(805) 687-1616

The Tee-off (a golf theme is carried throughout) has been at this upper State Street location for about 50 years. It has an old-fashioned steak house ambience, with plush booths and red leather bar stools. The menu fits the theme, with steak, prime rib (a favorite), chops, chicken, and seafood topping the list. It's the perfect place to unwind after a game of golf,

Word began to spread. Visitors and workers at Vandenberg Air Force Base began to tell other people about tri-tip, and soon, it was rumored, people from the San Joaquin Valley started coming over the hill to Santa Maria and buying tri-tip by the case, hauling it home for their own barbecues.

Once the secret was out, people started demanding tri-tip in grocery stores and meat markets all over the county. South County markets soon had tri-tip in their meat cases right along with those expensive cuts, sometimes premarinated and ready to put on the grill.

Soon caterers started serving tri-tip, and it was showing up at wedding receptions and church picnics. Certain groups—such as the Santa Maria Elks Club—developed reputations for being among the best tri-tip barbecuers in town and were in constant demand. They bought their own portable barbecue pits and charged to come out and put on a "Santa Maria–style barbecue" for special events and get-togethers. (To this day, tri-tip barbecuing seems to be a sort of male bonding experience, although women can do it just as well.)

Santa Marians show off a perfectly done piece of tri-tip: brown on the outside, pink on the inside, and generously sliced. COURTESY OF SANTA MARIA VALLEY CHAMBER OF COMMERCE VISITOR AND CONVENTION BUREAU

so order up a martini and a big juicy steak and enjoy. The Tee-off is open for dinner nightly.

Tupelo Junction Cafe $$
1218 State Street, Santa Barbara
(805) 899-3100
www.tupelojunction.com
Bon Appetit said Tupelo Junction Cafe, a Southern-style American restaurant, represents the "funky side" of Santa Barbara by pouring its coffee into country-style crockery mugs, mixing its mimosas in mason jars, and decorating with colorful fruit-crate labels. Amy Scott, proprietor, is the mastermind behind this restaurant, and she pulls it off, shall we say, with a Southern flair. Start your day with a buttermilk biscuit slathered in gravy or Mom's pumpkin oatmeal waffle top with carmelized bananas, candied pecans, and maple syrup. For lunch maybe it's a deep-dish cheddar and Gouda mac 'n' cheese you're hankering for or an Applewood smoked bacon and fried green tomato BLT. Dinner still says "Southern home cooking," with entrees of blackened molasses organic salmon and fried chicken salad with cornbread. Bring on the crawdads! Breakfast, lunch, and dinner are served on time every day. Momma would be proud.

Wine Cask $$$$
813 Anacapa Street, Santa Barbara
(805) 966-9463, (800) 436-9463
www.winecask.com

If you're a wine and food connoisseur, you'll be right at home at the Wine Cask, one of Santa Barbara's best (and most expensive) restaurants. Local bottles comprise almost a quarter of the 65-page wine list, and the experienced waiters will happily recommend the best wine to complement your meal. Wander through the fountain courtyard, and you'll enter the dramatic dining room, which exudes a warm and elegant European ambience with a baronial fireplace crackling on one side and antique hand-painted beams overhead. You can also dine alfresco on the stone patio—a lovely spot on warm summer days.

The food is outstanding. Depending on the season, you can choose from grilled Kobe beef top sirloin, organic king salmon, or miso-grilled black cod. Owner and founder Doug Margerum recently sold the Wine Cask after building it to excellence over 24 years. Bernard Rosenson, a health care magnate-turned-restaurateur, has taken over the helm, but Doug is still around as a consultant, so no outlandish changes are expected. The Wine Cask is open for lunch Monday through Friday and dinner nightly. Make sure you stop at the adjacent wine store on your way out—if not to buy a bottle then at least to check out the incredible inventory.

Woody's Bodacious Barbecue $$
5112 Hollister Avenue, Goleta
(805) 967-3775

The decor is strictly "old ranch house" at Woody's, one of only a few barbecue restaurants in Santa Barbara. Get ready to have your senses assaulted the minute you walk in the door.

First, there are those tantalizing smells, as the kitchen whips up chicken, ribs, tri-tip, and burgers. Then there's the noise. You might be sitting next to an entire kids' soccer team, a clanging video game, or a blaring television.

Everything from a full slab of beef or pork ribs to a Caesar salad is available for the asking, and there's a kids' menu, too. Just step on up to the counter and order your food (which comes in a pie tin), and pick it up when your number is called. Then settle yourself down at a table and dive into a huge platter of smoked barbecue, which comes with a ton of fries or a baked potato plus your choice of barbecued beans, coleslaw, tossed salad, or pasta salad.

Woody's also offers microbrewed draft beers and free refills on soft drinks and coffee. If you don't feel like going out, Woody's will cater or deliver.

Woody's is open for lunch and dinner daily.

Zookers Cafe & Juice Bar $$
5404 Carpinteria Avenue, Carpinteria
(805) 684-8893
www.zookerscafe.com

Cute and cozy Zookers Cafe & Juice Bar has added some zing to Carp's sleepy restaurant scene. This popular little neighborhood nook is a locals' favorite, serving affordable California cuisine (with a hint of granola). Wedged into an uninspiring strip mall, Zookers has the feel of a San Francisco college cafe—unpretentious and earthy. You can perch at the pine-wood bar, pick a rustic wooden table in the dining room, or sit street-side on the small patio. Zookers uses only fresh local organic greens for its flavorful salads and will gladly substitute tofu for chicken. In fact, the menu lists many mouthwatering meatless options. In addition to gourmet sandwiches, salads, quiche, and pasta, the menu includes zesty entrees like citrus beurre noisette glazed salmon, chicken breast stuffed with sage and prosciutto, cioppino, and seafood tostada. Daily specials of fresh fish, lamb, and pork broaden the already excellent selection. Cap your meal with a homemade dessert and a local bottle from the small but satisfying wine list (most are available by the glass), and you'll know what the buzz is all about. Zookers serves lunch and dinner Monday through Saturday (closed Sunday).

CHINESE

Empress Palace $$
2251 Las Positas Road, Santa Barbara
(805) 898-2238
www.empresspalace.net

For flexibility and price, you can't beat the Empress Palace, Santa Barbara's only fine dining Chinese restaurant. Set aside some time for a meal here; it will take you a while just to read the menu. More than 200 items are featured, including Cantonese and Szechuan dishes and classics like chow mein, imperial shrimp, and chop suey. For starters, the plump pan-fried pot stickers are a good choice, and the menu offers an expansive list of soups. Expanding the options even further are barbecue dishes, such as succulent roast duck and spare ribs. Lobster lovers can feast on a steamed whole specimen picked fresh from the tank and served with your choice of sauce, such as black bean and chile, butter, or ginger and green onion. With its large tables, roomy banquettes, and affordable prices, this is a great spot to come with a group or family. You're sure to find something appealing from the massive menu, and you can also order special meal selections designed for three, four, or five diners so you can taste and share a variety of dishes. Empress Palace is open for lunch and dinner daily.

Mandarin Palace $$
3955 State Street, Santa Barbara
(805) 683-2158

Sandwiched into the busy Five Points Shopping Center, the Mandarin Palace is always crowded with hungry shoppers as well as students from UCSB, a testament to the quality of its food.

You'll find a great selection of Chinese specialties here—the sauces are delicious, and the veggies are always done just right. The wine list includes about 10 wines, including an Asian plum wine. Takeout is available and very popular. The restaurant is open for lunch and dinner daily, and the lunch special is always a good buy.

Shang Hai $
830 North Milpas Street, Santa Barbara
(805) 962-7833

A family favorite for years, Shang Hai lends credence to the saying "Don't judge a book by its cover." Set in a strip mall in a less-upscale part of town, Shang Hai serves up the standard Chinese fare in a way that tastes anything but standard. The hot-and-sour soup and mu shu pork are our family favorites. (Just be sure to ask for an extra plum sauce for the pork.) Reputed to be the "best in town" are the egg rolls. Celebrities and famed directors from Montecito all make this their haunt. Just look at the wall or ask for the books of birthday celebration pictures, and you're sure to see a recognizable face. Shang Hai is open for lunch every day except Tuesday and Sunday, and it serves up dinner every day except Tuesday.

FRENCH

Pacific Crepes $
705 Anacapa Street, Santa Barbara
(805) 882-1123

From the first friendly "Bonjour" to the last decadent bite, we love this delightful little French creperie. You can't beat the prices here, plus you can polish your French and feel as if you've popped over to Brittany for a bite to eat. Sit out on the sunny, pink-hued patio, or dine inside amid antique French posters and Breton-style blue and gold linens. The menu features authentic French-style omelets and buckwheat crepes (called galettes in Brittany) with your choice of fillings. You can choose any combination of meat, eggs, vegetables, smoked salmon, and hard-to-find imported French cheeses, including Reblochon and Roquefort. Pacific Crepes is open for breakfast and lunch from 9:00 a.m. every day except Monday and serves dinner Wednesday through Sunday.

Restaurant Mimosa $$
2700 De la Vina Street, Santa Barbara
(805) 682-2272

Frequently voted Santa Barbara's best French restaurant in local newspaper polls, Restaurant Mimosa is an old favorite, serving delicious French food at affordable prices in an unremarkable uptown location. Retirees seem to love it, and our friends always celebrate special occasions here with their elderly relatives. The service is usually excellent, and though casual attire is fine here, you can also dress up and still feel quite comfortable. A balance between classic and country cooking styles, the "French casual" cuisine features mouthwatering meat, chicken, and seafood dishes.

FUSION

Couchez $$$
214 State Street, Santa Barbara
(805) 965-3585

Finding Couchez can be a bit tricky (it's 2 blocks from the pier), but once you do, you'll be glad that you did. Executive Consulting Chef Roberto Cortez displays his European training with his amazing dishes. To whet your appetite, order the silky white corn velouté or the carmelized onion-walnut brioche. His signature appetizer dish, the hot foie gras with a lemongrass gelée and peppercorn peaches, has already become the Santa Barbara rave. Organic chicken breasts, wild mushroom cappelletti, and a tender lamb sirloin give diners every option. The perfect complement of a robust red or refined white is chosen for each entree. Unlike more formal restaurants, you can dine while lounging on a sofa or at a bistro table. Dinner is served Wednesday through Sunday, and a brunch is served Sunday morning.

HEALTH FOOD

Dish Cafe $
5722 Calle Real, Goleta
(805) 964-5755

Using organic, unsprayed, and hormone-free products whenever possible and never using microwaves are just two of the rules Dish lives by. What could be yet another boring granola crunch or bland health food restaurant is actually an eclectic mix of dynamic food that will have you begging for more. The vegetarian rolls cut into triangles are so tasty, we ordered another plate of them. The brown rice salad, although upon presentation seemed boring, actually had a spicy kick to it, no doubt brought about by the guacamole, and the Thai papaya chicken salad has caused a local stir. There are plenty of menu choices for those with carnivorous desires. The buffalo burger is just one such treat. Breakfast, lunch, and dinner are served every day except Sunday.

The Natural Cafe $
508 State Street, Santa Barbara
(805) 962-9494

361 Hitchcock Way, Santa Barbara
(805) 563-1163

5892 Hollister Avenue, Goleta
(805) 692-2363
www.thenaturalcafe.com

The Natural Cafe serves up great-tasting health food for vegetarians and health-conscious carnivores alike (you won't find red meat here, just turkey and chicken). In past local polls, the cafes scored awards for best veggie burger and best health food. Pick a table, scan the extensive menu, and line up at the cash register to order your meal. When it's ready, one of the super-friendly, helpful staffers will deliver it to your table. There's something for everyone here: fish, chicken, pasta, vegetarian entrees, a kids' menu, a complete juice bar, beer, local wines, and desserts. All three locations of the Natural Cafe are open for lunch and dinner every day.

Sojourner $
134 East Canon Perdido Street,
Santa Barbara
(805) 965-7922
www.sojournercafe.com

Voted "Best Spot to Dine Alone" in past local newspaper polls, Sojourner has served up natural food in a cozy, relaxed setting since 1978. It's a stone's throw from the Old Presidio (across the street), just 2 blocks east of State Street. The menu includes mostly vegetarian dishes: soups, sandwiches, salads, pastas, polenta cakes, crispy tofu and onions, vegetarian stir fry, and lasagna.

For a protein pickup, try the Sojburger, a vegetarian protein patty with melted cheese, guacamole, sour cream, and sprouts. Beverages to complement your meal include juices, smoothies, chai, yogi tea, and vegan shakes. Sojourner also has an espresso bar, beer, local wines, and fantastic desserts. The "Soj" is open daily for lunch and dinner.

Spiritland Bistro   **$$**
230 East Victoria Street, Santa Barbara
(805) 966-7759
www.spiritlandbistro.com
This small restaurant maximizes its limited space with its big sophistication. Crisp white linens on carefully laid-out tables and an attentive, if not slightly flirtatious, waitstaff create an ambience of elegance that bespeaks a four-star restaurant rather than one that claims offerings of organic global cuisine. Chef Joel Koch's mantra is "Creative, flavorful, and pure," and he hits the note just right with his offerings of authentic ethnic cuisine. Try the Asian five-spice and sesame-crusted organic free-range chicken, the Hawaiian macadamia nut–crusted mahimahi, or the vegan Greek moussaka. The smells alone will send you around the world. Of special note: If you're allergic to milk or wheat or a practicing vegan, Spiritland Bistro has a meal for you, which is often not the case when people with special needs are dining out.

INDIAN

Spice Avenue   **$**
1027 State Street, Santa Barbara
(805) 965-6004
www.spiceavenuesb.com

In a great location amid State Street shopping, this welcome new addition has spiced up Santa Barbara's bland selection of Indian restaurants. It's also one of the best dinner buffet bargains in town. On Wednesday night, for $12.95 per person, you can heap your plate with all-you-can-eat curries, biryanis, and other Indian delights—including dessert. The lunch buffet is $7.95 daily. Fragrant aromas lure you through the perfect people-watching terrace into a warm and exotic dining room adorned with spice-colored Indian fabrics, gold-framed prints, and potted palms. The buffet is a great way to sample a variety of dishes, and vegetarians will find plenty of meatless options. Order some naan bread to mop up all the sauces, quench your thirst with a mango lassi, or sip a little self-serve burgundy, a chilled chablis, or imported beer, and you'll be in dining nirvana. Spice Avenue is open for lunch and dinner (and takeout) daily.

ITALIAN

Aldo's   **$$**
1031 State Street, Santa Barbara
(805) 963-6687
www.sbaldos.com
Popular with tourists, Aldo's is a quaint, old world–style restaurant in a nationally registered historic adobe built in 1857. Here you can sit by the fountain in the stone courtyard and pretend you're in a trattoria in Florence, sipping chianti and watching the world go by, or dine indoors by candlelight and tune out the world entirely. Wherever you choose to dine, you can order up traditional Italian seafood and meat dishes, pasta, salads, gourmet pizza, and local and Italian wines. Try Aldo's famous pork chops with various sauces, stuffed rigatoni with sea scallops, veal parmigiana, or one of the chef's daily specials. On weekends, guitar players and singers add to the Mediterranean ambience.

Aldo's is open for lunch and dinner daily, as well as for brunch on Saturday and Sunday.

Ca'Dario $$–$$$
37 East Victoria Street, Santa Barbara
(805) 884-9419
www.cadario.net

Ca'Dario is a self-proclaimed "unpretentious Italian neighborhood restaurant filled with aroma, clever waiters, good friends, and rowdy conversation." In other words, you can expect a lively atmosphere and some really good food. In fact, we know locals who wouldn't go anywhere else for authentic Italian cuisine.

Experienced chef Dario Furlati whips up succulent dishes—osso buco con risotto (braised veal shank with saffron arborio rice) and sella d'agnello (grilled rack of lamb basted with garlic, olive oil, and fine herbs), to name a few. The daily special and the fresh fish of the day, available at market price, are other great options. The wine list is excellent and heavy with Italian wines, and the service is attentive.

Whether you go for a meal or just to sip wine or cappuccino at the bar or the sidewalk tables, you'll be glad you discovered Ca'Dario. The restaurant is open for lunch Monday through Saturday and for dinner daily.

Emilio's Ristorante and Bar $$
324 West Cabrillo Boulevard, Santa Barbara
(805) 966-4426
www.emilios-restaurant.com

Cozy and convivial, Emilio's, located on Cabrillo Boulevard across from the beach, serves a seasonal menu of delicious European country–style food using fresh organic vegetables and herbs. The appetizers and entrees are supplemented by both Italian and Santa Barbara County wines, and the bar serves everything from drink-of-the-moment martinis to grappas, vodkas, and scotches. Breads, raviolis, and gnocchi are made on-site, and paella is a specialty. Open for dinner nightly, Emilio's is usually crowded.

Italian & Greek Delicatessen $
636 State Street, Santa Barbara
(805) 962-6815

Known affectionately as "Johnny's" to the locals, this unpretentious, family-run deli has been serving some of Santa Barbara's best sandwiches, salads, and Italian and Greek specialties since 1971. Locals frequently rate this the "Best Deli" in newspaper polls, and it's well deserved—co-owner "Johnny" always makes time to chat with the regulars and welcomes his customers with a warm, friendly smile. Since it's right downtown near Paseo Nuevo, you can pop in here for a quick bite to eat after shopping. The place gets packed at lunch. Everything is made fresh to order exactly how you like it, and the crusty sandwiches are huge, fresh, and filling. In addition to the usual lunch fare, Johnny's reputedly serves the best pastrami in town. The Greek salad is also a favorite, and you'll find everything from delicious dolmades, gyros, spanikopita, and melt-in-your-mouth moussaka to classic pizza and daily pasta specials. While you place your order at the counter, check out the rows of cheeses, meats, and other imported goodies on display. You can take your food to go, but we love to munch at one of the sandwich bars or red-checkered tables in back. Johnny's is open seven days a week and doesn't accept credit cards.

Olio e Limone Ristorante $$$
17 West Victoria Street, Santa Barbara
(805) 899-2699
www.olioelimone.com

Owned and operated by Chef Alberto Morello and his wife, Elaine, Olio e Limone serves up an imaginative menu of authentic Italian dishes—including a sprinkling of Sicilian specialties. Along with Bouchon (see separate entry), this sophisticated little eatery is one of a few culinary gems to sprout up in this part of town. The restaurant lies just around the corner from the Arlington Center for the Performing Arts and is often buzzing with the symphony crowd, which comes here to dine before performances. Tucked in a tiny space on Victoria Street, Olio e Limone feels like a cozy Florentine trattoria. Tables are set skirt by skirt, and passersby can peek in through the row of windows facing the street. The food is bright and fresh and bursting with flavor. Among the pasta dishes, you'll find surprises like the ribbon pasta with morel mushrooms, asparagus, and cream, and the house-made duck ravioli. Olio e Limone serves only beer and wine. It's open for dinner daily.

Pane e Vino $$$
1482 East Valley Road, Montecito
(805) 969-9274
We (along with practically everyone else in Santa Barbara) love the intimate atmosphere, charm, and high-quality meals at this small, authentic Italian trattoria. It's in the back of a shopping plaza parking lot in Montecito's Upper Village, but don't let the location fool you: This place is a romantic little gem. It's also a favorite with local and visiting celebrities.

You can choose a table in the softly lit interior or outside on the vine-draped, heated patio. Most of the waiters are Italian, and the Italian music that plays softly in the background enhances the aura of romance. The menu features rustic, Northern Italian foods: pasta, seafood, veal chops, and meats (rabbits, duck) roasted on a spit.

Pane e Vino is open for lunch and dinner Monday through Saturday (closed Sunday).

Pascucci $
729 State Street, Santa Barbara
(805) 963-8123
The lively, contemporary atmosphere, good food at unbelievably affordable prices (at least for downtown Santa Barbara), and convenience of Pascucci make it one of the most popular eateries in the Paseo Nuevo shopping area. It offers delicious pasta, soups, salads, sandwiches, appetizers, and pizzas—and many items are under $10. In fact, it often scores awards in local newspaper polls for offering the "Best Meal under $10." This is a

great place to stop in for some sustenance after a busy day of shopping. The garlic dinner rolls are addicting. You can dine in the cozy interior, perch at the bar, people-watch on the street-side patio, or order a glass of chianti and relax on a comfortable sofa by the fireplace. Pascucci is open for lunch and dinner daily.

Trattoria Mollie $$$
1250 Coast Village Road, Montecito
(805) 565-9381
www.trattoriamollie.com
From simply delicious pizzas to delectable homemade breads and pastas to knockout gelatos, Mollie delivers fabulous Italian cuisine in her stylish Montecito trattoria. Mollie Ahlstrand is originally from Ethiopia, but she trained at Arturo's restaurant in Rome and has learned the fine art of creating splendid dishes from Padua, Umbria, Bologna, and Rome.

Pizzas and breads are baked in a wood-burning oven, meat dishes are tender and juicy, and the seafood is impeccable. If you really know Italian food, you'll love Mollie's perfectly executed renditions. Dress up a bit, and you'll fit right in with the upscale crowd.

Not for the "faint of wallet," Mollie knows the worth of her expertise, and as a diner, it's worth every dime. Even Oprah loves Mollie's.

Trattoria Mollie is open for breakfast, lunch and dinner Tuesday through Sunday (closed Monday).

Via Vai Trattoria & Pizzeria $$
1483 East Valley Road, #20, Montecito
(805) 565-9393
An offshoot of Pane e Vino, Via Vai in the Montecito Village shopping center offers a variety of authentic Northern Italian dishes, with an emphasis on pizza and pasta. You'll find everything from pizze capricciosa to farfalle al salmone e piselli and salsiccia con polenta on the menu. The grilled meats and seafood are just as tasty. You can dine in the bright, cozy dining room or on the large

heated patio. Dress is casual here, and the restaurant is popular with local Montecitans. Via Vai is open daily for lunch and dinner.

JAPANESE

Arigato Sushi $$
1225 State Street, Santa Barbara
(805) 965-6074

In the heart of downtown, opposite the Granada Theater, trendy Arigato is still rolling out some of the freshest and best sushi in town. Voted the favorite Japanese sushi restaurant in a local poll, Arigato is best known for its wild combination rolls with equally wild names: California Sunset, Rock 'n' Roll, Swinging Roll, Wiki Wiki Roll, Wipeout Roll, and Sea Eel Goes Hollywood, to name a few. Can't choose? Get the "Whatever Roll," and your chef will prepare his favorite for the day. You can also get excellent soft-shell crab tempura and other traditional Japanese dishes. You can perch at the sushi bar, sit downstairs, or dine alfresco on the patio out front. The place is nearly always packed with young (20s and 30s), chic-looking diners. The beverage list offers more than 20 different types of hot or cold sake, imported Japanese beers, and some excellent wines—including the fruity plum wine. Arigato is open for dinner daily. Get there early if you can—the restaurant doesn't take reservations.

Kyoto $$
3232 State Street, Santa Barbara
(805) 687-1252

This serene Japanese restaurant on upper State Street between Alamar Avenue and Las Positas Road has been a popular neighborhood sushi spot for years. Kyoto's experienced chefs prepare generous proportions of high-quality traditional Japanese steak and seafood dishes, including sushi, sashimi, teriyaki, and tempura. People in their 20s and 30s seem to love Kyoto. It's a locals' gathering place for small celebrations. Planning a romantic meal? You can kick off your shoes

and get comfy in one of the private tatami rooms.

Kyoto serves lunch Tuesday through Saturday and dinner every day but Monday. Tip: The parking lot is tiny, so be prepared to park on the street or behind the restaurant.

Piranha $$
714 State Street, Santa Barbara
(805) 965-2980

Dressed in sleek black and metallic accents, Piranha is a popular and trendy Japanese restaurant with a really long sushi bar and excellent food. If you don't sit at the bar for a close-up view of the master sushi chefs, you can sit on barstools at one of the high tables lining the walls or at a lower table near the front windows. Piranha features numerous creative sushi combinations, plus everything from chicken teriyaki and sea scallops to grilled sesame and sweet soy-glazed tuna. You'll even find a coconut curry shrimp or chicken on the lunch menu. The soft-shell crab is also excellent. Piranha is open for lunch and dinner Tuesday through Sunday.

Sakana $$
1046 Coast Village Road, Montecito
(805) 565-2014

Just try and get a table at Sakana. The newest sushi place in town has seized the discerning Santa Barbara sushi crowd because of its classy but simple modern decor, artistic flair for culinary creations, and slightly higher but reasonable prices. From the moment you walk in, there's something that satiates the senses. That doesn't stop when the sushi arrives. One patron was even overheard to exclaim, "It's like eating a work of art." Cozy up to the bar, or settle into one of the white linen-draped tables. However you choose to dine, you won't be disappointed in the unbelievably fresh fish—so fresh you'd swear it was straight out of the harbor. Try the ahi carpaccio; it simply melts in your mouth. And the yellowtail melt, well, there's nothing like it. For lighter appetites, in case sushi isn't light enough, try the miso soup for the perfect melding of flavors, or the cucumber salad that puts a fresh satiation on any appetite. Sakana is open Tuesday through Friday for lunch and Tuesday through Sunday for dinner. The restaurant is closed on Mondays.

MEXICAN

Cafe Del Sol $$
30 Los Patos Way, Santa Barbara
(805) 969-3947

Cafe del Sol, in a pretty setting just across from the bird refuge, is an old Montecito favorite. Since 1965, this upscale Mexican eatery has attracted a loyal clientele of well-heeled locals who come here for the great food, earthy ambience, and friendly bar. You can dine on the sunny wraparound patio, in the evocative split-level dining room, or join the crowd of cheery locals sipping cocktails at the bar. Order up a bowl of fresh guacamole. Then kick-start your meal with a margarita. The menu offers a wide range of options. The food is reasonably priced, and the restaurant is always humming with lively conversation. Cafe del Sol serves up lunch and dinner daily as well as Sunday brunch.

Carlitos Cafe y Cantina $$$
1324-A State Street, Santa Barbara
(805) 962-7117

The big brother of Carlitos Cava (listed next), Carlitos Cafe serves the same sort of upscale Mexican and Southwestern specialties as the Montecito restaurant. Fresh, homemade tortillas, meats cooked over an open-fire grill, and fresh chiles and spices combine to make all of Carlitos' dishes a sensation.

Carlitos has a full bar, including a large selection of Blue Agave tequilas and liqueurs and the requisite list of imaginative margaritas. Eat on the patio if it's a sunny day and enjoy the bubbling fountain. This is a fun place to bring a group. Kids can keep busy with crayons at the table, and live entertainment is offered every evening.

Carlitos is open for lunch and dinner daily and for breakfast on Sunday.

Carlitos Cava Restaurant and Bar $$$
1212 Coast Village Road, Montecito
(805) 969-8500
www.cavarestaurant.com

"Cava," the more sophisticated little brother of Carlitos Cafe y Cantina (see previous entry), dishes up creative Mexican and Spanish cuisine in a cozy spot on Coast Village Road. Choose a table on the small patio (there's a bit of traffic noise), or snuggle up inside, where a Santa Fe–style fireplace invites you to linger over cocktails. Your friendly waiter will bring a complimentary basket of chips and fabulous salsa (all salsas are made fresh every day) for dipping while you peruse the menu.

No matter what you choose, your food will be spicy and delicious. Entrees are served on huge plates with hot black beans and rice made with vegetable puree and chiles. Try the hearty pozole soup or the Cava fajitas platter. For dessert, we loved the besito de Cava, a chocolate torte with coffee, raspberry, and mango syrup, topped with whipped cream. The restaurant is quite kid-friendly, with brown paper and crayons on the tables to keep little hands busy.

Cava is open for lunch and dinner daily and also serves breakfast on weekends.

La Playa Azul Cafe $$
914 Santa Barbara Street, Santa Barbara
(805) 966-2860

Family-owned and -operated La Playa Azul has offered first-rate Mexican cuisine since 1976. When renovation of the Old Presidio began a few years back, the restaurant building was torn down. Luckily for Santa Barbarans, La Playa Azul was able to move into another house on the same block. This one's larger and has a wonderful dining patio that's shaded by a colorful jacaranda tree.

La Playa Azul is best known for its fresh, high-quality ingredients, generous portions, and an intimate, slightly elegant atmosphere. It's also famous for its excellent Jose Cuervo margaritas. Specialties include shrimp and fish fajitas and chicken flautas.

La Playa Azul serves lunch and dinner every day.

Going Local?

A fast-growing food trend is already hitting Santa Barbara's restaurants. Started by a group of affectionately nicknamed "locavares" in San Francisco (www.locavores.com), this concept involves eating only locally grown or harvested foods from within a 100-mile radius of your hometown. The values behind this trend are ones of health, conservation, and economics. If the produce hasn't been picked green and then spent days traveling across the United States, it retains more body-loving vitamins and minerals. Local produce doesn't carry the cost of bicoastal or international transportation, a cost we all know is growing bigger by the day. Buying local also supports the local agricultural economy and, in Santa Barbara, the fishing community, too.

Santa Barbara restaurant proprietors Mitchell Sjerven of Bouchon and John Downey of Downey's are dedicated to providing menus that are "freshly Santa Barbara." In Santa Barbara, their task is much easier than in most towns. Farmers' markets occur six days a week, fishermen bring the catch of the day in the harbor, and the Santa Ynez Valley is bursting at the seams with local wines.

It's not just restaurateurs that are trying to follow this trend. Many Insiders are dedicating themselves to eating local by visiting farmers' markets or by accessing the organic sections of many markets, such as Lazy Acres.

Laurence Hauben (www.marketforays.com), a local slow-food guide, recently started a culinary experience for vegetarians and foodies who want to nosh on local fish and green foodstuffs. The adventure starts by shopping for ingredients at the Fisherman's Market at the Wharf, the farmers' market, C'est Cheese, and Our Daily Bread. Then, participants learn how to prepare a locally fresh and tantalizing lunch.

Besides the agricultural produce and locally focused restaurants in town, there are a few other businesses that are uniquely Santa Barbara County. To save you the time, here's a quick guide for snapping up some local goodies.

American Flatbread
225 Bell Street, Los Alamos
(805) 344-4400
www.foodremembers.com
Certified by California Certified Organic Farmers (CCOF), American Flatbread began in Vermont in 1985 and traveled west with its award-winning organic bread. Now also settled in Los Alamos, American Flatbread has a variety of pizzas, such as the Ionian Awakening and roasted tomato salsa, black bean, and corn, that are mouthwateringly tasty. American Flatbread is available in stores throughout Santa Barbara, such as Gelson's and Tri-County Produce.

Ingeborg Chocolates
1679 Copenhagen, Solvang
(805) 688-5612
www.ingeborgs.com/

These delicious Danish chocolates, created from old world recipes, are melt-in-your-mouth good. The treats are the work of Danish chocolate dipper Ingeborg Larsen, who formerly ran her own chocolate shop in Copenhagen. Don't miss out on the licorice or the factory tour.

Montecito Country Kitchen
597 Freehaven Road, Montecito
(805) 969-1519
www.montecitocountrykitchen.com
This *école de cuisine* specializes in cooking classes based on the food of Provence and the Italian countryside. The classes focus on cooking an entire meal. Mauviel copper cookware from Normandy is also for sale.

Olive Hill Farm
4801 Baseline Avenue, Santa Ynez
(805) 688-3700
www.olivehilloil.com
Over 1,400 Lucca olive trees on seven and a half acres are the source for this gold medal olive oil. It was selected by editors of *Santa Barbara Seasons* magazine as one of their nine favorite gifts.

Righetti Specialties, Inc.
7476 Garciosa Road, Santa Maria
(805) 937-2402
www.susieqbrand.com
Firing up the barbecue for a weekend party? Spice up your dishes with one of the most-beloved Santa Maria–style seasonings. Sauces and salsas, bean mixes, beef jerky, grilling wood, and pie mixes are also available.

Santa Barbara Olive Co.
12477 Calle Real, Santa Barbara
(805) 562-1456
www.sbolive.com
Order off the Web and you save 10 percent on this CCOF organic estate-grown extra virgin oil. Over 100 olives and olive-related products are brought to you by the great-great-grandson of the original commercial olive farmer, John Goux, who purchased and farmed olive trees on 100 acres in Santa Barbara County beginning in 1851.

Santa Barbara Pistachio Company
3380 Highway 33, Maricopa
(877) 766-8112
www.santabarbarapistachios.com
The high desert temperatures of the Sierra Madre Range in Santa Barbara County provide the perfect climate for this locally owned and family-

managed pistachio farm. You'll find the pistachios at the farmers' market on Saturday and in stores throughout Santa Barbara.

Santa Barbara Roasting Company
321 Motor Way, Santa Barbara
(805) 962-5213
www.sbcoffee.com
The only roasters in town, you can find these trendy, comfortable coffee spots by the harbor and downtown. This is truly delicious coffee.

La Super-Rica Taqueria $
622 North Milpas Street, Santa Barbara
(805) 963-4940
No credit cards

This small, unassuming taco stand with a canopied patio serves up some of Santa Barbara's best and most authentic Mexican cuisine. After earning a master's degree in Spanish linguistics at UCSB in the late 1970s, owner Isidoro Gonzalez decided to abandon academia and venture into the restaurant business. First, though, he went to Mexico to collect regional recipes from relatives and other chefs—recipes that still form the basis of his 20-item chalkboard menu.

When you place your order, you have a full view of the tiny kitchen. It's a delight to watch the cooks roll out tortillas from fresh dough and toss sizzling steaks, chicken breasts, pork, and veggies onto the grill.

In addition to various tacos and quesadillas, Super-Rica offers many dishes rarely found in other Mexican restaurants, including roasted pasilla chile stuffed with cheese and served with pork (the Super-Rica Especial), melted cheese with bacon cooked in Mexicanware (the Tocino Especial), and cup-shaped corn tortillas filled with chicken, cheese, and avocado (Sopes de Pollo). Drinks include sodas, Mexican beer, and horchata, a popular Mexican rice beverage. Thanks to rave reviews and glowing write-ups in *Sunset,* the *Los Angeles Times,* and other publi-

cations, Super-Rica has achieved widespread notoriety. During prime dining hours, the line of people waiting to order nearly always stretches out the door and down the street.

The restaurant is open Thursday to Tuesday for lunch and every night but Wednesday for dinner. Dine early or late if you want to avoid a 15-minute wait in the order line.

Rudy's $
305 West Montecito Street, Santa Barbara
(805) 899-3152

Paseo Nuevo Mall
811 State Street, Santa Barbara
(805) 564-8677

3613½ State Street, Santa Barbara
(805) 563-2232

5680 Calle Real, Goleta
(805) 681-0766

1001 Casitas Pass Road, Carpinteria
(805) 684-7839

The long list of Rudy's locations attests to the popularity of its food. It's a great place to stop for a quick lunch or dinner before a movie or to just call up and order takeout. Rudy's is particularly famous for its great burritos, flautas, chimichangas, chile rellenos, and tamales. It also has great burgers. Rudy's is open for lunch and dinner daily.

MOROCCAN

Chef Karim's Moroccan Restaurant $$$
1221 State Street, Santa Barbara
(805) 899-4780
Step into Chef Karim's dimly lit dining room and you step into another culture—a place filled with warm Moroccan hospitality, belly dancers, and belly laughs. It's a great choice if you're looking for an exotic culinary adventure and a fun night out with friends. As you sink into the comfy cushions amid jewel-toned tapestries and rugs, your Ceremonial Feast begins with the traditional orange-blossom hand-washing ceremony. It pays to partake because, as in Morocco, at Chef Karim's your fingers are your forks. Anchoring your multi-course Moroccan feast is your choice of 10 different entrees, such as lemon chicken, a vegetarian feast, succulent honey lamb, and the delicious white fish in red sauce. The meal begins with a hearty harira soup, Moroccan salads, and fresh-baked bread. But the highlight is the scrumptious cinnamon and sugar–dusted b'stilla. This filo pastry pie filled with chicken, eggs, and almonds (or vegetables, if you prefer) is a favorite with Chef Karim's guests. Then comes the entree, served up with a side dish of couscous and vegetables, followed by a dessert of honey-drizzled cookies, fruit, and nuts accompanied by Moroccan mint tea. You can also order imported Moroccan beer or wine and burn off the meal with some after-dinner belly dancing. Meals for children under 10 are half-price. If you're planning to bring a group, reserve the cozy private alcove. Chef Karim's is open for dinner Wednesday through Sunday.

SOUTH AMERICAN

Cafe Buenos Aires $$
1316 State Street, Santa Barbara
(805) 963-0242
www.cafebuenosaires.com
For a taste of tango, romance, and South American flavor without having to fly to Argentina, head for Cafe Buenos Aires, right across from the Arlington Center for the Per-

forming Arts. Owners Wally and Silvia Ronchietto, Argentine natives who have lived in Santa Barbara off and on for years, have managed to re-create not only the cuisine they grew up with but also the casual, yet elegant Latin-European atmosphere of Buenos Aires.

Our favorite place to dine is in the spacious courtyard, which centers around a fountain and old world streetlight. But we also love the beautiful interior, with hardwood floors that are perfect for tango dancing. The menu focuses on traditional Argentinean food plus popular dishes from Brazil and other South American nations. Definitely try the Argentine beef, which we think has more flavor than its typical American counterpart, or fill up on shrimp and fresh fish specials, Argentine barbecue meats, or hot and cold tapas (beef, chicken, and corn).

The cafe offers a great selection of South American wines and exotic mixed drinks from the full bar (try the tangy lime caipirinha, Brazil's national drink). It also has live Latin music (diners are welcome to dance) Thursday through Sunday. Cafe Buenos Aires is open for lunch and dinner daily.

THAI

Your Choice $$
3404 State Street, Santa Barbara
(805) 569-3730
www.yourchoicethairestaurant.com
Your Choice is a favorite uptown Thai restaurant. The spacious, contemporary dining room is always filled with the alluring aromas of coconut, lemongrass, and other savory Thai ingredients. The long menu features all sorts of appetizers, soups, salads, curries, seafood, beef, chicken, noodle, and rice dishes (the pad thai and the hot-and-sour soups are fantastic).

Your Choice serves dinner every day and lunch Tuesday through Sunday.

Your Place $$
22-A North Milpas Street, Santa Barbara
(805) 966-5151, (805) 965-9397
Your Place is Santa Barbara's oldest Thai

restaurant, and it's regularly voted the best Thai restaurant in town in local polls. The kitschy dining room is a treat in itself—you can gaze at the giant fish tank and the authentic Thai decorations while feasting on mouthwatering plates of exotic foods. Choose from more than 200 authentic Thai dishes, from satay and panang curry to coconut ice cream.

The restaurant sits right on Milpas Street, just a few blocks north of the freeway. It's open for lunch and dinner Tuesday through Sunday (closed Monday).

NIGHTLIFE

When the sun goes down, Santa Barbara nightlife ignites. The afterglow from spending a day at the beach or on the water converts to social energy—and you'll discover most of it centered between Stearns Wharf and the 1300 block of State Street. Even people who live in Goleta, Carpinteria, and Montecito head for downtown Santa Barbara just to be at the heart of the action.

Most dance clubs and bars catering to the younger crowd (early 20s) are between the 300 and 600 blocks of State Street. As you walk north from there and approach the "arts and culture district" that extends to the 1300 block, you'll find dozens of restaurants, bars, theaters, bookstores, and coffeehouses along the way. Santa Barbara's cultural events calendar is busy every month of the year (see The Arts chapter for a broad overview of your many choices).

Many Santa Barbara nightspots appeal to a wide cross section of people of all ages. We can, however, make a few generalizations: The middle-aged tend to go to the hotels; the college-aged tend to hang around the dance clubs on lower State Street.

At many places, the age group depends on the type of music played that evening. If a particular nightspot caters mostly to a single age group, we mention it in the listing. Otherwise, just pop your head in the door and find out whether the ambience suits your style.

Many bars and restaurants host live music performances on Thursdays, Fridays, and Saturdays and sometimes other weekdays as well. Cover charges vary.

In this chapter we've included some of the most popular nightspots in the area. We begin with our favorite bars, listed by geographic area. Then we list a few places

according to their specialties: sports bars, dance clubs, billiards, coffeehouses and bookstores, movie theaters, and social dancing (swing, ballroom, tango).

To find out what's happening on any given night, check the "Pop, Rock, & Jazz" or "The Week" sections of *The Santa Barbara Independent* (a free weekly paper that comes out on Thursday) or *Scene* magazine in the *Santa Barbara News-Press* (included in the Friday edition).

But before we send you on your nocturnal adventures, there are a few things you should know.

One of the most important is that California law forbids all smoking in bars and restaurants, so expect to stand outdoors if you wish to light up.

Bars in the state of California are bound by law to stop serving alcohol by 2:00 a.m., so don't argue when the bartender shuts down. The minimum drinking age in California is 21. Be prepared to show legal identification (driver's license, passport) if you look younger than 30 years old.

Last, but certainly not least, know that any driver with a blood-alcohol level of .08 or higher is considered legally drunk. If you're caught driving drunk, you will be handcuffed, taken to jail, fingerprinted, and thrown into a detox cell for at least a few hours, usually overnight. You will also lose your license for a while—the length of time depends on how many times you've been previously arrested for drunk driving.

So now you're ready to walk, crawl, or dance your way through the Santa Barbara night hours. Have fun, and be sure to tell us about any hot spots we might have missed.

BARS/LOUNGES
Downtown/Beachside Santa Barbara

Barra Los Arcos
633 East Cabrillo Boulevard,
Santa Barbara
(805) 564-4333
www.fpdtr.com

The DoubleTree is one of Santa Barbara's high-end hotels, and its Barra Los Arcos matches the casual, yet sophisticated, character of the rest of the hotel. The bar offers a full range of drinks and light music, with live jazz bands on Friday and Saturday evenings. Many hotel guests come to this soothing spot to wind down after a busy day of sight-seeing or business meetings.

Bistro Eleven Eleven
1111 East Cabrillo Boulevard,
Santa Barbara
(805) 730-1111

Bistro Eleven Eleven is a casual-to-slightly-dressy restaurant and bar at the Hotel Mar Monte. On Friday and Saturday nights, locals and visitors come to listen or dance to live music, which ranges from soft rock to rhythm and blues, and the musicians happily take requests. The musical entertainment usually starts up around 9:00 p.m. Happy hour is 4:00 to 7:00 p.m. seven days a week.

Blue Agave
20 East Cota Street, Santa Barbara
(805) 899-4694

We've noticed more than a few Hollywood celebrities popping into this small, two-story restaurant/bar with soft lights, contemporary decor, and a romantic ambience. This is a great spot to take a first date. On weekends the place is packed with chic singles and couples in their late 20s, 30s, and 40s. You can choose from various types of margaritas (Blue Agave has an extensive tequila selection) as well as excellent martinis. If you don't like standing, we suggest you go early for dinner—especially if you have a date—so you can snuggle up in one of the coveted booths or on a cozy couch by the fireplace.

Bricks Cafe
509 State Street, Santa Barbara
(805) 899-8855

Looking for the ultimate late-night munchy restaurant and bar? Then look no further than Bricks Cafe, a huge brick bar and restaurant more reminiscent of downtown Chicago than Santa Barbara. A quality $5 martini list, starter menu, late-night appetizers, nightly specials, and a live band serve as the perfect nightcap to your evening downtown. Open until 1:00 a.m.

Brophy Bros.
On the breakwater at the harbor,
Santa Barbara
(805) 966-4418

Brophy's overlooks the yacht harbor and the mountains and is one of our favorite restaurants and watering holes. Many locals, especially those from the harbor community, quench their thirst and satisfy their hankering for seafood at the long cocktail and oyster bar. If you're lucky, you might score a table with fantastic views. Sometimes you'll be lucky to sit at all—the place is nearly always crowded. It's not a late-night spot, though, since everything closes around 10:00 p.m. Sunday to Thursday and around 11:00 p.m. on the weekends.

Cafe Buenos Aires
1316 State Street, Santa Barbara
(805) 963-0242
www.cafebuenosaires.com

Tango and romance are always in the air at Cafe Buenos Aires, a Latin restaurant and bar with a casually elegant atmosphere. Sit at a table by the fountain in the spacious, open-air courtyard, sample exotic South American wine or mixed drinks, and let the live Latin music sweep you away to Argentina. Or choose an indoor table in the elegant dining room and tango the night away on the hardwood floors.

Wherever you're seated, you can dine on authentic traditional and new cuisine from

Argentina or order fantastic tapas. After a few mojitos and Pisco sours, you'll be tearing up the dance floor. Cafe Buenos Aires has somewhat flexible hours. It stays open as late as need demands—for example, after a symphony performance at the Arlington Center for the Performing Arts across the street. The restaurant presents live dance performances every Wednesday from 6:30 to 8:30 p.m. Guests can get up and tango at 9:00 p.m. (see the Social Dancing section later in this chapter).

Chad's
625 Chapala Street, Santa Barbara
(805) 568-1876
www.chadsrestaurant.com

Housed in a rambling old Victorian house, this popular restaurant and bar is one of Santa Barbara's happy hour hot spots—especially for young professionals. Wander past on a Friday night and you'll see the after-work crowd swelling out onto the heated patio sipping Moët and chocolate martinis (one of Chad's many martini specialties). The wine list focuses almost exclusively on California bottles. Happy hour runs Monday through Saturday from 4:30 to 6:30 p.m. with live music.

Dargan's Irish Pub & Restaurant
18 East Ortega, Santa Barbara
(805) 568-0702
www.dargans.com

Owned and run by some affable Irishmen, this bright, cheery, traditional Irish pub is one of our favorite bars in Santa Barbara. You can wander in here any night of the week and usually find a lively crowd chatting over a few pints and shooting some pool. We've also noticed people pouring in here after special events. This is the kind of place where anyone can wander in and feel perfectly comfortable; where the classic, foot-tappin' tunes are loud enough to enliven the crowd but not so loud that they drown out conversation. You can come here and play a game of foosball with your buds, kick back with a Guinness stout by the fireplace, and warm your belly with some hearty Irish stew. For easy access to Dargan's, park in Lot 10 on East Ortega.

El Paseo Restaurant
10 El Paseo, Santa Barbara
(805) 962-6050
www.elpaseorestaurant.com

In a historic building originally constructed in 1827 by one of Santa Barbara's founding fathers, El Paseo scores our vote as one of the most evocative spots to sip a margarita. The restaurant and bar are drenched in the spirit of Santa Barbara's Old Spanish days, and the place gets packed during Fiesta with locals who come here to crack confetti-filled cascarones and dance on the tables. On warm summer evenings, the retractable roof rolls back, and romance hangs heavy in the air. Settle down in a highback chair by the fountain, slurp some margaritas under the stars, and you'll be howling at the moon in no time. Happy hour is Tuesday through Friday from 4:00 to 6:00 p.m. with complimentary appetizers.

i If you've overindulged, call Rose Cab (805-564-2600), Yellow Cab (805-964-1111), or Gold Cab (805-685-9797).

Indochine
434 State Street, Santa Barbara
(805) 962-5516
www.indochinebar.com

Targeting the glamour crowd, this sophisticated champagne and cocktail bar sizzles on the State Street strip. Started by two enterprising brothers and their two friends, this bar was conceived after a late night at the Cannes Film Festival. Sporting stylish mosaic bars, candle-topped tables, red-leather banquettes, Asian-inspired motifs, and an impressive gilded ladies' restroom, Indochine strives to evoke a decadent brand of exotic elegance. After 11:00 p.m. the pocket-size space is packed with pouty young 20-somethings drinking big-ticket bubbly and designer cocktails. This is definitely a place where people come to be seen. The club has a mysterious dress code—denims are allowed; you just have to exude a certain hip je ne sais quoi.

Intermezzo
813 Anacapa Street, Santa Barbara
(805) 966-9463
www.winecask.com

The acclaimed Wine Cask Restaurant (which has a more upper-crust ambience) opened this relaxed, next-door bistro in 1997. It caters to the late-night crowd and offers bistro-style dining, a full bar, and fine cigars, which you can smoke on the patio. This is the type of place you go to before or after a concert or theater performance. Order a gourmet cheese platter, curl up on a leather couch, and sip a port by the crackling fire.

The James Joyce
513 State Street, Santa Barbara
(805) 962-2688
www.jamesjoyce.com

In this cozy bar, you can order a pint of Guinness just as Joyce's Bloom would have done in 1904 Dublin. The James Joyce is a very popular, traditional Irish pub with a stone fireplace and a good selection of Irish whiskeys, single-malt scotches, and cigars. It serves up a heartwarming Irish coffee, too. Come here to shoot some pool, spark up the jukebox, play darts, or relax and chat with your buddies. The James Joyce also hosts live jazz on other nights of the week. Call for details.

Joe's Cafe
536 State Street, Santa Barbara
(805) 966-4638

Joe's has been around forever (since 1928) and is said to be the longest running restaurant and bar in Santa Barbara. As a restaurant, it delivers mom-and-pop-style steak, seafood, and Italian meals to your table. The bar, however, is another animal. The bartenders are known to pour the strongest cocktails in town, so the bar is nearly always packed. Joe's is also a popular meeting place for native Santa Barbarans who come here to

catch up with old friends, spin some tunes on the jukebox, and prime themselves for a night on the town.

Mel's Lounge
Paseo Nuevo
6 West De la Guerra Street,
Santa Barbara
(805) 963-2211

A colorful cross section of locals and tourists (mostly in the 30-plus age group) have mixed at Mel's for 60-plus years. It often scores awards for best neighborhood bar in local newspaper polls. Happy hour runs from 4:00 to 7:00 p.m. Monday through Friday. You'll also find a pool table, jukebox, and, some say, a very liberal attitude toward beefing up the booze content on the mixed drinks. The Bloody Marys will knock your socks off. You'll find Mel's just a few doors down from State Street in one of the Paseo Nuevo courtyards.

The Press Room
15 East Ortega Street, Santa Barbara
(805) 963-8121

The Press Room, named for its location next to the *News-Press* building, is where local bartenders head as soon as they're off work. This small, cozy Brit-owned bar has a European feel and a great selection of beers. You'll find 12 brews on tap here, including Guinness and Fullers. Best of all, The Press Room opens at all hours of the morning for big international football matches. It's popular with locals and foreigners and a great little spot to chat about sports. It can get quite rowdy; a few barroom brawls have been known to break out.

Q's Sushi a Go Go
409 State Street, Santa Barbara
(805) 966-9177

Brimming with beautiful people (mostly in their 20s), clubby Q's is currently one of the hottest hangouts in the downtown area. The building dates back to 1899 and used to be a dinner theater, among other things. You can sink into the red velvet ambience on several levels surrounding a curtained dance stage, chow down on sushi and other nibbles from the S.O.S. (sick of sushi) menu, order any type of drink you like, and shoot some pool at one of the nine tables on the third floor. You can even watch major sports events on TV at the bars. Q's is open daily and has a smoking patio off the pool table level.

Rocks Restaurant and Lounge
801 State Street, Santa Barbara
(805) 884-1190

One of Santa Barbara's most popular nightspots, Rocks draws a hip, upscale crowd of locals and tourists who come here to dine on fantastic fusion cuisine and quaff lemon drop martinis. All age groups are represented here, from 20-somethings to 50-plus. You'll find it in a prime location at one of the entrances to Paseo Nuevo shopping mall. Pick a table for two on the terrace overlooking State Street (a perfect spot for people-watching), or sit inside amid the sleek contemporary decor. Live bands rock the place at least a couple of nights a week, a DJ spins tunes other nights, and the dance floor in the top-level nightclub sees plenty of traffic.

Roy
7 West Carrillo Street, Santa Barbara
(805) 966-5636

Roy is one of the few downtown restaurants that serves meals late in the evening (until midnight). It also offers late-night entertainment, usually on the weekends, featuring original compositions by folk, jazz, rock, and blues musicians. The food is delicious and inexpensive. Drinks are a bit less of a deal, but they're still affordable. Roy has a full bar, beer, wine, and great coffee. Get here early if you plan to eat on the weekend.

SOhO
1221 State Street, Santa Barbara
(805) 962-7776
www.sohosb.com

If you enjoy live music and want to get away from the hustle and bustle of lower State Street, chances are you'll love SOhO. Buzzing with a mainly 30-something crowd, SOhO is a casual restaurant serving California cuisine and loft-style bar up on the second floor of the Victoria Court shopping arcade. The site is ideal for all types of performances and dancing with high ceilings, rows of windows, red brick walls (like those in a Soho loft), and an outdoor patio/deck.

Live music fills the restaurant every night of the week. The musical variety ranges from blues, jazz, folk, funk, and reggae to rhythm and blues and rock 'n' roll. Many of the bands and entertainers are local talent.

The music usually starts at 7:30 or 8:00 p.m. during the week, and on Monday nights you can enjoy live jazz from 6:00 to 10:00 p.m. Weekend nights heat up with dance music. If you want to make sure to get a good seat (or any seat at all when popular bands are playing), we suggest you eat dinner here first.

Wildcat Lounge
15 West Ortega Street, Santa Barbara
(805) 962-7970
www.wildcatlounge.com

Rising from the ashes after a fire blazed through here, this old locals' favorite still attracts a flock of artsy college grads and hip 20-somethings. The dimly lit '50s decor is saturated in deep red and black, with a few prized plush booths and a spacious smoking patio out back. You can also play pool, but you need to get here early to score a coveted table. Call for a schedule of events, which usually includes live local and national touring acts and social nights with various drink specials.

Midtown/Upper State Street Area

Harry's Plaza Cafe
3313B State Street, Santa Barbara
(805) 687-7910

Harry's is an uptown version of downtown Joe's—a traditional, family-style restaurant with big booths and long tables. Like Joe's, it's a Santa Barbara institution. It's always lively and packed with locals, mostly age 30 and older. Be forewarned: The bartenders serve very strong drinks that pack a mighty punch.

Goleta

Beachside Bar-Cafe
5905 Sandspit Road, Goleta
(805) 964-7881
In a superb seaside location on Goleta Beach, this is a perfect spot for sunset drinks. Order up some oysters at the raw bar, relax in the contemporary dining room, or pick a popular spot on the glass-enclosed patio and lose yourself in the ocean views. Heat lamps and a well-stoked fire will keep you warm when the sea breeze picks up. The wine list spotlights local bottles, and the full bar has beers on tap and specializes in tropical cocktails. After your drinks, you can cap off the evening with a romantic, moonlit stroll along the pier. Come early on weekends, or you may have to wait.

To get here, take U.S. Highway 101 to the UCSB off-ramp (California Highway 217) and drive for about a mile to the Sandspit Road exit. Go left, then turn right into the Goleta Beach parking lot and veer left—you can't miss it.

Elephant Bar
521 Firestone Road, Goleta
(805) 964-0779
www.elephantbar.com
Elephant Bar is a lively, safari-style restaurant just off Hollister Avenue near the airport. It serves a varied menu for lunch and dinner, but at night most people come here for the action-packed bar scene and the jumbo-size drinks, like the African Queen Martini and the Jungle Colada.

Mercury Lounge
5871 Hollister Avenue, Goleta
(805) 967-0907
Warm, welcoming, and casual, this neighborhood retro '50s lounge is a local favorite. The Mercury serves a great range of beers and wines, including microbrews and imports. The affable owner will also let you bring in food from nearby restaurants. You can hang out and play pool, sip a cold beer on the outdoor patio, and meet some of the loyal regulars.

Montecito

Ty Lounge
1260 Channel Drive, Montecito
(805) 969-2261
www.fourseasons.com/santabarbara
The Ty Lounge at the posh Four Seasons Resort The Biltmore Santa Barbara is the best "cheap date" in town. Order a drink, blend in with the crowd, and listen (or dance) to live music Tuesday through Saturday, usually piano, swing bands, jazz, or salsa, depending on the schedule. And there's never a cover charge.

Lucky's
1270 Coast Village Road, Montecito
(805) 565-7540
Owned by the founder of Lucky Brand jeans, this swank cocktail bar and steak house on affluent Coast Village Road draws an upper-crust crowd of chic, well-coiffed couples and moneyed Montecitans. Just look for the parade of posh cars at the valet parking. Its name speaks for itself. You can perch at the sleek bar, sip a Cosmopolitan, and gaze at the old black-and-white photos of movie stars on the walls. Lucky's has its own wine cellar and plasma TV for sporting events.

Carpinteria

The Palms
701 Linden Avenue, Carpinteria
(805) 684-3811
www.thepalmsrestaurant.com
The casual Palms restaurant has long held the title of Carpinteria's main local hangout. The cocktail lounge brings in live music Friday and Saturday. Expect anything from rock 'n' roll and country music to covers of classic '60s and '70s tunes. Try the popular Tim's Titanic cocktail with Malibu rum and Midori, and if you feel like dancing, just get up and boogie on the large dance floor.

Up the Mountain

Cold Spring Tavern
5955 Stagecoach Road, Santa Barbara
(805) 967-0066
www.coldspringtavern.com

For a real adventure, drive up California Highway 154 about 20 minutes from Santa Barbara to Cold Spring Tavern. The rustic, 1865 cabin in the woods was once a stop on the main stagecoach route. Today it offers excellent food (fish, game, pastas, steaks), as well as a range of wines, beers, and mixed drinks. You'll always find a colorful crowd here—everyone from bikers and ranchers to wine-tasting tourists.

The tavern has live music Friday, Saturday, and Sunday nights. A tip: Designate a driver when you go here—Highway 154 has only two lanes in most places and is very curvy.

SPORTS BARS AND BREWPUBS

O'Malley's
523 State Street, Santa Barbara
(805) 564-8904

O'Malley's has been around for ages. It's in the heart of the downtown bar district and flaunts the requisite overhead TVs and sports memorabilia on the walls. This is the kind of boozy bar blaring loud rock where you can dress down and play up (and check the score of your big game if you can muster the concentration). If you want a quieter spot to sit and chat, head upstairs to the cozy lounge. A DJ spins tunes usually Thursday, Friday, and Saturday nights.

Santa Barbara Brewing Company and Restaurant
501 State Street, Santa Barbara
(805) 730-1040
www.sbbrewco.com

The bright and cheery "BrewCo" is the only combination microbrewery/restaurant in Santa Barbara County. It's a classy, American-style brewpub with eight large TVs broadcasting all major college and professional sporting events. Locals and travelers of all ages come

Need an affordable designated driver? Bill's Bus (805-284-BILL; www.billsbus.com) transports college students between Isla Vista and downtown Santa Barbara Tuesday, Thursday, Friday, and Saturday from 8:30 p.m. until 2:00 a.m. Call or check the Web site for details.

here to meet with friends and drink fresh-brewed beer while watching the big game. This is also a great spot for a casual lunch any day of the week. You can wash down some hearty traditional American fare with a variety of homemade ales and lagers, such as Santa Barbara Blonde, Rincon Red, Pacific Pale Ale, and State Street Stout.

DANCE CLUBS

The Sand Bar
514 State Street, Santa Barbara
(805) 966-1388

The Sand Bar is a casual restaurant, bar, and dance spot with a beachy theme. You can sit indoors or on the lush outdoor patio and dance until you drop—or until The Bar closes. Live reggae jams on Tuesday nights, and other nights it's funk, jazz, or blues. Happy hour is 4:00 to 7:00 p.m. Tuesday through Sunday.

Zelo
630 State Street, Santa Barbara
(805) 966-5792
www.zelo.net

In the heart of all the State Street action, this popular nightspot has been around for more than 20 years, and it's nearly always voted best dance club in local polls. Zelo has a split personality. Early in the evening, it tends to be quite calm and civilized, serving classic California cuisine in the cozy indoor booths and the tropical courtyard. Then after 10:00 p.m. it really starts hopping. Each night the club features a different music theme. Call or check the Web site for weekly schedules. Cover charges vary depending on the evening, but you won't pay more than $10.

BILLIARDS

Don Q Family Billiard Center
1128 Chapala Street, Santa Barbara
(805) 966-0915

Don Q is Santa Barbara's largest pool hall. It attracts billiards fans of all ages and serves beer to players 21 and older, as well as chips and sodas. Kids can play with video and pinball games if they don't want to play pool. Don Q has a room full of excellent tables, including tournament and snooker tables. Open from noon to 2:00 a.m. every day.

COFFEEHOUSE/ BOOKSTORES

Santa Barbara has a thriving coffeehouse culture. Bookstores and cafes serve as the main social hubs for many locals who seek alternatives to the bar scene. It's easy to find Starbucks, Peets, and other chain coffee shops: They're strategically located up and down all the popular shopping and restaurant streets.

Santa Barbara Roasting Company
321 Motor Way, Santa Barbara
(805) 962-0320

607 Paseo Nuevo
(805) 962-2070

Insiders call this large coffeehouse/coffee roasting company, and its sister store, "RoCo." It reminds us of the cozy coffeehouses where we used to meet friends and pretend to study when we were in college. RoCo is usually open until 11:00 p.m. daily.

MOVIE THEATERS

Moviegoing is one of Santa Barbara's favorite pastimes. Every day of the week you can choose from a wide range of new-release films shown in the afternoons, evenings, and sometimes in the mornings as well. Metropolitan Theatres owns all the theaters in the Santa Barbara area. You can call the Metropolitan Theatres Movie Hotline (805-963-9503) or visit the Web site at www.metrotheatres.com for locations and showtime information for all the following cinemas. If a theater also has a direct number, we've listed it.

Santa Barbara

Arlington Center for the Performing Arts
1317 State Street, Santa Barbara
(805) 963-4408

Fiesta 5
916 State Street, Santa Barbara

Metro 4
618 State Street, Santa Barbara

Paseo Nuevo
8 West De la Guerra Place (in the Paseo Nuevo Mall), Santa Barbara

Plaza de Oro
371 Hitchcock Way, Santa Barbara

Riviera Theatre
2044 Alameda Padre Serra, Santa Barbara

Goleta

Camino Real Cinemas
Camino Real Marketplace, Hollister and Stork Avenue, Goleta

Fairview Theatre
225 North Fairview Avenue, Goleta

SOCIAL DANCING

Cafe Buenos Aires
1316 State Street, Santa Barbara
(805) 963-0242
www.cafebuenosaires.com

You can tango under the stars in the courtyard or inside the beautiful restaurant at informal dances held at Cafe Buenos Aires every Wednesday at 9:00 p.m. throughout the year (dancing usually lasts about an hour to an hour and a half). An international dance teacher occasionally gives a seminar. Here's your chance to practice the Argentine tango, waltz, and Milonga. Call the restaurant for more information.

Carrillo Recreation Center Ballroom
100 East Carrillo Street, Santa Barbara
(805) 897-2519
The Carrillo Rec Center boasts one of the best dance floors anywhere—it's spring-loaded, which means you can dance for long periods of time without exhausting your leg muscles.

Practice your swing dancing every first and third Friday of the month. The night begins with a lesson from 7:30 to 8:15 p.m. Ballroom dancing also happens at this convivial venue. There is a price for admission.

SHOPPING

Santa Barbara has become synonymous with style. People come from all over the world to shop here, lured by that image of Santa Barbara chic, and many expect to find haute couture and sky-high price tags. Although it's true that you will find a sprinkling of big-ticket boutiques and other posh stores in our upscale shopping districts, you can also find some great bargains.

As you embark upon your shopping adventure, you'll discover an eclectic mix of large national and international retailers as well as many charming specialty shops selling unusual products and unique gifts that you won't find anywhere else. Most of these smaller shops have to keep their prices down to compete with the retail giants, so you're bound to unearth some great deals. In this chapter, you'll also read about homegrown Santa Barbara companies with outlet stores here offering fantastic savings—up to 80 percent off regular retail prices.

Santa Barbara also has some fabulous antiques shopping. You'll find a concentration of stores in downtown Santa Barbara, Summerland, and Carpinteria brimming with treasures from the past.

Perhaps what best defines shopping in Santa Barbara is the experience itself. Strolling the sunny outdoor paseos amid palms and fountains, people-watching at a sidewalk cafe, and sampling luscious local fruits at our friendly farmers' markets are all part of the Santa Barbara shopping experience. It's a browser's paradise.

In this chapter, we first give you an overview of the region's main shopping areas. Then we take you on a brief tour of major shopping malls and arcades and share a list of homegrown stores that are unique to the area. Finally, we depart from our usual geographic listing format to point out a few of the most popular specialty stores by category—from bookstores to surfwear to women's clothing. All stores are open daily unless otherwise noted.

If you're on a mission, take this book with you to save time. Need help making a selection? Ask one of our friendly shopkeepers. Most love to chat with customers and are happy to point out one-of-a-kind treasures. Finally, a few words of advice before you head out: Pace yourself, make sure you take time to stop and enjoy the scenery, and buy something special so you'll remember Santa Barbara long after you return home. Happy shopping!

SHOPPING AREAS

Santa Barbara

For the quintessential Santa Barbara shopping experience, head downtown to State Street. You'll find most stores concentrated on or near lower State Street, between the beginning of State Street at Stearns Wharf and the 1400 block. Popular palm-lined Paseo Nuevo Mall (651 State Street), in the heart of the downtown shopping district, is a great place to start your shopping marathon. It's the largest outdoor mall in this area, parking is plentiful in the underground parking structure (enter from Chapala), and from here you can stroll up and down State Street, browsing as you go.

While you're wandering, keep an eye out

i California sets its own trends when it comes to fashion—Santa Barbara even more so. Want to understand what we mean by "California casual"? Then log onto Paseo Nuevo's fashion blog at www.sbmall.typepad.com, where you'll discover for yourself what's new on Santa Barbara's fashion scene.

for the hidden paseos, or brick-paved shopping arcades, tucked back off State Street. *Paseo* comes from the Spanish word for "passage," and these cobbled shopping corridors will lead you to some delightful locally owned specialty shops and fountained courtyard cafes. Historic El Paseo lies across State Street from Paseo Nuevo and Victoria Court, and the charming La Arcada Court shopping arcades sit at the upper end of the district between the 1100 and 1200 blocks. You can read more about these paseos in the Shopping Malls and Arcades section. To access the State Street shopping district, park in any of the city lots along Anacapa and Chapala Streets. Before you head downtown, you might also want to check out the Santa Barbara Downtown Organization Web site at www.santabarbaradowntown.com for a list of shops and services in the area as well as printable maps of the downtown shopping district and parking lot locations.

On upper State Street, which starts at about the 3000 block and continues through the 4000 block, you'll find a long stretch of shops, services, and businesses. La Cumbre Plaza, another outdoor mall adorned with palms and fountains, is the main magnet in this area—it occupies the entire 3800 block of State Street.

You'll also find several strip malls here, as well as a few shopping centers anchored by supermarkets: Five Points (across from La Cumbre Plaza on the 3900 block of State Street), Loreto Plaza (at the intersection of Las Positas Road and State Street), and Ralph's (near the intersection of State Street and Alamar Avenue, between State and De la Vina Streets).

Goleta

Loads of stores, specialty shops, and services line both sides of Calle Real between Patterson and Fairview Avenues, considered the downtown area of Goleta. The main strip mall in the area is the remodeled Calle Real Center, with nearly 50 merchants. These include Patty Montana (unique women's clothing), gift shops, the wholesaler chain store Trader Joe's, and restaurants such as Outback Steakhouse. Parking is plentiful along the strip that fronts the stores.

The Camino Real Marketplace—the largest shopping mall and discount center on the South Coast—opened in 1999 at the intersection of Hollister Avenue and Storke Road. (See the Shopping Malls and Arcades section of this chapter for a detailed description.)

Montecito

The upscale shopping area of Coast Village Road lies parallel to U.S. Highway 101 between Hot Springs and Olive Mill Roads. You'll find a mix of galleries, high-end home stores, gift shops, and chic boutiques along here, as well as some popular restaurants. You can park in the designated lane fronting the stores. At the Hot Springs Road intersection, you'll find a large shopping center with a Vons grocery store and drugstore, a French bakery, a health food store, and other specialty shops.

Montecito Village, or what the locals call "The Upper Village" at the intersection of San Ysidro and East Valley Roads, is a collection of exclusive boutiques, specialty shops, antiques stores, restaurants, a bookstore, a grocery store, and the post office. Keep your eyes open if you're hoping to run into a film star or celebrity. Since many of them live nearby, this is where you're most likely to find one grabbing a cup of coffee, a newspaper, or a bite to eat, often at Pierre La Fonds or Via Vie Restaurant.

Carpinteria and Summerland

These two seaside enclaves south of Santa Barbara are best known for their quaint shops and friendly, small-town feel. Summerland is home to the popular Bikini Factory and Indian Summers boutique, and it's also a haven for antiques shopping. You'll find most of the stores concentrated along Lillie Avenue and Ortega Hill Road, and many are housed in colorful Victorian cottages. In Carpinteria you'll find some great surf shops, small boutiques, and local stores filled with antiques, collectibles, and gifts for the home and garden. Most shops are located in the business district, which consists of several blocks radiating south, east, and west from the intersection of Linden and Carpinteria Avenues. You'll also find a couple of strip malls off Casitas Pass Road, between U.S. 101 and Carpinteria Avenue. Parking is usually plentiful and easy to find.

SHOPPING MALLS AND ARCADES

Downtown

El Paseo
800 block of State Street, Santa Barbara
Historic El Paseo was reportedly California's first shopping center. It was built in the 1920s on the site of a historic residence that belonged to one of Santa Barbara's original Spanish families. Stroll through the cool courtyards with their fountains, tiles, and wrought-iron gates, and you'll feel as though you're in an old Spanish village. Once a breathtaking locale of elite shops, El Paseo now comprises two restaurants, an antiques store, a fine jewelry store, and a plethora of investment firms and local business offices.

La Arcada Court
1114 State Street, Santa Barbara
You'll know you're at the entrance to beautiful La Arcada Court when you see a giant clock on a pedestal in front of a broad, tiled walkway about a ¹/₂ block from the Museum of Art. The Spanish-Mediterranean ambience takes you back in time and makes you forget the hustle and bustle of adjacent State Street. Wander the cool paved corridors and you'll find art galleries, specialty shops, and coffee shops. In fact, the arcade is somewhat of a gallery in itself. Whimsical sculptures and life-size bronzes provide fun photo opportunities, and the sounds of bubbling fountains fill the air. Visit the old-fashioned barber shop, or browse the stores for top-of-the-line children's clothing, consigned women's clothing, contemporary furniture, and one-of-a-kind gifts.

Paseo Nuevo
651 State Street, Santa Barbara
(805) 963-2202
www.sbmall.com
Pretty palm-lined Paseo Nuevo is the star of the Santa Barbara shopping scene. Built in 1990, this stunning outdoor mall occupies 2 full city blocks in the heart of downtown near many of the most popular restaurants, cafes, clubs, and bookstores. Palms, fountains, and tropical flowers adorn the brick-paved courtyards, where shoppers dine alfresco and stroll in the sunshine. Nordstrom and Macy's anchor the mall, and in between you'll find more than 50 shops and restaurants, a five-screen movie theater, the Contemporary Arts Forum gallery, and the Center Stage Theater (see the Arts chapter for descriptions of the latter two). During the summer months and holiday seasons, you can enjoy live jazz, carolers, and other entertainment while you browse the shops.

Paseo Nuevo merchants include well-known chains (Victoria's Secret, Gap, Bebe, Banana Republic, and See's Candy), as well as a few that are unique to Santa Barbara and/or Southern California (for example, This Little Piggy Wears Cotton). You'll find plenty of parking underneath and adjacent to the mall (enter on Chapala Street) as well as in the city lots on Anacapa and Chapala Streets.

Victoria Court
1200 block of State Street, Santa Barbara
(805) 965-2216
Locals like the small-scale, cozy ambience of the two-story collection of shops and restaurants at Victoria Court. The SOhO nightclub is

---

i Not sure what to give that special someone who has absolutely everything? Purchase a gift certificate at the Paseo Nuevo Management Office (second floor, 805-963-7147; www.sbmall.com), open Monday to Friday from 8:30 a.m. to 4:30 p.m., and the recipient can redeem it at any store in Paseo Nuevo.

upstairs, and Santa Barbara Gift Baskets and Video Schmideo—with the best selection of foreign films and documentaries in town—are down below. Pick up a croissant and a cappuccino, find a table in the peaceful courtyard, and relax and watch the world go by.

Uptown

La Cumbre Plaza
3853 State Street, Santa Barbara
(805) 687-6458
www.shoplacumbre.com
La Cumbre Plaza is a convenient one-stop shopping venue. It's 3.5 miles north of downtown Santa Barbara, between U.S. 101 and State Street, bordered by Hope Avenue and La Cumbre Road. Completed in 1967, this complex was our only large-scale mall before Paseo Nuevo was built in 1990. Amble along the lovely outdoor walkway with its tiled fountains and colorful flowers. La Cumbre also attracts fewer tourists than State Street so it tends to be less crowded but parking can sometimes be a challenge.

Macy's and Sears department stores anchor the north and south sides of La Cumbre Plaza. In between you'll find well-known chain stores such as Williams-Sonoma, Ann Taylor, Talbots, Kay Bee Toys, Express, and a Pottery Barn.

Goleta

Camino Real Marketplace
Hollister and Storke Avenue, Goleta
(805) 685-3458
www.caminorealmarketplace.com
The biggest shopping attraction in Goleta is the Camino Real Marketplace, which opened in 1999. Located at the Hollister Avenue/Storke Road intersection, this sprawling "big box" mall introduced the first conglomeration of discount retail outlets to the region. With 83 acres and 3,000 parking spaces, it's also the most diverse shopping center on the South Coast. Though some residents wince at the increased traffic and loss of open space, most shoppers appreciate the discounted wares now available in our notoriously high-

priced region. In addition to well-known stores such as Costco, Staples, Home Depot, Comp USA, Borders Books & Music, and Linens 'N Things, the mall includes restaurants such as Kahuna Grill and Pascucci's, a multiplex theater, and baseball fields.

i Scoring a parking spot at La Cumbre Plaza, especially during the holiday season, can take more than a prayer to a parking god. Locals know that behind the mall (enter off Hope Avenue between Calle Real and State Street) there are usually spaces just waiting to be had.

UNIQUE SANTA BARBARA STORES

Santa Barbara is putting on the "dog"—the Big Dog that is. Big Dog Sportswear is just one of the many unique businesses that make their home in Santa Barbara. Deckers Outdoor Corporation (www.deckers.com), manufacturer of Uggs, Simple, and Teva outdoor wear, was started by a University of California at Santa Barbara surfer boy.

Big Dog Sportswear Factory Outlet
6 East Yanonali Street, Santa Barbara
(805) 963-8728, (800) 642-DOGS
www.bigdogs.com
As legend goes, a group of friends conceived the Big Dog idea in 1983 while on a river-rafting expedition. Before tackling the rapids, everyone received a pair of oversized, brightly colored shorts. They were a huge hit. One guy supposedly said, "Man, these puppies are big!" and that timely phrase launched Big Dog Sportswear, right here in Santa Barbara.

The Big Dog name and logo—a black-and-white Saint Bernard with a great big smile and bright red tongue—now appear on casual activewear and accessories for men, women, and children in the company's 200-plus stores across the United States. You can also buy Big Dog clothing through mail-order catalogs.

At the outlet store, which sits on the corner of State and Yanonali Streets just a few blocks up from Cabrillo Boulevard, you can pick up Big Dog items at greatly reduced prices. Big dogs (and little dogs) are also welcome in the store.

Crispin Leather
18 West Anapamu Street, Santa Barbara
(805) 966-2510
www.crispinleather.com
Since 1965, Crispin Leather has supplied Santa Barbarans and visitors from far and wide with top-quality leather goods. They specialize in "comfort footwear," carrying major brands (e.g., Birkenstock, Dansko, Born, and Teva). Locals shop here for quality hiking boots, belts, hats, wallets, and purses.

Jedlicka's Saddlery
2605 De la Vina Street, Santa Barbara
(805) 687-0747, (800) 681-0747
www.jedlickas.com
Bring out the wrangler in you with Jedlicka's, reknown for its cowboy boots and hats. Started by George (Jed) Jedlicka in 1932, this Western store provides "everything for you and your horse." This is where real ranchers outfit themselves. You'll have a great time looking through the authentic Western clothes, belt buckles, Stetson hats, custom-made saddles, and riding equipment for men, women, and children. Jedlicka's is closed Sunday.

Magellan's
110 West Sola Street, Santa Barbara
(805) 568-5400, (800) 962-4943
www.magellans.com
America's leading source for travel supplies is headquartered right here in Santa Barbara. You can visit the showroom and view all the unique travel products featured in Magellan's catalogs, from alarm clocks and luggage to rain gear and water filters. Access the Web site for great Web specials and travel advice. The store is closed Sunday.

Santa Barbara Gift Baskets
Victoria Court
1221 State Street, #13, Santa Barbara
(805) 965-1245
www.sbgiftbaskets.com
Tucked in a corner in Victoria Court, this small shop specializes in gift baskets featuring locally produced gourmet foods, wines, and gifts. Choose one of the prefilled baskets, such as the "Little Bit of Santa Barbara Basket" or the "Fiesta Bucket." Or you can custom-design a gift basket with your choice of local goods, such as honey, chocolates, wines, olives, marmalades, salad dressings, marinades, and notecards. Santa Barbara Gift Baskets also carries wedding, wine, and special-occasion gift items year-round, and they'll deliver them locally or ship nationwide.

Santa Barbara Outfitters
1200 State Street, Santa Barbara
(805) 564-1007
www.sboutfitters.com
Santa Barbara Outfitters is known more for its adventure programs, including mountain biking, river rafting, hiking, backpacking, and trips to the Channel Islands. Now, locals are turning to the huge Santa Barbara Outfitters store for their athletic needs. Name the sport, and you'll find the equipment or apparel required. Rumor has it that online shopping is just around the corner. When something's so good, why not share it with the rest of the world? The store's indoor climbing wall is open seven days a week and is the perfect place to let your kids test their adventurous spirit.

The Territory Ahead
515 State Street, Santa Barbara
(805) 962-5558, ext. 181
www.territoryahead.com
Many people know about this high-quality clothing company through its popular mail-order catalog. But here in Santa Barbara—the home of The Territory Ahead—you can try on and buy the clothes and accessories in the flagship store.

Territory Ahead designs and develops casual yet classy men's and women's clothing and accessories made from high-quality natural fiber fabrics and materials. These are the clothes you might wear while on safari or strolling the streets of Shanghai. For bigger savings, visit the Territory Ahead Outlet a few blocks down State Street, at 400 State Street. (See the Outlets section toward the end of this chapter for details.)

This Little Piggy Wears Cotton
311 Paseo Nuevo, Santa Barbara
(805) 564-6982
www.littlepiggy.com

One of our all-time favorite stores for children, "The Piggy" offers unique, top-of-the-line designer-style clothes for babies, boys, and girls. The quality and style are unsurpassed. The imported and domestic toys are also of the highest quality, and most are educational. Thanks to the store's success, the owners expanded and now have five "Piggys" throughout California, Arizona, and Oregon. This Little Piggy is a great place to shop for baby showers, birthdays, baptisms, and any occasion for which you can muster an excuse to lavish a child with "only the best."

ANTIQUES

Santa Barbara and its neighboring city, Summerland, have a variety of old Victorians brimming with antiques that lure people from far and wide. Take a walk down the quaint streets of yesteryear—Brinkerhoff Avenue in Santa Barbara and Lillie Avenue in Summerland—here you're sure to discover the perfect antique.

Antique Alley
706 State Street, Santa Barbara
(805) 962-3944

This antiques collective is jam-packed with all kinds of collectibles and bric-a-brac. The aisles resemble a giant estate sale, with antique furniture, estate jewelry, china, glassware, pottery, fine art, paintings, prints, and vintage clothes.

Brinkerhoff Avenue (between State, West Cota, West Haley, and De la Vina Streets), Santa Barbara

Stroll along this charming street, and you can shop for antiques and admire the beautifully restored Victorian cottages at the same time. Brinkerhoff Avenue was named for Samuel Brinkerhoff, Santa Barbara's first physician. All the original Victorian houses still stand, and the city of Santa Barbara has designated Brinkerhoff Avenue as a special historic district. A few of the houses are now charming shops with antiques, wood carvings, collectibles, and specialty gifts.

Brostrom's Antiques & Reproductions
539 San Ysidro Road, Montecito
(805) 565-0039

Mixed with Asian antiques (handpicked by owner Allen Brostrom during his shopping excursions to Asia) are some contemporary but equally as artful items, such as Mary Frances purses (if you've never seen them, they are simply divine!) and, during the holidays, Patricia Breen's designer Christmas ornament lines.

Europa Antiques & Fine Art
2345 Lillie Avenue, Summerland
(805) 969-4989
www.antiqueseuropa.com

Europa is easy to find: Just look for the enormous 17th-century Spanish wine vessels at its entranceway. You'll wend your way through rooms brimming with antiques, fine art, and garden objects from the 16th to 20th centuries.

The Gentlemen Antiquarians
El Paseo
Space 37 & 38, 812 State Street, Santa Barbara
(805) 965–5355

A plethora of antiques may be discovered in Santa Barbara. GREG PETERSON/SANTA BARBARA CONFERENCE & VISITORS BUREAU

The Gentlemen Antiquarians specializes in 18th- and 19th-century European furnishings, but you'll also find an eclectic mix of English, French, Oriental, and American antiques and accessories, Russian icons, and musical instruments. The store is open seven days a week.

Summerhill Antiques
2280 Lillie Avenue, Summerland
(805) 969-3366
Summerhill was established in 1977 as seaside Summerland's first antiques store. You can browse two floors filled with world-class antiques especially from the Edwardian and Victorian periods.

The Treasure House
1070 Fairway Road, Montecito
(805) 969-1744
Set on the Music Academy of the West campus, this high-end consignment shop sells

"antiques and fabulous things" to benefit the Music Academy of the West. You'll find everything from antiques, china, linens, and silver to furniture and paintings here. The Treasure House also gladly accepts donations. Open 1:00 to 4:00 p.m. Tuesday through Saturday.

BOOKSTORES

Bennett's Educational Materials
Magnolia Shopping Center
5130 Hollister Avenue, Santa Barbara
(805) 964-8998
www.BennettsEducational.com
Parents, teachers, and anyone looking for quality books, toys, and school supplies will love this store, which has been in business in Santa Barbara since 1972. Bennett's sells a diverse range of children's books, workbooks, teaching resources, developmental toys, posters, and puzzles with an emphasis on educational

items. The preschool section is particularly strong. Pop in and have a look. You're sure to find something fun and fascinating for your little ones.

The Book Den
15 East Anapamu Street, Santa Barbara
(805) 962-3321
www.bookden.com

The Book Den is Santa Barbara's oldest and best-stocked bookstore, with tens of thousands of new, used, and out-of-print books (mostly used). Consistently voted "Best Used Bookstore" in a local poll, this popular store also provides online out-of-print search services. The titles encompass a wide range of subjects, including California history and architecture and books in foreign languages. You can browse the virtual shelves at the Web site or wander in and look for yourself. To find the store, just walk across the street from the Museum of Art.

The Chandlery
132-B Harbor Way, Santa Barbara
(805) 965-4538
www.chandlery.com

If you're looking for maritime books, this is the place to go. Established in 1946, The Chandlery offers an array of fiction and non-fiction books, charts, and maps, all related to boating, sailing, and nautical themes. Looking for a cookbook to take on a cruise or a book on sailing rules, repairing a boat, or tying knots? You'll find them all here, plus expert staff members who can point you to the exact books and charts you need.

The Chandlery overlooks the Santa Barbara Harbor, between the Yacht Club and Brophy Bros. restaurant.

Chaucer's Books
Loreto Plaza
3321 State Street, Santa Barbara
(805) 682-6787
www.chaucer.booksense.com

Insider bibliophiles rank Chaucer's as the best independent bookstore in town. It has a huge

i Looking for a unique Santa Barbara souvenir or a special gift? Don't miss the Arts & Crafts show on Cabrillo Boulevard, where you can stroll along the waterfront and buy original artwork from more than 290 local artists. The show is held Sunday and special holidays from 10:00 a.m. until dusk. For more information, call (805) 897-1982.

selection of titles—all stacked sky-high on shelves, floors, and any available space in the relatively small quarters. Chaucer's has extremely knowledgeable staff, an incredibly diverse selection of books, an outstanding children's section, and regular book signings by famous authors. The store is in Loreto Plaza, at the intersection of Las Positas Road and State Street.

Front Page
5737 Calle Real, Goleta
(805) 967-0733

This small bookstore offers a great selection of magazines, newspapers, popular paperbacks, current best-sellers, maps, cards, and stationery. You'll also find postcards and a few children's titles.

Isla Vista Bookstore
6553 Pardall Road, Santa Barbara
(805) 968-3600
www.ivbooks.com

Conveniently situated just down the road from UCSB, Isla Vista Bookstore is a complete off-campus college store. It primarily sells used textbooks and educational paperbacks but also offers clothing, art, and school supplies.

Lost Horizon Bookstore
703 Anacapa Street, Santa Barbara
(805) 962-4606

Lost Horizon buys, sells, and appraises single copies and entire libraries of antiquarian books and maps. It has hundreds of books on the fine and decorative arts, monographs on artists, pencil-signed prints, paintings, and photographs.

Metro Entertainment
6 West Anapamu Street, Santa Barbara
(805) 963–2168
www.metroautographs.com
Kids clamor to go to Metro, which has every type of comic book published. It carries a full line of them, including Japanese anime, children's, and independents. It also has games, toys, and TV and movie merchandise and memorabilia.

Pacific Travelers Supply
12 West Anapamu Street, Santa Barbara
(805) 963-4438, (888) PAC-TRAV
www.sbtravelstore.com
Part of Nations! Travelstores, Inc., Pacific Travelers offers one-stop shopping for travel books, luggage, clothing, gifts, and accessories, but it's probably best known for its excellent maps. Whether you're headed to Antarctica, Italy, or Mozambique, you can order a map of your destination here. The expert staff will help you find everything you need.

Pacifica Graduate Institute Bookstore
249 Lambert Road, Carpinteria
(805) 969-3626, ext. 121
www.pacifica.edu/bookstore.html
Tucked in the renovated wine cellar of the former Fleischmann estate, the Pacifica Graduate Institute Bookstore carries titles related to psychology, mythology, religion, and philosophy in ancient cultures. The store also stocks tapes, cards, music, videos, drums, images, and jewelry.

Located on the campus that houses the Joseph Campbell Collection, it's between Summerland and Carpinteria; take the Padaro Lane exit, go south on Via Real, turn left on Lambert Road, and head toward the mountains. (For more information on the institute, see the Education and Child Care chapter.)

Paperback Alley Used Books
5840 Hollister Avenue, Goleta
(805) 967-1051

For more than 25 years, Paperback Alley has bought and sold thousands of fiction and non-fiction books, mostly paperbacks. You're bound to find something you like at an affordable price.

Paradise Found
17 East Anapamu Street, Santa Barbara
(805) 564-3573
www.paradise-found.net
If you're into metaphysics, you'll find paradise here in the form of metaphysical books, gifts, jewelry, incense, tapes, compact discs, and astrology charts. Listen to music, and savor the incense. An on-site intuitive reader or astrologer is often on hand. Call for an appointment.

Read 'N Post
1046-B Coast Village Road, Montecito
(805) 969-1148
An entire wall of the Read 'N Post is devoted to magazines of all types and sizes, including an abundant collection of French magazines. The store also carries a wide selection of newspapers, maps, and paperbacks. Buy a magazine or paper, drop off your mail (there's a post office here), then head next door to Starbucks for a cup of coffee—that's what many Montecitans do every day.

Sullivan Goss Books & Prints, Ltd.
7 East Anapamu Street, Santa Barbara
(805) 730-1460
www.sullivangoss.com
Sullivan Goss boasts one of the largest selections of books on art, architecture, and photography in the world. It buys and sells new, rare, and out-of-print books on architecture, art history, and photography, as well as artists' biographies and catalogues raisonnés.

Artists, collectors, gallery owners, and art lovers all shop here regularly. The store also offers vintage and contemporary paintings, prints, and photographs by California artists.

The Arts and Letters Cafe, in a beautiful courtyard at the back of the store, provides delicious gourmet meals and classical music entertainment (see the Restaurants chapter for details).

Tecolote Book Shop
1470 East Valley Road, Montecito
(805) 969-4977

When it first opened for business in 1925, Tecolote was a carriage-trade bookstore—the staff would bring books to the carriage to show the customers. Today the small, intimate Tecolote remains a favorite bookstore among Insiders. Choose from a diverse selection of books, and pay extra attention to the many unusual art and coffee-table books, especially those on Montecito and Santa Barbara history.

Tecolote sits on the edge of a green lawn with a fountain in Montecito's Upper Village, an ideal spot to rest, read, and regroup.

UCSB Bookstore
University Center
UCSB, Santa Barbara
(805) 893-3271
www.bookstore.ucsb.edu

Conveniently located on campus in the University Center, the UCSB Bookstore buzzes with students, teachers, and faculty members, and it's also open to the public. The store specializes in academic support materials, but you can also stock up on computer software, greeting cards, UCSB sweatshirts, gifts, and school and office supplies.

Vedanta Book Shop (Sarada Convent Books)
925 Ladera Lane, Montecito
(805) 969-5697

Part of the Vedanta Temple, this religious bookstore offers an impressive variety of books covering all major religions, including Buddhism, Hinduism, Native American religions, Islam, and Sufism. You'll also find a huge selection of deity statues, for example, Kuan Yen (a goddess of compassion), Buddha, traditional Christian statues, santos, and angels and gift items, such as jewelry and incense.

If you're heading out to the farmers' market, take a big basket or bag. It's easier to carry all the fresh fruit and vegetables in one large carrier than to juggle a bunch of plastic bags.

FARMERS' MARKETS

Santa Barbara Certified Farmers' Market Association
232 Anacapa Street, Suite 1A
(805) 962-5354
www.sbfarmersmarket.org

Sunset magazine selected the Santa Barbara farmers' market as one of the "Top 10 Farmers' Markets in the West." It was started in 1973 by a handful of Santa Barbara growers who sold their produce at the Mission Rose Gardens. Now it's a nonprofit association with more than 140 growers.

We love shopping at the farmers' markets every week for our fruits and vegetables (many are organic or not sprayed with pesticides), flowers, nuts, eggs, honey, cheese, and plants. They're also fun places to browse and people-watch. Bring lots of change and small bills as well as sacks or baskets for all your purchases.

The association currently sponsors the following local markets:

Saturday: Downtown Santa Barbara Market (this is the largest and most popular one) is at the corner of Santa Barbara and Cota Streets and is open Saturday from 8:30 a.m. to 12:30 p.m.

Sunday: Camino Real Marketplace, at the corner of Storke and Hollister Streets in Goleta, is open Sunday from 10:00 a.m. to 2:00 p.m.

Tuesday: Old Town Santa Barbara Market, in the 500 and 600 blocks of State Street, is open Tuesday from 3:00 to 6:30 p.m. (4:00 to 7:30 p.m. during the summer).

Wednesday: La Cumbre Plaza Market, inside the La Cumbre Plaza Shopping Center, is open Wednesday from 1:00 to 5:00 p.m. (2:00 to 6:00 p.m. during the summer).

Thursday: Goleta Market, in the 5700 block of Calle Real, is open from 3:00 to 6:00 p.m. year-round.

Thursday: Carpinteria Market, in the 800 block of Linden Avenue, is open from 3:00 to 6:00 p.m. (4:00 to 7:00 p.m. during the summer).

Friday: Montecito Market is in the 1100 and 1200 blocks of Coast Village Road and is open from 8:00 to 11:15 a.m.

Santa Barbara Fishermen's Market
Santa Barbara Harbor (in front of Brophy Bros. on the Navy Pier)
(805) 965-9564
www.sbfish.com

You can't get fish much fresher than this unless you catch it yourself. The market is usually held every Saturday from 7:30 to 11:30 a.m. You can buy only whole fish, so be prepared to feed a crowd or freeze what you don't eat. Take your fish to the adjacent Fish Market (run by the same association) at 117-F Harbor Way, and they'll fillet your fish so it's ready to cook.

If you're not an early bird or if it happens to be a day of the week other than Saturday, you can still purchase the association's fresh fish at the aforementioned Fish Market, which is open daily.

GARDEN DELIGHTS

Gallup & Stribling Orchids
3450 Via Real, Carpinteria
(805) 684-9842, (805) 684-1998
www.americanorchids.com

Gallup & Stribling Orchids is one of the world's largest wholesale orchid growers, but everyone is welcome to buy these tropical blooms in their excellent visitor center. Set on 48 acres in the foothills of Carpinteria, the nursery specializes in growing cymbidiums and phalaenopsis as cut flowers and pot plants. The visitor center displays many of the farm's prized specimens and a huge selection of these outrageously ravishing blooms.

Garden Market
3811 Santa Claus Lane, Carpinteria
(805) 745-5505
www.thegardenmarkets.com

From the front, Garden Market resembles a fruit market, with its baskets of avocados, papayas, and mangoes, but wander in and you'll find a cute little cafe, delightful gifts, and a courtyard nursery. Looking for a gift for the gardener in your life? Take a peek in the gardening shed out back, where you'll find books, gloves, accessories, and gift baskets.

Island View Nursery
3376 Foothill Road, Carpinteria
(805) 684-0324

Home store location
1036 Casitas Pass Road, Carpinteria
(805) 684-0363
www.islandviewnursery.com

You can travel the globe in a few hours strolling around this unusual nursery. Enter the 15,000-square-foot showroom through hand-carved Balinese temple doors, breathe in the fragrance of tropical blooms, and let your eyes lead you through lush palms to imaginative displays of imported furniture, art, and exotic plants from around the world. You can also browse the huge collection of orchids and other tropical blooms in the adjacent greenhouses. The outdoor gardens are equally inspirational. Wander the winding pathways and you'll discover rare palms, aloes, bamboo, and colorful annuals and perennials in a gorgeous garden setting adorned with pottery and hand-carved statues. The retail location is a fantastic place to buy unusual gifts or gather some ideas for a tropical home makeover.

Santa Barbara Botanic Garden
1212 Mission Canyon Road, Santa
Barbara
(805) 682-4726, ext. 127
www.sbbg.org
The Garden Growers Nursery at the Botanic Garden is a great source for native California and unusual drought-tolerant Mediterranean plants. It's staffed by volunteers from 10:00 a.m. to 3:00 p.m. daily and is open on a self-serve basis during the garden hours (see Attractions). You can also shop for books, crafts, gift items, cards, and posters at the Garden Shop, which is open daily during Botanic Garden hours.

i Santa Barbara is one of the nation's leading producers of orchids. If you'd like to tour an orchid-growing estate or buy a rare specimen, visit www.sborchidshow.com for information on growers, a history of orchid growing in the region, and the International Orchid Show.

Santa Barbara Orchid Estate
1250 Orchid Drive, Goleta
(805) 967-1284
www.sborchid.com
One of the world's largest collections of orchids is shown at the five-acre Orchid Estate, home of a vast selection of cymbidiums. A stroll through the grounds will surprise and delight the senses. You can purchase orchid plants and bulbs as well as cut flowers, and all can be shipped anywhere in the United States.

OUTLET STORES

Big Dog Sportswear Factory Outlet
6 East Yanonali Street, Santa Barbara
(805) 963-8728, (800) 642-DOGS
www.bigdogs.com
This popular factory outlet is a Santa Barbara institution. If you love bright, comfortable, casual clothing, stop in here and pick up some gear. You can't miss the bold Big Dog

logo. For more details, see the write-up under Unique Santa Barbara Stores earlier in this chapter.

Italian Pottery Outlet
19 Helena Street, Santa Barbara
(805) 564-7655
www.italianpottery.com
Less than a block up from the beach, between State and Anacapa Streets, is the largest selection of Italian ceramics in the western United States. You can buy all sorts of pottery firsts and seconds, from Sicilian folk art to classic designs, for up to 50 percent off retail prices. The store also carries other gift items from Italy.

Santa Barbara Ceramic Design
436 East Gutierrez Street, Santa Barbara
(805) 966-3883
www.sbceramic.com
Since 1976, this wholesale factory outlet has been dressing up homes and gardens nationwide with colorful ceramic art.

Best-sellers are the cheery address plaques and switch plates, but the store also sells other items, such as clocks, doorbells, platters, plates, and coffee cups. This is a great place to shop for gifts. The store now carries the unique line of Lolita martini glasses, which will have you sipping your Cosmopolitan in style.

The Territory Ahead Outlet Store
400 State Street, Santa Barbara
(805) 962-5558, ext. 185
This outlet store carries discontinued and discounted clothing and accessories—the same stuff you see in Territory's regular store a block up State Street, only a few months later and a lot cheaper. Expect discounts of 30 to 80 percent. Some of their best-sellers are seconds sold at cost—especially leather goods, such as shoes and jackets. See the store description in the Unique to Santa Barbara section earlier in this chapter.

A Garden of Eden for Organic Shopping

Forty years ago, "organic" was a word most people only heard in college chemistry classes. Today, organic labels are splashed across fruit, vegetables, meat, milk, and other products in markets across the nation. In health-conscious Santa Barbara, shopping for organic produce is an entrenched ritual for thousands of residents who care about their families' health and the health of the planet. Many also say organic food just tastes better. But if you're shopping for organic products, it helps to understand the different labels so you know exactly what you're buying.

In 2002, after a decade of heated debate, the U.S. Department of Agriculture (USDA) introduced federal regulations setting strict standards for organic food labeling. Under this new legislation, anything labeled "organic" must be produced without the use of pesticides, antibiotics, growth hormones, bioengineering, or ionizing radiation. The rules also require farmers to conserve soil and water and to treat animals humanely. A government-approved agency inspects and certifies organic products.

Now when you're shopping, you'll see one of three USDA-sanctioned labels on all organic products whether imported or grown in the United States:

- "100 Percent Organic" means that the product must contain only organically produced ingredients.
- "Organic" designates products made up of 95 percent or more organically produced ingredients.
- "Made with Organic Ingredients" means that the products must consist of at least 70 percent organic ingredients.

Foods that are 95 percent organic or more can display the green-and-white USDA organic seal.

All this is good news for organic food producers and consumers. The regulations help increase consumer confidence, boost sales, and, ultimately, lower prices, making organic products more affordable for everyone. Best of all, our planet will be a healthier place to live. If you're hunting for organic products here in Santa Barbara, you'll find an array of excellent health food stores and fruit and vegetable stands. Here are a few of our favorites:

For convenient one-stop shopping, go to **Lazy Acres Market,** at 302 Meigs Road (near the intersection of Cliff Drive) in Santa Barbara (805-564-4410; www.lazyacres.com). Lazy Acres carries high-quality organic produce, grains, and dairy products, as well as all-natural (haven't been pumped with hormones or antibiotics) fish, poultry, and meats, a deli counter, a bakery, gourmet treats, and all the usual things you would expect at a supermarket.

Lassen's Health Foods, at 5154 Hollister Avenue in Goleta's Magnolia Shopping Center (805-683-7696; www.lassens.com), and **Tri-County Produce Co.,** at 335 South Milpas Street in Santa Barbara (805-965-4558; www.tri

countyproduce.com), also offer a range of organic and natural products.

Weekly farmers' markets are great places to find fresh organic produce (see the Farmers' Market section of this chapter). You can also stop in at the following stands—most are open daily: **Fairview Gardens Farms,** 598 North Fairview Avenue, Goleta (805-967-7369; www.fairviewgardens.com. Many local residents invest in harvest "shares" of produce from mid-March through mid-November); **Lane Farms Green Stand,** 308 Walnut Lane, off Hollister Avenue, Goleta (805-964-3773); **Lane Farms-San Marcos Gardens,** 4950 Hollister Avenue, Goleta (805-964-0424); and **Mesa Produce,** 1905 Cliff Drive, Santa Barbara (805-962-1645).

Agriculture is one of SB County's largest industries. NIK WHEELER/SANTA BARBARA CONFERENCE & VISITORS BUREAU

SKATEBOARDS

Church of Skatan
26 East Gutierrez Street, Santa Barbara
(805) 899-1586
If you're obsessed with skateboarding, you'll be totally at home in this unusual shop housed in a building that was once a real church. It provides top-quality equipment for hard-core skateboarders, including a large selection of shoes.

SURF AND BEACHWEAR

If you want to look like a Santa Barbara Insider, you should wear the proper attire: shorts, T-shirts, sandals, bathing suits, hats, and sunglasses. Go to any of these shops and ask the staff for guidance—they'll be glad to deck you out in Santa Barbara style.

A-Frame Surf
3785 Santa Claus Lane
Carpinteria
(805) 684-8803
www.aframesurfshop.com
Run by two local brothers, this surf shop opened in 1999 on Santa Claus Lane. Heading for the waves and need some equipment? You can rent surfboards, body boards, wet suits, fins, and skim boards here, and surfing lessons are available year-round. The store also sells short boards from local designers such as Progressive and Clyde Beatty Jr., as well as some hard-to-find smaller lines of surf and beachwear for men, women, and children. You'll also find a large selection of Hawaiian shirts.

The Beach House
10 State Street, Santa Barbara
(805) 963-1281
www.surfnwear.com
Local teenagers love The Beach House, as do the young-at-heart. Santa Barbara's quintessential beach store sells long and short surfboards, boogie boards, beachwear, and accessories. If you want to learn more about surfing, check out the books, videos, and antique surfboards. The store also runs a great summer surf camp for kids. (See the Kid-stuff chapter.)

The Bikini Factory
2275 B Ortega Hill Road, Summerland
(805) 969-2887
The Bikini Factory is a funky little store just off the freeway exit in Summerland that has been saving women from the bathing suit blues for more than three decades. It has a fantastic selection of swimsuits and casual clothes for all ages and sizes. You can mix and match bikini tops and bottoms, and customize your own bathing suit.

Channel Islands Surfboards
36 Anacapa Street, Santa Barbara
(805) 966-7213
www.cisurfboards.com
The classic surf store specializes in high-performance short boards, but you can find a huge variety of surfboards here, all designed by Al Merrick, one of the best board designers and shapers in the surfing industry. You can also choose from a good selection of wet suits, shirts, shorts, sundresses, and sandals.

Surf Country
Calle Real Center
5668 Calle Real, Goleta
(805) 683-4450
www.surfcountry.net
Surf Country is a complete surf and skate shop, with a great selection of surfboards, wet suits, skateboards, and beachwear for children and adults. You'll also find clothes, watches, sunglasses, hats, and accessories, and the staff is happy to dispense information about the best surf and beach spots. Surf Country rents soft and hard surfboards and body boards; wet suits and surfing lessons are also available.

CLOTHING

Angel
1221 Coast Village Road, Montecito
(805) 565-1599
www.wendyfoster.com

At Angel, the younger and hipper sister store of Wendy Foster, you'll find a hand-picked selection of cool clothes and accessories from small designer labels. Montecito darlings shop here for special events, but the store stocks everything from bikinis, jeans, and trendy sportswear to chic evening dresses and accessories.

Blue Bee
923–925 State Street, Santa Barbara
(805) 897-1137
www.bluebee.com

Blue Bee's two owners moved to Santa Barbara five years ago and since then have taken the Santa Barbara clothing retail scene by "swarm." Blue Bee, the original store, is where hip teens shop for everything from casual wear to designer collections. Trying to decide on a gift for your discerning teen? You can't go wrong with a gift certificate to Blue Bee.

Blue Bee Jeans
915 State Street, Santa Barbara
(805) 882-2468

Right next door to Blue Bee is Blue Bee Jeans. This 5,000-square-foot space has become known for launching the latest in designer jeans.

Blue Bee Shoes
1102 State Street, Santa Barbara
(805) 965-1956

Blue Bee Shoes lets you step out in style, with its breathtaking display of Italian shoes. Sigerson Morrison, Moschino, Lucchese Boots, and Christian Lacroix are just a few of the makers of these luscious shoes. Don't miss the handbags by Escada and Marc Jacobs.

Blue Beetle
925 State Street, Santa Barbara
(805) 897-1137
www.bluebeemen.com

Men love to shop, too, and Blue Bee hasn't forgotten them, with their 2005 opening of Blue Beetle. The store showcases the swankiest of men's clothing.

Blue Bee Luxury
1100 State Street, Santa Barbara
(805) 965-1956

Is your head abuzz with the number of Blue Bee stores? We're not done yet. Blue Bee Luxury is the most exclusive of exclusive, offering everything from one-of-a-kind garments to unique jewelry. Looking for something sexy and fun? Try one of Nicole Miller's or Jenny Packham's chic dresses.

Diani
1324 State Street, Suite B, Santa Barbara
(805) 966-3114
www.dianiboutique.com

Caroline Diani displays a collection of sleek and timeless designer clothing in this soothing showroom of sea grass, potted palms, and blond woods. Inspired by her time in Kenya, the collections accent classic, understated style and include European and American labels .

Diani Essentials
1324 State Street, Suite H, Santa Barbara
(877) 342-6474

Right around the corner from the main boutique is Diani Essentials, which, as the manager says, "is like stepping into someone's closet and picking out the perfect thing." This tiny store is filled with seasonal "exclusives." This is the place for the woman in search of must-haves.

Diani Shoes
Diani Shoes stepped onto the scene in the fall of 2006, when the demand for high-end shoes prompted its opening. This delightful boutique, filled with unusual styles, is as relaxing

Shoppers come from far and wide to scout out Santa Barbara's garage sales. To get a jump start, check the Friday classifieds in the *Santa Barbara News-Press*.

as it is trendy. Browse among its high-fashion footwear. A sighting of Ferragamos or Tracy Reeses may just tempt a splurge.

Indian Summers
2275 Ortega Hill Road, Summerland
(805) 969-1162
This tiny gem of a boutique appeals to women of all ages looking for stylish, comfortable casual wear. The store carries collections from well-established and new designers, including Sue Wong dresses, JW Los Angeles, and clothing from the BCBG label. You'll also find handcrafted jewelry and other accessories, such as hats, shoes, leather totes, and purses. The store is closed Monday.

Patty Montana
5726 Calle Real, Goleta
(805) 683-2733
At Patty Montana, you'll find a great selection of casual contemporary attire, including dresses, separates, jackets, sweaters, and jewelry. The store offers a wide range of colors and styles and has an extensive lingerie collection.

Wendy Foster
833 State Street, Santa Barbara
(805) 966-2276

516 San Ysidro Road, Santa Barbara
(805) 565-1506
www.wendyfoster.com
The clothes in this upscale boutique reflect Santa Barbara's casually elegant style. The store stocks sportswear as well as dressier outfits from small labels—clothing you can't usually find in other shops. It's very expensive, but the quality is high, and the subdued colors and classic designs seem to stay in style. If you can't decide on a purchase, buy a gift certificate and give the gift of guilt-free shopping.

ATTRACTIONS

Santa Barbarans love showing visitors around their beautiful home. When you come here, you'll see why. For such a relatively small town, Santa Barbara offers an amazing diversity of things to see and do. Explore the region and you'll discover nationally acclaimed museums, wildlife sanctuaries, stunning gardens, fascinating historical sights, informative tours, and an exciting lineup of ocean adventures. Look around you. Chances are many of your fellow explorers are locals, who unabashedly proclaim that they'd rather spend their vacation discovering their own city than jet off to some exotic locale.

Of course, the locals have "been there, done that," but they know that new exhibits, expansions, and upgrades make Santa Barbara attractions worth visiting again and again. The Santa Barbara Art Museum, for instance, just received one of its most significant gifts of late-19th- and early-20th-century works by French, British, and American artists. Masterpieces by Mary Cassatt, Pierre-Auguste Renoir, Armand Guillaumin, and Berthe Morisot now hang proudly on the walls of this gem of an art museum. The continual changing and upgrading of existing attractions, along with the addition of new ones (such as the multimillion-dollar Maritime Museum), are why many Santa Barbarans are happy to spend their vacations at home.

If you're a history buff, you'll be pleased to know that most of the city's historical sights lie within a short stroll from each other in the downtown area. You can explore them in a couple of hours by taking the self-guided Red Tile Walking Tour (see the Close-up in this chapter), which begins at the County Courthouse, one of Santa Barbara's most famous landmarks.

If you're more interested in some seaside fun, head for Stearns Wharf and the Santa Barbara Harbor, where you can go for a stroll in the crisp sea air, grab some fresh seafood, and browse the specialty shops.

Tired of trying to see it all on your own? Let someone else show you around on a special tour by trolley, limousine, private car, or van. (We've listed a few of the best-known tour companies toward the end of this chapter.) Most will customize itineraries to suit your particular interests.

Finally, to save you time, we've designed a few itineraries featuring "must-do" Santa Barbara attractions. Flip to the end of this chapter and you'll find suggestions for one-, three-, and five-day stays. Use them as a guide. If you have a particular passion not covered in these suggestions, you can supplement or substitute them with other activities covered elsewhere in this book.

Attractions outside the greater Santa Barbara area are discussed in the Day Trips chapter, which covers destinations both north and south of the city. But we think you'll find enough right here to keep you happily occupied for quite a long time. Enjoy!

SANTA BARBARA

Cultural Attractions

Arlington Center for the Performing Arts
1317 State Street, Santa Barbara
(805) 963-4408
The Arlington Center is one of Santa Barbara's most beloved performance venues, and both its name and its location speak volumes about Santa Barbara history. In 1875 the tony Arlington Hotel occupied the current site of the Arlington Center. The hotel was a magnet for the rich and famous of the day, including several presidents, movie stars, military heroes, and foreign guests.

In 1909 a fire of undetermined origin burned the hotel to the ground. A "new"

Arlington was built on the site, but it never quite lived up to the original and was razed in 1925. In 1931 Fox West Coast Theatres built an impressive, Moorish-style movie palace on the site. That historic structure is now occupied by the Arlington Center for the Performing Arts.

The seats on the main floor of the elaborate theater provide the illusion of being under an open sky in the central courtyard of a Spanish village. Slanted tile roofs, arched doorways, and balconies surround the perimeter, and above the rooftops are mountain vistas and twinkling stars arranged as they might appear in the night sky. So realistic is this scene that Santa Barbarans have often been able to convince a newcomer that this is indeed an outdoor theater-under-the-stars.

These days, in addition to featuring first-run films, the Arlington is home to the Santa Barbara Symphony and hosts a plethora of other special events. No formal tours are offered, and the theater is open regularly to the public only during the screening of movies or other public events. Plan to go early so you can explore a bit before the lights go down.

Karpeles Manuscript Library Museum
21 West Anapamu Street, Santa Barbara
(805) 962-5322
www.rain.org/~karpeles

A small museum dedicated to historical documents, the Karpeles has a significant collection of rare manuscripts and original documents. Discover works from authors such as H. G. Wells, Mark Twain, Sir Arthur Conan Doyle, and John Steinbeck. In addition, the Karpeles has historical documents from the fields of history, music, science, and art, including works by Einstein, Darwin, and Newton. Since the Karpeles family's acquisitions are rather staggering, exhibits change periodically, so you may see new documents each time you visit. Occasionally, the museum hosts special events such as the Great Women in History exhibit. The museum is open daily from 10:00 a.m. to 4:00 p.m. Admission and all special events are free. You can read more about the museum in The Arts chapter.

Santa Barbara Museum of Art
1130 State Street, Santa Barbara
(805) 963-4364
www.sbmuseart.org

One of the top 10 regional museums in the country, the Santa Barbara Museum of Art has permanent collections of Asian, American, and European art, including works by such well-known artists as Thomas Eakins, Claude Monet, Marc Chagall, Pablo Picasso, and Georgia O'Keeffe. See the chapter on The Arts for more details.

Historic Places and Historical Museums

Carriage & Western Art Museum
129 Castillo Street, Santa Barbara
(805) 962-2353
www.carriagemuseum.org

When Santa Barbara's historic carriages and stagecoaches are not making their annual appearance in the Old Spanish Days parade (see our Annual Events chapter), they're housed at this museum, which contains one of the most extensive collections of antique carriages in the country.

You'll see a variety of horse-drawn carriages (sans the horses, of course), many owned by early Santa Barbara families and restored by the museum. The museum also houses an impressive collection of saddles, a horse-drawn fire truck, an antique hearse, and an old wine cask cart. Rumor has it the Carriage Museum may move to a site off Calle César Chávez while the city builds a new Carriage Museum by the railroad.

The Carriage Museum is open daily from 9:00 a.m. to 3:00 p.m. for self-guided tours. Docent tours are available without reservations on the third Sunday of every month from 1:00 to 4:00 p.m. Admission is free, but a donation to the nonprofit museum is appreciated.

El Paseo and Casa De la Guerra
15 East De la Guerra Street, Santa Barbara
(805) 965-0093
www.sbthp.org

Spanish Colonial Revival–style architecture is shown off beautifully in El Paseo, a small shopping complex (reportedly California's first "shopping center") built in the 1920s around the historic De la Guerra adobe, Casa De la Guerra. The adobe was built between 1819 and 1826 by Jose de la Guerra y Noriega, who was, at the time, commander of El Presidio de Santa Barbara. De la Guerra and his wife, Doña Maria Antonia, raised 12 children here, and the house was the social center of Santa Barbara for years.

The wedding reception of De la Guerra's daughter, Anita, took place at Casa De la Guerra in 1836 and was described in Richard Henry Dana's book, *Two Years Before the Mast*. In 1998 the Santa Barbara Trust for Historic Preservation restored the adobe house and opened an evocative little museum here filled with furniture and artifacts from the era and featuring rotating exhibits. You can visit the museum from noon to 4:00 p.m. Thursday through Sunday. Admission is $3 for adults; children 16 and under are free.

Today you can feel the history as you stroll El Paseo. Once filled with shops and galleries, El Paseo now houses mostly offices and restaurants. It's a fabulous spot for lunch. You can relax in the old world courtyard, sip a margarita at El Paseo restaurant, and imagine the Spanish dons and doñas mingling at the casa more than two centuries ago.

Browsing is free anytime at El Paseo. The main entrance is on the 800 block of State Street, but you can also access it from De la Guerra and Anacapa Streets.

El Presidio de Santa Barbara State Historic Park
123 East Canon Perdido Street, Santa Barbara
(805) 965-0093
www.sbthp.org

Sitting incongruously in the middle of bustling downtown Santa Barbara is a nearly block-long complex of stark adobe buildings that represent the city's beginnings. Founded in 1782 by Lieutenant Jose Francisco de Ortega, the Royal Presidio was the last military out-

> **i** The rear courtyard of El Presidio has become an archaeological dig. Students from Cal Poly–San Luis Obispo Continued Education and board members from the Santa Barbara Historic Trust joined together for investigations that have already unturned artifacts from Santa Barbara's Chinese, Spanish, and American periods. You can participate in history yourself by learning how to make adobe bricks. Call El Presidio at (805) 965-0093 for more information.

post of the Spanish Empire in the new world.

An ongoing restoration process by the Santa Barbara Trust for Historic Preservation has preserved the spirit of the place. The bell tower that was destroyed by an earthquake in the 19th century was replaced, along with two huge bells, one of which is believed to be the original Presidio Bell rung by Father Junipero Serra at the first mass said here in 1782. (See the History chapter for more information.) The careful restoration makes it easy to imagine the Spanish padres sitting in their sparsely furnished quarters or Santa Barbarans of 200 years ago worshipping in the Presidio Chapel, reconstructed on its original foundations.

Also of note here is El Cuartel, the guard's house. It's the oldest building in Santa Barbara and the second oldest in the state of California.

Visits to the site are self-guided, although groups may call to arrange a docent-led tour. A 15-minute slide show is well worth seeing, and a scale model of the Presidio offers a detailed look at life in Spanish California. The Presidio is open every day from 10:30 a.m. to 4:30 p.m. Admission is $3 for adults; children under 16 are free.

Fernald Mansion
414 West Montecito Street, Santa Barbara
(805) 966-1601
www.santabarbaramuseum.com

Next door to the Trussell-Winchester Adobe (see separate entry), the 14-room Fernald

Close-up

Adaptable Adobe

When you're exploring Santa Barbara's famous architectural landmarks, you'll come across the word *adobe* (ah-DOH-bee)—adobe buildings, adobe bricks, adobe clay. In fact, adobe is a large part of Santa Barbara's foundation. Not only is this humble, hard-packed clay one of the region's dominant soils, but it was also one of the city's first building materials, and volunteers are adapting the original recipe to restore historic landmarks today.

Mud buildings may seem primitive to us, but they made perfect sense for the Spanish and Mexican settlers—environmentally and economically. Instead of chopping down trees for lumber or using expensive materials, the settlers simply scooped up the earth beneath them, mixed it with straw and water, then shaped the mixture into large blocks using wooden molds. After the bricks baked in the scorching sun, the settlers used them to build Santa Barbara's first houses, forts, and churches. The adobes, as they are called, were extremely energy efficient. Fortified with thick, 2- to 5-foot (0.6- to 1.52-meter) walls, they adapted beautifully to the temperature extremes of the arid climate, staying cool in summer and warm in winter.

Today, adobe bricks are still made by hand in Santa Barbara, using much the same methods the Spanish and Mexican settlers used more than two centuries ago. Each year, volunteers get down and dirty during Adobe Days, making bricks to restore the structures at El Presidio de Santa Barbara State Historic Park (see the write-up in this chapter). The volunteers still use the traditional recipe—mud, straw, and water—but they adapt it slightly by adding a bucket of emulsified asphalt to help waterproof the bricks. Hardworking volunteers have made every brick used to restore these historic buildings for the last 25 years, re-creating Santa Barbara's rich history for all of us to enjoy.

To visit some of the city's historic adobes, take the self-guided Red Tile Walking Tour (see the other Close-up in this chapter). If you would like to take part in Adobe Days, call the Santa Barbara Trust for Historic Preservation at (805) 965-0093.

Mansion is one of only a few Victorian homes preserved in Santa Barbara. An example of the traditional Queen Anne–style Victorian, the gabled "gingerbread" mansion was built in 1826 by local lawman Judge Charles Fernald for his wife, Hannah.

The mansion was originally located on lower Santa Barbara Street but was moved to the Montecito Street address, where it is now a museum operated by the Santa Barbara His-

torical Society. The Fernald family's furnishings and personal effects are of interest, as are the hand-carved ornamentation, staircase, and wainscoting.

Guided tours are offered every Saturday at 1:00 and 2:00 p.m. Group tours are available by appointment. Admission is $5 for adults and $1 for children under 12. The mansion is not wheelchair accessible.

Lobero Theatre
33 East Canon Perdido Street, Santa Barbara
(805) 963-0761
www.lobero.com

When opera aficionado Jose Lobero set out to build his dream opera house in Santa Barbara, he had the financial backing and the necessary artistic flair, but he made a mistake when he chose the neighborhood.

When the opera house opened on February 22, 1873 (with the premiere of an opera written by Lobero), Santa Barbarans came in droves. But soon business dwindled due to the venue's proximity to Chinatown's opium dens and brothels. Eventually, Lobero lost the theater and committed suicide, and the building was razed in 1923.

The elaborate Spanish-style theater occupying the site today was built in 1924 and named in Lobero's honor. It's currently home to some of the area's leading arts organizations and performances, including UCSB Arts and Lectures, Santa Barbara Youth Ensemble, Sings Like Hell, Speaking of Stones, BOXTALES, Santa Barbara Chamber Orchestra, and the Music and Arts Conservatory. (See The Arts chapter for more information.) Oh, and the neighborhood's actually quite posh these days, so buy yourself a ticket and allow time to mingle in the new courtyard and enjoy the ambience. Tours are available by appointment only.

Mission Santa Barbara
2201 Laguna Street, Santa Barbara
(805) 682-4713
www.sbmission.org

Known as the "Queen of the Missions" for its beauty and hilltop setting, Mission Santa Barbara was the 10th of California's 21 missions founded by Franciscan friars and is the only one that has been continuously occupied by the Franciscan order since its founding.

Dedicated on December 16, 1786, the mission complex has undergone many changes since its humble beginnings as a small chapel and living quarters for missionaries and Chumash Indians. In December 1812,

a major earthquake nearly leveled the chapel and surrounding buildings. The present pink sandstone church—with one bell tower—was constructed around the old chapel and dedicated in 1820. The second bell tower was added more than a decade later.

In 1925 the mission suffered the shock of another major earthquake, and the towers and living quarters had to be repaired and reinforced. The building remained intact until the years following World War II, when deterioration called for complete reconstruction of the mission facade, which was done in the early 1950s. In future years, the mission will undergo further restoration as the soft stone and adobe bricks crumble with age.

Visit the mission today, and its graceful beauty will instantly impress you. Reportedly inspired by a drawing of a church designed by the Roman architect M. Vitruvius Polion in the first century B.C., Mission Santa Barbara has strongly influenced the architectural style of the city. As you wander through the grounds, notice the thick adobe walls, red-tiled roof, and open courtyards, features which are echoed in many of Santa Barbara's other public buildings. Inside, rooms are preserved in the style of the 1700s, with artifacts and displays relating to early mission life.

The self-guided tour includes eight museum rooms, the cloister gardens, the chapel, the cemetery, and the beautiful Moorish fountain and courtyard. You can also view a 20-minute video on mission history. Docent-led group tours must be arranged in advance. A gift shop near the entrance sells religious items and educational materials on Santa Barbara and the California missions. For a moment of quiet reflection after your tour, wander down to the beautiful Mission rose gardens. You can also explore the ruins of the old Mission aqueduct built by the Chumash in 1806—just wander across the street from the church. Mission Santa Barbara is open seven days a week from 9:00 a.m. to 5:00 p.m. Admission is $4 for adults, free for children 12 and younger.

Painted Cave
Off California Highway 154 on Painted Cave Road, Santa Barbara

This ancient, 22-foot (6.7-meter)–deep cave preserves brightly colored pre-Columbian pictographs inscribed by the Chumash, Santa Barbara's first residents. Unfortunately, unscrupulous marauders removed the cave's other Stone Age artifacts in the 1870s, including arrowheads, axes, and baskets. The rock paintings remain intact, now protected by a locked metal screen.

The cave is on the edge of the road, but you have to look carefully or you'll drive right by. Watch for the sign on Painted Cave Road off East Camino Cielo Road.

Santa Barbara County Courthouse
1100 Anacapa Street, at Anapamu Street, Santa Barbara
(805) 962-6464
www.sbcourts.org

Hundreds of historic courthouses grace this fair country, but it would be difficult to find another as stunning—both inside and out—as the Santa Barbara County Courthouse, a magnificent Spanish-Moorish structure that is one of the most photographed buildings in the nation. In 2003 it was declared a state historic landmark, and it's now well on its way to becoming a national landmark.

Completed in 1929 (fortuitously, just before the stock market crash), the ornate structure features handpainted ceilings, a spiral staircase, wrought-iron chandeliers, imported tiles, carved doors, and beautiful historical murals depicting early California history and Chumash life.

Outside, spacious lawns and swaying palm trees surround the building, set off by a beautiful sunken garden, which serves as an evocative venue for many weddings, community events, and concerts. In the words of Charles H. Cheney, who in 1929 wrote the preface to *Californian Architecture in Santa Barbara*, "romance ran riot" in the courthouse, an assessment that was not altogether a compliment, as Cheney deemed it too large and overdone to "belong" to what he viewed as the low-key, intimate style of the city.

Still, Cheney acknowledged the "extraordinary number of intriguing bits of design" found both inside and outside the structure, and it is these unique features that continue to draw visitors nearly 80 years after the building was completed.

Free hour-long guided tours are offered Monday through Saturday at 2:00 p.m., with an additional 10:30 a.m. tour on Monday, Tuesday, and Friday, or you can wander around on your own. Be sure to go to the top of the clock tower, which affords a panoramic view of the city. The courthouse is open weekdays 8:00 a.m. to 5:00 p.m. and weekends 10:00 a.m. to 5:00 p.m., but the doors close to new visitors at 4:45 p.m. Admission is free.

Santa Barbara Historical Museum
136 East De la Guerra Street, Santa Barbara
(805) 966-1601
www.santabarbaramuseum.com

Art, textiles, furniture, clothing, and other artifacts from Santa Barbara's rich, multicultural past have been preserved in this complex of adobe structures under the auspices of the Santa Barbara Historical Society. Step back in time as you view the collected remnants of the area's Spanish, Mexican, and American periods, or stroll the inner courtyard, which seems far removed from the busy streets that surround the museum and adjacent historical adobes (including Casa Covarrubias, constructed in 1817). You can browse on your own (all exhibits are carefully labeled) or book a guided tour.

The Gledhill Library, on the museum grounds, houses an impressive collection of books, maps, and photographs chronicling Santa Barbara's history. It's open to the public

i *Adobe* is the Spanish word for a sun-dried brick and for the clay soil used to make these bricks. Santa Barbara's best-known historical adobe dwelling is Casa De la Guerra in El Paseo.

Paseo comes from the Spanish *paso*, which means "passage," and *pasear*, "to take a stroll." In Santa Barbara, it refers to the quaint Spanish-style promenades and courtyards linking downtown streets.

10:00 a.m. to 4:00 p.m. Tuesday through Friday and 10:00 a.m. to 1:00 p.m. the first Saturday of the month. (An hourly library research fee applies if you are not a member of the Historical Society.)

The museum is open Tuesday through Saturday from 10:00 a.m. to 5:00 p.m. and Sunday from noon to 5:00 p.m. Admission is free, but a donation is appreciated. If you can't find a parking space on the adjacent street, watch for the small driveway next to the museum on De la Guerra Street; you'll find parking spaces in back.

Trussell-Winchester Adobe
412 West Montecito Street, Santa Barbara
(805) 966-1601
www.santabarbaramuseum.com

In 1853 the sidewheel steamer *Winfield Scott* sank off Anacapa Island. The ship's captain, Horatio Trussell, salvaged a ridge pole from its mast as well as other useful timber and brass and used the objects along with adobe bricks in the construction of this home, built in 1854. Later the home was occupied by Dr. Robert F. Winchester, a local physician, until his death in 1932.

Now under the auspices of the Santa Barbara Historical Society, the home is a small museum that includes period furnishings and other items used by the Trussell and Winchester families. The museum welcomes visitors for guided tours every Saturday at 1:00 and 2:00 p.m. If you would like to arrange a group tour at another time, call the Historical Society at the listed number to make a reservation. Admission is $5 for adults and $1 for children under 12.

Local Landmarks and Outdoor Attractions

Moreton Bay Fig Tree
Chapala Street at U.S. Highway 101, Santa Barbara

The Moreton Bay Fig Tree (and yes, everyone in Santa Barbara knows exactly which tree you are talking about when you say "the" Moreton Bay Fig Tree) was planted on July 4, 1876, by a young girl who had been given the seedling by a sailor fresh off the boat from Australia. A year later, when the girl moved away, she gave the little tree to a friend, who transplanted it to its current location. The rest, as they say, is history.

The tree is now huge (some say it is the largest specimen of *Ficus macrophylla* in the country), and it has had quite a life here in the fertile soil of Santa Barbara. In the 1930s the tree was nearly cut down to make way for a gas station until Pearl Chase (read all about her in the Close-up in the History chapter) put a stop to that nonsense.

In 1961 the Parks Department measured the tree and announced that more than 16,000 people could stand in the shade beneath the 21,000 square feet (1,951 square meters) covered by its outstretched branches. In the 1970s it was a home of sorts to the city's homeless people, who camped on the lawn until they were finally evicted. In 1982 it was declared a city landmark.

In recent years, the venerable tree underwent special treatment to ensure that it continues to flourish. Both the Santa Barbara Parks Department and the Historic Landmark Commission approved the installation of a chain barrier to keep people at a distance (branches have been broken by climbing children, and people have carved their initials in the trunk). Interpretive signs tell you about the tree and politely ask that you admire it from afar.

The Moreton Bay Fig Tree is always open, and admission is free.

Red Tile Walking Tour

If you're interested in Santa Barbara's famous architecture and fascinating history, we highly recommend the **Red Tile Walking Tour.** Named for the color of the roof tiles on many of Santa Barbara's downtown buildings, this self-guided tour takes you to some of the city's most important historic landmarks. Strolling around Santa Barbara in the sunshine on this 12-block tour is the best way to appreciate the city. The weather is almost always gorgeous, and you'll discover many sidewalk cafes, specialty shops, and hidden courtyards along the way. Below we've provided step-by-step directions to each attraction as well as must-see highlights. If you need more information, turn to the detailed write-ups in this chapter. So what are you waiting for? Get out there and explore. And don't forget your camera!

• Start your tour at the **Santa Barbara County Courthouse (1)** (1100 Anacapa Street; 805-962-6464). If you time it right, you can join a free hour-long guided tour starting in the Mural Room offered Monday through Saturday at 2:00 p.m. with an additional 10:30 a.m. tour on Monday, Tuesday, and Friday. Don't miss the view from the clock tower.

COURTESY OF THE SANTA BARBARA CAR FREE PROJECT AND THE SANTA BARBARA CHAMBER OF COMMERCE

• Cross Anacapa Street to the **Santa Barbara Public Library (2)** (40 East Anapamu Street; 805-962-7653). Here you can view art exhibitions at the **Faulkner Gallery** Monday through Thursday from 10:00 a.m. to 9:00 p.m., Friday and Saturday from 10:00 a.m. to 5:30 p.m., and Sunday from 1:00 to 5:00 p.m.

• Continue down Anapamu Street to the **Santa Barbara Museum of Art (3)** (1130 State Street; 805-963-4364; www.sbmuseart.org). One of the top 10 regional museums in the country, the museum displays Asian, American, and European treasures spanning more than 4,000 years. Don't miss the acclaimed *Portrait of Mexico Today* (1932), the only intact mural in the United States by renowned Mexican artist David Alfaro Siqueiros. You'll see it at the front entry steps.

• Stroll ½ block south on State Street and enter charming **La Arcada Court (4)** (1114 State Street) with a 16-foot (5-meter) clock at the entrance.

This quaint Spanish paseo and courtyard are filled with fountains, quaint shops, cafe-style restaurants, and a series of life-size bronze statuary that provide great photo ops.

• Wander south on State Street to Carrillo Street, then turn east toward the mountains to the **Hill-Carrillo Adobe (5)** (11 East Carrillo Street, 805-963-1873), dating from 1826. The first city council met here in 1850. It now houses the Santa Barbara Foundation, but you can admire the building from the outside.

• Return to State Street and walk south 2 blocks to **El Paseo (6)** (11–19 East De la Guerra Street). Built in the 1920s around historic **Casa De la Guerra,** this "Street in Spain" was reportedly California's first shopping complex. As you stroll along the cobbled flower-lined passageway, notice the graceful details of the Spanish Colonial Revival architecture. El Paseo Restaurant here is a great spot to sip a margarita. Across the street from El Paseo, you'll find palm-lined **Paseo Nuevo (7)** Mall, packed with specialty shops and sidewalk cafes.

• Continue through the passageway of El Paseo and enter the courtyard of **Casa De la Guerra (8)** (15 East De la Guerra Street, 805-966-6961). Built between 1819 and 1826, the adobe was originally home to Jose de la Guerra y Noriega, commander of El Presidio de Santa Barbara, and was the social center of Santa Barbara for years. Across the street, framed by date palms, is **De la Guerra Plaza (9),** site of the annual Fiesta downtown marketplace. Adjacent you'll see the Spanish Revival *Santa Barbara News-Press* building and City Hall.

• Turn left on De la Guerra Street, head toward the mountains to Anacapa Street, and you'll see the 1849 **Oreña Adobes (10)** (2729 East De la Guerra Street). Look for the plaque on the corner of De la Guerra and Anacapa Streets.

• Cross Anacapa Street and follow the hibiscus trees 1/2 block down De la Guerra Street to **Presidio Avenue (11),** the oldest street in Santa Barbara. At the corner, look for the plaque commemorating the guard's house built around the 1840s. If you enter the garden, you'll see a tranquil koi pond and elephant fountain.

• Return the way you came and cross De la Guerra Street to the **Santiago de la Guerra Adobe (12)** (110 East De la Guerra Street), one of the city's oldest structures. Next door, you'll find another historic home, the 1830 **Lugo Adobe (13)** (114 East De la Guerra Street) tucked in the pastel-hued courtyard of Meridian Studios.

• Stroll toward the mountains to the corner of De la Guerra and Santa Barbara Streets and visit the **Santa Barbara Historical Society Museum (14)** (136 East De la Guerra Street; 805-966-1601; www.santabarbaramuseum.com), where you'll see artifacts from Santa Barbara's multicultural past. The museum is open Tuesday through Saturday 10:00 a.m. to 5:00 p.m., and Sunday noon to 5:00 p.m. All exhibits are carefully labeled for self-guided tours.

• Turn right at the corner of De La Guerra and Santa Barbara Streets just past the Historical Society Museum, where you'll find 1817 **Casa Covarrubias (15)** (136 East De la Guerra Street; 805–966–1601) and the adjoining historic adobe. The peaceful oak-shaded courtyard graced by a fountain is a popular venue for special events.

• Leave the way you came, cross De la Guerra Street, and stroll up Santa Barbara Street to the pink-painted **Rochin Adobe (16)** (820 Santa Barbara

Street), made of salvaged bricks from the ruins of structures built against the South East Presidio walls.

• Continue north along Santa Barbara Street to Canon Perdido Street. At the corner is **El Presidio de Santa Barbara State Historic Park (17)** (123 East Canon Perdido Street; 805-965-0093; www.sbthp.org), site of the Presidio's founding in 1782. You can view a 15-minute slide show and take a self-guided tour of the Presidio every day from 10:30 a.m. to 4:30 p.m.

• Follow Canon Perdido Street toward State Street, where you'll find the reconstructed Presidio Chapel, the Canedo Adobe, and **El Cuartel (18),** all part of the Presidio barracks. Once the family home of the soldier entrusted with guarding the Presidio gate, El Cuartel is the oldest existing adobe in Santa Barbara and the second oldest in California.

• At the southeast corner of Canon Perdido and Anacapa Streets, you'll see the **Post Office (19)** (836 Anacapa Street), a mix of contemporary Federalist and Art Deco styles with a Monterey Revival wood shingle roof.

• On the northwest corner is the **Lobero Theatre (20)** (33 East Canon Perdido Street; 805-963-0761; www.lobero.com). Founded in 1873 by opera enthusiast Jose Lobero, this state historic landmark is California's oldest continuously operating theater. Continue north along Anacapa Street back to the Santa Barbara County Courthouse.

Santa Barbara Harbor and Breakwater
Entrance at Harbor Way, off Cabrillo Boulevard west of Castillo Street, Santa Barbara

We think Santa Barbara Harbor is a must-see attraction. In the 1920s Santa Barbara businessman Max Fleischmann funded its construction because he wanted a safe haven for his 250-foot yacht, the *Haida*. Tucked inside a protective breakwater, it's a great spot for a relaxing stroll, and you can't beat the salty ambience and stunning views of the mountains and sea. More than 1,000 boats bob in the slips here—from tiny rowboats to large luxury yachts like Fleischmann's. Paddling around in a kayak is a great way to explore the area, and you can rent them right on Harbor Way (see the Beaches and Watersports chapter.) Keep an eye out for harbor seals and sea lions. The breakwater, constructed in 1924, is paved and wide enough to accommodate you, your friends, and a baby stroller, so go for a walk (but watch out during rough seas).

At the east end of the harbor is SEA Landing, where the *Condor* departs for whale-watching excursions and Truth Aquatics' boats anchor (see the Beaches and Watersports chapter). The harbor is open every day, and there is no admission price for exploring.

Stearns Wharf
State Street and Cabrillo Boulevard, Santa Barbara
www.stearnswharf.org

When Santa Barbara lumberman John Stearns completed his namesake pier in 1872, he could hardly have imagined that more than 100 years later it would be the most visited landmark in town. For decades after its completion (it was then the longest deep-water pier between Los Angeles and San Francisco), the wharf was used for loading and unloading freight and passengers, but in 1941 The Harbor Restaurant was built, marking the beginning of the wharf's transition into a tourist attraction. Today its seaside location, restaurants, shops, and festive atmosphere draw visitors by the thousands. Limited parking (including valet parking) is available on the wharf itself, or you can park in the nearby public lots on Cabrillo Boulevard and walk the 1/2 mile (1 kilometer) to the end of the pier.

As you enter, stop for a look at the Dolphin Fountain, formally known as the Santa Barbara Bicentennial Friendship Fountain, which was created by local artist Bud Bottoms in 1982 under the sponsorship of the Santa Barbara/Puerto Vallarta Sister City Committee. A replica of the fountain adorns all of Santa Barbara's sister cities, including Puerto Vallarta, Mexico; Toba, Japan; and Yalta, Ukraine.

Continuing on, you'll find several popular seafood restaurants and shops selling confections, souvenirs, and sportswear. Parasailing trips and some harbor cruises depart from the pier, and you can even do a little wine tasting here. Stearns Wharf is always open, and admission is free.

Natural Attractions and Science Museums

Santa Barbara Botanic Garden
1212 Mission Canyon Road, Santa Barbara
(805) 682-4726
www.sbbg.org

In 1926, rather than see a pristine Santa Barbara canyon turned into a housing development, Anna Blaksley Bliss snapped up the land and declared it a botanical preserve in memory of her father, Henry Blaksley.

Today the 78 acres that make up the Santa Barbara Botanic Garden provide a superb setting for the study of native California flora. More than 5 miles (8 kilometers) of trails meander along the banks of upper Mission Creek and through the garden's meadows and canyons, which are planted with wildflowers, cacti, oak, sycamore trees, and more than 1,000 species of rare and indigenous plants. There's an entire section devoted to flora found on the Santa Barbara Channel Islands, as well as a forest of redwood trees and display areas

on the California desert and mountains.

The garden is best dressed in spring, when the wildflowers are in bloom, but it's the perfect spot for a peaceful stroll (or an invigorating hike) at any time of year. Although most plants are labeled, you may find it helpful to take a one-hour, docent-led tour, offered daily at 2:00 p.m. and also at 11:00 a.m. on Thursday, Saturday, and Sunday.

Of special interest to history buffs is the sandstone dam that spans Mission Creek near the redwood grove. Built in 1806 by Chumash to harness irrigation water for nearby grain fields, the structure remains intact. The gift shop has a particularly good collection of botanical books and offers handcrafted items for sale. The Home Demonstration Garden is dedicated to teaching groups and individuals about using and caring for California native plants in Southern California gardens. You can also visit an authentic Japanese tea house landscaped with California native plants in the Japanese style. One of the garden's biggest events is its fall plant sale held each October (see the Annual Events chapter).

The Botanic Garden is open 9:00 a.m. to 6:00 p.m. March through October and 9:00 a.m. to 5:00 p.m. November to February. Admission is $8 for adults; $6 for seniors 60 and older and for teens 13 through 17 and students with current ID; and $4 for children ages 2 through 12. Children younger than 2 are admitted free.

Santa Barbara Maritime Museum
113 Harbor Way
Santa Barbara Harbor, Santa Barbara
(805) 965-8864
www.sbmm.org

Opened in the summer of 2000, this impressive multimillion-dollar tribute to the sea is a treat for the whole family. The museum displays fascinating military history exhibits, model ships, fishing and diving equipment, antique instruments, rare artifacts, and historical photos. After reading about life on the sea, visitors can experience it through a host of fun, interactive exhibits. Spy through a real submarine

A walk along the breakwater at the Santa Barbara Harbor is a welcome diversion for Santa Barbara residents and visitors alike. Be careful, however, when the surf is high. More than one unsuspecting person has been doused when waves crashed over the wall. (The waves aren't dangerous—just wet and cold.)

periscope and see a 360-degree view of the harbor, learn to sail a yacht, explore shipwrecks, then "catch the big one" at the sportfishing exhibit. Shaped like a ship's hull, the 86-seat Munger Theater presents documentaries on nautical topics, such as the America's Cup, El Niño, and deep-sea archaeological expeditions and adventures. After your visit, browse the gift shop for maps, nautical books, clothing, toys, and gifts. The museum is closed Wednesday, but it's open every other day except major holidays from 10:00 a.m. to 6:00 p.m. during the summer (from Memorial Day to Labor Day) and from 10:00 a.m. to 5:00 p.m. during the rest of the year. Note that admission is free on the third Thursday of every month. Admission is $7 for adults; $4 for seniors, students, and kids ages 6 to 17; and $2 for children ages 1 to 5; children under 1 and members are free.

Santa Barbara Museum of Natural History
2559 Puesta del Sol Road, Santa Barbara
(805) 682-4711
www.sbnature.org

Tucked inconspicuously among the oaks in Mission Canyon, the Santa Barbara Museum of Natural History is thought by many to be one of the most beautiful small museums in the country. Founded in 1916 on the banks of Mission Creek, the low-roofed, Spanish-style structure includes several exhibit halls dedicated to the study of California and Santa Barbara County natural history.

Your adventure begins outside the entrance, where the magnificent 72-foot (22-meter) skeleton of a blue whale provides a perfect photo op. Pass through the entrance into a quaint courtyard, then follow the signs

to the areas that interest you most.

The museum is a treasure trove of Chumash artifacts (don't miss the baskets and the full-scale model of a Chumash canoe) and features small but impressive exhibits on mammals, birds, insects, reptiles (stop by the Lizard Lounge to visit live critters), gems and minerals, plants, and marine life. Kids love pushing a button to make a coiled rattlesnake's tail "rattle," and creating waves with the hands-on wave machine is a favorite diversion in the marine life exhibit hall.

In addition to its many permanent attractions, the museum offers a dynamic schedule of special exhibits and events for the whole family (see the Kidstuff chapter for details on activities of interest to children).

Gladwin Planetarium, on the grounds, features a changing lineup of programs reflecting the seasonal skies or other astronomical happenings and invites you to bring the whole family to survey the night sky through its high-powered telescope (dress warmly!). The museum gift shop sells books, jewelry, and lots of cool stuff for kids.

The museum is open 10:00 a.m. to 5:00 p.m. daily. Admission is $7 for adults; $6 for teens 13 through 17 and seniors 65 and older; and $4 for children ages 2 through 12. Admission is free to all on the last Sunday of each month except for September. There's a nominal charge in addition to the museum admission fee for planetarium shows.

Santa Barbara Zoo
500 Niños Drive, Santa Barbara
(805) 926-5339, (805) 962-6310, recorded information
www.sbzoo.org

Zoos and kids seem made for each other (and indeed, this one is amply discussed in the Kidstuff chapter), but the Santa Barbara Zoo is such a charming place that we think it's worth a visit whether you have the kids in tow or not. To begin with, there's a fabulous ocean view from its grassy hilltop, which is believed to have once been the site of a Chumash camp.

Long after the Chumash were gone, a

A Santa Barbara gem, the Santa Barbara Museum of Natural History. PROVIDED COURTESY OF THE SANTA BARBARA MUSEUM OF NATURAL HISTORY

grand mansion was built on the hill and was the centerpiece of a 16-acre estate. The original home was built by John Beale in 1896, but after his death in 1914, his widow, Lillian, married John Child, and the property became known as the Child Estate. After Mr. Child's death, the land was presented to the Santa Barbara Foundation, which in turn transferred management to the Child Estate Foundation.

In 1962 the land was cleared, making way for the very humble Child Estate Zoo, which opened in August 1963. A llama, two sheep, a goat, a turkey, and a pair of spider monkeys were the only inhabitants of the new zoo, but the community had a vision of what the zoo could become and set about making it a reality. In 1972 the zoo joined the Association of Zoos and Aquariums and has continued its development in keeping with the AZA's goals and objectives. In 1981 the zoo was accredited by the AZA—a status it currently maintains.

Over the years, Santa Barbara's zoo has added an impressive number of new animals and exhibits, and it continues to be dedicated to preserving a high-quality environment for both visitors and the zoo's permanent residents. More than 600 animals currently reside at the zoo, which attracts more than a half-million visitors every year, many of them long-time Santa Barbarans who go back often to see what's new.

Some of the most recent additions include the Channel Island fox exhibit; the Aquarium Complex, home to freshwater stingrays, a Malayan water monitor, and small sharks; Lorikeet Landing, where you can buy a cup of nectar and hand-feed these brilliantly colored parrots; and the Cats of Africa exhibit. An exciting project in the works is the California Condor exhibit. When completed, Santa Barbara will be one of only two zoos in the world where you can see these rare birds up close. One of the most popular exhibits is the Karisoke Research Outpost, a replica of Dian Fossey's gorilla research station in Rwanda, which overlooks the zoo's gorilla compound. Inside, you'll find information on gorilla conservation efforts and habitat preservation.

You can easily "do the zoo" in a few hours, but if you have kids, you may want to make a day of it. Don't miss the giraffe with the kinky neck (no, it doesn't hurt), the elephants, and the monkey island. And a stop at the gift shop is a must. The zoo is open every day (except Thanksgiving and Christmas) from 10:00 a.m. to 5:00 p.m., with ticket sales ending at 4:00 p.m.

Admission is $10 for adults, and $8 for children ages 2 through 12 and seniors 60 and older; tiny tots are admitted free of charge. Parking is $3 per vehicle.

Ty Warner Sea Center
211 Stearns Wharf, Santa Barbara
(805) 687-4711
When you enter the two-story glass foyer, a life-size 39-foot (12-meter) model of a California gray whale and her calf greets you. This interactive and downright fun sea center makes for a pleasant and educational morning. Children love crawling through the 1,500-gallon (5,600-liter) surge tank to get a real-life peek at happenings in the ocean, and they love testing their skills at being an oceanographer. Open daily from 10:00 a.m. to 5:00 p.m. Admission for adults is $7; $6 for seniors, teens ages 13 to 17, and students. Children ages 2 to 12 are $4, and children under 2 are free.

Whale Watching
Whale watching in the Santa Barbara Channel is one of the most popular family recreational activities in town. Several local companies offer trips from December through April, when California gray whales migrate along the coast, and from May through November, when blue and humpback whales come to feed in the channel. For details, see the Beaches and Watersports chapter.

GOLETA

South Coast Railroad Museum and Goleta Depot
300 North Los Carneros Road, Goleta
(805) 964-3540
www.goletadepot.org
The Goleta Depot, built in 1901, has been restored on this site, adjacent to the Stow House (see below). The museum is very small but includes railroad memorabilia, photos, and an extensive model railroad. Movies are screened in the theater room. You can send a telegraph or climb aboard the real caboose displayed on tracks outside.

A big draw is the miniature train that circles the grounds and offers rides Wednesday and Friday between 2:00 and 3:45 p.m. and Saturday and Sunday between 1:15 and 3:45 p.m. (see the Kidstuff chapter for details on train rides and birthday parties at the museum). A small museum shop sells gifts and educational materials with a railroad theme.

The museum is open 1:00 to 4:00 p.m. Wednesday through Sunday. Admission is by donation.

Stow House
304 North Los Carneros Road, Goleta
(805) 964-4407
www.goletahistory.org
The Stow House, a restored Victorian home built in the 1870s, is the oldest frame home in Goleta and is filled with furniture, clothing, kitchenware, and other items from the period. Its interior is especially charming when adorned for Christmas. A blacksmith's shop and other small outbuildings have also been preserved.

The grounds are lovely, with various exotic plantings (many labeled) and a wide expanse of shaded lawn that is often used for special events such as weddings, an annual Fourth of July celebration, and other community events. Lake Los Carneros, a small artificial lake located east of the house, is a popular site for walking or birding.

The Stow House is open from 2:00 to 4:00 p.m. Saturday and Sunday, with 30-minute guided tours beginning at 2:00 and 3:00 p.m.; it's closed in January. A $3 donation is requested. Children under 12 are free.

MONTECITO

Casa del Herrero
1387 East Valley Road, Montecito
(805) 565-5653
www.casadelherrero.com
Casa del Herrero (1925) is one of Santa Barbara's most underrated attractions. Listed in the National Register of Historic Places, this stunning home was designed by acclaimed architect George Washington Smith on a beautiful 11-acre estate in Montecito. Still under original ownership, it's one of the finest examples of Spanish Colonial Revival architecture and is now preserved as a museum. Inside you'll see an amazing collection of 13th- to 18th-century Spanish furnishings, decorative arts, extensive Mediterranean tilework, and other colorful architectural details, including a ceiling from a 15th-century convent. The 90-minute tour of the casa also includes a visit through the elaborate Moorish garden and adjacent workshop, where you can view an array of silversmithing tools. Tours are available from February through November, Wednesday and Saturday at 10:00 a.m. and 2:00 p.m. Reservations are essential, and a fee of $15 per person is payable when you reserve your space.

Ganna Walska Lotusland
695 Ashley Road, Montecito
(805) 969-9990
www.lotusland.org
Lotusland is a Santa Barbara gem. You have to do some planning in order see it, but you will never forget your visit. Overseen by the Ganna Walska Lotusland Foundation, the 37-acre estate is named for the sacred Indian lotus, which was planted there in the early 1890s by nurseryman R. Kinton Stevens.

In 1941 the estate was purchased by well-known Polish opera singer Mme. Ganna Walska, who shaped Lotusland into what it is today: a series of breathtaking theme gardens filled with rare botanical specimens that delight the eye and renew the spirit.

Your two-hour guided tour will take you through an imaginative Theatre Garden displaying 16th-century German and Viennese sculptures of dwarves and hunchbacks; the delightful Blue Garden, planted with blue fescue, blue Atlas cedars, and blue Mexican fan palms; a breathtaking Aloe Garden, with its centerpiece Shell Pond lined with abalone and South Sea Island giant clam shells; a forest of dragon trees from the Canary Islands; a serene Japanese Garden; and the second-finest collection of rare cycads in the world, including 11 of the 12 genres.

Other highlights include a working horticultural clock, a 12th-century baptismal font, and topiary, fern, palm, and succulent gardens. This is far more than an interesting tour for garden buffs; it is an invitation to the fascinating world of Mme. Walska and her botanical wonders. Don't miss it. Tours are

Lotusland. NANCY SHOBE

conducted Wednesday through Saturday at 10:00 a.m. and 1:30 p.m. from mid-February to mid-November.

Reservations can be made up to a year in advance; call between 9:00 a.m. and noon Monday through Friday to book. The reservation office is open year-round.

Admission is $35 for adults, $10 for children ages 5 to 18 and $5 for children under 5.

CARPINTERIA

Carpinteria Harbor Seal Colony
Below Carpinteria Bluffs

Carpinteria is home to one of only two publicly accessible harbor seal colonies in Southern California. To see these fascinating creatures, hike a 1/2 mile (1 kilometer) down the spectacular bluff-top trail at the southern end of Bailard Avenue. You'll see the viewing area perched on a bluff just before the

Venoco pier. For more information, see the Close-up in the Parks chapter.

Carpinteria Valley Museum of History
956 Maple Avenue, Carpinteria
(805) 684-3112
www.carpinteriahistoricalmuseum.org
Although it may not have the glamour of Santa Barbara, Carpinteria is a delightful little city with deep historical roots. Its small museum depicts the lives of Carpinteria's earliest residents, with exhibits on the Chumash, the city's pioneer families, and its agricultural history.

Furniture, clothing, farm tools, and other historical artifacts are on display, along with exhibits on oil production, an early-20th-century schoolhouse, and a quilt depicting local historical events.

The museum is open 1:00 to 4:00 p.m. Tuesday through Saturday. Admission is by donation.

SIGHT-SEEING TOURS

Architectural Foundation of Santa Barbara Walking Tours
(805) 965-6307
www.afsb.org

These educational 90-minute walking tours are one of the best sight-seeing deals in town. For a $5 donation per person (children under 12 are free), trained docents from the Architectural Foundation will guide you through the hidden courtyards and original adobes of downtown Santa Barbara, pointing out distinctive architectural features and sharing historical tidbits. The Sabado (Saturday) tour leaves from the steps of City Hall, De la Guerra Plaza, at 10:00 a.m. Along the way, you'll visit the historic De la Guerra Adobe, El Paseo, and some of Santa Barbara's earliest buildings as you explore the architectural legacy of the Spanish and Mexican settlers. You'll also learn about the giants of Santa Barbara design. The Domingo (Sunday) tour departs from the entrance of the public library at 10:00 a.m. This tour explores Santa Barbara's downtown art and architecture, as it was reborn after the 1925 earthquake. Reservations are only required for private groups and the physically challenged. Rain cancels all tours.

Personal Tours, Ltd.
P.O. Box 60109, Santa Barbara
(805) 685-0552
www.personaltoursltd.com

You get just what you'd expect from this well-established Santa Barbara company, which offers affordable, in-depth, private tours with a personal touch. All tours are custom designed to match your special interests. You can focus on Santa Barbara's estates and gardens, natural history, fine arts, real estate, or photography, or explore the hot shopping spots. If you're not sure what you want to see, call and chat with the friendly staff, and they'll happily recommend an itinerary to fit your time limitations and budget. Tours are priced according to the duration of the trip and the vehicle used but range from $105 for a basic tour in your own car to $375 for a

basic coach tour. You can also choose from sedans, convertibles, custom vans, and minibuses. Charter tours to out-of-town attractions, such as Hearst Castle, Big Sur, and Los Angeles events, are also available, and international language tours can be arranged with advance notice. Vehicles are equipped for the physically challenged, and all tours require reservations in advance.

Santa Barbara Old Town Trolley
22 State Street, Santa Barbara
(805) 965-0353
www.sbtrolley.com

Hop aboard the 30-passenger Santa Barbara Trolley for a 90-minute narrated tour of Santa Barbara City and all the major tourist attractions.

This is an affordable way to see the sights in one day, and it offers some flexibility so it's a great option if you have the kids in tow. The trolley tour includes 14 attractions, such as beautiful Butterfly Beach in Montecito, the Moreton Bay Fig Tree, and Santa Barbara County Courthouse. The only scheduled stop included in the 90-minute tour is at Mission Santa Barbara, where you can leave the trolley and stretch your legs for 15 minutes. If you want to spend more time at the other attractions, you can hop off anywhere along the route and explore on your own, then hop aboard again when another trolley comes by. The tours run daily every hour between 10:00 a.m. and 4:00 p.m. from Stearns Wharf. Admission is $16 for adults and teens and $9 for children 12 and younger.

Spencer's Limousine & Tours
(805) 884-9700
www.spencerslimo.com

Take a peek at gated movie-star estates on a celebrity tour of Montecito, explore the city's architectural gems, or visit top attractions on a Santa Barbara City tour, all in the comfort of a plush limousine or Lincoln Town car. Voted one of the top tour companies by local newspaper polls, Spencer's Limousine & Tours customizes all its tours based on your special

Close-up

Suggested Itineraries

So you can't choose from all the attractions in this chapter? To save you time, we've listed Insider recommendations for one-, three-, and five-day itineraries. If you're visiting, you can use them as a guide and tweak them to suit your interests and time limits. If you live here, they might come in handy when friends and family visit.

Need transportation? See the Getting Here, Getting Around chapter. For more information on each attraction, you can read the individual write-ups throughout this book. So pack your sunglasses and camera, slather on the sunscreen, and enjoy!

SNAPSHOT

Only have one day in paradise? The following itinerary will give you a taste of Santa Barbara's history, shopping, architecture, and waterfront.

• Visit the beautiful Mission Santa Barbara, "Queen of the Missions." Take the self-guided tour through the museum, cloister gardens, cemetery, and chapel. If you have time, stop to admire the roses in the beautiful Mission rose garden.

• Bike, bus, or drive downtown to State Street. Stroll amid the fountains and flowers of Paseo Nuevo Shopping Mall. Then wander 4 blocks up State Street, browsing the specialty shops and quaint Spanish-style paseos along the way (see the Shopping chapter).

• Enjoy an alfresco lunch in a street-side cafe. Continue up State Street (about 3 blocks) to Anapamu Street. Turn right, walk 1 block to Anacapa Street, and you'll see the magnificent Santa Barbara County Courthouse on the right-hand corner. Take a self-guided or docent-led tour (see the listing in this chapter), then climb up the clock tower and enjoy panoramic views over the red-tiled roofs of Santa Barbara to the sea.

• Bike, bus, or drive to Stearns Wharf. Browse the gift shops or sample some wines in the ocean-view tasting room. Bike or stroll ¼ mile west along the beachfront bike path to the Santa Barbara Harbor. (If you have time, visit the Maritime Museum.) Sip a cocktail at a waterfront restaurant (see the Restaurants chapter) and/or enjoy a fresh seafood dinner while you gaze out at the sunset and the silhouetted yachts.

SHORT AND SWEET

Our three-day itinerary captures the contrast between Santa Barbara's coastal attractions and the quiet countryside of the Santa Ynez Valley. You can mix and match these activities and swap the days depending on the weather. Remember, if it's foggy on the coast, it's usually warm and sunny in the wine country.

Day One
See the Snapshot itinerary above.

Day Two
Consider renting a limousine so you can sip your way through the Santa Ynez wine country in style (and safety). If you're driving, take San Marcos Pass over the mountains and into the valley. Linger for lunch in small-town Los Olivos or the quaint Danish village of Solvang. Then follow the Foxen Canyon Wine Trail through the oak-studded countryside, stopping to sample wines along the way. (See the Santa Barbara Wine Country chapter for information on tour companies, wineries, and restaurants.)

Day Three
Weather permitting, board a whale-watching cruise. In the winter, you can see migrating gray whales; in the summer, blue whales, humpbacks, and minkes. Summer cruises may include a brief stop at Santa Cruz Island in Channel Islands National Park. (See the Beaches and Watersports and Channel Islands National Park and National Marine Sanctuary chapter.)

and/or
Follow the self-guided Red Tile Walking Tour (see the Close-up in this chapter). If you did the Snapshot tour, you can skip the Courthouse, but be sure to stop at the Santa Barbara Historical Society Museum, El Presidio de Santa Barbara State Historic Park, El Paseo, and the Art Museum.

STAY AWHILE
Our five-day itinerary explores the ocean, history, shopping, architecture, and cultural arts of Santa Barbara with an optional side trip to Channel Islands National Park.

Days One to Three
Follow the Short and Sweet itinerary.

Day Four
Explore the Santa Barbara Zoo, Museum of Natural History, and/or the Santa Barbara Botanic Gardens.

Day Five
Take the scenic drive (see the map at the front of this book) and explore the affluent neighborhoods of Montecito and Hope Ranch.

or
Hop aboard a cruise to the unspoiled Channel Islands National Park. Spend the day hiking the Nature Conservancy trails, diving the kelp forests, or kayaking around the sea caves and rocky coves. (See the Channel Islands chapter.)

interests. Spencer Winston, a docent for the Santa Barbara Historical Society and avid historian, spices his narration with hot little tidbits along the way. Tours can be customized. Call for prices.

Spitfire Aviation
204 Moffett Place, Suite P, Santa Barbara
(805) 967-4373
www.flyspitfire.com

Unique to Santa Barbara, this touring company lets you see the city and environs from the sky, where you can really appreciate the area's dramatic topography. Board a four-seat Cessna at the Santa Barbara Airport for your tour, and you're up, up, and away! Lasting just over an hour, the excursion includes an aerial view of Santa Barbara, the coastline, the Santa Ynez Valley, and the mountains.

KIDSTUFF

Hey, kids! Welcome to Santa Barbara. Your assignment: to find out as much as you can about the city and its people. This will involve lots of hands-on exploration, like going to the younger natives' favorite beaches, playgrounds, and camps. It also means having lots of fun along the way.

Are you up for this action-packed adventure? Then let's get started! Don't forget to bring your parents along. They might come in handy when you're renting equipment and buying admission tickets.

First, we need to help you look and act like a Santa Barbara kid so you'll fit right in. Most local kids (both boys and girls) wear T-shirts, shorts, and sandals nearly every day. When it's too cold for shorts, they wear sweatshirts and jeans or cotton pants.

If you really want to look like a Santa Barbara kid, wear surfer-style flip-flops. (Tell your parents to check out the Surf and Beachwear section in the Shopping chapter to find stores that sell the proper attire.) A Santa Barbara kid wouldn't be caught dead with a bright-red sunburn, so make sure you slather on that sunscreen! Baseball caps and shades are always "in."

When it comes to language, Santa Barbara kids mostly speak just like everyone else in Southern California. Throw in the word *like* between lots of words (". . . and she's like swimming down at the . . . and then he's like mad . . . ") and you'll sound just like a young Insider.

WHAT'S HAPPENING IN SANTA BARBARA

Several publications have listings of the many daily, weekly, ongoing, and special events for kids in the Santa Barbara area. In the *Santa Barbara News-Press,* check out the events calendar.

The *Santa Barbara Independent,* a free weekly paper available at newsstands all over the county, also lists events for kids. Read the day-by-day listings in "The Week."

Santa Barbara with Kids! by Susan Applewood Cann is a locally produced and published book with comprehensive information about places to go and things to do with youngsters. It's available at most bookstores in the area as well as at many museums and attractions. A free monthly magazine, *Santa Barbara Family Life* (www.sbfamilylife.com), includes articles, parenting tips, book and software reviews, a calendar of events, and a section just for kids. You can find it at grocery stores, bookstores, the library, toy shops, and many other places frequented by families. Look up sbparent.com for everything happening with parents and kids in the area.

After you've done your prep work, you're ready to explore. Take this manual along—it has lots of tips about where to go and what to do.

THE FUN BEGINS!

In this chapter, you'll find information about Santa Barbara kids' favorite haunts and activities. Many of these also appear in more complete detail in other chapters, for example, Beaches and Watersports, Recreation, and Attractions. In these cases, we provide a brief description tailored for kids in this chapter and refer you to the appropriate chapter for other details.

Good luck and have fun. Don't forget to report back to us about what you see and do!

GETTING WET AND WILD

When the weather's warm (which is often), Santa Barbara kids like to cool off down by the ocean or in one of our many community pools.

Favorite Beaches

Most young Insiders hang out at the beach a lot. You'll always find a pack of them boogie-boarding and surfing at beaches every day during the summer and on warm-weather weekends the rest of the year. The following are their favorite beach haunts (see the Beaches and Watersports chapter for detailed descriptions). Lifeguards are generally on duty at these beaches daily from early or mid-June until Labor Day.

Santa Barbara

Arroyo Burro Beach
2981 Cliff Drive, Santa Barbara
(805) 687-3714
www.sbparks.org
This is the place to find Insider kids, who call it "Henry's" (spelled Hendry's) beach. Even when the surf's not up, dozens of children float around in wetsuits, hoping for a swell. Parents like to hang out at the Brown Pelican restaurant at the beach entrance, while kids line up at the snack bar. It's also a great beach for tidepooling when the tide is low, and you can reserve a group area here for birthday parties.

East Beach/Cabrillo Pavilion Bathhouse
East Cabrillo Boulevard near Niños Drive, Santa Barbara
(805) 897-2680
www.sbparksandrecreation.com
Although East Beach isn't the best beach for surfing and boogie-boarding, you can't beat the services and activities. There's a playground, snack shop/restaurant, bathrooms, showers, and volleyball courts. You can rent boogie boards, beach chairs, volleyballs, and more at the bathhouse.

Leadbetter Beach
Shoreline and Loma Alta Drives, Santa Barbara
(805) 897-2680
www.sbparksandrecreation.com
"Leds" is a broad stretch of sandy beach between the yacht harbor and Shoreline Park. Since it's a favorite local sailboarding spot, you can watch the sailboards and catamarans ply the waves while you're digging for crabs and building sand castles.

If you don't want to picnic, you can order great food at the Shoreline Beach Cafe, with tables either right in the sand or just above on the patio. The waves near the point are often ideal for pint-size surfers: not too big, but big enough for fun boogie-board and surf rides. Picnic and barbecue areas, restrooms, and outdoor showers are also available here.

Goleta

Goleta Beach County Park
5986 Sandspit Road, Goleta
(805) 967-1300
www.sbparks.org
This 29-acre county park is very popular with local families. It lies right near the entrance to UCSB and offers boating, fishing, restrooms, a playground, horseshoes, volleyball courts, and picnic and barbecue areas on a grassy expanse under a stretch of palm trees. Paved bicycle trails twist through the park, and you can fish off the Goleta Pier and munch on snacks from the snack bar.

The popular Beachside Bar-Cafe, located on the beach inside the park, provides excellent food and views in a casual atmosphere.

i Before you take the kids to a park or beach, check out www.sbparks.org and www.sbparksandrecreation.com for information on facilities, directions, and maps.

Summerland

Lookout Park/Summerland Beach
2297 Finney Road, Summerland
(805) 568-2460
www.sbparks.org
You'll find this scenic little park and beach between U.S. Highway 101 and the ocean, near the Summerland exit. The park provides spectacular cliff-top views over the sheltered beach to the distant Channel Islands. Romp in the large playground and picnic on the bluffs above the beach. When you're ready for a swim or a stroll along the shore, just head down the path to the beach. The park has barbecue facilities, restrooms, and on-site parking.

Carpinteria

Carpinteria City Beach
End of Linden Avenue, Carpinteria
(805) 684-5405
www.carpinteria.ca.us
This is billed as the "world's safest beach." That's because the natural reef breakwater along the shore tames large waves and eliminates rip tides. The gently sloping shore and mild waves make it a great beach for safe swimming, surfing, and boogie-boarding. You can rent bikes, kayaks, and other equipment, buy snacks and lunch at the snack bar, and play volleyball on one of the beach courts.

Carpinteria State Beach Park
Entrance at Linden Avenue near Sixth Street, Carpinteria
(805) 684-2811
www.parks.ca.gov
One of the most popular parks in California's state park system, this beautiful 48-acre stretch of coast is right next to the City Beach. You'll find day-use and camping facilities here and a visitor center with natural history exhibits and nature programs. It's a fantastic place to explore tidepools, watch birds, swim, fish, hike, picnic, and splash around. Keep an eye out for sea lions and dolphins, and you can view harbor seals thronging on the beach at the nearby rookery. (See Carpinteria Harbor Seal Colony in Walk on the Wild Side later in this chapter.) The

park also has an excellent swimming beach and a fairly good area for surfing.

For camping information, read the Camping section in the Recreation chapter.

Surf and Boogie Board Lessons

If you want to learn to surf or boogie board or just improve your skills, we recommend you take lessons from the experts. They'll teach you about safety, surf etiquette, and a whole lot more. See the Beaches and Watersports chapter for information on renting or buying boards, wet suits, and other equipment.

Santa Barbara

Davey Smith's Surf Academy
711 Palermo Drive, Santa Barbara
(805) 687-5436
www.surfinstruction.com
Davey offers a hugely popular surf camp during the summer (see the Summer Camp section later in this chapter). During the fall, winter, and spring months, however, he gives private lessons to kids of all ages. Call for prices.

Shoreline Park, just above Leadbetter Beach, is one of the best places to fly a kite when the breeze picks up.

Surf Happens Surf School
1117 Las Olas Avenue, Santa Barbara
(805) 966-3613
www.surfhappens.com
Surf Happens offers private instruction and runs popular year-round surf camps for kids (see the Summer Camps section), as well as after-school instruction and Saturday Surf Days with lessons, contests, and prizes. Instruction focuses on strengthening the fundamentals of surfing techniques and improving both mental and physical fitness. Lessons usually take place at Santa Claus Lane Beach in Carpinteria or Leadbetter Point in Santa Barbara and cost about $60 per hour, depending on the number of kids in the group. Everything is provided. All the kids have to do is show up in their swimsuits.

Goleta

Surf Country
5668 Calle Real, Goleta
(805) 683-4450
www.surfcountry.net
Sign up for Surf Country's lessons and learn
to paddle a board, maneuver it quickly, gain
balance, read a wave, and surf as safely as
possible. A 90-minute lesson costs $85 for
an individual and $75 per person for three
people. Winter rates are slightly cheaper for
individual lessons. The shop supplies the surfboard, wax, leash, and wet suit. Surf Country
offers lessons by appointment for all levels,
from beginner to advanced.

Swimming Pools

If you're looking for a cool spot on a hot day,
you can head to one of Santa Barbara's clean,
safe community pools. Lifeguards are always
on duty. The listings here are all outdoor
pools. Several private indoor heated pools,
however, are open for day use with limited
hours. Anacapa Dive Center (805-963-8917,
www.anacapadive center.com) offers open
swim sessions Monday through Thursday from
11:00 a.m. to noon and 1:00 to 2:00 p.m., Friday from 11:00 a.m. to noon, Saturday from
1:00 to 5:00 p.m., and Sunday 11:00 a.m. to
1:00 p.m. The cost is $3 per person (including
babies and children). You can also buy a swim
card for $30, which entitles you to 15 visits.
The Santa Barbara YMCA (805-687-7727;
www.ciymca.org) charges $15 for non-
member day use of their heated indoor pool
and $10 if you're accompanied by a member.
Call for hours. Several private organizations
also offer swim instruction for infants and children in warm indoor pools year-round. Call
Anacapa Dive Center (805-963-8917; www
.anacapadivecenter.com), Santa Barbara
Aquatics (805-967-4456), Santa Barbara YMCA
(805-687-7727; www.ciymca.org), or Wendy
Fereday Swim School (805-964-7818;
www.clubswim.com/directory).

Santa Barbara

Los Baños del Mar Pool
401 Shoreline Drive, Santa Barbara
(805) 966-6110
Built in 1914, this historic 50-meter pool is on
the waterfront next to West Beach at the harbor (where Castillo Street ends). From mid-
June to Labor Day weekend, the pool is open
for recreational swimming weekends from
1:15 to 5:00 p.m. and weekdays from 1:45 to
3:45 p.m. Fees are $4 for adults and teens, $1
for children 18 and younger. Parking is available in the harbor lot and on the street. (See
the Recreation chapter for information on
other Los Baños programs.)

Oak Park Wading Pool
Oak Park, Alamar and Junipero Avenues,
Santa Barbara
(805) 966-6110
A fountain sits in the middle of this large,
sparkling pool. You can splash and float here
if you're younger than 7. The pool is open
11:00 a.m. to 5:00 p.m. daily from the second
week of June through Labor Day; in May to
mid-June and from Labor Day to the end of
September it's open 2:00 to 5:00 p.m. on
weekdays and 11:00 a.m. to 5:00 p.m. on
weekends. Bathing suits are required, and
children who are not toilet trained must use a
nondisposable swim diaper. Admission is free.

West Beach Wading Pool
401 Shoreline Drive, Santa Barbara
(805) 966-6110
This spacious 18-inch-deep pool sits right
next to the "big" pool complex, Los Baños del
Mar. It's open to kids 7 and younger daily
from the second week of June through Labor
Day weekend from 11:00 a.m. to 5:00 p.m.
Bathing suits are required, and children who
are not toilet trained must use a nondisposable swim diaper. Park in the harbor lot or on
the street. Admission is free.

Goleta

University of California at Santa Barbara
Campus, Goleta
(805) 893-7619
UCSB opens its gorgeous outdoor pool complex to the public every afternoon during the summer months and on weekends during the school year. It includes a 50-meter pool, a diving pool, plus an additional lap pool with a shallow area for kids. The fee is $5 for adults and teens, $3 for kids younger than 18. Call for hours.

Carpinteria

Carpinteria Valley Community Swimming Pool
5305 Carpinteria Avenue, Carpinteria
(805) 566-2417
For just $1.50, kids younger than 12 can splash and play in Carpinteria's large outdoor pool every afternoon and evening during the summer and every afternoon the rest of the year. Adults pay $3.50. See the Recreation chapter for hours.

WALK ON THE WILD SIDE

Santa Barbara isn't just inhabited by people—lots of exotic animals, plants, and other natural wonders live here, too. Following are some of the best places to see, touch, feel, and experience all these things for yourself.

Santa Barbara

Santa Barbara Botanic Garden
1212 Mission Canyon Road, Santa Barbara
(805) 682-4726
www.sbbg.org
The Botanic Garden is much more than a collection of plants and flowers—it's a great place to dive headlong into the world of nature. Walk (or run) along the 5.5 miles (8.9 kilometers) of trails, and you'll discover a redwood grove, meadows, canyons, a historic dam, a Japanese Tea House, and a creek.

There's a picnic area and a gift shop filled with books, games, and interesting items for kids as well as adults.

The Botanic Garden also sponsors workshops and special events for children throughout the year. Call and ask for the Education Department for details, or visit the Web site. (Also see the Attractions chapter for additional details, hours, and admission fees.)

Santa Barbara Museum of Natural History
2559 Puesta del Sol Road, Santa Barbara
(805) 682-4711
www.sbnature.org
See a live tarantula, walk beneath a giant blue whale skeleton, and learn all about the Chumash, the Native Americans who lived in the Santa Barbara region for thousands of years. This museum has lots of exhibits on birds, marine life, mammals (including grizzly bears, coyote, and deer), shells, and lizards. Many of the exhibit halls feature interactive computers or displays.

You can explore the wonders of the universe in the museum's Gladwin Planetarium, which has regular shows throughout the year. Star parties (free admission) are held the second Saturday of every month from 8:00 to 10:00 p.m.

The planetarium was remodeled in 2005, resulting in a Digistar 3 SP full-dome digital projection system that takes visitors on a virtual flight through space. Be sure to stroll over to the creek and the picnic areas in the museum's backyard. It's a great place to hang out and watch squirrels, birds, and lizards in action. On your way out, you have to leave through the museum gift shop—a perfect time to ask for a souvenir from Mom and Dad.

The museum sponsors after-school and weekend workshops for kids and adults throughout the year. Call or visit the Web site for details. See the Attractions chapter for a full museum description, including hours and admission prices.

Santa Barbara Zoo
500 Niños Drive, Santa Barbara
(805) 962-5339
(805) 926-6310 recorded information
www.sbzoo.org
Get up-close and personal with lions, gorillas,

ℹ️ Taking the gang to the zoo? Rent a wagon for $7, pop the kids and your bags inside, and you can whiz around the exhibits with ease.

elephants, leopards, and other animals. Considered the finest small zoo in California, the Santa Barbara Zoo is as wild as Santa Barbara gets. It's also one of the best places for kids to spend free time on fair-weather days. Lots of Insider kids go there at least once a week year-round and attend a week or two of Zoo Camp in the summer (see the Summer Camps section later in this chapter).

Once part of a grand estate, the beautifully landscaped grounds include palm gardens, exotic plants, and an expansive hilltop knoll overlooking the ocean. More than 600 animals representing 160 species live amid the lush gardens—river otters, lions, leopards, giraffes, sea lions, and llamas, to name just a few. Most exhibits have low enclosures and windows or open space, so shorter visitors (even toddlers and babies in strollers) can easily see and interact with the animals. Don't miss the crooked-neck giraffe, the Cats of Africa exhibit, and the gorillas.

You can see nearly all the animals in an hour or two, but you'll probably want to spend at least a half-day just enjoying the grounds. Take a spin on the handmade Dentzel miniature carousel—you can ride on a sea serpent, unicorn, horse, pig, frog, rabbit, or fish. It's for kids only (sorry, Mom and Pop!) and costs only 75 cents. The carousel is open 11:00 a.m. to 2:00 p.m. daily.

You can also hop aboard one of the miniature C. P. Huntington trains that circle the zoo. Train tickets for kids ages 2 through 12 cost $1.50; adults and teens pay $2 a ride. From the train you can see toucans, giraffes, gibbons, behind-the-scenes areas, and the adjacent Andree Clark Bird Refuge.

If you're bursting with energy, head up to the zoo playground. During certain hours of the day, you can feed the llamas and sheep. When your own tummy growls, spread out a picnic lunch on the grassy knoll. Or you can buy salads, sandwiches, burgers, corn dogs, zoo fries, and other fare at a restaurant at the zoo entrance.

Don't leave without browsing the gift shop, which has everything from African artifacts, puzzles, books, and games to jewelry, clothing, and exotic stuffed animals.

During the school year, the zoo offers fun workshops for kids, adults, and families. One of the more popular kids' workshops is the Zoo Snooze, an overnight adventure where you learn all about animal nightlife.

For information on workshops, visit the Web site, or call (805) 962-5339 and ask for the Education Office.

Ty Warner Sea Center
211 Stearns Wharf, Santa Barbara
(805) 687-4711

"What's in all that water anyways?" Find out at the newly renovated and much improved Ty Warner Sea Center. Be an oceanographer for a day by taking water samples and analyzing them through video magnifiers, or learn about ongoing scientific research and try to beat the computers by giving the right answer. The live tide pools give kids a close-up view and hands-on experience with ocean creatures, and the video theater presents an engaging and awe-inspiring documentary on the wonders of our own Santa Barbara Channels. This is truly a fun way to spend a morning or afternoon. Don't forget to get a lip-sticking cotton candy or melt-in-your-mouth ice cream on Stearns Wharf on the way out.

Goleta

Ellwood Grove Monarch Butterfly Roosting Site
End of Coronado Street, Goleta

This dense eucalyptus grove is one of several places along the California coast that attract wintering monarch butterflies. The black-and-orange butterflies usually start to arrive in October, and you can see them hanging from the trees and fluttering about. Peak butterfly-watching season is midwinter.

The grove is in the Santa Barbara Shores neighborhood near the Winchester Canyon exit of U.S. Highway 101. To find it, drive along Coronado Street from Hollister Avenue toward the ocean. This will dead-end at the eucalyptus grove. Park on the street and follow the trail to the right about 100 yards. Look up in the trees—you can't miss them!

Wilderness Youth Project
5386-D Hollister Avenue, Goleta
(805) 964-8096
www.wyp.org
Nature is the greatest teacher, and nothing exemplifies this more than the Wilderness Youth Project. After-school, summer, and weekend programs for kids ages 4 to 17 have kids learning what's in the wilds of nature. Ever heard of the elderberry? Did you know it can be used to help the common cold or flu? Or how about a plantain (like a banana) salve? Wilderness Youth Project kids know it as the "Band-aid" plant because it's great for bee stings, cuts, and poison oak. Check out the Web site for full program details and costs of the program.

Carpinteria

Carpinteria Harbor Seal Colony
Carpinteria Bluffs
End of Bailard Avenue, Carpinteria
Want to see a real wild seal colony? Well, you're in luck, because Carpinteria is home to one of only two publicly accessible harbor seal rookeries in California. Best of all, the rookery is tucked in a cove below the beautiful Carpinteria bluffs—a fantastic place to hike and look for other wildlife, too. The best time to visit is from December 1 to May 31, when the seals haul out on land to rest, give birth, and nurse their pups. From January to May, volunteers are there to answer your questions. Visit from late February to April, and you might even be lucky enough to see a chubby little seal pup coming into the world.

To find the rookery, take the Bailard Freeway exit in Carpinteria, turn right, and park in the lot at the end of the street near the hot dog stand. Follow the path to the right along the ocean, and you'll see breathtaking views of Rincon Point to the east and the Channel Islands to the south. Watch for red-tailed hawks. They hover here looking for ground squirrels and gophers. But don't get too close to the edge; it's very steep.

About 1/2 mile (1 kilometer) down the track, you'll see the viewing area just before the pier. Dogs scare the seals, so if you happen to be walking one, tie it up before you enter the area. Shhh! Be very quiet. Creep up to the railing slowly, and you should be able to spot the seals way down on the beach below. Look for some in the water and on the rock. See how well their big, blubbery bodies blend with their natural surroundings? To find out more about the harbor seals—including what they eat and what eats them—see the Close-up in the Parks chapter.

North of Santa Barbara

Cachuma Lake
California Highway 154, 20 miles (32 kilometers) northwest of Santa Barbara
(805) 568-2460
www.sbparks.org
Take a cruise on Cachuma Lake and spot bald eagles, deer, and other animals. Park naturalists lead two-hour guided Eagle Cruise tours from November through February. When the eagles leave, you can still take the cruise to spot other wildlife. See the Parks and Recreation chapters for a detailed description of the lake.

Little Orphan Hammies
P.O. Box 924, Solvang 93464
(805) 693-9953
www.lilorphanhammies.com
This little piggy went to Solvang to see the potbellied pig rescue and sanctuary. This five-acre pig "pen" rescues, adopts, boards, and takes long-term care of potbellied pigs. Tours are offered to school-aged children.

A llama and alpaca farm in Santa Ynez Valley. GREG PETERSON/SANTA BARBARA CONFERENCE & VISITORS BUREAU

Ostrich Land
610 East Highway 246
P.O. Box 490, Buellton 93427
(805) 686-9696
www.ostrichland.com/comevisit.html
What is the world's largest bird? The ostrich, and there are plenty of them at Ostrich Land. Quick, how many toes do they have? Did you guess two? You're right. All other birds have three or four. Feeding the birds is allowed for $1 per sack. The bowl of feed is put on a finger-saving dustpan. Just lift the dustpan to the ostrich's mouth and watch the feed be gobbled down. Seeing ostriches in action can be quite a sight, as they can run up to speeds of 40 miles an hour. On this 33-acre breeding farm, the 50 or so ostriches can really kick it into action. Fifteen emus, the largest bird native to Australia, also call Ostrich Land home. Look for the small roadside shop selling fresh eggs, meat, feathers, and egg art. Open daily 10:00 a.m. to 6:00 p.m. Admission is $4.

Quicksilver Miniature Horse Ranch
1555 Alamo Pintado Road, Solvang
(805) 686-4002
www.syv.com/qsminis/
Kids can hardly believe their eyes when they see these little horses that were originally bred in Europe as pets for royalty. Patient and gentle, miniature horses are sometimes no bigger than a large dog. Aleck and Louise Stribling have been breeding these cute-as-a-button horses for years on their 20-acre high-tech training facility. Please note: The ranch doesn't offer rides in carts or petting pens. Open daily 10:00 a.m. to 3:00 p.m. Admission is free. Tours are available only by appointment. For tours of 20 or more, the cost is $3 per person.

"Return to Freedom" American Wild Horse Sanctuary
P.O. Box 926, Lompoc 93438
(805) 737-9246
www.returntofreedom.org
Meet Spirit, the horse who inspired Dream

Works' animated movie, at this nonprofit sanctuary for horses. It was schoolchildren, in the 1950s, who initially convinced government officials to enact laws protecting wild horses through a letter campaign they developed at the urging of Velma Johnson, known as "Wild Horse Annie." Now children can see the results of their predecessors' work at the sanctuary. The Children Living History Tours give a firsthand look at wild horse behavior for $20 per adult and $10 for children under 12. The sanctuary officially declares August Youth Month, which includes a volunteer day and an overnight camp experience. For future ranch hands, there's A Kid's Day at the Ranch, where children learn about the day-to-day operations of managing a horse and burro ranch. If you want to roll up your sleeves, pitch some hay, and also pitch in, there's the Youth Volunteer Weekends, where everyone helps around the ranch, then gathers around the campfire for late-night stories. The next morning, bright-eyed and bushy-tailed and with a feeling of satisfaction, everyone breaks down camp and heads home. Call for the available dates and pricing.

WIGGLE MODE

You've got the wiggles and you just can't sit still any longer. What's a kid to do? Luckily, there are many places in Santa Barbara where kids can run around and expend excess energy. Here are a few safe, fun ways to shake your sillies out and develop your motor skills.

Bowling

Zodo's Bowling & Beyond
5925 Calle Real, Goleta
(805) 967-0128

Open until 2:00 a.m., the smoke-free Zodo's Bowling & Beyond offers daily bowling and bumper bowling. It's a great place to let off steam, especially when it's cold, rainy, or foggy outside. Prices are $4 per person per game for adults Monday through Friday from 8:30 a.m. to 5:00 p.m. On weekends and weekday evenings, you'll pay $5.50 per person per game. Friday and Saturday evenings from 5:00 p.m. to 12:30 a.m. are $6.95 per person per game. Late-night pricing from 12:30 to 2:00 a.m. is $3.00 per person per game for Sunday to Thursday and $3.50 per person per game on Fridays and Saturdays. You can also pay on a per lane, per hour basis. Monday through Friday per lane, per hour is $22 from 8:30 a.m. to 5:00 p.m.; Saturday and Sunday from 8:30 a.m. to 5:00 p.m., and Sunday through Thursday from 5:00 p.m. to 12:30 a.m. is $28 per lane, per hour. Friday and Saturday evenings from 5:00 p.m. to 12:30 a.m. is $35 per lane, per hour. (Monday through Thursday from 5:30 to 9:00 p.m. are booked with leagues.) Summer specials starting in late June and continuing through September include one free game every day for kids 18 and under. Shoe rental is $4.00 for children and adults, $3.50 for Wednesday evenings after 9:00 p.m. Looking for some additional fun? Check out Rock and Bowl, Galactic Bowl, and Glow Bowl, with its disco strobes and luminous bowling balls. Special balls are provided for kids. There's also a cafe on the premises.

Indoor Play

Kindermusik
1213 State Street, Suite 1, Santa Barbara
(805) 884-4009

Carpinteria Women's Club
1059 Vallecito, Carpinteria

Kindermusik with Seniors
5486 Calle Real, Maravilla
www.kindermusikwithkathy.com

Kindermusik is extremely popular with Santa Barbara moms and their children. The director, Kathy Hayden, is a former preschool, kindergarten, and first-grade teacher who shares her passion for music with children from 3 months to 7 years. Depending on the age group, the sessions involve creative dance, instrument exploration, singing, and storytelling through music. Classes range from about $143 for a 15-week program for infants to $217 for young children. Materials for the classes, such as books, CDs, and instruments, incur an extra charge. Kindermusik is tucked back behind McDonald's near Victoria Court.

My Gym Santa Barbara
3888 State Street, Santa Barbara
(805) 563-7336
www.my-gym.com
Bury yourself in a sea of plastic balls, clamber over padded obstacles, swing from the trapeze, bounce on the trampoline, watch puppet shows, dance, sing, jiggle, wiggle, and just go crazy. In 2003 this colorful, music-filled children's gym opened a location in Santa Barbara, opposite La Cumbre Shopping Mall, and it's filled with active little Insider kids ages 3 months to 9 years.

2000 Degrees
1206 State Street, Santa Barbara
(805) 882-1817
2000 Degrees is a fantastic place for budding little artists to hang out—especially on rainy or foggy days. At this ceramics workshop, you purchase greenware (unfinished ceramics, such as cups, plates, and bowls), and paint it with your own creative designs. Prices range from $5 for a tile to $60 for a large platter. Not the artistic type? Don't worry. Experienced staffers are on hand to help you out. 2000 Degrees will do all the glazing and firing. They'll even ship the piece to you if you leave town before it's ready. This is a great place to make personalized gifts for friends and family.

i Looking for a creative weekend activity for the kids? Art from Scrap (302 East Cota Street, Santa Barbara), a program run by the Community Environmental Council (805-884-0459; www.community environmentalcouncil.org), runs Saturday workshops (10:00 to 11:30 a.m.) where kids can make jewelry, masks, puppets, robots, mosaics, and more from discarded material. Call or visit the Web site for details.

Playgrounds

The Parks chapter provides complete details on the area's best parks. Here, though, we'd like to point out a few of the local kids' favorite playgrounds. They're all in Santa Barbara, and they all have safe, modern play structures plus unique atmospheres that spark your imagination. Romp on!

Chase Palm Park Shipwreck Playground
Cabrillo Boulevard, between Santa Barbara Street and Calle Cesar Chavez, Santa Barbara
(805) 564-5418
www.sbparksandrecreation.com
Designed for toddlers through 12-year-olds, this amazing playground opened in May 1998, replete with spouting whales, a shipwreck village, talking tubes, and bridges. The 15,000-square-foot (1,394-square-meter) playground represents Santa Barbara, from the Santa Ynez Mountains (represented by a tall back wall) all the way to the Channel Islands.

Beneath the mountains stretches a cityscape—a series of arched facades adorned with Spanish/Mexican details. From the spongy "shore," a pier juts out in the sandy "ocean." A ramp leads to one of the coolest play structures around—a ship that appears to have crashed on rubber-coated rock.

Cross another couple of bridges and you come to an island—a mounded area with a deck and pole like Robinson Crusoe's. In the sand area, you can ride statues of whales, dolphins, and other sea creatures, as well as a spring-mounted raft and buoy.

Toddlers can make sand castles and dig around in a contained area shaped like breaking waves. Water mists sprinkle the sand (and any kids sitting nearby) every few minutes, timed by embedded computer chips. The playground also has picnic areas and restrooms.

Kids' World
Alameda Park, corner of Micheltorena and Garden Streets, Santa Barbara
(805) 564-5418
www.sbparksandrecreation.com
Sit on a shark, ride a whale, hide in the turrets of a magic castle, and race across suspension bridges. This one-of-a-kind playground is 8,000 square feet (743 square meters) of pure fun. It was designed by Santa Barbara children and constructed by community volunteers in 1993.

Very young children can scramble around in the toddler area, which has pint-size swings, slides, and climbing equipment. Older, more agile kids can tear through tunnels, slip through slides, swing on ropes, and generally have the time of their lives. (Be sure to wear brightly colored clothes so Mom and Dad can spot you between the wooden castle slats.)

Just across the street, at Alice Keck Park Memorial Garden, you can watch koi circle the pond and count the turtles basking in the sun.

Oak Park Playground
300 West Alamar Avenue at Junipero Street, Santa Barbara
(805) 564-5418
www.sbparksandrecreation.com
"Take me to the oak tree park!" Santa Barbara children make this request all the time. It has two great playgrounds—one perfect for toddlers and small children and another for the agile and daring. During the summer months, kids 7 and younger can cool off in the wading pool (see the Swimming Pools section earlier in this chapter). It has restrooms, shady picnic sites, and convenient parking in the lot or on the street.

Shoreline Park Playground
Shoreline Drive and San Rafael Avenue, Santa Barbara
(805) 564-5418
www.sbparksandrecreation.com
This small playground, near the parking lot and restrooms at the west end of Shoreline Park, is ideal for younger children. It's where

Insiders take their little ones to practice riding trikes and two-wheelers. From here you can take in fantastic views of the ocean and the Channel Islands. At certain times of year you can spot whales, and throughout the year you can often watch the schools of dolphins that regularly play nearby.

Stevens Park
258 Canon Drive, Santa Barbara
(805) 564-5418
www.sbparksandrecreation.com
Twenty-five-acre Stevens Park lies at the entrance to the foothills near the intersection of San Roque and Foothill Roads. Here you can picnic, go on short nature walks, and hike along creekside and canyon trails. It has swings and two play structures (one for toddlers and one for older kids), restrooms, barbecue and picnic areas, and on-site parking.

Challenge your parents to a climb— a climbing wall, that is. Open seven days a week at Santa Barbara Outfitters downtown store location (1200 State Street), this indoor wall is a treat for kids and parents alike. Who do you think will have the fastest time to the top?

Tar Pits Park
East end of Carpinteria State Beach
The Chumash built their canoes and boats here and caulked the planks with natural asphalt. You can see gooey black stuff oozing down the cliffs, plus lots of sea creatures on the reef. To get here, take Concha Loma to Calle Ocho. Park and walk over the railroad tracks to the lookout point. Walk down the steps to reach the beach. Make sure you wear old shoes and swimsuits—the natural asphalt can really stick to them.

In-line Skating/ Skateboarding
The best places to in-line skate or skateboard are along the Cabrillo Bike Path or Skater's Point Skate Park (see the listing below). You

i One of our favorite family activities is cycling along the beachfront on the Cabrillo Bike Path. Rent a family-size surrey and pedal together. Along the way, you can explore Andree Clark Bird Refuge, watch the pelicans on Stearns Wharf, and look for seals at the Santa Barbara Harbor. (For bike rentals see the Recreation chapter.)

can rent equipment at a number of beachside locations—see the Recreation chapter for details. No one's allowed to skate or skateboard on any public street or on many city sidewalks or public ways in the downtown and beach area. When you see signs with pictures of skates and skateboards with a big line painted through them, you'll know you're in a restricted area. When you rent or buy equipment, ask for information on prohibited areas.

Santa Barbara Hockey Association
In-line Hockey Rink
Earl Warren Showgrounds, 3400 Calle Real, Santa Barbara
(805) 564-2035
www.sbhockey.com
The nonprofit Santa Barbara Hockey Association runs this huge in-line hockey rink at Earl Warren Showgrounds, reputedly one of the best in Southern California. Kids of all ages can skate at open sessions during the daytime on weekdays or at the popular Saturday night session. The association also organizes hockey leagues for kids age 5 to 17 for all levels, from beginners to advanced. You'll have to bring your own equipment, and you might want to pack some snacks and drinks. To find the rink, enter Earl Warren Showgrounds through Gate C off Calle Real.

Skater's Point Skate Park
Chase Palm Park
236 East Cabrillo Boulevard (near Stearns Wharf), Santa Barbara
(805) 897-2650
www.sbparksandrecreation.com
Completed in 2000, this waterfront skate park is a popular hub for Santa Barbara's skating

community. You can't beat the location. It's right on the beachfront. Head toward Stearns Wharf, and you'll see it on the east side. Kids of all ages flock here to ride the 14,200 square feet (1,319 square meters) of ramps, bowls, ledges, pipes, and rails. While they're waiting, they can practice on Cabrillo Bike Path or watch all the action from the observation decks. The park is open daily from 8:00 a.m. to sunset. [Inexperienced skaters are encouraged to try out the park before 11:00 a.m. on the weekends.] Helmets and knee and elbow pads are required, and admittance is free.

Youth Sports

Santa Barbara offers countless opportunities for kids to participate in individual and team sports. The city's Parks and Recreation Department sponsors dozens of youth sports lessons and team programs for boys and girls; among them are aquatics, baseball, flag football, golf, softball, T-ball, tennis, track and field, and volleyball. Call (805) 564-5495 or (805) 564-5418 for information, or visit www.sbparksandrecreation.com.

The Santa Barbara Family YMCA (805-687-7727; www.ciymca.org) and the Montecito Family YMCA (805-969-3288; www.ciymca.org) also offer a range of youth sports programs. If you're interested in joining a sports league or would like private instruction, we recommend you call the Page Youth Center at (805) 967-8778 or visit www.pageyouthcenter.com. You can also look through the Yellow Pages and call for information. Popular youth

i Tee off in style at The First Central Coast's golf program for kids. Learn about the rules of the course and the rules of life with this character-building golf program designed for kids ages 7 to 17. Held throughout the year, the program is offered in summer sessions as well. Check out the Web site at www.thefirstteecentralcoast.org, or contact Twin Lakes Golf Course and Learning Center at (805) 964-1414, www.twinlakesgolf.com, for more information.

sports include Little League, BMX Motor Cross, football, roller hockey, soccer, swimming, diving, and water polo. A number of private organizations offer training and specialized instruction in gymnastics, martial arts, horseback riding, and tennis.

One club worth special mention is the Santa Barbara Sea Shell Association (www.sbssa.org), Santa Barbara's oldest youth sports club. It promotes the sport of sailing by teaching its members racing skills, seamanship, and the art of being a good sport.

THINKING MODE

Libraries

Nearly all branches of the Santa Barbara Public Library offer a weekly Preschool Story Time. They also sponsor many special events for children, for example, puppet and magic shows, films, and drumming workshops. You can pick up a monthly calendar of events at any branch. You can also check out videos and connect to the Internet at any branch.

If you have any questions or need help finding something, the experienced children's librarians are more than happy to help out. Hours vary by branch; call for information, or visit the library Web site at www.ci.santa-barbara.ca.us/departments /library. If the branch locations aren't convenient, you can always visit the Bookmobile, a huge traveling library that goes all over the city: to schools, shopping centers, retirement centers, and other locations throughout the community. Call the Goleta branch for schedules.

Having fun at Skater's Point Skate Park on Cabrillo Boulevard. NANCY SHOBE

Preschool Story Times

Santa Barbara Central Library
40 East Anapamu Street, Santa Barbara
(805) 962-7653
10:30 a.m. Tuesday and Thursday

Santa Barbara Eastside Branch
1102 East Montecito Street, Santa Barbara
(805) 963-3727
10:30 a.m. Wednesday, bilingual story times
10:00 and 10:30 a.m. Thursday

Goleta Branch
500 North Fairview Avenue, Santa Barbara
(805) 964-7878
10:30 a.m. Wednesday and Thursday

Montecito Branch
1469 East Valley Road, Santa Barbara
(805) 969-5063
10:30 a.m. Thursday

Carpinteria Branch
5141 Carpinteria Avenue, Santa Barbara
(805) 684-4314
10:30 a.m. Thursday

JUST PLAIN FUN

Goleta

South Coast Railroad Museum and Goleta Depot
300 North Los Carneros Road, Goleta
(805) 964-3540
www.goletadepot.org

Hop aboard a miniature train, clamber through a real caboose, and check out cool train artifacts from long ago. Built in 1901, the Victorian Goleta Depot is a historical landmark as well as a fun place to picnic and hang out. It's located at Lake Los Carneros County Park, right next to the historic Stow House (see the Attractions chapter). The museum is dedicated to the history and adventure of railroading, emphasizing American rural railroad stations.

The miniature train ride is by far the most popular attraction for children at the museum. It operates year-round on Wednesday and Friday through Sunday. The rides are usually offered from 2:00 to 3:45 p.m. during the week and from 1:00 to 3:45 p.m. on weekends.

It costs $1 for a single ride, $1.50 for two rides, and $2 for three rides. Ticket prices are usually higher during special events at Easter, Christmas, and other holiday times. Infants aren't allowed on the train; you have to be able to get on and off by yourself and be at least 34 inches tall. Parents may ride with their children.

Other popular attractions include an extensive HO-scale model railroad exhibit, working railroad communications and signaling equipment, a bay-window caboose, a station yard track, and a gift shop with train history–related gifts for all ages. On the third Saturday of every month, you can ride a handcar around the grounds. A minimum height of 48 inches is required.

The museum is open Wednesday through Sunday 1:00 to 4:00 p.m. Admission is free.

HUNGER MODE

Since Santa Barbara is such a laid-back place, many restaurants have children's menus, crayons, and comfortable seating for wiggly bodies. We want to tell you about a couple of our favorites—places where the food is great, kids won't get bored, and parents can relax, too. See the Restaurants chapter for the price code key.

Beach Grill at Padaro/Pizza Mizza $
3765 Santa Claus Lane, Carpinteria
(805) 566-3900
www.beachgrillpadaro.com

Bordering popular Santa Claus Beach, this friendly outdoor restaurant is a hands-down Insider family favorite. You can't beat the setting. Picnic tables dot nearly half an acre of beachfront lawn centered by a huge sandbox and play area packed with toys. While the kids are digging around in the sand, Mom and Dad can relax with a glass of wine and a burger. The lawn is separated from the beach by fenced-off train tracks, so the kids can't go wandering off the property, and they have plenty of room to run around. You'll find all the surfside classics on the menu, including burgers, sandwiches, pizzas, salads, pasta dishes, and house specialties, such as the fish tacos. Kids can refuel on hot dogs, grilled cheese sandwiches, burgers, chicken tenders, and spaghetti. Beach Grill at Padaro is open daily for lunch and dinner until 8:00 p.m. on Sunday through Thursday and 9:00 p.m. on Friday and Saturday. Brunch is served on weekends. Call for seasonal hours. Pooches are welcome on the street side of the lawn, but they must be leashed.

Longboards Grill $$
210 Stearns Wharf, Santa Barbara
(805) 963-3311

Perched high on Stearns Wharf overlooking the water, Longboards is a great hangout for little Insider surfer dudes and gals. It's also a great spot for Mom and Dad to sip a beer and watch the sunset. Relax on the ocean-view outdoor deck, or choose a surfboard-shaped table inside. While you wait for your meal, you can munch on free peanuts (throw the shells on the floor), check out the surfing memorabilia, watch videos of monster waves and wipeouts, or just gaze out at the ocean views

i Sign up for summer camp sessions as early as possible. The most popular camps fill up early, sometimes by May.

through the panoramic windows. The children's menu includes favorites such as grilled cheese sandwiches, corn dogs, miniburgers, and chicken tenders with fries. After the meal, well-behaved kids can pick a toy from the treasure chest as a special treat.

Woody's Bodacious Barbecue $
5112 Hollister Avenue, Goleta
(805) 967-3775
www.woodysbbq.com
Voted "Best Barbecue Restaurant" in a local poll for 19 years in a row, Woody's is a fun place to take the kids. The rugged Wild West decor (you wash your hands in a bathtub in the center of the room) and great kid's menu of dino ribs, chicken strips, hamburgers, and hot dogs are sure to be a hit with the young ones. Moms and dads will love the prices and the portions. The huge servings of succulent barbecue chicken, baby back ribs, and oak-smoked prime rib and duckling will satisfy even the hungriest of bellies. Vegetarians can graze at the salad bar. Woody's is open for lunch and dinner daily.

SUMMER CAMPS

The hardest task facing Santa Barbara kids every summer is deciding which camps to attend. Santa Barbara has dozens of day camps and a few overnight camps in the area. Some are general summer camps that typically offer arts and crafts, sports, and activities. Others focus on a particular theme or sport, for example, music, arts, sailing, basketball, or aquatic activities.

Your best bet for choosing a camp is to pick up a regional camp guide. *The Santa Barbara Independent* publishes an excellent summer camp/youth activity guide every spring. Another excellent resource is the City of Santa Barbara's *Parks & Recreation Guide*

(spring/summer issue). You can view the latest issue online at www.sbparksandrecreation .com, or call (805) 564-5418. The following camps are the most popular among Insider kids. Happy camping!

Santa Barbara
Davey Smith's Surf Academy
711 Palermo Road, Santa Barbara
(805) 687-5436
www.surfinstruction.com
Hundreds of youths ages 8 through 15 have honed their surf skills at Davey Smith's summer surf camp. The one-week sessions (Monday through Friday 9:00 a.m. to 4:00 p.m.) teach safety, etiquette on the water (for example, when to take a wave if others are waiting), style, and technique.

Davey usually offers about 11 sessions from mid-June to September. He sends out information at the beginning of March, and the sessions fill up fast. The sooner you can reserve a spot, the better. This is a mobile camp; the group meets at a designated location and heads for a beach that's conducive to the day's weather and swell. The academy provides wet suits and boards. Call for prices.

The First Tee Central Coast
P.O. Box 1611, Summerland 93067
(805) 684-2184
www.firstteecentralcoast.org
The First Tee Central Coast teaches more than just the game of golf to kids ages 11 to 17. It also teaches about the nine core values of honesty, integrity, sportsmanship, respect, confidence, responsibility, perseverance, courtesy, and good judgment and about maintaining a positive attitude, thinking through the consequences of decisions, and defining and setting goals. "It's the best ever," boasted one eager young player when asked about The First Tee. Held on public golf courses throughout Santa Barbara County, the local First Tee is located in Goleta at Twin Lakes Golf and Learning Center. Access The First Tee Web site for more information on this very affordable year-round golf program.

Santa Barbara Family YMCA
36 Hitchcock Way, Santa Barbara
(805) 687-7727
www.ciymca.org

The Santa Barbara YMCA has offered an affordable day camp for years. Activities typically include field trips, games, swimming, arts and crafts, drama, music, and sports. It's open to children in kindergarten through sixth grade, and campers are grouped by grade. Fees are $130 a week with a $50 registration fee. You can view a copy of the summer camp program online.

Santa Barbara Outfitters
Youth Adventure Camp
1200 State Street, Santa Barbara
(805) 899-3010

For kids grades three through six, this camp for young adventurers teaches them about sustainabililty and managing their impact on the environment. Surfing, boogie-boarding, sea kayaking, astronomy, rock climbing, and camping are all part of the weekly adventures. Camp counselor to camper ratio is six to one. Session 1 lasts for two weeks and includes overnight camping at Santa Cruz Island; the cost is $1,149. Session 2 lasts for one week and features a campout at Orella Ranch; the cost is $425. Enrollment forms are available online.

Santa Barbara Surf Adventures
10 State Street, Santa Barbara
(805) 963-1281
www.santabarbarasurfadventures.com

Run out of the Beach House in Santa Barbara, this popular one-week summer surf camp is geared to first-time and beginner surfers who want to brush up on their surfing skills. Classes, taught by professional lifeguards and experienced long-time Santa Barbara surfers, also cover beach safety, first aid, and marine biology. One-week Leadbetter Beach camps start at about $290 and include a soft surfboard, wet suit, and camp T-shirt. One-week travel camps cost about $330. Participants meet at Leadbetter Beach and venture to the day's surfing destination depending on swell and weather conditions.

ShowStoppers
(805) 682-6043
www.showstoppersproductions.com

ShowStoppers offers summer performance workshops for kids ages 7 through 14. Participants acquire musical theater skills through practical workshops where they learn to perform in a musical production. Call for more information. See the The Arts chapter for information on ShowStoppers' year-round programs.

Surf Happens Surf School
1117 Las Olas Avenue, Santa Barbara
(805) 966-3613
www.surfhappens.com

Each summer Surf Happens runs 11 weeks of surf camps beginning mid-June and running until the end of August. The camps teach fundamental movements, introduce surf etiquette, and help students overcome fear of the water. The series includes summer sleepover camps at El Capitan, travel camps when more advanced surfers scout the coast for the best waves of the day, international camps at surfing hot spots around the world, and day classes at Santa Claus Lane Beach. Call for details.

Youth Sailing/Kayaking Camp
Santa Barbara Harbor
(805) 962-2826, (800) 350-9090
www.sbsail.com

The Santa Barbara Sailing Center has offered these popular camps since 1962. Kids ages 8 to 15 can "learn the ropes" at the sailing camp, and 10- to 15-year-olds can practice paddling at the kayaking camp. The weeklong sessions (Monday through Friday) include 20 hours of hands-on instruction and are offered from mid-June to the end of August. Kayaking sessions are held from 8:30 a.m. to 12:30 p.m. Sailing sessions meet in the afternoons from 1:00 to 5:00 p.m. Sessions cost $140.

Zoo Camp
Santa Barbara Zoo
500 Niños Drive, Santa Barbara

(805) 962-5339
www.santabarbarazoo.org
Zoo Camp is regularly voted the "Best Kids' Camp in Santa Barbara" in local newspaper polls. It's open to all kids from ages 3 to 12. Campers are grouped by age or grade; group size ranges from 10 to 15 kids, with one counselor and two to four counselors-in-training per group.

Each weeklong session (Monday through Friday, 9:00 a.m. to 2:00 p.m. or 8:00 a.m. to 5:00 p.m. for the extended stay) focuses on a particular theme, for example, Habitats, Diversity, and Conservation. Themes are repeated every three weeks, and you can sign up for as many sessions as you like.

Each week's activities revolve around the theme of the week and include animal encounters, group play, behind-the-scenes visits, games, stories, educational activities, and art projects. Special field trips such as excursions to the beach or bird refuge are held every Friday. Contact the zoo for information on zoo camp fees and scholarships. Note that you can also buy a summer camp family membership for $40, which includes zoo camp discounts and free entry to the zoo for the entire summer.

Goleta

University of California at Santa Barbara Summer Camps
UCSB Campus, Goleta
(805) 893-3913
www.recreation.ucsb.edu
Since 1981, UCSB has provided excellent summer programs for local and visiting youth. The UCSB Day Camp is open to kids ages 5 through 14; it's led by UCSB coaches, local teachers, and students earning teaching credentials. The one-week sessions introduce kids to various sports, games, and activities appropriate for the specific age group and skill level.

Typical activities include arts and crafts, gymnastics, swimming, field trips, beach days, archery, and sports. Groups are sorted into four divisions: Freshman Camp (ages 5 through 6), Sophomore Camp (ages 7 through 8), Junior Camp (ages 9 through 11), and Senior Camp (ages 12 through 14). UCSB Day Camp costs between $110 and $130 a week.

UCSB coaches also run specialized volleyball and basketball camps for girls and boys (day and overnight). There are also tennis, golf, soccer, water polo, baseball, drama, and swing dance camps. UCSB Ocean Camps offer one-week surf and kayak sessions for boys and girls ages 9 through 15. Fees vary.

Montecito

Montecito Family YMCA
591 Santa Rosa Lane, Montecito
(805) 969-3288
www.ciymca.org
This camp is smaller than the one at the main YMCA—approximately 100 kids attend the camp at a time. The Y offers special activities such as off-site camping and horseback riding. Each session has a theme and lasts two weeks. Typical activities include arts and crafts, swimming, barbecues, and field trips to local parks and beaches. Fees range from $160 to $170.

Westmont College Sports Camp
Westmont College
955 La Paz Road
Montecito
(805) 565-6010
www.westmont.edu
Summer sports camps run by this Christian college are especially popular because camp leaders take a noncompetitive approach to the sports. Instead, the camps emphasize fun and help children develop confidence in their abilities. Kids from ages 5 through 16 can sign up for half-day programs in basketball, soccer, volleyball, tennis, track and field, archery, and general sports skills. Kids ages 5 through 14 can enroll in a full-day sports camp for basketball, soccer, or baseball. Age groups vary depending on the sport. Half-day sessions cost $160; full-day sessions, $200. Sessions last one week. Visit the Web site for online registration.

SPECIAL NEEDS

Camp Wheez
American Lung Association
1510 San Andres Street, Santa Barbara
(805) 963-1426
Held in August, this one-week free camp is for children with chronic asthma who are in grades one through six. Daily classes help children learn to better manage their disease.

Happy Adventure Summer Camp
Cornerstone House
(805) 684–5840
www.cornerstonehouse.org
This 15-year-old day camp offers two weeks of summer activities for developmentally disabled youth ages 5 to 18. It's run by Cornerstone House, a nonprofit. Call (805) 680-2538 for more details.

BEST PLACES FOR A BIRTHDAY PARTY

When the big day comes along, you can choose from dozens of places to celebrate with friends and family. During warmer months, parties take place at just about every park in the county (see the Parks chapter to review your options). Here are a few other Insider kids' favorite party locations.

Santa Barbara

Kindermusik
1213 State Street, Suite 1, Santa Barbara
(805) 884-4009
www.kindermusikwithkathy.com
Kids love music, and good tunes are sure to set the tone for a successful birthday party. Kindermusik will create a theme and design musical activities and creative games for your child's party. The birthday boy or girl can choose a theme that sparks his or her imagination, such as Thomas the Tank Engine, Bob the Builder, the Little Mermaid, kitty cats, doggies, or princesses. You can stage the event in the Kindermusik studio, or they'll come to you.

My Gym Santa Barbara
3888 State Street, Santa Barbara
(805) 563-7336
www.my-gym.com
Kids can go wild in this colorful, music-filled gym—swinging on trapezes, singing, dancing, climbing, bouncing, stomping, and jumping. Supervised by the friendly staff, the party includes organized games, puppet shows, songs, a "Space Flight," a special birthday march, and all the decorations, refreshments, and cleanup. All you have to do is send the invitations, select a cake, and show up. Parties for up to 20 kids cost $300 for members and $325 for nonmembers.

Santa Barbara Zoo
500 Niños Drive, Santa Barbara
(805) 962-5339 ext. 27, Birthday Party Hot line (805) 962-5339, ext. 54 (recorded message)
www.sbzoo.org
This is a favorite Insider venue for children's parties. Santa Barbara Zoo offers a great party package for a minimum of 10 children ages 2 to 12. The package includes a three-hour reservation at one of the zoo's seven scenic picnic sites, an animal demonstration with a zoo critter (such as a snake, lizard, or rabbit), animal-themed tableware, zoo souvenirs, activity booklets, and train tickets. When the kids are finished gobbling cake and candy, they can burn off their sugar buzz romping around the exhibits. The package costs $13 per person for members and $17 for nonmembers. For an additional fee, extra options such as special catering are available. If you don't want all the zoo goodies, you can reserve one of the sites for three hours at a cost of $40. Note that party reservations must be made at least two weeks in advance.

Goleta

South Coast Railroad Museum and Goleta Depot
300 North Los Carneros Road, Goleta
(805) 964-3540
www.goletadepot.org

Hop aboard the party train! The South Coast Railroad Museum offers a Party Pack, which lets you buy tickets for miniature train rides in advance and reserve a picnic area right near the boarding point so Grandma and Grandpa can sit and watch the kids ride the train.

Zodo's Bowling & Beyond
5925 Calle Real, Goleta
(805) 967-0128

Zodo's is a huge hit with kids of all ages—especially the Saturday Glow Bowling sessions. When the lights go down, the bowling balls light up, and fog machines swirl a spooky mist over the lanes. While the kids party the day away, parents can relax with a drink at the cocktail lounge. Make sure you book at least two weeks in advance. Minimum 10 guests; up to 50 may be accommodated.

ESPECIALLY FOR TEENS

BOXTALES Theatre Training
Marjorie Luke Theatre
721 East Cota Street, Santa Barbara
(805) 636-2015
www.boxtales.org

Learn to be a thespian under the footlights of the historical Marjorie Luke Theatre with this fun-loving theater group, BOXTALES. The three-week summer intensive teaches acting, movement, storytelling, music, and collaboration, plus it provides exposure to "in the business" guest speakers. It starts the last week of June and runs until mid-July. There's a $500 fee; the program is for teens ages 14 and up.

Brooks 5 @ 9
Brooks Institute
801 Alston Road, Montecito
(805) 966-3888
www.brooks.edu

Budding high school Ansel Adamses go on photo shoots during this summer workshop at one of the nation's renowned photography schools. Assignments are given that push creative buttons. Creating the perfect shot under studio lighting is taught, as well as how to enhance photographs in the digital lab workshop. The program costs $675, and lunch is provided. An advanced workshop is also available. Into music videos? Then check out the Music Video Workshop. This one-week program costs $675.

Junior Lifeguards
Santa Barbara Parks and Recreation
Cabrillo Bathhouse
1118 East Cabrillo Boulevard, Santa Barbara
(805) 897-2680
www.sbparksandrecreation.com
www.santabarbaraca.gov/summerfun/jr_lifeguards.htm

High schoolers are getting into the swim of things with the Junior Lifeguard Program. One of the coveted summer programs, it means something in Santa Barbara to say you're a junior lifeguard. Learn how to tower guard, rescue, and offer first aid and CPR. An overview of oceanography and marine biology is also taught. Check out the application process online, or call for more information. A tryout period before the summer is required.

Teen Center
1235 Chapala Street, Santa Barbara
(805) 882-1235
www.sbparksandrecreation.com

The Santa Barbara City Parks and Recreation Department sponsors Teen Programs for local youth ages 12 to 19. Activities are planned by teens themselves and include sports tournaments, drug-free and tobacco-free dances with DJs and live bands, special classes, field trips, teen-produced TV shows, murals, and conferences. The fee for each activity varies.

LIVING WITH MOTHER NATURE

With all of Santa Barbara's wonderful qualities, you wouldn't think there'd be anything to worry about besides high prices and an occasional foggy morning, but local residents know that Mother Nature occasionally imparts a cruel blow. Rather than burying our heads in the proverbial sand, we try to learn as much as we can about every possibility. Knowledge is power, as they say, and being prepared could literally save your life.

Visitors to California are probably more afraid of earthquakes than anything else. No matter how sophisticated the science of earthquake prediction has become, the fact is that no one knows exactly when a quake will hit—or how earthshaking it will be. Although you just never know when the ground underneath you will start heaving and jolting, we hope that reading this chapter will allow you to rest a little easier. In addition to earthquakes, the chapter deals with several other unsettling natural phenomena, including Santa Ana winds, brushfires, and El Niño, a warm ocean current that causes a huge increase in seasonal rainfall followed by inevitable floods, mudslides, and one great big mess. However, before you start panicking, remember that most of us have lived for decades in Santa Barbara without being directly affected by any of these natural disasters. And we've all survived an earthquake or two with nothing more than a few broken knickknacks and frayed nerves. So relax! We still think you'd be hard-pressed to find a nicer place to vacation—or live in—at any time of year.

ROCKIN' AND ROLLIN'

Santa Barbara has had its share of earthquakes, and we mean big earthquakes (as well as lots of little shakers). This is mostly because California's main earthquake fault, the San Andreas, sits right under the Santa Ynez Mountains, which border Santa Barbara to the north. It is along the San Andreas that seismologists have predicted the proverbial "Big One": that massive earthquake that is supposed to suddenly let loose after years of pressure buildup along the fault line. Of course, no one knows when this will happen, and predictions run the gamut, from "imminent" to "within the next 100 years." Even if a large quake does occur, the fault stretches from Southern California clear up to the San Francisco Bay Area, so the hardest hit areas could be anywhere along the fault line. While we're realistic about earthquakes, we like to think the Big One will leave Santa Barbara relatively unscathed.

The above philosophy might be wishful thinking, however, because Santa Barbara has been hit by large quakes before, both along the San Andreas Fault and on smaller faults in the area. Of course, back in the old days, structures were built of adobe bricks, which couldn't withstand the shaking. On the morning of December 12, 1812, for example, a major quake destroyed Mission Santa Barbara and the Presidio. It was more than a century before the next major quake struck, on June 29, 1925, destroying most of downtown Santa

i Until 1934, Santa Barbara had a record high temperature on the U.S. Weather Bureau's books. On June 17, 1859, a simoom (scorching wind) swept down from the northwest, and the mercury soared to 133° Fahrenheit (about 56° Celsius). Cattle dropped dead, and birds fell from the sky. The record was topped when the mercury hit 134° Fahrenheit (about 57° Celsius) in Death Valley in 1934.

Wildflowers bloom at the Santa Barbara Botanical Gardens. PROVIDED COURTESY OF SUSAN SHAPIRO

Barbara's buildings, cracking Sheffield Reservoir, and killing several people. The largest recent temblor to cause damage in Santa Barbara happened in 1978, when a fault under the Santa Barbara Channel gave way, rupturing to the northwest. Goleta sustained the most damage in the quake, which hurled one-third of the books in the UCSB library onto the floor, shattered windows, dislodged dozens of mobile homes from their supports, and derailed a freight train. Luckily, the 2003 6.5 magnitude Paso Robles quake did little damage to Santa Barbara, although it devastated our neighbor to the north and killed two people. The most famous of California's earthquakes in recent years is probably the Northridge quake of 1994, which killed 55 people and caused more than $9 billion in

Birding in Santa Barbara

If all you've been doing since you arrived is sunning yourself, going for strolls on the beach, and browsing museums, you've missed one of the activities for which Santa Barbara is renowned. We're talking about birding. More than 450 species of birds have been recorded in Santa Barbara County, making it one of the premier birding spots in the country. Santa Barbara's combination of ocean, coastal wetlands, freshwater marshes, coastal sage scrub, native grasslands, riparian woodland, oak woodland, chaparral, and pine forest make it a magnet for birds. Due to its location along the Pacific Flyway, a major avian migratory route, the area also sees large numbers of migrating birds in spring and fall, which is when you are most likely to see local birders out in force.

GETTING STARTED

The Santa Barbara Museum of Natural History (805-682-4711; www.sb nature.org) schedules birding classes and sponsors field trips. We also rec-ommend joining the Santa Barbara Audubon Society (805-964-1468; www.rain.org/~audubon/), which offers free field trips at least once a month and puts on monthly programs that cover all aspects of birding and nature in general. Introductory membership is $20 ($15 for seniors and students) and includes a subscription to El Tecolote, the monthly newsletter that lists all field trips and programs. If you are a member of the National Audubon Society, membership in the local chapter is free. Finally, every beginning birder needs a field guide. Two excellent choices if you're just starting out are Herbert Clarke's An Introduction to Southern California Birds and Roger Tory Peterson's A Field Guide to Western Birds.

Once you've mastered all the local species (give yourself a couple of years for this), you'll be ready to graduate to the National Geographic Soci-ety's more comprehensive Field Guide to the Birds of North America. Commonly referred to as the "Geo guide," this is the favorite of most birders and includes birds from all regions of the country. (Believe it or not, most of the eastern birds—especially the warblers—have made their way to Santa Bar-bara County at one time or another, causing no end of excitement for local listers.)

BEST BIRDING SPOTS

While you may not have to go looking for birds in Santa Barbara (there are usually plenty in your yard, especially if you have a feeder), there are a few local hot spots that are frequented by both local and out-of-town birders. Here are a few of our South County favorites.

Rocky Nook Park

With mature oaks and sycamores, as well as the riparian woodland border-ing Mission Creek, Rocky Nook Park, located just above Mission Santa Barbara in Mission County, is a great birding spot during every season. It's especially good in early spring, when warblers tend to gather before migration. Yellow-rumped, Townsend's, and black-throated gray warblers are usually singing by April, and warbling vireos, western tanagers, Bullock's and hooded orioles, Pacific-slope flycatchers, black-headed grosbeaks, and western kingbirds are always present in the spring. Oak titmice, wrentits, and several varieties of woodpeckers are just some of the species that inhabit the park year-round, and an occasional rarity, such as a black-and-white warbler, may lurk in the oaks.

Andree Clark Bird Refuge
At the east end of Cabrillo Boulevard, the refuge offers a close-up look at waterfowl as well as land birds that frequent the introduced trees and plants north of the refuge. This is one of the few places in the county where you can sometimes find great-tailed grackles and wood ducks, and you'll occasionally see eastern kingbirds on the islands during migration. Observation platforms along the north side of the refuge allow for clear viewing of the water, and a trail runs from the Los Patos Way parking lot west.

Garden Street Outfall
Where Garden Street meets Cabrillo Boulevard, the beachfront is especially good for spotting shorebirds, gulls, and terns. This is the favorite resting spot of black skimmers in the winter, and Santa Barbara's only recorded black-headed gull showed up at the outfall for several winters beginning in 1992.

Atascadero Creek
Atascadero Creek is accessible at the south end of Turnpike Road, Walnut Drive, Patterson Avenue, and Ward Memorial Drive. It is especially good in fall for migrating warblers and sparrows. Blue grosbeaks and lazuli and indigo buntings are often found in the weedy grasses here in fall, and occasionally a rarity, such as a painted bunting, bobolink, or dickcissel, turns up. It's an easy walk along the hard-packed dirt of the edge of the creek, and an adjacent bike trail runs the entire distance.

San Jose Creek
San Jose has been a favorite birding creek for years. Right on the border between Santa Barbara and Goleta, it offers the best birding between Cathedral Oaks Road and north Patterson Avenue and above and below the Berkeley Road bike bridge. During migration, it's especially good for warblers, tanagers, orioles, and hummingbirds, which frequent the bottlebrush trees along Merida Drive.

Stow House and Lake Los Carneros
Located off Los Carneros Road between Calle Real and Cathedral Oaks Road, this county park features exotic plantings, an artificial lake, and plenty of open space. One of the best places in the South County to see all the California specialties (wrentit, California towhee, California thrasher, and often

California quail), it is frequented by area birders. In the garden of Stow House, look for an abundance of orioles (both hooded and Bullock's) in the spring as well as hummingbirds, vireos, and warblers. Sparrows, including white-crowned, Lincoln's, and golden-crowned, are plentiful in winter, and berry-eaters such as cedar waxwings, American robins, and western tanagers feed in pyracantha and toyon. The lake affords views of a variety of wintering ducks and herons, egrets, and bitterns. You can hike around the lake and garden in about an hour, or stop on the footbridge at the north end of the lake and watch the reeds below for soras, Virginia rails, and least bitterns. In spring and fall, Lake Los Carneros is a perfect spot for observing seasonal comings and goings.

Central Coast Birding Trail

The National Audubon Society of California and the Santa Barbara and La Purisima local chapters became partners in forming the Santa Barbara County section of the Central Coast Birding Trail, which in its entirety runs from the northern edge of Ventura County up the coast to Monterey. A brochure outlining Santa Barbara County's best birding spots along the trail is available from the Santa Barbara Audubon Society. Some of the places we've mentioned previously are included, along with several North County sites.

CHRISTMAS COUNT

Every year, the National Audubon Society sponsors a Christmas Bird Count. The CBC happens during a designated two-week period from mid-December to early January, and each local Audubon Society chapter picks one day

property damage in the San Fernando Valley. Who can forget those news shots of a three-story apartment building that collapsed down to one story, killing 16 people who were asleep in their beds? Could the same thing be in store for Santa Barbara?

California is earthquake country. But before you panic, remember that the Hollywood film depictions of people being swallowed up by huge cracks in the ground during earthquakes take it to the extreme. Unless something falls on you or you go running around with no shoes through a room littered with broken glass, you'll probably be able to ride the thing out with no problem. Seismic

retrofitting (which is essentially strengthening buildings to withstand major quakes) is a continuous process in the city and the state, and most of our public buildings, highway bridges, and schools would be able to stand some pretty heavy shaking without falling down.

Around the house, we suggest protecting your family heirloom china by storing it in a box on the garage floor, or puttying it to pantry shelves. Bolt or strap heavy bookcases, cabinets, and water heaters to the wall so they don't fall on you. Some people go so far as to put latches on kitchen cabinets to keep dishes and food from spilling out onto the floor during a quake. Household chemicals

during the count period to stage its count. On that day, birders fan out over the designated count circle (each count must be conducted within the perimeter of a predetermined circle with a 15-mile [24-kilometer] diameter), recording every species and individual bird they see. Although it is impossible to be exact, data from counts held all over North America are used to determine the relative stability of certain species and the expansion or shrinking of their ranges. All of this scientific stuff aside, the CBC has evolved into a kind of Super Bowl of birding during which different count circles vie for the honor of recording the most species of birds. Santa Barbara inevitably does itself proud in this winter census, virtually always finding enough species to rate a place in the top five counts in the country. Nearly 500 species of birds have been counted in Santa Barbara—an amount that makes it one of the hottest birding spots in North America. Only experienced birders generally participate in the count, but feeder watchers can also contribute. Look for details in *El Tecolote*, the Santa Barbara Audubon Society's newsletter.

LISTING

Listing is big with birders. As the name implies, listing is simply keeping a list of all of the species of birds you've seen in a particular context. Most local birders keep a life list (a list of every species they've ever seen), a North America list, a California list, and a Santa Barbara County list as well as a yard list (a list of every species they've seen in or from their yard). Listing is made easier by the availability of checklists, which you will find in most field guides or can pick up from the local Audubon Society chapter. The checklist to the birds of Santa Barbara County, for example, has 445 species. It's available for a small fee from the Santa Barbara Audubon Society.

should be sealed tightly and stored so they won't tip over, and flammable liquids should be stored well away from your water heater if it has a pilot light.

For more tips on earthquake safety, contact the local office of the American Red Cross at (805) 687-1331. When you feel an earthquake happening (and yes, you'll know when it happens), here are a few basic survival tips: First, stay calm! (Okay, okay, we know this is pretty unrealistic.) If you are inside, stand under a doorway or take shelter under a sturdy desk or table away from windows or falling heavy objects or appliances. If you are outside, stand as far away as possible from

buildings (which usually fall outward if they are going to fall), trees, and telephone or electrical lines. If you are on the road, get away from overpasses, bridges, and tunnels and stop in a safe area, then stay in your car until the shaking stops and it is safe to proceed. If Santa Barbara is hit with a major earthquake, fire, or flood, possibilities include loss of electrical power and/or telephone service, evacuation, contaminated drinking water, and lack of access to retail stores. To prepare for such a state of affairs, you should have a basic emergency kit for your family. Suggested items include a portable radio with extra batteries; a flashlight for each member of the family plus

ℹ️ Lost electricity after a good-sized quake? Whatever you do, don't light a match. Gas lines may leak after a shaking, and striking a match may cause a "big bang."

extra batteries; a first-aid kit, including a book with instructions for dealing with injuries; enough bottled water to sustain your family for several days; canned and dried foods to sustain your family for a week (rotate these, making sure that shelf life is not exceeded); and a manual can opener. You can add other items you feel are appropriate for your family.

DEVIL WINDS

Nearly every year, in late fall and early winter, the wind pattern shifts ominously along the Southern California coast. Ocean breezes that keep us cool and gently sway the trees give way to hot, dry, and powerful Santa Ana winds out of the northeast. The change doesn't happen in an instant, and forecasters are usually able to see the winds coming, but they are stifling and unsettling at best, and the threat of wind-driven brushfires lingers oppressively on everyone's mind until the winds abate. Reportedly named for Santa Ana Canyon near Los Angeles, where they blow particularly strong, Santa Ana winds are created when high pressure develops over the Great Basin, forcing air downslope from the high plateau to the coast. The air warms as it rushes through the canyons of Southern California, and it also picks up speed. Temperatures may rise into the 90s or 100s, and winds typically gust between 15 and 40 miles (24 and 65 kilometers) per hour, with isolated gusts reaching hurricane force. The winds tend to blow hardest at night and in the early morning, rattling nerves as they play havoc while you're trying to sleep.

It is during the ferocious Santa Ana wind storms that the California fire season roars into everyone's consciousness. Chaparral-covered hillsides that have dried out through the summer are tinder-dry in fall, and all it takes is a careless moment to ignite a wind-driven fire that can be virtually unstoppable.

See the next section for suggestions on how to protect yourself and your property from fire damage. Thus prepared, the next time those devil winds come thundering down the canyons, perhaps you can relax on your deck with a tall glass of iced tea.

FIRE!

Santa Barbara is no stranger to fires. Many neighborhoods in the city have either been destroyed or threatened, and homes in the brushy canyons are especially vulnerable. One of the most devastating fires in Santa Barbara's history happened in June 1990, when an arsonist hurled an incendiary device into the dry brush above Painted Cave Road. Driven by gusting Santa Ana winds, the blaze swept down the canyon and threatened to torch its way to the sea. Exclusive homes burned to the ground as residents barely escaped with their lives, and horses and other animals wandered the streets, dazed and confused. When the winds finally died down and fire crews extinguished the blaze, it had destroyed more than 450 homes and consumed nearly 5,000 acres, leaving a black scar on the hills above Santa Barbara for years. If you are lodging along the coast or live in the midst of a well-populated area free of brush and chaparral, brushfires are not much of a threat. But if you live in the foothills or canyons above the city, you should protect yourself against fires and prepare for a possible evacuation.

First, remove all hazardous brush to within 100 feet of your house and any outbuildings. If you have a wooden shake roof (which is a veritable fire trap), replace it with fire-resistant roofing material. Ask your contractor or a building supply store for options. If you have a swimming pool, buy a pump that will divert water into a hose for firefighting. Since people tend to panic in emergencies, make a prioritized list now of what you want or need to take

ℹ️ On the prowl for species rare in these parts? Call the Santa Barbara Audobon Society's Rare Bird Alert hotline at (805) 964-8240.

with you if you have to evacuate suddenly. Post it in a convenient place (like on the inside of a cupboard door), and make sure the items listed are easily accessible. During periods of high fire danger, keep your car's gas tank at least half full so you don't have to stop and get gas to evacuate the area. Also, have at least two sets of keys for each vehicle, and leave one set at home and easily accessible so you can move parked cars out of harm's way. Finally, be careful out there! Do not discard lighted cigarettes carelessly, never set off personal fireworks, and be extremely careful when using outdoor machinery that could send sparks flying into dry brush. The neighborhood you save may be your own.

AND—WOULD YOU BELIEVE—FLOODS!

If you've never lived in California, you might not have heard of Santa Ana winds, but we'd bet our bottom dollar you've heard of El Niño. This benignly named weather phenomenon has wreaked havoc on the world a couple of times in the last several years and has been blamed for floods, droughts, fires, and just about every other natural disaster, including the plunge of the stock market (well, maybe that's a slight exaggeration). El Niño, which is a Spanish name used in reference to the Christ child, was originally recognized by fishermen off the coast of South America. Since it tended to show up near the Christmas holiday, it was given the name of the baby whose birth is celebrated at that season. Over the years, however, El Niño has lost whatever innocent connotation it once had and tends to strike fear into the hearts of just about everyone who has something to lose from its effects.

El Niño is quite a complex phenomenon, but basically it has to do with the interaction between the atmosphere in the tropical Pacific and the surface layers of the ocean. That somehow results in warmer temperatures at the surface of the ocean off Southern California, which causes storms to be warmer, resulting in a lot more rain than normal. Also, it causes big waves that tend to take out piers

i Be prepared with an out-of-state emergency contact. Every family member should have Grandma's number in Michigan, because local lines get shut down for emergency services. Grandma can manage the communication, so everyone will know how everyone's doing.

and crash through the windows of beachfront homes. While it's interesting to read about the causes of El Niño, people are more concerned about the impact it will have in their own backyard. In fall 1997, scientists started warning Californians that the winter of 1997–98 was going to be a big El Niño season. Everyone got all worked up, and creeks were cleared, the harbor was dredged, sandbags were amassed, roofs were replaced, emergency agencies planned their strategies, and then . . . nothing. Halloween and Thanksgiving came, and went and hardly a drop fell from the sky. And then, just when everyone was on the verge of gleefully declaring that the scientists were wrong, a major storm slammed Santa Barbara in early December. "Not an El Niño storm," said meteorologists. "Just wait." The rest of December and nearly all of January were practically bone dry.

We were almost out of the woods. Then, in February, El Niño hit with a vengeance. High waves ripped 150 deck planks off Stearns Wharf and loosened 50 foundation pilings, requiring $500,000 in repairs. Then the rains pounded Santa Barbara, sometimes dropping 4 or 5 inches (10 to 13 centimeters) per storm. Near the end of the rainy season, Santa Barbara had already received nearly 47 inches (121 centimeters), beating the former record of 45.2 inches (116 centimeters) in the 1940–44 season. As a result, the hotel occupancy rate dropped, rain-soaked hillsides slid onto roads and houses, and floods drenched many areas of the city and county. Everything was, in short, a great big mess. Luckily, El Niño only comes around every three to seven years. But no one knows for sure when the next one will hit, so all we can do is batten down the hatches and be prepared.

SANTA BARBARA WINE COUNTRY

Are you a wine lover in search of a Santa Barbara excursion? Just hop in your car and drive north, and within 45 minutes of leaving downtown Santa Barbara you'll land smack dab in the heart of one of California's premier wine regions.

The North County (which is how most Santa Barbarans refer to the region on the north side of the Santa Ynez Mountain range) is a tranquil and beautiful area, with scenic roads that wind through rolling, oak-studded valleys and mountains. Reminiscent of old rural California, it's home to ranchers, farmers, and, in recent years, more than a few celebrities escaping the glare of Hollywood.

Agriculture dominates the North County scene, and much of Santa Barbara County's produce originates here. Strawberries and broccoli almost always rank in the top three of the county's most valuable cash crops. The other top crop is wine grapes.

Once a sleepy little enclave on the other side of the mountain, the Santa Ynez Valley is now recognized internationally for its premium wine production. The demand has been so great that a million-plus cases of reds and whites are produced each year. Production yields over $360 million a year—one third of which comes from the grapes alone.

FROM MISSIONS TO MAVERICKS

Santa Barbara County's wine-making and grape-growing history spans more than 200 years. It started in 1782, when Father Junipero Serra carried grapevines from Mexico all the way to Santa Barbara. Mission Santa Barbara maintained several vineyards, and there was even a winery on Santa Cruz Island. Justinian Caire planted 150 acres with imported French grape slips and shipped his wines up the coast to San Francisco for bottling.

By the 1920s, wine grapes grew on about 250 acres of land until Prohibition effectively shut down all winery operations in the area. It took more than 30 years for the industry to rebound. But it did so with a vengeance.

In the early 1960s, researchers at the University of California at Davis discovered that the unusual geography, topography, and climate of the Santa Barbara County region held great promise for growing wine grapes. This substantiated the suspicions of several wine-making pioneers, who were already scoping out the region for places to plunk their vines.

Time for a geography lesson. (Don't yawn—it's important!) By now, you're probably used to hearing about the unusual east-west orientation of the Santa Barbara coastline. Well, the Santa Ynez and San Rafael mountain ranges also run east-west. In fact, they are the only mountain ranges running in this direction (most run north-south) along the entire West Coast of North America (except in parts of Alaska). Another unusual geographical feature of Santa Barbara County is that the valleys between these local mountains run perpendicular to the coast, sucking cool ocean breezes and fog inland during late afternoon and evening. The result: hot sunny days and cool nights—perfect conditions for growing wine grapes.

The region is basically a grower's paradise: All the classic grape varieties thrive here, thanks to the numerous microclimates and the long, cool growing season. The region is far enough south to avoid the early winter storms that sometimes threaten late harvests up north. And since the winters are usually temperate, bud break on the vines occurs much earlier than up north. The grapes here hang on the vines longer, which allows them to develop rich, intense, concentrated flavors.

In 1962 Pierre Lafond established Santa Barbara Winery, the first commercial winery in Santa Barbara County since Prohibition. Stearns Wharf Vintners followed suit in 1965. The 1970s gave birth to several more fledgling wineries, including Firestone Vineyard, Rancho Sisquoc Winery, Zaca Mesa Winery, and The Brander Vineyard.

By the 1980s, the buzz about Santa Barbara's viticultural promise lured more winemakers to the region, and the industry's roots were firmly entrenched in local soil. Today you can tour more than 80 wineries in Santa Barbara County. Most are small operations, run by families or individuals rather than large corporations.

Until just a few years ago, the majority of grapes grown here were shipped to wineries outside the county. That trend is now reversed—the grapes are mostly being used by wineries within Santa Barbara County or by wineries outside the county that own vineyards here, such as Kendall-Jackson and Robert Mondavi in Northern California.

GREAT GRAPES

Nearly everyone here grows and produces Chardonnay—it's the area's signature wine. But Santa Barbara County has also been singled out for producing world-class Pinot Noir—a fragile, delicate varietal that requires not only ideal growing conditions, but also careful management. Other popular Santa Barbara County wines include Riesling, Sauvignon Blanc, Syrah, Merlot, Cabernet Sauvignon, and Gewürztraminer.

While great grapes form the basis of great wines, they wouldn't amount to much without the expertise of an experienced winemaker. The winemakers of Santa Barbara County have earned a reputation in the wine world not only as wizards in the technical sense but also as creative innovators who aren't afraid to experiment with new methods and varietals. Here, you'll notice some unique and

i Throwing a party? Plan for one bottle of wine for every two and a half guests.

intriguing blends that you won't find anywhere else.

Santa Barbara County wines have earned great respect in the wine world and won numerous awards in regional, national, and international competitions. Once you taste them, you'll be raving, too.

WINE COUNTRY INFORMATION

Santa Barbara County Vintners' Association
(805) 688-0881, (800) 218-0881
www.sbcountywines.com
The Santa Barbara County Vintners' Association is a nonprofit organization founded in 1983. It supports and promotes Santa Barbara County as a premium wine-producing and wine grape–growing region. It also strives to enhance the position of Santa Barbara County wines in the world marketplace. Current members include 80 wineries, 25 independent vineyards, and several vineyard consultant/management companies.

The Vintners' Association sponsors festivals, seminars, and tastings and provides information to the media and consumers. Call or visit the association's Web site for specific information about wineries and events and to request a current Santa Barbara County wine country map.

TOURING AND TASTING THROUGH WINE COUNTRY

Santa Barbara wine country is not Napa or Sonoma, but we think that's a blessing. It's not nearly as touristy or crowded, and we think the wines rank up there with the best.

When you go touring here, you can relax and enjoy gorgeous scenery and outstanding wines without the crowds and the hype. Many wineries welcome visitors year-round, most on a daily basis and others at least on weekends.

Tasting rooms range from cozy spaces in historic farmhouses and rustic cabins to spacious, contemporary buildings. You can try the wines and buy a few bottles (or cases) to bring home, and at some wineries you can sample and purchase gourmet foods, such as pasta sauces, salsas, grapeseed oils, and other winery products.

Several wineries offer tours of the wine-making facilities and/or caves, and one or two will take you through the vineyards at certain times of year. Reservations for tasting and tours are usually required for groups of 10 or more—you'll need to call ahead and make an appointment.

Most Santa Barbara County wineries lie along three scenic wine routes: the Santa Ynez Valley Wine Trail, the Foxen Canyon Wine Trail, and Santa Rita Hills loop (see the Wineries section of this chapter). You can also visit a few tasting rooms in Los Olivos and the Danish village of Solvang. If you can't make it out to the wine country, don't worry. You'll find several tasting rooms in downtown Santa Barbara by the beach.

In this chapter, we give you an overview of most of the area's main tasting rooms. We also let you know about a few of our favorite hotels, inns, and restaurants in Santa Barbara wine country. If you'd like someone to guide you through the wine country—and do all the driving—we recommend a few tour companies.

If you need more information on what to see and do while on a day trip to Solvang and other parts of the North County, be sure to read the Day Trips chapter. Have a wonderful time tasting your way through Santa Barbara County!

In the summer, when it's foggy and cool on the coast, it's usually hot and sunny in the wine country. So if you're heading to the valley for a day of wine tasting, dress in cool, light clothing. But bring a light sweater. It cools off at night.

HOW TO GET THERE

Before heading out on your wine-tasting adventure, be sure to get an up-to-date wine touring map featuring all Vintners' Association member wineries, restaurants, lodgings, wine shops, and touring services. The association is adding members all the time, and it produces a new map at least once a year, sometimes more often. You can pick up the map at winery tasting rooms, visitor centers, restaurants, and hotels throughout Santa Barbara County and by calling the Vintners' Association at (805) 688-0881 or (800) 218-0881. You can also view a PDF version of the map online at www.sbcountrywines.com.

From Santa Barbara, you have two travel options. The first (and our favorite) is the "scenic" or "mountain" route along California Highway 154 (San Marcos Pass), which drops dramatically into the Santa Ynez Valley. Drive carefully. The road twists and turns over mountain passes and can be a little tricky—especially on wet or foggy days. From downtown Santa Barbara, take U.S. 101 to the State Street/Highway 154 exit and take Highway 154 up the mountain. As you descend, you'll see spectacular views of the Santa Ynez Mountains, the Los Padres National Forest, and Cachuma Lake.

About 40 minutes after leaving Santa Barbara, you'll arrive at the point where Highway 154 intersects with Highway 246. Turn left to visit historic Santa Ynez or the Danish village of Solvang, or continue on about 5 miles (8 kilometers) to charming Los Olivos. All are great points to stock up on picnic items and gas before you head out on the wine trails.

The second option is the coastal route, which offers great views of some of the last remaining unspoiled tracts of coastline in California. Drive north along U.S. 101 about 45 miles (73 kilometers) to Highway 246 in Buellton. Head west if you want to visit the wineries in the **Santa Rita Hills** region. Otherwise head east. We suggest you begin your tour by stopping at the historic town of Santa Ynez about 10 miles (16 kilometers) east of U.S. 101. From there it's a short drive to many of the wineries on the **Santa Ynez Valley Wine Trail.** If you're planning to take the **Foxen Canyon Wine Trail,** you should continue driving north on U.S. 101 past Buellton, up to the HIghway 154 turnoff. Turn right and head east a few miles to Foxen Canyon Road.

TOURS AND TRANSPORTATION SERVICES

Taking an escorted tour is a great way to cruise through wine country. Just sit back, relax, and sample wine without worrying about driving.

Breakaway Tours and Event Planning
3463 State Street, Suite 141, Santa Barbara
(805) 783-2929, (800) 799-7657
www.breakaway-tours.com
Specializing in seriously fun and educational tours, Breakaway Tour guides really know their stuff. Much more than someone just driving you to your destination, the guides are passionate about wine—so passionate that they'll share information about the grape-growing region and teach you how to read a wine label. Breakaway gives you the best kind of break away—they do all the planning. Call for tour details and prices.

| i | For a contrast in scenery, take the mountain route on the way to the |

For a contrast in scenery, take the mountain route on the way to the wine country and the coastal route on the return journey (or vice versa).

Cloud Climbers Jeep Tours
(805) 646-3200
www.ccjeeps.com
Looking for a wilder kind of wine country tour? Cloud Climbers will pick you up from your doorstep in a six-passenger canopy-covered Jeep and whisk you away on a six-hour back-country safari to four of the region's best wineries. Along the way, you'll explore rugged mountain trails; learn about local history, flora, and fauna; and pass by the former Reagan Ranch. Tours include a gourmet deli lunch at a private vineyard picnic area, water and soft drinks, a logo wine glass, tasting fees, and a professional guide or naturalist. This is a great tour if you're looking for a little adventure and hate being cooped up in a crowded coach. Prices start at $104. The tour starts at 10:00 a.m. A deli lunch is included.

Personal Tours Ltd.
P.O. Box 60109, Santa Barbara 93160
(805) 685-0552
www.personaltoursltd.com
This excellent local company will customize a wine country tour to suit your needs. All tours are narrated, so you'll learn some interesting tidbits about the vineyards, celebrity ranch estates, and other attractions in the area. Vehicles range from sedans, convertibles, and custom vans to minibuses and motor coaches with restrooms. The company also provides step-on guide service (aboard your own vehicle). Call for prices.

Santa Barbara Old Town Trolley
(805) 965-0353
www.sbtrolley.com
If you have a group of 10 or more people and you want a private, narrated tour of the wine country by trolley, this is the company for you. Along the way, you'll visit Buttonwood Farm Winery, Bridlewood, Sunstone, and Rideau vineyards. Tours include a gourmet deli lunch and wine-tasting fees. Champagne and hors d'oeuvres are also provided on the trolley, so you can relax, sip some bubbly, and learn a bit about the region's wine-making history without having to worry about driving. Customized tours are also available. Call or visit the Web site for more information.

Santa Barbara Wine Country Cycling Tours
3640 Sagunto Street, Santa Ynez
(805) 686-9490, (888) 557-8687
www.winecountrycycling.com
Imagine escaping to the wine country on two wheels instead of four. Santa Barbara Wine Country Cycling Tours is an innovative touring company that offers half-day or full-day

guided tours. Half-day tours are $75 per person or $60 per person for four or more. If you add in lunch, it's $125 per person or $110 per person for four or more. Full-day tours are $150 per person and for four or more, $125 per person. Self-guided tours are $35 for a half day and $45 for a full day. Rates are cheaper if you BYOB (bring your own bike).

Spencer's Limousine & Tours
(805) 884-9700
www.spencerslimo.com
Regularly voted one of the top Santa Barbara tour companies in local polls, Spencer's offers wine tours in the comfort of a plush limousine or Lincoln Town car. Spencer is an avid historian, so you can expect fascinating narration along the way. Tours are customized to suit your taste in wines and places of interest and include tastings at six different wineries. You'll find a lunch menu in the car, and Spencer will pick up your gourmet selection at a local Italian deli on the way so you can picnic at one of the wineries. Tours range from five to eight hours. Call for prices.

SuperRide Shuttle & Tours
(805) 683-9636, (800) 977-1123
www.SuperRide.net
SuperRide specializes in customized narrated tours of Santa Barbara County wineries and attractions. This means you and your group will be the only clients on the tour, and the company will pick you up at your hotel and take you to the wineries of your choice. If you're not sure where to go, ask SuperRide to suggest an itinerary based on your special interests. Depending on the size of your group, you can choose from a Lincoln Town car, passenger van, minibus, or luxury coach. All tours include a gourmet picnic lunch and as much bottled water as you need. Make sure you book at least 24 hours in advance.

WINE'edVENTURES
(805) 965-9463
www.welovewines.com
If you want to feel as though you've learned something about wine before you start sipping, these narrated tours are an excellent choice. The owner, Dusty Rhodes, was involved in wine country tours in Napa and Sonoma for more than 20 years before establishing WINE'edVENTURES in 1999. At the moment, they are the only company in Santa Barbara running daily tours to the wine country. Hop aboard the 24-passenger air-conditioned mini-coach and you'll learn all about wine country history, stagecoach trails, prohibition, wine lingo, and local tidbits. The Deluxe Excursion costs $105 per person and includes visits to four wineries, tasting fees, an oversized wine glass, a wine production tour, and a picnic lunch. Vineyards include Brander, Carina Cellars, Koehler, Lucas & Lewellen, Mandolina, Melville, Presidio, Rusack, Shoestring, Sunstone, and Zaca Mesa. Tours depart between 9:00 a.m. and 9:45 a.m. from major hotels, including Best Western Pepper Tree Inn, Colonial Beach Inn, Fess Parker's DoubleTree Resort, Hotel Mar Monte, Harbor View Inn, Holiday Inn Express—Santa Barbara, Holiday Inn Express–Solvang, and the Solvang Visitor's Center.

TASTING IN LOS OLIVOS

Los Olivos is a quaint, historic town at the north end of the Santa Ynez Valley Wine Trail and near the beginning of the Foxen Canyon Wine Trail. It's a great place to stop for a snack or a meal or to shop for high-quality art at its famous galleries.

The downtown area covers just a few square blocks, so you can park your car and walk wherever you need to go. You can taste an array of local premium wines right in town at tasting rooms on Grand Avenue, the main street in Los Olivos. Some of the rooms offer wines made by wineries without visitor facilities, and several are part of the Santa Ynez Valley Wine Trail.

Here are two independent tasting rooms that give you the chance to sample various local wines.

Los Olivos Tasting Room and Wine Shop
2905 Grand Avenue, Los Olivos
(805) 688-7406
www.losolivoswines.com
Here you can sample various wines from wineries that either don't have their own tasting rooms or have limited quantities of wine or limited tasting room hours—including Au Bon Climat, Lane Tanner, Foxen, Edge, Fiddlehead, and Hitching Post. Ten different wines are always uncorked and ready for tasting. The tasting room is open from 11:00 a.m. to 6:00 p.m. daily (last tasting at 5:30 p.m.).

Los Olivos Wine and Spirits Emporium
2531 Grand Avenue, Los Olivos
(805) 688-4409, (888) SB-WINES
www.sbwines.com
The Los Olivos Wine and Spirits Emporium represents many of the area's smaller premium wineries that produce wine in limited amounts. Most of these wineries do not have their own tasting rooms. You can taste the quality wines of Whitcraft, Qupé, Lane Tanner, Jaffurs, Fiddlehead Cellars, and many others.

You can also purchase wines as well as brandies, distilled agave, small-batch bourbons, and other spirits. The emporium is open daily from 11:00 a.m. to 6:00 p.m. You'll find it in the middle of a field just 1/2 mile (1 kilometer) south of the town of Los Olivos (look for the windmill).

THE WINERIES

Now that you're familiar with the area, you're ready to start your wine-tasting tour. Following are brief descriptions of the main wine trails and the wineries along them, including tasting room hours. Some tasting rooms offer 5 to 10 free samples of wines, but most charge a nominal tasting fee (usually $5 to $6 per person), which typically includes a logo wine glass. Some also offer you the chance to taste special reserve wines for a fee.

It's best to devote at least a day to each trail so you can take your time tasting, relaxing, and taking in the views. Also, you should eat a bit before each session and remember to drink lots of water—wine can dehydrate you quickly, especially in warm weather.

Foxen Canyon Wine Trail

The beautiful, bucolic Foxen Canyon Wine Trail connects two wine-growing regions: the Santa Ynez Valley and the Santa Maria Valley. The trail begins on Foxen Canyon Road, just north of Los Olivos. From there, the road twists and turns through 20 miles (32 kilometers) of gently rolling hills and vineyards until it reaches Santa Maria, the northernmost area of the county. (We personally think that Foxen Canyon Road is one of the most scenic country roads in the state.)

As you drive, you can stop at trail wineries along the way. This is a fantastic tour if you want to feel as if you've stepped back in time and left the workaday world far behind.

Addamo Vineyards
400 East Clark Avenue, Santa Maria
(805) 937-6400
www.addamovineyards.com
David Addamo has always had a passion for wine and well he should. His grandparents owned a small production facility in Sicily, and his parents owned acres of Cabernet Sauvignon in Hollister, California. Addamo moved his family onto 120 acres in Orcutt in 2000. He successfully produces and grows eight varietals of all estate wine. The 2005 Delcetto was a bronze medal winner, and the 2005 White Riesling earned a silver medal at the Santa Barbara County Fair competition. The tasting room is open Tuesday through Sunday from 11:00 a.m. to 7:00 p.m.

Bedford Thompson Winery & Vineyard
448 Bell Street, Los Alamos
(805) 344-2107
www.bedfordthompsonwinery.com
In late 2003 Bedford Thompson opened a tasting room in historic downtown Los Alamos with a lovely courtyard for picnics.

Santa Ynez valley. NANCY SHOBE

Established in 1994, the small winery on Alisos Canyon Road produces 5,000 to 7,000 cases a year of Chardonnay, Pinot Gris, Grenache, Mouvedre, and Gewürztraminer, but it's best known for its Syrah and Cabernet Franc. The tasting room on Bell Street is open from 11:00 a.m. to 5:00 p.m. daily.

Cambria Winery and Vineyard
5475 Chardonnay Lane, Santa Maria
(805) 937-8091, (888) 938-7318
www.cambriawines.com
From its name, many people assume this winery is located in the coastal town of Cambria (see the Day Trips chapter if you're interested in visiting the town, not the winery). Actually, Cambria Winery is located about 12 miles (19 kilometers) east of downtown Santa Maria, at the base of Tepusquet Canyon, a former Chumash encampment.

This was the original vineyard in the area, and as Tepusquet Vineyard it produced top-quality wine grapes from the early 1970s to the mid-1980s. Katherine's Chardonnay, Julia's Pinot Noir, and Tepusquet Syrah and other flagship wines make up 90 percent of production.

The winery tasting room is open 10:00 a.m. to 5:00 p.m. Saturday and Sunday and weekdays by appointment.

Costa de Oro Tasting Room and Gold Coast Marketplace
1331 South Nicholson Avenue, Santa Maria
(805) 922-1468
www.costadeorowinery.com
This brand-new tasting room showcases Costa de Oro's award-winning wines, along with Gold Coast produce and gourmet food selections. Gary Burk, winemaker, made his

way into the wine business through the music business, but that's a whole other story. He struck the right cord with his wine making, having received 90 points or higher from *Wine Spectator* and *Wine and Spirits* magazines. His wines have also appeared in the top 100 lists in respected wine magazines. His most recent wine accolades were winning "Best of Show" at both the Orange County and Santa Barbara County fairs.

Cottonwood Canyon Vineyard & Winery
3940 Dominion Road, Santa Maria
(805) 937-9063
www.cottonwoodcanyon.com
Cottonwood Canyon is a small ultra-premium winery specializing in Estate Chardonnay, Pinot Noir, and Syrah. It was founded in 1988 by the Beko family, and you can sample their wines here in the vineyard tasting room.

The winery sits on a hilltop overlooking the valley, and the picnic area boasts fantastic views of the northern end of the Foxen Canyon Wine Trail. Tours of the wine caves, which are dug into the hillside, are offered on Saturday and Sunday at 11:00 a.m. and 1:00 and 3:00 p.m., midweek by appointment only. The tasting room is open from 10:30 a.m. to 5:30 p.m. daily.

Curtis Winery
5249 Foxen Canyon Road, Los Olivos
(805) 686-8999
www.curtiswinery.com
Curtis Winery opened in April 1998 right next door to Firestone (see subsequent listing). Winemaker Chuck Carlson selects handpicked grapes from estate vineyards and various Santa Barbara County vintners with a focus on the Rhone Varietals.

Sheltered by oaks in a cool, white adobe, the tasting room is usually set with at least one Viognier, a Viognier blend, a Heritage rose, a Syrah, and a Syrah blend. Curtis is also producing small lots of wine in a gravity-flow facility. The winery is open for tours, tasting, and sales from 10:00 a.m. to 5:00 p.m. daily, and you'll find some shaded picnic tables near the tasting room.

Fess Parker Winery & Vineyard
6200 Foxen Canyon Road, Los Olivos
(805) 688-1545, (800) 841-1104
www.fessparker.com
Fess Parker (a.k.a. Davy Crockett) and his family own this large, contemporary winery. Fess, the founding visionary, turned the reins over to his son and daughter. In fact his son, Eli Parker, is the winemaker. The vast tasting room is set amid 700 acres of vineyards, lawns, manicured rose gardens, and winery facilities. Step inside and you can browse the antiques and Hollywood memorabilia or relax by the massive stone fireplace.

Several of Fess Parker's Syrahs, a Pinot Noir, and a Chardonnay scored over 90 on Robert Parker's list. The gift shop offers gourmet items, signature winery merchandise, picnic snacks, and Davy Crockett and Daniel Boone items, including Fess's trademark coonskin caps and coonskin bottle toppers.

Tastings and sales are available from 10:00 a.m. to 5:00 p.m. daily.

Firestone Vineyard
5000 Zaca Station Road, Los Olivos
(805) 688-3940 ext. 31
www.firestonewine.com
Founded in 1972, Firestone is the oldest estate winery in the county. It sits atop a secluded mesa overlooking the valley and vineyards and is best known for its excellent Chardonnay. The winery also makes award-winning Cabernet Sauvignon, Merlot, Syrah, Sauvignon Blanc, and Riesling.

You can picnic in a secluded courtyard or in a picnic area on the hillside overlooking the scenic valley below. Firestone is open for tours, tasting, and sales from 10:00 a.m. to

i Fill up your gas tank before you drive the Foxen Canyon Wine Trail. You won't find any services along the way, and it can take up to an hour just to drive along this winding road, so make sure you leave enough time to visit the final winery on your list before they cork the bottles.

5:00 p.m. daily. Tours are at 11:15 a.m. and 1:15 and 3:15 p.m. Don't miss the vineyard tours during harvest time.

Foxen Vineyard
7200 Foxen Canyon Road, Santa Maria
(805) 937-4251
Foxen Vineyard's small, rustic winery and tasting room are in a 100-year-old-plus converted barn and other historic buildings right off the side of the road. Foxen makes small amounts of handcrafted Chenin Blanc, Chardonnay, Pinot Noir, Cabernet Sauvignon, Cabernet Franc, Merlot, Syrah, Viognier, and Sangiovese using traditional French methods. It's open for tasting and sales 11:00 a.m. to 4:00 p.m. daily.

Koehler Winery
5360 Foxen Canyon Road, Los Olivos
(805) 693-8384
www.koehlerwinery.com
In 1997 Peter Koehler purchased this property, hired winemaker Doug Scott, and decided to use the high-quality grapes grown on the 30-year-old vines to make his own wines. Cabernet Sauvignon, Chardonnay, Sauvignon Blanc, Riesling, Syrah, Sangiovese, Grenache, and Viognier all flourish on this 100-acre estate, and you can sample some of the wines in the tasting room from 10:00 a.m. to 5:00 p.m. daily. The shaded picnic tables are a pretty spot to enjoy lunch.

Rancho Sisquoc Winery
6600 Foxen Canyon Road, Santa Maria
(805) 934-4332
www.ranchosisquoc.com
This rustic winery on a 37,000-acre cattle ranch uses only the finest grapes from its 308-acre estate vineyard—one of the oldest in the county. When you arrive at Rancho Sisquoc, you really feel like you're out on a homestead in the Old West—there's nothing around for miles except pastures, vineyards, and a few ranches and farms. The picnic tables on a grassy area are a great spot to relax and eat.

In the tasting room, you can sample various Rancho Sisquoc wines, such as Sauvignon Blanc, Chardonnay, Sylvaner, Riesling, Merlot, Cabernet Sauvignon, and a Meritage blend. The Rancho Sisquoc tasting room is open from 10:00 a.m. to 4:00 p.m. daily. Keep an eye out for the redwood chapel at the entrance, which is also featured on the wine label. In 1966 it became the first official landmark in Santa Barbara County, and in 1975 it was dedicated as a State Historical Landmark.

Zaca Mesa Winery
6905 Foxen Canyon Road, Los Olivos
(805) 688-9339, (800) 350-7972
www.zacamesa.com
Spanish settlers called this area *la zaca mesa* (the restful place), and the name truly fits the bill. This is one of our favorite wineries, not just for its fantastic estate-bottled wines but also for the gorgeous natural setting—an unobtrusive, environmentally correct building that blends perfectly with the surroundings.

The 750-acre property includes 240 acres of mesa vineyards, tranquil dirt roads, nature trails, herb gardens, and native landscaping. You can picnic at tables in the grassy courtyard picnic area or up on the nature trails.

Established in 1972, Zaca Mesa produces about 30,000 cases of wine a year with an emphasis on Rhône varietals, including Viognier, Syrah, and Roussanne. The winery is known as a trendsetter because of its unique blends of Rhône varietals, including the Z Cuvée, a blend of Grenache, Mourvedre, Syrah, Cinsant, and Counoise.

Zaca Mesa is open for tasting from 10:00 a.m. to 4:00 p.m. daily, with extended hours (from 10:00 a.m. to 5:00 p.m.) on weekends during summer.

Santa Ynez Valley Wine Trail

The Santa Ynez Valley Wine Trail winds through the southern end of Santa Barbara wine country, where most of the population lives. You'll see horse farms and orchards, historic towns, and the quaint Danish village of Solvang.

The trail is a loop that takes you to all the

major wineries in the Santa Ynez Valley. You can start in Buellton, then head over to Santa Ynez, go up to Los Olivos, and wind back through historic Ballard to Solvang. Or follow the route in reverse.

Either direction you take, you can spend a day (or longer) stopping at the premium wineries along the trail.

Artiste Winery
3569 Sagunto Street, Studio 102, Santa Ynez
(805) 686-2626
This is truly the most interesting of the area wine-tasting rooms. Bion Rice, proprietor, seems to have gotten it right when he combined his obvious passion for all things beautiful in both wine and art. He extended this love onto the wine bottle labels, too, as each production carries the artwork of a specially commissioned piece. Fill a glass with Artiste's delicious Syrah or Chardonnay, then grab a brush and sweep your own broad brush strokes onto the community canvas located inside the tasting room.

The Brander Vineyard
2401 Refugio Road, Los Olivos
(805) 688-2455, (800) 970-9979
www.brander.com
Suffused with old world charm, The Brander Vineyard was established in 1975 by Argentinean-born Fred Brander, and has always been acclaimed as a top producer of premium Sauvignon Blanc. Along with the Sauvignon Blanc, Brander makes a Bouchet (a blend of red Bordeaux varietals), Merlot, and Cabernet Sauvignon. Its sister winery, Domaine Santa Barbara, produces Chardonnay, Pinot Gris, Cabernet-Syrah, and Pinot Noir, and you can taste these wines at Brander. Housed in a European-style, small pink chateau, the tasting room is open daily from 10:00 a.m. to 5:00 p.m. during the summer and 11:00 a.m. to 4:00 p.m. the rest of the year.

Bridlewood Estate Winery
3555 Roblar Avenue, Santa Ynez
(800) 467-4100, ext. 216

Surfer boy/winemaker David Hopkins is as mellow as his wine. He insists he blends for "character and balance," not the AVA (American Viticultural Areas) label, and we believe him. Under the red-tiled roof of this elegant and stately winery, you'll feel a world away from all that matters. After a few sips of the tasting room pour, you'll feel it even decidedly more so.

Bridlewood is the quintessential wine-tasting experience. The tasting room is open from 10:00 a.m. to 5:00 p.m. daily.

> **i** The term *estate winery* means the winery uses it own fruit to make the wines rather than purchasing it from other vineyards. This gives the vintner greater control over the wine-making process from the vine to the bottle.

The Gainey Vineyard
3950 East California Highway 246, Santa Ynez
(805) 688-0558
www.gaineyvineyard.com
The *Los Angeles Times* has written that "Gainey Vineyard is one of the most beautiful wineries in the world." It's part of the 1,800-acre Gainey Ranch in the Santa Ynez Valley, and the location has been used for a number of Hollywood films and TV shows.

Run by the father-son team of Daniel J. and Daniel H. Gainey, it's one of only a few wineries in Santa Barbara County to own vineyards in both warm and cool microclimates: one for top-quality Bordeaux varietals and the other for Burgundian varietals. It produces about 18,000 cases annually. Varietals include Sauvignon Blanc, Chardonnay, Riesling, Merlot, Pinot Noir, and Cabernet Franc.

Rising at the end of a long drive lined with pepper trees, the beautiful Spanish-style tasting facility was built in 1984. Within its cool tiled interior, you can taste and purchase the wines and buy delicious tapenades, pasta, gourmet vinegars, and bread-dippers. Be sure

Close-up

What's in a Name

Ever looked at bottles of wine from Santa Barbara County and wondered about the different regions on the labels? These appellations, also known as American Viticultural Areas (AVAs), can divulge much about the character of the wine you are about to drink. If a label says "Santa Ynez Valley," this means at least 85 percent of the grapes were grown in that federally recognized region. It's a guarantee of geographic origin. Once you know a bit about the growing conditions in these areas, you'll have a richer appreciation for the differences in climate and soils that create the flavor of the wine. California has 69 appellations, three of which belong to Santa Barbara County. We've described these three AVAs briefly below so you can impress your friends next time you buy a bottle.

Santa Rita Hills—In 2001 the Bureau of Alcohol, Tobacco, and Firearms approved this AVA to differentiate wines made from grapes grown in the cooler western edge of the Santa Ynez Valley. Conditions here mirror those found in Reims in Champagne, France. Morning fog is frequent, winds are strong, and soils typically contain less clay and more calcium than those in the eastern Santa Ynez Valley. World-class Pinot Noir and Chardonnay are produced in this region, which encompasses most of the vineyards lying west of U.S. Highway 101.

Santa Ynez Valley—Lying predominantly east of Highway 101, this region is generally warmer than the Santa Rita Hills area with well-drained soils ranging from sandy loams and clay loams to shaly and silty clay loams. The area primarily produces high-quality Cabernet Sauvignon, Cabernet Franc, Merlot, Syrah, Grenache, and Sauvignon Blanc.

Santa Maria Valley—This funnel-shaped region in the northern part of Santa Barbara County has a cool climate, thanks to its prevailing ocean winds, and enjoys one of the longest growing seasons of any viticultural area in the world. The area's well-drained soils range from sandy loam to clay loam, and its cool temperatures make it one of California's best AVAs for Pinot Noir and Chardonnay. Rhone varietals also thrive here, showing great clarity and depth of fruit.

to pick up some of the complimentary gourmet recipe sheets near the counter. If you're looking for a place to eat lunch, you can relax and dine at picnic tables overlooking the vineyards. Each year the winery hosts an extensive program of events, including cooking classes, outdoor concerts, winemaker dinners, and an annual harvest "crush party." The tasting room is open 10:00 a.m. to 5:00 p.m. daily (last tasting at 4:45 p.m.). Free tours begin at 11:00 a.m. and 1:00, 2:00, and 3:00 p.m.

Kalyra Winery
343 North Refugio Road, Santa Ynez
(805) 693-8864
www.kalyrawinery.com

Fact: Santa Barbara County is home to one of the few wine regions in the world with easy access to great surf breaks. What does this have to do with making wine, you may ask? It's what lured Aussie-born winemaker Mike Brown to Santa Barbara County to pursue his passion for crafting fabulous wines (with a little surfing on the side). With more than 20 years of wine-making experience under his belt in both California and Australia, Mike opened the Kalyra Winery and tasting room in 2002 with his younger brother Martin. *Kalyra* is a translation from an Australian aboriginal language meaning "a wild and pleasant place," and you'll find the tasting room fits this description well. Aboriginal art adorns the walls, Aussie salsas are set out for tasting, and the friendly staff and great tunes enhance the lively ambience. The winery produces a Sauvignon Blanc and Chardonnay, but it's best known for its dessert wines, including a tawny port, orange muscat, and black muscat. You can also taste wines under the M.Brown label here, including an excellent Australian Shiraz and Riesling. The tasting room is open from 10:00 a.m. to 5:00 p.m. daily, and you can enjoy a picnic lunch on the scenic deck or at the tables on the lawn.

Sunstone Vineyards and Winery
125 Refugio Road, Santa Ynez
(805) 688-WINE, (800) 313-WINE
www.sunstonewinery.com

Sunstone's name comes from its sun-colored stone embankment overlooking the Santa Ynez River Valley, and it's one of the most beautiful wineries and tasting rooms in the area. Completed in 1993, the spacious, Provençal-style facility offers an elegant tasting bar, stone floors, an arbored porch, beautiful landscaping with French lavender and rosemary, a courtyard with umbrella tables, and a unique stone cave dug into the hillside and packed with French oak barrels filled with aging wines. You can also purchase gourmet pasta sauces, vinegars, and grilling oils from

Bien Nacido Winery in Santa Maria Valley. KIRK IRWIN/SANTA BARBARA CONFERENCE & VISITORS BUREAU

the display in the rustic tasting room.

The winery uses only organically grown grapes. Its signature wine is Merlot, but it also makes excellent Cabernet Sauvignon, Syrah, Viognier, Sauvignon Blanc, Chardonnay, and Muscat Canelli. The tasting room is open from 10:00 a.m. to 4:00 p.m. every day.

i Heading out for a day of wine tasting? Appoint a designated driver before you begin the tour and take a bottle of water. Sipping wines in the sun all day can leave you feeling dehydrated.

Santa Rita Hills Loop

Home to some of Santa Barbara's wine-making visionaries, this cooler region of the Santa Ynez Valley, tucked behind the coastal mountains, is Santa Barbara County's newest AVA. The cooler microclimate here produces world-class Pinot Noir and Chardonnay. You can drive along a scenic 34-mile (55-kilometer) loop to explore the area and visit some of the wineries. Along the way, the road carves through wide-open countryside rimmed by rugged mountains, and you'll see some of the most unspoiled scenery in the Santa Barbara Wine Country. Starting from U.S. Highway 101, you can either take Santa Rosa Road west and loop back on Highway 246 or vice versa. Although Mosby Winery isn't technically in the Santa Rita Hills AVA, you have to drive right by it when you take Santa Rosa Road, so we've included it in this section.

Alma Rosa Winery & Vineyards
201-C Industrial Way, Buellton
(805) 688-9090
www.almarosawinery.com
The indefatigable Richard Sanford is an icon in the world of wine. A near-native of the valley, Sanford came to the valley 35 years ago to create wines that would rival France. His pioneering paid off. With the first planting of Pinot Noir vines, Sanford became successful and established quite a reputation. Perhaps

Sanford's greatest feat is still yet to come with this new venture of wine-making combined with organic farming and sustainable agriculture methods. Continuing in his renowned tradition, Sanford is still putting out the most excellent of Pinot Noirs and Chardonnays. The tasting room is open daily from 11:00 a.m. to 4:00 p.m.

Babcock Vineyards
5175 East Calif. Highway 246, Lompoc
(805) 736-1455
www.babcockwinery.com
Dentist Walt Babcock and wife, Mona, established this winery in 1984, and son Bryan has been making highly lauded premium, hand-crafted wines ever since. The *Los Angeles Times* named him one of the "10 Best Winemakers of the Year." Babcock is known for its Chardonnay, Pinot Noir, Syrah, Gewürztraminer, and Pinot Grigio, making it one "taste test" you really shouldn't miss. The newly remodeled tasting room is so beautiful and inviting that a family of birds has taken up residence in one of the planters. The Babcock tasting room is open daily from 10:30 a.m. to 4:00 p.m.

Foley Estates, Vineyard & Winery
6121 East Highway 246, Lompoc
(805) 737-6222
www.foleywines.com
How does William Foley II, the founder and CEO of Fidelity National Finance Corp., have enough time to be a vintner? Who knows, but Foley's passion for wine drove him to purchase the former J. Carey Cellars in 1997. He promptly changed the name to Lincourt, a combination of the names of his two daughters. In 1998 he purchased Rancho Santa Rosa and planted 230 acres of Pinot Noir, Chardonnay, and Syrah. He named that venture Foley Estates. Visit the unbelievably huge tasting room and event center there. It's as impressive as the wine. Open daily from 10:00 a.m. to 5:00 p.m.

Lafond Winery & Vineyards
6855 Santa Rosa Road, Buellton
(805) 688-7921
www.lafondwinery.com

French Canadian-born Pierre Lafond founded Santa Barbara's first post-Prohibition winery, Santa Barbara Winery, in 1962 (see separate entry) and is one of the valley's viticultural pioneers. In 2001 he opened this new estate winery and vineyard to visitors, specializing in vineyard-designated Pinot Noir, Syrah, and Chardonnay. You can sample the wines daily from 10:00 a.m. to 5:00 p.m. in the tasting room designed by Pierre Lafond himself (who also happens to be an architect). From here you can see all the working areas of the winery. If you bring lunch, you can picnic at tables on the lawn.

Melville
5185 East Highway 246, Lompoc
(805) 735-7030
www.melvillewinery.com

At the northern end of the Santa Rita Hills loop near Babcock Vineyards, Melville is a relatively young estate winery, specializing in Pinot Noir, Chardonnay, and Syrah. Set in a gorgeous Mediterranean-style villa surrounded by poplar trees, oaks, and sprawling vineyards, the winery eschews competitions but wins high praise for its wines. It's a beautiful winery to visit and enjoy a picnic on the patio and lawn. You can sample the wines—including some limited bottlings from the small lot collection available only through the tasting room—Monday through Friday from 11:00 a.m. to 3:00 p.m. and Saturday through Sunday from 11:00 a.m. to 4:00 p.m.

Mosby Winery
9496 Santa Rosa Road, Buellton
(805) 688-2415, (800) 70-MOSBY
www.mosbywines.com

Although Mosby Winery isn't technically in the Santa Rita Hills AVA, it lies just off Highway 101, and you can easily pop in here on your way to the other wineries in the region. This 46-acre vineyard and winery was once part of the old Rancho de la Vega land grant and has been owned and operated by Bill and Jeri Mosby since 1975. The rustic, restored 1860s carriage house now serves as the tasting room. No other Santa Barbara County winery produces as many Italian varietals or brandies as Mosby.

It's mainly known for its Pinot Grigio, Sangiovese, and brandies, which include Grappa di Traminer (from estate-grown Traminer), Distillato di Prugne Selvaggie (made from wild Pacific plums), and Acqua di Lampone (made from Oregon raspberries). It's also one of the few wineries in the country to produce Teroldego and Cortese. Mosby also produces an award-winning Dolcetto, a dry, medium-body red wine. The tasting room is open Monday through Friday 10:00 a.m. to 4:00 p.m. and Saturday through Sunday 10:00 a.m. to 5:00 p.m.

Sanford Winery
7250 Santa Rosa Road, Buellton
(805) 688-3300, (800) 426-9463
(toll-free in California only)

Sanford is one of our favorite wineries. It's a little farther out than some of the others, but we think it's worth the drive for the breathtaking scenery, rich historic ambience, and fantastic wines. You'll find Sanford Winery just outside Buellton, 5 miles (8 kilometers) west of U.S. 101 on Santa Rosa Road.

The winery site, part of the original Santa Rosa land grant, is a 738-acre property known as Rancho El Jabali. Look carefully for the small sign near a cactus garden lined with California poppies, then follow the drive 1/2 mile (1 kilometer), over a tiny stream, to the tasting room.

Established in 1981 by Richard and Thekla Sanford, the winery was the first in Santa

i If you have time while you're exploring the Santa Rita Hills region, visit La Purisima Mission (805-733-3713; www.lapurisimamission.org), the most fully restored of all California's missions, near the Lompoc end of the Santa Rita Hills loop.

Barbara County to have its estate vineyards certified as organic. It currently produces Chardonnay, Sauvignon Blanc, and Pinot Noir Vin Gris. Surrounded by golden meadows and geranium gardens, the tasting room is in a rustic but beautiful building that was artfully converted from an old milking shed in 1983. A small herd of goats can be found wandering around the hills. The tasting room and adjoining picnic facilities are open daily from 11:00 a.m. to 4:00 p.m. and from 11:00 a.m. to 5:00 p.m. in the summer. Tours of the adobe winery are available by appointment.

Solvang

If you want to sample wines and soak up some Danish culture at the same time, stop by Solvang while you're in the wine country. In recent years several tasting rooms have popped up amid the windmills and pastry shops. Following are two Insider favorites. (For information on hotels and attractions in Solvang, see the Day Trips chapter.)

Lucas & Lewellen Vineyards
1645 Copenhagen Drive, Solvang
(805) 686-9336, (888) 777-6663
www.LLwine.com
In 1996 veteran viticulturalist Louis Lucas and Judge Royce Lewellen teamed up with winemaker Dan Gehrs to focus on making fine, food-friendly wines at affordable prices. The results are drawing accolades. Visit their huge tasting room in downtown Solvang, where you can sample wine under three different labels. The namesake label features Rhône, Bordeaux, and Burgundy varietals; the Mandolina label offers award-winning Italian varietals such as Dolcetto, Barbera, Nebbiolo, Pinot Grigio, and Rosato; and the Virgin label includes an unwooded Sauvignon Blanc and Chardonnay. Lucas & Lewellen is also the only

winery producing champagne and one of the few producing Cabernet Sauvignon. The tasting room is open from 11:00 a.m. to 5:30 p.m. daily. You can also purchase clothing, wine accessories, and ceramics.

Presidio Winery Tasting Room
1603 Copenhagen Drive, #1, Solvang
(805) 693-8585, (888) 930-9463
www.presidiowinery.com
Founded in 1991, Presidio Winery produces premium handcrafted Pinot Noir (the signature wine), barrel-fermented Chardonnay, Merlot, and Late Harvest Zinfandel as well as a few wines that are only available in the tasting room, such as a Chenin Blanc and Syrah. The tasting room opened in 2003 on the corner of Mission Drive and Atterdag Street in downtown Solvang and is open from 11:00 a.m. to 6:00 p.m. daily. Feel free to ask questions—the friendly staff encourages your curiosity. You can also purchase wine gifts and accessories, clothing, and gourmet food items.

Santa Barbara

If you can't make it over the mountains to the North County, you can sip wines by the beach at two of the oldest wineries in the country.

Santa Barbara Winery
202 Anacapa Street, Santa Barbara
(805) 963-3633, (800) 225-3633
www.sbwinery.com
Established in 1962 by Pierre Lafond (see Lafond Winery), Santa Barbara Winery is the oldest winery in the county. It produces Chardonnay, Pinot Noir, Sauvignon Blanc, Syrah, Zinfandel, and Cabernet Sauvignon wines. The vineyard is up in Santa Ynez, but the winery is down by the beach, on the corner of Yanonali and Anacapa Streets, just 2 blocks north of Cabrillo Boulevard and 1 block east of State Street.

You can sample the wines in the tasting room from 10:00 a.m. to 5:00 p.m. daily and browse the gift shop for wine accessories, gourmet specialty food, and gifts.

i Experienced wine tasters recommend choosing one or two varietals to taste and compare so you don't confuse your palate.

Stearns Wharf Vintners
217G Stearns Wharf, Santa Barbara
(805) 966-6624
www.silcom.com/~ricky/vintners.html
Perched over the Pacific on historic Stearns
Wharf, this scenic tasting room opened in
1981. Here you can sample Stearns Wharf
Vintners wines (including Chardonnay, Pinot
Noir, Muscat Canelli, and Merlot) and other
wines while taking in wonderful views of Santa
Barbara, the ocean, and the islands. The room
is open for tasting from 9:00 a.m. to 8:00 p.m.
daily (9:00 a.m. to 6:00 p.m. in the winter).

RESTAURANTS

Wine tasting works up an appetite, so following are a few of our favorite wine country
restaurants and cafes. You can relax and
enjoy a gourmet meal at one of the fine dining
restaurants, feast on steaks and fries at a rustic tavern, or pick up some sandwiches and
salads from a local deli and picnic at one of
the wineries. If you're looking for food in an
area not listed here, ask a North County
Insider. They'll be happy to help.

Price Code

For your convenience, we've included typical
pricing for a dinner for two, excluding such
extras as appetizers and dessert, tax, and tip.
These codes are general guidelines only.

$ . . . . **Less than $20**
$$ . . . . **$20 to $40**
$$$ . . . . **$41 to $60**
$$$$ . . . . **$61 and more**

Ballard

The Ballard Inn Restaurant $$$
2436 Baseline Avenue, Ballard
(805) 688-7770
www.ballardinn.com
Taken over by new owners in 2004, this ele-
gant but unpretentious country restaurant at
The Ballard Inn is a great spot for a romantic
meal. The wine list spotlights bottles from
Santa Barbara County, and Executive Chef

Budi Kazali has crafted a menu focusing on
Asian-influenced French cuisine featuring
seafood, grilled meats, and fresh local pro-
duce. Pan-seared Maine scallops with lemon-
grass risotto is just one of the tempting
dishes on the menu. Cuddle up by the fire in
the intimate dining room or dine alfresco on
the patio in summer. The restaurant serves
dinner Wednesday through Sunday. Reserva-
tions are highly recommended.

Buellton

The Hitching Post II $$$
406 East Highway 246, Buellton
(805) 688-0676
www.hitchingpost2.com
Where do local and visiting vintners head
when they want a great Santa Maria–style
steak, interesting company, and robust wines
all in one place? The Hitching Post II, a casual
cowboy-style steakhouse and bar, is at the
top of the list. It's been written up in *Gourmet,* the *Los Angeles Times,* and other publications, and restaurateurs and vintners from
around the world rave about the quality of the
meat, cooking, and service.

Choose the cut and size of steak you'd
like (all are from Midwestern corn-fed beef,
and nearly all are certified Angus), and the
cook will grill it to perfection over an open fire
of red oak. Reviewers also rave about the
wine list, which features Santa Barbara
County wines, of course, including those
made by the owner and main chef, Frank
Ostini.

Complete steak dinners include a fresh
vegetable tray, choice of soup or bay shrimp
cocktail, organic mixed green salad, choice of
rice pilaf, baked potato, or french fries, salsa,
and garlic bread. Prices vary by the steak's

i Rent the Oscar and Golden
Globe–winning movie *Sideways* by
Alexander Payne, then go have dinner at
the Hitching Post II. Rex Pickett, author of
the novel *Sideways,* hung out at the Hitching Post II while he was writing the book.

size and type. You can also order combination meals of steak with quail, shrimp, or duck.

Don't worry if you're not a beef eater—the menu also features pork ribs and chops, seafood, quail, turkey, ostrich, and various other entrees. You can also order a children's meal of steak or chicken for $8.

The Hitching Post II is conveniently situated right off Highway 246, just 1 mile (1.6 kilometers) or so east of U.S. 101. You can't miss it: look for the sign that says WORLD'S BEST BBQ STEAKS.

Los Olivos

Brothers Restaurant at Mattei's Tavern $$–$$$
2350 Railway Avenue, Los Olivos
(805) 688-4820
www.matteistavern.com

When the stagecoach pulled out from Cold Spring Station, it rolled down the hill, forded the Santa Ynez River, and eventually arrived in Los Olivos, home of Mattei's Tavern, established in 1886.

Today you can enjoy a surreal experience here at Brother's Restaurant, dining on fresh California cuisine in the rustic Old West atmosphere. The namesake chefs, brothers Matt and Jeff Nichols, owned a popular restaurant in Solvang before moving here in 2002, and they're still drawing raves for their food. Matt was the kitchen manager at Spago Hollywood, and Jeff worked in Paris, so you can expect crisp dishes drizzled with decadent sauces. If you sit inside amid the old black-and-white photos and Western-style furniture, you can watch them work their magic in the exhibition kitchen. You can also dine on the outdoor patio—a lovely spot on warm nights. Dishes range from roast chicken breast stuffed with goat cheese to prime rib with garlic mashed potatoes, and horseradish-crusted Irish salmon. Save room for the chocolate truffle cake with berries—it's a favorite. The wine list spotlights Santa Barbara County wines. After dinner you can swig a nightcap with the locals in the Western-style bar. Brothers Restaurant is open for dinner

nightly. Dress is casual, and reservations are highly recommended.

To get to Mattei's, take Highway 154 and turn west onto Grand Avenue in Los Olivos. Take an immediate right on Railway Avenue and just head north a few blocks.

Los Olivos Cafe $$–$$$
2879 Grand Avenue, Los Olivos
(805) 688-7265
www.losolivoscafe.com

On the main street in the heart of Los Olivos, this cute Mediterranean-style cafe is a popular spot with the locals. Featured in a scene in the movie *Sideways*, what was a thriving cafe is now a virtual hot spot. Sauteed wild king fillet of salmon on a warm spinach salad is a must, and so is the deliciously decadent Chocolate Scream. If you're planning a picnic lunch, you can order food to go. Los Olivos Cafe is open for lunch and dinner daily.

Wine Cask Los Olivos $$$
Fess Parker's Wine Country Inn & Spa
2860 Grand Avenue, Los Olivos
(805) 688-7788, (800) 436-9463
www.winecask.com

The Wine Cask has been in business for 24 years and has a sterling Santa Barbara reputation. Before restaurateur Doug Margerum sold the Wine Cask, he first birthed its sister, the Wine Cask in Los Olivos. Large picture windows bathe the room in natural sunlight during the day. Cozy up in front of the welcoming fireplace and drink in the ambience while you enjoy one of the selections from the long list of local wines. Going local is one of Wine Cask's menu trends, as its seasonal offerings change according to what's at the farmers' market or down at the Santa Barbara harbor. We've heard the Hawaiian ahi carpaccio is quite good, and you can never go wrong with oysters on the half shell. Potato-crusted pheasant and juniper berry duck breast are a few of the chef's originals. Dinner is served daily.

Off San Marcos Pass

Cold Spring Tavern $$–$$$
5995 Stagecoach Road, Santa Barbara
(805) 967-0066
www.coldspringstavern.com

More than a century ago, when stagecoaches pulled up to the Cold Spring relay station at the top of San Marcos Pass, travelers could always count on a delicious Old West meal at the tavern. It's still a great place to stop on the way to or from the wine country. You can dine by romantic lamplight in the rustic cabin or snuggle up by the wood-burning fireplace and order some unusual cuisine.

The hearty lunch choices include buffalo burgers, venison sausage burgers, and venison steak sandwiches. For dinner, you can stick with traditional favorites like rack of lamb, fresh fish, roast chicken, steaks, and pasta. Or, if you're daring, go for the wild game: medallions of rabbit, stuffed pheasant breast, or wild boar tenderloin. Wind up the meal with Jack Daniel's pecan pie or apple cobbler just like Mom used to make.

Cold Spring Tavern is open for lunch and dinner daily and for country breakfast on Saturday and Sunday. To get there, take U.S. 101 to Highway 154 and head up the mountain (it's about 7 miles [11 kilometers] to the top). Once you start downhill on the valley side, continue about 1 mile (1.6 kilometers) and turn left onto Stagecoach Road. Take a direct right and go down the canyon about 1.5 miles (2.4 kilometers) to the tavern. If you're coming from the opposite direction, turn right on Stagecoach Road, take another immediate right, and follow the road about 1/4 mile (0.4 kilometer).

Santa Ynez

Trattoria Grappolo $$
3687 C Sagunto Street, Santa Ynez
(805) 688-6899
www.trattoriagrappolo.com

Using fresh local ingredients, Chef Leonardo Curti whips up delicious Italian cuisine at this family-run local favorite. Popular dishes are the rollino appetizers (pizza crust wrapped around smoked mozzarella and raddichio topped with fresh tomatoes) and entrees such as the cioppino and tortelloni (homemade ravioli stuffed with spinach and ricotta cheese in a butter sage sauce). Locals love to sit inside and chat with the friendly staff or perch at the wine bar inside and watch the chef work his magic, but you can also sit outside on the patio. The restaurant serves beer and a large selection of wines from around the world. Trattoria Grappolo is open every day for dinner and Tuesday through Sunday for lunch. Reservations are recommended.

The Vineyard House $$
3631 Sagunto Street, Santa Ynez
(805) 688-2886
www.thevineyardhouse.com

Next door to the elegant Santa Ynez Inn, tucked in a beautiful old Victorian house, Vineyard House serves hearty American and international cuisine, using fresh produce from local farmers and herbs straight from the garden. You can dine inside or on the romantic outdoor deck. Lunch dishes include salads, burgers, pastas, and sandwiches. The dinner menu offers a choice of meat, fish, chicken, and pasta entrees. The Vineyard House is open daily for lunch and dinner. It's closed on Tuesday.

Solvang

Cabernet Bistro $$–$$$
485 Alisal Road, #L2, Solvang
(805) 688-8871
www.cabernetbistro.com

If you want a European alternative to the Danish smorgasbords at the tourist joints, you can't go wrong with Cabernet Bistro. Experienced restaurateurs Jacques and Diana Toulet opened this fine dining restaurant and have drawn rave reviews for their French "comfort" cuisine. Take a seat amid the antiques, chandeliers, and pink linen in the cozy wood-beamed dining room and choose an award-winning local wine or an imported French vintage to complement your meal. The restaurant is best known for its roast duck served with a choice of sauce—Cassis, cherry, amaretto, Grand Marnier, or green peppercorn. You can also choose from seasonal dishes such as sand dabs sautéed in a white wine lemon butter sauce and French classics like escargot. Cabernet Bistro is open for dinner Tuesday through Sunday, and reservations are recommended.

ACCOMMODATIONS

After a day in the North County, you can easily drive back to Santa Barbara—it's just an hour or less down U.S. 101. But if you'd like to spend more than a day or two exploring wine country, we recommend staying overnight at a hotel or bed-and-breakfast inn. (After a day of sampling wine in the sun, most people just want to take a nap rather than a long car ride.)

If you stay, you can choose from a number of fine lodging places. Unless otherwise noted, the accommodations below provide at least one specially equipped room for the physically challenged. A few allow small dogs in certain rooms.

To make quick arrangements, call a free reservation service: Santa Barbara Hotspots (805-564-1637 or 800-793-7666; www.hotspotsusa.com) or Coastal Escapes (805-684-7679 or 800-292-2222; www.coastalescapes.com). They'll be happy to provide information on availability and rates and make your reservations. You can also call the Solvang Conference and Visitors Bureau at (805) 688-6144 or (800) 468-6765, or visit www.solvangusa.com.

Price Code

Prices for these accommodations are based on a one-night, double-occupancy stay in the high season and do not include taxes and fees for added services. Remember that these are just averages—some rooms may be more expensive (especially suites), while others may cost less.

$.	$100 to $120
$$	$121 to $170
$$$	$171 to $225
$$$$	$226 and more

The Day Trips chapter also offers suggestions on places to stay and dine in Solvang and other nearby towns. Here, we'll tell you about a few of our favorite wine country inns and resorts. Some are a bit pricey but well worth the money spent.

**The Alisal Guest Ranch and Resort $$$$
1054 Alisal Road, Solvang
(805) 688-6411, (800) 4-ALISAL (from outside the 805 area code)
www.alisal.com**
This exclusive 10,000-acre resort and working cattle ranch has 73 comfortable California ranch–style cottages, studios, and suites, each with a wood-burning fireplace. Voted one of the "50 Best Dude Ranches in the West" by *Sunset* magazine, this popular resort has been pampering guests—many of them loyal returnees—since 1946. The resort hosted an impressive list of celebrities ever since Clark Gable and Lady Ashley exchanged vows here back in 1949 in the original library. Today, it is a favorite hideaway for active couples and families who enjoy all the cozy comforts of home but want to remain incommunicado for a while—all the rooms are telephone- and television-free. The room rate ranges from $465 to $595 a night and includes breakfast and dinner. The resort offers an incredible array of recreational facilities, including seven tennis courts, two 18-hole golf courses; a private 100-acre spring-fed lake for boating and fishing; guided horseback rides; a ropes course; and miles of spectacular nature trails. At certain times of the year, the resort offers a special package that includes unlimited horseback riding on scheduled trips, golf, tennis, and fishing.

Dining in the Ranch Room is reserved for guests, and you'll have to dress up in the evening—dinners are formal and men require a jacket and tie. The Alisal's River Grill over-

Horses in Santa Ynez Valley. GREG PETERSON/SANTA BARBARA CONFERENCE & VISITORS BUREAU

looking the public course is open to the public for breakfast, lunch, and dinner, and the Ranch Grill on the private golf course serves breakfast and lunch.

The Ballard Inn $$$–$$$$
2436 Baseline Avenue, Ballard
(805) 688-7770, (800) 638-2466
www.ballardinn.com

Fronted by picket fences and fragrant rose gardens, this charming inn on a quiet street in the tiny town of Ballard is a popular getaway for couples seeking a romantic weekend retreat. All of the 15 comfy guest rooms are uniquely decorated with themes reflecting the region's colorful history. Davy Brown's Room feels like a cozy wood cabin with its stone fireplace and wood-paneled walls, the Western Room has a cowboy theme, and the larger-but-pricier Mountain Room boasts a small balcony overlooking the street. Typical appointments include antique furnishings, king-size beds, and hand-pieced quilts or down comforters. Phones and televisions are available upon request, but most guests here don't want them. All rooms have full private baths and seven rooms have wood-burning fireplaces.

Rates include a full cooked-to-order breakfast and afternoon wine and hors d'oeuvres. The inn's restaurant serves dinner Wednesday through Sunday (see the Restaurants section of this chapter). Although the Ballard is a nonsmoking inn, smoking is permitted on the veranda.

Pets are allowed in designated rooms.

Fess Parker Wine Country Inn
& Spa $$$$
2860 Grand Avenue, Los Olivos
(805) 688-7788
www.fessparker.com

Tucked behind olive trees on the main street in
Los Olivos, this posh bed-and-breakfast–style
hotel has beautifully appointed rooms, a pool,
a spa, and a fleet of bicycles for your use. Fess
Parker (a.k.a. Davy Crockett) purchased the
hotel in summer 1998 and remodeled it to
reflect a wine country theme. You might even
bump into him during your stay, as he regularly pops in to shake hands with the guests.
Fess's wife, Marcella, infused a personal touch
by decorating each room differently. Some are
bright and airy, with potted palms and light
color schemes; others are warm and cozy. All
the rooms have antique furnishings, gas fireplaces, down comforters, TVs in armoires, wet
bars, hair dryers, and plush robes. One room
in the complex across the street is equipped
with a Jacuzzi tub. A new annex with additional rooms is planned. If you really want to
pamper yourself, go to Fess's DiVine spa for all
sorts of rejuvenating facial, body, and massage therapies. The resort also offers meeting
space with audiovisual equipment. Downstairs
is the Wine Cask Los Olivos. (See the Restaurants section in this chapter.) Room rates start
at $300 per night during weekdays and $495
on weekends, including in-room continental
breakfast and nightly wine and cheese reception.

Santa Ynez Inn $$$$
3627 Sagunto Street, Santa Ynez
(805) 688-5588, (800) 643-5774
www.santaynezinn.com

Opened in the fall of 2001, this $2 million
Victorian-style boutique hotel in the Old West
town of Santa Ynez is a fresh choice for visitors seeking luxury accommodations in the
wine country. The elegant two-story inn offers
14 plush guest rooms and suites, a fitness
facility with sauna, an outdoor heated
whirlpool and sun deck, meeting rooms,
catering facilities, and extensive gardens.

Each room is uniquely decorated. Expect
antique furnishings, queen- or king-size beds,
TVs with DVD/CD entertainment systems, coffeemakers, hair dryers, robes, and thoughtful
touches such as fresh-cut flowers. Some
rooms also come with gas fireplaces, balconies or patios, double steam showers, and
whirlpool tubs. Rates are around $400 per
night and include a full gourmet breakfast,
afternoon tea, evening wine, hors d'oeuvres,
and desserts.

Santa Ynez Valley Marriott $$–$$$
555 McMurray Road, Buellton
(805) 688-1000, (800) 638-8882
www.santaynezhotels.com

This midsize Mediterranean-style Marriott
offers good-value accommodations in a convenient location, just north of the U.S. 101
Highway 246 intersection. It's right next to the
freeway, but you really don't hear much of the
traffic when you're indoors. The hotel offers
deluxe guest rooms and two-room executive
suites, a swimming pool, and tennis, racquetball, and squash courts, as well as several
restaurants. Room rates vary, depending on
the time of your visit.

FESTIVALS

Santa Barbara wine country takes advantage
of every opportunity to host a celebration.
(Wouldn't you if you had such great wine and
food to serve?) Dinners, concerts, open
houses, harvest parties, and other special
events take place at various wineries practically every month of the year.

For a current schedule of events, contact
the Santa Barbara County Vintners' Association at (805) 688-0881 or (800) 218-0881, or
visit www.sbcountywines.com. Also watch for
announcements in the Santa Barbara Independent or the Santa Barbara News-Press.
The following are brief descriptions of two
major events that almost always sell out
beforehand. Get your tickets early! Call (800)
218-0881 for information; also see the Annual
Events chapter.

Santa Barbara County Vintners' Festival

This extravaganza is one of the most popular annual events in the valley. Member wineries dispense their wines, and picnic lunches are prepared on-site (or you can bring your own). The main event is usually held in mid-May in a beautiful outdoor setting, such as River Park in Lompoc.

Visitors spend the afternoon sampling fine wines, watching demonstrations (for example, wine barrel building), and listening to live music. The festival usually takes place from 1:00 to 4:00 p.m. on a Saturday. The admission fee covers all tasting and entertainment.

A Celebration of Harvest

This colorful festival is held the second weekend in October at Rancho Sisquoc Winery in Santa Maria. It showcases wines grown and produced in Santa Barbara County. Celebrate the grape harvest with local vintners, taste fine wines, and fill up on gourmet treats. The celebration also features music, demonstrations, and exhibits. Tickets must be purchased in advance from the Vintners' Association. Call for a schedule of events.

DAY TRIPS

With all the people coming to Santa Barbara to escape the rigors of big-city life, you wouldn't think Santa Barbarans would be looking for a getaway of their own. The fact is, even we enjoy a change of scenery every now and then.

There are basically two choices for a day trip or getaway out of Santa Barbara: drive north or drive south.

If you head north on U.S. Highway 101 (which will eventually take you to San Francisco), you're basically eschewing the big city and looking for some peace and quiet in northern Santa Barbara County or in the little beach towns that dot the coast between here and Monterey. This drive is far less hectic than the southbound route and avoids most of the L.A. traffic that tends to rattle the nerves of Santa Barbarans. We'll give you a peek at the charming Danish town of Solvang in the Santa Ynez Valley plus some information on the Morro Bay area and one of the Central Coast's most popular attractions, Hearst Castle.

Traveling south on U.S. 101 will take you to Los Angeles, where you'll find all the sights and entertainment you've come to expect from a large cosmopolitan city. We've included information on some of the most-visited attractions in L.A. as well as a look at the artsy and rural town of Ojai, an off-the-beaten-path destination south of Santa Barbara with a Bohemian feel.

No matter which way you decide to go, there are plenty of options within a few hours' drive of Santa Barbara's borders for daylong or weekend adventure.

HEADING NORTH

Velkommen til Solvang!

Solvang, one of the most popular day trip destinations with Santa Barbarans, is just a 45-minute drive up the coast. From either U.S. 101 or California Highway 154, take California Highway 246 into the heart of this self-proclaimed "Danish Capital of America."

Here you can get a good look at Danish-style architecture (including windmills), check out the **Hans Christian Andersen Museum** at 1680 Mission Drive (805-688-2052; www.solvangca.com/museum) and the **Elverhoj Museum of History & Art** at 1624 Elverhoj Way (805-686-1211; www.elverhoj.org), or allow yourself to be seduced by the smell of *abelskivers*, small, round Danish pancakes smothered in raspberry jam with a dusting of powdered sugar.

The specialty and gift shops are fabulous, and the art galleries and antiques stores make browsing irresistible. All of these attractions draw hordes of tourists, so plan to wade through the crowds at this Disneyesque Danish town, especially on weekends and during the summer. If you really want to get a taste of Denmark, visit during the Danish Days celebration in September (see the Annual Events chapter).

Solvang is particularly charming when decorated for Christmas (see the Winterfest listing in the Annual Events chapter), which is a great time to shop and pick up some incredible Danish pastries to tempt Santa. (First you have to get them home without devouring them—quite a challenge for most of us.) Summertime brings the **Pacific Conservatory of the Performing Arts Theaterfest** (805-922-8313; www.pcpa.org), the central coast's professional resident theater company, to Solvang, and several productions are staged in the city's outdoor **Festival Theatre** each season from June through October. This is not small-town entertainment by any means. Well-known professional actors are often in the cast, and productions are always first-rate.

Santa Barbarans frequently make a round-trip excursion to Solvang on a summer evening to eat dinner and catch a show.

Golfers will love the beautiful **River Course at the Alisal** (805-688-6042; www .rivercourse.com), a public 18-hole championship course on the banks of the Santa Ynez River near the exclusive 10,000-acre Alisal Guest Ranch and Resort, at 1054 Alisal Road (805-688-6411, 800-4-ALISAL from outside the 805 area code; www.alisal.com; see the Santa Barbara Wine Country chapter).

You'll find the city's recent face-lift has changed Solvang's former hotel names, like the Vagabond Inn and Chimney Sweep Inn, to upscale names, like the Wine Valley Inn and Cottages (1564 Copenhagen Drive, Solvang; 805-688-2111; 800-824-6444; www.winevalley inn.com) and Hadsten House Inn and Spa (1450 Mission Drive, Solvang; 805-688-3210; 800-457-5373; www.hadstenhouse.com), a sure reaction to the influx of trendy tourists. Contact the Solvang Conference and Visitors Bureau, at the corner of Mission Drive and Highway 246 (805-688-6144, 800-468-6765; www.solvangusa.com) for information.

Also in Solvang is **Mission Santa Inés,** on Mission Drive just east of Alisal Road (805-688-4815; www.missionsantaines.org). The 19th of California's missions, founded in 1804, it's worth a look (if you can tear yourself away from the sights and smells of downtown Solvang).

You can also explore the nearby wineries and sample wines at the tasting rooms in downtown Solvang (see the Santa Barbara Wine Country chapter).

More of the North County

Just a hop, skip, and jump from Solvang (3 miles [4.8 kilometers] to the east on Highway 246 to be exact), is the **Chumash Casino** (800-248-6274; www.chumashcasino.com), operated by the local Chumash tribe. Touted as "the best place to play from L.A. to the Bay," the casino has become a gambling and entertainment hot spot, offering a large range of gaming options and big-name entertainment.

i Chumash Casino offers free daily return shuttles from Santa Barbara to the casino. You can hop aboard at Milpas/Calle Puerta Vallarta across from the DoubleTree Inn by the beach or at Camino Real Marketplace behind Linens-n-Things in Goleta. Call (800) CHUMASH for details and schedules.

Five miles (8 kilometers) northwest of Solvang is **Lompoc** (correctly pronounced LOM-poke), where flower seeds are a blooming business. More than 15 miles (24 kilometers) of private flower fields bloom in the summer, including wide expanses of sweet peas, lavender, marigolds, calendula, and larkspur. You can get a map of the flower fields from the Lompoc Valley Chamber of Commerce at 111 South I Street (805-736-4567, 800-240-0999; www.lompoc.com). Also in Lompoc, along Highway 246, is **La Purisima Mission State Historic Park** (805-733-3713; www.lapurisimamission.org). La Purisima was the 11th of the 21 Spanish missions built in what became California. All of the main buildings are filled with furniture and other artifacts. Candlelight tours, concerts, and crafts are just some of the activities here.

In downtown Lompoc, it's hard to miss the dozens of murals depicting the city's culture and history. You can drive by and admire them, or call the Chamber of Commerce for information on walking tours.

Also here is **Vandenberg Air Force Base** (www.vandenberg.af.mil), where missile launches often light up the sky. Public tours are offered the second Wednesday of each month. Two-week advanced reservations are required. There is a 9:45 a.m. check-in. For up-to-date information, call (805) 606-3595. The base's main gate is at the end of Highway 1.

Approximately 80 miles (129 kilometers) north of Santa Barbara on U.S. 101 is **Santa Maria,** home of the Santa Maria–style barbecue known as tri-tip (see a brief discussion of this delicacy in the Restaurants chapter) and the Santa Barbara County Fair (see the Annual Events chapter).

i Want a little more nature? Check out Cachuma Lake Wildlife Cruises. You'll spend two hours cruising Lake Cachuma in a 45-foot (14-meter) passenger pontoon boat. A naturalist navigates you through the wilds while regaling you with stories. Cruises are available on Friday, Saturday, and Sunday from March through October. Call (805) 686-5054 for more information, or check out the Web site at www.cachuma.com.

The Central Coast

Just north of Santa Maria, you'll cross the line into San Luis Obispo County, which marks the halfway point between Los Angeles and San Francisco. As you meander along U.S. 101, you'll come to the small beach towns of **Grover Beach, Pismo Beach, Shell Beach,** and **Avila Beach** just before the freeway makes a wide curve inland.

Any of the beach cities are good places to stop for a bite to eat or a seaside stroll. **F. McLintocks Saloon and Dining House** (805-773-1892; www.mclintocks.com), just off U.S. 101 on Mattie Road in Shell Beach, is a popular stopping-off point for steaks and seafood, and there's a great kids' menu, too.

Pismo has a great family beach and some good seafood restaurants with excellent clam chowder and fish and chips. Just south of Pismo Beach is **Oceano Dunes State Vehicular Recreation Area** (ohv.parks.ca.gov), the most extensive coastal dunes in California. Off-road vehicles have access to the expansive sand dunes.

Stay on U.S. 101 and you'll come to the city of San Luis Obispo. Just outside the city limits, you'll pass the famous **Madonna Inn** (805-543-3000, 800-543-9666; www.madonnainn.com), a fantasy lodging built in 1959. Every room is uniquely decorated at this hotel—and we don't mean with a different color of chintz. The list of imaginative theme rooms includes the Cave Man Room, which is carved out of stone.

San Luis Obispo is home to the Central Coast campus of **California Polytechnic State University** ("Calpoly"), at the north end of Grand Avenue, and is a pleasant mix of college town and historic California. You can take a campus walking tour (805-756-5734; www.calpoly.edu/visitors), visit the city's historical sights, including **Mission San Luis Obispo de Tolosa** at 751 Palm Street (805-781-8220; www.missionsanluisobispo.org), or pick up some of the local bounty at the Thursday night farmers' market, held downtown (www.downtownslo.com/farmers.html). Stop by the Chamber of Commerce Visitor Center at 1039 Chorro Street (805-781-2670; www.visitslo.com) for maps and complete information on local sights and celebrations.

Take Los Osos Valley Road west through Los Osos and you'll come to the beautiful 8,000-acre **Montaña de Oro State Park** (805-528-0513, 805-772-7434, www.parks.ca.gov), with its rugged coastal beaches, large eucalyptus groves, and miles of hiking, biking, and horseback-riding trails. Check in at the park headquarters in the old Spooner Ranch House just above Spooner's Cove for information about camping, nature walks, and other park activities.

Morro Bay

If you take scenic Highway out of San Luis Obispo, you'll soon find yourself in Morro Bay, a beautiful little town by the sea. The waters of Estero Bay lap at the shore, providing more than 2,000 acres of mudflats, eelgrass beds, tidal wetlands, and open water. As you might imagine, the birding is excellent here, and there are plenty of opportunities for kayaking, fishing, surfing, and boating.

Morro Rock, a volcanic remnant that towers more than 575 feet (175 meters) above the bay, looms over the harbor and is a wildlife preserve and home to nesting peregrine falcons. If you watch the waters at the base of the rock, you may get your first glimpse of some delightful Central Coast characters, the California sea otters—so bring your binoculars and camera.

On Main Street on the south side of the city is **Morro Bay State Park** (805-772-2560), which includes a great blue heron rookery, a Museum of Natural History (805-772-2694), and plenty of opportunities for birding (pick up a birding guide at the museum), hiking, and camping.

If roughing it isn't your idea of a good time, consider a stay at **The Inn at Morro Bay** (60 State Park Road; 805-772-5651, 800-321-9566; www.innatmorrobay.com), a Cape Cod–style inn overlooking the bay at the park's entrance (and right across the street from a golf course).

Even if you're not into birding, you'll find plenty to do in Morro Bay, from watching the fishing boats come in to browsing the unique shops on the Embarcadero to lingering over some delicious seafood at one of the local restaurants. In October the dockside Harbor Festival is a great excuse for a weekend getaway.

Contact the Morro Bay Chamber of Commerce, 845 Embarcadero, #D (805-772-4467, 800-231-0592; www.morrobay.org) for complete information on things to do, local festivals, and lodging and dining options.

Cambria

Once you've had your fill of Morro Bay, continue up Highway 1 to the little village of **Cambria,** a great getaway spot for Santa Barbarans (it's a little more than two hours from home) and beginning to catch on with L.A. residents as well.

This is too bad in a way, for sleepy little Cambria used to be a true respite from the world; now it's crowded on weekends, and you can scarcely get a room reservation unless you call weeks ahead. This situation does little to deter Cambria lovers, however, so plan ahead if you want to spend the weekend.

Lodging choices on Moonstone Beach Drive will put you across the street from the beach and just a few steps from a romantic evening stroll at sunset, but you'll pay less for a room in town. Also, although fog may blanket the coast in winter and early spring, you'll save money by visiting in the off-season. Besides its

appealing shops and art galleries, Cambria has some excellent restaurants, including the eclectic **Robin's,** 4095 Burton Drive (805-927-5007; www.robinsrestaurant.com), with a wonderful international menu; **The Brambles Dinner House,** 4005 Burton Drive (805-927-4716; www.bramblesdinnerhouse.com), an award-winning restaurant that offers steak, seafood, and prime rib; and **The Sow's Ear Cafe,** 2248 Main Street (805-927-4865; www.the sowsear.com), touting a menu of "American country and contemporary cuisine."

Just a few miles up the coast from Cambria is **San Simeon,** home of William Randolph Hearst's lavish castle on the hill. Now one of the most popular tourist attractions in California, **Hearst Castle** (www.hearstcastle .org) (its official name is La Cuesta Encantada, "The Enchanted Hill") is now a State Historical Monument overseen by the California State Parks system.

It took almost 28 years to build Hearst's magnificent estate, which has 165 rooms and 127 acres of gardens, terraces, pools, and walkways. Spanish and Italian antiques fill the rooms, and the pure opulence of the place is staggering.

Except for marveling at the sheer size of the thing as you gaze up from Highway 1, you can't get near the castle without a ticket for one of the tours. Four daytime tours are offered daily beginning at 8:20 a.m., with the last tour scheduled for about 3:20 p.m. Each tour focuses on different areas of the castle, but first-time visitors usually choose The Experience Tour, which includes the main

i For a real National Geographic experience, stop by the Piedras Blancas elephant seal rookery along scenic Highway 1, the Pacific Coast Highway. About 8,000 seals come here to mate, molt, and give birth on the beach 4.4 miles (7.1 kilometers) north of Hearst Castle and 11.7 miles (18.9 kilometers) north of Cambria. For more information and maps, visit www.elephantseal.org, or call (805) 924-1628.

We're Off to the Spa . . .

For centuries, vacationers have "taken to the waters." The crisp oceanic air and the salty waters promised healing effects to those who partook. This demand for "a cure" from daily stressors soon evolved into European indoor wellness centers and spas. As with most European trends, it didn't take long for the trend to make a transatlantic crossing, and, in this case, a transcontinental one, to Santa Barbara. In the last 10 years, there has been an explosion of new spas in Santa Barbara, so much so that there are far too many to list. Here's a sample of our Insiders' favorites.

Avia Spa
350 Chapala Street, Santa Barbara
(805) 703-7303
www.aviaspa.com
The minute you walk through the door, you transcend into another place, a place that's reminiscent of Bali. This East/West sanctuary is no ordinary spa, with its thatched roofed treatment rooms, bamboo fountains, and a lounge that serves organic teas. While waiting for your spa specialist, which is never more than a few minutes, you can catnap on the teak loungers and listen to the sound of the flowing fountain. Let yourself be talked into the Myofascial Release, a therapeutic stretching treatment with relaxation effects that last for over a week. The Hawaiian-inspired Lomi Lomi Massage rocks you like a gentle wave; for those seeking decadence, there's the Buddha-ful package. Facials, waxes, herbal wraps, and salon services are all available at this delightfully perfect full-service spa. This is truly one of our favorites.

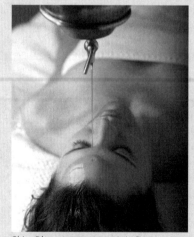

Shiro Dhara treatment at Avia Spa. TYSON ELLIS, COURTESY OF AVIA SPA

Cielo Spa Boutique
1725 State Street C, Santa Barbara
(805) 687–8979
www.cielospasb.com
Cielo means "heaven" in Spanish, and you'll sure get a taste of it at this quaint spa and boutique. Owner and masseuse Roxanne Zbinden seems to understand best how to relax mothers, being a mother of three young children herself. The boutique is filled with artistic creations including handmade bibs and diaper bags and the pure organic line of Aromababy products. (This is the perfect place to buy that baby shower gift.) Don't miss out on the signature Champagne Facial and Body Treat, which uses the yeast of the Pinot Noir grape

to regenerate and boost your body. Had a little too much of the California sun? The Rose Quartz Facial and Body Treatment will soothe the burn.

Crimson Day Spa and Boutique
31 Parker Way, Santa Barbara
(805) 563-7546

Tucked away on a little street is a spa whose presence is not to be overlooked. Crimson's decor and staff (which has to be the nicest spa staff in town) make you feel immediately relaxed. Sink into the comfy couch while waiting, or peruse the boutique and discover owner Jeanine Guerra's passion for the organic. Yoga wear and soaps are just a few of the things artfully displayed. The Parisien-line Yonka is her product of choice, a plant-based product that matches Guerra's refined tastes for quality and aromatherapy. A house specialty is the detoxifying Warm Seaweed Wrap, a treatment "no person should do without," declares Guerra.

Peaches Skin Care
104 West Mission Street, Santa Barbara
(805) 563-9796
www.peachesskincare.com

The first thing you smell when you walk into this quaint upstairs spa is—you guessed it—peaches. The artistically designed spa hails the ambience of yesteryear, right down to owner Nicole Jordan McGinnis's Lucille Ball–type head wrap. (Perhaps the spa's stagelike appearance is due to the influence of Nicole's theatrical husband, who danced for years on Broadway in *The Lion King*.) The pampering packages of "Come Fly With Me," "Oh Look at Me Now," and "The Good Life" leave you with a peaches-and-cream glow that will make you come back begging for more. Nicole is a strong proponent of oxygen facials, so strong that she adds oxygen to each one of her facial treatments. This is an experience not to be missed. After the massage, waxing, facial, or other spa treatment, Nicole offers a glass of blueberry-infused antioxidant water that tops off the experience in a most refreshing way.

The Spa
Chumash Casino
3400 East Highway 246, Santa Ynez
(800) 248-6274, ext. 1755
www.chumashcasino.com

Voted "Best Spa of the Valley" by *Santa Ynez Valley News'* readers, the Chumash Spa is always a winner. If you're tired of the Chardonnay and ready for the bubbly, then bathe in the afterglow of the Champagne Salt Scrub Wrap, a treatment that includes Pinot Noir grape yeast. Looking for something a little more homegrown? Then taste the fruits of the Santa Ynez Baked Apple. Well, not literally taste, but try this exfoliation treatment that combines the natural acidic properties of apple with sugar and cinnamon.

The Spa
Four Seasons Resort The Biltmore Santa Barbara
1260 Channel Drive, Montecito
(805) 969-2261
www.fourseasons.com/santabarbara

It's difficult to decide which offers more tranquility—the spacious and luxuriously appointed massage rooms, with fireplaces, bathtubs, and rain showers, or the meditative rose garden and Pacific Ocean the rooms overlook. The $30 million renovation of The Spa (and the $100 million-plus renovation of the rest of this property) makes it a serious contender for one of the finest spas in the world. At The Spa, no lavish stone has been left unturned by the artful Ty Warner and his design group. Chilled towels await you at every turn. There are private locker rooms with punch-in codes, so you're not left fumbling with a key. You can stuff your swimsuit into a locker bag designed for wet clothes after you've dipped into the mineral water pool set to a tepid 94° Fahrenheit (34° Celcius). Still a little too cold? Then dip into the 104° Fahrenheit (40° Celcius) pool. (We're not even going to mention the now-patented iridescent tiles that Warner had designed so the pools would shimmer.) If you think a spa is a spa is a spa, then you will be pleasantly pleased with this one.

Spa de Menicucci
Fess Parker's DoubleTree Resort
633 East Cabrillo Blvd., Santa Barbara
(805) 564-4333
www.fpdtr.com

Currently undergoing a remodel led by the indefatigable Julie Menicucci, director of spa remodels around town, Fess Parker's new four-room facility spa will host intimate, beautifully appointed rooms different from the "big hotel" type of spa. Designed to help you decompress, the new outdoor waiting patio (an indoors waiting room will also be available) will allow you to sip a glass of Chardonnay while soaking your feet in a hot bath. If you desire a day away, you'll be able to indulge in the Boreh Wrap Package ($395), a three-hour special consisting of a gentle buffing and polishing of your skin with a delightfully scintillating mix of cloves, cinnamon, and ground rice scrub, a scalp treatment, foot reflexology, and face and neck massage. The pampering tops off with a 60-minute European facial.

house and gardens, the Assembly Room, the Refectory, the Morning Room, the Billiard Room, and the Theater featuring the film *Hearst Castle—Building the Dream*.

Tours last just over two hours, and each requires a 1/2-mile (1-kilometer) walk and climbing 150 to 400 stairs, depending on the tour you choose. Special evening tour times vary. Reservations are strongly recommended and can be made by calling (800) 444-4445 (major credit cards are accepted). You can also make reservations online—just visit

> **i** The ladies and many of the gents of Santa Barbara know that for an in-and-out manicure or pedicure (for nearly half the price), nothing beats Tina's Nail Salon (201 South Milpas Street, #103; (805) 730–1023). You don't even need to make an appointment, although appointments are recommended. It's such a local secret that we feel like a traitor even talking about it.

www.hearstcastle.org and click on "Tours." You can also buy tickets at the Hearst Castle ticket office when you arrive, but you'll be lucky to find a vacancy. Some of the tours sell out months in advance.

Prices range from $20 to $30 for adults and $10 to $15 for children ages 6 through 17. Children 5 and younger are admitted free. Wheelchair-accessible tours may be arranged by calling (805) 927-2115 or (800) 444-4445. For more information on Hearst Castle, as well as directions and a map, see www.hearst castle.org.

HEADING SOUTH

Ojai

Ever heard of the 1930s film *Lost Horizon*? Well, if you have, you can be in Shangri-la within 45 minutes of leaving downtown Santa Barbara. The famous movie was filmed in Ojai (pronounced OH-hi), a lush valley surrounded by vast groves of orange trees, the majestic Topa Topa Mountains, and millions of acres of Los Padres National Forest lands. It's one of the most scenic spots in all of California (besides Santa Barbara, of course) and an ideal destination for a day trip.

Ojai resembles Palm Springs in some ways: It's a resort town (population 7,800) where you can golf on championship courses, pamper yourself with an enticing array of spa treatments, and shop for quality artwork and antiques. But it's also a Shangri-la for artists and for outdoor-recreation and nature lovers. You can hike along hundreds of miles of trails

and go mountain biking, horseback riding, boating, fishing, and camping. Ojai is home to a number of unique centers of philosophy and spirituality—in fact, it's a New Age capital of sorts.

To get to Ojai, just drive south from Santa Barbara about 12 miles to Carpinteria. At the Ventura/Santa Barbara County line, you'll see an exit for Highway 150. If the road is open (mudslides sometimes close this scenic country road during the winter months), you can take it all the way to Ojai, about 20 miles (32 kilometers) to the southeast (just follow the signs).

Call the Ventura CalTrans office at (213) 897-3656 before setting out to find out whether the road is open. If it's not, you need to drive another 20 or so miles to Ventura, then take the Highway 33 exit and head up to the mountains for 11 miles (18 kilometers). Along the way you pass through a few small towns: Casitas Springs, Oak View, and Mira Monte. The road forks just a mile or two before downtown Ojai. Just keep heading east. The road will become a combination of Highway 33 and Highway 150 for a while.

Just before you reach downtown Ojai, you'll come to another major intersection: the "Y." This is where Highway 33 turns to continue its trek over the mountains to the northwest. To reach downtown, though, you should veer right and stay on Highway 150 heading east. First, we recommend you stop in at the **Ojai Valley Chamber of Commerce,** at 201 South Signal (805-646-8126; www.ojai chamber.org), where you'll find maps and tons of information on accommodations, restaurants, special events, things to see and do, shopping, and art galleries.

It's fun to walk around the small, quaint town of Ojai. Many people drive hundreds of miles just to poke around the galleries and antiques shops, which are said to be among the best in Southern California. Ceramicists know Ojai as the home of the now-deceased bohemian artist, craftsperson, and writer Beatrice Wood. Visit the incredibly art-worthy **Beatrice Wood Center for the Arts** at 8560

Ojai-Santa Paula Road (805-646-3381; www .beatricewood.com). It's open Friday, Saturday, and Sunday from 11:00 a.m. to 5:00 p.m. and by appointment. For information on local artists and events, contact Ojai Studio Artists (www .ojaistudio artists.com). Be sure to browse at **Bart's Books,** which sets out more than 100,000 used books on tree-shaded patios. You'll find it 1 block north of Ojai Avenue on the corner of Cañada and Matilija Streets (805-646-3755). Bart's is closed Monday.

The **Ojai Valley Museum,** 130 West Ojai Avenue (805-640-1390; www.ojaivalley museum.org), is a fun place to explore if you're interested in finding out about the colorful local history. Admission is $3 for adults and $1 for children 6 to 18. Children under 6 are free. Hours are 1:00 to 4:00 p.m. Monday through Thursday and 10:00 a.m. to 4:00 p.m. on Saturdays. Guided tours are available on Wednesdays.

It's easy to get around Ojai—just hop aboard the air-conditioned, wheelchair-accessible **Ojai Trolley Service,** which traverses the valley's main strip Monday through Friday from 7:08 a.m. to 5:53 p.m., and Saturday and Sunday from 9:08 a.m. to 4:53 p.m. The one-hour town ride costs only 25 cents, and if you're 65 or older or younger than 2, you ride free. The trolley stops near most of the hotels, motels, restaurants, and shops. Note that it does not operate on major holidays.

Ojai offers a jam-packed year-round calendar of events, and many visitors arrange their visits to coincide with them. A few major events include the **Ojai Music Festival** (www.ojaifestival.org), a renowned series of classical music concerts that usually takes place over three days at the end of May or the beginning of June; the **Ojai Wine Festival** (www.ojaiwinefestival.com), an afternoon in early June that you can spend tasting wines, sampling cuisine from Ojai Valley restaurants, and browsing through displays of works by local and regional artists and artisans; and the **Ojai Shakespeare Festival** (805-646-9455; www.ojai shakespeare.org), which takes place in August.

Fifteen-acre **Libbey Park,** in the center of town, is the site of many special events. The park includes the Libbey Bowl (where most performances take place), picnic areas, tennis courts, and a playground.

If you've come to Ojai to enjoy the great outdoors, you have many options. The scenic, 9-mile (14.5-kilometer) **Ojai Valley Trail** has wide pathways for horseback riding, biking, walking, and jogging. It links Ventura's Foster Park (7 miles [11 kilometers] north of Ventura near Casitas Springs) to Ojai's Soule Park, at the eastern edge of town, so you can park your car at Foster Park and ride your bike to Ojai, if you wish. Dogs are allowed on leashes only. Ask for a trail map at the Chamber of Commerce. You can rent bikes at **Bicycles of Ojai,** 108 Cañada Street (805-646-7736).

Hiking in the mountains near Ojai can be sheer bliss—the vistas from the peaks over the valley, ocean, and islands below are spectacular. At the **Ojai Ranger Station,** 1190 East Ojai Avenue (805-646-4348), you can pick up free maps of dozens of backcountry hiking and mountain-bike trails in the Los Padres National Forest. Note that the ranger station is closed on weekends. To make camping reservations, call (877) 444-6777, or visit www.reserveusa .com.

Adventure Passes are required if you want to park in the Los Padres National Forest. You can purchase them at the ranger station. A day pass costs $5; an annual pass is $30.

Horses and equestrian trails abound in Ojai. **Western Trail Riding** (805-640-8635) offers guided trail rides for one or two people (maximum) and lessons, and **Ojai Valley Inn's Ranch and Stables** offers guided trail rides, western riding lessons, pony rides, and western hoedowns. Call (805) 646-1111, or contact www.ojairesort.com for information.

Hoping for a few hours trolling for trout in a beautiful lake? Head for the **Lake Casitas Recreation Area,** 11311 Santa Ana Road, just 5 miles (8 kilometers) southwest of Ojai. In 1984 the Olympic rowing and canoeing events were held here. You can rent boats (805-649-2233, 805-649-1122 for reservations; www.lakecasitas.info) and fish for bass, catfish, trout, and crappie from sunrise to sunset.

If golf is your game, you can tee off at the legendary par-70 PGA course at the **Ojai Valley Inn & Spa,** 905 Country Club Road (805-646-1111; 888-697-8780; www.ojairesort .com), or the **Soule Park Golf Course,** an 18-hole, par-72 public course at 1033 East Ojai Avenue (805-646-5633; www.soulepark.com).

Ojai is where Insiders go for an ultimate pampering experience—for a birthday, wedding, or anniversary treat, or just for a massive dose of R&R. The most exclusive, Five Diamond spa is the **Spa Ojai,** at the Ojai Valley Inn & Spa, 905 Country Club Road (805-646-1111, 888-697-8780; www.ojairesort.com).

Rated as one of the best spas in the country, Spa Ojai offers innovative treatments and programs for creativity, self- discovery, and fitness. Step inside and you'll find 28 treatment areas (some with fireplaces), a cardiovascular fitness center, a weight room, a pool, an art studio, and a hair and nail salon. Take your pick of massages, body treatments, facials, and fitness programs in an elegant setting.

Another famous spot is **The Oaks at Ojai,** a residential health spa where you can check in to lose pounds and inches and indulge in facials, body scrubs, and paraffin treatments. It was voted one of *Travel & Leisure*'s "10 Best Destination Spas." It's at 122 East Ojai Avenue (800-753-6257; www.oaksspa.com).

Anyone interested in philosophy and spiritual traditions may want to check out a couple of renowned centers located here. The **Krishnamurti Library,** at 1070 McAndrew Road (805-646-4948; www.kfa.org), has a comprehensive collection of the writings and tapes of philosopher J. Krishnamurti. Open Wednesday through Saturday 1:00 to 5:00 p.m. Closed Mondays and Tuesdays.

The **Krotona Institute of Theosophy,** at 46 Krotona Hill (Highway 33 at Hermosa Road; 805-646-2653), includes a library, bookstore, and school of theosophy. The public is invited to check out the institute's beautiful grounds—a 115-acre wooded estate with Spanish-style buildings, lily ponds, and magnificent views. The Krotona Institute is open daily; call for hours.

For one of the most beautiful views in the valley, visit **Meditation Mount,** at 10340 Reeves Road (805-646-5508; www.meditation .com), home to Meditation Groups Inc., a nonprofit organization dedicated to improving life on this planet for everyone through meditation. You are invited to stop by the complex and meditation room between 10:00 a.m. and sunset daily.

Another popular visitor site is the **Old Creek Ranch Winery,** 10024 Old Creek Road in Oak View (805-649-4132; www.oldcreek ranch.com), which offers wine tasting Saturday and Sunday from 11:00 a.m. to 5:00 p.m.

Where to Eat in Ojai

If all the beautiful scenery, spirituality, and spa treatments make you hungry, Ojai has a great selection of restaurants that range from the ultimate gourmet experience to excellent taco stands and pizza parlors. You can pick up a detailed restaurant list from the Chamber of Commerce.

The area's most famous restaurant is **The Ranch House,** on South Lomita Street (805-646-2360; www.theranchhouse.com), which offers gourmet dining in a gorgeous garden setting with meandering streams. It's open for dinner Tuesday through Sunday and for brunch on Sunday (closed Monday).

Another famous gourmet spot is **Suzanne's Cuisine,** at 502 West Ojai Avenue (805-640-1961; www.suzannescuisine.com). Suzanne's is open for lunch and dinner every day except Tuesday.

A more casual local's favorite is **Boccali's Restaurant** at 3277 Ojai-Santa Paula Road (805-646-6116; www.boccalis.com). The owners use fresh-picked produce from their nearby ranch for the pizza and pasta dishes. On a warm day, the oak-shaded outdoor patio is a serene spot to sit and gaze out over the orchards. Boccali's is open every day for dinner and Wednesday through Sunday for lunch.

Now that the Ojai Valley Inn & Spa, at 905 Country Club Road (805-646-1111, 888-697-8780; www.ojairesort.com), has become the place to be, so has its dining venues. **Jimmy's Pub** hosts a casual atmosphere with a wood-burning brick pizza oven and a myriad of draft beers and Central Coast wine offerings. It's open daily from 11:00 a.m. to 1:00 p.m. **Maravilla,** the inn's upscale award-winning restaurant, highlights the region's fresh foods. Marvilla is open Wednesday through Sunday from 6:00 to 10:00 p.m.

Where to Stay in Ojai

Although you can easily return to Santa Barbara (it's just 45 minutes away), you might be tempted to overnight in Shangri-la. For accommodation arrangements, contact the **Ojai Valley Chamber of Commerce** (805-646-8126; www.ojaichamber.org) for an Ojai Valley area accommodations guide.

If you're looking for a luxurious resort, you can't go wrong by choosing Ojai's most famous hotel: the **Ojai Valley Inn & Spa**, 905 Country Club Road (805-646-1111, 888-697-8780; www.ojairesort.com). It's a full-service, 220-acre luxury resort with spectacular views, 304 deluxe guest rooms and suites, an 18-hole championship golf course (site of many Senior PGA events), and two heated swimming pools, including a 60-foot (18-meter) lap pool.

The inn offers tons of activities—horseback riding, tennis, swimming, hiking, biking, and jeep tours—along with a children's program, a golf academy, and a fitness center. The Spa Ojai (see spa description above) has a huge range of services. Call for rates.

Slightly more affordable is **The Oaks at Ojai,** 122 East Ojai Avenue (800-753-6257; www.oaksspa.com), a resident fitness spa. It has 46 rooms, including cottages and a main lodge plus a pool. It also offers massages, facials, and a hair and nail salon.

For a bed-and-breakfast experience, try the **Theodore Woolsey House,** 1484 East Ojai Avenue (805-646-9779; www.theodore woolseyhouse.com), a historic bed-and-

breakfast inn on a seven-acre estate in a peaceful, secluded setting. Room rates start at $85 and go up to $175 per night.

The **Blue Iguana Inn** is an affordable, artsy place to hang your hat and explore. This Southwestern-style villa is right on Highway 33 at 11794 North Ventura Avenue (805-646-5277; www.blueiguanainn.com), 2 miles (3.2 kilometers) west of downtown Ojai. It has single rooms, one- and two-bedroom suites, and two-bedroom bungalows. Room rates start at $99 and go up to $229 for a two-bedroom bungalow.

Los Angeles

We Santa Barbarans hate to admit it, but Los Angeles does have some attractions well worth getting in the car and driving two hours for. Where else in Southern California can you find such a high concentration of world-class museums, concerts, and performances? Los Angeles County—a huge metropolitan area with nearly 10 million people—is just 90 miles (145 kilometers) south of Santa Barbara on U.S. 101. There's so much to see and do there, we can't possibly tell you about everything, but we'll point out some sources of general information and highlight our favorite places to visit. We'll also give you pointers about when and how to travel to L.A.—the freeways can be confusing, not to mention super-crowded.

If you want to find out what's happening in the Los Angeles area, be sure to pick up a copy of the Sunday *Los Angeles Times,* available at newsstands and supermarkets around Santa Barbara County. The weekly "Calendar" section gives detailed information on current

---

i The Santa Barbara Airbus arranges a regular schedule of day trips to popular L.A.-area destinations, for instance, the Getty Center, Dodger games, and the Los Angeles County Museum of Art. Call (805) 964-7759 or (800) 423-1618, or visit www.sbairbus.com for fares and schedules.

performance and exhibition schedules for art, music, theater, dance, theme parks, and much more. Listings include information on where and how to purchase tickets.

For general tourist information on the greater Los Angeles region, contact the Los Angeles Convention and Visitors Bureau, 333 South Hope Street, 18th Floor, Los Angeles; (213) 624-7300 or (800) 228-2452; www.lacvb .com. They'll send you an information packet with suggestions for entertainment, lodging, dining, special events, and more. If you're already in L.A., stop by the visitor information centers in downtown Los Angeles, 685 South Figueroa Street, (213) 689-8822; or in Hollywood, 6541 Hollywood Boulevard, (213) 689-8822.

Getting There

To get to Los Angeles from Santa Barbara, just drive south on U.S. 101, which becomes the Ventura Freeway as soon as you cross the southern Santa Barbara County line. Drive for 90 miles (145 kilometers), and you'll be at the edge of the city of Los Angeles. From there, you have a mind-boggling array of freeway choices, depending on where you're going. We suggest you purchase a good map of the Los Angeles–area freeway system before heading south—they're available at most gas stations and convenience stores.

If you're going to the Westwood–Beverly Hills–Los Angeles Airport region, take Interstate 405 south. If you're heading for downtown Los Angeles or Hollywood, just continue on U.S. 101 until you see signs for the Hollywood Freeway, then go south (it will still be U.S. 101).

If you have time and would like to follow a less stressful, scenic route to the city, you can take Highway 1, the Pacific Coast Highway (PCH), which follows the coastline through Malibu. Watch for the Highway 1 signs as you enter Oxnard, about 40 miles (64.5 kilometers) south of Santa Barbara. The highway winds through the city of Oxnard until it reaches the coast. Follow the road all the way to Santa Monica, where you'll take U.S. High-

i Enjoy over 30 Los Angeles attractions for much less with the L.A. All Access Pass. Call the Los Angeles Convention and Visitors Bureau at (213) 624-7300 or (800) 228-2452, or visit the Web site at www.seemyla.com. Adult passes are $109, and children 12 and under are $89. The pass includes up to three visits at each attraction.

way 10 east to reach I-405, Beverly Hills, and downtown Los Angeles.

We Insiders carefully plan our departures to and from Los Angeles. Most of us hate sitting in bumper-to-bumper traffic and heavy congestion, which is pretty much a given during rush hours and a possibility at any time of day or evening because of freeway construction, accidents, and other factors.

On weekdays, it's best to leave Santa Barbara either very early in the morning (5:00 a.m.) or wait until about 8:30 a.m. When returning to Santa Barbara, it's best to get back on the freeway before 2:00 p.m. or to have dinner and wait until 7:00 or 8:00 p.m. Otherwise, you're risking a severe bout of frustration while stuck in gridlock and traffic that moves at a snail's pace. Another alternative is to make it to Highway 1 on the coast before 3:00 p.m., then head back north. Weekend traffic can be worse—especially in the summer months when you should avoid, for the sake of your own sanity, traveling southbound from Santa Barbara on a Sunday afternoon. But you never know when or if you'll run into traffic, so always leave plenty of time to arrive at your destination.

Unfortunately, Los Angeles is a car-oriented city, and public transportation pales in comparison with systems in other cities its size. But from Santa Barbara you can take an Amtrak train to historic Union Station in downtown Los Angeles (800-872-7245; www.amtrak.com)—there are about six trains every day.

Once you arrive, you can walk around or hop on the Metro Red Line, which makes three stops on its way through downtown to

MacArthur Park. The Metro Blue and Red Lines will take you to Long Beach and to Redondo Beach and eastern suburbs, respectively, but they don't really stop close to many major tourist attractions. For more information, contact the Metropolitan Transportation Authority (800-COMMUTE; www.mta.net).

i Avoid the freeways Friday afternoons and any afternoon preceding a major holiday. Also, U.S. 101 is nearly always packed with visitors headed for L.A. on Sunday afternoons, so try and avoid the southbound lanes.

Things to See and Do

Among all the things to see and do in Los Angeles, here's a rundown of our favorite museums and attractions.

Los Angeles boasts excellent museums, and many are situated on Museum Row on Wilshire Boulevard, between I-405 and downtown Los Angeles.

The **Los Angeles County Museum of Art**, 5905 Wilshire Boulevard (323-857-6000; www.lacma.org), has more than 100,000 works of art and is one of the largest art museums in the country. It features impressive permanent collections, special exhibitions, lectures, films, and concerts. The museum is closed Wednesday.

The **Natural History Museum of Los Angeles County,** 900 Exposition Boulevard (213-763-3466; www.nhm.org), is a great place to see dinosaurs, fossils, gems, minerals, animal exhibits, and pre-Columbian artifacts. Open Monday through Friday 9:30 a.m. to 5:00 p.m. and Saturday and Sunday 10:00 a.m. to 5:00 p.m.

Another fascinating museum focusing on natural history is the **George C. Page Museum of La Brea Discoveries,** on Museum Row at 5801 Wilshire Boulevard (323-934-7243; www.tarpits.org). This museum houses prehistoric fossils recovered from the La Brea Tar Pits, the world's richest source of Ice Age mammal and bird fossils. You can view some of the pits up-

close and personal (from behind a fence, of course).

We think that if everyone visited the **Museum of Tolerance,** war would disappear from the planet. Conveniently situated at 9786 West Pico Boulevard, on the corner of Pico and Roxbury Drives, just south of Beverly Hills, this high-tech, hands-on experiential museum focuses on two themes through interactive exhibits: the dynamics of racism and prejudice in America and the history of the Holocaust.

Although the themes of this museum may sound depressing, parts of it are actually very uplifting, as they focus on courageous acts of people fighting against intolerance. It's an eye-opening experience for anyone 8 and older. (Younger children are welcome, but they probably won't absorb the full impact of the exhibits.)

The museum is closed Saturday and on major Jewish holidays. Call (310) 553-8403 for information, or visit www.museumoftolerance.com. Advanced reservations are recommended.

The fabulous **Getty Center** sits on a hill overlooking Brentwood, Beverly Hills, and the sprawling city of Los Angeles. It includes the J. Paul Getty Museum plus a host of organizations funded by the J. Paul Getty Trust. Take a tram ride to the summit, then visit the museum, which consists of five two-story pavilions housing the permanent collection.

The museum presents an awesome collection of Western art from the Middle Ages to the present.

The Getty Center, at 1200 Getty Center Drive, opened in early 1998 and has been absolutely packed with people ever since. To get there, take U.S. 101 to I-405, then head south just a few miles and exit at Getty Center Drive. The museum is closed Monday and major holidays.

Admission is free, but you do have to make a reservation for parking and pay an $8 parking fee. If you arrive by taxi, bus, motorcycle, or bicycle, you don't need a reservation, but you may not be admitted due to site capacity restrictions. Parking on surrounding streets is restricted— residents of this posh neighborhood do not enjoy having the public hanging about near their properties. To make a parking reservation or for more information, call (310) 440-7300 or visit www.getty.edu.

Museums appeal to our intellectual sides. Now we'll tell you about the Los Angeles attractions that provide high-charged entertainment for visitors of all ages who just want to have some fun.

We start off with what is probably the main attraction in all of Southern California—**Disneyland** (www.disneyland.com). If you have children and they discover Santa Barbara is just two and a half hours from the Magic Kingdom in Anaheim, they'll probably never forgive you if you don't make the effort to take them there—especially now that Disneyland's new neighbor, **California Adventure,** has opened its doors. Launched in February 2001, this new Disney venture boasts a bevy of adrenaline-pumping attractions, like Soarin' Over California, which gives riders the sensation of hang-gliding over forests, mountains, and oceans, and the California Screamin', a knuckle-clenching roller-coaster ordeal. You'll also find plenty of opportunities to experience the glamorous world of the silver screen.

Both Disneyland and California Adventure are open daily. Admission for a day at one of these parks (which includes all the rides) is $63 for adults and children ages 10 and older, and $55 for children ages 3 through 9. Children younger than 3 get in free. If you want to visit both parks, you have to buy a one-day Park Hopper Ticket, which will set you back $83 for adults and children ages 10 and older, and $73 for children ages 3 through 9. Call (714) 781-4565, or visit www.disneyland.com for hours and all other information.

To get to the parks, take U.S. 101 south to Interstate 5 and continue south. Exit at Harbor Boulevard and go southwest (just follow the signs to the parks).

Although you could conceivably drive to one of the parks, spend the day, then head back to Santa Barbara, it would be an exhausting enterprise. It's easier to stay at the **Disneyland Hotel, Disney's Grand Californian Hotel & Spa,** or **Disney's Paradise Pier Hotel,** right next to the parks. The hotel rates are not cheap, but you can't beat the convenience. Check out online reservations at www.disneyland.com for package prices. Drive from Santa Barbara the night before, check into the hotel, get up early, ride the monorail to the park, and do Disneyland or California Adventure with as little stress as possible.

For more theme-park fun, head to **Six Flags Magic Mountain** (www.sixflags.com/magicmountain). It's an amusement park with 100 acres of rides, shows, and entertainment, including lots of roller coasters. You'll find it at 26101 Magic Mountain Parkway, off I-5 near Valencia. Admission is $44.99 for adults and $29.99 for children 4 feet tall (1.2 meters) and shorter. Children 2 and younger are free. Call (661) 255-4100, or visit www.sixflags.com/magicmountain for hours.

Next door to Magic Mountain is **Six Flags Hurricane Harbor Water Park.** It's a pirate's dream come true: lagoons, ruins, and more than 20 water slides. Younger children will like Castaway Cove, which has waterfalls and slides perfectly sized for little ones. Admission is $29.99 for adults and $20.99 for children 4 feet (1.2 meters) tall and shorter. Children 2 and younger are free. Visit www.sixflags.com/parks/hurricaneharborla for hours and information. A Magic Mountain Hurricane Harbor Two-Park Combo is $69.99

At **Universal Studios Hollywood,** you can take a thrilling tour through the 420-acre Universal Studios complex—the largest TV and film studio in the world. The tour lasts five to seven hours, so plan on a full day. Go behind famous movie scenes, ride through Jurassic Park, meet King Kong, and watch a Flintstones show. Call (818) 508-9600, or visit www.universalstudios.com for more information. Universal Studios is located just off U.S. 101; either the Universal Center Drive exit or the Lankershim Boulevard exit.

ANNUAL EVENTS

Santa Barbara loves a party. Really. No matter what month of the year, you'll find enough galas, fund-raisers, benefits, ethnic festivals, and celebrations to keep you busy every weekend. Luckily, the local press does a great job of publishing calendar listings, so you can look ahead and pick and choose events that appeal to you.

As you glance through our list, you'll notice that many events are related to the local agricultural bounty. For example, there's the International Orchid Show (March), the Lompoc Flower Festival (July), the California Lemon Festival (October), the California Avocado Festival (also in October), and a host of festivals and parties celebrating the local wine-making industry.

A colorful lineup of ethnic festivals also graces the list. Many of these have become Santa Barbara perennial favorites mostly because they are fun, free, offer fabulous food, and have a delightful international flavor. Many of the fund-raisers involving wine and wine tasting are expensive. Although you might think $50 is a bit steep for a few hours of sipping wine and eating hors d'oeuvres, these events are extremely popular with Santa Barbarans, and nobody minds the cost because the money goes to worthy causes (besides, you can fill up on excellent wine and hors d'oeuvres). If you can't afford fancy wine dinners, you'll find plenty of events to attend that are inexpensive and even free. In addition to the ethnic and agricultural festivals noted above, many family-oriented events offer free admission.

i For a list of upcoming festivals and events, visit the Santa Barbara Chamber of Commerce Web site at www.sbchamber.org/calendar_select.php and click on the Calendar of Events link.

In general, casual dress is acceptable everywhere unless you're attending a fancy "gala" of some sort. If you have any questions about what to wear or are concerned about any aspect of the event, by all means call and ask.

The following listings are in alphabetical order under each month. Unless indicated otherwise, admission to all events is free (although you'll probably have to pay for food and maybe some activities). Prices listed are correct as we go to press, but they have a tendency to creep up from year to year. The events that cost are always worth the money. Enjoy!

JANUARY

Airsports Hang Gliding and Paragliding Festival
South side of Elings Park
Cliff Drive, Santa Barbara
(805) 965-3733
www.flyaboveall.com/newyear1.htm
If you're not into football, spend a pleasant New Year's Day afternoon observing experienced hang glider and paraglider pilots maneuver their crafts down one of the oldest training hills in the country. This is a grassroots, low-key, no-frills festival. No rides are given to the uninitiated.

For the best viewing, enter the park at the Cliff Drive entrance located on the north side of Cliff Drive. Bad weather cancels the festival, but if the weather holds, most gliders are launched between noon and 4:00 p.m.

Organizers encourage a donation to the nonprofit Elings Park Foundation.

Santa Barbara International Film Festival
Various locations, Santa Barbara
(805) 963-0023
www.sbfilmfestival.org

Usually held at the end of January and running into February, this local film festival, in its second decade, has received worldwide acclaim for its diverse programming and screenings of more than 200 films from around the world. It has a strong local following, and enthusiastic fans, industry professionals, and celebrity guests take part in an exciting 11 days of screenings and other special events held all over town.

Independent films made in the United States and abroad are screened at local theaters, and workshops and symposiums focusing on films and filmmaking are held at various venues in the city.

A well-known film professional (such as actor Will Smith or director Peter Jackson) is feted each year, and many celebrities come to town to join in the festivities, which include a star-studded opening night. You'll find schedules for all festival events on the Web site and at local hotels; you can also check listings in the local newspapers or call to get on the mailing list.

You can purchase special passes, which allow admission to all festival events, or you can buy single film tickets. Get tickets early for the special events, as they often sell out ahead of time. For details, call or visit the Web site.

FEBRUARY

American Riviera Wine Auction and Dinner
Santa Barbara County Vintners' Association
P.O. Box 1558, Santa Ynez 93460
(805) 688-0881
www.sbcountywines.com
Tux and maybe even tails are definitely in order for this exclusive wine auction that raises funds for the Santa Barbara–based nonprofit Direct Relief International. The multi-course gourmet dinner features celebrity chefs and wines that are perfectly married with the cuisine. Hosted at the ritzy Bacara Resort & Spa, there's always a bidding frenzy for the plethora of auction items. Tickets are between $100 and $200.

Amgen Tour of California
www.tourofcalifornia.com
The world's top international professional cycling teams compete in this 700-mile (1,129-kilometer), eight-day race, which spans the California redwoods to Long Beach. Locals sit on the sidelines and cheer on the cyclists, who travel through Solvang and then on to Santa Barbara.

Harbor Seals Birthing
Carpinteria Bluffs
Bailard exit off Highway 101
In February and March, the harbor seals birth their adorable pups. This is one of only two places along the Southern California coastline that offers public access to the harbor seal colony. Take pictures, ooh and aah, but don't touch them or make loud noises. Barking dogs are especially forbidden, as they can scare off the mother seals, which results in the abandonment of the pups. Harbor seals are federally protected, and any infringement on their colony results in a $10,000 fine.

MARCH

Holistic Living Expo
Sacred Productions
Earl Warren Showgrounds
Highway 101 at Las Positas Road
www.holisticlivingexpo.com
Make an interdimensional shift by attending the Holistic Living Expo. The metaphysical is ever-present in Santa Barbara, no more so than at this unique fair that offers spiritual readings, presentations, workshops, and speakers on healing the mind, body, and soul. Admission is $5 or $8 for two, $3 for seniors and teens. Children are free.

Santa Barbara International Orchid Show
Earl Warren Showgrounds, U.S. Highway 101 and Las Positas, Santa Barbara
(805) 969-5746
www.sborchidshow.com
Santa Barbara produces more orchids than any other region of the country, and local growers introduce their finest blooms at this

three-day event, which is the longest-running orchid show in the state. The show features the largest collection of specimens brought in by more than 50 exhibitors from around the world. Booths are designed around each year's theme, and both commercial and private growers compete for the top awards.

A selection of blooming plants, corsages, supplies, commemorative pins, and limited-edition posters are on sale. In conjunction with the show, many local growers host open houses and greenhouse tours. Admission is $10 for adults; $8 for seniors 65 and older and students with ID; children 12 and under are admitted free. Buying tickets in advance saves you a few dollars.

APRIL

Easter Bunny Express
South Coast Railroad Museum
300 North Los Carneros Road, Goleta
(805) 964-3540
www.goletadepot.org
All aboard at Wabbit-Twacks Station for a trip around the South Coast Railroad museum on a miniature train. Stops at Harvey's House (for a cookie and beverage), Easter Bunnyville (to meet the Easter Bunny and get a surprise), Jack-Rabbit Junction (to enter a drawing), and What's Up Doc (for a souvenir) make for an egg-cellent Easter adventure. Tickets are $4 for adults and children.

Garden Egg Hunt and Children's Festival
Santa Barbara Botanic Garden
1212 Mission Canyon Road, Santa Barbara
(805) 682-4726
www.sbbg.org
It's an eggstravaganza! The garden staff dyes eggs donated by local markets and tucks them into nooks and crannies throughout the expansive grounds. Kids are taken on a nature walk, then turned loose for the egg hunt, which is followed by refreshments and activities. Proceeds go toward the garden's children's programs. The egg hunt takes place the Saturday before Easter. Call for times and ticket prices.

Kids Draw Architecture
Architectural Foundation of Santa Barbara
Mission Rose Garden/Santa Barbara Junior High
(805) 965-6307
www.afsb.org
Two free Saturday sessions offer kids the chance to sketch Santa Barbara's famous landmark buildings. Drawing materials are provided, and architects and artists are on hand to offer their guidance and expertise.

Presidio Days
El Presidio de Santa Barbara
123 East Canon Perdido Street, Santa Barbara
(805) 965-0093
www.sbthp.org
The place where Santa Barbara began celebrates the city's birthday with a reenactment of the founding of the Presidio. Come down and take a look at Santa Barbara as it once was and indulge in its annual birthday cake. Presidio and Chumash descendants usually ring the bells in the bell towers. Multicultural dance and music performances begin the festivities.

Santa Barbara Fair & Expo
Earl Warren Showgrounds
U.S. Highway 101 and Las Positas, Santa Barbara
(805) 687-0766
www.earlwarren.com
Held in April, the city's annual Fair & Expo is five days (usually Wednesday through Sunday) of fun with an old-fashioned county-fair ambience. Exhibits, crafts, art, games, animals, and carnival rides, along with live entertainment and food booths, are the hallmarks of this event.

A special area is dedicated to the younger set, offering puppet shows, jugglers, a petting zoo, and pony rides. Teenagers will enjoy the thrill rides, while smaller kids can find tamer fare at the Kiddie Carnival. A Junior Livestock Auction happens on Saturday afternoon, and there are special exhibits aimed at young adults. Tickets are $5 for adults, $4 for seniors

Santa Barbara Fair & Expo. NANCY SHOBE

55 and older, and $3 for kids 6 through 12. Children 5 and under are admitted free.

Santa Barbara County Vintners Festival
River Park, Lompoc
(805) 688-0881
www.sbcountywines.com
Meet the region's vintners at this dynamic wine-and-dine festival. Wander around and taste delectable samples from local restaurants and catering companies. Local artists display their works, and live music provides the perfect accompaniment. Call for admission prices and tickets.

Santa Barbara Kite Festival
Santa Barbara City College
"Great Meadow"/West Campus Lawn
(805) 682-2895
www.sbkitefest.com
The kite festival has been a tradition in Santa

Barbara for over two decades. Held during National Kite Flying Month, this family affair is filled with high-flying events like tail chase and sports flying.

South Coast Earth Day Festival
Santa Barbara County Courthouse Sunken Gardens
(805) 963-0583
www.communityenvironmentalcouncil.org
In 1969 an oil rig ruptured off the coast of Santa Barbara, spewing 200,000 gallons of crude oil into the sea. The spill devastated marine habitats and fueled an environmental movement that culminated in the designation of Earth Day in 1970. Hosted by the Community Environmental Council and University of California at Santa Barbara's Donald Bren School of Environmental Science and Management, the festival includes live music, the Green Car Show and Advanced Transportation

Marketplace and Energy Village. Kids will love the children's activities.

Wheels and Waves Car Show
De la Guerra & State Streets
(805) 683–3869
www.wheelsandwaves.com

Cruising up and down State Street are 400 of the nation's finest hot rods and classics. Rev up your engines for the live music, good drink, and tasty food. Who knows? Maybe your own personal favorite may just win the prize.

MAY

Bonsai Weekend at the Garden
Santa Barbara Botanic Gardens
1212 Mission Canyon Road, Santa Barbara
(805) 682-4726
www.sbbg.org

The art of miniature trees and landscapes is presented in this weekend of Japanese cultural activities hosted by the Santa Barbara Botanic Gardens and the Bonsai Club of Santa Barbara. Guided tours of the garden's Japanese Tea House, along with teachings of an authentic Japanese tea ceremony, accentuate the weekend's activities. The event is free with botanic garden admission.

Children's Festival
Alameda Park West
Micheltorena and Anacapa Streets, Santa Barbara
(805) 965-1001
www.fsacares.org

You'll find free entertainment as well as a ton of fun stuff to do all day long at the Children's Festival. The most popular activity is the pony ride, which usually has a long line of would-be cowboys and cowgals waiting for their turn. There's also face painting, kids' crafts, carnival games, magicians, clowns, and Sportsworld, with games to test athletic skills in kids ages 6 and up. Food booths tempt you to splurge on a variety of treats. The festival is always held the Saturday after Mother's Day, with proceeds benefiting the Family Service Agency of Santa Barbara.

Cinco de Mayo
Various locations, Santa Barbara
(805) 965-8581

Several local venues have Cinco de Mayo celebrations to mark the anniversary of the Mexican defeat of the French at the city of Puebla.

Food booths and entertainment are offered at De la Guerra Plaza (on De la Guerra between State and Anacapa Streets).

Some activities are held on the day of Cinco de Mayo (May 5), while others are scheduled on the closest weekend. Check the newspaper, as times and events vary.

Downtown Art and Wine Tour
Downtown Organization
27-B East De la Guerra Street, Santa Barbara
(805) 962-2098, ext. 22
www.santabarbaradowntown.com

Sip a local red or a delicate white and nibble on tasty tidbits while touring the downtown art scene. An absolute sell-out every year, the $50 tickets are definitely a prebuy must. Proceeds benefit such events as the Downtown Childrens' Holiday Parade.

I Madonnari
Mission Santa Barbara
Laguna and Los Olivos Streets, Santa Barbara
(805) 964-4710, ext. 4411
www.imadonnarifestival.com

Held annually on Memorial Day weekend, I Madonnari is a charming Italian street-painting festival held in the Mission courtyard. More than 200 artists get down on their hands and knees to create colorful chalk masterpieces on the asphalt and cement.

Spectators stroll the courtyard at their leisure, then walk down to the lawn, where an "Italian marketplace" features food booths and entertainment. After the festival is over, the street paintings remain, so you can browse later if you don't want to brave the crowds on the weekend (parking is a pain). If there's rain in the forecast, of course, the paintings are in danger of becoming chalk puddles, so don't wait too long.

I Madonnari Italian Street Painting Festival. GREG PETERSON/SANTA BARBARA CONFERENCE & VISITORS BUREAU

Pearl Chase Society Historical Home Tours
Various locations
www.pearlchase.org
One of our favorites, the historical home tour showcases up to nine houses on a weekend in mid-May. Downtown, uptown, or winding through Montecito, you can lookey loo at homes you'd probably never be invited in to see. George Washington Smith, Mary Craig, and many other renowned architects designed these homes into a perfection that still exists today. Tickets are around $50 and well worth the price of admission.

Presidio Pastimes
El Presidio de Santa Barbara State Historic Park
123 East Canon Perdido Street, Santa Barbara
(805) 965-0093
www.sbthp.org
Want a taste of Santa Barbara's history? Participate in archaeological digs and crafting early California goods. Learn how to cook delicious tortillas and craft adobe bricks. The fort's uniformed soldiers are on hand to give you and your family a look at what life in Santa Barbara used to be.

Steelhead Trout Festival
Stearns Wharf
(805) 963-0583, ext. 116
www.communityenvironmentalcouncil.org
It was over a decade ago that steelhead trout were declared an endangered species. What does Santa Barbara do when something's endangered? Raise money to help out, and in a creative way. This exuberant festival does just that with a steelhead sculpture art exhibit on State Street, a 5-kilometer fun run mimicking the path of a steelhead trout, and live music and fun on Stearns Wharf. The giant fiberglass trouts, painted by local artists such as Rebecca Stebbins, are displayed on State Street after the festival.

JUNE

Big Dog Parade & Canine Festival
De la Guerra Plaza, Santa Barbara
(805) 963-8727, ext. 1398
www.bigdogs.com
Ever had a secret urge to dress up your puppy in a ridiculous outfit? This is your chance. Enter Fido in the annual Big Dog Parade and Canine Festival; make him look really silly, and you might even win a prize. More than 2,000 participants (people and pooches) strut down State Street in this popular event, and prizes are awarded for the Best in Parade, Best Costume, and Most Humorous. Enjoy live music and great food while possibly winning a trip to Mexico, a new dog bed, or a year's supply of doggie treats. It costs $15 to enter the parade. Proceeds go to the Big Dog Foundation to help children, dogs, and dogs helping people. If you just want to turn up and have a giggle on the sidelines, it's free.

Lompoc Flower Festival
Various locations, Lompoc
(805) 735-8511
www.flowerfestival.org
The Lompoc Valley, known for its thriving flower seed industry, turns into splashes of vibrant color during June, July, and August. This self-proclaimed "greatest little free festival in the West" celebrates the valley's blooming harvest with a weekend's worth of arts and crafts, flower field tours, and—what festival would be without it?—lots of delicious food.

A parade features floats decorated with local flowers, a carnival offers rides and attractions for the whole family, and you'll find free entertainment at several local venues.

The festival's highlight is the flower show, which has been judged one of the highest ranking shows in the state and is held at the Veterans Memorial Building. More than 200 amateur flower arrangements and 500 specimens are on display, and there are arrangements by commercial growers and a children's section. (Needless to say, it all smells heavenly!)

Other events held in conjunction with the festival include guided bus tours departing from Ryon Park and rolling past 1,000 acres of local flower fields (a nominal fee is charged), where you can buy seeds directly from farmers, and an arts and crafts show displaying the works of artists and artisans.

Santa Barbara Writers Conference
Fess Parker's DoubleTree Resort
633 East Cabrillo Boulevard, Santa Barbara
(805) 964-0367

Smash through writer's block with a source of literary inspiration by indulging in this week-long Santa Barbara Writers Conference. This internationally renowned event, run by Marcia Meier, is open to the public and includes workshops on biography, humor, nonfiction, fiction, screenwriting, poetry, science fiction, mysteries, children's books, and more. Such literary luminaries as T. C. Boyle, Jane Smiley, Pico Iyer, and Ray Bradbury have been guest speakers in the past.

A highlight of the event is Agents and Editors Day. For $35 each, writers are able to pitch their stories in 15 minutes or less to a bevy of nationally known agents and editors. Many budding authors have reveled in their success when an agent or editor has asked to have the full manuscript sent to him or her.

The cost for the event is $625 through March 1 and $825 afterwards, not including lodging. For those not able to escape for a week or for those on a writerly budget, try the "Taste of the Conference" for $475.

Summer Solstice Celebration
State Street and Alameda Park, Santa Barbara
(805) 965-3396
www.solsticeparade.com

If you're looking for Spanish dancers and historical parades here, forget it. Summer Solstice, held at high noon on the Saturday nearest June 21, is when the city throws its distinguished past out the window and goes completely wacko. A whimsical theme is chosen for the parade each year, and participants

> **i** The Summer Solstice Parade is only half the fun. After the parade, head to Alameda Park for the wild free party with food, drink, and dance.

walk, cycle, in-line skate, or use some other creative form of transportation (no motorized vehicles or live animals are allowed) up State Street dressed in imaginative and colorful costumes that relate to the theme. (Well, actually, some people ignore the theme, using the occasion to parade around half-dressed and body-painted, or just half-dressed, period.) After the parade, the whole party moves up the block to Alameda Park for a free celebration with food, drink, and dance that continues for the rest of the afternoon.

This is Santa Barbara's largest single-day arts event, and it's about as wild and unpretentious a parade as you can get. Everyone has fun at Summer Solstice, and parade-watchers are often as wild and crazy as the participants. If you don't have a thing to wear or want to design your own float, sign up for the public workshop held in the weeks prior to the parade and make your own ensemble with the help of artists-in-residence.

JULY

French Festival
Oak Park
300 West Alamar Avenue, Santa Barbara
(805) 564-5418
www.frenchfestival.com

Say *bonjour* to this fete française, the largest French celebration in the western United States. Held to coincide with Bastille Day (July 14), it features everything from a French poodle parade to a miniature Eiffel Tower. Entertainment includes can-can dancers and live music, and the food is wonderful. French pastries, fresh croissants, savory hunks of French bread, and a variety of French wines are on the menu, and all can be enjoyed at a European-style outdoor cafe. With the puppet shows, storytellers, and wading pool, there's plenty to keep the kids entertained too. Admission is free.

Greek Festival
Oak Park
300 West Alamar Avenue, Santa Barbara
(805) 683-4492
www.saintbarbara.net/GreekFestival.htm
Always held the week before Fiesta (which can land it in late July or early August), the Greek Festival is far and away the favorite ethnic festival of Santa Barbarans. Who can resist the moussaka, shish kebob, and baklava, not to mention that infectious music? You'll be dancing like Zorba by the time you leave. It's great fun and always crowded. Admission is free.

Independence Day Parade and Celebration
(805) 961-2556
www.spiritof76sb.org
The grand march of this parade celebrating July 4 begins at 1:00 p.m. on the corner of Micheltorena and State Streets. It ends at Cota, where an exhibit of vintage military vehicles is on display. There's partying all day long at Chase Palm Park on the waterfront, then an explosion of fireworks at the end of the breakwater starting at 9:00 p.m. Reputed to be the largest fireworks display between Los Angeles and San Francisco, the fireworks are never disappointing. (Note: All personal fireworks are illegal in Santa Barbara.)

Santa Barbara County Fair
County Fairgrounds
937 South Thornburg Street, Santa Maria
(805) 925-8824
www.santamariafairpark.com
A local tradition for more than 110 years, the Santa Barbara County Fair is an old-fashioned kind of celebration. You'll find kids auctioning off stock, displays of local agricultural bounty, exhibits galore, top-flight entertainment such as Kenny Loggns and Pat Benatar, Circus Vargas Non-Animal Circus, Dog and Horse Shows, and a popular carnival midway in addition to a plethora of food. Lots of fun is in store for the whole family. Preadmission is $5 for adults, $3 for children 6 to 11, $18 for carnival wrist bracelet, $15 for destruction derby, and $10 for general admission.

Santa Barbara National Horse Show
Earl Warren Showgrounds
U.S. Highway 101 and Las Positas, Santa Barbara
(805) 687-0766
www.earlwarren.com
This national horse show is a long and distinguished Santa Barbara tradition. The National Horse Show draws horses from eight western states and riders from around the world, making it one of the top multibreed shows in the nation and the only one in the West to appear on the American Horse Shows Association's short list of "Major National and International Equestrian Competitions."

The two-week-long show features Paso Fino horses, Morgans, Hackney Ponies, Roadsters, Tennessee Walking Horses, and Welsh ponies and cobs the first week and jumpers and hunters the second. Ages of the participants vary from 5 to 85, making this a decidedly family event. Even if you don't understand a thing about horse shows, the arena performances at this one are both entertaining and enjoyable.

Semana Nautica
Various locations, Santa Barbara, Goleta, and Carpinteria
www.semananautica.com
A full summer sports festival that spans both sides of the July 4 holiday, Semana Nautica offers for your participation or observation just about every sport you can imagine, from beach volleyball to spearfishing tournaments to cartwheel-a-thon (okay, so some of them aren't exactly sports). More than 30 events are scheduled at venues throughout the South County, including swimming, kayaking, in-line hockey, softball, cycling, and running. Get off that couch and start training! Schedules are available starting June 1. There is a small fee for participation in each event, but the spectating is free.

AUGUST

Old Spanish Days
Various locations, Santa Barbara
(805) 962-8101
www.oldspanishdays-fiesta.org

Old Spanish Days (the locals call it "Fiesta") is quintessentially Santa Barbara. A distinguished annual tradition that began in 1924, the five-day event is a colorful feast for the eyes, ears, and palate as residents and thousands of tourists celebrate the city's Spanish roots.

So many things happen around town in conjunction with Fiesta that you need a program to keep track of them all including the not-to-be-missed Kiwanis Pancake Breakfast at Alameda Park, which is in its fifth decade of flipping flapjacks for Fiesta revelers. The *Santa Barbara News-Press* and the *Santa Barbara Independent* both publish annual Old Spanish Days special editions that list virtually everything, allowing you to pick and choose.

Some of the most popular events are the two parades, El Desfile Historico (The Historical Parade) and El Desfile de los Niños (The Children's Parade); Las Noches de Ronda, a free program of dance and music held every evening in the sunken gardens of the Santa Barbara County Courthouse; the two Mercados (marketplaces), one in De la Guerra Plaza downtown and one at MacKenzie Park on upper State Street, where vendors sell everything from Mexican food to T-shirts; the Competencia de los Vaqueros, a stock horse show and rodeo held at Earl Warren Showgrounds; and Celebración de los Dignitarios, a fun-filled evening of wine and finger foods held hilltop at the Santa Barbara Zoo.

Some locals steer clear of downtown during Fiesta, especially during the parades, because of the traffic snarls, parking problems, and crowds, but most look forward to it. Wander down to the Mercado at lunch and you'll see locals in business suits snacking side-by-side with the tourists. You haven't really done Santa Barbara until you've done Fiesta, so pour yourself a margarita, grab your castanets, and party! Oh, and watch out for those cascarones, decorated eggs filled with confetti that are sold on the street. You haven't been initiated into Fiesta until someone has cracked one over your head, spilling colorful confetti right into your hair and down your back, and into your clothes, your car, your house, and . . . well, you get the picture. Admission to most of the public events is free. (Also see the Close-up on Fiesta in this chapter.)

Santa Barbara Triathlon
Various locations
(805) 682-1634
www.santabarbaratriathlon.com

This is considered by many to be one of the most beautiful and most challenging triathlon courses in the country. Some 900 triathletes compete on the long course, which involves a 1-mile (1.6-kilometer) swim, a 34-mile (54.8-kilometer) bike race, and a 10-mile (16.1-kilometer) run. The women's only sprint and coed sprint attracts around 400 athletes competing in a 500-yard (457-meter) swim, a 6-mile (9.7-kilometer) bike race, and a 2-mile (3.2-kilometer) run. Want to get back in shape? Training for the Santa Barbara Triathlon is guaranteed to do it.

SEPTEMBER

ArtWalk
Santa Barbara Museum of Natural History
2559 Puesta del Sol, Santa Barbara
(805) 682-4711
www.sbnature.org

Truly one of our favorite events and a major fund-raiser for the museum, the ArtWalk opens on Friday night with a reception, then proceeds with two days of art exhibitions and a juried fine arts show and sale. Paintings,

i Best warm summer night hangout during Fiesta: the Santa Barbara County Courthouse. Bring a blanket, a picnic dinner, and binoculars for a close-up view, and enjoy a (free!) evening of Spanish, Mexican, and Indian dance, music, and song.

jewelry, glass, photographs, and ceramics by more than 100 artists from California and the West line the museum grounds. It's a beautiful weekend wandering through the Mission Creek outdoor setting while sipping a glass of Merlot and talking to the artists. Celebrity artists are featured each year in a special indoor show. Admission is $7 and $50 for the Friday night Artist and Patron Reception.

Danish Days
Various locations, Solvang
(800) 468-6765
www.solvangcc.com
It's almost as good as being in Denmark when you visit the annual Danish Days festival held in mid-September in Solvang. Folk dancing, music, parades, storytelling, demonstrations of Old World Danish crafts, and plenty of good food (we recommend the deliciously delectable *aebleskivers* smothered in raspberry jam and powdered sugar) contribute to the charm of this weekend festival. Everyone dresses up in native costumes, and a roving beer wagon adds to the ambience.

Even if you find ethnic festivals ho-hum, the *aebleskivers* alone make this one worth attending.

Santa Barbara Book and Author Festival
Santa Barbara Central Public Library Gardens
Anapamu and State Streets
www.sbbookfestival.org
Designed for readers who want to explore new books and feed their bibliomania, this festival highlights local authors and story-tellers and their books. Santa Barbara is teeming with literary talent possessing

i If you have kids and fancy a taste of Fiesta but want to avoid the downtown crush, head to El Mercado del Norte at MacKenzie Park off Las Positas Road in Santa Barbara. You'll find the same food booths as well as live music and dance and a host of kid-friendly attractions, including a petting zoo, rides, and a miniature train.

international acclaim. Wander booth to booth and get inspiration from successful authors. Just like any other Santa Barbara festival, there's also an assortment of food and drink.

Taste of the Town
Riviera Park and Gardens
2030 Alameda Park Serra, Santa Barbara
(805) 653-4685
www.arthritis.org
Santa Barbarans love to eat and drink. The Arthritis Foundation joined the bandwagon by creating this sell-out event. Taste of the Town truly showcases the finest of Santa Barbara food, wine, and beer and appeals to culinary lovers.

OCTOBER

California Avocado Festival
Linden Avenue, Carpinteria
(805) 684-0038
www.avofest.com
The South Coast's largest free festival will have you turning green—avocado green, that is. Forty entertainment acts (dubbed guac 'n' roll) appear on three stages, 30 foods booths and 30 commercial vendors line the streets, and over 70 arts and crafts vendors displaying their wares make this three-day festival a whole lot of fun. Think you've probably eaten everything avocado—from guacamole to spooning it out from around the pit? Well, we bet you haven't indulged in avocado ice cream, a tasty treat that's dished up by the scoopfuls. And there's nothing quite like sitting in the "love pit," a papier-maché avocado.

California Lemon Festival and Goleta Fall Classic Car, Motorcycle and Hot Rod Show
Girls Inc. 5k Run
Girsh Park
Storke and Phelps Roads, Goleta
(805) 967-4618, (800) 646-5382
www.lemonfestival.com
The California Lemon Festival has pucker power! Lemonade, lemon cakes, lemon bars, lemon tacos, and lemon meringue pies satiate

your appetite at this two-day event devoted to the citrus crop that's been the staple of Goleta's economy for years. Too bad lemon juice can't fill the tanks of the eye-catching assortment of classic cars, motorcycles, and hot rods. Pony rides, moon bounces, laser tag, and a petting zoo are just a few (and we mean only a few) of the exciting activities. "Safety Street," a large gathering of safety professionals, is a big hit with the children. They can sit in a fire truck or take a peek into the back of an ambulance.

Celebration of Harvest
Rancho Sisquoc Winery, 6600 Foxen Canyon Road, Santa Maria
(805) 688-0881
www.sbcountywines.com/festivals.htm
Local vintners celebrate the grape harvest at this fall festival held on the second Saturday of October from noon to 4:00 p.m. Similar to the Santa Barbara County Vintners' Festival held in April or May, the Celebration of Harvest features local wines, picnic lunches, taste testing, and a silent auction. Tickets go on sale at the end of July and must be purchased in advance from the Santa Barbara County Vintners' Association.

Santa Barbara Harbor and Seafood Festival
Santa Barbara Harbor
(805) 897-1962
www.santabarbaraca.gov
Lobster, crab, mussels, clams—you name it. Whatever seafood you're hankering for, it's guaranteed fresh off the boats. Don't know a thing about cooking seafood? Demonstrators will show you how. There are also interactive maritime and children's activities, boat rides, and the most amazing of tall ships for everyone to see. This is one festival that will really "float your boat."

Santa Barbara Smooth Jazz Festival
Santa Barbara Zoo
500 Niños Drive, Santa Barbara
(805) 962-5339
www.santabarbarasmoothjazzfestival.com

Chris Botti, Michael Lington, Ray Parker Jr., and Julia Fordham are just a few of the headliner acts at this awesome festival that's an absolute must for any jazz lover. The melodic sounds of the nation's top jazz artists entertain the crowd from 3:00 until 8:00 p.m. Local artists and culinary crafters enhance the ambience with their works. Tickets are $38 for general admission and $58 for VIP, which means near-the-stage seating.

NOVEMBER

Santa Barbara National Amateur Horse Show
Earl Warren Showgrounds
U.S. Highway 101 at Las Positas, Santa Barbara
(805) 687–0766
www.earlwarren.com
Always held around Thanksgiving (thus the nickname "Turkey Show"), this major event is an important training show for future Olympian equestrians. Junior and amateur riders compete in English and Western divisions. In addition to the equestrian highlights, turkey dinners are sponsored, and barns compete for the best-dressed Thanksgiving table.

DECEMBER

Downtown Holiday Parade
State Street, Santa Barbara
(805) 962-2098
www.santabarbaradowntown.com
Many local kids strut their stuff in this traditional holiday parade, with bands playing Christmas songs and a few floats, one carrying a smiling Santa Claus.

It's no coincidence that this parade winds its way down State Street, where most of Santa Barbara's retail stores are located, so after the parade, browse the shops and spend some money. Christmas is coming, after all! The parade usually starts at 6:30 p.m. For more information, visit the Web site and click on "What's Happening?"

Spirit of Fiesta

Every year, on a warm summer night, thousands gather beneath the steps of Mission Santa Barbara. As the moon rises from the lavender peaks, and the crowd falls silent, a proud senorita lights up the stage. She stands tall. Her gaze fixed, her chin up, she stretches her slender arms to the sky. Guitars strum a crisp glissando, and with a swirl of her skirt and a staccato of clicks from her castanets, flamenco fills the air. This is Fiesta Pequeña, "Little Fiesta," prelude to the annual five-day Old Spanish Days celebration ("Fiesta" to the locals), and this beautiful senorita dances for all Santa Barbara. Tomorrow she will lead the parade, smiling and waving in her white satin dress. But tonight she dances in the footsteps of three generations. She is an ambassador picked for her passion and poise. She is the Spirit of Fiesta.

For many Santa Barbarans, Fiesta means a five-day margarita fest. It means fat burritos in El Mercado, long bar lines, late nights, and cracking *cascarones* (confetti-filled eggs) on the heads of unsuspecting friends. Some think it's too commercialized, but to most Santa Barbarans, Fiesta is a proud tradition. It's one of the few times of the year when the community comes together to celebrate its diverse heritage regardless of social status, religion, or race.

Like the celebration today, the first Fiesta was spawned from a mix of history, art, and commerce. The descendents of the families who first settled in Santa Barbara wanted a way to preserve the gracious Old Spanish Days culture of the past. Old Spanish Days refers to the Rancho Period of the early 19th century, when Santa Barbara was an isolated patchwork of pueblos and ranches under both Mexican and American rule. By all accounts, the residents of Santa Barbara during this time lived in harmony, and the spirit of charity and hospitality was strong. *Rancheros* (ranchers) welcomed visitors into their homes and shared their food and friendship—"*mi casa es su casa*" (my home is your home) was the popular sentiment of the time. It was a life less hurried, when the arrival of visitors or the return of old friends and family prompted huge celebrations. It was a life of simplicity, generosity, and warmth. This romantic notion of the past hung heavy in the minds of the descendents of these *Californianos*, as they were called. So they organized special festivals such as La Primavera (the spring party) with colorful costumes, music, and dance to keep the spirit of the Old Spanish Days alive.

Against this background of nostalgia came the imminent opening of the new Lobero Theatre. It was 1924. The theater had just been restored, and civic leaders wanted to celebrate its debut with a gala event, something the whole community could enjoy. With this in mind, the Community Arts Association conceived an idea. Why not organize a festival to mark the occasion? Representatives from Community Arts shared the idea with the merchants' association and received an enthusiastic response. For years, the business folk in town had dreamed of staging an annual summer festival to entertain and attract tourists in the relatively quiet warmer months. Celebrating the opening of the Lobero was the perfect occasion.

As a result of these mixed motivations, representatives from three diverse groups—art lovers, businesspeople, and descendents of early Spanish settlers—all came together and formed a committee to plan the celebration. Working side by side with a budget of only $5,000, they came up with many ideas of their own and decided to incorporate elements of La Primavera as well. They wanted the five-day celebration to include food stalls, a Western rodeo, activities for children, an arts and crafts fair, and free nightly performances of music, song, and dance. The committee also envisioned a large parade as a critical component of the celebration and enlisted Dwight Murphy, a noted horseman of Santa Barbara, to organize the event.

Endowed with a modest $200 budget, Dwight met with other members of the community and came up with the idea of having a historical theme for the parade. To learn more about the old way of life, they met with descendents of the Spanish settlers, the De le Guerra and Ortega families, who shared their history, culture, and traditions with the men. Dwight then appointed committees to arrange floats, carriages, horsemen, and costumes.

That first Fiesta Parade was a walking history book, albeit a romanticized version. Chumash, Spanish explorers, and soldiers marched down State Street reenacting important events from Santa Barbara's past. The arrival of the Spanish pioneers, the founding of the Presidio and the Mission, the raising of the Mexican flag, and the Gold Rush, among other events, were all represented in the parade. Golden palominos, saddled in silver, pulled the beautifully decorated floats. Spectators dressed in the colorful costumes of Old Spanish Days, and a spirit of unity prevailed. The festival was a huge success.

Today, the Historical Parade (El Desfiles Histórico) is the biggest equestrian parade in the United States, and most of the elements of that original festival still survive. Visit Santa Barbara in the first week of August (when Fiesta traditionally takes place) and you can still enjoy the free nightly entertainment with costumes, song, and dance (known today as Las Noches de Ronda), a children's parade (El Desfile de los Niños), open-air marketplaces filled with the aromas of authentic Old Spanish Days cuisine (El Mercado), an arts and crafts show, and a

The graceful senorita named "Spirit of Fiesta," who leads the Old Spanish Days Fiesta Parade.
MICHAEL D. ROBERTSON, COURTESY OF OLD SPANISH DAYS

Western rodeo (Competencia de los Vaqueros), the same events that brought thousands of locals and visitors together over 80 years ago.

Over the years, Old Spanish Days/Fiesta has evolved and expanded. Two years after the first Fiesta celebration, Dwight Murphy was elected as the first "El Presidente" of the Old Spanish Days festival. In this role, he presided over its organization and acted as spokesperson for all the events. This custom continues today. Each year, the volunteer board of directors selects a respected member of the community to act as El Presidente or La Presidente. He or she is honored at many of the Old Spanish Days events and acts as an ambassador to visitors and residents.

La Fiesta Pequeña also originated two years after the original festival. In 1925 a massive earthquake rocked Mission Santa Barbara, but it was restored by the following year. So on a warm summer's night in 1926, on the eve of Old Spanish Days Fiesta, the people of Santa Barbara gathered beneath the steps of the Mission to celebrate its restoration. Today this event, known as "Little Fiesta," is the official opening of the five-day celebration. It's a night of blessings, dance, music, and song. For the next five days the community will come together to celebrate and recapture the rich traditions and culture of the past.

As you sit sipping your margarita, watching the beautiful senorita twirl across a moonlit stage, think of the true spirit of Fiesta. It's not just the costumes, the crowds, and confetti. It's a ritual that reflects the friendliness of the people of Santa Barbara. It's a time to share our love of music, art, and dance. But most importantly, it's the gracious spirit of old Santa Barbara passed from generation to generation, a spirit of tolerance, hospitality, and warmth. Viva La Fiesta!

Folk and Tribal Arts Marketplace
Santa Barbara Museum of Natural History
2559 Puesta del Sol, Santa Barbara
(805) 682-4711
www.sbnature.org
You can shop the world in a weekend at this three-day arts and crafts marketplace, which is usually held the first weekend in December in the museum's auditorium. It's the perfect place to find an unusual gift for the holidays, with booths featuring jewelry, baskets, clothing, art, and other objects from around the world. Highlights include textiles from Guatemala, carvings from Africa and Asia, and jewelry from India. Prices for the art and crafts range from as low as 50 cents up to $500 for more elaborate pieces. Admission is free.

The Nutcracker
Arlington Theatre
1317 State Street, Santa Barbara
(805) 963-4408
A Santa Barbara tradition for more than 20 years, the enchanting Nutcracker ballet is presented each December by the Santa Barbara Festival Ballet and the Santa Barbara Ballet Center, with celebrated guest artists and imaginative sets and costumes. Take your budding little ballerina and watch her eyes shine.

Performances are usually on a Saturday and Sunday, with matinees both days and an evening performance on Saturday. Call for ticket prices.

Parade of Lights at the Harbor
The waterfront off Stearns Wharf, Santa Barbara
(805) 564-5531
www.santabarbara.ca.gov

This Yuletide evening parade features dozens of boats adorned with holiday lights and other festive decorations cruising around Stearns Wharf and the local waterfront. There's a theme chosen for the parade each year, and entries range from the whimsical to the elaborate. If swells are high, the boats cruise around inside the harbor. Make sure you bundle up—it's chilly near the water.

Santa Barbara Trolley Christmas Lights Tours
Around town
(805) 965-0353
www.sbtrolley.com

All aboard for this magical Christmas tour of lights on the Santa Barbara trolley. It's true that many Santa Barbarans have holiday fever and overindulge in holiday lights. Some neighborhoods even hold contests for decorations. The Santa Barbara Trolley geniuses scope out

i What are the best seasonal events in Santa Barbara? According to a local poll, Summer Solstice and Fiesta take the top honors for summer, while the Parade of Lights and the Christmas Parade are the winter favorites.

the homes and create 90-minute tours showcasing the displays. This tour is guaranteed to wow.

Winterfest (Solvang)
Various locations, Solvang
(805) 688-6144, (800) 468-6765

The Danish town of Solvang is appealing at any time of year, but it's especially delightful when dressed up in twinkle lights for Christmas. The Winterfest celebration is marked by millions of lights adorning the downtown area, live entertainment, and special events.

A tree-lighting ceremony kicks off the monthlong celebration. There's a Christmas Tree Walk led by Santa and Mrs. Claus, a Christmas parade, the Nativity Fest, and the Danish Christmas Celebration at the Elverhoj Museum of History and Art. Now that you're in the Christmas spirit, stop in at the city's many unique shops in search of that special Christmas gift—and don't forget to sample the fabulous Danish pastries and cookies.

THE ARTS

The Santa Barbara arts scene has been hopping since the 1870s. Spurred by reports of the glorious climate and gorgeous scenery, wealthy families from the East, South, and Midwest began moving here in droves in the late 1800s and the first half of the 20th century. Rather than do without the established opera houses, museums, theaters, and orchestras to which they were accustomed, they decided to bring world-class culture right here.

Numerous patrons poured large amounts of money into local community groups. (The Fleischmanns, Peabodys, McCormicks, and Ridley-Trees, as well as Lotte Lehmann, Michael Douglas, and Michael Towbes, are just a few of the many generous financial supporters of Santa Barbara arts over the years.)

These groups in turn developed arts schools, theater and dance companies, orchestras, and other performing arts groups. They also invited the world's best performers, teachers, musicians, and writers to Santa Barbara.

This tremendous local support continues to this day and is largely responsible for the big-city variety and quality of arts and culture in our relatively small community. We have our own symphony, two chamber orchestras, choral groups, a professional ballet company, and several theater companies presenting everything from Shakespeare and Broadway-style musicals to contemporary dramas and comedies.

You can also explore several major art museums, a natural history museum, and a number of historical museums.

The area's institutions of higher education also contribute to the rich variety of community arts. The dance, music, theater, and art departments at the University of California at Santa Barbara, Westmont College and Santa Barbara City College present regular concerts, exhibits, and events showcasing student talent. Aspiring professional photographers from the Brooks Institute of Photography exhibit their thought-provoking pieces at various locations on the institute's two campuses and around town.

For more than 50 years the Music Academy of the West has brought together master musicians and talented music students for a summer of intensive study—and a popular eight-week festival that wows the public year after year.

A great thing about Santa Barbara is that you don't have to travel far to enjoy performances by world-class artists. Instead, they come here, and they don't seem to need much convincing. Santa Barbara is a perfect stopover on a trip to Los Angeles or San Francisco. And who wouldn't want to hang out on the beach or stroll the streets of our beautiful town between performances?

The area's stimulating intellectual environment has attracted both emerging artists and those whose names are already internationally renowned. Just sit for a while in a downtown cafe and look around. You're bound to see budding photographers, screenplay writers, artists, and musicians. You might also run into one of our many resident celebrities, including film stars, directors, producers, and novelists.

It's tough to be an artist just starting out here—the cost of living isn't exactly cheap. Also, the Santa Barbara audience as a whole

i For a calendar of Santa Barbara performances, check out the Santa Barabara Performing Arts League Web site at www.sbperformingartleague.org.

is highly educated and culturally diverse—it can be very critical and demanding of artistic quality.

Still, many young people manage to eke out a living in our fair city and establish a foundation for a future career in their chosen artistic field. In fact, Santa Barbara currently enjoys an international reputation as a destination point for vanguard art.

Our thriving rock 'n' roll scene serves as a case in point. Agents come regularly to Santa Barbara to check out new Santa Barbara bands, which have established a national reputation for creating cutting-edge music. Many local bands have signed contracts with major agencies in past years, including Toad the Wet Sprocket (now disbanded), Nerfherder, Dishwalla, Jack Johnson, and the up-and-coming (no doubt soon-to-be signed) Tripdavon.

While we couldn't possibly include everything related to the arts in this chapter, we've tried to give you a good idea of the depth and breadth of our cultural offerings. The chapter isn't arranged geographically because nearly all the groups and venues are in Santa Barbara.

To find out what's happening in Santa Barbara while you're here, we recommend you pick up any of the following publications. The *Santa Barbara Independent* is a free weekly newspaper that comes out every Thursday and includes a detailed events calendar for the entire week. It also has a popular arts section with reviews, information, and gallery listings. The *Santa Barbara News-Press* features a daily listings calendar. The Friday issue includes a special *Scene* magazine with a day-by-day events listing for the week as well as reviews and other arts information. The *Santa Barbara Performing Arts Guide* is a weekly pamphlet that includes complete local theater, event, and gallery listings.

ONE-STOP CULTURAL SHOPPING

Santa Barbara has a number of arts organizations and centers that sponsor a wide range of exhibits, events, programs, and activities throughout the year.

Cabrillo Pavilion Arts Center
1118 East Cabrillo Boulevard, Santa Barbara
(805) 564-5418
www.sbparksandrecreation.com
On East Beach overlooking the sand and sea, the Cabrillo Arts Center presents a range of art exhibits at the pavilion and organizes a variety of fun classes and events at other sites around town. All are sponsored by City Parks and Recreation. Visit the gallery at the Art Center itself and you'll see a new exhibit each month by a local group or organization, such as the Santa Barbara Art Association and the Los Padres Watercolor Society. The center also presents special art exhibits coinciding with ethnic and cultural celebrations like African American, Hispanic, and Native American Heritage Months. The Arts Center gallery is open Monday through Friday 9:00 a.m. to 5:00 p.m. Admission is free.

In July and August, you can attend free concerts hosted by the Department of Parks and Recreation in Alameda Park on Sunday afternoons and music concerts at Chase Palm Park on Thursday evenings. You can also book the Cabrillo Pavilion Arts center for private special events.

Channing Peake Gallery
County Administration Building
105 East Anapamu Street, Santa Barbara
(805) 965-9044
www.sbartscommission.org
Hidden away in the County Administration Building is a treasure trove of art. The exhibits here seem to be an Insiders' secret, but they are out in the open now. After visiting the Channing Peake Gallery, head across the street to the Faulkner Gallery at the Santa Barbara Central Public Library, where four galleries are brimming with art. Admission is free. Open Monday through Friday from 8:00 a.m. to 5:00 p.m.

Faulkner Main/East and West and Townley Room Gallery
Santa Barbara Central Public Library
40 East Anapamu Street, Santa Barbara
(805) 564-5608, (805) 962-7653
Local sculptors, printmakers, and visual artists display their works at one of the four galleries located at the Santa Barbara Central Public Library. Walk through during library hours, or attend one of the special evening art openings. Admission is free. Call for hours.

Gallery 113
La Arcada Court
1114 State Street, Studio 8, Santa Barbara
(805) 965-6611
www.sbartassoc.org
Santa Barbara is not short on original artwork. Gallery 113 is a cooperative gallery where local sculptors, fine artists, ceramicists, jewelers, and other artists of the Santa Barbara Art Association display and sell their original works. Artists are often on hand to discuss their work. You won't be disappointed in the quality or the diversity of the collection. Don't forget to go upstairs; it's worth the climb. The gallery is open Monday to Saturday from 11:00 a.m. to 5:00 p.m. and Sunday from 1:00 to 4:00 p.m.

Santa Barbara Arts and Crafts Show
Chase Palm Park, along Cabrillo
Boulevard east from State Street, Santa Barbara
(805) 897-1982
www.sbaacs.com
You can shop for culture here—literally. Established in 1965 by local artists, the Santa Barbara Arts and Crafts Show is called the "Art Center of the West." Sponsored by City Parks and Recreation since 1966, the show is now the only continuous, nonjuried arts festival of original drawings, paintings, sculpture, crafts, and photography in the world. Approximately 250 Santa Barbara County resident artists display their own works in an informal atmosphere under the palms of Chase Palm Park. All items are original art, created by the artists you meet. The show is held on all fair-weather Sundays and Saturdays of holiday weekends from 10:00 a.m. until dusk.

Santa Barbara Contemporary Arts Forum
653 Paseo Nuevo, 2nd floor, Santa Barbara
(805) 966-5373
www.sbcaf.org
Founded in 1976, CAF presents provocative, innovative contemporary art that explores aesthetic and social issues of our time. It has earned an international reputation as a leading alternative art space and is the primary contemporary arts center on California's Central Coast.

CAF presents the work of local, regional, national, and international artists as well as a broad variety of performance and media art. In addition, it operates extensive education and outreach programs, including classes in contemporary art, lectures, poetry readings, panel discussions, workshops, catalogs, video programs, artists' gallery talks, and mentorship programs.

The Santa Barbara Contemporary Arts Forum is located in a striking second-story space in the Paseo Nuevo Mall and is open to the public Tuesday through Saturday from 11:00 a.m. to 5:00 p.m. and Sunday noon to 5:00 p.m. Admission is free.

University of California at Santa Barbara Arts and Lectures
UCSB Campus, Goleta
(805) 893-3535
www.artsandlectures.ucsb.edu
For nearly 50 years, the UCSB Arts and Lectures program has brought a unique and lively array of performing arts, films, lectures, and writers' readings to the university campus—and to the entire Santa Barbara community.

Performances feature world-class touring artists: dance companies, chamber musicians, theater companies, and traditional musicians from all over the world. Examples of the diverse range of invitees include the Silk Road Ensemble and Yo-Yo Ma, Madeleine

Peyroux, and the Lyon Opera Ballet.

Arts and Lectures also presents international cinema, rarely seen documentaries, independent films, and top Hollywood movies. Lectures and readings bring distinguished people from every area of public life to the stage, for example, Madeleine Albright, Gary Trudeau, the Dalai Lama, and Garrison Keillor.

Most events are presented in the 860-seat Campbell Hall on the UCSB campus, although recently productions and programs have been making more frequent appearances in downtown venues such as the Lobero Theatre and Arlington Center (see the Venerable Venues section later in this chapter).

BELLS ON THEIR TOES

Dance in all its forms is a favorite Santa Barbara activity. Although many talented local dancers have found it difficult to earn paychecks for their expertise, they have found numerous ways to practice dance and create high-caliber performance groups. The Santa Barbara Dance Alliance (805-966-6950; www.sbdancealliance.org) arranges for the country's best choreographers to visit the city and promotes local choreographers and dancers.

A number of local amateur dance companies—Ballet Santa Barbara (805-682-6872; www.balletsantabarbara.org), Santa Barbara Ballet Center (805-966-0711; www.santa barbaraballetcenter.com), and West Coast Ballet (805-687-6086) give seasonal performances.

Are you "over" the plié and ready for something different? Then check out Irish step at Claddagh School of Dance (805-672-0167; www.claddaghdance.com) or Polynesian dance classes with Hula Anyone? (805-451-0589; www.hulaanyone.com).

State Street Ballet
322 State Street, Santa Barbara
(805) 965-6066
www.statestreetballet.com
This professional ballet company made its

i Your foot is tapping, but you don't know the steps? Check out Santa Barbara Dance Alliance's Web site, www.sbdancealliance.org, for a complete listing of studios and schools offering dance lessons. By the way, ballroom dancing has become the local rage. Could it have to do with the television program *Dancing with the Stars?*

debut in 1994 and has succeeded in its goal of bringing the Santa Barbara community "high-quality ballet with a flair." The company strives to present energetic contemporary ballets mixed with the classics. It tours nationally but is in residence at the Lobero Theatre, with performances from September through April.

State Street Ballet manages to attract top-notch dancers thanks to the extensive dance-world contacts of its founder, Rodney Gustafson. Gustafson is a former American Ballet Theatre dancer who first came to Santa Barbara while on tour with the ABT in the 1970s. He noticed Santa Barbara was rich in all the arts except professional ballet. The beauty and potential of the area drew him back here in 1993 to start a professional company.

THE CAMERA'S ROLLING ALL OVER TOWN

Since it's only 90 miles (145 kilometers) from Hollywood, Santa Barbara attracts not only celebrity residents from the motion picture industry but also visiting film crews. While you're here, you might even see a group filming a scene at the beach, the zoo, on the courthouse lawn, or on State Street.

At one time, Santa Barbara was the film capital of the world. In 1912 the Flying A Studio built the best-equipped and most innovative motion picture studio in the nation on the corner of Mission and State Streets. Flying A produced hundreds of films—from westerns to dramas set on tropical islands and the Arabian desert. At one point, nearly one film per day was being produced in Santa Barbara.

Hollywood eventually succeeded in drawing the motion picture industry farther south, and grand-scale film production in Santa Barbara ceased by 1921. Today you can satisfy your appetite for great film at a number of Santa Barbara movie theaters, film festivals, and other venues.

Movie Theaters

Metropolitan Theatres has a monopoly on just about all the movie theaters in this town. All theaters show the usual Hollywood releases as well as a few major foreign films. The Riviera Theatre tends to present popular artsy foreign films. The less popular or more off-beat films are often sent to Plaza de Oro.

Call the Metropolitan Theatres Movie Hot line, (805) 963-9503, for locations and show-time information for all the following cinemas or purchase tickets online at www.metro theatre.com. Santa Barbara Fiesta 5, 916 State Street; Metro 4, 618 State Street; Paseo Nuevo, 8 West De la Guerra Place (in the Paseo Nuevo Mall); Riviera Theatre, 2044 Alameda Padre Serra; Arlington Center for the Performing Arts, 1317 State Street (805-963-4408); Plaza de Oro, 371 Hitchcock Way; Camino Real Cinemas, Camino Real Market-place, 7040 Marketplace Drive, and Fairview Theatre, 251 North Fairview.

Film Festivals and Other Movie Venues

Santa Barbara International Film Festival
1528 Chapal Street, Santa Barbara
(805) 963-0023
www.sbfilmfestival.org
Every January Santa Barbara turns into a mini Cannes, with film professionals, celebrities,

i In the mood for a flick? Guarantee yourself a ticket (movie theaters are very crowded at night in Santa Barbara) by preordering your tickets by phone at (805) 963-9503 or visiting Metropolitan Theatres Web site at www.metrotheatre .com.

press, and thousands of fans dashing from screen to screen for 11 straight days. Best known for its international films, panels of film professionals, and educational seminars, the Santa Barbara International Film Festival continues a tradition of diverse programming, showcasing independent films from around the world. It presents more than 200 international films to an audience of over 60,000.

University of California at Santa Barbara
Arts and Lectures
UCSB, Goleta
(805) 893-3535
www.artsandlectures.ucsb.edu
The UCSB Arts and Lectures program sponsors a series of excellent films from around the world—internationals, documentaries, and independents—as well as top Hollywood movies.

GALLERY GAZING

Architectural Foundation Gallery
229 East Victoria Street, Santa Barbara
(805) 965-6307
www.afsb.org
This tiny gem of a gallery is not to be forgotten when wandering around town looking for free things to do. Oils by B. J. Staphens and Fred Sweeney are just a few of the works that have been known to hang on the walls of this cute gallery housed in the historic Acheson House. Where else but perhaps the Santa Barbara Museum of Art do you get to see the art of architecture (the gallery is in a Victorian Italianate residential designed house) and artworks all at once? Hours are Monday through Thursday from 9:00 a.m. to 2:00 p.m. or by appointment.

Atkinson Art Gallery
Santa Barbara City College
721 College Drive, Santa Barbara
(805) 965-0581, ext. 3484
www.sbcc.edu/art/website
Located on the beautiful Santa Barbara City College campus, this gallery hosts seven exhibits of contemporary art a year. In spring,

the gallery showcases student works. Gallery hours are Monday through Thursday 10:00 a.m. to 7:00 p.m. and Friday and Saturday 10:00 a.m. to 4:00 p.m.

Brooks Institute of Photography Galleries
Jefferson Campus (main gallery)
1321 Alameda Padre Serra, Santa Barbara
(805) 966-3888

Montecito Campus
801 Alston Road, Montecito
(805) 966-3888
www.brooks.edu

Brooks Institute of Photography is an internationally renowned school for professional photographic education. Brooks hosts numerous cultural events for the Santa Barbara community, including exhibits by world-renowned photographers, international multimedia slide shows, student film festivals, undersea slide shows, and educational lectures. The public is invited to tour the campuses and view the numerous photographic images produced by students, faculty, and alumni. Admission is free.

Delphine Gallery
1324 State Street, #D, Santa Barbara
(805) 962-6625
www.delphinegallery.com

You'll find Delphine Gallery in Arlington Plaza, across the street from the Arlington Center for the Performing Arts. The gallery showcases the work of California artists (most of them modern) and is open Tuesday through Friday from 10:00 a.m. to 5:00 p.m. and Saturday from 10:00 a.m. to 3:00 p.m.

The Easton Gallery
557 Hot Springs Road, Montecito
(805) 969-5781
www.eastongallery.com

Ellen Easton's gallery focuses on contemporary landscapes by local artists. Easton represents the artists involved in The Oak Group, a local group of plein air artists. The gallery is open weekends from 1:00 to 5:00 p.m. and by appointment weekdays.

East/West Gallery
714 Bond Avenue, Santa Barbara
(805) 963-4041
www.eastwest-gallery.com

An exhibition of photographic works by iconic photographer Horace Bristol (1908–1997) launched this gallery in December 2006. Henri Bristol, gallery owner, is the son of the famous photographer. Since its inception, exhibitions have included photographs with fine art, assemblage, surf culture, and ceramics. The gallery is open Tuesday through Saturday. Exhibits run for a month and a half, with a 15-day downtime between shows. Slated for fall 2008 is a retrospective of Horace Bristol's work to commemorate the 100th anniversary of his birth.

Faulkner Main/East & West Gallery and Townley Room Gallery
Santa Barbara Public Central Library
40 East Anapamu Street, Santa Barbara
(805) 564-5608, (805) 962-7653

Select art groups can book this gallery for monthlong shows. All types of art are shown here, including weaving, sculpture, and ceramics. Call for gallery hours. Admission is free.

Gallery 113
1114 State Street (La Arcada Court), Santa Barbara
(805) 965-6611
www.gallery113.com

The Santa Barbara Art Association runs this cooperative enterprise, which is billed as Santa Barbara's oldest fine art gallery. Founded in 1973, the gallery presents a new show every month featuring a local artist. Shows represent a variety of art forms, including sculpture, painting, jewelry, and ceramics. It's open Monday through Saturday 11:00 a.m. to 5:00 p.m., Sunday 1:00 to 4:00 p.m.

Maureen Murphy Fine Arts
1187 Coast Village Road, Suite 3A, Montecito
(805) 969-9215
www.mmfa.com

Nearly a Montecito institution, Maureen Murphy Fine Arts has been displaying an impressive collection of early California artists since 1986. *Plein air,* a French term meaning "in the open air," is one of the collected styles. Local resident Meredith Brooks Abbott, a contemporary impressionist painter, is well represented at this gallery. The gallery is open Tuesday through Sunday from noon to 5:00 p.m.; closed on Mondays.

Peregrine Galleries
1133 Coast Village Road, Montecito
(805) 969-9673
www.peregrinegalleries.com
Collectors of plein air art, Jim and Marlene Vitanza have been showcasing the finest in art to Santa Barbara residents for over 20 years. In addition to paintings, Bakelite jewelry from the early 1930s and antique silverwork from masters William Spratling, Hector Aguilar, and Georg Jensen are also represented. The galleries are open from noon to 5:30 p.m. Monday through Saturday and 11:00 a.m. to 4:00 p.m. on Sunday.

Reynolds Gallery
Westmont College
955 La Paz Road, Montecito
(805) 565-6162
www.westmont.edu
Reynolds showcases all types of art by local and national artists. It offers a number of shows throughout the year, including an invitational theme show, a faculty show, a holiday show, and an end-of-year senior exhibit. It also has an annual show with judging, in which the entire community is invited to exhibit. Reynolds is open Monday through Saturday from 11:00 a.m. to 5:00 p.m. Closed on college holidays.

Ro Snell Gallery
Hotel Andalucia
31 West Carrillo Street, Santa Barbara
(805) 569-3059
www.andaluciasb.com/thegallery
Ro Snell has made a name for herself in the Santa Barbara art scene and elsewhere with her keen eye and excellent taste for contemporary art. Paintings, sculpture, mixed media, photography, and sculpture are all represented in the beautiful space located at the breathtaking Hotel Andalucia. The gallery is open daily from 9:00 a.m. to 9:00 p.m. and is situated at the landing of the spiral staircase located off the hotel lobby.

Sullivan Goss Books & Prints Ltd./Arts & Letters Café
7 East Anapamu Street, Santa Barbara
(805) 730-1460

1266 Coast Village Road, Montecito
(805) 730-1460
www.sullivangoss.com
These two excellent galleries exhibit the works of America's great artists, focusing on Californian artists from the middle of the 19th century to the present. Visit the galleries to view important sculptures and oil paintings as well as revolving exhibitions. The Santa Barbara combination bookstore/cafe/gallery also houses one of the largest art book collections in the world. You can enjoy lunch by the fountain in the lovely courtyard, and the summertime Opera under the Stars dinners on Thursday evenings are always sellouts (see the Restaurant chapter for details).

i If you want to visit the studios of some of our talented local artists, call Santa Barbara Studio Artists at (805) 898-4471, or visit www.studioartists.org and arrange a guided tour.

UCSB's Women's Center Art Gallery
Women's Center
University of California at Santa Barbara
Santa Barbara
(805) 893-3778
This art gallery of ever-changing exhibits highlights art that specifically addresses women's issues. Mixed media art is presented throughout the gallery and usually carries very

thought-provoking messages. Gallery hours are Monday through Thursday 10:00 a.m. to 9:00 p.m., and Friday 10:00 a.m. to 5:00 p.m. Admission is free, but a parking permit is required for parking on campus. The permit can cost $5 to $7 for three to four hours.

Waterhouse Gallery
1114 State Street, Suite 9, Santa Barbara
(805) 962-8885
www.waterhousegallery.com
Established galleries abound in Santa Barbara, and Waterhouse Gallery has developed quite a reputation for its showing of renowned Western painters, including artists from the California Art Club and Oil Painters of America. Conveniently located by the Museum of Art, this gallery is a must-see. Open 11:00 a.m. to 5:00 p.m. daily

A WORDSMITH'S WONDERLAND

Writers abound in Santa Barbara. The literary community sparkles with the extraordinary talents of novelists, poets, and screenwriters, including T. C. Boyle, Fannie Flagg, Sue Grafton, and Dennis and Gayle Lynds. Famous authors of children's books associated with the area include Audrey and Don Wood and Lee Wardlaw. Santa Barbara also has more small publishers than almost any other U.S. region of its size.

Nearly every day brings a reading, lecture, or book signing at bookstores, cafes, colleges, and libraries. The *Santa Barbara Independent* also includes book signings and other literary happenings in the weekly events listings.

If you're moving here and want to get involved in a writer's group, we suggest you attend a reading at one of the locales listed below and speak with other writers. They can point you in the right direction. You can also meet other budding scribes through Santa Barbara City College adult education classes. Each year, the continuing education division offers excellent writing courses in a number of different genres. After attending these courses,

many students get together and form their own writers' groups. (See the Education Chapter for more information on this program, or visit www.sbcc.net/continuingeducation.)

Here are a few highlights of our literary scene.

Santa Barbara Writers Conference
Fess Parker DoubleTree Resort, Santa Barbara
(805) 964-0367
www.sbwritersconference.com
Nationally renowned, this conference is now hosted at the spectacular Fess Parker Double-Tree Resort located right across from the beach (see listing in Hotels and Motels). The conference aims to sharpen the skills of aspiring writers and launch them on the path to publication. Registrants attend the full week (usually at the end of June) of writing workshops, evening lectures by literary celebrities, and private writing sessions. Guest speakers have included Amy Tan, Sue Grafton, Gail Tsukiyama, and Carolyn See. Registration is $825 for the conference, $625 for the early-bird registration before March 1, and $475 for a "Taste of the Conference," which allows attendees to "taste" the first four days of the conference.

Small Publishers, Artists & Writers Network (SPAWN)
(818) 886-4281
www.spawn.org
SPAWN is a nonprofit organization providing education, information, resources, and a supportive networking environment for artists, writers, and other creative people interested in the publishing process. The organization participates in book festivals, arranges occasional seminars, and holds field trips to areas of literary interest such as book manufacturing facilities. SPAWN membership dues are $45 per year and include market updates, printed member directory, a personal Web page, a health benefit program, member book listings, and steep discounts at several literary organizations as well as seminars and

workshops. You can also subscribe to a free newsletter online. The newsletter is the best source of information, but you can also access schedules for upcoming events at the organization's Web site.

Speaking of Stories
Lobero Theatre
33 East Canon Perdido Street, Santa Barbara
(805) 966-3875, (805) 963-0761
Lobero Theatre Box Office
www.speakingofstories.org
Pages come alive on stage during these magical evening performances, when professional actors read classics and short stories to a captivated audience. In the past, performers have included celebrities such as John Cleese, Jane Seymour, Jeff Bridges, and talented local actors.

Readings are offered from January through May at the Lobero Theatre (805-963-0761). You can also attend special presentations at other times of the year. Tickets range form $13 to $35. Season subscriptions are also available for $69 to $134.

TREASURES FROM ART AND NATURE

Art in a variety of guises can be found in several Santa Barbara museums.

Karpeles Manuscript Library Museum
21 West Anapamu Street, Santa Barbara
(805) 962-5322
www.rain.org/~karpeles
The Karpeles Library is the world's largest private holding of important original documents and manuscripts. David and Marsha Karpeles established the library because they wanted American children to gain a sense of destiny and hope for the future. They believe this can be achieved by helping people look closely at important accomplishments in various disciplines—particularly history, literature, science, government, art, and music. They opened the original Manuscript Library

Museum in Montecito in 1983 but now operate out of the above location.

In addition to the Santa Barbara location, the library now operates museums throughout the United States.

The library features rotating exhibits that focus on about 25 documents at a time. Topics are drawn from fields of history, music, science, literature, and art. Highlights of the museum's permanent collection include the original draft proposal for the U.S. Bill of Rights and documents penned by such stellar scientists as Einstein, Galileo, Darwin, and Newton.

Past exhibits include "Anne Frank in the World 1929–1945," "Space," and "Great Women in History." Every three months the museum features different painting and photography exhibits showcasing the works of the community. The museum is open daily 10:00 a.m. to 4:00 p.m., and is closed on Christmas. Admission is free.

Santa Barbara Historical Museum
136 East De la Guerra Street, Santa Barbara
(805) 966-1601
This fascinating museum will give you a sense of what it was like to live in the Santa Barbara of yesteryear. The Santa Barbara Historical Society constructed this museum, and for more than four decades it has celebrated Santa Barbara's artistic and cultural heritage through displays of unique artifacts, photographs, furnishings, and textiles dating as far back as the 15th century.

Artifacts from the Chumash, Spanish, Mexican, American, and Chinese cultures attest to Santa Barbara's multicultural heritage. The museum library holds rare literary and visual documents, including 30,000 historic photographs. Adjacent to the museum are two early-19th-century buildings, the 1817 Casa Covarrubias and the 1836 Historic Adobe. The Gledhill Library is brimming with rare literary and visual documents, including 50,000 historic photographs.

Santa Barbara Museum of Art. PROVIDED COURTESY OF SANTA BARBARA MUSEUM OF ART

Museum hours are Tuesday through Saturday 10:00 a.m. to 5:00 p.m., Sunday noon to 5:00 p.m. You can also book a docent-led tour. Call for details. The museum is closed Monday. Admission is free, but a donation is appreciated. (See the listing in the Attractions chapter for more information).

Santa Barbara Museum of Art
1130 State Street, Santa Barbara
(805) 963-4364
www.sbmuseart.org
Santa Barbara's Museum of Art ranks among the top 10 regional museums in the country. Its permanent collection includes Asian, American, and European treasures spanning more than 4,000 years, from ancient bronzes to vanguard contemporary art.

American art ranges from early portraits through 19th- and 20th-century landscapes, still life, and portraiture to Modernist painting and sculpture. The Asian collection encompasses the art of China, Japan, India, Tibet, and Southeast Asia.

While roaming the halls, you can view works by numerous well-known artists such as Eakins, Monet, Chagall, Picasso, and O'Keeffe. The museum also exhibits the acclaimed Portrait of Mexico Today (1932), the only intact mural in the United States by renowned Mexican artist David Alfaro Siqueiros, and touring exhibits are on display several times a year. Kids will love the interactive children's gallery (open Tuesday through Sunday noon to 5:00 p.m.). You'll also find a cafe and gift shop on the premises. The Constance and George Fearing Library stocks a wide range of reference books, art periodicals, and art exhibition and auction catalogs. Library hours vary, so call before you visit.

Museum hours are Tuesday through Sunday 11:00 a.m. to 5:00. It is closed on Mondays. Admission is $9 for adults, $6 for seniors/students with ID and children ages 6 to 17; children under 6 are admitted free. Admission is free on Sunday.

Susan Quinlan's Doll and Teddy Bear Museum
122 West Canon Perdido Street, Santa Barbara
(805) 730-1707
www.quinlanmuseum.com

Susan Quinlan grew up taking art classes at the Cleveland Museum of Art. Upon earning her degree in library science, she became a librarian for the Cal State University system for over 30 years. During those years, she must have focused an inordinate amount of time on collecting, because she amassed one of the largest displays of dolls and teddy bears in the United States, perhaps in the world. Three thousand of her historical and contemporary dolls and teddy bears are on display at the museum's three galleries. The gift shop has numerous one-of-a-kind and limited edition items and out-of-print books. The museum is open 11:00 a.m. to 5:00 p.m. Friday through Monday. It is closed Tuesday through Thursday and on holidays. Admission is $6.50 for adults, $3.50 for preteens.

University Art Museum
UCSB, Goleta
(805) 893-2951
www.uam.ucsb.edu

Established in 1959, the University Art Museum is known for its creative programs focusing on vanguard contemporary art. The museum's 7,000-object fine art collection ranges from antiquity to the present. Of special note is the Sedgwick Collection of Old Master Paintings and the Morgenroth Collection of Renaissance Medals and Plaquettes. Modern holdings include sculpture by Henry Moore, Sam Francis, and George Rickey; paintings by Joan Mitchell and Robert Therrien; and works by Georgia O'Keeffe and Jean Tinguely.

One of the museum's particular strengths is works on paper, with drawings by Jonathan Borofsky and prints by Jean Arp, Richard Diebenkorn, and 1930s WPA artists. You'll also find more than 300 paintings and drawings by early-20th-century Santa Barbara artist Fernand Lungren and a substantial group of 19th- and 20th-century photographs here.

The museum's architecture and design collection, which focuses on the work of Southern California–based architects and designers, is considered one of the most comprehensive of its type in the country. It includes more than 750,000 historic drawings and related documents such as correspondence and writings, photographs, models, casts, and furniture.

A diverse educational outreach program of lectures, tours, films, performances, and symposia is scheduled throughout the year, and special educational programs are offered for school children. In addition, the Museum Store offers an array of unique art, design, and fashion items that reflect the museum's changing exhibitions. For information about current exhibitions and programs, call the numbers above or visit the museum's Web site. The museum's hours are noon to 5:00 p.m. Wednesday through Sunday. The museum is closed Monday and Tuesday. Admission is free. A parking permit is required for parking on the campus. It can cost from $5 to $7 for three to four hours.

Wilding Art Museum
2392 Jonata Street, Los Olivos
(805) 688-1082
www.wildingmuseum.org

Out of town but worth every minute of travel is the Wilding Art Museum, which is dedicated to the art of America's wilderness. Housed in the historic Keenan-Hartley House, the museum presents four exhibits a year, along with a series of art classes, lectures, field trips, and programs. Enjoy a picnic lunch in the garden after your visit and before your afternoon of exploration of the quaint country town of Los Olivos. The museum is open Wednesday through Sunday from 11:00 a.m. to 5:00 p.m. The suggested donation is $2 per adult. Children and members are free.

THE SCINTILLATING SOUNDS OF MUSIC

Camerata Pacifica Santa Barbara
(805) 884-8410, (800) 557-BACH for information
www.cameratapacifica.org
A sonorous little Santa Barbara gem, Camerata Pacifica is a chamber music ensemble with a refreshingly relaxed approach and a sharp sense of humor. The ensemble's concert series is often spiced with witty banter between the group's founder/director Adrian Spence and the other musicians. Performances range from The Lunchtime Series of casual performances to more formal special events. They are staged at the Lotte Lehmann Hall at the Music Academy of the West and various venues in L.A. The group's diverse repertoire includes the classics as well as more obscure musical treats and contemporary pieces.

Community Arts Music Association (CAMA)
111 East Yanonali Street, Santa Barbara
(805) 966-4324; tickets for individual performances through the Arlington Box Office, (805) 963-4408 or the Lobero Box Office, (805) 963-0761
www.camasb.org
Founded in 1919, CAMA is the grande dame of Santa Barbara arts groups. It's devoted to bringing the world's greatest symphony orchestras, maestros, and soloists to Santa Barbara's balmy shores.

The roster of artists and orchestras presented by CAMA over the past 85 years represents a who's who of music in this century: Horowitz, Rachmaninoff, Segovia, Mehta, the New York and Berlin Philharmonics, and the Concertgebouw Orchestra, to name just a few. The Los Angeles Philharmonic has performed in Santa Barbara every year since 1920.

CAMA's season runs November through May, and concerts tend to sell out quickly; in fact, it's sometimes hard to get tickets to certain performances at all unless you're a season subscriber. Call right away if you have any interest in attending a performance. All concerts are held at the Arlington Center for the Performing Arts, at 1317 State Street or the Lobero Theatre at 33 East Canon Perdido Street.

Music Academy of the West
1070 Fairway Road, Montecito
(805) 969-4726, (805) 969-8787 box office
www.musicacademy.org
The Music Academy of the West is internationally renowned and widely considered one of the finest summer music festivals and schools in the country. Every summer it offers eight weeks of richly varied music performed by exceptional musicians—much to the delight and benefit of Santa Barbara residents and visitors.

The academy was established in 1947 by a group of dedicated arts patrons and celebrated musicians, including legendary German opera singer Lotte Lehmann and Dr. Otto Klemperer, music director of the Los Angeles Philharmonic from 1933 to 1939. The group wanted to create a summer music academy on a par with such East Coast institutions as Juilliard and Tanglewood.

The academy has provided gifted young musicians with the opportunity for advanced study and performance under the guidance of internationally known faculty artists (including Metropolitan Opera star Marilyn Horne, director of the Music Academy's voice program, and piano pedagogue Jerome Lowenthal).

In 1951 the academy took up permanent residence at Miraflores, an elegant, Mediterranean-style estate on a bluff overlooking the Pacific Ocean. Today the campus occupies nine acres of wooded, beautifully landscaped grounds and gardens.

Events are open to the public during the academy's Summer Festival, which starts in mid-June and ends in mid-August. Picnic Concerts at the Miraflores campus are popular events. Concertgoers enjoy a picnic supper in the gardens followed by a concert showcasing brilliant young musicians in Abravanel Hall.

Masterclasses—the academy's signature program, in which faculty artists give feedback to students after they perform—are held in piano, strings, brass, winds, percussion, and voice and are open to the public. Call or visit the above Web site for more information. Also, free community-outreach concerts are presented at various locations around town, including the Santa Barbara Museum of Art and the Presidio. Some of the Summer Music Festival events are free of charge. For those that aren't, subscriptions are available or you can purchase single tickets from the Music Academy Box Office (805-969-8787).

Opera Santa Barbara
123 West Padre Street, Suite A, Santa Barbara
(805) 898-3890, (800) 563-7181
www.operasb.com
When this nonprofit organization opened its first official season in 1996, it was the first opera company in the region in nearly 35 years.

Opera Santa Barbara is the dream child of opera singers Marilyn Gilbert, a lawyer by profession, and her husband, Nathan Rundlett, a retired teacher. They wanted to bring opera on a grand scale back to town and started making the dream a reality in 1993. They staged five full operas and countless operatic excerpts at many locations to build an audience. A following emerged, and the company opened its first official season in fall 1996.

Opera Santa Barbara attracts first-rate singers, technical staff, conductors, and stage directors. Many of the stars sing with major opera companies, for example, the Metropolitan, San Francisco, and Munich operas. The orchestra is composed of professional players from Santa Barbara and Los Angeles.

i If you like the blues, visit www.sbblues.org and sign up for the free Blues Lovers e-mail updates. You'll receive all the latest information on blues events in Santa Barbara.

Productions are fully staged, thanks to set designers from California and New York, choreographers, award-winning costume designers, and a large chorus. The season runs from September through March. For tickets, call the Lobero Theatre Box Office (805) 963-0761, or visit www.lobero.com.

Santa Barbara Blues Society
(805) 897-0060
www.sbblues.org
Founded in 1977, Santa Barbara Blues Society is the oldest society of its kind in the United States. This nonprofit organization sponsors and produces regular performances of well-known blues musicians—such as Sonny Rhodes, Robert Cray, and Etta James—at various locales around town.

Santa Barbara Chamber Orchestra
(805) 966-2441
www.sbco.org
Directed by renowned violist Heiichiro Ohyama, this acclaimed orchestra consistently presents classical chamber music of the highest standards and spotlights world-renowned guest soloists.

The orchestra's season runs fall through spring, with concerts taking place on Tuesday evenings. Seats are almost always sold out through season subscriptions, but when they are available, individual tickets can be ordered through the Lobero Theatre Box Office (805-963-0761). To order subscriptions, call the Santa Barbara Chamber Orchestra at the number above.

Santa Barbara Choral Society
(805) 965-6577
www.sbchoral.org
The Santa Barbara Choral Society, founded in 1948, is the oldest performing arts organization in Santa Barbara. It's renowned for the high quality and discipline of its singers and its challenging, innovative repertoire. Composed of about 100 members, the society aims to open up avenues for study and performance

to all qualified singers and to encourage public interest in choral music. The society has presented several world premieres and devotes a significant number of its programs to 20th-century music by American composers.

Santa Barbara Master Chorale
(805) 967-8287
www.sbmasterchorale.org
Created in 1984, Santa Barbara Master Chorale performs major choral works primarily in the oratorio tradition. The professional orchestra and soloists, conducted by Phillip McLendon, present concerts three or four times a year.

Santa Barbara Symphony
1900 State Street, Suite G, Santa Barbara
(805) 898-9626, season tickets;
(805) 963-4408, Arlington Center box office
www.thesymphony.org
Led by internationally renowned music director Nir Kabaretti, the Santa Barbara Symphony performs traditional symphonic, choral, and popular music.

An annual seven-concert subscription series forms the core of the symphony's offerings, and internationally recognized musicians and conductors often participate in the series as guest artists. Most performances take place at the Arlington Center for the Performing Arts. The Symphony's New Year's Eve Concert is always popular. The symphony also presents free outdoor performances such as the annual July 4 concert in the courthouse sunken gardens, and it offers a range of valuable educational programs and special events geared toward families. For more information, call the number above or visit the symphony's Web site. You can also order both season tickets and single concert tickets online.

Sings Like Hell
Lobero Theatre
33 East Canon Perdido Street, Santa Barbara
(805) 963-0761
www.singslikehell.com
The promoters call this year-round series of monthly performances "very hot music in a really cool place." Top singers/songwriters come to the Lobero Theatre to play a range of music, from folk, rock, jazz, reggae, and pop to hip-hop and country. The targeted audience is people who want to listen to live contemporary music concerts in a comfortable theater setting rather than a bar. Typically, hip 30- to 60-year-olds attend.

Performers in this radical series are chosen for their talent, regardless of fame or fortune. In the past they have included Peter Case, Tom Russell, The Persuasions, David Crosby, Tracy Chapman, Charlie Musselwhite, Greg Brown, Laura Love, and Shawn Colvin. Season ticket holders receive a backstage pass for a meet-the-artist reception after each show. Tickets are available at the Lobero Theatre Box Office (see above) or online at www.lobero.com.

CURTAIN CALL

It's not New York, but Santa Barbara comes pretty darn close to offering a similarly wide range of high-quality dramas, musicals, contemporary plays, and offbeat comedies.

Circle Bar B Dinner Theater
Circle Bar B Guest Ranch
1800 Refugio Road, Goleta
(805) 967-1962
www.circlebarb.com
The Circle Bar B Guest Ranch in the mountains northwest of Santa Barbara hosts a lively dinner theater every Friday and Saturday evening and Sunday afternoon from April through November. Tickets cost $40 for general admission, $32 for seniors (Sunday only), and include the show plus a tri-tip barbecue dinner served family-style. Vegetarian meals are also available with advance notice, and the dinner theater has a full bar.

The theater usually offers four shows every season, typically comedies, farces, and musical comedies.

Ensemble Theatre Company of Santa Barbara
(805) 962-8606, box office
www.ensembletheatre.com

Founded in 1979, the award-winning Ensemble Theatre Company is Santa Barbara's longest-running professional theater group. ETC has built an excellent reputation for producing a range of classic and modern comedies, dramas, and premieres. It produces five fully staged productions each season from October through June. ETC's professional company members have performed on Broadway and appear regularly in film and television. Guest directors come from major regional theaters, and set designers work in regional theater, film, and television.

Outside the mainstage season, ETC presents annual short-run experimental productions by local and emerging playwrights. It also offers a Storybook Theatre, which stages two original musical plays for children every year. The company resides at the intimate 140-seat Alhecama Theatre in the Presidio State Park. Call the number above for tickets.

Pacific Conservatory of the Performing Arts Theaterfest
(805) 928-7506, box office; (805) 922-8313
www.pcpa.org

This unique regional theater group is not technically within the geographic region we're focusing on in this book. However, many Santa Barbarans head up to Solvang and Santa Maria in the North County for the excellent performances of comedies, dramas, and musicals.

PCPA is based at Allan Hancock College in Santa Maria and appears at three different North County facilities, the closest being the 700-seat Solvang Festival Theatre, an outdoor amphitheater. PCPA is the only training program of its kind in the country offered by a community college. It supports a unique, fully accredited vocational training program for aspiring actors and theater technicians.

PCPA Theaterfest is home to a core company of resident and visiting professionals. Past productions include such classics as

To purchase tickets in advance for many events, visit TicketMaster at www.ticketmaster.com, or access Ticket-Master at the Arlington Theatre, Macy's at La Cumbre Plaza, or Wherehouse Records.

42nd Street, The Tempest, My Fair Lady, Rope, and *On Golden Pond.* You can order season subscriptions òr tickets to individual performances from the PCPA Web site or by calling the box office number above. Note that arrangements for patrons with special needs are subject to availability and must be made in advance.

VENERABLE VENUES

A number of area arts centers, auditoriums, theaters, and halls host a wide range of performances by local and traveling companies and troupes.

Alhecama Theatre
914 Santa Barbara Street, Santa Barbara
(805) 962-8606

The Alhecama, a cozy 140-seat theater next to the Old Presidio, was originally the centerpiece of the Santa Barbara School of the Arts. The school, which was a branch of the Community Arts Association, boasted a powerhouse teaching staff of nationally known artists, including Buckminster Fuller, Carl Oscar Borg, Ed Borein, and Colin Campbell Cooper. The school closed when its director died in 1932, and the association handed over the property to a bank during the Depression to pay off creditors.

Philanthropist and civic leader Alice Schott saved the arts complex from becoming a parking lot when she bought the property in 1939. She renamed the property and the theater Alhecama—a word coined from the first two letters of her four daughters' names: Alice, Helen, Catherine, and Mary Lou. Later she deeded the property to what's now called the Adult Education Program, which held well-attended classes there from 1945 to 1981.

The California Department of Parks and Recreation purchased the property in 1981, handing management over to the Santa Barbara Trust for Historic Preservation. Today the theater is home to the Ensemble Theatre Company. The facilities feature a climate-control system and free parking next to the theater.

Arlington Center for the Performing Arts
1317 State Street, Santa Barbara
(805) 963-4408
This exquisite city landmark is probably the most unusual theater you'll ever visit. It's also Santa Barbara's main performing arts venue, and it has held that title for more than 50 years. It's built on the site of the grand Arlington Hotel, which opened in 1875. Arlington was the name of the Virginia mansion owned by Robert E. Lee and later used by General Ulysses S. Grant, and the posh hotel was so named to appeal to post–Civil War sympathizers of both the North and the South.

The hotel burned to the ground in 1909, and a new Arlington rose from the ashes in 1911. Bad luck befell that building too, as it was heavily damaged in the 1925 earthquake and subsequently demolished.

The site lay as a patch of weeds until Fox West Coast Theatres erected the third and present structure as a showcase movie house in 1930–31. The stunning tile-roofed building was designed to resemble the Moorish kings' Alcazar in Seville. The unique architectural style is actually a combination of numerous styles from Spanish architecture. The Andalusian exterior features a tall spire and an arched courtyard with fountains.

The interior is adorned with sweeping staircases of glazed Tunisian tiles, antique chandeliers, and iron lanterns that are copies of Catalonian street lamps from the 14th through the 16th centuries. The walls depict authentic Spanish villages, each building completely detailed with roof, chimney, lighted windows, balconies, stairways, and ironwork. The ceiling boasts a moonlit sky and twinkling stars. Metropolitan Theatres Corporation

restored the Arlington as a center for the performing arts in the mid-1970s, increasing the seating capacity in the process to attract top artists. It opened in 1976 with Benny Goodman and the Santa Barbara Symphony Orchestra as featured performers. Many famous artists and groups have performed here since, including the Vienna Choir Boys, The National Theatre of the Deaf, Mummenschanz, Maya Angelou, and Fiona Apple.

Campbell Hall
UCSB, Goleta
(805) 893-3535
Opposite the University's Cheadle Hall administration building, Campbell Hall is the main venue for Arts & Lectures performances by comedians, musicians, dance troupes, and all types of touring artists. This 860-seat facility on the UCSB campus was originally designed as a recital hall, and the acoustics and sight lines are excellent.

Center Stage Theater
751 Paseo Nuevo, Santa Barbara
(805) 963-0408
www.centerstagetheater.org
When negotiating permission from the city to build the Paseo Nuevo Mall, mall developers agreed to provide space for the visual and performing arts. The intimate Center Stage Theater now occupies some of this space on the top level of the mall. The theater is a great little black-box venue. Because of its diminutive size (it seats a maximum of only about 150 people), you're always close to the action on stage. At intermission, you can sip drinks in the Spanish-style courtyard out front overlooking the palms and fountains of the mall below. It's a lovely spot to gather on warm summer evenings. Center Stage Theater is run by Santa Barbarans for Santa Barbarans. The main mission is to provide an accessible venue for performances, 90 percent of which are local theater, dance, and music groups that rent the space. Top professionals appear at Center Stage only about 12 weeks a year. Tickets are usually very reasonable.

El Capitan Canyon
U.S. Highway 101 North to El Capitan State Beach
(805) 685-3887

Historic groves of oaks and sycamore trees surround you in this outdoor luxury camp-ground site, where a summer concert series offers families a night of rocking-good fun. For a $10 admission, local bands play every Satur-day night from April through October. Adults, kids, and young-at-hearts dance on the Creek-side Greens near a blazing fire pit and under a canopy of twinkling stars. Barbecue dinners with humongous portions of chicken, salad, beans, and garlic bread are offered for $18, or you can bring your own picnic and drink.

i Parking at the Granada Theatre is easy with the new parking struc-ture, but be careful on your way in. Errant planning forgot to include a turn lane, so the city has erected a funky barrier that creates confusion when people are enter-ing the parking garage.

Granada Theatre
1216 State Street, Santa Barbara
(805) 899-3000
www.grenadasb.org

Currently undergoing a $40+ million restora-tion, the Granada Theatre is destined to be one of the premier entertainment venues on the South Coast. Seating for 1,550 patrons will include loge and balcony sections, plus eight side boxes. The Granada Theatre's origi-nal chandelier is being unpacked, dusted off, and restored for installation. The parking garage behind the Granada (once an open-air lot) is now upscale, with its computerized dis-plays of available parking spaces. The antici-pated reopening of the Granada is slated for March 2008.

Lobero Theatre
33 East Canon Perdido Street, Santa Barbara
(805) 966-4946
www.lobero.com

In the 1870s there were no opera houses in California south of San Francisco. A Santa Bar-bara opera aficionado named José Lobero changed all that by establishing the first opera house in Southern California. He raised money and built the original theater—supposedly the largest adobe structure in existence at the time—in 1873. It soon became a major cul-tural center, attracting traveling shows, vaude-ville, and performances by community groups.

Unfortunately, Lobero eventually went bankrupt and, unwilling to live without money and in poor health, committed suicide. The building fell into disrepair and was condemned in 1922. The Community Arts Association pur-chased the structure and tore it down. The group then contracted famous local architects George Washington Smith and Lutah Maria Riggs to design the "new" Lobero, a stately Spanish Revival structure with soaring columns, graceful arches, and a red tile roof. The new theater opened in August 1924.

Today the Lobero Theatre is not only a major performing arts center for the commu-nity but also a city and state historic landmark that enjoys the title of California's oldest con-tinuously operating theater. The nonprofit Lobero Theatre Foundation has operated the 680-seat theater since 1938. It provides an inti-mate setting for many types of performances and events, from chamber music, ballet, and opera to lectures, contemporary music, and children's theater.

Marjorie Luke Theatre
Santa Barbara Junior High School
721 East Cota Street, Santa Barbara
(805) 884-4087, ext. 1
www.luketheatre.org

This theater is named in honor of the late Marjorie Luke, the well-loved former perform-ing arts instructor at Santa Barbara Junior High School. The theater's Spanish Colonial Revival architecture, similar to the courthouse and Mission Santa Barbara, provided a perfect framework for the $4 million renovation (2003) that created this stunning 812-seat space. Features include vaulted wood ceilings, ornate relief work, handmade tiles, and hand-forged wrought iron. Santa Barbara Junior High students use this theater, as do community arts organizations. Mentoring and technical workshops are held here.

Santa Barbara Bowl
1122 North Milpas Street, Santa Barbara
(805) 962-7411
www.sbbowl.com

The newly renovated (and continuing to be improved) Santa Barbara Bowl is one of our most evocative venues. Music lovers of all types flock to the Bowl to see top performers and internationally acclaimed acts from April through October. Built in 1936 of local stone, the 4,562-seat outdoor amphitheater in the Riviera foothills provides an outrageously scenic setting for rock bands, symphonies, and singers of all stripes. The sloped seating makes for fantastic views. On clear evenings, you can see the ocean shimmering in the distance, and with the stars glittering above and on stage, you can't beat the bowl for ambience.

Itzhak Perlman, Joan Baez, Jimmy Buffet, Bruce Springsteen, and James Taylor have performed here. In recent years, the Bowl has hosted a long list of popular stars, including Sting, Sheryl Crow, Alanis Morisette, Bob Dylan, the B-52s, the Gypsy Kings, Tom Petty and the Heartbreakers, and Toad the Wet Sprocket (our most famous local band, which has since disbanded).

Marjorie Luke Theatre foyer. KEN CHEN

ART FOR KIDS
(AND GROWN-UPS, TOO)

2000 Degrees
1206 State Street, Santa Barbara
(805) 882-1817

At this ceramics workshop you can choose from more than 200 pieces of bisqueware, then paint it, bake it, and take it home. Prices for the pieces (cups, plates, platters, and more) range from $2 to $60. Your purchase allows you to select up to four colors for each piece from a palette of 60 hues.

For a small fee, you can paint as long as you want. When you're done, the staff coats the piece with a high-gloss finishing glaze and fires it in the kiln. Pieces are ready for pickup in one to four days; you can have them shipped if you won't be in town when they're done.

Art from Scrap
302 East Cota Street, Santa Barbara
(805) 884-0459
www.artfromscrap.org

Art from Scrap is a fun place where children and adults can transform springs, foam rubber, plastic neon-colored squigglies, yarn, paper, and all sorts of industrial doodads into works of art. An educational program of the nonprofit Community Environmental Council, Art from Scrap promotes conservation and reuse of discarded materials through hands-on exploration. Regional businesses and manufacturers donate materials.

i Drop your kids off at Art from Scrap on Saturday mornings from 10:00 a.m. to noon while you shop for fresh fruits and veggies at the nearby farmers' market.

Art from Scrap Fun Workshops have varying themes and are offered every Saturday from 10:00 to noon. The cost is $6 per person. Art from Scrap's office and retail store are open Tuesday, Wednesday, and Friday from 10:00 a.m. to 2:00 p.m., Thursday 10:00 a.m. to 6:00 p.m., and Saturday 10:00 a.m. to 3:00 p.m.

BOXTALES Theatre Company
Marjorie Luke Theatre
721 East Cota Street, Santa Barbara
(805) 636-2015
www.boxtales.org

Voted "Best Children's Theatre Group" by the Santa Barbara *Independent Reader* polls in 2003 and 2005, BOXTALES is a unique theater that presents international myths and folktales. A three-week summer theater intensive program is available for teens ages 14 and up. Teens gain confidence and training in acting, movement, collaboration and storytelling. Call for more details on dates, hours, and cost.

Patricia Henley Foundation
Marjorie Luke Theatre
721 East Cota Street, Santa Barbara
(805) 963-0761

Children ages 11 to 17 get to unglue themselves from the television set and computer monitors and partake in this new six-week theatrical extravaganza. The summer 2007 launch of the Henley Foundation theater experience was "A Tribute to the Musical," a musical performance in which kids and theater professionals presented 22 outrageous, toe-tapping numbers. Guest speakers from the entertainment industry give informative and inspirational speeches to the kids, and other nonprofit arts organizations collaborate in the fun.

Santa Barbara Museum of Art
Ridley-Tree Education Center at the
McCormick House
1600 Santa Barbara Street, Santa Barbara
(805) 962-1661
www.sbmuseart.org
Young Michelangelos and unrealized creative adults will revel in the inspired classes taught at the Ridley-Tree Education Center. The quarterly Artventure programs cover sculpture, painting, drawing, ceramics, collage, and architecture. Some of the classes are geared to parents and children, which makes for a perfect morning or afternoon of creative bonding. Call for more details and information, or download the brochure from the Santa Barbara Museum of Art Web site.

PARKS

It's true that Santa Barbarans love their beaches, but eventually we all get a hankering for a change of scenery, a wide expanse of green grass, and a shady grove for picnicking. Luckily, maintaining a thriving system of parks has always been a high priority in Santa Barbara, and whether you're looking for a tranquil garden or a rugged spot to hike, you'll find enough wide-open spaces to fit your every mood (not to mention plenty of room for the kids to run around).

In this chapter, we show you the best of our beautiful parks, covering Santa Barbara first, then heading west to east from Goleta to Carpinteria. Next, we'll go inland for a look at Cachuma Lake Recreation Area, one of the county's most popular parks. City, county, and state parks are listed according to the geographical area in which they are found, along with their major features and other useful information.

For information about parks within the city of Santa Barbara, contact Santa Barbara Parks and Recreation (805-564-5418; www.sbparksandrecreation.com), which administers the daily workings and programs at more than 55 parks citywide (a total of 1,764 acres). The Adapted Programs Office (805-564-5421) can answer questions about wheelchair accessibility to the parks; call between 8:00 a.m. and 5:00 p.m. weekdays.

All city parks are open from sunrise until a half hour after sunset, except where posted otherwise. During summer daylight saving time, many parks remain open until 10:00 p.m., but be sure to check the posted hours when you arrive. All city park restrooms are closed at dark, and no overnight camping is allowed.

Reservations for city park facilities such as ballfields or group picnic areas with barbecue pits are taken on a first come, first served basis and can be made up to 30 days before an event by calling Parks and Recreation at (805) 564-5418. You can also make reservations online at www.sbparksandrecreation.com. Fees vary according to the facility you wish to rent, with charges for staff services, group-picnic-site maintenance, and recreational facilities. If you want to take your chances and not make a reservation, the area is yours if you show up first and no one else has reserved it, but popular areas are often reserved ahead, so don't count on one being available.

If you're planning a big party, be aware that consumption of alcoholic beverages in city parks is prohibited at all posted sites, and you should apply in advance for a special permit if you're planning to haul along a cooler full of beer. Call for information on the city ordinance that may cut into the fun unless you know how to get around it (legally, of course).

More than 20 county parks (900 acres) fall under the auspices of the Santa Barbara County Park Department (805-568-2460; www.sbparks.org), headquartered at Rocky Nook Park in Mission Canyon. You can make reservations for facilities at any county park by calling (805) 568-2465. You can also read about park facilities or download printable maps at the department's excellent Web site at www.sbparks.org. Park hours are from 8:00 a.m. to sunset year-round.

Southern Santa Barbara County has four California state parks on the beach. We include a short write-up on each in this chapter, but refer to the Beaches and Watersports and Recreation chapters for complete information on facilities and camping. A parking fee between $4 and $14 a day for use of all state parks; it's payable at the entrance kiosk. (If you pay an entrance fee to one state park, you can use the permit to enter another park the same day.)

Annual passes ($125 a year) are also available and entitle you to unlimited passenger-vehicle or motorcycle entry and parking at any state park for a 12-month period. Discount passes are available for the disabled and for seniors 62 and older. For complete information on all California state park passes, call (916) 653-4000, visit www.parks.ca.gov, or write to P.O. Box 942896, Sacramento, CA 94296-0001. The Channel Islands National Park and Marine Sanctuary are so spectacular, they get their own separate chapter in this book—don't miss it!

If Fido is part of the family outing, you'll want to make a note of these rules. Dogs must be on a leash at all times in county parks, and there are only three leash-free areas in the city of Santa Barbara: the Douglas Family Preserve, the area east of the slough at Arroyo Burro (Hendry's Beach) Park, and a posted off-leash area of Elings Park with a special permit. The dog's human companion must be at least 18 years of age, be able to leash the dog immediately if there are any signs of trouble, and keep the dog out of picnic sites, sports fields, and playgrounds. Any damage done to a park by an unleashed dog is the owner's responsibility, and doggie messes must be cleaned up immediately using "poop station" supplies, which are found in most city and county parks.

You can bring your dog with you to a California state park, but you must be able to show the dog's rabies vaccination certificate or license. During the day, dogs must be on a leash no more than 6 feet long, and they are not allowed on trails, on the beach, or in buildings unless they are seeing-eye dogs.

SANTA BARBARA

Alameda Park
1400 Santa Barbara Street, Santa Barbara
(805) 564-5418
www.sbparksandrecreation.com
One of the city's oldest parks, Alameda is best known today as the site of Kids' World (see the Playgrounds section in the Kidstuff chap-

i For a taste of quintessential Santa Barbara, check out the free summer music concerts from June through August at Alameda Park on Sunday afternoons and Chase Palm Park on Thursday evenings. Pack a picnic, round up the family, kick back, and enjoy some great tunes while the kids run wild. For more information, call (805) 897-1982, or visit www.sbparksandrecreation.com.

ter), a very cool 8,000-square-foot fun zone for—who else?—kids. But while the kids are playing, Mom and Dad will appreciate the park's unique collection of more than 70 species of trees, the gazebo, and the acres of shady lawn. Since this park is close to downtown, it provides a good respite from the hustle and bustle, even though the street-only parking can sometimes present a problem. Many downtown workers grab lunch, hoof it over from their offices, and relax in the shade.

Alice Keck Park Memorial Gardens
1500 Santa Barbara Street, Santa Barbara
(805) 564-5418
www.sbparksandrecreation.com
A relative newcomer on the city parks scene, Alice Keck Park Memorial Gardens is a gorgeous 4.6-acre sanctuary right in downtown Santa Barbara. With the focus on an impressive botanical collection complemented by a koi-filled lily pond and small streams, the park has an especially tranquil feel. It's the perfect spot to contemplate the meaning of life. A Sensory Garden for the visually impaired, with audio posts and interpretive Braille signs, is one of few such areas on the Central Coast. Within the garden, visitors can touch trees and bubbling water as well as smell the flowers and enjoy other nonvisual experiences. Alice Keck also boasts a low-water demonstration garden. Pick up a pamphlet here and you'll find lists of all the plant species used in its creation. Parking is on the street.

Andree Clark Bird Refuge
1400 East Cabrillo Boulevard, Santa Barbara
(805) 564-5418
www.sbparksandrecreation.com
Once a tidal marsh known as the Salt Pond, the bird refuge was donated to the city in 1909. Mary Clark, a local philanthropist, had the pond drained and converted to a freshwater lake, then named it after her deceased daughter, Andree. You can ride your bike to the refuge, which sits at the east end of Cabrillo Boulevard. Be sure to pack your binoculars. This is one of the best spots in town for observing waterfowl, migrating songbirds, and resident species that thrive in the water and surrounding foliage. Stroll around the pond and you'll find interpretive signs and observation platforms. It's an easy walk.

Although the city has done its best to remove domesticated fowl from the refuge, there are always a few hanging around, and you should be aware that feeding the birds here is against the law (not to mention unhealthy for the birds). If you choose not to walk or bike, you can park your car in the small lot on Los Patos Way.

Arroyo Burro (Hendry's Beach) Park
2981 Cliff Drive, Santa Barbara
(805) 687-3714
www.sbparks.org
Better known as Hendry's Beach, Arroyo Burro is one of the most popular county parks in Santa Barbara. It was part of the original lands that the king of Spain granted to Santa Barbara in 1782. You can walk your dog off leash here in the area east of the slough as long as you remain within voice control range. For more information on recreational facilities, see the Beaches and Watersports chapter.

Chase Palm Park
East Cabrillo Boulevard, Santa Barbara
(805) 564-5418
www.sbparksandrecreation.com
Named in honor of the venerable Pearl Chase (see the Close-up on Miss Chase in the History chapter), Chase Palm Park stretches along the beachfront from Stearns Wharf to East Beach. The 35 acres include a bike path and walkway, large stretches of lawn, a soccer field, and restrooms.

Once consisting mainly of just palm trees and grass, the park seems to be ever evolving. Across the street, Chase Palm Park Expansion, completed in early 1998, includes a fantastic children's playground with a nautical theme (read more about it in the Playgrounds section of the Kidstuff chapter), a carousel, and a public pavilion. Arts and crafts booths line the park each Sunday and holiday, and the rest of the time you'll see people of all ages enjoying the lovely seaside setting.

The only problem is—you guessed it—parking. Parking is found along the street or in city lots, but on weekends and holidays, it can be difficult to find a space.

Douglas Family Preserve
End of Linda Road on the Mesa, Santa Barbara
(805) 564-5418
www.sbparksandrecreation.com
Overlooking Arroyo Burro (Hendry's Beach), the Douglas Family Preserve is one of the last undeveloped pieces of oceanfront property in Santa Barbara. At one point developers wanted to change that, but in late 1996 the citizens of Santa Barbara had a chance to save the property from development when the owners, tired of trying to get financing, offered to sell it for $3.5 million.

The fate of what was formerly known as the Wilcox Property (it was once owned by nurseryman Roy Wilcox) had been a subject of public debate for years, and preservation-minded Santa Barbarans were not about to let this chance go by. So they started sending in money. Cash, checks, and even pennies from children's piggy banks flooded in from all parts of the city and county.

When the total didn't quite add up to enough, actor and local resident Michael Douglas chipped in $600,000 to put the fundraising campaign over the top. On March 1, 1997, the 70-acre Douglas Family Preserve,

Douglas Family Preserve. PROVIDED COURTESY OF SUSAN SHAPIRO

named by the largest contributor in honor of his father, Kirk, became the property of the City of Santa Barbara.

Truly a "people's park," it's basically undeveloped, but it's a good place for a solitary stroll on bluffs overlooking the ocean, and it's one of only two parks in the city where dogs can run free. Park on the 300 block of Linda Road and enter through the metal gate, or park at Arroyo Burro and walk up the newly developed path access. There are no restrooms or recreational facilities.

i If you want to take a walk in the park and enjoy spectacular Santa Barbara views, Shoreline Park, Franceschi Park, and Douglas Family Preserve are the best picks. Don't forget your camera.

Elings Park
1298 Las Positas Road, Santa Barbara
(805) 569-5611
www.elingspark.org
Run by the Elings Park Foundation, which has donated untold amounts of money and time to make it one of the city's most beloved recreational areas, beautiful Elings Park comprises 230 acres and is the largest public green and recreational space in Santa Barbara City. Of these, 135 acres remain undeveloped. Facilities include three lighted fields, two soccer fields, a BMX track, a radio control car track, mountain bike trails, jogging and hiking trails, picnic and barbecue facilities, a playground, and restrooms. Stand on the hilltops here and you can breathe in panoramic views of the city and ocean.

The undeveloped south part of the park boasts the area's best hang gliding and paragliding training hill and is the site of the annual New Year's Day Hang Gliding and Paragliding Festival (see the Annual Events chapter). Soaring gliders are a common sight in this area of the park, and you are welcome to watch.

If you're planning a get-together, you can reserve one of two picturesque special event

areas. Godric Grove, especially for weddings, boasts a 300-seat amphitheater, a sprawling lawn, and a deck area shaded by oak trees. Singleton Pavilion, also for weddings, has a lovely gazebo in the middle of a meadow as well as picnic tables tucked in a grove of liquid amber trees. Three picnic venues include Cappello Picnic Area, with a canopy top, Fenton Davison Picnic Area, with horseshoe pits and barbecue, and Pine Grove Picnic Area, with a large barbecue. These areas are often booked on weekends, so be sure to make a reservation well in advance (up to a year ahead if you want a group area on a weekend during the months of June, July, August, and September). Parking is usually ample, but when several events are going on at once, cars can spill out onto the adjoining streets.

The park is one of only two in Santa Barbara that allow off-leash dogs in certain areas. But you'll need to pay for a permit and tags. The yearly fee is $60. For information, e-mail the Elings Park Dog Owners Group (EPDOG) at epdog@cox.net.

Park hours vary depending on the time of year but are generally from sunrise to sunset. Office hours for reservations are from 9:00 a.m. to 5:00 p.m. Once you've enjoyed this wonderful place, you might be moved to make a donation to the Elings Park Foundation, which will gladly accept your contribution. Just walk into the office and write a check, or send your donation to the foundation at 1298 Las Positas Road, Santa Barbara 93105. Overnight camping is not allowed.

Franceschi Park
1510 Mission Ridge Road, Santa Barbara
(805) 564-5418
www.sbparksandrecreation.com
Named for Francesco Franceschi, who made a name for himself in horticulture, the 18-acre park actually encompasses a portion of a nursery he owned until 1925.

In addition to an impressive botanical collection, the park offers a panoramic view of the city and ocean from its lookouts and winding walkways. Of special interest is Franceschi's

i Try to find the likeness of Francesco Franceschi, an Italian botanist, carved into stone at Franceschi Park. His serene face gazes out toward the Pacific Ocean. (Hint: It's easier to see it from Mission Ridge Road.)

home, built in 1905 and still within the park's boundaries. Plans are currently in the works for house and park restoration. In the meantime, check out the 63 medallions (see if you can find them all!) placed around the house by a previous wealthy owner. The medallions pay tribute to places and people, although no one knows for sure what the meaning is behind them. You'll also find a small picnic site and restrooms within the park, and it has its own parking lot. This is not necessarily a good "kid" park, however, as there is no play area and no lawn for romping. It is an excellent place for romance, though, as it has one of the best views in town.

MacKenzie Park
State and De la Vina Streets, Santa Barbara
(805) 564-5422
www.sbparksandrecreation.com
MacKenzie Park, the site of El Mercado del Norte (the Northern Marketplace) during the annual Old Spanish Days celebration (see the Annual Events chapter), is fairly busy the rest of the year, too. In addition to one of the city's few lawn-bowling greens, plus an adjacent clubhouse, the nine-acre park has a playground, baseball diamonds, picnic areas with barbecues, and restrooms.

A recreational building in the park has a kitchen, fireplace, barbecue pit, and large patio and is available for meetings or other functions. Parking is available in an on-site lot.

Mission Rose Garden
Los Olivos and Laguna Streets, Santa Barbara
(805) 564-5418
www.sbparksandrecreation.com
Tended carefully by local volunteers, the Mission Rose Garden and surrounding grassy area provide a popular place to toss the Frisbee around, stretch out for a nap, or literally stop and smell the roses. Inhale the fragrance of more than 1,500 rose plants in the garden, which is across the street from Mission Santa Barbara (see the Attractions chapter). You can also walk along the paths to the ruins of old aqueducts, a reservoir, a grist mill, and even a jail. This is a must for rose lovers. Park on the street.

Oak Park
300 West Alamar Avenue, Santa Barbara
(805) 564-5418
www.sbparksandrecreation.com
Oak- and sycamore-studded Oak Park, bisected by Mission Creek, plays host to all the city's ethnic festivals, and it's one of the most visited parks in the city. It also provides a few extras, such as a raised dance floor where dancers from the festival of the moment can entertain the crowds.

When the park is not full of festival-goers, you'll find folks playing tennis on two public courts and kids splashing in the wading pool (open May through September) or romping on the playground. You can also play a serious game of horseshoes in the lighted horseshoe pit. The park has plenty of places to picnic and barbecue. Restrooms and a parking lot are also available.

Orpet Park
Alameda Padre Serra and Moreno Road, Santa Barbara
(805) 564-5418
www.sbparksandrecreation.com
This charming park on the Riviera is filled with exotic plants and trees and is a good place for birding in the fall and spring. Park on Alameda Padre Serra, then meander along the footpaths and enjoy the botanical wonders.

Pershing Park
100 Castillo Street at West Cabrillo Boulevard, Santa Barbara
(805) 564-5422
www.sbparksandrecreation.com

Known for its lighted ballfields and eight lighted tennis courts, Pershing Park is doesn't have much more in the way of recreational facilities, but you can spread a blanket out on the lawn and picnic. Restrooms are on-site, and there's a parking lot, but it fills up fast on weekends so you may have to park on the street.

Rocky Nook Park
610 Mission Canyon Road, Santa Barbara
(805) 681-5650
www.sbparks.org
Donated to Santa Barbara County in 1928, 19-acre Rocky Nook Park is a charming spot for a stroll along the banks of Mission Creek or a quiet lunchtime picnic. Studded with oaks and sycamores and dotted with boulders, the park is almost completely shaded, which makes it a cool respite from the heat during the summer. It's also a great place for birding, especially in spring, when migrating birds gather in the dense foliage.

You'll find two large group picnic and barbecue areas here as well as several smaller picnic sites, and a small playground for the kids. Permanent restrooms are on-site, and parking is plentiful. After a relaxing picnic lunch, you can pop across the street to the Santa Barbara Museum of Natural History or stroll to Mission Santa Barbara, which is also within walking distance. You won't find any expansive lawns here, but that's part of the charm of this little "rocky nook."

Skofield Park
1819 Las Canoas Road, Santa Barbara
(805) 564-5418
www.sbparksandrecreation.com
High in the Santa Barbara foothills, oak-studded Skofield Park is just below the trailhead for Rattlesnake Canyon Trail, the most popular hiking trail in Santa Barbara (and yes, you do need to watch out for rattlers in the spring and summer). You'll find lots of other trails here for mountain biking, walking, or hiking. Group picnic and barbecue facilities, restrooms, and on-site parking are available.

Skofield has a more rugged feel than some of our parks, but there is a wide expanse of lawn for those who don't want to rough it. Reservable camp areas are available for nonprofit groups dedicated to youth. One caution: Because of its foothill location, temperatures in the park during the day are often much warmer than those down below in the city, so dress accordingly.

Shoreline Park
Shoreline Drive and La Marina, Santa Barbara
(805) 564-5418
www.sbparksandrecreation.com
One of the most popular parks in Santa Barbara, Shoreline Park encompasses 15 manicured acres that overlook the beach just west of the Santa Barbara City College campus. It's the perfect place to fly a kite, or you can gaze out toward the Channel Islands and maybe see a whale swimming by (a bronze whale's tail marks the best vantage point for whale-watching).

You can access the beach by going downstairs to the sand, or you can opt to relax in the park's grassy areas, which include facilities for picnics and barbecues. Kids will love the playground here, and you'll find restrooms on-site. The park has a fairly generous parking lot, so you usually don't have to go looking on the street.

Stevens Park
258 Canon Drive, Santa Barbara
(805) 564-5418
www.sbparksandrecreation.com
Tucked into the foothills at the end of Canon Drive, Stevens Park is another great spot for

i Some of Santa Barbara's parks are favorite weddings spots. Among the most popular are the oceanview bluffs of Shoreline Park, the Rose Garden near the Mission, Alice Keck Memorial Garden with its koi-filled lily pond, Chase Palm Park by the beach, and the panoramic hilltop at Elings Park.

hiking, birding (white-throated swifts can be found here almost all year long), and picnicking. A small playground sits along the banks of a creek, and the park has barbecues and restrooms. Parking is available in a small lot at the entrance. If you're going to hike, watch out for rattlesnakes, especially in spring and summer.

Tucker's Grove Park
805 San Antonio Creek Road at Cathedral Oaks, Santa Barbara
(805) 967-1112
www.sbparks.org
Tucker's Grove is hugely popular with large groups, partly because of its easy access and partly because it has group picnic areas that can accommodate up to 400 people.

The lower portion of the park is almost completely level and covered with lawn, which means that it's easy to keep an eye on the kids, and they aren't likely to go climbing off someplace where you can't find them. On this level there's a large playground area, a volleyball court, horseshoe pits, and lots of picnic areas for large or small groups.

Kiwanis Meadow, the upper area of the park, also has a very large group picnic area with a barbecue, play equipment, a ballfield, and a volleyball court. From Kiwanis Meadow you can hike up San Antonio Creek Canyon on foot or ride up on horseback (although you're responsible for getting the horse) all the way to San Marcos Pass Road. Both areas have permanent restrooms and parking lots, although the lots may fill up during large group events or on holidays.

GOLETA

Evergreen Open Space
Evergreen Drive and Brandon Drive, Goleta
(805) 568-2460
www.sbparks.org
A greenbelt area in west Goleta, Evergreen has tennis courts and playground equipment and is a great spot for a picnic. It's the home of the only official 18-hole Frisbee (or "disc")

golf course between here and Los Angeles. If that's your game, this is your place! Parking is on the street, and there are no restrooms.

Goleta Beach County Park
5986 Sandspit Road, Goleta
(805) 967-1300
www.sbparks.org
Located just east of the University of California at Santa Barbara campus, Goleta Beach sits at the entrance to the Goleta Slough, which makes it a great birding spot as well as a first-rate day-use facility for sunbathing, swimming, or fishing off the pier. A playground, restrooms, and ample parking are onsite, and the excellent Beachside Bar and Cafe (805-964-7881) sits right on the sand (see our Restaurants chapter). For more information about the park, see the Beaches and Watersports chapter.

Lake Los Carneros Park
Los Carneros Road and Calle Real, Goleta
(805) 568-2460
www.sbparks.org
Lake Los Carneros, bounded by Los Carneros Road, Covington Way, Calle Real, and La Patera Lane, is a hidden jewel in the center of busy Goleta. The grounds include the lovely Stow House (see the Attractions chapter) and outbuildings, the restored Goleta Train Depot, which houses the South Coast Railroad Museum (also listed in the Attractions and Kidstuff chapters), and a 25-acre artificial lake that has been declared a natural preserve.

Pathways (either dirt, decomposed granite, or wood-chip-covered) circle the lake, making it easy to do the loop on foot or on a bike. At the north end of the lake, a wooden footbridge crosses the channel, offering the perfect vantage point for observing the birds, turtles, frogs, and other fauna that populate the area.

The garden around the Stow House, planted with a variety of exotic plants, is also a wonderful birding spot, especially in spring. Fish inhabit the lake, and local anglers swear that some of these are big, but we've never seen anything bigger than a large minnow. Still, you can take your chances by casting off the bank if you want. No swimming is allowed in the lake.

Near the railroad depot is a small picnic area, but people often eat lunch on the Stow House lawn, stretching out in the shade to enjoy the sights and sounds of nature. The park is a perfect place to exercise your dog, but please remember that pets need to be on a leash and should never be allowed to disturb the local wildlife by leaping into the lake.

You can park on any of the streets that border the park, but most people opt to use the parking lot on Los Carneros Road, between Cathedral Oaks and Calle Real. Restrooms are on-site.

Stow Grove Park
580 La Patera Lane, Goleta
(805) 961-7500
www.sbparks.org
Truly unique for the Santa Barbara area, this Goleta City park is dominated by a large grove of California coastal redwood trees that tower over wood-chip-covered walkways lined with low wooden fences. Also scattered throughout the park are mature sycamores, oaks, and eucalyptus, and a small grove of giant sequoias grows north of the children's play area.

The south section of the park is newer, with a large redwood play area, lots of picnic tables, and a wide lawn sheltered by oaks and pines. The north section includes group picnic areas, a smaller playground, two volleyball courts, horseshoe pits, and a softball diamond. Stow Grove has a permanent restroom, and parking is available in the on-site lot. If the lot fills up, park on La Patera Lane or on the street north of Cathedral Oaks Road.

MONTECITO

Manning Park
449 San Ysidro Road, Montecito
(805) 568-2460
www.sbparks.org

Divided into two distinct sections—upper and lower—Manning Park is a lovely shady spot in the middle of Montecito. It's a popular site for weddings and family celebrations. All the vegetation in the park has been introduced, and California live oaks as well as native plant species such as toyon, coffeeberry, and maple trees have been planted.

In addition to the charm of its terrain, the park offers many recreational facilities, including three group picnic areas with barbecues (the largest accommodating up to 250 people), a softball field, a tennis court, a volleyball court, four horseshoe pits, and a playground. The upper park has a permanent restroom, while the lower park offers only a chemical toilet. Small parking areas are scattered throughout the park, or you can park on School House Road, which borders the southwest side of the upper park.

SUMMERLAND

Lookout Park
2297 Finney Road, Summerland
(805) 969-1720
www.sbparks.org
Known for its spectacular view of the ocean and the Channel Islands, four-acre Lookout Park is perched above the sea just north of Carpinteria. The beach below (you must descend a steep hill to reach the sand) has a secluded feel to it, and it's a great spot for swimming, surfing, or surf fishing. In the park area, you'll find two large picnic areas with a barbecue, a playground on a sand surface, volleyball courts, and restrooms.

Toro Canyon Park
576 Toro Canyon Road, Summerland
(805) 568-2460
www.sbparks.org
You are miles from the beach at this county park, but the rugged oak woodland provides a pleasant change of scenery. The 74 acres remain in their natural state, with only a small, 1-acre grassy area breaking up the chaparral, oak, manzanita, sage, and other indigenous plants.

Toro Canyon has two main parking areas, three large group picnic areas (one accommodating more than 200 people), and a network of paths and hiking trails throughout, one of which will reward you with an overlook gazebo at the end. Recreational facilities include horseshoe pits, and a playground.

A park ranger lives here year-round.

Note: Fire danger can be extremely high here during the summer and fall.

CARPINTERIA

Carpinteria Bluffs Nature Park
Bailard Avenue, Carpinteria
(805) 684-5405

Perched high above the sparkling Pacific, this stunning expanse of wilderness is one of the largest tracts of open space left along the county's south coast. In October 2000, after a passionate fund-raising campaign by a local group known as Citizens for the Carpinteria Bluffs, this 52-acre property was officially deeded to the City of Carpinteria to be protected as a natural open-space preserve. Stretching west from Bailard Avenue, the bluffs encompass a spectacular area of quiet meadows, thick eucalyptus groves, and rugged sea cliffs. As you stroll along the hiking trails, you'll be treated to gorgeous views of the Carpinteria Valley, the Santa Ynez Mountains, and the Santa Barbara Channel. It's also a fantastic place to hike and look for wildlife. In a rocky cove below the bluffs lies one of only two publicly accessible harbor seal colonies in Southern California (see the Close-up in this chapter). To access the bluffs, take the Bailard Avenue exit, turn right, and park in the lot at the end of the street.

Carpinteria Salt Marsh Nature Park
Ash Avenue and Sandyland Road
(805) 684-5405

A remnant of a wetland that once extended from the Santa Ynez Mountains to the Pacific, this newly restored 230-acre reserve is one of the largest remaining coastal estuaries in California. A few years ago, this vast wetland resembled little more than a wasteland, but it's made an incredible comeback. Native plants are flourishing, halibut and other marine and estuarine fish nurseries are thriving in the channel, and waterfowl flock to the fish-rich waters. Not surprisingly, birding is excellent. Visitors have spotted more than 200 species here, including ospreys, long-billed curlews, pelicans, egrets, and endangered species such as Belding's savannah sparrow and the light-footed clapper rail. To access the park, exit U.S. Highway 101 at Linden Avenue and drive south less than a mile (1.5 kilometers). Just before the avenue hits Carpinteria Beach, turn right on Sandyland Road. Continue 3 blocks to the park entrance on Ash Avenue, and park along the street. Near the entrance, you'll find an amphitheater, interpretative signs, and restrooms. For a relaxing mile-long stroll, follow the nature trails to the edge of the channel, where you can watch fish jumping and waterfowl stalking the banks. You can join a 90-minute docent-led tour at the park entrance on Saturday at 10:00 a.m.

Carpinteria State Beach
Linden Avenue and Sixth Street, Carpinteria
(805) 968-1033

In addition to camping spaces, this 48-acre park has a mile of beachfront perfect for swimming, fishing, tidepooling, surfing, beach volleyball, and soaking up the sun. If you'd rather not get sand in your shorts, there's a grassy play area that's relatively sand-free. Nearby, seals and sea lions are often visible, and occasionally you can even spot a whale swimming by. Stop by the visitor center to view natural history exhibits or take one of the scheduled nature walks.

El Carro Park
El Carro Lane and Namouna Street, Carpinteria
(805) 684-5405
www.ci.carpinteria.ca.us

This small neighborhood park has a playground for the kids, a picnic area with a barbecue, a multiuse field, and restrooms. It's a

Sealing Their Future

As our human population swells, wildlife habitats shrink, so it's exhilarating to know wild places can still thrive in our midst. If you visit small-town Carpinteria, on the eastern reaches of Santa Barbara, and hike along the spectacular oceanview bluffs, you can see one of these last fragile places. Tucked deep within a rocky cove is one of only two publicly accessible harbor seal colonies in Southern California.

Harbor seals are perhaps the most easily seen of all Santa Barbara's six species of seals. On land, however, they're extremely skittish, so you need to approach the viewing area with care. If you visit the sanctuary in December through January, you will see expectant mothers resting on the shore. In February to early May, the chubby doe-eyed pups are born and suckled amid the mossy rocks on the beach. By the end of May, the pups are independent. They are swimming and fishing on their own, ready to face a life of uncertainty in the sea.

Every year, more than 10,000 people come to the colony to see this cycle of life unfold. We've listed some of the questions most frequently asked of the volunteers who staff the colony. We hope the answers enhance your appreciation of these gentle creatures.

How do I get to the colony?

Going south on Highway 101, take the Bailard exit. Turn right and park in the lot at the end of the street near the hot dog stand. Follow the path west along the bluffs for approximately 1/2 mile (0.8 kilometer) until you see a viewing area just before the pier. If you have a dog with you, tie it up before you enter the area. (Dogs scare the seals into the water.) Slowly and quietly approach the viewing area. You can usually spot the seals lying on the beach, playing in the surf, or resting on the large rock. Don't forget your binoculars, so you can see them up close and personal!

From the Carpinteria State Beach Campground, hike along the bluff-top trail parallel to the beach for about 1/4 mile (0.4 kilometer). When you arrive at the private Venoco parking lot, follow the blue seal markers on the ground.

What are harbor seals?

Harbor seals are mammals. They are called pinnapeds (Latin for "fin-footed ones") and belong to the group of seals known as phocids, or true seals. On land, phocids crawl on their stomachs like giant caterpillars instead of using their flippers for mobility as sea lions and fur seals do. Look closely at their heads and you'll also notice that they lack external ear lobes.

When is the best time to see the seals?

Your best chance to spot the seals is from December through May, when the beach is closed to the public and the seals feel safe enough to rest on shore.

If you visit the Carpinteria seal colony between February and May, you may witness the birth of a harbor seal. BRIAN HASTINGS

From January to May, volunteers are there to protect the seals from any disturbances. Try to visit at low tide during these times.

Why is the beach closed?
From December 1 through May 31, the beach is closed so that the pregnant seals can haul out on land to rest, give birth, and nurse their pups. Disturbances such as a loud noise, a sudden movement, or a dog barking can frighten the seals and send them crawling into the water. When this happens, spontaneous abortions can occur, and any young pups left on shore are extremely vulnerable to predators. If separated for too long from their mothers, the pups are orphaned and can starve to death. Disturbances may also result in relocation of the colony.

What work are the volunteers doing?
Volunteers are there to protect the seals, inform the public, answer questions, monitor the impact of disturbances, and collect data. Every 30 minutes the seals are counted.

Can I go onto the beach and touch the seals?
No. The seals are protected by both local and federal law. Under the Federal Marine Mammal Protection Act, you can be fined up to $10,000 for disturbing the seals. Dog owners are also liable for any injury inflicted by their pets.

Are the seals here year-round?
Yes. Unlike some other species of seals, harbor seals are nonmigratory, so they use this cove as their home base throughout the year. However, they're difficult to see when the beach is open in summer and fall because people and animals frighten them into the water. Your best bet for spotting them at this time of the year is to visit the colony early in the morning.

Where else are they found?
Harbor seals are found throughout the northern hemisphere in the Atlantic and Pacific Oceans. In the northeast Pacific they range from the Bering Sea to Baja. They also breed and give birth on some of the Channel Islands.

How many seals live in this colony?
More than 300 seals have been counted here, but numbers fluctuate depending on the tides, the weather, and local disturbances.

How big do they get?
Adult males can grow up to 6 feet (1.83 meters) in length and weigh up to 300 pounds (136 kilograms). Females are slightly smaller.

How long do they live?
Harbor seals can live to be 30 to 40 years old.

Why are they different colors?
It's a matter of genetics. Just as people are born with different hair color, seals are born with different-colored coats and variations in mottling. Some are a beautiful silvery gray or dark brown with many dark splotches. Others are cream, caramel, or white, with few markings. You can only see their colors on land when their coats are dry. In the water they all look shiny and black.

What do they eat?
The diet of harbor seals consists mainly of fish, but they also eat shrimp, squid, crayfish, and crab. They can dive as deep as 600 feet underwater to find prey on the ocean floor, staying down for up to 20 to 30 minutes.

What eats them?
In the water, killer whales and sharks—especially great white sharks—are common predators. On land, coyotes, domestic dogs, and eagles prey on juveniles or pups. For centuries, humans slaughtered harbor seals for meat and for their thick pelts, but the animals have been protected in the United States since 1972. Unfortunately though, we are still killing them indirectly. Ocean pollution has led to an increase in the incidence of disease, and in this colony, it's the most common cause of death.

How big are the pups when they are born?
At birth, harbor seal pups weigh about 12 to 18 pounds (5.5 to 8.2 kilograms).

When can the pups swim?
Since they are born in intertidal zones, the pups can swim almost immediately after birth. They will spend roughly half their lives in water and half on land.

How long do the pups stay with their mothers?
Harbor seal pups usually stay with their mother for about four to six weeks until they are weaned. After this they must find their own food and fend for themselves.

Are there any males in this colony?
Yes, but since the difference in size between males and females is slight, they are difficult to identify.

Where do they sleep?
Harbor seals prefer to sleep on land; however, they are occasionally forced to sleep in the water during high tides or when hauling grounds are in short supply.

Do the seals ever have twins?
Harbor seals rarely give birth to twins. When they do, however, the chances of both pups surviving to adulthood are slim.

How do seals communicate with each other?
Harbor seal pups sound a little bit like human babies. They make a bleating noise that sounds like "maaaaaaa, maaaaaaa," which helps their mothers identify them. The adults, while not as vocal as other species, communicate by grunting, yelping, growling, snarling, and making deep belching noises. They probably wouldn't make the best dinner-party guests!

What should I do if I find a harbor seal on the beach?
The first thing you should do is leave it alone. If it's a pup, chances are its mother is in the water searching for food or waiting for you to leave so she can reunite with her baby. Staying too close to seal pups can result in them being orphaned. Also, you should never pour water on seals. Note the exact location of the animal and call the Marine Mammal Center Hotline at (805) 687-3255.

great place to spread out a blanket, and there's plenty of room to run on the expansive lawn.

Monte Vista Park
Bailard Avenue and Pandanus Street, Carpinteria
(805) 684-5405
www.carpinteria.com/activities/parks/MonteVista

One of Carpinteria's most popular parks, its open spaces encourage soccer games. A jogging trail, multiuse field, and playground are also in the park. The park is set back behind some condominiums outside the city of Carpinteria, just above the Ventura County line.

WEST OF GOLETA

We mention El Capitan, Gaviota, and Refugio beaches briefly here. For detailed information (including camping information) see the Recreation and Beaches and Watersports chapters.

El Capitan State Beach
Off U.S. Highway 101, 17 miles (27 kilometers) west of Santa Barbara
(805) 968-1033
www.parks.ca.gov

One of our favorites, El Cap is open from dawn to dusk year-round and offers swimming (the beach is accessible via a stairway on the bluffs), fishing, picnicking, and camping as well as tidepooling and birding. The bike trail here connects with Refugio State Beach, 2.5 miles (4.0 kilometers) up the coast. Along the bike trail are some lesser known but very rewarding accesses to the beach.

Gaviota State Park
Off U.S. Highway 101, 33 miles (53 kilometers) west of Santa Barbara
(805) 968-1033
www.parks.ca.gov

Made up of 2,700 acres that rise from sea level to the top of Gaviota Peak, Gaviota is a popular park for swimming and camping. Anglers,

divers, and surfers can use the pier at the west end of the beach. In addition to the normal beach activities, the park has great hiking trails, including one that takes you to Gaviota Hot Springs, and it's a beautiful spot for a picnic. High winds can sometimes be a problem so be prepared. Nearly half the campsites can now be reserved ahead of time from the end of May through August.

Refugio State Beach
Off U.S. Highway 101, 23 miles (37 kilometers) west of Santa Barbara
(805) 968-1033
www.parks.ca.gov

Just 2.5 miles (4.0 kilometers) west of El Capitan State Beach, Refugio is an excellent spot for surf fishing, picnicking, camping, and hiking. The waters off Refugio also offer some great swimming and diving, with reefs and kelp beds to explore.

SANTA YNEZ VALLEY

Cachuma Lake Recreation Area
Calif. Highway 154, 20 miles (32 kilometers) northwest of Santa Barbara
(805) 686-5054
www.sbparks.org

Although the Santa Ynez Valley is technically out of Santa Barbara proper, we include this county park because it's a local favorite and less than an hour's drive from Santa Barbara. It's especially popular for fishing and camping (see the Fishing and Recreation chapters for details) as well as for boating and wildlife viewing.

You can rent boats (with or without motors) at the lake on a daily, weekly, or monthly basis, and private boat-launching facilities are also available. (Canoes, kayaks, and other boats less than 10 feet in length are not allowed on the lake.)

Because Cachuma is a domestic water reservoir, swimming, wading, waterskiing, sailboarding, and any other bodily contact with the water are not allowed, but there's a swimming pool in the campground that's

El Capitan Beach. NANCY SHOBE

open during the summer months. You can also rent a bike or arrange for horseback riding in the vicinity.

The Cachuma Lake Nature Center features displays of local flora and fauna as well as Chumash artifacts (the Chumash Village of Ah-ke-tsoom once thrived in the area, but the site was covered with water after the construction of Bradbury Dam in 1953). For a fun family outing, join in the nature walks scheduled every Saturday from 10:00 to 11:30 a.m. Some of the animals you might expect to see around the lake are deer, wild pigs, bears, and as many as 275 species of birds.

Cachuma is especially proud of its small but permanent American bald eagle population, and this is the only place in the county where you can reliably spot this majestic symbol of America. To get a close-up look at the eagles and other wildlife, we recommend taking a two-hour, naturalist-led Eagle Cruise aboard the *Osprey*.

The 45-passenger *Osprey* departs from the marina Wednesday through Sunday at 10:00 a.m., with additional trips Friday and Saturday at 2:00 p.m. The cost is $15 for adults; $7 for children 12 and younger. Be sure to make a reservation (805-686-5050), and bring your binoculars and a warm jacket, as it can be quite chilly on the lake. Because you are riding on a relatively flat surface, seasickness is generally not a problem.

Cachuma Lake is open for day use from 8:00 a.m. to sunset; admission is $6 a vehicle. Plenty of parking is scattered throughout, and restrooms (or chemical toilets) are available in each camping area, at the marina, and near the pool.

CHANNEL ISLANDS NATIONAL PARK AND NATIONAL MARINE SANCTUARY

The Channel Islands are less than 30 miles from the mainland, but they're an entire world apart. When you step ashore, you feel as if you've traveled a century back in time to the pristine California land and seascapes that once dominated the coast. You won't see hotels, restaurants, and museums lining the shores. Instead, you'll find spectacular white-sand beaches, sea caves and hidden coves, vast grasslands, barren mountains, rocky reefs, and incredibly clear water.

Eight islands in the waters off Southern California make up the Channel Islands. Often referred to as "America's Galapagos," these remote islands and the waters surrounding them are filled with unusual flora and fauna, dramatic geological formations, rare archeological finds, and other oddities that occur nowhere else on earth.

One reason the channel is so unique is because it's an unusual transition zone called the Southern California Bight. At Point Conception, the islands and the mainland run east-west rather than north-south. The waters lying between the islands and the mainland form the Santa Barbara Channel—a melting pot of currents from different directions. The California current brings cold waters from the Arctic into the channel from the north. Warm currents from Mexico come in from the south, carrying more subtropical marine life along with them.

The result of this complex blend of currents is an exceptional variety of cold-water and warm-water plants and animals, including giant kelp forests, sea birds, whales, seals, and sea lions. In addition, the remoteness of the islands has allowed plants and wildlife to evolve in isolation. This is the only part of the world where you'll find the Santa Cruz Island scrub-jay, the Channel Island fox (see the Close-up in this chapter), the Anacapa deer mouse, and many other endemic species.

FROM ISOLATED ISLANDS TO PROTECTED SANCTUARIES

For more than 11,000 years, the Chumash, or "island people," lived on these islands, regularly traversing the channel in swift canoes called *tomols* to trade with mainland Indians. They lived in peaceful isolation on the islands until 1542, when explorer Juan Rodriguez Cabrillo cruised through the channel while leading an expedition for Spain. He supposedly fell on San Miguel and died as a result, but his body has never been found.

The 1700s and 1800s brought more explorers and eventually fur traders, hunters, settlers, and ranchers—all of whom threatened the Channel Islands' resources and habitats. It wasn't until the late 20th century that the incredible biodiversity, important cultural artifacts, and stunning natural beauty of the islands triggered a succession of moves to protect the region. In 1980 Congress officially recognized the significance of the region's natural and cultural resources and declared five of the islands—San Miguel, Santa Rosa, Santa Cruz, Anacapa, and Santa Barbara—and their surrounding 1 nautical mile of ocean as the Channel Islands National Park. Later that year, 1,252 nautical miles of ocean extending from mean high tide to 6 nautical miles offshore around each of the islands in the park were designated a National Marine Sanctuary.

The islands themselves fall under the jurisdiction of the National Park Service, while the National Oceanic and Atmospheric Administration (NOAA) administers the marine sanctuary program, and the National Park Service and the National Marine Sanctuary share jurisdiction of the nautical mile closest to the island shores. (In this chapter, Channel Islands National Park and Channel Islands National Marine Sanctuary are often referred to collectively for easier reading.)

CONTINUED CONSERVATION

In 1988 The Nature Conservancy, a nonprofit international environmental organization, acquired the western 90 percent of Santa Cruz Island from a private owner and formed the Santa Cruz Island Preserve. The National Park Service continued to own and manage the remaining eastern side of the island. Then in August 2000, The Nature Conservancy transferred 8,500 acres of its holdings on Santa Cruz Island to the National Park Service, a donation designed to reinforce the partnership between the two organizations. Since the transfer, the Conservancy owns and manages the western 76 percent of the island, while the eastern 24 percent is owned and managed by the National Park Service.

The 8,500 acres of Santa Cruz Island donated by The Nature Conservancy to the National Park Service adjoin the park's western boundary and includes the 5-mile-long narrow section of the island called the isthmus. The land transfer was great news for visitors to Santa Cruz Island, who now have much more land to explore. The public can come ashore on the isthmus at Prisoners' Harbor, hike the trails, explore the beach, and camp in the designated areas. The Nature Conservancy limits public access to the Santa Cruz Island Preserve due to recovering ecosystems in this part of the island. See the Santa Cruz Island Project section below for more information.

BACK IN THE NEST

In the early and mid-1900s, the national bald eagle population declined by nearly two thirds.

The pollution of DDT and other pesticides was to blame. The Channel Islands were not exempt from this decline. The previously plentiful bald eagles became completely extinct by the early 1960s. Chemical pollution caused the birds to lay thin-shelled eggs. Thankfully, the subsequent banning of toxic pesticides allowed the islands to slowly recover to their natural state. With the islands in a healthier condition, bird restoration began.

In 2002 funding from the Montrose Settlements Restoration Program and its partner, the Institute for Wildlife Studies, allowed for the reintroduction of 61 young bald eagles to the northern Channel Islands. In spring 2006, efforts paid off when the first bald eagle chick hatched (unaided by humans in over 50 years) on the islands. This important conservation event made national headlines. It was so big that federal agencies joined together to set up a webcam (chil.vcoe.org/eagle_cam.htm) to live feed the action to the entire country. (In fact, the chick identified as A-49 was recently tracked flying over the mainland near Santa Barbara.)

Spring 2007 brought yet another birth of a bald eagle chick on Santa Cruz Island, an extremely positive indicator that the islands are one chick closer to recovering their bald eagle population. Currently, over 30 bald eagles are in residence.

Bald eagles aren't the islands' only comeback chicks. Another is the peregrine falcon. It, too, disappeared from the islands in the mid-20th century. Scientists recently discovered the first pair of peregrine falcon chicks in over 50 years, all signs of good things to come.

A WEALTH OF NATURAL RESOURCES

In the areas of the Channel Islands that are currently protected, scientists have been following a remarkable comeback by Mother Nature. Native flowers and plants are beginning to bloom anew after years of grazing by cows and sheep. Sea lions and seals are multiplying, and fish are restocking their schools.

People come from all over the world to see and experience the wonders of the Channel Islands. The national park is home to more than 2,000 terrestrial plants and animals, and 145 of these are found nowhere else on earth. Thousands of sea birds nest on the islands because there are few other creatures to prey on them.

The marine life surrounding the Channel Islands is equally amazing. The giant kelp forest alone supports more than 800 species of marine life. Key species in the sanctuary include the California sea lion, elephant and harbor seals, blue and gray whales, dolphins, and the blue shark, brown pelican, western gull, abalone, garibaldi, and rockfish.

Pinnipeds (seals and sea lions) were once hunted nearly to extinction for their meat, fur, oil, and ivory. But the Marine Mammal Protection Act passed in 1972 made it illegal to kill, harm, or capture any kind of marine mammal without a permit. Six species of pinnipeds live and breed on the Channel Islands and in the surrounding waters.

More than 27 species of cetaceans (whales and porpoises) inhabit the sanctuary during the year. From December through April, thousands of gray whales swim through the channel on their annual migration from Alaska to Mexico and back. (See the Whale-Watching section of our Beaches and Watersports chapter if you'd like to go on a whale-watching trip). In the last decade, increased numbers of more unusual whales have shown up in the channel, including blue, minke, and humpback.

The common dolphin practically owns the channel. They travel in large groups and love to play and surf in the wake of passing boats. Sometimes you can spot a Dall's porpoise or Risso's dolphins. Other dolphins here include the Pacific white-sided and bottlenose dolphins.

More than 25 species of sharks have been sighted in the channel, but some only vacation here from time to time. Resident sharks include the giant basking, leopard, thresher, blue, horn, and Pacific angel.

We humans are invited to experience this natural wonderland in all its splendor—as long as we respect and care for its precious resources.

THE NATIONAL PARK, MARINE SANCTUARY, AND NATURE PRESERVE

The National Park Service, the National Marine Sanctuary, and The Nature Conservancy all work to protect the fragile ecosystems of the islands and the sea, while educating the public about the plants, animals, marine life, and other natural phenomena. Following are descriptions of the special services each provides.

Channel Islands National Park Headquarters and Robert J. Largomarsino Visitor Center
1901 Spinnaker Drive, Ventura
(805) 658-5730
www.nps.gov/chis
The Channel Islands National Park Headquarters and Visitor Center is in Ventura, 35 miles southeast of Santa Barbara. Although it's not technically in the geographic area covered by this book, we do need to tell you about the visitor center, which is not only a one-stop resource for information about the islands but also a fun and fascinating place to visit. Wander inside and you'll find a museum, a bookstore, a living tidepool and interactive touch-screen exhibit, telescopes, and other interesting displays. You can also see a 25-minute movie in the auditorium. The visitor center is open daily 8:30 a.m. to 5:00 p.m.; it's closed on Thanksgiving and Christmas.

On weekends and holidays at 11:00 a.m. and 3:00 p.m., park rangers offer free public programs about park features such as tidepools and recreational opportunities within the park.

i The most complete skeleton of a pygmy mammoth was discovered on Santa Rosa Island in 1994. The mammoths roamed the Channel Islands during the Pleistocene epoch.

Channel Islands National Marine
Sanctuary
113 Harbor Way, Suite 150, Santa Barbara
(805) 966-7107
www.cinms.nos.noaa.gov
The Channel Islands National Marine Sanctuary is one of only 13 National Marine Sanctuaries in the United States. Sanctuary programs are designed not only to protect the waters but also to promote public awareness of marine issues and make the area available for recreational activities.

Diving trips, underwater photography, whale-watching, and fish surveys are all offered.

Santa Cruz Island Project of The Nature
Conservancy
(949) 263-0933, information
www.nature.org
The Nature Conservancy is a private, international nonprofit membership organization. Its mission is "to preserve the plants, animals, and natural communities that represent the diversity of life on Earth by protecting the lands and waters they need to survive."
The Nature Conservancy currently owns and manages the Santa Cruz Island Preserve, which comprises 76 percent of the island.

The organization also offers a variety of daylong and occasional overnight educational trips to the preserve through local concessionaires and museums. Call for more information.

WHAT TO SEE AND DO

If you're looking for direct interaction with nature, you'll love the Channel Islands. They offer a fantastic array of recreational opportunities amid gorgeous scenery. You can hike, fish, camp, dive, snorkel, and even surf within the park. You can go diving, birding, whale-watching, and sailing, explore tidepools, and lounge on the beaches, which locals think are among the most beautiful in the world.

From certain overlooks on some islands, you can observe hundreds of seals and sea lions hauling onto the beaches. You can kayak in coves, sea caves, and lagoons or go on a ranger-led hike and discover the island's human history. Many Santa Barbara companies offer scuba diving, kayaking, and sailing trips—see our Beaches and Watersports chapter for details on specific sports. You'll also find complete information on angling in our Fishing chapter.

If you're interested in kayaking, contact the Channel Islands National Park and Robert J. Largomarsino Visitor Center at (805) 658-5730 and request its special sea kayaking information brochure. For guided camping adventures and customized tours, contact Santa Barbara Adventure Company (805-898-0671, 888-773-3239; www.sbadventureco.com).

Camping

You can camp year-round in National Park Service–managed campgrounds on all five islands, but no camping is allowed in the Santa Cruz Island Preserve. Beach camping is allowed on Santa Rosa Island.

Camping reservations are required for all campgrounds and can be obtained by calling (800) 365-CAMP, visiting the National Park Service online Reservation Center at reservations.nps.gov or through Biospherics, Inc. at (800) 365-2267. Before you can reserve a campsite, however, you are required to arrange your transportation. That's because the boats tend to fill up before the campgrounds.

The camping fee is $15 per campsite per night, with most of the money covering maintenance of the camping facilities as well as monthly water monitoring. Reservations can be made no more than five months in advance, and we recommend that you reserve well ahead of time, not only to ensure that you get a site but also to allow time for the permit to travel in the mail. When you call, you will need to have some information at hand: camping dates, transportation information, and number of campers.

Facilities are very primitive. You will need to bring all your own water and food. You also have to carry your gear from landing areas to the campgrounds, so don't go overboard when packing. All campgrounds have picnic tables and pit toilets. Fires are not permitted. Bring along an enclosed camp stove for cooking.

On Santa Rosa Island and Scorpion Ranch on Santa Cruz Island, you can enjoy the luxury of running water. Santa Rosa even has an outdoor cold-water shower. But, to be safe, you should only use this water for cooking and washing—you should still bring your own drinking water or a water filter.

Fierce winds often blast the campgrounds on Santa Rosa and San Miguel Islands. The National Park Service has built windbreaks to shield campers from their full force. You won't blow away, but your maps and lightweight items might, so stow them tightly away.

The National Park Service can send you detailed camping information specific to each island as well as suggested packing lists. Call (805) 658-5730, or visit the camping Web site at www.channelislands.national-park.com/camping.htm.

Diving

The National Park and the Marine Sanctuary form one of the most fascinating dive destinations on the planet. Divers from all around the nation and the world come to explore the magnificent kelp forests and the incredibly diverse marine life. Visibility here is usually much better than off the mainland beaches.

Fall is usually the best time to explore the waters. At this time of year, seas are smoother, water temperature hovers in the higher ranges, and sunshine lights up the water. Visibility also tends to be better during the fall.

If you're a diver, contact the Channel Islands National Park or the Marine Sanctuary for special pamphlets on diving and shipwrecks you can visit. Permits to dive are not required. For information on diving excursions, refer to the Diving section of the Beaches and Watersports chapter. In the

meantime, here are a few guidelines to keep you safe in the sometimes-treacherous channel waters.

- Use standard safe diving procedures.
- Know the area.
- Be aware that changing weather affects currents and surge.
- Never dive alone.
- Always fly the diver's flag when underwater.

ISLAND BY ISLAND

Although the Channel Islands have a lot in common with each other, each has distinct features that set it apart. Here are brief descriptions of each island. You also can request a detailed guide for each island from the Channel Islands National Park Visitor Center in Ventura (805-658-5730).

Note that there are no food and drink concessions on the islands. When you visit, you must bring all your own supplies, including drinking water. You will also need to pack out all your trash.

Anacapa Island

Anacapa Island's name is derived from the Chumash word "Eneepah," which means island of deception or mirage. That's because the island gives the illusion of changing shape when the weather is foggy or very warm. Anacapa is actually a chain of three small islets (East, Middle, and West Anacapa) connected by shallow sandbars. It's not very big—5 miles (8 kilometers) long and 1/4 mile (0.4 kilometer) wide—and the land area totals just 1 square mile. Since this island is closest to the mainland (Ventura), it's also the most visited. It's only about 90 minutes by boat from the mainland and is a good choice if you're visiting the islands for the first time.

Anacapa has 130 sea caves, 29 Chumash archeological sites, and towering cliffs. The

i The lighthouse on Anacapa Island was the last permanent lighthouse built on the West Coast.

islands attract large populations of sea birds, including California Brown Pelicans and the largest breeding colony of Western gulls in the world. Tidepooling is also excellent—the best area is said to be near Frenchy's Cove on the southeastern tip of West Anacapa.

Almost all trips to Anacapa are to East Anacapa Island, where you'll find ranger residences, a visitor center, a lighthouse, and a churchlike building containing two 50,000-gallon redwood water tanks, all built before 1932. Until 1990, the lighthouse had a handmade Freshnel lens. It now uses a modern lighting system, but you can see the original lead crystal lens in the visitor center.

You can hike on about 1.5 miles (2.4 kilometers) of trails on East Anacapa. During the summer, the park rangers offer daily guided nature walks. A self-guided trail booklet is available at the visitor center trailhead. Picnic tables for day use are available in three areas on East Anacapa. You can snorkel and swim in the Landing Cove, but you might want to wear a wetsuit—the water's cold, even in summer.

Santa Cruz Island

Santa Cruz is the largest and most topographically diverse of all the Channel Islands. It's about 24 miles (39 kilometers) long, with a total of 60,645 acres of mountains, valleys, grasslands, woodlands, beaches, and dunes. Most visitors hike, camp, picnic, and explore on the eastern end of the island, which is managed by the Channel Islands National Park. Be prepared for a skiff landing on the beach—there are no piers at any of the landings.

A number of rugged hiking trails and roads lead you to bluffs and mountaintops for spectacular views, and along the coastline are sea caves, rocky ledges, reefs, and tidepools. On land, the island supports an exceptional array of flora and fauna. More than 600 plant types flourish here, and eight types are found only on Santa Cruz Island. The most famous endemic plants include the Santa Cruz Island ironwood and the island oak.

More than 260 species of birds inhabit the island, including the endemic Santa Cruz

i Santa Cruz Island is home to the largest and deepest known sea cave in the world—Painted Cave. Named for the colorful rocks and lichens covering its surface, the cave is 160 feet (49 meters) high at its entrance and extends a quarter of a mile into the side of the island. In the spring a waterfall cascades down through its mouth. Depending on conditions, you might be able to visit the cave on a summer whale-watching cruise aboard the *Condor Express*. (See the Beaches and Watersports chapter.)

Island scrub-jay—a bigger, bluer version of its mainland cousin. The Channel Island fox is the most famous mammal in these parts, next to the seals and sea lions that bask and play in the coves.

The island is a superb destination for swimming, snorkeling, diving, and kayaking. It lies right in the transition zone for warm currents from the south and colder currents from the north, so this is where you'll find a mingling of marine species.

If you're in any type of kayak or a private boat and want to land or hike in the Nature Conservancy–owned preserve, you must apply for a day-use landing permit in advance. See the Permits and Regulations section later in this chapter.

Santa Rosa Island

Santa Rosa is the second-largest island in the park (53,000 acres, or 84 square miles). It's also one of the most remote, which means you won't run into many people. Because of its size and seclusion, Santa Rosa is a great choice for multiday visits. Or you can take a day trip over to fish for surf perch and halibut off the windswept beaches or wander the rugged trails. The island's many landscapes—mountains, canyons, sand dunes, grasslands, woodlands, and freshwater marsh—make hiking along the dirt roads and trails a real treat.

We've visited Santa Rosa in the summertime and enjoyed walking along the beautiful

Blue Whales—Repeat Visitors to the Channel Islands

At one time of year or another, 27 species of cetaceans (whales and porpoises) visit the Channel Islands National Marine Sanctuary. Among these are the rare and magnificent blue whales—the largest animals to ever exist on Earth.

Blue whales (*Balaenoptera musculus*) have been on the endangered species list since 1966. Before the whaling industry severely depleted their numbers, about 300,000 blue whales cruised the world's oceans. Today, there are fewer than 10,000. About 2,000 are found off the coast of California—the greatest concentration of blue whales in the world.

In 1992, for reasons still not entirely understood by marine experts, blue whales began coming in increasing numbers to feed in the Channel Islands National Marine Sanctuary, usually from late May through October. Approximately 200 blue whales have been sighted at the peak of the feeding season, which is an incredibly large number considering that blue whales are usually very shy, very fast, and as a result, seldom seen. Also, they generally travel alone or in pairs, and their migratory patterns are not entirely predictable.

The whales that feed near the California coast typically go south in the winter (usually to Mexico) to breed and give birth. In the summer, they return to California to feed, traveling wherever they can find abundant krill, which are small, shrimplike crustaceans found mostly near continental shelf waters. It seems as though blue whales have discovered a sumptuous krill buffet in the Channel Islands National Marine Sanctuary, and they keep coming back for more.

Blue whales are truly amazing creatures. When a calf is born, it already weighs 2 to 3 tons and is 20 to 24 feet long. Adults weigh approximately 150 to 200 tons, which is equal to about 30 elephants, or 1,600 people. They reach about 80 to 100 feet in length. An adult blue whale's heart is about the size of a VW Beetle, and its tongue is heavier than an African elephant.

Despite their weight and girth, blues are incredibly fast swimmers, traveling at speeds of 8 to 25 knots. They can also dive up to 630 feet. When a blue whale blows, the spout rises up to 50 feet.

The jury's still out on why the blue whales have decided to become regular vacationers in the Santa Barbara Channel. One thing's for certain, though—they do like the gourmet krill the channel serves up. During the spring and summer months, there's something of a "krill machine" phenomenon in the channel, out near a deep canyon close to the Channel Islands. The winds cause an upwelling of dense, cold water that is rich in oxygen and nutrients. When the strong summer sunlight hits this nutrient-rich water, it triggers photosynthesis. The miniscule plants that result attract tiny, but slightly larger, animals such as krill, which feed on the plants. Two hundred krill weigh about one ounce, and it takes about 3,200 to top a pound. They float around in swarms measuring about 330 by 660 feet. Blue whales simply flap their flukes, open their jaws wide, and swim fast through the swarm, and in a short time they pick up literally tons of krill and other marine life that happens to be in the way. One adult blue whale can eat up to 4 tons of krill a day.

Blue whales are particularly sensitive to low-frequency sound. They can hear certain frequencies, including the ones produced by the testing, for thousands of miles. The government ceased seismic testing in 1989, and, lo and behold, in 1992 the blue whales in the vicinity increased in number.

Could it be the lack of disturbance or a larger volume of krill that lured the blue whales back? No one knows for certain, but in the meantime, wildlife enthusiasts are trying to see them while they can.

You can view a 67-foot skeleton of an adolescent blue whale outside the Santa Barbara Museum of Natural History. But if you'd like to see the real thing, make a point of taking a whale-watching cruise sometime during the blue whales' June through October feeding season. See the Whale-Watching section in the Beaches and Watersports chapter for details.

Whale-watching on the Condor Express. FRED BENKO, COURTESY OF THE SANTA BARBARA CONFERENCE ANAD VISITORS BUREAU

i Archaeologists believe the 13,000-year-old bones from an ancient woman discovered on Santa Rosa Island in 1959 are the oldest known human remains in North America.

windswept beaches and up to the grove of Torrey pines—one of the rarest trees in the world. The only other Torrey pines on this half of the planet are found near San Diego, at the Torrey Pines State Reserve. Three native terrestrial mammals make their home on the island—the Channel Island fox, spotted skunk, and deer mouse, all of which are endemic to the Channel Islands.

Santa Rosa is also famous for its remains of the pygmy mammoth, a miniature mammoth that roamed the island during the Pleistocene era. A fossil skeleton of a pygmy mammoth discovered in 1994 on Santa Rosa is the most complete specimen ever found.

Santa Rosa Island was long home to a commercial cattle ranch, Vail & Vickers Company, which began ranching here in 1902. In 1986 the company sold the island to the National Park Service and negotiated a special-use permit allowing it to continue the business until 1998, when the last of the cattle were removed. Currently, the company holds a special-use permit allowing it to hunt introduced species such as deer and elk for a few months of the year.

Other characteristics unique to Santa Rosa include six endemic plant species that occur nowhere else on earth and extensive archaeological findings that divulge much about the Chumash, who thrived on this island for thousands of years. Santa Rosa is the only island that allows backcountry beach camping at certain times of the year. Call the visitor center for more information.

San Miguel Island

San Miguel lies closest to Point Conception, the westernmost end of the channel. Since it is more exposed to prevailing northwest winds and blasting Pacific storms, this island is more barren and weather-beaten than the others. It's often foggy and windy, but if you can put up with the less-than-perfect weather, you'll be rewarded with scenes of wildlife you won't find anywhere else.

Animals like their privacy, and they know that San Miguel is about as private as you can get among the northern Channel Islands. San Miguel's major draw is the Point Bennett rookery and haul-out spot for pinnipeds (sea lions and seals), including Northern fur seals, California sea lions, elephant seals, and harbor seals. At certain times of year, more than 30,000 of these pinnipeds crowd the beach, creating one of the largest congregations of wildlife in the world.

Another unique thing about San Miguel is its caliche forest. Sort of a petrified forest in sand, it was formed by caliche (calcium carbonate) casts around plant roots and trunks. The plants are gone, but you can still see the very strange stone forms that enveloped them.

Between 1948 and 1970 the U.S. Navy used San Miguel as a bombing range, which didn't exactly do much for its natural environment. But Mother Nature has made a huge comeback on the island, and it's now a fertile and scenic preserve for many species of animals and plants. Whales (gray, killer, and blue), dolphins, and porpoises grace the surrounding waters, and zillions of birds, including western gulls, cormorants, pelicans, and auklets fill the skies during the spring and summer months.

Hiking is a fantastic way to experience San Miguel. However, if you leave the Cuyler Harbor and ranger station area, a park ranger must lead you.

Santa Barbara Island

Santa Barbara Island lies much farther offshore than the other islands in the park, so be prepared for a longer boat ride (four or more hours). It's also the smallest of the group—only 1 square mile, or 640 acres. Most of the island is a giant mesa, surrounded by steep cliffs.

Although the island is small, it offers a surprisingly rich array of wildlife and scenery.

We once asked a ranger which island she preferred in the park, and she named Santa Barbara as her perennial favorite.

Santa Barbara Island is most famous for its large sea lion rookery, and you can observe the seals and sea lions from a number of excellent overlook spots. More than 11 species of seabirds nest along the steep cliffs, making the island excellent for birding. The island is also an outstanding destination for snorkeling, swimming, diving, and kayaking.

PERMITS AND REGULATIONS

To protect the delicate resources of the National Park and Marine Sanctuary, all visitors are required to follow specific regulations and obtain appropriate landing, day-use, and camping permits. Here's an overview.

Permits

Channel Islands National Park

Landing and hiking on the islands is limited, and in most cases (except day use on Anacapa and Santa Barbara Islands), you will need a permit to access an island beyond the beaches. All permits are issued free of charge and are available at the park's headquarters and visitor center in Ventura or by calling (805) 658-5730.

Santa Cruz Island Preserve

Access to the preserve is limited, and commercial vessels or commercial charter parties are not allowed to land or let passengers off here. However, if you go by private boat, you can apply for a permit that allows you to land and hike on this part of the island. Contact The Nature Conservancy at (949) 263-0933 to get an application and a list of the strict rules governing activity on the island. The Conservancy issues permits to owners or captains of private charter boats but not to commercial vessels. Permits cost $60 for a calendar year or $20 for 30 consecutive days. You can also sign up for one of the naturalist-led day trips to the island scheduled throughout the year or, if you represent an educational, research,

or nonprofit organization, you can organize a charter day trip. Contact Island Packers at (805) 642-1393, or www.islandpackers.com (see the listing under By Boat in this chapter).

Rules and Regulations

Going out to the National Park and Marine Sanctuary is a fantastic way to view wildlife up close and personal. But you have to remember that all the island's natural resources are protected. The National Marine Sanctuary Program Synopsis of Regulations brochure summarizes the rules all visitors must follow. It's available at the National Park Service Visitor Center in Ventura or the Marine Sanctuary office in Santa Barbara.

Following are a few of the major regulations you should know about.

You may not feed, collect, harass, or otherwise harm the wildlife, plant life, or other natural and cultural resources of the Channel Islands National Park. That means you may not bring back any shells, plants, feathers, animals, Chumash artifacts, or other things you might be tempted to stash in your backpack. When you're tidepooling, don't collect anything. Take only pictures, and leave everything else where it is.

The water, too, is protected, so don't dump any type of refuse in the ocean.

Under federal law, it is illegal to disturb and/or harm marine mammals and seabirds in the National Park or the Marine Sanctuary at any time. They are very sensitive to any type of human disturbances, especially during nesting and pupping seasons. Kayakers, hikers, and other visitors should stay at least 100 yards away from marine mammals, both in the water and on the beaches.

Fishing in waters within the park and sanctuary requires a California fishing license. You can get one at any bait and tackle shop or onboard a Truth Aquatics vessel (see subsequent listing under By Boat). You can check out the Fishing chapter for more specifics on licenses.

The waters 1 nautical mile around Anacapa, San Miguel, and Santa Barbara

Islands are California State Ecological Reserves, where special fish and game regulations apply. In some areas marine life is totally protected—you can't fish or take game at all.

Abalone is now endangered and totally off-limits to everyone for an indefinite period of time. Hands off!

Pets are not allowed onshore on any of the islands.

GETTING THERE

The easiest way to get to the Channel Islands is to hop aboard a commercial passenger boat operated by one of the two official park concessionaires. You can also fly to Santa Rosa Island or catch a ride on a private charter boat.

By Boat

For years, Island Packers Company in Ventura was the sole concessionaire providing public boat transportation to the islands. In recent years the National Park Service added another, Truth Aquatics, located right in Santa Barbara, making it easier for locals and visitors to get out to the islands.

Island Packers Company
1691 Spinnaker Drive, Suite 105B, Ventura
(805) 642-1393 reservations
www.islandpackers.com
Island Packers offers various trips to Anacapa and Santa Cruz Islands year-round, to Santa Barbara and Santa Rosa Islands from April through October, and to San Miguel in May through October. Trips include half-day cruises, all-day excursions, nature discovery tours, and transportation for campers and kayaking expeditions.

Weekend and holiday trips fill quickly during the spring and summer months, so you should make your reservations at least two weeks in advance. Fees range from $42 for a half-day trip to Anacapa Island to $102 for a two-day visit to San Miguel Island.

Truth Aquatics
SEA Landing, 301 West Cabrillo Boulevard, Santa Barbara
(805) 962-1127, (805) 963-3564
www.truthaquatics.com
Truth Aquatics has three fully equipped dive boats and has been taking divers on regular excursions to the Channel Islands for years. It started its official island transportation service in April 1998 and takes passengers from Santa Barbara Harbor to the islands year-round, usually several times a month from September through May and more often during the summer. You don't have to be a diver. Anyone can hop aboard.

You can take a two-day weekend trip, for example to Santa Rosa and San Miguel. The boat departs from Santa Barbara early morning. You reboard the boat for evening activities, slide shows, videos, or education workshops. After sleeping onboard, you wake up and spend the day exploring another island before returning to Santa Barbara. At times, campers can board the boat and hop off for two to six or more days of camping, depending on when the boat is scheduled to pick them up.

A two-day trip to Santa Rosa and San Miguel, including meals, costs $330 for adults and $230 for children 12 and under and seniors. Private charters may be arranged for one-day trips.

Other Commercial and Private Boats

A number of commercial and private boats offer island excursions—see our Beaches and Watersports chapter for an overview of your boating options. If you plan to take your own boat out to the islands, you can find navigational information in NOAA charts 18720, 18727, 18728, 18729, and 18756. If you need emergency assistance, call the Coast Guard on Channel 16 of your marine band radio. National Park Service patrol vessels regularly monitor the channel.

By Air

Channel Islands Aviation
Camarillo Airport, 305 Durley Avenue,
Camarillo
(805) 987-1301
www.flycia.com
If you really can't face being on a boat or your time is limited, just cruise to the islands by air in only 25 minutes. Channel Islands Aviation offers year-round departures from Santa Barbara Airport (six-passenger minimum, day trips only) and Camarillo Airport. It provides camper transportation, day trips, and one-day and weekend camping and surf fishing safaris to Santa Rosa Island.

Camper transportation costs $159.

RECREATION

For a city its size, Santa Barbara has an incredible number of recreational opportunities. Part of this is due to the number of tourists who come to town looking for fun, but it's also a result of the Santa Barbara lifestyle, which places a heavy emphasis on being health-conscious, active, and fit. We think you'll find just about everything you'd ever want to do listed below, but if you wake up one morning and get the urge to do something spur-of-the-moment, pick up the Santa Barbara News-Press and look in the "Public Square" section for a listing of the day's activities and events around town.

On Sunday look for the "What's Doing on the South Coast" calendar, which includes everything happening in the upcoming week. Also check "The Week" listings in *The Santa Barbara Independent* (distributed free each Thursday). Remember that facilities such as tennis, volleyball and basketball courts, gyms, pools, and running tracks at local colleges may be available for limited public use. Call UCSB, (805) 893-3738, the Santa Barbara City College Community Services Department, (805) 965-0581, ext. 2726, or the Westmont College Athletic Department, (805) 565-6010, for information.

This chapter begins with a list of local sports and recreation companies, facilities, and organizations, then covers area sports and activities alphabetically. The chapter ends with a list of local athletic clubs.

ORGANIZATIONS AND FACILITIES

The following companies, organizations, and facilities sponsor a variety of sports and recreational programs and events in Santa Barbara.

Louise Lowry Davis Recreation Center
1232 De la Vina Street, Santa Barbara
(805) 897-2568

Carrillo Recreation Center
100 East Carrillo Street, Santa Barbara
(805) 897-2519
www.santabarbaraca.gov/resident/
recreation_and_sports/seniors
Headquarters for the Senior Citizens Information Service, the Louise Lowry Davis Center offers weekday recreational activities for adults, with many programs specially designed for the older set. The center offers bridge, Scrabble, Italian and French classes, bingo, "stretch-and-tone" classes, porcelain painting, yoga, crochet, and knitting. The Carrillo Recreation Center also offers many classes for adults, including dance and fitness. Both centers are run by the Santa Barbara Parks and Recreation Department. You can pick up activity schedules for both centers at either location.

Santa Barbara Adventure Company
(805) 898-0671, (888) 773-3239
www.sbadventureco.com
Launched in 1998, Santa Barbara Adventure Company offers a range of guided outdoor adventures. Trips are tailored to your interests, with activities ranging from kayaking, biking, hiking, surfing, and rock climbing to camping adventures, Channel Island trips, and wine country tours. The emphasis is on escaping crowds and getting back to nature. One of the most popular trips is the coastal kayaking excursion. Experienced guides lead kayakers along the spectacular Gaviota coast while sharing their knowledge of the area's natural history and marine ecology. Multisport

adventures are also available (biking and kayaking, for example). Prices range from $85 per person for a two-hour kayaking tour to about $495 per person for a fully outfitted multisport three-day adventure. All trips include qualified guides, equipment, transportation, and any necessary permits. Day trips require advance reservations. For overnight trips, book at least two weeks in advance. Call or visit the company's Web site for more information.

Santa Barbara City College Adult Education Program
310 West Padre Avenue, Santa Barbara
(805) 687-0812

300 North Turnpike Road, Santa Barbara
(805) 964-6853
www.sbcc.net/continuingeducation

This comprehensive program of inexpensive classes is a huge hit with Santa Barbarans, who anxiously look forward to the quarterly Adult Ed schedule (it comes in the *Santa Barbara News-Press* or can be picked up at Adult Ed offices).

In addition to business classes, computer courses, lectures, foreign-language classes, and self-improvement courses, Adult Ed offers a plethora of recreational and arts classes, including dance, fitness, ceramics, drawing, painting, quilting, cooking, birding, nature walks, and music. We can only scratch the surface of the possibilities here, so call for a copy of the schedule of classes and tempt yourself to try something new.

Santa Barbara Outfitters
1200 State Street, Santa Barbara
(805) 564-1007
www.sboutfitters.com

Santa Barbara Paddle Sports
117B Harbor Way, Santa Barbara
(805) 899-4925
www.kayaksb.com

Hailed as a year-round indoor playground, Santa Barbara Outfitters retail store's claim to fame is its huge indoor wall for rock-climbing enthusiasts. It's open Monday through Saturday from 10:00 a.m. to 8:00 p.m. and Sunday from 11:00 a.m. to 6:00 p.m. The equally popular Y.A.C. summer youth camps offer a menu of thrilling outdoor adventures for children grades three to six. The Outfitters' sister location, Santa Barbara Paddle Sports, focuses on kayaking adventures to the Channel Islands and in and around the Santa Barbara waters. For full details, visit both Santa Barbara Outfitters' and Santa Barbara Paddle Sports' Web sites.

i If you live in the city of Santa Barbara, sign up for the City of Santa Barbara Parks and Recreation Resident Discount Card. You'll score 20 percent off the regular fees for activities, programs, and facility rentals. For details, call (805) 564-5418, or visit www.sbparksand recreation.com.

Santa Barbara Parks and Recreation Department
620 Laguna Street, Santa Barbara
(805) 564-5418
www.sbparksandrecreation.com

The Santa Barbara Parks and Recreation Department organizes a wide range of recreational activities for the whole family. Among these are the city's youth and adult sports leagues, dance classes, dog-obedience training, teen programs, fitness classes, aquatics, tours, and special programs for seniors (to name a few).

Information on all of the programs can be found in the free *Parks & Recreation Activity Guide*, which is issued twice a year (spring/summer and fall/winter); it's distributed inside *The Santa Barbara Independent* and the *Santa Barbara News-Press* and is also available at the Parks and Rec office. Fees vary according to the class or activity you choose but are generally very affordable. Special needs persons need not feel left out of the local recreation scene. In addition to hundreds of other events,

Parks and Recreation sponsors adapted programs such as adapted bowling, aquatic programs, and the Blaze Sports Club program. Call (805) 564-5421. You can register online for most recreational classes. Visit the Web site listed above and click on "e-Recreation."

Santa Barbara Semana Nautica Association
P.O. Box 5001
Santa Barbara, CA 93150
(805) 897-2680
www.semananautica.com

Back in the mid-1930s, five Navy battleships were moored outside the Santa Barbara Harbor, filled with bored crew members. The locals hit upon an idea: Why not challenge the sailors to a series of contests on our beach, just for the fun of it?

Originally dubbed "Fleet Week," the celebration still happens every year, now a month long in June and July, but with a new name to honor Santa Barbara's Spanish heritage.

This festival draws crowds of spectators, but we list it here for those of you interested in participating. With contests as diverse as swimming, tennis, yachting, cycling, softball, running, racquetball, paddleboarding, volleyball, Cartwheel-a-thon, Ironman inline hockey tournament and tug-of-war—to name a few—you're sure to find something you're good at. Designed for people of all ages and skill levels, the contests appeal to both serious athletes and weekend warriors, plus kids and older adults. Most events require entry fees, which vary widely depending on the event. For a brochure listing all events and relevant phone numbers, contact the Santa Barbara Semana Nautica Association at the address listed above or visit the Web site.

The East Beach Bathhouse, 1118 East Cabrillo Boulevard (805-897-2680), and the Santa Barbara Parks and Recreation Department, 620 Laguna Street, (805-564-5418), also have Semana Nautica brochures. This is Santa Barbara–style recreation par excellence, so start getting in shape now!

Santa Barbara Sports Leagues
(805) 564-5422
www.sbparksandrecreation.com

The Santa Barbara Parks and Recreation Department organizes city leagues in a variety of sports, including volleyball, basketball, soccer, softball, and tennis. Men's, women's, and coed leagues are available, so get your friends together and join the fun. Registration fees vary depending on the type of league you join. Call for further information.

University of California at Santa Barbara
Off Highway 217, Goleta
(805) 893-3738
www.recreation.ucsb.edu

UCSB's Exercise and Sports Studies Recreation offers a packed schedule of recreational programs and classes held on the campus or nearby. Most are excellent, and all are open to the public, although you'll have to pay more if you're not a student (and you'll also have to pay for parking). Especially popular are the Leisure Arts classes (805-893-3738), which include everything from aquatics, dance, and group fitness to martial arts, sailing, and kayaking. Call for a current brochure or visit the department's Web site for information.

BIKING

As you might expect in a fitness-conscious city like Santa Barbara, there are miles of bike trails that will literally take you from the mountains to the sea (or from downtown Santa Barbara to Goleta). Nearly all county roads have bike paths marked by a solid white line on the right side of the road. These lanes must be kept clear of vehicular traffic, and by the same token, bikes are expected to stay out of the vehicle lanes.

A good investment is Map No. 7 of the Santa Barbara County Recreational Map Series, "Santa Barbara Road Bicycling Routes," available for about $3.50 from bookstores and bike shops (we suggest Bicycle Bob's, 15 Hitchcock Way [805-682-4699]; Open Air Bicycles, 224 Chapala Street [805-962-7000]; or Velo Pro Cyclery, 633 State

Mountain biking. NIK WHEELER/SANTA BARBARA CONFERENCE & VISITORS BUREAU

For free biking resources, including scenic South Coast bike tours, maps, and information on bike shops, bike safety, and cycling events, contact the Santa Barbara Bicycle Coalition (805-568-3046; www.sbbike.org), a county-wide biking advocacy group.

Street [805-963-7775] or 5887 Hollister Avenue, Goleta [805-964-8355]). City maps are available at these locations for free. You can also receive a free map by calling Traffic Solutions at (805) 963-SAVE or by visiting its Web site at www.trafficsolutions.info and sending an e-mail request.

One of the favorite in-town spots to bike is the two-lane Cabrillo Bike Path, which spans the entire waterfront from Leadbetter Beach to the east end of Cabrillo Boulevard. This path is open to bicycles, quadracycles, and in-line skaters, so it is often crowded, and you never know who you might (literally) run into.

Caution is the byword here, especially on weekends or holidays, when massive numbers of bikers and skaters (as well as many pedestrians who walk across bike paths) make for a harrowing ride. Of course, in addition to casual biking, many Santa Barbarans love cycling the county's rugged hills and canyons. To get the buzz on what's hot for training or racing, ask at any of the bike shops.

Outfitters

The following companies organize biking trips.

Pedal and Paddle of Santa Barbara
(805) 687-2912
www.nvstar.com/pedpad
Judy Keim, a local naturalist, leads bike and kayak excursions from Carpinteria to Gaviota. (See our Beaches and Watersports chapter for details on the paddle activities.) You can choose from several standard tours, or you can customize a tour if you wish.

Santa Barbara Adventure Company
(805) 452-1942, (888) 773-3239
www.sbadventureco.com

Bike through the back streets of town, cycle around the wine country across rolling hills and farmland, or bump your way along a rugged single-track forest trail. Santa Barbara Adventure Company offers a range of excursions for bikers of all levels, and they'll customize tours to suit your skills and interests. If you don't want to break a sweat climbing any hills, choose the Mountains to the Shore trip and zoom downhill with the wind in your hair. Prices range from $115 per person (four-person minimum) for the mountains to the shore trip to $155 per person for a wine country bike tour.

Santa Barbara Wine Country Cycling Tours
P.O. Box 1439
3630 Segunto Street, Santa Ynez 93460
(805) 557-8687
Tim Gorham and Corey Evans are the quintessential hosts on biking tours around the breathtakingly beautiful Santa Ynez Wine Country. Half-day guided tours begin at $135 per person (four-person minimum). If you'd rather bike to the beach, you can try the "Bike to the Beach" tour from Santa Ynez to Refugio Beach. The tour includes a gourmet picnic and is $175 per person (two-person minimum). Still looking for more touring action? Multiday trips and customized trips are also available.

Rentals

Wheel Fun Rentals
23 East Cabrillo Boulevard, Santa Barbara
(805) 966-2282

Santa Barbara Electric Cars and Scooters
101 State Street, Santa Barbara
(805) 962-2585

Fess Parker's DoubleTree Resort
633 East Cabrillo Boulevard, Santa Barbara
(805) 966-2282

Hotel Mar Monte
1111 East Cabrillo Boulevard, Santa Barbara
(805) 966-2282
www.wheelfunrentals.com

Quadracycles, cruisers, mountain bikes, and tandem bikes are offered at this lower State Street rental shop just a half-block from the beach and the waterfront bike paths. Rental prices range from $24 for two hours for single quadracycles (surrey) to $44 for one hour for a trible surrey (nine person).

BOWLING

Zodo's Bowling & Beyond
5925 Calle Real, Goleta
(805) 967-0128
www.zodobowl.com
Open until 2 a.m., Zodo's Bowling & Beyond is the only bowling alley located in the South County. With 24 lanes, bumpers for kids, and the popular Glow Bowl (five days a week), and College Night on Wednesdays, it's a popular place for birthday parties and recreational bowling. In addition, Zodo's organizes a variety of leagues, including men's, women's, mixed, and senior. Z's Taphouse & Grill is also in the bowling complex.

CAMPING

Camping is a fantastic way to experience Santa Barbara's famed natural beauty. Few things are more exhilarating than waking up in the morning to the call of the birds and wildlife, then going for an early morning hike or walk along the beach, with views of the ocean, islands, and mountains everywhere you look.

Santa Barbara doesn't have many campgrounds, but they all offer excellent camping facilities as well as incredible scenery. Nearly all are situated on or near a beach, and several let you experience both the mountains and the beach at the same time.

One thing we can't emphasize enough: make reservations as early as possible. The state park campgrounds fill up very quickly, especially during the summer months and on holiday weekends. Many people make their summer reservations at least six months in advance.

Los Padres National Forest also has a number of campgrounds. Many of these sites are available on a first come, first served basis with varying fees depending on the facility. You will, however, need a permit to park or camp at most of these sites. For reservations, call (877) 444-6777 or visit www.reserveUSA .com. If you have any questions, you can call the Los Padres National Forest Service headquarters (805-968-6640) or the Santa Barbara Ranger District (805-967-3481). For a truly unique camping experience, try one of the Channel Islands. You'll find detailed information in the Channel Islands National Park and Marine Sanctuary chapter.

State Parks

Four state parks with year-round campgrounds are in the area covered in this book. Three of them—El Capitan, Refugio, and Gaviota—occupy prime beachfront along the scenic coastline that stretches northwest between Goleta and Gaviota. The fourth, Carpinteria State Beach, lies on the shores of Carpinteria, just 12 miles (19 kilometers) south of Santa Barbara. Each welcomes hundreds of thousands of day-use visitors and campers every year.

To reserve a site at El Capitan, Refugio, or Carpinteria, call Parknet (800-444-7275) or visit www.reserveamerica.com. We highly recommend reserving your campsite well ahead of time. You can make reservations up to seven months in advance (but do so at least two days before your planned arrival). Gaviota does not accept reservations; sites are available on a first come, first served basis. Note that a $7.50 reservation fee will be added to the campsite cost.

You can camp in these parks for up to seven days from March 1 through November. At other times of year you can stay longer—up to 14 days. During the off-season and on weekdays, you might be able to get a campsite without advance reservations, but don't count on it—these parks are amazingly popular, even during the winter months. Lifeguards are generally on duty at state beaches from mid-June through Labor Day weekend.

Keep in mind that all California state parks have strict regulations regarding noise, curfews, parking, trail access, and litter (you will be advised of these regulations when you arrive). Dogs are allowed on a 6-foot leash, but you may not take them on trails or beaches. Be prepared to pay a fine if you do. And don't forget to clean up after your pets!

El Capitan State Beach
Off U.S. Highway 101, 17 miles northwest of Santa Barbara
(805) 968-1033
www.parks.ca.gov for information
(800) 444-7275
www.reserveamerica.com for reservations
"El Cap" ranks among the most beautiful state parks in Southern California. The 133-acre park was formerly the site of a large Chumash village. Today it features 130 developed campsites and four group sites, restrooms, a snack bar, showers, barbecue grills, and open fire pits. Trailers up to 27 feet in length and campers to 30 feet in length are allowed to park here, but there aren't any hookups.

Rates start at $25 per night for a standard site. There's a lot to see and explore at El Cap. Walk down a path from the bluffs and you'll arrive at the sandy beach, where you can sunbathe, fish, sailboard, and explore tidepools. You can hike along nature trails or along the bluffs—and if you take the blufftop trail just 2.5 miles (4.0 kilometers) west, you'll end up at Refugio State Beach. From June 19 through Labor Day, lifeguards patrol daily.

Gaviota State Park
Off U.S. Highway 101, 33 miles
(53 kilometers) west of Santa Barbara
(805) 968-1033
www.parks.ca.gov
This sprawling, 2,700-acre park is smaller and a bit more primitive than El Capitan and Refugio, but it offers fantastic views from mountainside trails. It lies near where the coastline turns north at Point Conception. Thirty-nine developed sites are available on a first come,

first served basis; 18 of these can now be reserved in advance. You'll need to bring your own drinking water.

Park facilities include pay showers, food service, restrooms, and picnic areas. You can swim, fish off the pier, and hike on numerous trails, including one that leads to Gaviota Hot Springs. U.S. Highway 101 cuts across the park. So does a railroad trestle (down by the day-use parking lot). Trailers up to 25 feet and campers as long as 27 feet may park here, but there are no hookups.

Camping fees start at $25 per site per night year-round.

Refugio State Beach
Off U.S. Highway 101, 20 miles northwest of Santa Barbara
(805) 968-1033
www.parks.ca.gov for information
(800) 444-7275
www.reserveamerica.com for reservations
Palm trees line the beach and campgrounds at Refugio, so the place looks like a picture-postcard scene from Hawaii. The park offers 66 developed campsites and one group site, many picnic areas, excellent coastal fishing and nature trails, and a seasonal kiosk. Trailers up to 27 feet and campers up to 30 feet in length may park here, but there aren't any hookups.

Depending on the time of year, camping fees start at $25 per night.

Refugio is a great place for picnicking, diving, snorkeling, and exploring nature trails. A 2.5-mile (4.0-kilometer) bike trail connects Refugio with its neighboring state park, El Capitan.

Carpinteria State Beach
5361 Sixth Street, Carpinteria
(805) 968-1033
www.parks.ca.gov for information
(800) 444-7275
www.reserveusa.com for reservations
Because of its excellent facilities and programs, Carpinteria State Beach is almost always booked to capacity throughout the summer and on every major holiday. The park

has a visitor center with natural history exhibits and nature programs as well as a convenience store. Birding, swimming, fishing, hiking, surfing—you name it—are popular activities here. You can also spot harbor seals nearby from December through May.

The 48-acre park has more campsites and facilities than any other state park in the region. Each of the 213 narrow family campsites has a parking space, picnic table, and fire ring. Restrooms in each campground feature hot showers. Drinking water is available nearby. You'll find sites here for tents as well as campers, trailers, and motor homes up to 30 feet. Water, sewer, and electrical hookups are available in one of the campgrounds.

Adults and kids alike can sign up for naturalist-led nature walks to the shore and tidepools. Check the schedule at the visitor center. The park is about 12 miles (19 kilometers) south of Santa Barbara off U.S. Highway 101. Take the Casitas Pass exit to Palm Avenue and follow it 3 blocks into the park.

Other Public Camping Areas

Cachuma Lake Recreation Area
Highway 154, northwest of Santa Barbara
(805) 688-4658 recorded information
(805) 686-5054, (805) 686-5055
www.cachuma.com

Cachuma Lake is a 3,200-acre county reservoir and recreation area in the Santa Ynez Mountains about 20 miles (32 kilometers) northwest of Santa Barbara. It's the pride and joy of the Santa Barbara County park system, and you can count on friendly staff, gorgeous scenery, and diverse wildlife in the area at any time of year.

Tent and RV campsites are available year-round on a first-come, first-served basis. More than 420 regular campsites are available, each with a picnic table and barbecue pit.

i When hiking in the county, it's possible to run into a rattlesnake, especially in the spring and summer. So watch your step!

Ninety sites have full electrical, water, and sewer hookups; 38 have electrical and water. All campsites are close to showers, restrooms, and water. You can stay up to 14 days in the summer and up to two months in the winter. Group sites for 32 to 120 people can be reserved up to a year in advance; call (805) 686-5050 for information.

For an unusual camping experience, you can reserve a yurt (pronounced YOORT), which is basically a tent covering the frame of a round cabin, for $45 to $65 per night. Fees vary, depending on the yurt size and season. Each yurt is insulated and has bunk beds, a skylight, and a wooden deck. The yurts are very popular with families and can be reserved up to a year in advance. There is a two-night minimum weekend stay and three-night minimum stay for holidays. Call (805) 686-5050 for reservations.

Cachuma Lake recently added three private, one-bedroom cabins with a full bathroom, kitchenette, electricity, living room, private patio, and picnic table. These can be reserved for $145 to $165 a night.

Cachuma Lake provides numerous facilities, including a fully stocked general store, a gas station, a Laundromat, a snack bar and grill, a marina, a bait and tackle shop, bike rentals, boat rentals, and an RV dump station. You're allowed to bring a dog as long as it stays on a leash. You'll need to pay a $3 daily pet fee and show proof of rabies vaccination.

If you're looking for a place to pursue lots of different recreational activities while camping, you can't go wrong by choosing Cachuma. It's a recreational paradise, with boating, fishing, naturalist programs, wildlife and eagle cruises, and trails for horseback riding and hiking.

However, swimming, waterskiing, sailboarding, or any bodily contact with the lake is strictly forbidden because it's a reservoir, and much of the water ends up in someone's home down the mountain.

Rates range from $18 to $25 per night, depending on the type of site. A second vehicle at the same site costs an additional $8 (maximum two vehicles and eight people per

Hiking on Grass Mountain in Santa Ynez. NANCY SHOBE

site). If you're going to visit Cachuma more than once, you might consider buying a season pass at the entrance. The Parks chapter contains a complete description of the Cachuma Lake Recreation Area.

Los Padres National Forest
Various campsites off Calif. Highway 154, about 20 miles (32 kilometers) northeast of Santa Barbara
(805) 968-6640 headquarters
(805) 967-3481 Santa Barbara Ranger District Office
(877) 444-6777
www.reserveusa.com for reservations
Los Padres National Forest is a huge region (nearly 2 million acres) stretching across the coastal mountain ranges from Los Angeles County in the south to Monterey County in the north. You'll find 16 developed family campgrounds in the Santa Barbara Ranger

District of this national forest; the closest to the city of Santa Barbara lie near Highway 154, near Paradise Road, the upper Santa Ynez River, and Cachuma Lake. Amenities at each site vary from rustic campgrounds with toilets (but no piped drinking water) to full-service sites with piped water, fire pits, toilets, paved roads, picnic tables, and stoves. You can also camp by permit in designated back-country areas.

Reservation sites are Upper Oso, Paradise, and the group area at Sage Hill. All the other sites are available on a first come, first served basis, and the fees are about $15 per night. It costs around $75 for a group and $5 for rustic campgrounds with an adventure pass. You will, however, need a permit to park and/or camp at most of these sites. For information, call the Forest Service office, 6755 Hollister Avenue, Suite 150, Goleta, at (805) 968-6640 or (805) 967-3481.

Private Campgrounds

Sunrise RV Park
516 South Salinas Street, Santa Barbara
(805) 966-9954, (800) 345-5018

Sunrise is the only private RV park in Santa Barbara, and it's only 13 blocks from East Beach, 1.5 miles (2.4 kilometers) from State Street, and 2 blocks from a bus stop. It has been in operation for more than 50 years and has 33 RV sites. Each site offers full hookups (water, 50-amp electricity, sewer, and even cable TV). The park has four restroom areas with free hot showers, free wireless Internet service, and laundry facilities.

Rates start at $50 per night per person in an RV up to 30 feet in length. Each additional person costs $5 per night. If your rig is longer than 30 feet, you pay extra for each additional 5 feet. You can stay for as long as 28 days. After that, you can request an extension, which is sometimes available during the off-season. The ultimate maximum length of stay is six months.

Sunrise RV Park is booked year-round. Advance reservations are highly recommended. Pets are welcome as long as they remain leashed and owners clean up all pet messes.

DANCING

The Santa Barbara Parks and Recreation Department offers an impressive lineup of dance lessons and dances, including swing, salsa, Argentine tango, folk dancing, ballet, tap, and hip-hop. After you practice, show off your steps at the Carrillo Recreation Center, at 100 East Carrillo Street (805-965-3813). The center's ballroom is one of only two spring-loaded dance floors in the country. Ballroom dances are scheduled here every Saturday evening (except the last Saturday in a five-Saturday month). An optional $5 lesson from 7:00 p.m. to 7:40 p.m. is available. For $9 ($10 for nonmembers), you can dance to a live ballroom orchestra from 8:00 to 11:00 p.m.

For a schedule of dance programs, pick up an *Activity Guide* from Santa Barbara Parks and Recreation (see the listing at the beginning of this chapter) or download one at the department's Web site, www.sbparksandrecreation.com. You can also contact the Santa Barbara Country Dance Society (www.sbcds.org) for contra and English country dance schedules and information. See the Nightlife chapter for more information on dancing.

HANG GLIDING AND PARAGLIDING

Hang gliding and paragliding are alive and well in Santa Barbara, and an active association in town promotes the sports. If you're new to gliding, you can take lessons (it costs about $200 for an introductory lesson) using the company's equipment. After that you'll have to decide whether to buy a glider, as they are usually not rented.

Local launch points include La Cumbre Peak, the Douglas Family Preserve, and the beloved 200-foot training hill—which is considered one of the best in the country—in an undeveloped area on the south side of Elings Park. Contact Fly Away Hang Gliding (805-957-9145) or Fly Above All AirSports (805-965-3733; www.flyaboveall.com) to talk to real enthusiasts of the sport who are anxious to tell you all about it. (Also see the listing for the New Year's Day Hang Gliding and Paragliding Festival in our Annual Events chapter.)

HIKING

Santa Barbara is a haven for hikers. In fact, hiking is one of our most popular weekend recreational activities. With miles of scenic trails accessible year-round, you'd be hard-pressed to find a better place to explore the wilderness.

Maps and information (as well as permits needed for backcountry hiking) can be found

i For quick information on Santa Barbara hikes, log on to Santa Barbara Hikes at www.santabarbarahikes.com.

at the Los Padres National Forest Headquarters, 6755 Hollister Avenue, Suite 150, Goleta (805-968-6640). Or you can pick up a copy of the *Santa Barbara Trail Guide* at a local bookshop or outdoor equipment store; it lists 25 hiking trails in the Santa Barbara area, including trail ratings, access information, descriptions, maps, and trail logs.

Santa Barbara Day Hikes by Raymond Ford Jr. and *Day Hikes around Santa Barbara, 2nd: 82 Great Hikes* by Robert Stone are also good resources, as is Map No. 2 in the Santa Barbara County Recreational Map Series, titled "A Hiker's Guide to the Santa Barbara Front Country." Trail maps are also available at Pacific Travellers Supply, 12 West Anapamu Street, Santa Barbara (805-963-4438). If you'd rather not wander off by yourself, the Sierra Club (805-966-6622) sponsors a variety of day and evening hikes that range from easy to strenuous. These and other local club hikes are usually listed in the "Events Today" or "What's Doing" sections of the *Santa Barbara News-Press* or in *The Santa Barbara Independent* under "The Week."

One of our favorite easy hikes is Rattle Snake Canyon, a serpentine trail with waterfalls, pools, and plenty of shady picnic spots. The moderately easy Cold Springs Trail is also popular. Once a stagecoach route, this trail begins in the shade by a cool running creek and ends with a steep and rocky climb up the mountain.

i There's nothing like springtime at Figueroa Mountain in the Santa Ynez backcountry. Blue lupine, chocolate lilies, purple shooting stars, and orange poppies create a panorama of colorful wildflowers. Don't forget to bring a picnic lunch!

HORSESHOES

Horseshoe courts are available in the following parks: Monte Vista Park, Bailard Avenue and Pandanus Street, Carpinteria (one court);

Manning Park, San Ysidro and East Valley Roads, Montecito (four courts); Oak Park, West Alamar Avenue and Junipero Street, Santa Barbara (one lighted court); Goleta Beach Park, Sandspit Road, Goleta (four courts); Stow Grove Park, La Patera Lane and Cathedral Oaks Road, Goleta (two courts); Tucker's Grove Park, San Antonio Creek Road and Cathedral Oaks, Santa Barbara (eight courts); Toro Canyon Park, Toro Canyon Park Road (two courts).

HORSEBACK RIDING

Circle Bar B Stables and Guest Ranch
1800 Refugio Road, Goleta
(805) 968-3901
www.circlebarb.com
Well known for its riotous dinner theater, the Circle Bar B, 20 miles (32 kilometers) north of Santa Barbara, offers 90-minute horseback rides at 9:30 and 11:30 a.m. and 2:00 and 4:00 p.m. daily. The cost is $30 per person, and reservations are required. Children must be at least 7 years old to participate.

Half-day rides with views of the local canyons, the ocean, and the Channel Islands are also available and last from 9:00 a.m. to 1:00 p.m.; they cost $65 per person, including lunch. Groups can also be accommodated.

From U.S. 101, take the Refugio State Beach exit and drive 3.5 miles (5.6 kilometers) toward the mountains. A large sign will be clearly visible on your right.

El Capitan Ranch
Off U.S. Highway 101, 20 miles (32 kilometers) north of Santa Barbara
(805) 685-1147
www.elcapranch.com
Twenty miles north of Santa Barbara, horseback riding means galloping through natural canyons of caramel-colored grasses, along cobbled arroyos, and trotting along the sands of windswept beaches. El Capitan Ranch offers a slate of scenic rides. "The Hidden Grove Road" trail ride has you guiding your steed through a lush avocado grove for one

hour. Ride times are at 11:00 a.m. and 3:00 p.m. daily and the cost is $47 per person. The two-hour "Pacific Ridge Ride" takes you along the stunning Gaviota coastline. The rides start at 9:00 a.m. and 1:00 p.m. every day and cost $75 per person. The all-time favorite "Canyon Summit Lunch Ride" is a three-hour ride with a trailside picnic complete with glistening ocean views. The rides start at noon daily and cost $115. Reservations are necessary.

Los Padres Wilderness Outfitters
(805) 331-5252
www.lospadresoutfitters.com
Whether its horseback riding in the mountains or along the beaches, Los Padres Wilderness Outfitters really knows how to make it an unforgettable experience. Half-day and two-hour rides are available as well as full-day rides with a delicious lunch. The full-day ride is $195 per person with a two-person minimum. For a true taste of the backcountry, a two-, three-, and four-day pack or hike trip is a must (or you can customize it to the amount of days you would like). Rates range from $120 per person a day for hikers to $250 per person a day for packers. Pack trips can cost from $475 to $575 per person. Call for details.

Rancho Oso Stables and Guest Ranch
3750 Paradise Road, Santa Barbara
(805) 683-5686
www.rancho-oso.com
You'll be riding into history at this old ranch, once a Spanish land grant in the local mountains. Rancho Oso offers trail riding starting at $35 for a one-hour ride. Little cowboys and cowgirls ages 7 and younger can practice their skills on hand-led pony rides. On the weekends, the chuckwagon food service lets you refuel after your ride. Rancho Oso offers equestrian group camping as well as overnight accommodations in cabins and covered wagons. Reservations are required, so call ahead. Beginners and children are welcome. Take Highway 154 to Paradise Road and look for the sign approximately 5.5 miles (8.9 kilometers) from the turnoff.

JOGGING

The beach is the most popular jogging site in Santa Barbara, either on the sand, along the Cabrillo bike path, or along Shoreline Drive. If you're looking for something away from the coast, head for one of these parks, which have jogging trails: Monte Vista Park, Bailard Avenue and Pandanus Street, Carpinteria; and Elings Park, Las Positas Road and Jerry Harwin Parkway, Santa Barbara. If you're into serious running, see the listing for Adventours Outdoor Excursions in the Organizations and Facilities section at the beginning of this chapter.

LAWN BOWLING

Santa Barbara has two lawn bowls greens, and free instruction is offered at both. Since they are open on alternate days, it's possible to play every day if you're so inclined.

MacKenzie Park Lawn Bowls Club
State Street at Las Positas Road, Santa Barbara
(805) 563-5494
www.mackenzieparklbc.org
This club has two greens, which are open to visitors as well as club members. Call the club to arrange a one-hour free lesson. (After your lessons, you'll need to buy your own bowls.) Walk-ins are welcome. The club is open Monday, Wednesday, and Friday from 9:00 a.m. to 3:00 p.m., and Saturday from 9:00 a.m. to noon. Join in at the noon game (sometimes there is a a 2:00 p.m. game, as well). From May to October, Twilight Bowl occurs Tuesday and Thursday from 5:30 to 7:30 p.m.

Santa Barbara Lawn Bowls Green
1216 De la Vina Street, Santa Barbara
(805) 965-1773
santabarbaralbc.org
The two greens here are open to club members and novices, who learn to bowl during a short training course. Out-of-town visitors need to be a member of a lawn bowls club to play and pay $2 per game. Walk-ins, either

beginners or experienced lawn bowls club members, are welcome. Free lessons are given on Tuesdays, Thursdays, and Saturdays.

Open bowling times are 10:00 a.m., noon, and 2:15 p.m. Sunday games are at noon.

MARTIAL ARTS

Whether it's karate, tae kwon do, kung fu, t'ai chi, or sambo, you can find a variety of local schools willing to teach you the skills you seek. We've included a few and suggest you check the Yellow Pages of the local phone directory for others. Call for complete information on class schedules and prices, which vary widely.

Aikido with Ki
255 Magnolia Avenue, Goleta
(805) 967-3103
www.west.net/~aikido
Learn aikido (mind and body coordination) and judo from a master at this small school, which has been in Goleta for more than 40 years. There's a free introductory lesson, and classes for men, women, and children are available.

Macomber Martial Arts Training Center
5950 Hollister Avenue, Goleta
(805) 683-6617
www.macomberkarate.com
Macomber is a family martial arts center offering a range of classes for preschoolers, children, and adults. The specialized curriculum combines techniques from Korean Tang Soo

Do, American Kenpo, and Okinawan Kobudo (weapons) as well as ground fighting and grappling skills. An introductory three half-hour lessons for $29.99 is offered. Call for information.

Santa Barbara Academy of Martial Arts
3122 State Street, Santa Barbara
(805) 687-1514
www.sbmartialarts.com
The Martial Arts Academy offers instruction in rising phoenix kung fu, hapkido, kenjitsu, kickboxing, and grappling. Free introductory classes are available.

The Wu Shu Studio
23A West Gutierrez Street, Santa Barbara
(805) 965-5316
This is the oldest martial arts studio in Santa Barbara and is consistently voted the best martial arts studio in local newspaper polls. You'll find a good range of martial arts taught here, including kenpo, kickboxing, kung fu, and tai-chi. There are classes for adults, children, seniors, and disabled persons.

SKATING

"Skating" is a rather passé term these days, as those clumsy old roller skates have given way to high-tech skateboards and in-line skates. Although Santa Barbara has no skating rinks, in-line skating is one of the most popular activities along the Cabrillo Boulevard waterfront. If you don't have your own, you can rent them from the places listed below. (Just remember to stay out of the way of bikes and quadracycles as you zip along the bike path.) All rentals include protective gear.

Wheel Fun Rentals
23 East Cabrillo Boulevard, Santa Barbara
(805) 966-2282

Santa Barbara Electric Cars and Scooters
101 State Street, Santa Barbara
(805) 962-2585

i Need some exercise? Sign up for the popular Nite Moves Summer Sunset Series, and you can walk, run, jog, or swim with other fitness enthusiasts every Wednesday evening at beautiful Leadbetter Beach. After your workout, stick around for the sunset party and awards ceremony with a free dinner buffet, drinks, and live entertainment. Kids are welcome. For details, call (805) 564-8879 or visit www.runsantabarbara.com.

Fess Parker's DoubleTree Resort
633 East Cabrillo Boulevard, Santa Barbara
(805) 966-2282

Hotel Mar Monte
1111 East Cabrillo Boulevard, Santa Barbara
(805) 966-2282
www.wheelfunrentals.com
Rent your skates from this location, and you're a glide away from Cabrillo Boulevard. In-line skates cost $7 for an hour, $10 for two hours, $12 for 3 to 5 hours, and $20 for 24 hours.

ROCK CLIMBING

Set against the rugged backdrop of the Santa Ynez Mountains, Santa Barbara has some great crags for climbing. From huge boulders and steep sandstone cliff faces to dramatic overhangs and bluffs, avid climbers will find plenty to challenge them. If you're serious about the sport, we suggest you pick up a copy of *Rock Climbing: Santa Barbara and Ventura* by Steve Edwards. It lists more than 1,000 climbing routes in the area.

One of the most popular climbing spots in Santa Barbara is Gibraltar Rock. It's easily accessible and offers routes for climbers of all levels. To get there, wind up Mountain Drive past Sheffield Reservoir, veer left, and turn right on Gibraltar Road. Continue about 5 miles (8 kilometers) up Gibraltar Road and you'll see the rock on the left hand side. Painted Cave has some of the best bouldering in Santa Barbara. The boulders hang over Painted Cave Road off Highway 154. You'll find them about a mile before the Chumash Painted Cave Historical Park.

If you're just starting out in the sport or want to brush up on your skills, UCSB Adventure Progams (805-893-3737; www.recreation .ucsb.edu) offers instruction for climbers of all levels—from total beginners to more advanced climbers. Start out your climbing expedition at the indoor Adventure Climbing Center, with the reputed "largest imprint wall on the West Coast." The 30-foot main wall has a dedicated bouldering section, top rope climbing, lead bolts, three crack features, and more. It's the perfect place for beginning learners or for those attempting to bone up on their skills. The center is open daily starting at 11:30 a.m. Harness or rock shoes may be rented at the center. A day pass or membership is required. If you're ready for a bona fide course, take a class at the university. Beginning to advanced rock-climbing classes are taught for around $109. Belay and rescue classes are also available.

An outdoor climbing rock can be discovered at Trigado-Pasado Park at 6633 Pasado, Isla Vista (805-564-1007).

Santa Barbara Outfitters at 1200 State Street also has an indoor wall with routes for all skill levels—from children to more experienced climbers. Rates are $5 per adult visit, $3 per child, or $30 for an unlimited monthly pass, and you can call the store to arrange climbing instruction (805-564-1007). Goleta Valley Athletic Club, 170 Los Carneros Way, has an outdoor wall which nonmembers can use for $12 a day. Certified belayers are on duty Monday through Thursday from 5:30 to 8:00 p.m. and Sunday from 2:00 to 5:00 p.m. Call (805) 968–1023 or visit www.gvac.net for details. If you're interested in guided outdoor climbs, Santa Barbara Adventure Company (805-452-1942, 888-773-3239; www.sbadventureco .com) offers guided climbs and instruction for all skill levels.

SKIING

Although the nearest ski slopes are several hours away from Santa Barbara, you might want to contact the Santa Barbara Ski Club (P.O. Box 6751, Santa Barbara, CA 93160; 805-687-3363; www.sbski.org), a member of the Far West Ski Association. The club is open to people 21 and older, with annual dues of $50 for individuals, $90 for couples.

Meetings are held the first and third Wednesdays of the month during the ski season at the Chase Palm Park Center, and the club plans regular excursions to destinations such as Lake Tahoe, Vail, Jackson Hole, and Mammoth.

i Looking for a spot to kick a soccer ball, flick a Frisbee, or hit a few tennis balls? Visit www.totalsantabarbara .com. The site lists neighborhood parks, complete with colorful keys to all their facilities. Once you've found your destination, you can click on the link for maps and directions.

SOCCER

Soccer is one of the fastest-growing sports in Santa Barbara. There are countless leagues (both adult and children's—see the Youth Sports section in our Kidstuff chapter for information on children's leagues), and hard-fought matches take place all over town on just about any weekend. Soccer fields (called "multiuse" fields because they also accommodate a good old American football game as well as Ultimate Frisbee) are found in Santa Barbara at Chase Palm Park, East Cabrillo and Santa Barbara Street; Dwight Murphy Field, Por la Mar Drive at Niños Drive; Elings Park, Las Positas Road and Jerry Harwin Parkway; MacKenzie Park, State Street and Las Positas Road; Pershing Park, Castillo Street and West Yannonali Street; Shoreline Park, Shoreline Drive; Girsh Park, Phelps Road, Goleta; Children's Park, Picasso Road, Isla Vista; Estero Park, Camino del Sur and Estero Road, Isla Vista. In Carpinteria, a field is located at Monte Vista Park, Bailard Avenue and Pandanus Street.

SOFTBALL

Softball is actually more popular than baseball around here, and a number of city leagues (see the earlier Santa Barbara Parks and Recreation listing) take to the fields during the spring and summer season.

Even if you don't join a league, if the ballfields are not occupied by league play, you're welcome to round the bases at these locations in Santa Barbara (all fields are lighted): Cabrillo Ball Park, Cabrillo Boulevard; Dwight

Murphy Field, Por la Mar Drive at Niños Drive (one field); Girsh Park, Phelps Road; Elings Park, Las Positas Road and Jerry Harwin Parkway (three fields); Ortega Park, East Ortega Street and Calle Cesar Chavez (one field); and Pershing Park, Castillo Street and West Cabrillo Boulevard (two fields).

Other area venues include El Carro Park, El Carro Lane and Namouna Street, Carpinteria (one field); Toro Canyon Park, Toro Canyon Park Road, Summerland (one field); Manning Park, San Ysidro and East Valley Roads, Montecito (one field); Stow Grove Park, La Patera Lane and Cathedral Oaks Road, Goleta (one field).

SWIMMING

With all our sunshine and warm weather, swimming is a popular form of aerobic exercise in these parts, and there are a couple of public pools to choose from. For information on children's wading pools, see the "Swimming Pools" section of the Kidstuff chapter.

Los Baños del Mar Pool
401 Shoreline Drive, Santa Barbara
(805) 966-6110
This 50-meter, seven-lane outdoor pool, opened in 1914 and formerly called "The Plunge," accommodates up to 300 swimmers every day.

Especially popular with lap swimmers, the pool is used for Parks and Recreation programs such as year-round noon lap swims, adult swim lessons, aquamotion sessions, and coached morning and evening workouts. It is heated to 79 to 80° Fahrenheit (26 to 27° Celsius). Adult visitors are $5 and drop-in Masters workouts are $6. Los Baños is open to the public only during limited summer afternoon hours.

Carpinteria Valley Community
Swimming Pool
5305 Carpinteria Avenue, Carpinteria
(805) 566-2417
www.carpinteria.ca.us

Aqua aerobics, master classes, Aquacamp, and children's swim lessons are just some of the activities and classes held at this community pool. Walk-ins are welcome for most classes, and lap swimming usually goes on all day (6:00 a.m. to 8:00 p.m. Monday through Friday and noon to 6:00 p.m. on Saturday and Sunday). Recreational swimming is available from noon to 5:00 p.m. Monday through Friday and on Saturday and Sunday. Admission is $4 for an adult, $3.50 for a youth, $4 for seniors, and $7.50 for the master's day pass. Annual memberships are $450 for individuals and $600 for families.

TENNIS

In addition to its swanky private tennis clubs, the Santa Barbara area has 28 public courts that are available on a first come, first served basis. Seventeen of the courts are lighted until to 9:00 p.m. Contact (805) 564-5573 or www.santabarbaraca.gov/resident/recreation _and_sports/tennis for more info.

Santa Barbara

In the city of Santa Barbara, permits are required for most public courts. They may be purchased on-site or from the Parks and Recreation Department at 620 Laguna Street. Daily permits are $5 per person; $4 with Resident Discount Card; students 18 and older with a student ID are $4. Annual permits are $125 ($105 with Resident Discount Card) for adults and $105 ($95 with resident Discount Card) for seniors 60 and older. Teens and children 17 and younger play free and do not need a permit. For information on any courts in the city of Santa Barbara, as well as on lessons, leagues, or local tournaments sponsored by the city, call (805) 564–5517.

The largest tennis facility in Santa Barbara is the Municipal Tennis Courts complex, at 1414 Park Place. You'll find 12 courts here, and the 1,000-seat center court stadium is the main venue for local tournaments. Open from dawn to dusk, the center has lockers, showers, restrooms, and equipment rentals.

Three courts are lit until 9:00 p.m. Monday through Friday.

The Las Positas facility, at 1002 Las Positas Road, includes six lighted courts, backboards, showers, and restrooms, and is open until 9:00 p.m. nightly. The only other lighted courts in the city are at Pershing Park, 100 Castillo Street. The eight courts here (four lighted) are used by the Santa Barbara City College tennis team and are open to the public only on weekends and on weekdays after 5:00 p.m. Play is available until 9:00 p.m. Monday through Friday. Oak Park, at 300 West Alamar Avenue, has two unlighted courts open for public use daily from dawn to dusk. You can also play on six hard courts at Santa Barbara High School (1031 Nopal Street) after 5:00 p.m. weekdays and all day on weekends and during school holidays.

Montecito

Montecito has one public court in Manning Park, at San Ysidro and East Valley Roads. You can play for free here.

Goleta

In Goleta you'll find two courts at the Evergreen Open Space, in the 7500 block of Evergreen Drive; two at the Emerald Terrace Open Space, at Berkeley Road and Arundel Road; four at the Kellogg Tennis Courts, in the 600 block of Kellogg Avenue; and two in the Stow Open Space, located in the 6200 block of Stow Canyon Road.

ULTIMATE FRISBEE

Santa Barbara has been described as a hotbed of Ultimate Frisbee. In fact, UCSB's team, the

i **Tennis anyone? The Santa Barbara Parks and Recreation Department** offers classes and lessons and organizes singles, doubles, and team tennis leagues. For details, call (805) 564-5573 or visit www.sbparksandrecreation.com.

Black Tides, has captured the National Championship six times. Check out www.santabarbara ultimate.com for more information. There's also a Frisbee Golf course in Goleta at the Evergreen Open Space, in the 7500 block of Evergreen Drive.

VOLLEYBALL

Volleyball is big in Santa Barbara, especially on the beach, where you can show off your tan (and your body) while getting a good workout. The East Beach volleyball courts on East Cabrillo Boulevard (there are 14 of them) are the most popular venues for beach volleyball, and they are generally available on a first come, first served basis (although Courts 9 through 14 are reserved from noon to 1:30 p.m. weekdays for the Parks and Recreation Noontime Volleyball program).

Most major tournaments are held here, and tournament or league play sometimes takes up most of the courts, but you're welcome to snag one if it's free. Several other local beaches and parks have volleyball courts, including Manning Park in Montecito (one court); Leadbetter Beach in Santa Barbara (two courts); and Goleta Beach Park (one court), Stow Grove County Park (two courts), and Tucker's Grove Park (two courts) in Goleta. Other locations include Lookout Park in Summerland and Toro Canyon Park in Carpinteria.

Men's, women's, and coed indoor volleyball leagues are organized by Santa Barbara Parks and Recreation, with games at Santa Barbara City College and the Goleta Valley Youth Center. Call (805) 564-5418 for information.

YOGA

Santa Barbara Yoga Center
32 East Micheltorena Street, Santa Barbara
(805) 965-6045
www.santabarbarayogacenter.com
You'll find more than 100 yoga classes a week at this busy center, including gentle yoga,

Ashtanga, pre- and postnatal yoga, and Restorative Yoga, just to name a few. Introduction to Yoga workshops are scheduled twice a month. Prices range from about $10 for a community class to $275 for a 90-day, 24-class pass.

Source Yoga Studio
1911 De La Vina Street, #G, Santa Barbara
(805) 569-2505
www.sourceyogastudio.com
Say "om" to peace and restoration. Vinyasa, restorative, and core strength are just a few of the styles of yoga taught at the Source. Class costs are $13 per adult, $10 for seniors and students. A $125 pass entitles you to an unlimited number of classes in a month's period.

Yoga Soup
28 Parker Way, Santa Barbara
(805) 965-8811
www.yogasoup.com
Eddie Ellner is quite locally renowned for offering mind, body, and spirit-bending yoga classes. His classes are usually packed with yoga-loving individuals who are trying to detox from the stresses of everyday. Because of Ellner's own inability once-upon-a-time to pay for yoga classes, he and fellow teachers at his studio offer classes on a donation basis, with a suggested donation of $14 a class. This studio is in a pleasingly rejuvenated part of downtown. You can even book a facial or a massage afterwards at Crimson Day Spa & Boutique right across the street. For easy parking, park in the public lot on the corner of Gutierrez and State Streets.

ATHLETIC CLUBS

The greater Santa Barbara area has a large number of health and fitness clubs with varied programs and facilities. Most will not quote membership prices over the phone but require you to come in, take a tour, and then choose from several membership options.

Generally, individual and family memberships are offered at each club, and special packages and discounts are often available, so be sure to ask if you are considering joining. Many clubs also allow a complimentary session to familiarize you with the facilities. If you're in town for a few days, ask about day-use fees, which are also commonly available.

Santa Barbara

East Beach Bathhouse
1118 East Cabrillo Boulevard, Santa Barbara
(805) 897-2680
Open 8:00 a.m. to 5:00 p.m. Monday through Friday and 11:00 a.m. to 4:00 p.m. on weekends, the bathhouse is situated right on the beach and offers weight rooms, beach volleyball courts, lockers, showers, and beach supplies and rentals. Best of all, there's no membership fee, and you can choose to pay a small fee or for a number of visits.

Santa Barbara Athletic Club
520 Castillo Street, Santa Barbara
(805) 966-6147
www.sbathleticclub.com
Aerobics, yoga, and self-defense classes are available here as well as an outdoor lap pool, a weight room, squash and racquetball courts, an outdoor workout center, and spinning and Pilates studios. You'll also find saunas, steam rooms, cafe and spas, plus a child care facility. A free towel and a locker are provided on each visit. The SBAC is open 5:00 a.m. to 10:30 p.m. Monday through Thursday, 5:00 a.m. to 10:00 p.m. Friday, 7:00 a.m. to 10:00 p.m. Saturday, and 7:00 a.m. to 8:00 p.m. Sunday.

Santa Barbara Family YMCA
36 Hitchcock Way, Santa Barbara
(805) 687-7727
www.ciymca.org
The usual family-oriented YMCA atmosphere prevails here, with classes and activities for the young and old. Serious fitness buffs will appreciate the circuit, free-weight, and cardio-training equipment, racquetball and tennis courts, and aerobics classes as well as the large pool, which is open for lap swimming, water aerobics classes, and recreational swimming.

The kids can take swim lessons, romp in the fantastic Kids' Gym, or join in group recreational programs. Child care is available. The Y is open weekdays 5:30 a.m. to 10:00 p.m., Saturday 6:30 a.m. to 7:00 p.m., and Sunday 10:30 a.m. to 7:00 p.m. Membership fee is $150, with a monthly fee of $54 per adult, $93 per family, and $45 for seniors.

Spectrum Athletic Club
21 West Carrillo Street, Santa Barbara
(805) 965-0999, (888) 867-5851

3908 State Street, Santa Barbara
(805) 563-8700, (888) 867-5860
www.spectrumclubs.com
Voted the top club in Santa Barbara, Spectrum has state-of-the-art weight-training equipment, nationally certified trainers, cardio machines with personal televisions, and a host of exercise classes. The club is open Monday through Thursday from 5:00 a.m. to 11:00 p.m., Friday from 5:00 a.m. to 9:00 p.m., and Saturday and Sunday from 7:00 a.m. to 8:00 p.m. (Club hours may vary according to location. Call first.)

World Kickboxing Gym
29 West Anapamu Street, Santa Barbara
(805) 963-7736
www.worldkickboxinggym.com
Specializing in kickboxing, boxing, muay thai, sambo, and tae kwon do, the World Kickboxing Gym features a full weight room, boxing ring, and plenty of punching bags. It also has Stairmasters, treadmills, locker rooms, and showers. The gym is open 9:00 a.m. to 9:00 p.m. Monday through Friday and 11:00 a.m. to 5:00 p.m. Saturday and Sunday.

Goleta

Cathedral Oaks Athletic Club
5800 Cathedral Oaks Road, Goleta
(805) 964-7762
www.wcaclubs.com

This popular family swim, tennis, and athletic club features a full fitness area with Stairmasters, treadmills, stationary bikes, and free weights; two outdoor heated pools; a Jacuzzi; and 12 tennis courts, eight of which are lighted. Also available are aerobics, step aerobics, aqua aerobics, and yoga classes, plus a variety of programs for children and teens, including child care at the Kids' Club.

There's a definite family feel here. It's open 5:30 a.m. to 9:30 p.m. Monday through Friday and 8:00 a.m. to 9:30 p.m. weekends.

Goleta Valley Athletic Club
170 Los Carneros Way, Goleta
(805) 968-1023
www.gvac.net

One of the largest fitness clubs in town, the Goleta Valley Athletic Club offers aerobics classes, fitness and cardiovascular equipment, free weights, handball, racquetball, yoga, kickbox aerobics, self-defense classes, and senior fitness classes. In addition, it has an outdoor lap pool, indoor and outdoor whirlpools, a sauna, and facilities for massage and yoga. Rock climbing and volleyball are also available. Hours are 5:00 a.m. to 11:00 p.m. Monday through Thursday, 5:00 a.m. to 9:00 p.m. Friday, and 8:00 a.m. to 8:00 p.m. weekends.

Spectrum Athletic Club
6144 Calle Real, Goleta
(805) 964-0556
www.spectrumclub.com

This 15,000-square-foot space offers everything a fitness buff is looking for. Weight-training equipment, yoga and Pilates classes, nationally certified trainers, and cardio machines with personal televisions are just a few of its amenities. Club hours are Monday through Thursday from 5:00 a.m. to 11:00 p.m., Friday from 5:00 a.m. to 9:00 p.m., and Saturday and Sunday from 7:00 a.m. to 8:00 p.m.

Montecito

Montecito Athletic Club
40 Los Patos Way, Montecito
(805) 969-4379

This 3,500-square-foot facility opened in February 1998 to rave reviews. Facilities include state-of-the-art Life Fitness equipment, free weights, a Pilates studio, custom-designed men's and women's locker rooms, and a second-floor mezzanine with the latest cardiovascular equipment. Hours are 3:30 a.m. to 9:00 p.m. Monday through Friday, 7:00 a.m. to 5:00 p.m. on weekends.

Montecito Family YMCA
591 Santa Rosa Lane, Montecito
(805) 969-3288
www.ciymca.org

The family-friendly atmosphere of the Y appeals to many, and you'll find a full lineup of youth lessons, classes, and sports, as well as facilities for adults who are serious about keeping fit. Facilities include a large pool, free weights, and cardio training equipment, as well as tennis and handball courts. Pilates, yoga, aerobics, and aqua aerobics are offered, and child care is available. The Y is open 6:00 a.m. to 9:00 p.m. Monday through Friday, 7:00 a.m. to 6:00 p.m. Saturday, and noon to 6:00 p.m. on Sunday.

Carpinteria

Carpinteria Sports and Wellness Center
4945 Carpinteria Avenue, Carpinteria
(805) 566-1003

This newly named wellness center features Nautilus equipment, Jazzercise, a cardiovascular room, massage studio, free weights, yoga, spinning classes, and tanning. The club is open from 5:00 a.m. to midnight Monday through Friday and 6:00 a.m. to 9:00 p.m. on the weekends.

GOLF

In a golf survey conducted by *Golf Digest*, golfers rated where they played as more important than how they played, which makes it clear why Santa Barbara is one the world's top destinations for golf. Over six public 18-hole courses, three 9-hole courses, and a variety of private courses in Santa Barbara provide for excellent golf accentuated by a backdrop of pristine natural beauty.

Tee off on one of Sandpiper Golf Course's six holes perched above the Pacific Ocean (now, there's a water trap!). This championship course was rated as one of the top 25 public courses in the country by *Golf Digest*. Or play on the Rivers Course in Solvang amid the caramel landscape dotted with dark green oaks.

Ty Warner has snapped up several of the courses in the last few years, which means only one thing: He'll continue his quest to take great things and make them even greater. His holdings now include the public Sandpiper Golf Course, Rancho San Marcos Golf Course, and Montecito Country Club.

Driving ranges abound in Santa Barbara. You'll discover them at Glen Annie, La Purisima, Rancho San Marcos, Alisal River Course, Sandpiper, Santa Barbara Golf Club, Tee Time Driving Range, and Twin Lakes.

Greens fees can be pricey, but discounts are offered during the week, later in the afternoon, or at one of the more affordable public courses. Note that all fees listed here include the use of a cart so you can save money if you walk the course. Most courses offer discounts to Santa Barbara residents and seasonal specials. Be sure to inquire when you call.

Now, pick up your bag and get ready to enjoy a day of golf. We'll provide the views and the excellent greens. The rest is up to you!

SANTA BARBARA

Hidden Oaks Golf Course
4760 Calle Camarada, Santa Barbara
(805) 967-3493

This picturesque little nine-hole, 1,027-yard course is almost literally hidden in the oaks south of Hollister Avenue. Once a lemon orchard, Hidden Oaks is a rather hilly par 27, and you play the whole course with irons. This is a great little practice course, especially for chipping and putting. The longest hole is 173 yards. Fees are $12 on weekdays, $14 on weekends for adults. Students ages 18 to 24 and seniors are $9 on weekdays and $11 on weekends. Juniors ages 17 and under are $6 on weekdays and $7 on weekends. Monthly passes and 10-play discount cards are available. No electric carts are available, but you can rent a pull-cart if you wish. Hidden Oaks operates on a first come, first served basis. Note that credit cards are not accepted.

Santa Barbara Golf Club
Las Positas
3500 McCaw Avenue, Santa Barbara
(805) 687-7087
www.sbparksandrecreation.com

One of the most popular courses in town, the par-70, 18-hole Santa Barbara Golf Club is owned by the City of Santa Barbara. In addition to public golf, the 6,037-yard course offers many activities including leagues for men, women, and couples. The club also sponsors a junior golf program in conjunction with the city's Parks and Recreation Department.

This course has been called the most affordable course of its quality in town, so it's definitely worth checking out. Also on-site are Mulligan's Cafe (with a banquet room), a putting green, and a 19-stall driving range with

Sandpiper Golf Course. NIK WHEELER/SANTA BARBARA CONFERENCE & VISITORS BUREAU

ocean views. Fees are $35 on weekdays ($28 with Resident Discount Card) and $45 on weekends ($32 with Resident Discount Card), with reduced twilight fees ($22 on weekdays and $25 on weekends with Resident Discoount Card) available after 2:00 p.m. from April 2 to September 30, 1:00 p.m. from February 1 to April 1, and 12:30 p.m. from October 1 to January 31. Soft spikes are required on the course. Reservations are recommended.

Nine-hole rounds are also an option. Golf carts are available.

GOLETA

Glen Annie Golf Club
405 Glen Annie Road, Goleta
(805) 968-6400
www.glenanniegolf.com
An environmentally friendly course supporting habitats for endangered wildlife, the 6,420-yard, par 71 championship Glen Annie Golf Course was expertly designed by Damian

Pascuzzo and Robert Muir Graves and is a local favorite. Snuggled into the foothills in west Goleta, it offers panoramic views and a large variety of unusual and personal services.

Your clubs are picked up when you arrive in the parking lot and are loaded into a cart, which will be ready to go when you reach the clubhouse. After you finish play, staff will whisk the clubs away and clean them for you.

Among the more challenging holes are the par-5 10th, which is the longest at 577 yards (uphill). A lake and 10-foot waterfall are visible on holes 4, 17, and 18.

In addition to a pro shop, a 32-spot driving range, and other amenities, the club boasts an excellent restaurant, the Frog Bar & Grill (see the Restaurants chapter).

Fees for tri-county residents are $59 Monday through Friday ($39 for residents), $74 on weekends ($49 for residents). Proof of residency is required. Twilight rates represent a significant savings over regular greens fees.

Soft spikes are required on the course. A monthly pass is now available for unlimited golf and cart with driving range privileges for $250 per month Monday to Friday or $325 per month Monday to Sunday. Family passes are also available. Check out the discounted "Stay and Play," which lets you check into a hotel, play golf, and have the golf outing conveniently billed back to your hotel. The packages range from economy to higher end hotels, such as the Fess Parker DoubleTree Resort. Call for details.

Ocean Meadows Golf Club
6925 Whittier Drive, Goleta
(805) 968-6814
A nine-hole, par-36, 3,250-yard course that has been operating in Goleta for more than 30 years, Ocean Meadows needs a bit of sprucing up, but it offers one of the most affordable games in town, and you'll rarely have to wait for a tee time. There are two par-5 holes and two long par 3s, with water at the sides of most holes. Since the course borders Devereux Slough, you might even see some wildlife. Ocean Meadows has a driving range, putting and chipping greens, and sand bunkers for practicing, and you can arrange a lesson if you want to improve your game. Fees are $20 on weekdays and $22 on weekends for nine holes. Student, junior, and senior discounts are available, as are twilight rates.

Sandpiper Golf Course
7925 Hollister Avenue, Goleta
(805) 968-1541
www.sandpipergolf.com
In 2003 local billionaire hotel magnate Ty Warner purchased this stunning championship course, which occupies a prime oceanfront location next to the Bacara Resort & Spa. Santa Barbara golfers were thrilled as Sandpiper was in need of some serious TLC. *Golf Digest* has rated Sandpiper among the top 25 courses in the country, and many locals say this seaside course provides the

i Save up to 20 percent on activities offered by the Santa Barbara Parks and Rec (such as golf at the Santa Barbara Golf Club) with your Resident Discount Card. Stop by the Parks and Recreation Administration Building at 620 Laguna Street; Carillo Recreation Center at 100 East Carillo, Cabrillo Pavilion Bathhouse at 1118 East Cabrillo Boulevard, or Los Banos Pool at 401 Shoreline Drive, to obtain your photo-id card.

ultimate golfing experience. Designed by William Bell and opened in 1972, the course is 7,068 yards, and the back nine is literally on the edge of the Pacific. Fees are $124 Monday through Thursday and $144 Friday through Sunday and holidays. Carts are $16. Junior golfer and twilight fees are also available. If you want to swing your clubs here, you'll have to look the part. No jeans or denim are allowed on the course. Men must wear collared shirts, and so must the ladies if they're wearing sleeveless tops. Soft spikes are required.

Twin Lakes Golf Course and Learning Center
6034 Hollister Avenue, Goleta
(805) 964-1414
www.twinlakesgolf.com
Twin Lakes, which sits near the bank of a Goleta creek, is a nine-hole, 1,501-yard executive course. It has several challenging holes with water and tight dogleg turns, and a mere slip of the wrist may put you out of bounds.

Twin Lakes boasts one of the best driving ranges in the greater Santa Barbara area, with 30 high-tech driving stations that are lighted at night. In fact, it is estimated that almost 50 percent of the golfers who come to Twin Lakes do so for instruction and practice.

Greens fees are very affordable—$12 on weekdays and $12 on weekends. Cart rental is an additional $8 for one person and $13 for two. This is an Insiders' favorite for hitting a bucket of balls.

Alisal Golf Course Rivers Course. GREG PETERSON/SANTA BARBARA CONFERENCE & VISITORS BUREAU

CARPINTERIA

Carpinteria doesn't have a golf course, but its Tee Time Driving Range, at 5885 Carpinteria Avenue (805-566-9948), is open for practice from 8:00 a.m. to dusk daily. The lighted range includes sand traps and putting greens, so you can practice all your skills. Golf lessons are also available. Fees are $12 per hour, $18 for an hour and a half, and $24 for all day.

OVER THE PASS

La Purisima Golf Course
3455 State Highway 246, Lompoc
(805) 735-8395
www.lapurisimagolf.com
Dubbed by *Golf Digest* as the 33rd-toughest course in America, this 18-hole championship 7,105-yard course is one with which to be reckoned. Not only is it difficult, but it was also rated 4.5 stars by *Golf Digest* and voted "Best Value" and "Best Conditioned" course by Southern California golfers.

A picturesque 45-minute drive from downtown Santa Barbara, La Purisima was designed by renowned architects Robert Muir Graves and Kenneth Hume Hunter Jr. What began as 300 acres became an architecturally landscaped course that continues to draw rave reviews and attention.

Beginners needn't sweat. Even though the course is challenging, it's also accessible and rewarding for novices.

Fees are $60 in the morning, $45 after 2:00 p.m., and $30 for twilight Monday through Thursday. Friday through Sunday and holidays are $78 for morning, $60 after 2:00 p.m., and $40 for twilight. Cart fees are $17. Call for details about the Golf Getaway packages, with golf and hotel stays are given at a discounted price.

River Course at the Alisal
150 Alisal Road, Solvang
(805) 688-6042
www.rivercourse.com

The soft caramel yellows and the deep oak greens of the valley and the Santa Ynez Mountains create a stunning vista for the River Course, which features four lakes and, for the most part, follows the path of the Santa Ynez River. The 6,830-yard championship 18-hole course (rated 73.1) is a local favorite.

Although the course is challenging, it isn't unforgiving, except maybe at the seventh hole, known for its multiple challenges. You can easily sink your ball into a vineyard, bounce it off a tree, or land it into the lake.

The Monday through Friday rates are $60 and $72 for Saturday and Sunday; seniors and students are afforded generous discounts, and twilight play after 2:30 p.m. offers discounts, too.

The River Course is part of the striking Alisal Guest Ranch, known as a destination resort getaway. Horseback riding, tennis, and fly fishing can be added to your menu of weekend activities.

Rancho San Marcos Golf Course
4600 Highway 154, Santa Barbara
(805) 683-6334, (877) 776-1804
www.rsm1804.com
The newly renovated, recently acquired Ty Warner property, Rancho San Marcos Golf Course, re-opened in the fall of 2007. Previously rated as one of the top 10 courses in California by *Golf* magazine, the original 18-hole, 6,817-yard championship course was designed by renowned golf architect Robert Trent Jones Jr. More than 1,700 valley oaks dot the course, many of them two centuries old.

An already excellent course has been renovated into an outstanding one. Changes include: the reestablishment of greens and bunkers on Hole #1, new green and bunkers at Hole #3, refurbishment of all bunkers, new bunkers at fairways #17 and #11, new target greens on the practice range, opened up site line on fairway #18 and hole #15, and a new cart path and bridge from green #3 to tee #4. Perhaps best of all, Rancho now serves cold beer and wine.

FISHING

Santa Barbara has some great spots to cast a line. It doesn't compare with some of the more famous sport-fishing areas of the world, for example Cabo San Lucas or the Florida Keys. We don't have many marlin, tuna, or dorado (although sometimes warm-water El Niño conditions send them this way). But the area does offer excellent opportunities to catch a wide variety of fish in the ocean as well as in freshwater streams and artificial lakes.

Santa Barbara has always been blessed with an abundance of fish, mollusks, crustaceans, and other forms of marine life. The Chumash Indians found fish aplenty in the channel, rivers, and creeks, and for more than a century, successful commercial fishing enterprises have supplied area homes and restaurants with a wide range of tasty bounty.

Given this bounty, angling is a cherished local pastime. You can cast your line from a party boat near the islands, off the Breakwater, into the surf, or beneath the calm waters of Cachuma Lake. And if you don't catch "the big one," you can at least enjoy a few relaxing hours surrounded by incredibly beautiful scenery.

A CHANNEL FULL OF SURPRISES

Santa Barbara County is the northern part of what's called the Southern California Bight. From Point Conception about 50 miles to Ventura, the coastline stretches east-west rather than following the north-south orientation that dominates the rest of the California coast.

About 25 miles (40 kilometers) off the coast lie the Santa Barbara Channel Islands, which also stretch from east to west. This unusual orientation has created the Santa

Barbara Channel, an area often protected from the larger ocean swells of the open Pacific.

The channel is a crossroads where cold water masses from the north converge with warmer masses from the south. North of Point Conception, the water is cold most of the year because the prevailing northwest winds cause an upwelling of water. South of the point, ocean waters gradually warm, although Santa Barbara waters are cool most of the year.

As the channel waters warm and cool with the seasons, game fish from the north and south migrate in and out of the area, resulting in an incredible diversity of species. At certain times of year, for example, you might catch warm-water barracuda and cold-water king salmon on the same day. This is one of the only places in California where you'll find such a mix.

USEFUL GUIDES

Pick up a free copy of the California Department of Fish and Game's *Guide to Ocean Sportfishing in Santa Barbara and Ventura Counties*. This clear, easy-to-read booklet is useful for any angler, but it especially targets novices and people who are unfamiliar with channel resources. It gives a general description of popular fishing sites, catch species, and fishing techniques. You can also pick up the *Guide to California Marine Fish Identification*. These guides are available at the Department of Fish and Game's office at 1933 Cliff Drive, Suite 9, Santa Barbara (805-568-1231), and you can access a PDF version of it at www.dfg.ca.gov.

To learn more about Pacific Ocean fish, you can purchase *Probably More than You Wanted to Know About the Fishes of the*

Pacific Coast: A Humorous Guide to Pacific Fishes by Milton Love. It's available at most local bookstores.

FISHING LICENSES AND REGULATIONS

Anyone 16 or older needs a sport-fishing license to take any fish, including mollusks and crustaceans, from California waters. However, you do not need a license to take fish from a public pier. Everyone must adhere to catch and season restrictions and size limits. Ask for a current list of regulations when you buy your license.

Fishing Licenses

Annual: $37.30 for residents, $100.00 for nonresidents

Ten-day nonresident sport-fishing: $37.30 (valid for 10 consecutive days from purchase date)

One-day sport-fishing: $12.10 for residents and nonresidents (valid for fishing in both inland and ocean waters)

Two-day sport-fishing: $18.65 for residents and nonresidents (valid for fishing in both inland and ocean waters)

By state law, you must display your valid sport-fishing license by attaching it to your outer clothing at or above the waistline so that it is plainly visible. If you're diving from a boat or shore, you may leave your license on the boat or within 500 yards of shore. Don't be caught fishing without a license. The fine is expensive.

Licenses can be obtained at authorized bait and tackle stores, most sporting goods stores, SEA Landing and Harbor Tackle at the harbor, and most county and state campgrounds.

The *California Sport Fishing Regulations* book provides details on the seasons, limits, and sizes allowed for each fish species. You should also ask about any supplements to this manual, as the state often issues periodic updates to be used in combination with the larger publication. Both books and supplements are available at bait and tackle shops and sport-fishing enterprises.

For more information regarding regulations and licenses, call or write the California Department of Fish and Game, 1933 Cliff Drive, Suite 9, Santa Barbara (805-568-1231). Better still, visit the Web site at www.dfg.ca.gov.

WHERE TO FISH

To help you become more familiar with the different places you can fish around Santa Barbara, we've divided this section into five areas: the Coast, the Islands, Pier Fishing, Surf Fishing, and Freshwater Fishing.

The Coast

The three main habitats along the Santa Barbara coast are the kelp beds, sandy bays and beaches, and open waters up to several miles from shore.

The main characteristic of our coastal waters is the presence of giant kelp (actually an algae) that grows in waters from 20 to 80 feet deep. Although rooted mainly to rocky bottoms, kelp can take root in soft bottoms in the more protected regions of the coastline.

Giant kelp can create dense underwater forests that provide shelter for a variety of marine life. The tops of the kelp canopies look like glassy brown patches spread along the surface of the water. While a source of many catches for anglers, kelp beds can also be a huge source of frustration. Lines often get tangled and break in the rubbery strands.

i The weather in the channel often turns nasty in the afternoon, when the winds pick up. Be sure to tune in to your weather radio or the Weather Channel (46 on the local Santa Barbara cable system) to get the latest forecast, especially if you're going out in a private boat.

Santa Barbara Marina. GREG PETERSON/SANTA BARBARA CONFERENCE & VISITORS BUREAU

Stretches of sandy beaches break up the kelp beds along the coastline, giving you a chance to troll freely for bottom species. Open waters generally encompass areas up to several miles offshore and provide an ideal home for pelagic species.

In the kelp beds, the kelp (or calico) bass reigns as king of the coast. They are generally found in dense kelp beds but also make their home in rocky reefs. You can catch calicos many ways; the most common is casting with scampi lures or live anchovies. Calicos are present just about any time of year but seem to be most active during summer and fall months.

Other edible species you can catch in the kelp bed areas include cabezon, sheepshead, a variety of rock fish, sculpin, and lingcod. The prime season to catch each species varies, but most are generally available year-round.

The California halibut is probably the most sought-after prize in Santa Barbara coastal waters. This flat fish tends to dwell on wide expanses of sandy bottoms, but you can also find it on sand patches in kelp forests. Although fish in excess of 40 pounds (18 kilograms) have been taken, large halibuts these days average about 25 pounds (11 kilograms). The sweet, flaky flesh of this hard-fighting fish makes for excellent dining.

To maximize your chance of catching halibut, you should troll on the bottom with a salmon-type rig—a large flasher baited with an anchovy and weighted with a one- to two-pound sinker. Drifting and casting with a small flasher and anchovy or live anchovy can also produce a good catch. The best time of year to catch halibut is during the spring and summer, when the water warms and the fish begin to spawn.

Other fish inhabiting the sandy coastlines include barred sand bass, corbina, and barred surf perch.

In the open waters offshore, you can catch pelagic species. One of the most popular is the Pacific bonito, but its numbers have seriously declined in recent years. You can catch it on live anchovy or by trolling a variety of lures, including green gobblers or "Cojo" flies.

Although smaller than its Atlantic cousin, the California barracuda still puts up a good fight and can weigh up to 15 pounds. You'll have the best luck catching this fish with live anchovies, but you can also achieve success by trolling with a bright lure. The peak season for most pelagic species is during the summer and early fall.

Every few years during the spring, migrating salmon can be found in the waters off the Santa Barbara area. King and silver salmon are the two most common species. These elusive fish usually appear when the local water is coldest. When a salmon run arrives, Santa Barbaran anglers hit the water en masse.

About the only way to catch these fish locally is to use a salmon rig with a flasher and a one- to two-pound weight with a quick release and baited with an anchovy. The slow troll required for salmon fishing can be extremely boring, but the rewards are more than worth the effort.

Occasionally during summers with very warm water temperatures, such as those produced by El Niño, tropical species can visit the coast of Santa Barbara. The most consistent visitor of this group is the yellowtail, a member of the jack family. It's the sign of a landmark season when anglers can catch these prized fish within several miles of the coastline. Yellowtail range from 10 to 30 pounds (4.5 to 14.0 kilograms), but the larger ones can reach a weight of 45 pounds (20 kilograms) or more.

The preferred areas for yellowtail fishing include the offshore oil rigs near Naples reef (west of Santa Barbara) and Carpinteria. Use live bait, such as squid, mackerel, or anchovy, for the best shot at catching these fish. However, you can also catch them by trolling white feathers and larger lures that look like mackerels.

The Islands

Before you head out to the islands, you need to know about the marine reserves. A new ruling establishes 110.5 square nautical miles as marine reserves and 1.7 nautical miles of marine conservation. If you're caught fishing in one of these reserves, you can be fined a hefty sum, so we recommend you contact the Department of Fish and Game (805-568-1231; www.dfg.ca.gov or the Channel Island Marine Sanctuary Web site at www.cinms.nos.noaa .gov/marinere/mail.html) for a map of restricted areas before you venture out on your own. That said, you'll still find plenty of fruitful fishing areas around the islands. Best of all, the "spillover" effect from the new reserves should help boost fish populations in other areas of the channel.

Four islands in the Santa Barbara Channel Island group run in an east-west chain about 25 miles offshore from the Santa Barbara coast: Anacapa, Santa Cruz, Santa Rosa, and San Miguel. In general, these islands offer better fishing than along the mainland due largely to the diversity of habitats and lower fishing impact. This windswept region of rock and water is famous for bottom fishing, and anglers routinely come home with a gunnysack full of fish.

Species include several types of rockfish. The most popular species include the vermilion rockfish or red snapper (the meat-and-potatoes of island fishing), lingcod, ocean white fish, cabezon, sheepshead, and sculpin. It's not uncommon to see anglers reel up a rock cod rig of six hooks from the depths with a fish on each hook.

The peak season for bottom fishing is usually during the winter months, but any time of the year can be fruitful. Halibut fishing along some of the sandy stretches of the islands during the warmer months can produce trophy-size fish.

If you don't have your own boat, the only way to access the islands from Santa Barbara Harbor is aboard Captain Bacon's custom sport fisher *WaveWalker* (805-964-2046; 805-895-3273; www.wavewalker.com). However, be prepared for cold temperatures and rough seas, as the exposed outer channel is typically much windier than the coastal waters.

Pier Fishing

The traditional roots of most local anglers are in pier fishing. You can cast a line off Stearns Wharf or the Breakwater at the Santa Barbara Harbor. Licenses are not required unless you step out onto the sand and/or use live bait. You can also pier fish at Goleta and Gaviota Beaches, about 10 and 30 miles (16 and 48 kilometers) west of Santa Barbara, respectively. Both piers lie on sandy bottoms.

Off the pier, you're most likely to reel in barred surf perch, with a sprinkling of halibut, mackerel, jack smelt, white croaker, yellowfin, and spotfin croaker.

Surf Fishing

Casting from shore is a popular form of fishing, both at sandy beaches and rocky coastlines. Some of the best sandy beaches for surf fishing include Goleta, Jalama, and Gaviota Beaches, and Carpinteria.

The main catches at these beaches are barred surf perch and an occasional halibut. You can also catch cabezon in the rough waters of Jalama and the scrumptious corbina (whose northern range is Santa Barbara) in Carpinteria. The best bait for these fish varies, but sand crabs, which can be dug from these beaches, usually bring the most success. Fly-fishers are an increasingly common site along the beaches in Santa Barbara and Carpinteria. If you want to try your luck with a fly line, you'll find that surf perch, halibut, yellowfin croaker, and corbina are especially partial to clouser minnow flies, sand crab imitations, and surf rat flies.

ℹ️ For local saltwater fly fishing information, surf-fishing clinics, and monthly fishing reports, check out the Web site of fly fishing guide Gary Bulla at www.garybulla.com. You can also purchase flies specially designed to lure local species on the site.

The rocky coastlines in the region can offer some profitable fishing for rockfish, calico bass, and cabezon. The reefy areas near Gaviota and Goleta, about 10 miles (16 kilometers) west of Santa Barbara, are prime spots. Many of the fishing techniques used for kelp beds apply here.

California grunion ranks as one of the wonders of the Southern California marine world. This member of the silversides family has the unique habit of coming ashore through the surf onto sandy beaches to mate and bury its eggs. Between March and September, these fish spawn three or four nights following each full or new moon and then for a one- to three-hour period immediately after high tide.

Females swim onto the beach and dig themselves into the sand to lay their eggs, while males flop next to them and fertilize the eggs. They achieve all this in a matter of seconds, then ride back into the ocean in a passing wave.

Grunion fishing (or hunting, as many locals call it) has been equated to snipe hunting, as a person can search for a lifetime and never experience this amazing phenomenon. Many people claim that the whole thing is really a hoax. In reality, grunion running does occur, but mainly on the darkest nights and on the darkest beaches away from human development.

In the Santa Barbara region, the best places to see grunion runs are Goleta Beach and beaches in the Carpinteria area. It is legal to take grunion by hand. However, just seeing a grunion run is reward enough for most people, as very few can truthfully say that they've seen this remarkable quirk of nature.

Freshwater Fishing

Drive 35 miles (56 kilometers) northwest of Santa Barbara and you'll come across Cachuma Lake (805-686-5054; www .sbparks.org)—the best freshwater fishing area in the county and one of the best bass fishing lakes in Southern California. Cachuma was created when the Bradbury Dam was built in the 1950s on the Santa Ynez River.

Surrounded by the Santa Ynez Mountains, the lake offers spectacular scenery as well as great fishing. On the shores you can spot many types of wildlife, from mountain lions, mule deer, and endangered pond turtles to osprey, kingfishers, and golden eagles. At certain times of year, you can also view several pairs of nesting American bald eagles and their offspring.

The lake water provides plenty of action for serious and not-so-serious anglers. Here you can find trout, small- and largemouth bass, catfish, bluegill, crappie, and redear perch. The lake is stocked with trout from October through May. Approximately 150,000 rainbow trout are planted annually. Licenses, bait, and tackle are available at the marina along with fish-cleaning stations. You can also rent a boat by the hour or day (see the Charter/Party Boats section below).

If you're into stream trout fishing, you'll find a few opportunities at the Los Padres National Forest north of Santa Barbara. The main fishery is in the Santa Ynez River above Cachuma Lake, where trout are stocked occasionally during the cooler months of the year. Other smaller streams in the backcountry offer small trout, but expect to hike a long distance to reach many of the more productive areas.

All forms of fishing appear to result in some success, for example, using flies, spinners, and natural baits. A small steelhead trout fishery once existed below Bradbury Dam on the Santa Ynez River, which created Cachuma Lake. Due to dwindling numbers, however, no fishing is permitted on any rivers from the coastal peaks to the ocean. That means no casting for any species, and steelhead are now protected—so hands off! Although Lake Casitas in Ventura County lies outside the geographic region covered in this book (it's about 20 miles [32 kilometers] east of Santa Barbara), it merits mention because it's one of the best spots in California for catching trophy-size largemouth bass. It's also a great place for trout, catfish, bluegill, crappie, and redear perch. Call the Lake Casitas Marine Bait & Tackle Shop at the lake for more information, (805) 649-2043.

CHARTER/PARTY BOATS

If you want to fish the coastal waters and don't have access to a private boat—or you just want the luxury of having someone else do the driving—Santa Barbara offers the party/charter boat *Stardust* and the charter sport fisher *WaveWalker*. Oxnard, about 30 miles (48 kilometers) south of Santa Barbara, also offers party boat operations. Call Captain Hook's Sportfishing, (805) 382-6233, www.captnhooks.com, and Channel Islands Sportfishing Center, (805) 382-1612, (805) 985-8511, www.channelislandssportfishing .com, in Channel Islands Harbor, for details.

Santa Barbara

Stardust
SEA Landing, 301 West Cabrillo Boulevard, Santa Barbara
(805) 963-3564
www.stardustsportfishing.com
Depending on the time of year, the 65-foot *Stardust* offers half-day, three-quarter day, and twilight deep-sea fishing trips. From Monday through Thursday half-day trips are from 9:00 a.m. to 3:00 p.m., Friday and Sunday three-quarter day trips are from 7:00 a.m. to 4:00 p.m. Two Saturday half-day trips happen from 7:00 a.m. to noon and 12:30 p.m. to 5:30 p.m. Twilight trips occur Friday and Saturday from 6:00 p.m. to 9:30 p.m. On board, you'll find a custom sundeck and a galley serving breakfast, lunch, and beverages—including beer. Prices vary from $40 for adults and $32 for children under 12 on a half-day trip to $56 for adults and $42 for children on a three-quarter day trip. Twilight trips are $30 for adults and $25 for children. Senior and children rates are available on weekdays only. Rod and tackle rental is available, and you can also charter the *Stardust* for group fishing trips.

i Tide books are available free at all local tackle shops and many other stores in Santa Barbara.

WaveWalker Charters

Marina 3 Gate at the harbor, Santa Barbara
(805) 964-2046 home
(805) 895-3273 cellular phone
www.wavewalker.com

Seasoned skipper and writer Captain David Bacon and his custom Grady-White sport fisher *WaveWalker* are available for charter for small groups of four to six passengers. Fees are $550 for a half-day morning or twilight trip, $700 for a three-quarter day, and $850 for an all-day coastal or island trip.

Cachuma Lake

Cachuma Boat Rentals

Cachuma Lake Marina
(805) 688-4040

If you're planning to fish at Cachuma Lake, you can rent boats right at the marina. Motorboat rates range from $45 an hour for a four-passenger, 6-horsepower boat to $120 for a full-day rental of a six-passenger, 9.9-horsepower boat. Boats without motors are $30 an hour. Patio deck boats start at $110 an hour for a 10-passenger, 25-horsepower boat to $288 for a full day on a 14-passenger boat.

BAIT AND TACKLE SHOPS

You can find bait and tackle shops near any of the piers, at the harbor, at charter boat landings, and at Cachuma Lake and Lake Casitas—here are three of the more popular ones in town.

Angel's Bait & Tackle

230B Stearns Wharf, Santa Barbara
(805) 965-1333

Conveniently located right on Stearns Wharf, Angel's sells salt- and freshwater tackle, live bait, and cold drinks and snacks. You can also rent fishing rods here. Once you've caught the "big one," you can bring your fish to Angel's for filleting and vacuum sealing.

Hook, Line and Sinker

4010 Calle Real, #5, Santa Barbara
(805) 687-5689

Hook, Line and Sinker is regularly named "Best Bait and Tackle Shop in Santa Barbara" in local media polls. It's conveniently situated near the intersection of State Street and Highway 154, which is right on the way to Cachuma Lake.

SEA Landing

301 West Cabrillo Boulevard, Santa Barbara
(805) 963-3564
www.sealanding.net

Heading out for some saltwater fishing? The SEA Landing has everything you need and is open seven days a week between 7:30 a.m. and 6:00 p.m.

BEACHES AND WATERSPORTS

When you think of Santa Barbara, the first thing that probably comes to mind is "beach." For most of us, the beaches, bluffs, and the blue channel waters are a recreational and spiritual rejuvenation. Here we take long walks, sunbathe, frolic, relax, and pursue our favorite watersports, which run the gamut from boating to surfing.

Thanks to the temperate climate, Santa Barbarans can enjoy the outdoors most of the year. It's a great feeling to think about the rest of the country in the dead of winter, locked in the icy grip of subzero temperatures, while we frolic on the beach in shorts, T-shirts, and bathing suits.

But there is a slightly less-than-perfect side to our waters you should probably know about before you plunge into the ocean. The water temperatures are not like those off the shores of the Caribbean or Mexico, where they average in the upper 70s (20s Celsius). During the summer months, water temperatures here tend to be in the mid-to-high 60s (teens Celsius). During the winter months, they drop about 10 degrees to the mid-50s (teens Celsius).

Many people wear wet suits or surf shirts so they can stay in the water for hours. Some hardy souls, however, dive and dip without any extra coverage every month of the year. If you find the water a bit cold for your taste, remember that these very temperatures allow for the incredible diversity of marine life in the channel.

In this chapter, we give you an overview of where you can go and what you can do in, on, under, over, and next to the water. We start with descriptions of our most popular beaches and places where you can rent or buy beach equipment. Then we highlight the area's major watersports, listed alphabetically: boating (including sailing), boat excursions/sightseeing, diving and snorkeling, kayaking, jet-skiing, kiteboarding, parasailing, whale-watching, and surfing.

If you're visiting between February and the end of April, you might want to check out the Whale-Watching section of this chapter right away. You won't want to miss the chance to view one of nature's most amazing events—the annual gray whale migration. You can view blue whales, humpback whales, and other types of marine mammals year-round. Whatever time of year you're here, our beaches and waters beckon you to enjoy and explore.

PARKING

Before you set out on your waterfront adventures, you have to actually get to the beaches and watersports within the Santa Barbara city limits. Which means you must find parking. Looking for a vacant, affordable spot can be a real frustration during the summer and on busy holiday weekends. Here are a few pointers.

The city operates a number of parking lots along the beach side of Cabrillo Boulevard: near East Beach, Chase Palm Park, Garden Street, at the harbor, and at Leadbetter Beach. Although these lots are extremely convenient (who wants to cross Cabrillo Boulevard with beach equipment and children in tow?), they can also be expensive if you park there for more than a few hours.

On off-season weekdays (November through April) you can park for free in the lots

> **i** If you're headed out for a whale-watching or fishing trip from SEA Landing, ask for a parking validation when you check in for the trip, and you'll score free parking in the harbor lot.

at Leadbetter, Garden Street, and Chase Palm Park. But from May through September, during holiday seasons, and on weekends you will have to pay an hourly or day rate. In the Cabrillo East, Cabrillo West, and Harbor West lots, the honor system applies year-round and parking fees are slightly cheaper. Look for the signs directing you to the collection boxes and drop your fee in the one that corresponds with your parking stall. The harbor lot is open 24 hours, so if you need to leave your car overnight while you're out on a boat, you don't have to worry. The Harbor Patrol cruises the lot regularly.

If you're going to be here for a while, we recommend buying an annual parking permit, which allows you to park free at any of the beachfront city lots except on Stearns Wharf. The permit (a sticker that goes on your windshield) costs $80 a year and is valid from January through December. Buy your permit on December 1 when they go on sale, and it will be valid for 13 months of parking. Buy it midway through the year and the fee will be prorated. They're available from the kiosks at the parking lot entrances or at the Harbor Patrol Office above the Chandlery on the harborfront. For waterfront parking information, call (805) 564-5523 or (805) 897-1965.

BEACHES

The Santa Barbara coastline stretches more than 50 miles (80 kilometers) between Gaviota and Carpinteria, and you'll find many excellent beaches all along the way. Some are ideal for a family day at the beach—they have full facilities, including restrooms, playgrounds, restaurants, snack bars, and showers. Others have no facilities but boast great tidepools, perfect surfing waves, and wide stretches of sand for sunbathing.

Even if the weather isn't conducive to sunbathing, our beaches can be fantastic places to enjoy the natural surroundings. Here we describe most of our favorite beaches. A few others are not listed because they have very limited parking in residential areas and/or

difficult-to-explain access by trails or paths through private property. Besides, you can reach most of these "secret" beaches by walking from the beaches described here at low tide.

Lifeguards are on duty at most of the beaches daily from Memorial Day weekend (or mid-June) through Labor Day weekend. They are also on duty other weekends in May and September and sometimes in October if warm weather prevails. If lifeguards are not available at a beach, we've noted it in the description.

Please keep a few rules in mind during your day at the beach. Bottles are not allowed on Santa Barbara city beaches (cans are fine). The same goes for open fires and burying coals. Use the designated barbecue pits if the beach has them. Dogs are not allowed at all on most city beaches, which include East Beach, West Beach, and Leadbetter Beach. Nor are they allowed on the beaches in the state parks including El Capitan, Gaviota, and Refugio Beaches. However, you can walk your dog on a county beach, as long as it's on a leash. Dogs are also allowed off leash east of the slough at Arroyo Burro Beach Park.

With that said, we wish you many happy hours in the sun, sand, and sea!

Santa Barbara

Arroyo Burro Beach Park
2981 Cliff Drive, Santa Barbara
(805) 687-3714
www.sbparks.org

Most Insiders call this "Hendry's Beach," and it's one of our favorites. It stretches beneath the bluffs of Hope Ranch and continues for nearly 2 miles (3.2 kilometers) west toward Goleta and a short way east toward the Mesa. It's a great place to surf, sailboard, fish from the shore, watch dolphins swim by, and look at tidepools. From February through May you might also spot some gray whales passing by (bring your binoculars).

At low tide you can walk or run as far as Goleta Beach Park to the west and Shoreline Park to the east. At high tide, especially during the winter, you might not be able to walk as far, but the views are still wonderful. You're allowed to walk dogs here off leash east of the slough as long as you keep your pet within voice control range. At all other areas, dogs must be leashed. Lifeguards are on duty every day from mid-June through Labor Day.

Arroyo Burro has restrooms, outdoor showers, public telephones, and a grassy area with picnic tables. The Brown Pelican Restaurant offers beachside seating, ocean views, good food, and a lively bar. It serves breakfast, lunch, and dinner and a popular Sunday brunch inside or on the patio. There's also a snack bar window outside the restaurant.

The beach parking lot lies about a half-block west of the Cliff Drive/Las Positas Road intersection.

East Beach
East Cabrillo Boulevard, Santa Barbara
(805) 897-1983
www.sbparksandrecreation.com
East Beach, with a wide swath of glorious sand that stretches from Chase Palm Park toward the Bird Refuge and numerous facilities, is one of the most popular beaches in Santa Barbara. It's often acclaimed in various magazines as one of the best beaches in the nation. Unfortunately, it often scores high for bacteria counts, so make sure you check the beach status report before you go swimming. Call the Beach Hotline at (805) 681-4949, or visit www.sbcphd.org.

Volleyball courts dominate the east end of the beach. This is where world-renowned beach volleyball champ Karch Kiraly (a native son) practiced and played for years. Big-time beach volleyball tournaments often take place here.

At the East Beach Bathhouse (beneath the Cabrillo Arts Pavilion) you'll find public restrooms, cold-water outdoor showers, equipment rentals (chairs, umbrellas, volleyballs, beach-friendly wheelchairs, etc.), and East Beach Grill, a casual restaurant/snack bar (see Best Breakfasts in the Restaurants chapter). The beach also has a large picnic ground

and playground. There's virtually no surfing here, but sometimes you can enjoy decent boogie boarding.

Park in one of the city lots on either side of the Cabrillo Arts Pavilion.

Leadbetter Beach
Shoreline Drive at Loma Alta Drive, Santa Barbara
(805) 897-2680
www.sbparksandrecreation.com
"Leds" is a fantastic family beach tucked between the harbor and Shoreline Park. The waves are usually small except at the point near Shoreline Park, where beginner and intermediate surfers and boogie boarders can usually count on catching some rides. When the breeze picks up, it's great fun watching the colorful sailboards, catamarans, and sailboats whiz by.

Volleyball courts, restrooms, outdoor showers, and a grassy expanse with family picnic areas and barbecues are all available here. You can enjoy breakfast, lunch, dinner, and drinks at the Shoreline Beach Cafe with your toes in the sand. Park in the city lot right at the beach.

West Beach
West Cabrillo Boulevard, Santa Barbara
(805) 897-2680
www.sbparksandrecreation.com
If you walk directly west on the sand from Stearns Wharf toward the marina, you'll be treading across West Beach. This small, quiet expanse has hardly any waves (it's at the entrance to the harbor) and is ideal for swimming and watching the boats cruise in and out of the harbor. Several kayak rental outfits

i For beach status reports, call the Santa Barbara County Environmental Health Services Beach Hotline at (805) 681-4949. To be safe, try to avoid contact with ocean and creek water for at least three days after a storm, when runoff pollutes the water.

park themselves on West Beach during the summer (see the Kayaking section of this chapter for information).

If the kids get tired of the beach, they can head over to the nearby playground and wading pool (open in the summer only) next to the Los Baños del Mar pool. Park in the harbor parking lot and walk toward Stearns Wharf to reach the beach.

West of Goleta

The following three state beaches are just off U.S. 101 near Gaviota. They all have camping facilities and are very popular. Day-use parking fee is $8. See the Camping section of the Recreation chapter for camping information.

El Capitan State Beach
Off U.S. Highway 101, 17 miles (27 kilometers) west of Santa Barbara
(805) 968-1033
www.parks.ca.gov
El Capitan was once the site of an extensive Chumash village, and it's easy to see why the Chumash chose to live in this area for so long. This is one of our all-time favorite beaches. At "El Cap" you can spend many hours exploring rocky tidepools, spotting sea lions and seals, and relaxing on the beach. The stands of sycamore and oak trees form a beautiful backdrop for swimming, fishing, surfing, and walking. From February through May you might even spot the gray whales swimming close to shore.

You can hike the nature trails in the adjacent park, and if you walk or ride a bike just 2.5 miles (4 kilometers) west, you'll arrive at Refugio State Beach. If you wander off the trail at designated places, you'll find public accesses to the beach that are relatively unused.

Gaviota State Park
Off U.S. Highway 101, 33 miles (53 kilometers) west of Santa Barbara
(805) 968-1033
www.parks.ca.gov
This huge, 2,700-acre park lies close to where the coastline turns north at Point Conception.

It has a cove at the mouth of a creek where you can fish, swim, and picnic. You can also fish off the pier or hike up to Gaviota Hot Springs. Facilities include food service, restrooms, and picnic areas. (See the Parks chapter for more details.)

Refugio State Beach
Off U.S. Highway 101, 23 miles (37 kilometers) west of Santa Barbara
(805) 968-1033
www.parks.ca.gov
If you saw a picture of Refugio, you might think it was a tropical beach on a Hawaiian island because of the many palm trees planted along the beach and camping area. The beach stretches for 1.5 miles (2.4 kilometers) along the coast, next to a 39-acre park. It's a great place for picnicking, diving, swimming, snorkeling, and exploring nature trails.

Refugio lies just 2 miles (3.2 kilometers) west of El Capitan State Beach—a bike trail along the bluff connects the two.

Goleta

Goleta Beach County Park
5986 Sandspit Road, Goleta
(805) 967-1300
www.sbparks.org
This 29-acre county park has long been a favorite destination for families and UCSB students. A palm-lined grassy expanse fronts the mile-long sandy beach. Waves tend to be small here, which makes the beach ideal for children and beginning surfers. You can fish off the pier (no license necessary), play volleyball on a court in the sand, and toss horseshoes in a designated area. Children can romp in the playground.

The park also has picnic facilities, barbecue areas, pay phones, dressing rooms, restrooms, and a snack bar. The Beachside Bar–Cafe serves lunch and dinner and drinks daily.

To reach the park, take the Ward Memorial Freeway from U.S. Highway 101 toward UCSB. You'll see the Goleta Beach exit just before you get to campus. Park in the free parking lot at the beach.

Montecito

Butterfly Beach
End of Butterfly Lane, Montecito
(805) 568-2460
Butterfly Beach is one of the few west-facing beaches, and it lies across the street from the posh Four Seasons Resort The Biltmore Santa Barbara. If you're hoping to run into celebrities, you have a fairly good chance here. This is where many Montecito residents take beach walks because it's one of the only places along the shore where you're allowed to walk your dog.

Lots of celebrities also stay at the Four Seasons and head to the beach for a few moments of R and R. It's a great beach for swimming and sunbathing, and when the tide is low, you can walk to East Beach. You won't find any facilities here, but the Coast Village Road shopping area is just a few blocks away. If you do spot a celebrity, we recommend you do what Insiders do—leave him or her alone.

Summerland

Summerland Beach
2297 Finney Road, Summerland
(805) 568-2460
www.sbparks.org
Summerland Beach is quiet and clean and a great place for families to spend the day. Lookout Park sits on the bluffs above the beach. There you'll find picnic tables, barbecue areas, restrooms, telephones, a volleyball court, and a playground. Walk down the steep, asphalt path from the parking lot to reach the sand, where you can swim, sunbathe, and stroll along the shore.

Take the Evans Avenue exit from U.S. 101 and head toward the ocean. You'll dead-end into the free parking lot.

Carpinteria

Carpinteria City Beach
End of Linden Avenue, Carpinteria
(805) 684-5405

> **i** Remember, all "private" beaches are public below the mean tide line. You're free to be there, as long as you don't trespass on residents' property. Use the legal access trails to get there.

The City of Carpinteria's beach is very popular with families, since it was once billed as the "world's safest beach." Protected by a natural reef breakwater, the beachfront waters are ideal for swimming, bodysurfing, and boogie-boarding. One word of caution: Stingrays also love this area—especially where Franklin Creek meets the beach—so be sure to shuffle your feet when wading along the shore toward Sandy Point; this scares them away. You can rent bikes, kayaks, and other equipment, buy snacks and lunch at the snack bar, and play volleyball on one of the beach courts.

Carpinteria State Beach
Linden Avenue and Sixth Street,
Carpinteria
(805) 684-2811
www.parks.ca.gov
Nearly 800,000 visitors trek to this 48-acre beach park every year to enjoy the glistening sands, tidepools, and campgrounds. You'll find day-use and camping facilities here (restrooms, picnic areas, and telephones) and a visitor center with natural history exhibits and nature programs.

This is a fantastic place to watch birds—in fact, it's one of the best birding spots in the area. You can also swim and fish at the shore, hike on the beach and nature trails, and picnic in the grassy play area. There's an excellent swimming beach and a designated area for surfing. For camping information, see the Camping section of the Recreation chapter.

Rincon Beach Park
U.S. Highway 101 at Bates Road,
Carpinteria
(805) 568-2460
www.sbparks.org

The point at the east end of this beach is world famous for its excellent surf waves (see the Surfing section of this chapter). But during the warmer months, when the waves are smaller, Rincon is a great beach for sunbathing and cooling off in the water, as long as you steer clear of the rocky point.

Rincon has public telephones, restrooms, and picnic tables. But bring your own picnic—there's no snack bar here.

To find Rincon, drive 3 miles (4.8 kilometers) east of Carpinteria and turn toward the ocean at the Bates Road exit, right at the Santa Barbara/Ventura County line. Park for free in the upper or lower Rincon Beach lots.

BEACH SUPPLIES

We've included specialized stores (dive shops, kayak specialists) in their respective categories later in this chapter. Here, though, are a few shops that rent a variety of equipment you'll find useful at the beach. Smaller kiosk-type rental shops are located at some beaches.

A-Frame Surf
3785 Santa Claus Lane, Carpinteria
(805) 684-8803
www.aframesurfshop.com
Run by two local brothers, this surf shop opened in 2000 right by Santa Claus Beach. You can wander in here and rent surfboards, body boards, wet suits, and skim boards, then stroll back out to the beach and hit the waves. Call for prices.

The Beach House
10 State Street, Santa Barbara
(805) 963-1281
This classic Santa Barbara surf shop is conveniently located near the intersection of Cabrillo Boulevard and State Street, right by the beach. You can rent soft surfboards, boogie boards, and wet suits here.

Santa Barbara East Beach Bath House
1118 East Cabrillo Boulevard, Santa Barbara
(805) 897-2680

The Bath House is situated right on East Beach. Although it doesn't have beach equipment like surfboards and wet suits for rent, it does rent out volleyballs for use on the beach and is the only place we know that provides beach-friendly wheelchairs. You can also use the showers for a small fee ($4) and stash your belongings in the lockers. It's open 8:00 a.m. to 5:00 p.m. Monday through Friday and 11:00 a.m. to 4:00 p.m. on weekends.

Surf Country
Calle Real Center
5668 Calle Real, Goleta
(805) 683-4450
www.surfcountry.net
Surf Country is a complete surf and beach shop with soft and hard surfboards, body boards, and wet suits for rent. It also sells a variety of other beach gear, such as clothes, sunglasses, hats, and accessories for men, women, and children.

BOAT EXCURSIONS/ SIGHTSEEING TRIPS

Most of these boats also offer special whale-watching excursions. (See the Whale-Watching section later in this chapter.) Schedules and excursions vary, depending on the season, so it's always best to call ahead for current departure times. The schedules in this section reflect summer options and rates, unless otherwise indicated. We recommend you wear rubber-soled shoes and try to dress in layers so you're prepared for sudden changes in weather. Remember to bring a sweater, hat, sunglasses, sunscreen, and your camera. If you have binoculars, bring those, too, for a close-up glimpse of the wildlife.

AKA *Sunset Kidd* Sailing
125 Harbor Way, Santa Barbara
(805) 962–8222
www.sunsetkidd.com
The *Sunset Kidd* is a 41-foot Morgan Out Island Ketch, Coast Guard–certified for 18 passengers who seek a truly tranquil sailing experience. Narration is kept to a minimum. *Sunset*

Lil' Toot Water Taxi. GREG PETERSON/SANTA BARBARA CONFERENCE & VISITORS BUREAU

Kidd takes people out on romantic sundowner cocktail cruises, two-hour coastal excursions, and overnight Channel Island trips. Morning and afternoon two-hour trips along the coast cost $35 per person. The romantic sunset-twilight sail also costs $35 per person. You can quench your thirst at the full-service bar on board, then relax and enjoy a quiet glide along the coast. *Sunset Kidd* is located at Cabrillo Landing in front of the Santa Barbara Maritime Museum at the harbor.

Condor
SEA Landing
Cabrillo Boulevard at Bath Street, Santa Barbara
(805) 882-0088, (888) 77-WHALE
www.condorcruises.com
Watch the sunset and dine, dance, and drink cocktails on the new 149-passenger high-speed catamaran *Condor Express*. It's the perfect party boat. You can charter the *Condor Express* for group sunset cocktail and dinner cruises or for a Pelagic bird trip. The boat has

a large galley that will provide anything from light hors d'oeuvres to three-course meals, and the full bar keeps guests well imbibed. Bands and DJs can also be arranged. Rates for summer party cruises are about $30 per person including hors d'oeuvres (but not including drinks), and prices for private charters start at $950 per hour on weekends and $850 per hour during the week with a two-hour minimum.

Double Dolphin/Santa Barbara Sailing Center
Next to the boat launch ramp at the harbor, Santa Barbara
(805) 962-2826, (800) 350-9090
www.sbsail.com
Sail in style on the 49-passenger *Double Dolphin,* a 50-foot catamaran. The *Double Dolphin* offers coastal trips, sunset champagne cruises, cigar cruises, jazz cruises, weekend dinner cruises, and Channel Island safaris. During the summer, coastal cruises are scheduled Monday through Thursday at 1:00 and 3:30 p.m., except Wednesday, when there's

only a 3:30 cruise, and the sunset champagne cruises are at 6:00 p.m. The cost is $35 for adults and free for children 12 and under. The two-hour trips include a narrated tour of the harbor, then a cruise past Stearns Wharf along the coastline towards Montecito. Jazz cruises are scheduled on Friday evenings mid-May to mid-September and cost $40 for adults and free for children 12 and under. Dinner cruises are available on Saturday and Sunday from 6:00 to 8:00 p.m. during the summer months. Fares are $55 for adults, $28 for children 12 and younger. Whale-watching and trips to the Channel Islands are also offered.

BOATING/SAILING

Santa Barbara Harbor

If you're moving to Santa Barbara and want a permanent slip for your boat, we have bad news for you. There's a very long waiting list for permanent slips in the 1,133-slip harbor—in fact, at the time of this writing, the wait list was closed. Most people sell their boat and their permit together, so the list rarely shrinks. However, in the near future the list will be reopened as the Waterfront Development branch refines the way in which the waiting list is comprised and utilized. Call the Waterfront Department (805-564-5531) to find out the latest developments.

If you're just visiting the area with your boat, you'll have better luck. Guest slips are available on a first come, first served basis. Call Visitor Slip Information, (805) 564-5530, regarding visitor slip assignments. Availability depends on the type of vessel.

If you arrive in Santa Barbara by boat and the marina is full, you can be added to a waiting list and then drop anchor in the open anchorage area to the east of Stearns Wharf. The list is updated daily.

Slip fees are payable in advance. The base rate for the first 14 days is 60 cents per linear foot per 24-hour day; the rate doubles after 14 days. The permit is valid until noon of the last day paid for. You can renew it by contacting the Harbormaster's Office (805-564-5530) before 11:00 a.m. of your checkout day.

You'll pay a $35 fine if your visiting vessel is tied up without permission and $5 per day for not paying for your visitor slip permit in advance. If you leave the harbor owing visitor fees, you pay $10 plus double the amount you owe.

Alcoholic beverages are permitted in marinas but not on public sidewalks. Pets must be confined aboard your boat. Dogs must be leashed when walking to and from your boat. Parking (maximum vehicle length 20 feet) costs $1.50 an hour ($9 maximum per day). No in-and-out privileges. Boat trailers in the launch ramp cost $1.50 an hour ($6 maximum per day). Three-night maximum stay.

Useful Numbers

These numbers might come in handy if you're boating or sailing in the Santa Barbara area:

Santa Barbara Marine Emergencies: 911

Coast Guard/Search and Rescue: (800) 221-8724, (310) 732-2044

Waterfront Department: (805) 564-5531

Harbor Patrol: (805) 564-5530 24-hours a day/7 days a week

Marine Weather: (805) 897-1942

Public Boat Ramps

If you have a boat and want to put it in the water, you have only a few choices. The Santa Barbara Harbor maintains a boat launch ramp that can handle most types of boats. It's at the east end of the harbor parking lot, near the intersection of Cabrillo Boulevard and Bath Street.

There's a small-vessel launch in Carpinteria off Ash Avenue. You'll need to go to the Santa Barbara Harbor if you have a real boat.

The piers at Goleta and Gaviota have winches from which you can launch boats up to two tons.

Power Boat Rentals

Sailing Center of Santa Barbara
Next to the boat-launching ramp in the harbor, Santa Barbara
(805) 962-2826, (800) 350-9090
www.sbsail.com

The Sailing Center rents three 13-foot Boston whalers, one 17-foot Boston Whaler with a center console, as well as 36- to 50-foot yachts with skippers by the hour and day. Prices start at $30 an hour for the smaller boats and range up to more than $1,000 a day for the large yachts with skippers.

Sailing

Sailing the Santa Barbara Channel can be an incredible experience. As you cruise along the coastline, you'll see the Santa Ynez Mountains looming beyond the bluffs and the Channel Islands shimmering on the horizon. Although infrequently windy, the area has a wide range of challenging conditions.

Breezes along the coastline average 10 to 15 knots, and swells average 2 to 4 feet during most of the year. Out in the channel, especially close to the islands, it's very common to experience light winds in the morning and winds of 20 to 30 knots in the afternoon.

If you have any questions regarding sailing in the Santa Barbara region, you can call the Sailing Center of Santa Barbara or The Chandlery marine supply store (see subsequent listings). They both have expert sailors on staff who can help you navigate a safe course through our waters.

Sailing Center of Santa Barbara
Next to the boat-launching ramp in the harbor, Santa Barbara
(805) 962-2826, (800) 350-9090
www.sbsail.com

The Sailing Center of Santa Barbara is one of the largest sailing schools on the West Coast.

The center offers one-stop shopping for sailboat rentals, group charters, cruises, and more. Its many other services include sailing lessons, from basic learn-to-sail classes to bareboat chartering certification; skippered and bareboat charters; and single- and multiple-day trips to the Channel Islands. Call for information and rates.

To rent a smaller boat, you'll need to pass a short checkout to show that you won't hurt yourself or others and that you know how to get back to the dock. If you plan to rent a larger boat to sail to the islands, you'll need to complete a four-hour checkout. To access the Sailing Center, park in the Harbor lot and walk to the center's docks by the boat launch ramps.

Marine Supply Stores

The Chandlery
132-B Harbor Way, Santa Barbara
(805) 965-4538
www.chandlery.com

Since 1946, The Chandlery has provided a full range of top-quality marine supplies. It's open daily and carries navigational maps and charts, marine hardware and electronics, rigging, installation, clothing, gifts, and just about everything related to the sailing and boating worlds, including new and used sailboats and power boats. You'll find The Chandlery on the breakwater at the harbor, near the Yacht Club.

West Marine
132C Harbor Way, Santa Barbara
(805) 564-1334

26A South Calle Cesar Chavez, Santa Barbara
(805) 564-1005
www.westmarine.com

West Marine offers all types of boating, nautical, fishing, and navigation equipment, and marine-oriented clothing. Hours are from 8:00 a.m. to 6:00 p.m. Monday to Saturday and 9:00 a.m. to 5:00 p.m. Sunday.

DIVING

The Santa Barbara Channel is one of the world's top spots for scuba diving. There's an incredible diversity of marine life, and many species are found nowhere else on earth.

Along the coastline you can explore the kelp forests and shallow reefs. Many divers from all over the world head out to the Channel Islands Marine Sanctuary, which surrounds the Channel Islands (see the Channel Islands National Park and National Marine Sanctuary chapter). The experts at the following dive shops and companies are your best bet for getting the scoop on where to dive.

Anacapa Dive Center
22 Anacapa Street, Santa Barbara
(805) 963-8917
www.anacapadivecenter.com
Lacy Lee Taylor and Michael Taylor own this full-service PADI dive center. Lacy is a NAUI instructor with training in both recreational and commercial diving, and Michael is an experienced PADI instructor, so you'll be in good hands here. The center is 1 block from the beach in downtown Santa Barbara and offers instruction in the on-site heated pool as well as beach dives. Classes range from resort scuba courses and open-water SCUBA certification to more advanced courses. SCUBA courses for disabled divers are also available. In addition, Anacapa Dive Center rents and sells equipment, provides expert service, and arranges local and international dive trips. The center is open daily.

Santa Barbara Aquatics
5822 Hollister Avenue, Goleta
(805) 967-4456
www.sbaquatics.com
Santa Barbara Aquatics has been around for more than 20 years. It offers a full range of classes, plus equipment sales and rentals for scuba diving, kayaking, surfing, and swimming. You can take SSI, NAUI, or PADI courses in just about every type of diving: night, deep, dry suit, kayak and boat diving, navigation, search and recovery, rescue, assistant instructor, dive master, and instructor.

The shop also sells wet suits and dry suits; rents skin-diving gear and assorted watersport accessories (but no masks, snorkels, or fins); and operates a repair station.

Dive Boats

Nearly all the aforementioned dive shops and other groups arrange frequent trips along the coast and out to the Channel Islands. Just call any of them to find out what's on the schedule. The following company offers regular trips for all types of divers throughout the year.

Truth Aquatics
301 West Cabrillo Boulevard, Santa Barbara
(805) 962-1127
www.truthaquatics.com
Truth Aquatics operates three excellent dive boats from SEA Landing at the Santa Barbara Harbor: *Truth, Conception,* and *Vision.* All were designed and custom-built for divers. Truth Aquatics runs one- to five-day excursions to the Channel Islands year-round. A great thing about this company is that you can show up in just a bathing suit, and the staff will outfit you with everything you need.

One-, two-, and multiday dives are scheduled throughout the year. Trips may be customized for your diving pleasure. Kayaking, hiking, and Channel Island trips are also provided by Truth Aquatics—their three boats may be chartered for groups for up to five days.

JET SKIING

Santa Barbara Jet Boats
SEA Landing
301 West Cabrillo Boulevard, Santa Barbara
(805) 570-2351
www.sbjetboats.com
Santa Barbara Jet Boats operates during the summer out of the harbor, next to the boat-launch ramp near SEA Landing. You can rent a Sea-Doo jet boat (seats up to four, $225 per hour), a WaveRunner III (seats one to three people, $135 per hour), or the *Challenger* (seats up to seven people, $235 per hour). All prices include fuel, life vests, wet suits, and safety orientation. You must be at least 18

years old to rent any watercraft, and a $500 security deposit with a credit card is required. Reservations are essential.

KAYAKING

The following firms offer kayak rentals and/or guided tours along the coast or out to the Channel Islands. Ocean kayaks are much more stable than the narrow, tippy river kayaks, so you don't need much experience to use one effectively. They're a fantastic way to explore the Santa Barbara coastline and marine world.

Aquasports
111 Verona Avenue, Goleta
(805) 968-7231, (800) 773-2309
www.islandkayaking.com
In business since 1988, Aquasports rents sea kayaks for groups and will deliver them to

beaches from Goleta to Leadbetter Beach in Santa Barbara. Rental fees include an introductory lesson—no experience is required.

Aquasports also offers guided kayak trips along the Santa Barbara coast. Launch the kayak near Stearns Wharf and paddle out into the open ocean along the coastal bluffs for a two- to three-hour round-trip. Prices are about $79 per person for a group of four. Another trip takes you along the spectacular Gaviota coastline, a succession of small, secluded coves about 15 minutes west of Santa Barbara. This is a more remote experience—some of the beaches along here can only be accessed by kayak, so you'll really feel like you're getting back to nature. This trip costs about $89 per person for a group of four paddlers.

Guided kayak trips to the Channel Islands are one of the most popular excursions (you cross the channel by power boat, then kayak off the islands). No special athletic ability or prior sea-kayaking experience is required.

Kayaks. GREG PETERSON/SANTA BARBARA CONFERENCE & VISITORS BUREAU

You can arrange custom trips with advance notice.

Captain Jack's Santa Barbara Tours, LLC
(888) 810-8687
www.captainjackstours.com

Captain Jack's boasts that it provides more tours than anyone else and, you know what? We think they're right. Their plentiful menu of adventurous tours leaves you wanting to book not one, but at least two or more. Here's a sample of what they have to offer: A two-hour harbor introductory kayak tour for $35 with a two-person minimum or $60 with an individual lesson beforehand; an Evening Champagne/Harbor Tour for $50 per person with a two-person minimum; the popular Gaviota Kayak/Hot Spring Hike Tour, a six-hour trip that costs $175 per person or $260 for two people; and the glider/kayak tour and horseback/kayak/wine-tasting tour. Phew. The choices just keep going on and on. Check out the Web site for more information.

Paddle Sports
117-B Harbor Way, Santa Barbara
(805) 899-4925, (888) 254-2094
www.paddlesportsofsantabarbara.com

Owned by a local kayak enthusiast, Paddle Sports is the oldest and largest kayak shop on the central coast of California. The convenient Santa Barbara Harbor store rents all types of kayaks, both singles and tandems, as well as kayak-related gear (helmets, wet suits, paddles, etc.). You can launch your kayak on flat water a short stroll from the store. The store also sells kayaks and accessories, and when the weather's fine, it rents kayaks on the beach between the Harbor and Stearns Wharf. A single-person kayak rents for $20 for the first two hours and $5 for each additional hour. Rates for tandem kayaks are $30 for the first two hours and $5 per hour thereafter. Day, week, and group rates are available. The State Street store, called Santa Barbara Outfitters (1200 State Street; 805-564-1007), sells an extensive selection of kayaks and accessories including colorful outdoor clothing and camping gear. The staff are experts in the sport and will outfit you with everything you need to get on the water.

Paddle Sports has years of experience guiding kayakers in local waters. During the summer, the store offers guided trips to the Channel Islands National Park and along the coast (call the harbor store).

Pedal and Paddle of Santa Barbara
(805) 687-2912
www.floweringdesign.com

Instructor/leader Judy Keim has been exploring the coastline by kayak and bike since 1974. She loves to share her knowledge of nature with others and specializes in the coastline from Gaviota to Carpinteria.

If you're not sure where you want to paddle, Judy will customize tours to your interests and skill level. She can also arrange overnight tours; for example, you can paddle from Gaviota to El Capitan, stay overnight at the campgrounds, and then paddle down to Goleta Beach. Pedal and Paddle also offers kayak/bike combination tours and bike-only tours (see the Recreation chapter for biking tour info). Judy's guiding fee is $45 per person for two hours, $72 for a half day. Equipment rental is extra, but Judy will facilitate this for you through local outfitters.

Sailing Center
Next to the boat-launching ramp in the harbor
Santa Barbara
(805) 962-2826, (800) 350-9090
www.sbsail.com

The Sailing Center rents kayaks and all the accessories starting at $10 per hour for a single kayak and $15 for a tandem with a two-hour minimum (add tax and insurance). Full-day rentals are $40 and $60, respectively. The center also offers an Olympic-style rowing scull for $20 an hour or $80 per day.

Santa Barbara Adventure Company
(805) 452-1942, (888) 773-3239
www.sbadventureco.com

Launched in 1998, Santa Barbara Adventure Company offers a wide range of kayaking excursions led by experienced and knowledgeable guides. Choose from coastal paddling adventures along the spectacular Santa Barbara and Gaviota coasts, evening stargazing trips, and full- or multiday paddles around the sea caves and secluded coves of the Channel Islands. As you paddle, the guides share their knowledge of the area's natural history and marine ecology, so you'll enrich your mind as well as your spirit. The company will also customize trips to suit your skills and interests. Prices range from about $85 per person for a four-hour paddle to $175 per person for a one-day paddle around Santa Cruz Island. If you're not completely confident on a kayak, sign up for a lesson. Santa Barbara Adventure Company offers kayak instruction for beginners as well as kayak surfing classes for more advanced paddlers. All trips include qualified guides, equipment, transportation, and any necessary permits. The company operates on an open calendar, so day trips require advance reservation. For overnight trips, book at least two weeks in advance. Call or visit the company's Web site for more information.

Santa Barbara Aquatics
5822 Hollister Avenue, Goleta
(805) 967-4456
www.sbaquatics.com
Santa Barbara Aquatics sells and rents kayaks and accessories. Rentals average $40 a day for a single kayak and $55 a day for a tandem, including life vests and paddles.

KITEBOARDING

Gaze out at the water from East Beach when the wind picks up and you might see brightly colored kites flying through the air with bodies attached. Kiteboarding is one of the fastest growing extreme sports in the world, and it's making a huge splash in Santa Barbara. Prevailing light, steady breezes make ideal conditions, and our wide-open beaches provide safe landing sites. In the right wind conditions, pilots can launch themselves from flat water and reach speeds of up to 20 to 30 miles (32 to 48 kilometers) per hour. East Beach is the most popular venue due to its wide landing area, but you can also kiteboard at Leadbetter Beach, and in the winter Arroyo Burro (Hendry's Beach) and Isla Vista offer challenging conditions for more experienced pilots.

Salt Air Kiteboarding
(805) 698-0432
www.saltairkiteboarding.com
A new sport is flying high in Santa Barbara. From May to mid-September, you can check out kiteboarding with PASA-certified kiteboarders like Ammy Naff. Amy and her crew teach you all about this unique sport that combines kite flying, wakeboarding, windsurfing, and surfing all into one. At least four 3-hour lessons are recommended for beginners. Learning is best done in pairs, and partnerships will be created for solos. Salt Air also has a supply of kites, kiteboards, and other gear available online for purchase. Call for more details and pricing.

SURFING

The Santa Barbara coast is one of California's premier surfing areas. The best waves hit the coast in the winter and fall, but good wave conditions for beginner to advanced surfers roll in regularly just about every month of the year.

The Channel Islands help protect the Santa Barbara coast from storm winds and create manicured conditions during strong winter swells. Unfortunately, these islands also block the coastline from almost all southerly swells, which tend to dominate during the warmer months. So from about May through September, the surf along the Santa Barbara coastline is typically quite small—perfect for beginners or intermediate surfers, but less than thrilling for experts.

Most local surfers are reluctant to share

their favorite secret spots with anyone—crowds reduce their chances of catching the best waves. But we'll share a bit of Insider surf knowledge anyway, as long as you promise to adhere to local surf etiquette. Usually the first person who catches the wave or is closest to the white water at the shoulder of the wave has the right-of-way. Most local surfers passionately enforce this unwritten rule. Be patient and wait your turn when it's crowded. And give a few waves away to be polite—you might be on the receiving end the next time.

Now for the surf scoop. Here's a brief overview of the main surf spots along the Santa Barbara coast, from east to west. We've tried to give you a good idea of their locations and basic information about access. For surf instruction and for more details on the local surfing scene, call one of the surf shops listed after the surf spots—they can arrange lessons and point you toward the best wave conditions for the day. Santa Barbara Adventure Company also offers surfing instruction. Call (888) 773-3239, or visit www.sbadventureco.com for the sample schedule of the one-day lessons that cost $110 per person, with a two-person minimum.

By the way, you will need a full-length wet suit most of the year, although you can usually get away with a spring suit during the warmer months.

Rincon Point

The Rincon is internationally renowned in the surfing world. It's located a few minutes' drive to the east of Carpinteria, right at the Santa Barbara/Ventura county line. Sometimes called the "Queen of the Coast," this wide, cobblestone point offers long, classic California point-break waves. It's mainly a winter break, and waves during the cooler months are often excellent.

Since Rincon has a rocky bottom along most of the break, and conditions are often very crowded, this break is most appropriate for intermediate to advanced surfers.

You can easily access the spot from the U.S. 101 Bates Road off-ramp. Park in the county or state parking lot.

Leadbetter Point

You'll find this small point at the west end of Leadbetter Beach, just below Shoreline Park. It typically has small waves that break on a rocky bottom into a sandy beach. It's an excellent spot for beginner and intermediate surfers. You can access the break from the Leadbetter Beach parking lot on Shoreline Drive.

Arroyo Burro (Hendry's Beach)

This beach-and-reef break sometimes creates some decent surf waves during small to medium-size swells. It's also a good wind-swell spot (typically in the afternoons) and a fun spot for kids to catch some waves. Park in the Arroyo Burro parking lot off Cliff Drive. The break is directly in front of the parking lot and the Brown Pelican restaurant and snack bar.

Campus Point

Campus Point is a large point break named after the UCSB campus, which sits along its shore. It's one of the best breaks in Santa Barbara, with three or four sections that are good in nearly all conditions. Consequently, it offers great surfing for beginners to advanced surfers. However, it does have a rocky bottom, so it's not the safest place for beginners. It can also be packed with UCSB students.

To access Campus Point, take the Ward Memorial Freeway from U.S. Highway 101 to the UCSB campus gate, where you will need to pay a parking fee on weekdays. Once you're inside the gate, turn left. On weekends you can park in the first parking lot to the left. On weekdays, you're only allowed to use visitor parking spots, which are quite a distance from the beach.

Another approach is to take the Goleta Beach off-ramp, just before the entrance to UCSB. Park in the beach lot and walk west along the coast about 1/2 mile (1 kilometer).

Sands Beach

You'll find this sandy reef break just west of Isla Vista, the densely populated student community adjacent to UCSB. Sands offers very nice surfing experiences in a beautiful location. You can expect to find small to medium surf; the best conditions occur during wind swells. The only negative here is that you often have to put up with tar globs in the water and on the beach, thanks to offshore oil seeps.

To reach Sands Beach, take Del Playa Road to its west end, then walk about 1/2 mile (1 kilometer) to the trail, just past Devereaux Point (also a decent surf spot on occasion).

El Capitan State Beach

The point at El Capitan ranks among the most beautiful surf spots along the Santa Barbara coastline. A small rocky point that ends in a sandy bay, this spot can have excellent and hollow surf. Follow U.S. 101 north from Santa Barbara about 17 miles (27.4 kilometers) and take the El Capitan State Beach off-ramp. Go through the park gate (the day-use fee is $8), then take the beach trail east of the parking lot.

Hollister Ranch

Known by name to most surfers on the planet, "The Ranch" has some of the best surf in California. It's located about 30 miles (48 kilometers) west of the city of Santa Barbara and stretches from Gaviota State Beach to Point Conception. Unfortunately (or fortunately for those lucky enough to get to surf there), access to this stretch of coastline is very limited. There are only two ways to get there: by boat or by driving through private, gated Hollister Ranch property.

Boaters usually launch their crafts from the winch at the end of the Gaviota Beach pier, just east of the ranch property. As you motor westward, you'll run into several breaks with varying surf conditions. Recent subdivision of ranch property has substantially increased the number of property owners (many of whom buy pieces of land just to have surf access) and the number of people who are allowed to drive to the pristine beaches by vehicle. Local surfers frequently try to cajole, entice, and bribe their fortunate friends who own ranch property to drive them into the ranch for a session.

Jalama State Beach

Although not in the geographic area covered in this book, Jalama State Beach is often frequented by Santa Barbara surfers. This coastal area is well exposed to the open Pacific waters, and unlike Santa Barbara, it catches swells from southerly to northerly directions. With often windier, colder, and rougher surf, Jalama challenges even the most experienced surfer. Beach and reef breaks occur all along this stretch of wild and scenic coastline.

To access the area, take U.S. 101 to just north of Gaviota, then take the Calif. Highway 1 turnoff. From there, go about 8 miles (13 kilometers) to the Jalama Road turnoff on the left, then follow this winding road 12 miles (19 kilometers) to the beach. The state campground offers day-use facilities as well as dozens of overnight camping spots.

Surfing Equipment & Lessons

A-Frame Surf
3785 Santa Claus Lane, Carpinteria
(805) 684-8803
www.aframesurf.com
Run by two local brothers, this surf shop opened in 1999 right by Santa Claus Beach. The store sells short boards from local designers such as Progressive and Clyde Beatty as well as some hard-to-find smaller lines of surf- and beachwear for men, women, and children. You can also rent surfboards, body boards, wet suits, fins, and skim boards here, and surf lessons are available year-round, but you should book at least a week in advance and two weeks in advance during the summer. Surf lessons are $75 per person for 90 minutes, $65 per person for two people, and $55 per person for three people.

Channel Islands Surfboards
36 State Street, Santa Barbara
(805) 966-7213
www.cisurfboards.com

Tourists and surf experts alike shop at Channel Islands Surfboards. This is where you can find surfboards by Al Merrick, one of the best board designers and shapers in the surfing industry. You can also purchase a range of other surfing equipment and apparel.

Surf Country
Calle Real Center
5668 Calle Real, Goleta
(805) 683-4450
www.surfcountry.net

This complete surf and beach shop is a good place to pick up Insider information on the best surf and beach spots. It rents soft or hard surfboards, body boards, and wet suits. Rates for surfboard rentals are $30 a day and $15 for each additional day. Surfing lessons are also available.

Surf Happens Surf School
(805) 966-3613
www.surfhappens.com

Founded in 2003, this local surfing organization offers personal instruction for surfers of all ages, including year-round surf camps for kids, family surf camps, international surfing safaris, and free surfing competitions around the world. The school takes a martial arts approach to instruction, teaching discipline and focusing on both mental and physical fitness. Lessons cost about $60 an hour depending on the number of people in the group. Surf Happens provides all the equipment, including wet suits and sunblock—all you have to do is show up in your swimsuit.

WHALE-WATCHING

Every year in late September, about 28,000 Pacific gray whales begin migrating south from Alaska to the warm lagoons and bays in Baja California, where they mate and give birth. In early February, the adult males, preg-

nant females, and a few juveniles start heading back north to their summer Arctic feeding grounds. The new mothers and their calves hang around the lagoons a bit longer before following along.

This migration—among the longest of any mammal's—is one of nature's most incredible spectacles, and you can get a ringside seat to watch it right here in the channel.

Going south, most of the gray whales pass between Santa Rosa and Santa Cruz Islands. On the way back north, usually from February through mid-May, they tend to hug the Santa Barbara coastline, typically swimming from 1 to 5 miles (1.5 to 8.0 kilometers) offshore. Mothers and calves sometimes stay within a few hundred yards of the shoreline. It's truly amazing to watch these 80,000-pound giant mammals gracefully breach, spout, and smack their flippers on the water's surface.

You also have an excellent chance of spotting whales at other times of year. If you take a cruise out to the islands from July through September, you're almost guaranteed to spot humpback and blue whales, which often come through the channel, close to the islands, to feed on the krill. In fact, the largest concentration of blue whales in the world regularly visits local waters. Dolphins are a common sight at any time of year, and if you're lucky, you might also spot minke, pilot, or basking whales.

Orcas, also known as killer whales, inhabit the channel throughout the year, occasionally thrilling wildlife lovers with their antics. Shocked whale watchers on local boats have actually witnessed these seemingly benign creatures attacking gray whale calves and sea lions right by the boat. Of course, this doesn't happen every day, but it's a welcome reminder that we have a wonderful underwater wilderness on our doorstep.

i If you're heading out for a whale-watching trip, dress in layers with flat-soled shoes and take a windbreaker. It's cold on the water even in summer. Also, bring binoculars, if you have them, for a close-up view of the wildlife.

The following is a list of boats that will take you out to watch the whales and give you a bit of whale education in the process. It's a good idea to call to verify the current schedule, as departure days are often added or dropped, depending on how many whales are in the channel that week. All these boats work as a team. If one boat is enjoying a spectacular appearance by a whale or pod of whales, the captain will radio other whale-watching boats in the vicinity and share the sighting.

AKA *Sunset Kidd* Sailing
125 Harbor Way, Santa Barbara
(805) 962–8222
www.sunsetkidd.com
Sunset Kidd is probably the least touristy of the whale-watching trips. This excursion is for those who love sailing and prefer the tranquility of gliding up to the whales on a wind-powered vessel (the motor is used as little as possible). Narration is kept to a minimum. The *Sunset Kidd,* a 41-foot Morgan Out Island Ketch, takes up to 18 passengers on two-hour whale-watching cruises twice daily from mid-February through May. The fare is $35 (no discounts for kids or seniors).

Captain Don's Whale Watching
219 Stearns Wharf #G, Santa Barbara
(805) 969-5217
www.captdon.com
Captain Don's power yacht, the 149-passenger *Rachel G,* has a full galley and bar, an upper deck with great views and seating, and a lower deck with indoor seating, air-conditioning, and heating.

The boat goes out twice daily (12:00 and 3:00 p.m.) Monday to Friday and three times daily (9:00 a.m., noon, and 3:00 p.m.) from

i A giant sperm whale washed ashore in Isla Vista, near the University of California at Santa Barbara, in April 2007. This uncommon whale to Santa Barbara waters was believed to have been snacking on giant squid, cephalopods that were once minimal in our waters but are now abundant along the Central Coast.

February through the end of the migration in May. Trips last about two and a half hours.

From June through September, the *Rachel G* takes passengers out to the Channel Islands to visit with giant blue whales. Please call for prices and reservations.

Condor Express
SEA Landing
301 West Cabrillo Boulevard at Bath Street, Santa Barbara
(805) 882-0088, (888) 77-WHALE
www.condorcruises.com
The 75-foot, 149-passenger high-speed catamaran *Condor Express* is the only whale-watching vessel offering a whale-watch guarantee. If you don't see whales or exceptional sightings of other marine animals on your trip, the captain will issue a free trip on another excursion during the same season. All cruises include informative narration about the whales and other wildlife you might encounter on the trip. Check out the southern gray whale migration from December through early February, the gray whales northerly migration from mid-February through early May, and the humpbacks and blue whales from May to November (nearly 100 percent guaranteed whale sighting on these cruises). Call for prices and reservations.

Double Dolphin/Santa Barbara Sailing Center
Santa Barbara Harbor near the boat-launch ramp
133 Harbor Way, Santa Barbara
(805) 962-2826, (800) 350-9090
www.sbsail.com
The *Double Dolphin,* a 50-foot catamaran, takes up to 49 passengers out for two-and-a-half-hour narrated whale-watching cruises at 9:00 a.m., noon, and 3:00 p.m. from mid-February through mid-May during the gray whale migration. Rates are $35 for adults, free for children 12 and younger. On Sunday during the summer, the *Double Dolphin* runs full-day island safaris to Santa Cruz Island, and the boat often encounters whales during the Channel crossing. See the Boating section in this chapter for details.

SPECTATOR SPORTS

Although Santa Barbara's cultural and arts scene displays big-city sophistication, when the subject turns to professional sports, you're still talking small town.

While this may be a disappointing fact for big-league sports fans, you can see all the pro sports in Los Angeles—just a few hours away—including Dodgers and Angels baseball, Lakers and Clippers basketball, Kings and Anaheim Ducks ice hockey, and the renowned L.A. Marathon.

Not that Santa Barbara hasn't had big-league sports on its mind a time or two. Back in October of 1924, for example, Babe Ruth and Lou Gehrig were just a few of the players who came to Peabody Stadium (which now belongs to Santa Barbara High School) for a game that drew 2,000 fans. Tickets were a pricey $1.50, plus $1 for parking and a 10 percent war tax, but Santa Barbarans were more than ready to ante up for a big-time baseball game. Four years later, Laguna Park, a full-size major league ballpark, was built on East Cota Street in an effort to bring major league baseball to Santa Barbara on a permanent basis, and in 1941 a farm team of the Los Angeles Dodgers, the Santa Barbara Saints, began playing there. The park was closed down for a while at the beginning of World War II, and later the Dodgers moved their farm team to Bakersfield, which marked the beginning of the end for Laguna Park. After years of deterioration, it was torn down in 1970.

There's still some good baseball being played in Santa Barbara, though. The Santa Barbara Foresters, a semipro team in the California Coastal Collegiate League, play a June-through-August season at UCSB.

Football in Santa Barbara pretty much consists of local college and high school games, but don't underestimate the thrill of a good contest between crosstown rivals such as San Marcos and Dos Pueblos High, San Marcos and Santa Barbara High, or Carpinteria and Bishop Garcia Diego High. Santa Barbara City College also fields a good football team.

Horse racing was big in Santa Barbara in the mid-1850s, when Thomas Hope laid out California's first flat course for trotters and pacers at Hope Ranch. The first hurdle race in the state took place at Hope's track, which ran around the shores of Laguna Blanca. After his premature death in 1875, Hope's land was divided up, and Laguna Blanca later became the centerpiece of an 18-hole golf course at the La Cumbre Country Club, which opened in 1935.

Below are some of the local possibilities for spectating, along with some phone numbers for contacting L.A. teams about tickets and schedules. You can also check out the daily Sports section of the *Santa Barbara News-Press*.

PROFESSIONAL SPORTS

Santa Barbara Breakers
City College Sports Pavilion
Santa Barbara City College
721 Cliff Drive, Santa Barbara
(805) 965-4667
www.sbprohoops.com
Santa Barbara welcomes its first professional minor-league team in a very long time with the International Basketball League's (IBL) franchise—the Santa Barbara Breakers. Curt Pickering, known locally as the former director of operations for the Santa Barbara Islanders during their one-year stint with the Continental Basketball Association, is back as owner/head coach. The inaugural 20-game schedule for the 2007 season ran from April through June so as to not interfere with high school and college play. The IBL rules are

slightly different than the NBA, in that there are fewer timeouts and immediate inbound plays. The average IBL league points scored during 2005 and 2006 was around 126, which promises an action-packed season for Santa Barbara. Tickets are sold through Ticketmaster or by calling (805) 963-4408.

SEMIPRO SPORTS

Santa Barbara Foresters
Caesar Uyesaka Stadium
UCSB, Santa Barbara
(805) 684-0657
www.sbforesters.org
The Foresters are Santa Barbara's next best thing to professional baseball. Part of the Coastal Collegiate League, the Foresters play at UCSB's Caesar Uyesaka Stadium in a June-through-August season. Players come from college teams all over the country, including UCSB, USC, UCLA, Stanford, Florida State, and Wichita State. The Foresters are good, too. The team is a 12-time California Coastal Collegiate League winner and 7-time California State Champion. The team also is a two-time national champion, having won in 2003 and 2006.

There's an old-time family atmosphere at Foresters games, with promotions, contests, and races between innings, so bring the kids and enjoy.

Tickets are available at the gate. Season and family passes are available online, making this a great deal for summertime family fun.

COLLEGE ATHLETICS

Although nationally ranked teams and overflowing stadiums are not the rule in Santa Barbara, we're proud of our local schools and love to cheer them on. If there's a hot contest going, Santa Barbarans turn out in droves to support the home team, and everyone gets into the spirit. The cost for watching college athletic events varies—some events are free and others require an admission fee. Only UCSB offers tickets in advance, with Santa

Barbara City College and Westmont selling tickets at the door or gate.

Santa Barbara City College
721 Cliff Drive, Santa Barbara
www.sbcc.edu/athletics
SBCC has fielded some fine football, volleyball, and basketball teams, and the public is always welcome to attend any sports event on campus. The Vaqueros' football team, which plays in La Playa Stadium across from the beach, holds great promise with a new coach.

SBCC also fields baseball and softball teams and has men's and women's golf, soccer, tennis, and volleyball teams. Tickets to all SBCC athletic events can be bought at the door or gate and are not available in advance.

University of California at Santa Barbara
Athletics Ticket Office
(805) 893-8272
www.ucsbgauchos.cstv.com
UCSB's Gauchos, who play in the Big West Conference, host a variety of sports events that are open to the public. The Lady Gauchos basketball team won the Big West Conference regular season title for eight straight seasons and received the conference's automatic NCAA Tournament bid for seven straight years.

The men's basketball team is blazing a trail to victory under coach Bob Williams as the 2002 Big West Tournament Champions and 2003 Big West regular season champions. Join the Gauchos in the "Thunderdome," so named because the thousands of stomping feet during a tight game rumble like thunder.

UCSB almost always has great men's and women's volleyball teams. In the past, the men's team has ranked among the top five teams in the nation. Other spectator sports on campus include baseball, softball,

i For a chance to see some future major league baseball stars, check out a UCSB Gaucho game. More than a few players have been plucked from the team's ranks in major league drafts.

swimming, soccer, tennis, track, and water polo. You can buy tickets to Gaucho games on the Web site or by calling the number above.

Westmont College
955 La Paz Road, Santa Barbara
(805) 565-6010 (athletics)
www.westmont.edu/sports

The Westmont Warriors invite the public to basketball, soccer, volleyball, tennis, and other spectator sports events played by its six men's and six women's teams. Part of the Golden State Athletic Conference, the Warriors have won 48 conference titles in the past 18 years. Westmont has also claimed seven NAIA national championships, including titles in women's soccer in 2001, 2002, and 2003. Westmont Field & Track won the women's marathon and NAIA Outdoor Track and Field Championships in 2007. In addition, the men's basketball and soccer teams, plus the women's volleyball squad, have been highly ranked in recent years. When athletic events have an admission fee, tickets are sold at the gate or the door.

POLO

Santa Barbara Polo and Racquet Club
3375 Foothill Road, Carpinteria
(805) 684-6683
www.sbpolo.com

The public is invited to watch Sunday afternoon matches during the polo season, which runs from April through October. Matches are played at 1:00 and 3:00 p.m., and admission is $10 at the gate for adults (children under 12 are free). Food and beverage service is available, or you can bring your own picnic.

SATELLITE WAGERING

Earl Warren Showgrounds
U.S. Highway 101 and Las Positas Road,
Santa Barbara
(805) 687-0766
www.earlwarren.com

Although you can't enjoy the thrill of the race in person unless you drive to Los Angeles,

Earl Warren Showgrounds (affectionately called "Earl's Place" in this particular context) is open at 10:00 a.m. for satellite wagering on all race days. Races from several tracks, including Los Alamitos, Santa Anita, and Hollywood Park in the Los Angeles area, as well as some Eastern imports, are beamed down via satellite—you can even wager on the Kentucky Derby. Call (805) 682-2187 for schedules. Food and bar service are available. General admission is $5, $4 for seniors and students with ID. Seniors over 55 are admitted free on Thursday.

THE REAL THING— L.A. PRO SPORTS

For big-city spectator sports, you'll have to drive to the Big City—Los Angeles in this case. Expect a two- to three-hour drive to L.A., and plan to arrive at least 30 minutes before the game begins, as you may have to negotiate parking, crowds, and long lines at ticket windows and/or food stands.

Many teams offer advance ticket sales through TicketMaster, and the number is listed where appropriate. Note that the TicketMaster number listed is a local call from Santa Barbara, but you can get tickets from any TicketMaster outlet (www.ticketmaster.com). Tickets are also sold at the gate for most events. Toll-free numbers with the 800 or 888 prefix are listed when available, but you often need to make a toll call to reach the L.A. ticket office.

Baseball

The Anaheim Angels play American League baseball at Edison International Field, Anaheim, April through September. Information: (714) 663-9000, TicketMaster (805) 583-8700; www.losangeles.angels.mlb.com.

The Los Angeles Dodgers are the city's National League baseball team. They play at Dodger Stadium April through September. Information: (866) DODGERS; www.dodgers.com.

Basketball

The Los Angeles Clippers play NBA basketball at the Staples Center from October through May. Information: (213) 742-7555, TicketMaster (805) 583-8700; www.nba.com/clippers.

The Los Angeles Lakers (www.nba.com/lakers) also play NBA basketball at the Staples Center in October through May. TicketMaster (805) 583–8700.

Horse Racing

L.A. racetracks: Hollywood Park, Inglewood (310-419-1500; www.hollywoodpark.com); Santa Anita Park, Arcadia (626-574-7223; www.santaanita.com); Los Alamitos Race Course, Los Alamitos (714-995-1234; www.losalamitos.com).

Ice Hockey

The Los Angeles Kings play NHL hockey at the Staples Center from October through April. Information: (888) KINGSLA, TicketMaster (805) 583-8700; www.kings.nhl.com.

The Anaheim Ducks, another NHL hockey team, take to the ice at Honda Center, Anaheim, from October through April. Purchase tickets at the door, or call TicketMaster, (805) 583-8700; www.anaheimducks.com.

Running

The Los Angeles Marathon takes place in March. Information: (310) 444-5544; www.lamarathon.com.

RELOCATION

Santa Barbara isn't just a popular vacation destination; it's also one of the most desirable residential areas in the country. If you've ever visited, you'll know why. Where else can you bask in sunshine more than 300 days a year, spend one day bronzing on golden beaches and the next hiking in the mountains or sailing to unspoiled islands? In Santa Barbara we have access to top-notch educational institutions and high-quality health care. We enjoy a year-round calendar of theater, art, music, and dance, and if we want to, we can dine at a different gourmet restaurant every night of the week. And remember, Santa Barbara isn't a big, bustling city with high crime and high pollution. It's a small, safe Southern Californian beach town. It's also friendly, relaxed, and ravishingly beautiful. Let's face it, Santa Barbara has it all.

No wonder so many people are scrambling to buy a house or condo here. But as always, there is a downside to this incredible desirability. Consider the age-old formula of supply and demand. As more and more people want to move here, real estate prices skyrocket, leaving the average home buyer standing on the pavement with a serious case of sticker shock. There's just no way to sugarcoat Santa Barbara's housing situation. Sure, you'll find the home of your dreams. But the question is, can you afford it?

In this chapter, we'll help prepare you to make a decision. First, we'll take you on a tour of the area's neighborhoods, point out some landmarks and attractions, and give you a broad idea of home prices. While you're touring, we also suggest you refer to other chapters in this book with information pertinent to relocation—including Kidstuff, Recreation, Shopping, Parks, and Education and Child Care. Once you have a good feel for the different neighborhoods, continue on to the Real Estate section for the inside scoop on the local market, how to choose an agent, and a list of local real estate companies that can help you find your dream home.

If you absolutely can't afford a permanent real estate commitment in Santa Barbara, check out the Vacation Rentals chapter and line up a condo for the summer. It's the next best thing to living here!

NEIGHBORHOODS

Santa Barbara

If all you've ever seen of Santa Barbara is the touristy beachfront area, you've missed the flavor of the charming neighborhoods that make up our beautiful city. In fact, as you cruise the leafy streets of Santa Barbara, you'll discover many highly desirable residential areas—probably more than you'd expect for such a small town. Scenic enclaves such as the Mesa, downtown Santa Barbara, Mission Canyon, and the Riviera all evoke contrasting images for Insiders, and each is worth exploring. But let's start with an overview of the beachfront strip. Then we'll venture farther afield.

The Beachfront

The Santa Barbara beachfront area along Cabrillo Boulevard is the most tourist-oriented section of the city. State Street and Stearns Wharf divide this strip into East Beach and West Beach, our classic palm-fringed stretches of sand. Not surprisingly, hotels and motels line the street opposite the beach on the north side of Cabrillo. If you're not walking to the beach from one of these nearby accommodations, you will find parking a nightmare along here, especially on weekends when the Sunday Santa Barbara Arts and Crafts show is set up along East Cabrillo Boulevard. A few public parking lots are available if you're willing to pay; if not, get there early or park on a side street and walk.

East Beach has volleyball courts on the sand and is the site of many local tournaments. Across the street from these you'll notice some upscale condos.

West Beach includes the area west of Stearns Wharf to the Santa Barbara Harbor. This wide expanse of sand is home to beach-rental and kayaking concessions as well as a calm area for swimming. Across the street, motels and restaurants are jammed in from one end of West Beach to the other, drawing hordes of tourists during the summer. If you continue to the far west end, you'll hit SEA Landing, the boarding point for whale-watching trips.

The Mesa

Heading west up the hill from the harbor lies the Mesa (Spanish for "table"), a large, family-oriented residential neighborhood bisected by Cliff Drive. Properties here range from Mediterranean and ranch-style homes to contemporary dwellings and shingled cottages with prices starting at about $1 million for small single-family homes and reaching up to more than $2 million for larger homes on prime property with ocean views. You'll also find many apartments here rented by Santa Barbara City College students.

A thriving shopping district sits at the intersection of Meigs Road and Cliff Drive, and Mesa residents head to Shoreline Park for recreation. This 15-acre stretch of rolling lawns, on a bluff overlooking the ocean, is a favorite venue for family outings and picnics.

i The Santa Barbara Chamber of Commerce (805-965-3023; www.sb chamber.org) offers two relocation packets. For $25 ($30 mailed) you can order a personal packet with a map and real estate and demographic information. The $40 business packet contains an economic profile, contacts for commercial real estate, a calendar of events, and information on arts and cultural activities.

It's also one of the best places in Santa Barbara to watch the sunset and fly a kite. Perched on a Mesa bluff top to the east of Shoreline, you'll find Santa Barbara City College, which arguably has the best panoramic view of any educational institution in the country; its La Playa Stadium is directly across the street from beautiful Leadbetter Beach and the Santa Barbara Harbor.

Downtown

The retail center of downtown Santa Barbara lies on "lower" State Street, between Stearns Wharf and Carrillo Street. Its busy shops, restaurants, sidewalk cafes, theaters, and the palm-lined Paseo Nuevo outdoor mall are a natural draw for visitors.

On the outskirts of this downtown area is a mix of gorgeous historic homes, smaller single-family dwellings, apartment and condo complexes, and small California cottages. Especially lovely are the old Victorian homes and gardens interspersed throughout the city. To give you an idea of prices, small bungalows on the more affordable west side of the city start at $800,000, while many grand old Victorian homes closer to the city center may soar into the millions.

Downtown Santa Barbara contains a large number of tourist attractions, including the Santa Barbara County Courthouse, the Presidio, and the Santa Barbara Museum of Art, so it's easy for a visitor to shop, dine, and see the sights within a fairly compact area. If you want to explore this historic district, we recommend the Red Tile Walking Tour (see the Close-up in the Attractions chapter for more details). Downtown always seems to be decked out with banners or decorations of some sort, adding to the neighborhood's festive feel. If you want to explore this area, your best bet is to nab a spot in a public parking lot and explore on foot. Better still, you can take the electric shuttle, which will whisk you around the downtown area for less than you'd spend to park in one of the pay lots. (See the Getting Here, Getting Around chapter for more information on local parking and transportation.)

Upper State Street

If you continue your drive up State Street, you'll reach Mission Street, the beginning of the "upper" State Street district, a mix of commercial and residential properties extending to La Cumbre Road. Unlike the downtown area, upper State lacks the Spanish ambience and has a much more modern feel. An exception is La Cumbre Plaza mall, which was revamped in an upscale Mediterranean style.

San Roque

San Roque, between upper State Street and the foothills, is another charming residential neighborhood populated by a mix of families with young children and older retirees. Despite its close proximity to a busy shopping and commercial district, it manages to retain a quiet and secluded feel. Meticulously maintained homes with well-manicured lawns line the sunny streets, and you'll notice a variety of architectural styles, from imitation Tudor cottages and Spanish haciendas to classic ranch-style homes. Real estate (you're probably getting used to this by now) is expensive, and a small three-bedroom house can sell for more than $1 million. Smaller two-bedrooms may go for just around $1 million.

Mission Canyon

Mission Canyon is the quiet, thickly wooded neighborhood around Mission Canyon Road and the adjacent foothills. It's a beautiful area of old oaks and sycamores, rocky streams, and hiking trails. Lured by the area's natural beauty, many artists, writers, and musicians make their home here. It's only a 10-minute drive to downtown, but the rugged wilderness makes it feel more remote. In lower Mission Canyon you'll find the Santa Barbara Museum of Natural History, Rocky Nook Park, and Mission Santa Barbara, while upper Mission Canyon is home to the Santa Barbara Botanic Garden. Architecture in the area tends to be more contemporary in style. Real estate prices are $950,000 in Mission Canyon Heights to well over $3 million for more exclusive homes secluded in the woodlands.

The Riviera

Driving up from Mission Canyon on meandering Alameda Padre Serra (Insiders call it "APS") puts you on the sunny Santa Barbara Riviera, with its magnificent views of the ocean, the Channel Islands (on a clear day), and the city of Santa Barbara. Not all the homes on the Riviera are large, but their location makes them expensive, with prices ranging from $1.2 million to well over $8 million. The main campus of the Brooks Institute of Photography resides on prime property here, and just above Alameda Padre Serra you'll find the newly renovated El Encanto Hotel and Garden Villas, with its Mediterranean-style restaurant and spectacular views of the city and sea (find out more in the Hotels and Motels and Restaurants chapters).

Goleta Valley

The Goleta Valley ("Go-LEE-ta," from the Spanish word for "schooner"—and yes, we know that's not the correct Spanish pronunciation) is the fastest growing area on the South Coast. In 2001, after years of struggling to control the area's future, voters created a new City of Goleta stretching roughly from Patterson Road in the east to the western Urban Rural Boundary Line at the Bacara Resort. Many of the 29,000 residents of this new city are committed to curbing the huge boom in development that has changed the face of the Goleta Valley in the last 40 years. Once home to lemon groves and wide-open spaces, the area is now sprouting major high-density housing developments and apartment complexes. The Goleta Valley also has more high-tech firms than any other area in the county. Development aside, the new City of Goleta has one of the lowest crime rates in the state and nation for its size and attracts many families looking for a safe and relatively affordable place (by Santa Barbara standards) to raise their children.

The unincorporated area of the Goleta Valley includes Isla Vista (pronounced "EYE-la VIS-ta"—and yes, we've tweaked the Spanish pronunciation again), where thousands of UCSB students cram into several square blocks of rental complexes. You'll also find the Santa Barbara Airport here, although it technically sits on a patch of the City of Santa Barbara (just to complicate things).

The Goleta Valley has its own county beach, and you'll find several excellent golf courses here, including the celebrated Sandpiper Golf Course and the Glen Annie Golf Club. Camino Real Marketplace, a massive new retail center at Hollister and Storke Roads, draws throngs of bargain shoppers, and the Bacara Resort and Spa, a $200 million beachfront property, is one of Santa Barbara's most upscale resorts.

Other attractions in the area include the historic Stow House, a two-story Victorian home built in 1872; the Goleta Lemon Festival held each October on the Stow House grounds; and, of course, the cultural and educational offerings of UCSB. (See the Arts and Education and Child Care chapters for more information.)

The Goleta Valley's popularity with home buyers is pushing prices up here, too. At the low end, you might find an older two-bedroom tract home for about $800,000, depending on the neighborhood, while three-bedroom homes in the area are now selling for $900,000 and up.

Hope Ranch

Isolated between the area west of Modoc Road and the ocean, Hope Ranch, an affluent Santa Barbara County neighborhood, is like a community unto itself. Sprawling ranch-style homes and secluded mansions line the main thoroughfare of Las Palmas Drive, and the scores of winding, maze-like roads make it easy to get lost if you don't know where you're going. This is probably just fine with Hope Ranch residents, who value their privacy and employ their own security police.

Homes here sell for very big bucks, with low-end properties in the $1.5 million range and the most extravagant estates zooming upwards of $10 million.

You won't find any commercial businesses or tourist attractions in Hope Ranch,

but we recommend taking at least one sightseeing tour on Las Palmas Drive just to get a feel for the place. As you enter Las Palmas from Modoc Road (under the famous Hope Ranch gateway), to the left you'll see Laguna Blanca, a small lagoon that's part of the private La Cumbre Country Club. Originally the lagoon was surrounded by a horse-racing track designed by Thomas Hope, an Irishman who was granted the land in 1870.

You'll also notice a lot of bridle trails. Riding, as well as raising and showing horses, is a popular Hope Ranch pastime. Residents have access to bridle paths and a horse show ring as well as a private beach and tennis courts.

Montecito

Lying between Carpinteria and the city of Santa Barbara, Montecito has a well-deserved reputation as an enclave of the rich and famous. Unfortunately for the curious, most of the wealth is hidden behind massive gates or at the end of long, winding drives lined with trees or other lush vegetation. Movie stars do live here, but you'll be lucky to catch a glimpse of them unless you see them out shopping or browsing the local market.

Montecito's sense of elegance and seclusion is carried over into its luxurious lodging places, including the exclusive San Ysidro Ranch, built in the 1930s and a vacation retreat for the likes of John and Jacqueline Kennedy, Jean Harlow, and Katharine Hepburn, and the posh Four Seasons Resort The Biltmore Santa Barbara, a beautifully landscaped complex of elegant rooms and cottages constructed in 1927 and perched just above Butterfly Beach (for more details, see the Hotels and Motels chapter).

Shopping tends to be upscale and exclusive here, with two main shopping areas, the "lower village," along Coast Village Road, and the "upper village," at San Ysidro and East Valley Roads, which contain galleries, high-end real estate offices, and restaurants. In our opinion, the most rewarding attraction in Montecito is Lotusland, a stunning collection of wildly imaginative gardens and exotic plants created by the eccentric Polish opera singer Mme. Ganna Walska. (See the Attractions chapter for more details.)

The highly respected Westmont College and Music Academy of the West are located within the boundaries of Montecito. Many families with young children also hope to buy homes in Montecito because of the two excellent public elementary schools—Cold Springs and Montecito Union—but unless you have big bucks, there's probably not much of a chance you'll be living here. Home prices range from about $1.5 million way on up to the mega-millions. In fact, Montecito has always vied with Hope Ranch for the most stratospheric estate sales. In 2001 Oprah Winfrey snapped up a 42-acre estate here for a reported $50 million, giving Montecitans cause to gloat over their lattes again. Not only is this a record real estate sale for the county, it's also one of the biggest real estate transactions for a private home in U.S. history.

Summerland

Rambling up the hillsides on the north side of Highway 101, between the exclusive enclave of Montecito and laid-back Carpinteria, sits a community of funky Victorian-style houses, antiques stores, restaurants, and brightly painted cottages. Blink and you might miss it. But in recent years, this cute little coastal enclave has become quite a hot spot. Home buyers are scrambling for a prime piece of ocean-view property here, and its diminutive nature is a big part of its charm.

Tinged with a faintly bohemian air, Summerland (or "Spookville," as it was once called) used to be a stomping ground for spiritualists, who gathered here for séances in the late 1800s. Today it's a popular hangout for

i Find out about Summerland's "ghostly" past by purchasing local author Rod Lathim's book, *The Spirit of the Big Yellow House: A History of Summerland's Founding Family*. It can be purchased at the Santa Barbara Airport and at local bookstores.

antiques shoppers, surfers, and a steady gush of tourists who flock here on weekends to enjoy its quaint bed-and-breakfasts and friendly cafes.

Carpinteria

An incorporated city located about 12 miles south of Santa Barbara, Carpinteria has a friendly, small-town feel. Named for the Chumash carpenters that Gaspár de Portol encountered here on a 1769 expedition, "Carp" (as the locals call it) contains acres of flower fields, greenhouses, and avocado groves. The annual California Avocado Festival is held here each October (see the Annual Events chapter), and a weekly farmers' market also shows off the local bounty.

Carp's main attraction is its natural beauty, but it does maintain a small historical museum and boasts the area's only polo fields, just north of the city at the Santa Barbara Polo & Racquet Club. The downtown area, situated around the intersection of Linden and Carpinteria Avenues, has small shops and restaurants. A strip mall with more modern businesses occupies both sides of Casitas Pass Road. The area is especially good for antiques hunting, and the city has an excellent beach, once dubbed "The World's Safest Beach," with a wide sandy stretch and relatively riptide-free waters. Carpinteria State Beach Park is visited by about a million people annually. It boasts 4,000 feet of ocean frontage for swimming and tidepooling as well as facilities for picnicking, hiking, and surf fishing (see the Parks chapter).

Because everything is cheaper in Carpinteria, many families choose it over Santa Barbara for vacations, especially because it offers easy beach access, numerous motels, and better odds of finding a vacation rental. Historically, housing prices tend to be lower here than in Santa Barbara, but now Carpinteria is also expensive, with an older three-bedroom home selling for more than $800,000, and lavish homes on the beach or in the foothills running as high as $5 million or more.

Close-up

Beautiful Homes, Bargain Prices

High on a grassy knoll in the coastal hamlet of Summerland sits a cluster of charming new houses and condominiums with sparkling Pacific vistas. This upscale housing project, known as The Cottages at Summerland, consists of 20 deluxe single-family homes, most of which sold for more than $1 million. Adjacent, 10 similarly designed condos with the same million-dollar views started at $67,800. How can this be? It's all part of a creative approach to Santa Barbara's housing crisis. In exchange for permission to build more units than current zoning laws allow, the county requires developers of housing projects to add affordable units to the mix. These units sell for less than they cost to build, but the developers make up the loss by selling the extra luxury units at market prices. This isn't the first project of its kind in the area. Goleta is home to several others, and another exclusive Mediterranean-style development in mega-bucks Montecito with seven affordable housing units sent would-be first-home buyers into a frenzy. Think you want to be in on this deal? Good luck! Prospective home buyers must meet strict low-income criteria, live in the county, and enter a lottery for the privilege of purchase.

REAL ESTATE

In 1974 a struggling young couple with a down payment provided by their parents bought a three-bedroom, 20-year-old Santa Barbara tract home for $36,500. Making the payments was a stretch, but they managed, even while the mother stayed home to raise the kids.

More than 30 years later, the same home, with only a new coat of paint and some new carpet, sells for more than 25 times that amount. Mom and Dad, still living in the house, could not afford to buy it today, nor could they afford the mortgage payments, even though they're both working now. As for their grown-up children, they have to pack up and move out of town to be able to afford a home of their own.

And so it goes in Santa Barbara. Residents joke that they could sell their houses and buy mansions elsewhere, but the same scenario almost never happens the other way around. Facing a job transfer or other reason for relocation, many Santa Barbarans rent out their homes rather than sell and risk cutting off any chance of being local homeowners again if they ever come back. This tendency to hang on to local real estate is bad news for home buyers. Demand far exceeds supply. Adding to the fierce competition for housing in recent years is the tech effect. As advances in technology allow more businesses to operate away from big cities, high-tech companies and workers migrate to small towns like Santa Barbara, where crime rates are low and the quality of life is high. And then there are all those ripe-aged, wealthy baby boomers looking for a quiet place to retire. For them, Santa Barbara has it all: sun, sea, surf, and fabulous golfing.

With such high demand for property, median home prices are zooming to record highs in Santa Barbara. The median price marks the point at which half the homes on the market sell for more and half sell for less. Of course, all those multimillion-dollar estates in Hope Ranch and Montecito skew the figures a bit (we hear you can't even find a

ℹ New to Santa Barbara? Join the 400-member Newcomer's Club. This dynamic group plans social functions so you can get to know the area and the people. Hospitality coffees for prospective members are held the first Monday of the month at Fess Parker's DoubleTree Resort. Visit the Web site at www.sbnewcomers .org, or call (805) 564-2555 for more information.

decent estate around there for a measly $3 million anymore), but even at the lower end, homes in Santa Barbara are out of reach for many buyers.

To qualify for a loan of $800,000 for a house in Santa Barbara (which is way below the current South Coast median), your household income needs to be at least $195,000 a year. Considering Santa Barbara's median income hovers in the mid-$50,000 range, it's not surprising home buyers are frustrated. At this rate, most renters can only dream of owning a home in the area.

Some government officials say the solution to high-cost housing is simple: build more houses! This scenario makes conservation-minded Santa Barbarans (and there are a lot of them) cringe. So when will the real estate rocket ride end? Historically, the market moves in cycles. But even during the dips here, demand remains relatively strong and prices are still high. After all, there's only one Santa Barbara in the world, and so many people want to live here.

around for decades and have sterling reputations, while others are part of respected national chains. Several individually owned firms have also found their niche and are doing well.

The Internet has made a significant impact on the real estate market. Most of Santa Barbara's real estate firms have an Internet presence, but simply looking online for a firm and listings isn't enough. The personal guidance and services of a seasoned real estate professional is what's required to snatch up your ideal home, especially in this market of multiple offers and relatively quick turnovers. Sotheby's International Realty agent Maureen McDermut said, "According to the California Association of Realtors, 80 percent of all buyers start searching for real estate and agents on the Internet. Buying or selling a home is a complex process involving, perhaps, your largest financial asset. To have the best possible results, you should involve a professional Realtor to help you negotiate the ideal purchase price (or sale price) for your home."

Nearly all real estate companies offer some type of relocation services. The large firms associated with national chains often have relocation departments or specialists, but independent Realtors work hard to meet relocation needs as well.

The companies below represent a partial list of real estate firms located in the greater Santa Barbara area. They are generally considered to have experienced agents who have good track records in assisting both buyers and sellers.

Real Estate Firms

Whether you rent or buy, housing in Santa Barbara will take a tremendous toll on your budget. So it's important to find someone you trust to assist you in the process of home-finding. Santa Barbara is a relatively small town where everyone knows nearly everyone else in real estate, so word gets around fast if anything unscrupulous is going on—which is not often.

Many local real estate firms have been

Century 21
A Hart Realty Incorporated
3412 State Street, Santa Barbara
(805) 687-7591, (800) 350-2733
www.century21ahart.com
This well-respected office of more than 30 agents has won the coveted Centurion Award for outstanding customer service every year since 1983. The office specializes in residential real estate, but it also handles commercial and investment properties in all areas of

greater Santa Barbara. This office is independently owned but offers the benefits of affiliation with a large chain, such as Century 21's national relocation program.

Century 21
Butler Realty
1635 State Street, Santa Barbara
(805) 563-2121, (800) 421-4452
www.c21butler.net
In addition to being the top-producing Century 21 office in Santa Barbara, Century 21 Butler Realty offers a property management and vacation rental division. This division, founded and run by Eric Penner for over 10 years, is an excellent resource for vacation rentals. Insiders know that it is the first place to turn to for their vacation rental needs.

Coastal Properties
1086 Coast Village Road, Montecito
(805) 969-1258

5030 Carpinteria Avenue, Carpinteria
(805) 684-8777
www.coastalrealty.com
In business since 1995, Coastal Properties has turned its extensive knowledge of the upscale vacation rental market into a successful "boutique" real estate venture. Specializing in Montecito, Hope Ranch, Santa Barbara, Carpinteria, and beach properties, the company's agents deal in everything from low-end condos to multimillion-dollar estates.

Coldwell Banker
3902 State Street, Santa Barbara
(805) 682-2477

1290 Coast Village Road, Montecito
(805) 969-4755

1498 East Valley Road B, Montecito
(805) 969-0900
www.coldwellbanker.com, www.cbso
cal.com, www.previewsestates.com
Frequently voted Santa Barbara's best real estate company in local newspaper polls, Coldwell Banker is a distinguished firm that sells multimillion-dollar estates as well as lower-priced family homes. The company has been in Santa Barbara for more than 30 years and has over 150 experienced agents. Coldwell Banker also has a national and international relocation department, a commercial division, an REO department, and a concierge service to help smooth your transition.

Maizlish Realtors, Inc.
1514 Anacapa Street, Suite B, Santa Barbara
(805) 963-9555, (888) 963-9556
www.maizlish-sb.com
Co-owners Morton and Alicia Maizlish are both brokers and the sole employees of this independent firm established in 1980. They believe in the single-agency approach, which means the company will only represent one party in a transaction. Recently they have been specializing in downtown, upper east, and Riviera properties. The Maizlishes deal with a full range of real estate, from condos to estates, and limit transactions to between 20 and 25 a year in order to provide personalized service.

Prudential California Realty—Santa Barbara
3868 State Street, Santa Barbara
(805) 687-2666, (800) 326-3483

1150 Coast Village Road, Montecito
(805) 969-5026, (800) 201-4364

527 San Ysidro Road, Montecito
(805) 969-1520
www.prudentialcal.com
Doing business in Santa Barbara since 1950 (and voted the best local real estate company five years in a row in past *Santa Barbara News-Press* polls), Prudential California Realty–Santa Barbara has more than 80 agents working out of two local offices. The company deals in all

i Santa Barbara's strict building design guidelines arose from a stroke of Mother Nature's wrath. After a devastating earthquake in 1925, planners rebuilt the city in Spanish-Mediterranean style.

i Yammering loudly on your cell phone in public is considered big-city behavior in this laid-back town. If you want to look like a local, you might want to tone it down a notch.

types of properties including residential, commercial, and investment properties and specializes in helping first-time home buyers break into the market. Prudential's worldwide network of offices provides relocation assistance.

RE/MAX Santa Barbara
1715 State Street, Santa Barbara
(805) 687-2600

1205 Coast Village Road, Montecito
(805) 969-2282
www.remax-santabarbara.com
Part of a large national chain, this firm is a full-service agency handling a range of properties throughout the greater Santa Barbara area. Special divisions include estates, restaurants, residential, commercial, and investment properties. The company's broker has held many prestigious positions in the industry, including president of the California Association of Realtors. About 85 agents work out of two offices.

Sotheby's International Realty
1436 State Street, Santa Barbara
(805) 963-1961

1165-K Coast Village Road, Montecito
(805) 969-1133

1482 East Valley Road, Montecito
(805) 969-5005
www.socalsir.com
Sotheby's displayed its brilliance when it moved into town by snapping up the local real estate giant Pitts and Bachmann. Adding Pitts and Bachmann real estate locations and agents to the firm really created a Santa Barbara presence. It doesn't matter whether the estate or house is large or small, Sotheby's realtors handle the transactions with professional aplomb.

Village Properties
1250 Coast Village Road, Montecito
(805) 969-8900

4050 Calle Real, Suite 120, Goleta
(805) 681-8800
www.villagesite.com
Established in 1996, Village Properties is a locally owned and operated independent agency. Founded by Ed Edick and Renee Grubb, the company specializes in residential properties, including beachfront homes, estates, and new homes, but it also has experts in relocation, commercial properties, senior housing, affordable housing, and creative financing. More than 40 experienced agents with an average of 20 years' experience serve Santa Barbara, Montecito, Goleta, Carpinteria, and the Santa Ynez Valley. Village Property hosts a Teachers' Fund, which allocates dollars to teachers in the community.

Other Resources for Finding a Home

The real estate pullout section in the Sunday *Santa Barbara News-Press* is a great resource; it's published in cooperation with the Santa Barbara Association of Realtors. *Casa,* a free tabloid, features real estate ads and photographs of homes for sale as well as a schedule of open houses for the week and a few classified ads for rentals. It's available in real estate offices and at more than 250 street stands in Santa Barbara.

Homes & Land runs photos of listed properties along with ads for the real estate companies that are listing them, as does the glossy new *Real Estate* magazine. Ads for fancy estates on the market in Montecito and Hope Ranch can be found in the slick quarterly *Santa Barbara Magazine,* which often shows both interior and exterior shots. Price tags on these homes are seldom below $1 million and are occasionally as high as $20 million.

THE RENTAL SCENE

If you can't afford to buy, you may have to rent, but don't expect to get off without paying a lot of money. (Hey, this is Santa Barbara!) Home rentals start at about $1,500 a month, and there is literally no ceiling, with large mansions and beachfront properties renting for $20,000 a month or more.

Use whatever network you have in place, as word of mouth is often the best way to find out what's available. Tell everyone you know that you're looking, and follow up on every lead. If you are a college student looking for an apartment or room to rent, your best bet is the student housing office at the college or university you will be attending.

Most Realtors, who have many local contacts, will gladly advise you on rentals, but bear in mind that in Santa Barbara a Realtor gets no

i Housing prices in the North County (including Santa Maria and Lompoc) are lower than those in the South County (greater Santa Barbara), but consider the cost of gasoline and the extra driving time before you buy.

commission on rental property. Whether you're looking for a house or an apartment, landlords are choosy about their tenants, so you'll need to be organized. Pick up a rental application from a local real estate office, fill it out accurately and completely, and when you visit a potential rental, leave a copy with the landlord if you're interested. Make copies so you don't have to fill out a new application each time you apply. Finally, you'll need cash in the bank to cover required security and cleaning deposits, usually payable before you take occupancy.

RETIREMENT

When people dream of retirement, they often envision a comfortable home in a warm, dry climate, a region with plenty of social, recreational, and cultural opportunities, excellent health care, friendly people, and inspirational scenery. Santa Barbara, by all accounts, matches this dream. For more than a century, countless seniors and younger retirees from around the United States and the world have packed their belongings and moved to Santa Barbara. In this chapter, we focus on seniors, since they comprise the majority of retired folk in Santa Barbara.

The over-60 crowd makes its presence known everywhere. They play a major role in politics, the arts and culture scene, and adult education classes. Senior volunteers serve as docents at the museums, the zoo, the botanic garden, and other attractions; as helpers at our numerous service agencies; as tutors, teachers, guides, and mentors to younger Santa Barbarans. Our seniors also tend to stay active as long as possible. Folks from age 60 to 100 regularly attend fitness classes—it's not unusual to see a grandmother "crunching abs" right next to a 20-year-old. They walk, jog, play tennis and golf, attend concerts, travel, study, and read.

When seniors are no longer able to venture out as much as they'd like, Santa Barbara makes great efforts to bring services and

activities to senior residences throughout the community.

Sound perfect? Well, there's one catch. As we've mentioned elsewhere in this book, the cost of living here is exorbitant. In fact, it's virtually impossible to live here on Social Security alone, and seniors on limited incomes find it extremely difficult to meet the costs of daily life. Housing and services for lower-income seniors have limited availability and long waiting lists.

Affordability aside, Santa Barbara offers many advantages to retired residents. In this chapter we give you a sampling of our services and programs for seniors—with a special focus on those that can help stretch limited dollars.

We start with general information resources; then move on to senior centers; ways to nourish the body and mind; recreation; employment and volunteer opportunities; retirement communities; and housing. For information on Santa Barbara's extensive health care system, see the Health Care and Wellness chapter.

TAPPING INTO THE SENIOR NETWORK

Your best resource for finding out about senior services and programs is the Santa Barbara County Senior Resource Directory. It includes listings of nearly all nonprofit and government agencies that provide services to senior citizens. Its contents are the foundation of this chapter, and you won't find a more comprehensive compendium of information for seniors anywhere else in the county. To receive a copy, call the nonprofit Central Coast Commission for Senior Citizens at (800) 510-2020 in California or visit the Web site at centralcoastseniors.org.

i Do you love to read? Santa Barbara's new Web-based library reservation system makes hunting down that special book a breeze. Simply go to www.ci .santa-barbara.ca.us/departments/library and search by author, title, subject, or keywords. You can also browse through more than 800 magazines and medical journals and track down CDs, videotapes, and large-type books.

Senior Resources

The following organizations provide information on a variety of topics of interest to seniors.

American Association of Retired Persons (AARP)
Santa Barbara Chapter #72
333 Old Mill Road, #263, Santa Barbara
(805) 964-3943,
(916) 446-AARP, regional headquarters
www.aarp.org
AARP is the nation's leading organization for people age 50 and older. AARP's motto, "The power to make it better," reflects its commitment to preserving the independence and autonomy of all older persons. It serves the needs of seniors through advocacy, research, and consumer information. An extensive network of local chapters and volunteers provides educational programs and community services for our nation's older population.

Local Santa Barbara Chapter #72 holds meetings the first Monday of each month at 2:00 p.m. at 1232 De la Vina Street, Santa Barbara.

Area Agency on Aging/Central Coast Commission for Senior Citizens
528 South Broadway, Santa Maria (headquarters)
(800) 510-2020, (805) 925-9554
www.centralcoastseniors.org
The Older Americans Act (1965) and its subsequent amendments in 1973 gave birth to Area Agencies on Aging, a network of federal, state, and local agencies, all working together to help seniors maintain independence and dignity in the environments they choose. At the local level, the Area Agency on Aging works in tandem with other public and private agencies to provide senior citizens with a wide range of services.

The Area Agency on Aging for the Santa Barbara region is the Central Coast Commission for Senior Citizens. The organization, which is based in Santa Maria, provides information over the phone and through its Web site and publishes the Senior Resource Directory. Its programs include home-delivered meals, senior lunches, in-home support services, respite for caregivers, information and referral, transportation services, legal assistance, senior day care services, senior citizen centers, home repair, and peer counseling.

Senior Connection is a special service of the Area Agency on Aging. The staff can give you information, refer you to appropriate programs and services, and help you with just about any question you have relating to senior citizens.

Family Service Agency Senior Outreach Program
123 West Gutierrez Street, Santa Barbara
(805) 965-1001
www.fsacares.org
FSA is Santa Barbara County's oldest nonprofit human service agency. If you're older than 60 and live in Santa Barbara, Carpinteria, or Goleta, Family Services will send a professional counselor to your home to assess your needs. Then it will connect you with the appropriate community resources. FSA will also provide individual, group, and family counseling if you so desire.

FSA also sponsors SAIL—Seniors Aimed at Independent Living. Through SAIL, seniors and disabled persons receive help with home repairs and maintenance. Donations are accepted on a sliding scale based on monthly income. SAIL workers assist with general house upkeep, make safety modifications, and build wheelchair ramps. Seniors can also take advantage of the Homemaker Program, which provides assistance with meal preparation, cleaning, and grocery shopping.

Santa Barbara County Geriatric Assessment Program (GAP)
345 Camino del Remedio, third floor, Santa Barbara
(805) 681-5266
www.sbcphd.org
Are you over 60 and experiencing difficulty in your present living situation? Registered nurses will come to your home to assess your

social, environmental, psychological, and health needs. They will also develop a care plan and consult with family members, caregivers, and professionals about ways to preserve your independence.

Frequently Called Numbers

Santa Barbara's senior citizens have access to a wealth of resources. Here's a list of telephone numbers that you'll probably want to have on hand for quick and easy reference.

American Association of Retired Persons (AARP), (805) 964-3943

The Eldercare Locator, (800) 677-1116

Family Service Agency, (805) 965-1001

Senior Connection, (800) 510-2020

Senior Information and Referral Help Line, (805) 884-9820

> **i** Need assistance with a critical but nonemergency issue? Call 211, the help line established by Family Service Agency to help unburden the 911 lines.

SENIOR CENTERS

All the area community senior centers provide a vast range of information and resources, and each center offers different types of services. Typical examples are lunch programs, community education, recreational activities, music, health screenings, arts and crafts classes, computer training, and health insurance counseling. Senior centers are excellent places to meet with other seniors and stay active.

Carrillo Recreation Center
**100 East Carrillo Street, Santa Barbara
(805) 897-2519**
Active seniors love the Carrillo Recreation Center, with its Active Adult Club of stretch-

and-tone and Jazzercise classes. Known for its spring-loaded dance floors, this center bursts with all kinds of dance classes for seniors, including tap, salsa, folk, and tango. The next-door Carrillo Street Gym offers table tennis and weight conditioning.

**Louise Lowry Davis Recreation Center
1232 De la Vina Street, Santa Barbara
(805) 897-2568**
The Louise Lowry Davis Recreation Center is one of the most popular senior centers in the city. Located downtown on the corner of De la Vina and Sola Streets, the center serves as headquarters for the Senior Citizens Information Service. On fair-weather days, you can always see groups of smiling, laughing seniors bowling on the adjacent lawns. You can walk in and join various activities (e.g., chess and bridge) or sign up for weekday recreation programs. The center has a kitchen area, serving area, meeting rooms, restrooms, and on-site parking.

Other Senior Centers

Other area senior centers also provide social, educational, and recreational services and facilities.

Santa Barbara

Franklin Neighborhood Community Center
**1136 East Montecito Street, Santa Barbara
(805) 963–7605**

Lower Westside Center
**629 Coronel Place, Santa Barbara
(805) 963-7537**

Westside Community Center/Senior Center
**423 West Victoria Street, Santa Barbara
(805) 963-7567**

Goleta

Goleta Senior Center
**5679 Hollister Avenue, Goleta
(805) 683-1124**

Carpinteria

Community Action Senior Center
941 Walnut Avenue, Carpinteria
(805) 684-6090

NUTRITION
Grocery Resources

Call the Senior Connection at (800) 510-2020 for a list of stores in your area that deliver or for the names and phone numbers of services that will do your shopping for you.

Meals Delivered to Your Home

Community Action Commission Mobile Meals
5681 Hollister Avenue, Goleta
(805) 692-4979
www.cacsb.com
For a suggested donation of $2.25, Mobile Meals delivers a hot meal Monday through Friday from 10:30 a.m. to 2:00 p.m. to home-bound seniors ages 60 and older. Frozen meals for weekends and holidays are also available. The delivery area includes Santa Barbara, Goleta, and Carpinteria.

Meals-on-Wheels
(805) 683-1565
Meals-on-Wheels delivers hot midday meals to homebound seniors every day year-round, including holidays. They charge a modest fee for each meal—call between 9:00 a.m. and noon for more information.

Senior Brown Bag Program
4554 Hollister Avenue, Santa Barbara
(805) 967-7863
A project of the Santa Barbara County Food Bank, Brown Bag distributes market-size bags of groceries twice a month to six different sites in Santa Barbara, Goleta, and Carpinteria. The bags are meant to supplement seniors' grocery shopping and include a variety of food items, including produce and bread. To be eligible for this free program, you must be 60 or older, have a limited income, and be

i Need help picking up your groceries? Call the Market Van at (805) 965-1531. If you're 60 or older, of limited income, and have impairments that make it difficult for you to shop alone, the van will pick you up at your home every Friday for a $10 monthly donation. Call for details on eligible areas.

in an independent-living situation. Singles or couples may apply.

Dining with Friends

Cliff Drive Senior Luncheon
1418 Santa Fe Place, Santa Barbara
(805) 965-4286
Join other seniors for lunch the first and third Thursday of the month (from 11:00 a.m. to 1:00 p.m.) in the recreation room across the road from the Free Methodist Church. A $3 donation is suggested. The program doesn't operate in August.

Community Action Commission Senior Nutrition Sites

If you're 60 or older, you're eligible for hot lunches at a nutrition site. You need to make reservations 24 hours in advance. Meals are free, but donations are suggested. If you need a ride to the site, transportation may be available. Call the commission headquarters for information and to make reservations at any of the following sites. It's located at 5681 Hollister Avenue in Goleta (805-692-4979; www.cacsb.com).

Santa Barbara

Franklin Senior Center
1136 East Montecito Street, Santa Barbara

Presidio Springs
721 Laguna Street, Santa Barbara

Westside Senior Center
423 West Victoria Street, Santa Barbara

Lawn bowling—a popular past time for retirees. BRIAN HASTINGS

Goleta

Goleta Senior Center
5679 Hollister Avenue, Goleta

Carpinteria

Carpinteria Senior Center
941 Walnut Street, Carpinteria

RECREATION

Santa Barbara's recreational opportunities are available to active people of every age. See our Recreation chapter for a detailed overview of your many options. Many facilities offer senior discounts—be sure to ask whenever you inquire for information or pay fees.

Senior Recreation Services Club
Santa Barbara Parks and Recreation
100 East Carrillo Street, Santa Barbara
(805) 897-2519, (805) 965-3813
www.sbparksandrecreation.com
If you're 60 years of age or older, you can join the Senior Recreation Services Club for only $38 a year ($53 per couple). If you're a resident of Santa Barbara City, you can apply for a resident discount card and join the club for $32 ($44 per couple). You'll receive a monthly newsletter with details on classes, special events, and an extensive tour and travel program. Club members are eligible for discounts on tours and free admission to a range of fitness and personal-enrichment classes.

Most fitness activities take place at the Carrillo Recreation Center, 100 East Carrillo

Street, and Louise Lowry Davis Center, 1232 De la Vina Street.

Fitness activities include yoga, badminton, table tennis, various exercise classes, t'ai chi, dancercise, slow-pitch softball, lawn bowling, and horseshoes. The stretch and tone class is particularly popular. Personal enrichment classes and social events include dances, bingo, movie days, social luncheons, language classes, ceramics and painting classes, support groups, chess, and bridge games.

EDUCATION

There's no age limit for expanding the mind, and Santa Barbara offers an extraordinary array of educational opportunities (see the Education and Child Care chapter for more information). You'll find a variety of lectures, classes, forums, field trips, and poetry readings. Here we'd like to highlight one of Santa Barbara's shining stars—the Adult Education Program—which actually targets seniors and provides special educational programs just for the over-50 set.

Santa Barbara City College Continuing Education Division
Alice F. Schott Center
310 West Padre Street, Santa Barbara
(805) 687-0812
www.sbcc.net/continuingeducation
The Continuing Education Division of Santa Barbara City College, a.k.a. Adult Ed, offers an incredible range of noncredit and community service classes. During fall, winter, spring, and summer sessions, classes meet weekday mornings, afternoons, and evenings as well as Saturdays. More than 42,000 people enroll in adult ed classes every year.

Most classes take place at the Alice Schott Center. Others meet at the Selmer O. Wake Center, 300 North Turnpike (805-964-6853), and at more than 100 locations in the greater Santa Barbara area. Most classes are free, with occasional minimal fees for materials.

Many of the classes are specially designed for seniors. Subjects include the arts, business, finance, real estate, job training, computers, cooking and wine, crafts, current events and world affairs, literature, writing, home and garden, humanities, languages, music, and photography. The Omega Program (www.sbcc.edu/omega.htm), developed especially for seniors and frail elderly community residents, offers classes and workshops related to the subject of aging. The Omega Program fosters self-esteem and dignity and helps seniors develop an appreciation of their past roles. Examples of classes include Body/Mind Awareness; Our Lives and Times; Music for All Seasons and Reasons; and Words for Thought. For more information, call (805) 964-3714.

If you enjoy traveling, sign up for some of Adult Ed's popular trips and tours. Local trips enabled groups to explore the new Getty Center museum in Los Angeles and to visit Casa del Herrera, Santa Barbara's premier Spanish Colonial Revival residence. Trips abroad are sometimes offered as well.

EMPLOYMENT

AARP Foundation/Senior Community Service Employment Program
301 South Miller, #110, Santa Maria
(805) 922-7966
www.aarp.org
AARP Foundation is a special, separate branch of the AARP, the American Association of Retired Persons. It arranges hiring, training, and placement of seniors in part-time paid positions in public and private nonprofit agencies. You must be at least 55 years old and meet limited-income requirements.

VOLUNTEER OPPORTUNITIES

Give the gift of your talent, skills, and time to the community. Many human service agencies such as hospitals, museums, homeless shelters, children's programs, wildlife agencies, and libraries depend on volunteers to keep things running smoothly. Here are two clearinghouses for volunteer opportunities. You can also try calling specific programs directly—the *Santa Barbara News-Press* publishes a feature called "Lighting the Way" in the Sunday "Life" section that highlights volunteer opportunities and includes a partial list of non-profit organizations in Santa Barbara County.

Retired Senior Volunteer Program (RSVP)
Santa Barbara
35 West Victoria Street, Santa Barbara
(805) 963-0474
RSVP places seniors in volunteer positions at schools, hospitals, service agencies, senior centers, and other senior programs.

A ROOF OVER YOUR HEAD

It's very difficult for anyone to find affordable housing in Santa Barbara County. Low-cost rentals for seniors are available, but they are in extremely high demand and have long waiting lists. If you have a large nest egg put aside, you may be able to buy or rent a home in your choice of neighborhoods (see the Relocation chapter).

If you're like many seniors, you may be seeking the security and comfort of a retirement community where you can socialize with peers and take advantage of services that ease the challenges of daily life. All the retirement communities below offer, at the minimum, 24-hour security and housekeeping services. We've focused on communities with independent-living residences, although many of these also offer facilities for assisted living as well as skilled nursing.

People who opt for assisted living don't need full-time nursing care, but do need some help with dressing, bathing, eating, taking medications, and mobility. Assisted living facilities provide these services while allowing residents to retain privacy and independence.

We do not cover skilled nursing homes here. We recommend that you call Central Coast Seniors at (800) 510-2020 if you need information about this level of care in the community. If you're not sure what type of residence is best for you, just ask for guidance. The experienced staff will be more than happy to help.

Continuing Care Retirement Communities

These facilities offer a continuum of care: independent residential apartments or homes and separate facilities for assisted-living and skilled-nursing care. Costs vary significantly. Some require hefty entry fees plus monthly payments for services. At others, you pay month to month without a significant entry fee or endowment. Be sure to inquire about all the financial requirements when you request information.

Santa Barbara

The Samarkand
2550 Treasure Drive, Santa Barbara
(805) 687-0701, (800) 370-5357
www.covenantretirement.com
This Christian continuing care retirement community is situated on a 16-acre, centrally located campus in a residential neighborhood bordered by Oak Park, Las Positas Road, and State Street. The Samarkand property was originally a boys' school, which closed in 1920. The land was then subdivided, and the complex became a resort hotel, which was named after the capital city of the Mongol conqueror Tamerlane. A group of local businessmen converted the property to a retirement community in 1955 and sold it to the Evangelical Covenant Church in 1966.

Today the Samarkand is one of 14 Covenant Retirement Communities run by a nonprofit corporation of the Evangelical Covenant Church. The Samarkand campus has about 400 residents in independent living apartments ranging from 220 residential independent living studios to two-bedroom units, 55 assisted living units, and 63 beds in skilled nursing. Amenities include a 24-hour emergency call system, housekeeping, linen service, three meals a day, comprehensive health services, and much more.

Residents of Samarkand have access to many recreational amenities. The grounds encompass a lovely swimming pool and Jacuzzi, exercise room, library, billiard room, woodworking workshop, and hobby room, and residents can participate in organized activities and adult education programs. Community areas include a 220-seat fellowship hall, a private lounge for small groups, a dining room, and a chapel.

The Samarkand also has scheduled transportation for church, shopping, and appointments, as well as a gift shop, chaplain services, and a barber/beauty shop.

Valle Verde Retirement Community
900 Calle de Los Amigos, Santa Barbara
(805) 687-1571
www.valleverdesb.com

Valle Verde's 65-acre campus rests in the hills of the serene Hidden Valley neighborhood near Hope Ranch and Arroyo Burro (Hendry's Beach). It's owned and operated by American Baptist Homes of the West, a nonprofit corporation that has provided retirement housing and health care services since 1949. Valle Verde opened in 1966 and today offers several levels of care.

Many residents ride bikes, golf carts, or enjoy strolling around the flat, sprawling campus, which seems like a country club on a golf course. Amenities include a solar-heated pool and Jacuzzi, library, theater, private dining room, beauty/barber shop, and a convenience store. It also has a craft room and hobby shop, putting green, fitness center, hiking trails to the surrounding foothills, coach service, and city bus service. Activities include adult education and exercise classes.

All the apartments are ground-floor units with private patios and feature an emergency call system that connects directly with Valle Verde's Health Center, where registered gerontology professionals are always available. The wellness department offers a daily nursing clinic and the dietary department can design a special diet if required.

If your needs change, you can move to assisted living accommodations in Quail Lodge or to the Health Care Center, a skilled nursing facility. Each spacious suite in Quail Lodge has a living area and private bath,

along with a call bell system that connects you with staff 24 hours a day. The lodge serves three meals a day in a private dining room, and meals are tailored to the individual dietary requirements of each resident. It also provides housekeeping and maintenance services as well as activities. At the Health Center, licensed nurses and certified nursing assistants are on duty around the clock, providing postoperative and rehabilitative care and other support services.

Valle Verde also provides enhanced care for residents with Alzheimer's and other mild dementia in private apartments with specially trained staff available 24 hours a day.

Valle Verde welcomes pets.

Villa Santa Barbara
227 East Anapamu Street, Santa Barbara
(805) 963-4428

Villa Santa Barbara is located just a few blocks from the heart of downtown Santa Barbara's arts and culture district. Residents can walk to the Arlington Theatre, cafes, restaurants, the central library, bookstores, movie theaters, shopping, churches, and the Museum of Art.

Villa Santa Barbara's spacious apartments are available for rent on a monthly basis, with no initial investment other than a nonrefundable service fee. The monthly fee covers 24-hour staffing, tableside dining service (three meals a day, plus a 24-hour snack and beverage bar), housekeeping and linen services, transportation, and a full recreation program. Activities such as t'ai chi and craft classes, international dinners, and beach walks are available on-site or within walking distance.

Choose from studio alcove or one-bedroom apartments, some with a kitchenette and a terrace overlooking the garden. On-site facilities include a hair salon for both men and women, a library, a TV room, billiards, a theater/music room, and a roof-garden terrace. Villa Santa Barbara is located near doctors' offices, Cottage Hospital, and Sansum Medical Clinic; the staff provides transportation to appointments. It also provides Alzheimer's care.

Vista del Monte

3775 Modoc Road, Santa Barbara
(805) 687-0793, (800) 736-1333
www.frontporch.net

Vista del Monte is owned and operated by Front Porch, a not-for-profit organization that grew from a California teacher's service program established in 1928. Opened in 1964, this serene complex features beautiful landscaping, expansive lawns, and stately pines, and the entire complex has been vigorously refurbished to keep the buildings looking fresh and new. It's open to anyone 62 and older. The complex is located next to affluent Hope Ranch, near the Santa Barbara community golf course, hiking trails, and popular Arroyo Burro (Hendry's Beach).

Vista del Monte offers spacious independent-living and assisted-living apartments, a skilled-nursing facility, and specialized care for Alzheimer's patients. Residents also have access to a fitness and aquatic center with an excellent therapy pool, an adult education program, and an active residents' association. If you need limited assistance with daily activities, you can arrange for a home attendant to come to your residence. In assisted-living apartments, staff is available to help around the clock.

Montecito

Casa Dorinda
300 Hot Springs Road, Montecito
(805) 969-8011
www.casadorinda.com

This lush retirement community on 48 beautifully landscaped acres is the ultimate place to spend your golden years. It originally operated as a for-profit institution, but since 1988 it's been owned and operated by the Montecito Retirement Association, a community-sponsored, not-for-profit corporation serving seniors through estate retirement living.

Casa Dorinda was originally designed by Carleton Winslow for Anna Dorinda Bliss and her husband, William, wealthy New Yorkers who relocated to Montecito in the early 1900s. The grand mansion had more than 80 rooms surrounding a central patio and was once a focal point of Montecito social life. It opened as a retirement community in 1975. Today, more than 300 residents enjoy one of four levels of retirement care, from independent living to hospital care.

Casa Dorinda offers an on-site swimming pool and Jacuzzi, croquet, lawn bowling, a fitness center, transportation services, food service, maintenance, housing care, health care, and walking trails through 24 acres of sycamore and oak groves. A full-time activity director plans trips to the theater, symphony, and other cultural events, including excursions to the Los Angeles area. Beaches, bikeways, and mountain trails are all nearby.

The wide selection of apartments ranges from studios to two-bedrooms, all professionally updated and prepared for each resident. You can use the reception rooms for your own parties and to entertain guests. Other facilities include a nursing center, a separate clinic for everyday matters, a Personal Care Unit, and a state-of-the-art medical center. You must be at least 62 years old at time of entry and meet the entry requirements.

Senior Apartments

These comfortable apartments appeal to active seniors who want to maintain total independence in a community with their peers.

Rancho Franciscan Apartments
221 Hitchcock Way, #107, Santa Barbara
(805) 563-0343
www.towbes.com/residential/franciscan

Rancho Franciscan apartments are open to seniors only (minimum age 62). Built in 1988, the Spanish-Mediterranean–style complex is located in the upper State Street area. It's right next door to the Santa Barbara YMCA, which offers Rancho Franciscan residents discounted senior memberships, and it's a few short blocks to grocery stores, La Cumbre Plaza Mall, movie theaters, and restaurants. The MTD bus stops in front.

Rancho Franciscan's 111 units are divided among four stucco buildings with red-tile roofs.

You can choose from one- and two-bedroom apartments in two- and three-story buildings (three of the buildings have elevators). Each apartment has a private veranda and modern kitchen facilities.

Shared amenities include a Jacuzzi, a recreation center, and outdoor barbecue grills. A full-time social director organizes activities such as movie screenings, visits to local art galleries, and picnics.

Shepard Place Apartments
1069 Casitas Pass Road, Carpinteria
(805) 684-5589
www.towbes.com/residential/shepardplace
This senior apartment complex is owned by the same people who own Rancho Francis-can. It features 169 garden-style apartments (one- and two-bedroom), a swimming pool, a spa, and activities. Shepard Place is within walking distance of downtown Carpinteria and the beach. Residents sign a 12-month lease, then rent on a month-to-month basis after the lease expires. Monthly fees range from $1,065 to $1,130 for one-bedroom apartments and $1,360 to $1,405 for two-bedroom units.

DOOR-TO-DOOR TRANSPORTATION

Easy Lift Transportation
53 Cass Place, Suite D, Goleta
(805) 681-1181
www.easylift.org
Easy Lift is a nonprofit organization providing curb-to-curb, wheelchair-accessible van trans-portation service for frail elderly and handi-capped people who cannot ride the bus. Service is available Monday through Friday from 5:25 a.m. to midnight, Saturday from 6:00 a.m. to 11:20 p.m., and Sunday from 6:20 a.m. to 10:00 p.m. The cost is $2 per one-way trip (exact change is required).

HEALTH CARE AND WELLNESS Ⓗ

Illness and injury are never on anyone's agenda, but if the unexpected happens while you're in Santa Barbara, it's reassuring to know you have quick access to first-rate health care. The city offers the best concentration of health care facilities on the California coast between Los Angeles and the San Francisco Bay area. Every day, people from all parts of the state—and other areas of the country and the world, for that matter—come to Santa Barbara seeking quality health care services. Many of our hospitals and clinics date back a century or more, and our physicians and other health care practitioners rank among the best in the nation.

About the only medical services you won't have access to here are treatment for serious burns and organ transplants, and even those types of care can be found at highly rated institutions just an hour or two south of the county line.

Our community emphasizes preventive health care and offers many classes and services designed to promote good health. A "Health Calendar" with an extensive listing of nearly all wellness programs, support groups, and services appears every Tuesday in the *Santa Barbara News-Press*.

Most hospitals and clinics accept major insurance plans. However, health maintenance organizations (HMOs) are growing rapidly in the area, and along with the growth have come many changes, especially regarding physician choice. It's best to call and check beforehand with the individual hospital, clinic, or physician and your insurer to discuss coverage.

We begin this chapter with an overview of our main hospitals and affiliates, followed by descriptions of major clinics and alternative health care resources. We've also included handy lists of walk-in clinics, emergency numbers, and support services.

HOSPITALS

Cottage Health System

The nonprofit Cottage Health System (www.cottagehealthsystem.org) consists of Santa Barbara Cottage Hospital, Goleta Valley Cottage Hospital (both described below), and Santa Ynez Valley Cottage Hospital. Together they are the largest health care provider on the California coast between Los Angeles and the San Francisco Bay area.

Until the mid-1990s, the system's hospitals were all separate institutions. Santa Barbara Cottage Hospital merged with the smaller, community-based facilities so they could share services, save money, and expand their lists of health insurance providers. So far the merger has proved very successful, and you can count on excellent care at all affiliated centers.

In 2003, Cottage purchased the beloved but fiscally beleaguered St. Francis Medical Center. There are plans to turn it into residential housing for doctors. Cottage Health System is undergoing renovation on its main facility on Santa Barbara's Westside and is looking at the possibility of joining forces with the Rehabilitation Institute located in Santa Barbara.

The Cottage System presents a year-round wellness program (as do many of the facilities described below). The program's many offerings include Stop Smoking courses, depression screenings, flu shots, community CPR classes, mobile mammography, and tot safety classes.

Santa Barbara Cottage Hospital
Pueblo at Bath Street, Santa Barbara
(805) 682-7111, (805) 569-7210 emergency department
www.cottagehealthsystem.org
Cottage Hospital is Santa Barbara's oldest and

largest hospital. In the 1880s a group of civic-minded women came up with a radical concept for the times: a group of small cottages, each housing a separate medical department. Together they would provide medical care in a cozy, homelike atmosphere that would help patients recover faster. They decided to call it Santa Barbara Cottage Hospital. Although the cottage-style construction never happened (a single building was constructed instead), the name stuck.

Since 1888, Cottage has grown from a 25-bed facility to a nearly 500-bed, nonprofit acute-care medical center and teaching hospital that admits over 20,000 patients a year. Cottage has been nationally recognized for superior service, and it has one of the only graduate medical education programs between the San Francisco Bay area and Los Angeles, with sought-after residencies in internal medicine, general surgery, and radiology.

Cottage Hospital's services run the gamut. The hospital has a Level II Trauma Center and provides 24-hour in-hospital coverage for illness and accidents as well as complete outpatient services for psychiatric and chemical-dependency services. About 500 specialists in all major clinical areas make up the hospital's medical staff. Cottage is particularly renowned for its cardiac care (including open-heart surgery), as well as its pediatric and maternal/child services.

Cottage Children's Hospital includes a Childbirth Center (where some 2,500 babies are delivered each year) with a comprehensive maternal/child health program, neonatal and pediatric intensive-care units, a perinatal center for high-risk pregnancies, a perinatal/pediatric ambulance, pediatric surgery, a pediatrics unit, and pediatric gastrointestinal and pediatric hematology/oncology departments. Outpatient services include cardiac care (a chest pain center, cardiac electrophysiology, heart catheterization labs, and cardiac rehabilitation), an eye center, an outpatient surgery center, and diagnostic ultrasound, CT body scanning, and magnetic resonance imaging. The laboratory, radiology, and physical therapy services offer convenient extended hours. Over the next several years, the majority of the hospital's buildings will be upgraded to meet strict new seismic standards, and existing facilities will be improved in the process.

Goleta Valley Cottage Hospital
351 South Patterson Avenue, Goleta
(805) 967-3411
www.cottagehealthsystem.org
Many residents love this small, neighborhood hospital for the friendly, personalized care it has offered since 1966. Formerly called Goleta Valley Community Hospital, the 122-bed institution joined forces with Santa Barbara Cottage Hospital in 1996 but maintains its intimate, community-based character and services. About 1,500 patients check into the hospital every year.

Goleta Valley Cottage Hospital offers a full range of services, including a 24-hour emergency department and heliport, a Level IV trauma center, a comprehensive critical care unit, a subacute unit, specialized medical/surgical services for both inpatients and outpatients, a breast care center with specialized diagnostic and treatment programs, and an occupational health center. The comfortable, homey Birth Center at Goleta Valley attracts many women with low-risk pregnancies (about 300 babies are born here every year). In fact, Goleta Valley is one of only a handful of hospitals in the United States to receive a Baby-Friendly designation from the U.S. Committee for UNICEF. That's largely because the maternity nurses offer an optimal level of lactation care. They help new moms breastfeed their babies right from the start, and they even visit moms and babies at home to ensure continued breastfeeding success.

Other Area Hospitals
The Rehabilitation Institute at Santa Barbara
2415 De la Vina Street, Santa Barbara
(805) 687-7444, ext. 2317
www.risb.org
This beloved, nonprofit community institution

has cared for thousands of patients with major disabilities as well as their families. The institute's goal is to return patients to maximum independence. Established in 1967, it provides specialized inpatient, outpatient, and community-based programs for people with brain injury, spinal cord injury, stroke, neurological and orthopedic problems, and other disabling conditions resulting from injury or illness.

The institute's brain injury, spinal cord injury, and comprehensive rehabilitation programs are accredited by the Commission on Accreditation of Rehabilitation Facilities, the Joint Commission on Accreditation of Healthcare Organizations, and California Children's Services.

The institute is the only freestanding rehabilitation facility between Los Angeles and San Francisco. Therapy schedules are individually tailored to the particular medical condition. Each patient has a treatment team composed of physicians, a rehabilitation nurse, an occupational therapist, a psychologist/neuropsychologist, a case manager, a physical therapist, a recreation therapist, and a speech/language pathologist as appropriate. Families are also involved in education and treatment.

As a "hospital without walls," the institute provides a continuum of treatment, delivering various levels of care in many settings. The continuum begins with acute rehabilitation at the institute's 38-bed main hospital, coordinated by board-certified physicians who specialize in physical medicine and rehabilitation and internal medicine.

Outpatient services are also provided at the Keck Center (805-569-8900) at the main institute site. An affiliate of the institute, The Coast Caregiver Resource Center, at 1528 Chapala Street, Suite 302, Santa Barbara (805-967-0220; www.coastcrc.org), assists caregivers of adults with brain impairment.

Institute programs also extend to rehabilitation services in retirement communities and skilled-nursing facilities.

CLINICS

Cancer Center of Santa Barbara
300 West Pueblo Street, Santa Barbara
(805) 682-7300
www.ccsb.org

This nonprofit cancer treatment center, founded in 1949, offers radiation therapy, chemotherapy, and nuclear medicine for cancer patients. It also provides extensive support services for cancer patients and their families and friends. All support services are free and include counseling, home visits, a patient library, relaxation and stress management, support groups, and visitors programs.

Sansum–Santa Barbara Medical Foundation Clinic
Corporate Office: 470 South Patterson Avenue Santa Barbara
(805) 681-7500
www.sansum.com

In October 1998, Santa Barbara witnessed the merger of two of the oldest medical groups in the region: Sansum Medical Clinic and Santa Barbara Medical Clinic. The parent organization is now called Sansum–Santa Barbara Medical Foundation Clinic and serves in an administrative capacity for the newly formed medical group of more than 140 physicians.

Sansum Medical Clinic was established in 1924 by William David Sansum, M.D., who is widely credited as the first American to successfully isolate, produce, and administer insulin to treat diabetes. For decades, Sansum Medical Clinic has enjoyed a local, regional, national, and international reputation as a leading health care provider for medical evaluation, diagnosis, and treatment.

Santa Barbara Medical Clinic was founded in 1921 by three physicians. They succeeded in forming a carefully designed group practice to

> **i** Preferential hotel and transportation rates in Santa Barbara are available to Sansum-Santa Barbara Medical Clinic patients and guests. Visit www.sansum.com for a list of participating providers

make comprehensive specialty care available to all segments of Santa Barbara at a time when solo practitioners provided most of the care. In 1973 the physician-owners entrusted the clinic's assets, buildings, administrative operations, and contractual agreements to the non- profit Santa Barbara Medical Foundation Clinic. The physician group kept the name Santa Barbara Clinic, Inc., and was retained by the foundation as a multispecialty physician group to administer health services.

In a nutshell, the merger of these two groups means that you are likely to find excellent health care that matches your needs, no matter what ails you or what type of health plan you have.

Sansum–Santa Barbara Medical Foundation Clinic operates the following facilities in Santa Barbara's South Coast region:

Sansum Multi-Specialty Clinics

51 Hitchcock Way, Santa Barbara
(805) 563-6100, main number
(805) 563-1994, pediatrics, community medicine
(805) 563-6100, urgent care
(805) 563-6190, Center for Wellness

215 Pesetas Lane, Santa Barbara
(805) 681-7500

317 West Pueblo Street, Santa Barbara
(805) 682-2621, (805) 898-3479, (800) 472-6786

Sansum Specialty Clinics

Family Medicine
1919 State Street, Santa Barbara
(805) 563-6120

Obstetrics/Gynecology
515 West Pueblo Street, Santa Barbara
(805) 681-8911

Ophthalmology/Optometry
29 West Anapamu Street, Santa Barbara
(805) 681-8950, main number
(805) 681-8969, Laser Eye Care Center

i Sansum Diabetes Research Institute, under the leadership of Dr. Lois Jovanovic, has received international acclaim for its medical progress on healthy babies being born to women with diabetes, type 2 diabetes in children, and methods for the detection and progress of diabetes.

Physical Therapy
27 East Canon Perdido Street, Santa Barbara
(805) 681-1711

Physical Therapy
41 Hitchcock Way, Santa Barbara
(805) 681-7781

Pulmonary/Critical Care Medicine
301 West Pueblo Street, Santa Barbara
(805) 898-3291

Psychiatry/Psychology
1525 State Street, Suite 103, Santa Barbara
(805) 681-7517

Goleta Specialty Clinics

Family Medicine
122 South Patterson Avenue, Goleta
(805) 681-7500

Occupational Medicine
101 South Patterson Avenue, Goleta
(805) 898-3311

Physical Therapy
334 South Patterson Avenue, Goleta
(805) 681-1860

Carpinteria

Family Medicine, Internal, Pediatrics, Urgent Care
4806 Carpinteria Avenue, Carpinteria
(805) 566-5080

i Sansum–Santa Barbara Medical Foundation Clinic offers free flu shots in October and November. A $5 donation is requested. For more details, call the Influenza Hotline at (805) 681-7500.

Planned Parenthood of Santa Barbara
518 Garden Street, Santa Barbara
(805) 963-5801
www.ppsbvslo.org
The local Planned Parenthood center offers complete and confidential family-planning services at affordable rates. Services include pregnancy testing, counseling, birth control, testing and treatment for sexually transmitted infections and HIV, gynecological services, and education programs.

WALK-IN CLINICS

Urgent care centers are located throughout Santa Barbara County. These smaller medical facilities provide services for a range of health and wellness needs. They are usually open every day and often have extended hours, typically 8:00 a.m. to 8:00 p.m. weekdays and shorter hours on weekends.

In most cases, you can just walk in—no appointment necessary. If you need quick treatment for minor accidents and emergencies or general family medical care, these are convenient facilities.

Sansum–Santa Barbara Medical Foundation Clinic Urgent Care Centers
51 Hitchcock Way, Santa Barbara
(805) 563-6100
4806 Carpinteria Avenue, Carpinteria
(805) 566-5000

MedCenter
2954 State Street, Santa Barbara
(805) 682-7411

MedCenter
319 North Milpas Street, Santa Barbara
(805) 965-3011

MedCenter
271 North Fairview Avenue, #101, Goleta
(805) 681-7411

ALTERNATIVE MEDICINE

Many Santa Barbarans regularly turn to alternative medical treatments, and they don't have to go far to find them. You can find skilled practitioners in nearly every area of alternative health care, including naturopathy, homeopathy, clinical nutrition, acupuncture, and herbology. There are also numerous therapists with years of experience in massage, rolfing, shiatsu, and all types of bodywork therapy.

The weekly *Santa Barbara Independent* is a great resource for alternative medical services. You can also consult the Yellow Pages for listings.

PHYSICIAN REFERRAL SERVICES

Call any of these numbers to find out which physicians or dentists meet your particular medical and insurance needs.

Dental Society of Santa Barbara-Ventura County, (805) 656-3166
www.sbrcds.org

Santa Barbara County Medical Society Physician Referral, (805) 683-5333

NUMBERS TO CALL

Refer to this list if you are experiencing an emergency situation or need information and assistance regarding community resources. Crisis lines are answered 24 hours a day.

Emergencies, 911

Fire Stations
Santa Barbara, (805) 965-5254
Gaviota, Goleta, and Isla Vista, (805) 681-5500

Carpinteria, (805) 684-4591
Montecito, (805) 969-7762
Summerland, (805) 684-4591

Police or Sheriff Departments
Santa Barbara, (805) 897-2300
Gaviota and Goleta, (805) 681-4100
Montecito, Summerland, and
Carpinteria, (805) 681-4100

American Cancer Society, (805) 963-1576

California HIV, AIDS, and Sexually Transmitted Disease Hot Line, (800) 367-AIDS

California Poison Control, (800) 222-1222

Cottage Hospital 24-Hour Psychiatric/Substance Abuse Hotline, 211

Crisis/Suicide Intervention 24-Hour Helpline, 211

Coalition to End Family Violence 24-Hour Hotline, 211

Hospice of Santa Barbara, (805) 563-8820

Pollen and Mold Spore Hot Line, (805) 961-3951

Santa Barbara Rape Crisis Center 24-Hour Hotline, (805) 564-3696

Santa Barbara Council on Alcoholism and Drug Abuse, (805) 963-1433

Child Abuse Reporting Hot Line, (800) 367-0166

24-Hour Anger Management Hotline, (805) 656-4861

EDUCATION AND CHILD CARE

Given the intellectual atmosphere of the town, it should come as no surprise that Santa Barbarans have always placed great emphasis on high-quality education. For a relatively small community, Santa Barbara offers incredible educational breadth and diversity. If you're moving here, you'll have access to excellent schools, educational facilities, and programs for all ages, from preschool through retirement years.

At the preschool, elementary, and high school levels, parents have many choices for their children within the public and private sectors. At the higher education level, Santa Barbara is home to a University of California campus; Brooks Institute, one of the world's top photographic schools; Westmont College, a highly rated Christian college; and the prestigious Music Academy of the West. Santa Barbara also has one of the nation's leading community colleges as well as a number of continuing education and professional schools.

This chapter provides an overview of the many educational options available in Santa Barbara. We begin with elementary and high school education (public and private), then describe our higher education institutions, including schools that specialize in photography, music, law, and other fields. Finally, we give you a brief overview of resources for finding appropriate child care and preschools for infants, toddlers, and pre-kindergartners.

PUBLIC ELEMENTARY AND HIGH SCHOOLS

About 25,000 students are currently enrolled in public schools in South Santa Barbara County, the area of focus in this book. Despite the funding cuts that have affected virtually every public school in California over the last 20 years, Santa Barbara's public schools have managed not only to stay afloat but also, in many cases, to thrive. At schools where "extra" programs have been eliminated, parents and local school districts have rallied to find innovative ways to raise funds to support them. Hardly a week goes by without a car wash, a jog-a-thon, an auction, or some other form of fund-raising event for local schools.

Many of our schools have earned California Distinguished School status over the years—a designation awarded to only 4 percent of all public schools in the state of California. It's a sure sign of excellent and innovative programs. A high proportion of our schools have also earned the prestigious National Blue Ribbon Award in the last five years (see the individual school districts below). Only about 200 schools in the United States achieve this prestigious designation following a rigorous application and screening process.

Most schools and/or districts in the area also offer GATE (Gifted and Talented Education), and all schools have special education programs. Santa Barbara also has four charter schools—public schools that operate free of many state statutes and regulations—and an Open Alternative School with an alternative curriculum and structure.

Legislation passed in July 1996 provides California public schools with incentive funding to reduce class size in the primary grades to improve instruction and student performance. The law made funds available to elementary schools so that they can reduce class size to 20 students or fewer in first and second grades and then in either kindergarten or third grade, at the school's discretion. Most elementary schools in the county, seizing the opportunity to create smaller classes, quickly arranged for extra classrooms and teachers. At nearly all schools, you can count on classes of 20 or fewer in kindergarten through third grade. Class sizes for grades four to six are typically 26 to 28 students.

If you're researching public schools in the area, be sure to call individual schools and request their School Accountability Report Card. School boards issue the Report Card annually across the state. It provides information about each school's resources, operations, successes, and areas of growth and improvement. Contents include a school profile, student achievement statistics, class sizes, budgets, expenditures, and other useful information. Most of the school districts in Santa Barbara County also post their report cards on the Web. Go to www.sbceo.org/schools and click on the "School Accountability Report Card" link.

Current Issues in the Public School System

The biggest issue Santa Barbara public schools face today is declining enrollment—especially in our elementary schools. Combine this with statewide budget cuts, and our schools are grappling with serious fiscal challenges. Both Santa Barbara and Goleta elementary schools are experiencing a decline in student enrollment that began almost a decade ago, and the districts expect this trend to continue. Recently, the Carpinteria Unified District also reported declines in student populations to the point where they may close one of the elementary schools.

It's not the quality of education that's affecting enrollment. So why are students leaving? Apart from lower birth rates, many blame the high cost of living on the South Coast. With the median home price hovering around $1 million, lower income families are forced to settle in more affordable satellite suburbs. At the same time, those who can afford to live here often choose to enroll their children in private schools or the more affluent public school dis-

i Researching Santa Barbara schools? Check out the Santa Barbara County Education Web site at www.sbceo.org. You'll find links to public and private schools, as well as API reports, School Accountability Report Cards, STAR test results, and other resources for parents, teachers, and students.

tricts. Goleta Union receives funds from the surrounding property tax base, but both the Santa Barbara and Carpinteria Union districts operate on a per-student funding allocation. When enrollment declines, these districts have less money to meet fixed expenses, and deficits can and do result.

Faced with tough budgetary decisions, Santa Barbara school boards have so far managed to find creative ways to cut costs without sacrificing the quality of education. Parents rally to raise funds, and local businesses donate generous amounts of money and materials to schools in need. Of course, everyone has the best interests of the students at heart, and as long as this continues to drive future budgetary decisions, Santa Barbara public schools should continue to enjoy their excellent academic track record.

Public School District Overview

In this section we focus on the major school districts on the South Coast: Santa Barbara and Hope in Santa Barbara; Carpinteria; Cold Spring and Montecito Union in Montecito; and Goleta Union.

Santa Barbara

The Santa Barbara Elementary School/High School districts are separate districts governed by a single Board of Education. Under the California Education Code, the board operates independently from city or county governments. It has adopted an open-enrollment policy, meaning parents may enroll students at the school of their choice as long as space permits.

Santa Barbara Elementary School District
720 Santa Barbara Street, Santa Barbara
(805) 963-4338
www.sbsdk12.org

The Santa Barbara Elementary School District covers about 22 square miles in the City of Santa Barbara—and provides instruction for children in kindergarten through sixth grade. It serves more than 5,900 students in 13 schools, including three charter schools (public schools that operate free of many state statutes and regulations) and an Open Alternative School (kindergarten through eighth grade), which has an open structure and curriculum. Some of the schools in this district have earned California Distinguished School status, an award which honors only the most exemplary of schools. In the past few years, Adams, Monroe, Roosevelt, and Washington Elementary and Peabody Charter School have received this prestigious award. In 2002 Adams was also the first school in Santa Barbara County to be recognized as a Title Achieving School for its success in meeting the needs of a diverse student population.

Seventy percent of the district's student enrollment is Hispanic, 25 percent is White, and the remaining enrollment comes from a variety of ethnicities.

In 1999 the district opened Santa Barbara Community Academy, a year-round elementary school requiring uniforms, which now enrolls about 300 students in kindergarten through sixth grade. The academy emphasizes a challenging academic curriculum, including foreign-language instruction starting in the early grades. If the number of applicants exceeds available space, students are selected via a lottery system.

In the fall of 2000, the Cesar Estrada Chavez Dual Language Immersion Charter School opened its doors. The school uses a 50-50 balance of both English and Spanish to teach a curriculum that meets state standards in all subjects. Most schools in the district offer a number of special programs, including GATE, Mentor Teacher programs, and After-school Enrichment Classes. On average, the district's student-to-teacher ratio is 20 to 1 in kindergarten through grade three, and 27 to 1 in grades four through six. Since about 45 percent of students do not speak, read, or write English proficiently, the district provides specialized programs such as English as a Second Language to help these students improve their English language skills.

Santa Barbara High School District
720 Santa Barbara Street, Santa Barbara
(805) 963-4331
www.sbsdk12.org

The Santa Barbara High School District serves approximately 10,600 students in grades 7 through 12. This district covers a much wider region than the elementary district—about 136 square miles—and draws students from all neighborhoods stretching from Goleta to Montecito. The district schools include five junior or middle schools (La Cumbre, La Colina, Santa Barbara, Santa Barbara Charter, and Goleta Valley), three high schools (Dos Pueblos, San Marcos, and Santa Barbara), and one continuation high school. About 18 percent are English Language Learners. Forty percent of the student enrollment is Hispanic, 47 percent is White, and the remaining enrollment comes from a variety of ethnicities.

Each school offers a comprehensive curriculum that meets all state and district standards. GATE, Advanced Placement, and ESL classes are available, and many of the schools have earned distinguished awards. In the past few years, La Colina Junior High, Goleta Valley Junior High, Santa Barbara Junior High, and San Marcos High School attained California Distinguished School status. Dos Pueblos High and Goleta Valley Junior High also received the illustrious National Blue Ribbon Award.

Consistently a standout in this impressive lineup of schools is Dos Pueblos High. For the past several years, students from the school earned the highest average SAT scores in the county: 119 points higher than the state average and 113 points higher than the national average. The Academic Performance Index places Dos Pueblos in the top 10 percent of all high schools in the state. Average scores at the other local high schools are slightly lower but also well above the national average.

Over the last few years, the district has launched some innovative on-campus academies or "school-within-a-school" programs. These academies are designed to prepare students for various careers. Santa Barbara High School has two on-campus academies for the visual arts and multimedia arts. In the fall of 2001, San Marcos High School introduced a Health Careers Academy, and Dos Pueblos High School launched an Engineering Academy in 2002 and the prestigious International Baccalaureate academic program in 2003. This pre-university course provides students ages 16 through 19 with a liberal arts curriculum to help them gain admission to top colleges and universities. Students wishing to enroll in these programs must submit an application for review.

All schools in this district offer a full range of athletic and extracurricular activities and are fully wired for the computer and Internet age. The student-teacher ratio is about 30 to 1 in grades seven and eight and 32 to 1 in grades nine through 12. In grade 9, the student-to-teacher ratio for reading and mathematics is 20 to 1, in high school Advanced Placement, academies, and reading for Success classes have a student-to-teacher ratio of 25 to 1.

Hope School District
3970 La Colina Road, Santa Barbara
(805) 682-2564
www.sbceo.k12.ca.us/~hopesd/
With approximately 1,350 students enrolled in kindergarten through grade six, this small district consists of three excellent elementary schools in the Hope Ranch/San Roque/La Cumbre area: Monte Vista, Hope, and Vieja Valley. Hope Elementary School reopened in September 1997 after being closed for more than 20 years. Monte Vista and Vieja Valley have both been named California Distinguished Schools in the last decade, and

Monte Vista was recognized as a National Blue Ribbon School in 1997. To receive this award, a school must demonstrate a strong commitment to educational excellence for all students. At these schools, median test scores in reading, math, and language in grades two through six regularly rank in the high 70th to 80th percentiles nationally.

The Hope District provides a number of special programs, including GATE, Esperanza, and assistance for students with learning differences. Each school has computer labs with networked computers, and every classroom has a Macintosh computer with CD-ROM capabilities. The average number of students per teacher is 20 for kindergarten through grade three and 27 for grades four through six.

Goleta

Goleta Union School District
401 North Fairview Avenue, Goleta
(805) 681-1200
www.goleta.k12.ca.us
The Goleta Union School District has nine schools with more than 3,500 students enrolled in kindergarten through grade six. Class size is under 20 in grades K to 3 and 24 in grades 5 to 6. Approximately 35 percent of students are English Language Learners. Unlike other districts in the county, and most in the state, Goleta Union schools receive funds directly from the surrounding property tax base rather than on a per-student basis, so declining enrollment doesn't negatively impact school budgets. The district has nationally recognized programs in bilingual education, composition, computer literacy, and mathematics. All the district's schools offer technology programs as well as music, art, and physical education. GATE is offered in grades four, five, and six, and special education programs are available throughout the district. All schools have a computer center, and all classrooms are wired for high-speed communications.

Goleta Union parents and community members are very supportive and active participants in the schools, and the students' academic performance reflects this involvement. The district ranks consistently above the national average and state average in academic tests. In 2001 Mountain View was designated a Blue Ribbon School, the highest national honor bestowed upon a public or private school, and in El Camino School and Kellogg School attained California Distinguished School status. El Camino also has a state preschool program known as the Children's Center for income eligible 4-year-olds. All the schools in this district have undergone extensive refurbishments in recent years. The Goleta community passed a $26 million school construction bond measure in November 1996, and the money was used to repair and upgrade school infrastructures, build new classrooms and libraries, and replace the oldest school (Isla Vista) with a new facility for 700 students.

Montecito

Cold Spring School District
2243 Sycamore Canyon Road, Montecito
(805) 969-2678
www.coldspringschool.net

Tucked in the lush foothills of Montecito, Cold Spring School is a one-school district serving approximately 200 students in kindergarten through sixth grade. Student academic performance at this excellent school consistently ranks in the top 5 percent to 10 percent of all elementary schools in California. Cold Springs School earned the California Distinquished School title in 1986 and was deemed a coveted Blue Ribbon School in 1997. In addition to its core teaching staff, the school employs a technology specialist; resource specialists for reading, special education, and language; and professional musicians and artists who provide instruction in visual arts, ceramic sculpture, drama, and music. The school has a tech lab with 28 computers, and if they wish, students can participate in an after-school enrichment program. The school has also established a working relationship with nearby Westmont College, whose students serve as teacher's aides for extracurricular activities. Average number of students per teacher is 20 or fewer for kindergarten through grade three and 25 in grades four through six.

Montecito Union School District
385 San Ysidro Road, Montecito
(805) 969-3249
www.sbceo.k12.ca.us/~montecit/

Set on a beautiful eight-acre site in an exclusive neighborhood, Montecito Union is a highly regarded one-school district with grades kindergarten through six. Approximately 420 students are currently enrolled in the district, which has an outstanding academic record. Montecito Union remains as one of the top 100 high-performing schools in California. In 1998 the school was awarded California Distinguished School status. It was one of only two schools in California to receive a perfect score on all 11 areas of evaluation. Montecito Union offers a GATE program and hires specialists to teach computer sciences, music, art, Spanish, physical education, and library. In 2000 the district upgraded the campus, adding seven new classrooms and replacing six portable ones. Parents can expect an average of fewer than 20 students per teacher in kindergarten through grade three, and 22 students per teacher in grades four through six.

Carpinteria

Carpinteria Unified School District
1400 Linden Avenue, Carpinteria
(805) 684-4511
www.cusd.net/home

Carpinteria Unified serves the communities of Carpinteria and Summerland from the Rincon to Ortega Ridge Road and the Pacific Ocean to the Los Padres National Forest. The district's nine schools include five elementary schools, one middle school, one high school and two alternative schools. About 3,000 students are enrolled in grades kindergarten through 12, and more than a third are classified as English Language Learners. In 2001 Carpinteria Middle School received the prestigious California Distinguished School award for the 2000–2001 school year, and Main Elementary and tiny 60-student Summerland Elementary received the award in 2002. Carpinteria High School has six academies— Academy of the Media Arts, Culinary Arts Institute, Agriculture Science Technology Academy, Construction Technology, AVID, and Virtual Enterprise.

The district places a strong emphasis on integrating the tools of technology into its academic programs. Special education programs include GATE and assistance for those challenged in areas of learning, communication, and physical abilities. In addition, all English Language Learners receive primary language support through their core academic classes. Average number of students per teacher for the district is 20 for kindergarten through grade three, 30 for grades four through five, and 28 for grades six through 12.

PRIVATE SCHOOLS

Santa Barbara's private schools range from small, affordable, nonsecular schools to very expensive high schools that prepare students for entry into the best universities in the country. If you're looking into private schools, you'll have no trouble finding one that suits your children's academic interests and personalities. It might be difficult, however, to find one that pleases your pocketbook.

Typical annual tuition at private elementary schools can reach as high as $18,000 a year. Parochial schools are sponsored by parishes and usually cost considerably less. Many private schools offer some form of financial aid for qualified students—be sure to ask for information if your funds are limited.

Before you begin your search, be forewarned that application to one of Santa Barbara's private schools does not guarantee admission. The most sought-after schools typically have only one or two classes per grade and are flooded with applicants. Some schools can have as many as 100 applications

for a single, 20-student kindergarten class, which is often already filled with siblings of older students.

We recommend you apply to several schools to widen your options. At most independent schools, a child must be at least 5 and sometimes 5.5 years by September 1 in the year he or she enters kindergarten.

Santa Barbara also has a number of parish-supported elementary schools (Catholic, Episcopalian, and other denominations). Tuition at these schools is generally more affordable than at other independent schools. Keep in mind, however, that admission preference is given to registered active members of the parish. If you're interested in enrolling your children in a particular parochial school, we suggest you contact the parish directly.

Following is a roundup of many of the finest private schools in the area. All are coeducational. You can also check the Yellow Pages under "Schools" for a comprehensive list of local educational institutions.

Santa Barbara

The Anacapa School
814 Santa Barbara Street, Santa Barbara
(805) 965-0228
www.anacapaschool.org
The Anacapa School is a college-prep day school for grades 7 through 12. Founded in 1981, the school is very small, so students receive a great deal of personal attention. The student-to-teacher ratio is 6 to 1, and class sizes average 12 students.

The curriculum emphasizes critical thinking, writing skills, creativity, and personal integrity and offers a wide range of classes from core academics to electives such as animation and organic gardening. Students go on regular field trips, day excursions, and two camping trips a year. Almost 100 percent of Anacapa graduates continue on to college, and many have gained admission to some of the nation's top tertiary institutions.

The school is located right in downtown Santa Barbara, so visits to the main library, the Museum of Art, the Courthouse, and other downtown facilities are incorporated into the school's activities schedule.

Bishop Garcia Diego High School
4000 La Colina Road, Santa Barbara
(805) 967-1266
www.bishopdiego.org
Bishop Garcia Diego is a Catholic high school (grades 9 through 12) with an enrollment of approximately 300 students. It was founded in 1940 as Santa Barbara Catholic High and was later renamed to honor California's first bishop, Francisco Garcia Diego y Moreno. It operates in the Catholic tradition, teaching moral virtues and stressing a philosophy of scholarship and Christian service. The academic program offers a traditional, challenging, and comprehensive college preparatory curriculum. Advanced Placement classes are available to qualified students in English, American history, calculus, and Spanish. In recent years, 100 percent of Bishop graduates were accepted at colleges and universities throughout the country. The school also offers a state-of-the-art technology program as well as courses in the creative arts. Average class size is 16 students, and the student-to-teacher ratio is 11 to 1.

Bishop Garcia Diego is Santa Barbara's only Christian high school and admits students of all races, religions, and ethnic origins.

Laguna Blanca School
4125 Paloma Drive, Santa Barbara
(805) 687-2461
www.lagunablanca.org
Founded in 1933, Laguna Blanca School is a top-notch college-preparatory day school for students in kindergarten through grade 12. In 2000 the kindergarten through grade four classes moved to the former Howard School campus at 260 San Ysidro Road in Montecito. Grades five through 12 remain on the school's 29-acre campus in the heart of the affluent Hope Ranch neighborhood. Since the move, most of the extra space on the Hope Ranch

grounds has been converted to a middle school campus and additional facilities such as a state-of-the-art computer lab, an additional classroom, a student store, offices, and a new art room. The school offers advanced placement courses, an outstanding visual and performing arts program, a community-service component, interscholastic athletic competitions, student exchange opportunities, and a host of extracurricular activities. Not surprisingly, admission to Laguna is highly competitive. The school has a total capacity of about 425 students (325 in Hope Ranch and 100 in Montecito) with a maximum class size of just 13 students. Each year 100 percent of Laguna graduates are accepted to college.

Marymount of Santa Barbara
2130 Mission Ridge Road, Santa Barbara
(805) 569-1811
www.marymountsb.org
A member of the National and California Association of Independent Schools, Marymount is set on 10 acres of wooded grounds that once belonged to an old Riviera estate. The school enrolls about 243 students and welcomes qualified applicants of good character from all religious traditions, races, and ethnic origins for grades kindergarten through eight.

Marymount was founded in 1938 by the Religious of the Sacred Heart of Mary. Today it's a nonprofit corporation governed by a board of trustees and is one of the oldest and most respected private schools in Santa Barbara. Its two-track religion program (Catholic studies and religious studies) grows from the Judeo- Christian tradition and emphasizes moral development and community service. Students may choose an appropriate track, depending on their religious backgrounds.

The strong academic curriculum and small classes are designed to promote self-esteem and the love of learning in each student. The school has an iMac computer lab and employs a learning specialist for students with special needs, a reading specialist, and a school counselor. In 2003 the school added a new middle school facility to its leafy grounds. Academic performance consistently ranks in the 50th percentile and above among the nation's independent schools. Marymount encourages creative expression and emphasizes physical fitness and good sportsmanship.

Santa Barbara Christian School
3723 Modoc Road, Santa Barbara
(805) 563-4770
www.santabarbarachristian.com

Established in 1960, the Santa Barbara Christian School provides a program of high-quality, nondenominational Christian education. The curriculum focuses on helping students (grades kindergarten through eight) attain a balance of rigorous intellectual competence, healthy character development, and a personal commitment to Jesus Christ. Children from both Christian homes and those with no church affiliation are welcome.

The school emphasizes biblical doctrine, spiritual lifestyle, and excellent academics. It also provides instruction in art, music, foreign language, and athletics, and students have access to a computer lab. Although the school offers no special education programs or GATE, students are tested for learning differences, and the school works with private tutors. In 2004 the school moved from interim housing to a new campus at Emmanuel Lutheran Church in Santa Barbara at 3721 Modoc Road. Total enrollment is around 100 students. Classes average about 18 students per teacher.

Santa Barbara Middle School
2300-A Garden Street, Santa Barbara
(805) 682-2989
www.sbms.org

Founded in 1976, Santa Barbara Middle School spans grades six through nine and seeks to develop well-rounded and well-grounded teenagers through an innovative curriculum incorporating outdoor team trips. On a typical day, students attend challenging academic classes in the morning and engage in creative arts and sports activities in the afternoon. In addition, they participate in three "rite of passage" field trips a year linked to their academic course of study. The fall and midyear trips are usually a week in length. The end-of-year trip lasts from 10 days to two weeks.

In the Rite of the Wheel portion of the program, for example, students bicycle more than 1,500 miles (2,400 kilometers) in seven states during the course of their enrollment. They hike and backpack, travel, eat, and camp with their headmaster and teachers. The annual trips teach students about the history, culture, and geography of a particular region and help them learn teamwork, self-confidence, and self-reliance (for example, they learn to repair their own bikes).

Advanced Placement classes are offered in all core subjects. The school also boasts an excellent drama department and supplements its challenging academic curriculum with technology courses in computers, digital animation, and digital filming. It also provides a Learning Difference program for special needs students. The 165 students enrolled at the school are organized into age-appropriate academic villages with an average class size of about 16. Students also participate in a Career Study Week, during which students are exposed to career opportunities and are involved in community service.

The Waldorf School of Santa Barbara
Main Campus: 401 North Fairview, Goleta
(805) 967-6656
Early Childhood Campus: 5679 Hollister
Avenue, Goleta

The Waldorf School of Santa Barbara is one of at least 1,000 Waldorf Schools. It opened in 1984 and is now a complete elementary school with about 95 students in prekindergarten through grade eight. The six-acre campus lies on a beautiful historical site between Mission Santa Barbara and the Natural History Museum.

The school's approach to education is based on the principles of Waldorf Education, as initiated by Rudolf Steiner (1861–1925), an

Austrian philosopher/ teacher. The role of teachers is to inspire imagination and intuition in the students so that they may develop their intellectual, creative, and social capacities. The curriculum integrates traditional academic subjects with the arts in a structured program tailored to the developmental age of each child. Subjects include math, science, music, art, foreign languages, humanities, handwork, dramatic arts, biodynamic gardening, and physical education. Children with learning differences receive educational support. The school also aims to foster gratitude and reverence for the world, its cultures, diversity, and nature. Grade classes average about 12 to 15 students.

Goleta

Montessori Center School
401 North Fairview Avenue #1, Goleta
(805) 683-9383
www.sbceo.org/~mcssb
Founded in 1965, The Montessori Center School is a nonprofit organization offering preprimary, primary, and elementary education for approximately 300 students from 18 months of age through grade six.

Set amid beautiful gardens, the school adheres to the Montessori curriculum, which emphasizes hands-on, progressive, self-paced learning. Students work with specially designed learning materials at an early age to experience concrete principles and then move to greater complexity and abstraction. Montessori advocates believe these methods foster self-awareness, leadership, teamwork, and creative thinking. Most classes incorporate three different age or grade levels, which allows children to learn from one another and creates a "family" atmosphere. The school fosters environmental and global awareness as children participate in gardening, hiking, science and camping trips, peace education, and world cultural studies. Spanish, art, music, and fitness are taught to children at a very young age, as well as theater and library for elementary students. Extracurricular classes range from sign language to t'ai chi. The school also serves children with special needs and offers before- and after-school care. Adult-to-child ratios are 1 to 6 in pre-primary classes and 1 to 12 thereafter. In annual standardized tests, MCS elementary students consistently average results between two and three years above their grade level, and graduates generally enroll in GATE or honors programs at middle and high school.

Montecito

Crane School
1795 San Leandro Lane
Montecito
(805) 969-7732
www.craneschool.org
Set on 11 beautiful acres in affluent Montecito, Crane School offers a challenging academic curriculum for grades kindergarten through eight. The school was established in 1928 and has an excellent reputation. Crane's teachers encourage independence and creativity while helping students use their education to become kind and responsible human beings. The school teaches a traditional curriculum using a stimulating and innovative approach. Art, drama, music, and athletics are critical facets of the syllabus, and the school offers a selection of special programs in areas such as technology, library media, visual arts, and physical education. The eighth-grade class trip to Bajia de los Angeles to work on a sea turtle preservation farm is something Crane alumni remember forever.

Total enrollment is 230 students. Grades kindergarten through five have a maximum of 20 students per class, and grades six through eight are divided into sections of 12 to 16 students. Because Crane insists on small class sizes and has only one class per grade level, admission is extremely competitive.

Carpinteria

Cate School
1960 Cate Mesa Road, Carpinteria
(805) 684-4127
www.cate.org
Cate School is regularly ranked among the top college-preparatory boarding schools in the nation. The four-year high school (grades 9

through 12) was established in 1910 and boasts a gorgeous, 150-acre campus set on a mesa overlooking the ocean and the Carpinteria Valley.

About 270 students from all over the world are enrolled at Cate, and approximately 220 of them live on campus. Average class size is 10 to 12 students, and the school offers Advanced Placement courses in more than 19 subjects.

Admission is competitive and nearly 30 percent of the student body receives financial aid. In recent years Cate students have won National Merit Scholarships, National Science Scholarships, and numerous other awards. One hundred percent of Cate graduates go on to four-year colleges and universities such as Stanford, Harvard, UC Berkeley, and Brown.

The Howard School
5315 Foothill Road, Carpinteria
(805) 745-8448
www.thehowardschool.org
Known as Santa Barbara's oldest private school, this school was once located in Montecito but now is situated on the property of Girls Inc. in Carpinteria. The Howard School teaches the tools necessary for a comprehensive classical education. Its curriculum is based on the Carden method, established by Mae Carden in 1934. Joel Reed, the school's headmaster, personally greets each student as he or she arrives on campus each morning and starts the morning assembly with the Pledge of Allegiance and the Lord's Prayer. The approximately 80 preschool to eighth-grade students are taught in classes of no more than 15 students.

HIGHER EDUCATION

University of California at Santa Barbara (UCSB), Santa Barbara
(805) 893-8000
www.ucsb.edu
UCSB is one of the 10 campuses that form the University of California system—widely regarded as the nation's leading public sys-

i Counseling and Career Services at UCSB are not just for campus-related problems. If you're a student of the university and are having trouble with relationships, stress, homesickness, or depression, they can help. Call (805) 893-4411, or visit the office in Building 599.

tem of higher education. UCSB is unquestionably the academic jewel of the Santa Barbara area. Its presence extends well beyond the campus, influencing community arts, athletics, the intellectual scene, politics, and more.

Recently ranked one of the "hottest" colleges in the nation by *Newsweek,* UCSB offers 200 majors, degrees, and credentials. The campus includes three colleges: Letters and Science, Engineering, and Creative Studies. It's also home to two professional schools: the Graduate School of Education and the School of Environmental Science and Management.

The university "family" includes about 18,000 undergraduates, 2,800 graduate students, and more than 1,050 faculty members. About 2,500 students live on campus, and most of the others live in adjacent Isla Vista, a high-density student community with shops, restaurants, and a zillion bicycles.

Since the campus consists of nearly 1,000 acres of prime coastal property on the edge of the Pacific, overlooking palm-lined beaches, lagoons, and some fantastic surf breaks on its doorstep, one might wrongly assume that academics are a low priority. On the contrary—since UCSB was founded in 1944, it has firmly established itself as a world-class research center and teaching institution.

A recent national study of America's top research universities ranks UC Santa Barbara as one of the top public universities nationwide based on criteria such as research dollars, prestigious fellowships, and number of publications.

UCSB is also an elected member of the Association of American Universities, which includes 62 leading institutions of higher learning in the United States and Canada, including

Stanford, Harvard, and UC Berkeley. The Carnegie Foundation for the Advancement of Teaching also ranks UCSB as one of America's top research institutions.

The university is best known for interdisciplinary research. It's small enough for different colleges and departments to collaborate, which leads to more important discoveries. This makes it easier to obtain funding, which in turn attracts experts in various fields. In recent years UCSB's faculty members dazzled the academic community by winning five Nobel prizes in chemistry, economics, and physics. The faculty also includes fellows of the National Endowment for the Humanities, recipients of the National Medal of Science, and members of the National Academy of Arts and Sciences, the National Academy of Sciences, the American Association for the Advancement of Science, and the National Academy of Engineering.

UCSB has 11 national research centers and institutes, including the Kavli Institute for Theoretical Physics, the Materials Research Laboratory, and the Southern California Earthquake Center. Eight of the centers are sponsored by the National Science Foundation.

UCSB was selected for the California Nanosystems Institute, one of the first California Institutes of Science and Innovation. This research partnership between UCLA and UCSB is providing scientific advances that are critical to the California economy.

Not surprisingly, undergraduate admission to UCSB is highly competitive. Today more than 30 percent of all applicants have a high school grade point average of 4.0 or higher, and in 2007, UCSB received 48,728 applications. Considering the university's excellent academic reputation (not to mention its palm-studded setting), it's no wonder students are scrambling to sign up.

COMMUNITY COLLEGES AND CONTINUING EDUCATION

Santa Barbara City College (SBCC)
721 Cliff Drive, Santa Barbara
(805) 965-0581, ext. 7222
www.sbcc.net

Widely regarded as one of the leading two-year community colleges in the state and the nation, seaside SBCC offers more than 90 degree and certificate programs to over 12,000 students from Santa Barbara, virtually every state in the country, and more than 60 countries worldwide. The college also boasts one of the most breathtaking settings of any educational institution in the country. It's set high on bluffs overlooking the Santa Barbara Harbor.

Credit programs are open to any student who is at least 18 years of age or has earned a high school diploma or the equivalent. Students can receive an associate's degree; develop vocational, technical, and career skills; or prepare for transfer to a four-year university.

Nonresidents of California may attend City College, but they have to pay higher fees. To establish residency in California, you must be physically present in California for one year plus one day prior to the start of the semester and prove that you intend to make California your permanent place of residence.

To prove intent, you need to provide documentation, for example, California State Income Tax returns, voter registration dates, California driver's license and registration, and W-2 forms with a California address. You will have to complete and file a residency questionnaire, a statement of financial independence, and evidence of permanent California residency no later than two weeks prior to your registration date.

SBCC was recently named a top community college for Hispanics. Out of 109 California community colleges, it ranked third in transfers of Mexican-American students to UC campuses.

Santa Barbara City College Continuing
Education Division
Alice E. Schott Center
310 West Padre Street, Santa Barbara
(805) 687-0812

Selmer O. Wake Center
300 North Turnpike Road, Goleta
(805) 964-6853
www.sbcc.net/continuingeducation
"Adult Ed" (as the Continuing Education Division of Santa Barbara City College is more
commonly known) is one of the best educational resources in Santa Barbara and one of
the nation's leading adult education programs. It offers an incredibly wide range of
noncredit and community services classes,
and they're usually free, with occasional minimal fees for materials.

Subjects include the arts, business,
finance, real estate, job training, computers,
cooking and wine, crafts, current events and
world affairs, literature, writing, home and
garden, humanities, languages, music, and
photography.

More than 42,000 people enroll in classes
every year—an amazing number, since that's
about one out of every three residents in the
greater Santa Barbara region. During fall, winter, spring, and summer sessions, classes
meet weekday mornings, afternoons, and
evenings as well as Saturdays.

University of California at Santa Barbara
Extension
6950 Hollister Avenue, Goleta
(805) 893-4200
www.unex.ucsb.edu
UCSB Extension offers university-level certificate programs, seminars, and online courses
designed for professional training and career
advancement. The wide range of courses
includes art and design, business and management, computers and technology, education, legal studies, and mediation.

Through the UCSB Extension, you can
earn university credits and certificates and fulfill professional continuing education and reli-

censure requirements. Courses are offered
every quarter, year-round.

Private Colleges, Universities, and Specialty Schools
Santa Barbara
Antioch University Santa Barbara
801 Garden Street, Santa Barbara
(805) 962-8179
www.antiochsb.edu
Antioch University Santa Barbara is an extension of Antioch University, which was founded
in Yellow Springs, Ohio, in 1852. The Santa
Barbara campus opened in 1977. Most of the
students enrolled at Antioch are working
adults who wish to earn an undergraduate or
graduate degree. The average student is 35
years old, and many of the students receive
financial aid. Antioch offers a B.A. program in
Liberal Arts and M.A. programs in organiza-
tional management, education and teaching,
clinical psychology, and social justice and educational leadership. You can also sign up for
the weekend college courses in management
offered once a month.

Fielding Graduate Institute
2112 Santa Barbara Street, Santa Barbara
(805) 687-1099, (800) 340-1099
www.fielding.edu
Founded in 1974, Fielding Graduate Institute
is a regionally accredited graduate school
offering doctoral and master's degree programs and continuing professional education
in the fields of psychology, human and organi-
zational development, and educational leadership and change. Fielding's postgraduate
certificates include neuropsychology and
respecialization in psychology and clinical
psychology.

Also home to the Alonso Center for Psy-
chodynamic Studies, this institute is perhaps
best known for its innovative and flexible curriculum designed to serve mid-career professionals juggling work, family, and community
commitments. The institute's supportive com-
petency-based approach to learning and

assessment combines both theory and practice. Students build on their existing knowledge and professional experience and self-direct their learning through a mix of independent study, structured course work, and face-to-face and online collaboration with an extensive network of scholars, faculty members, and practitioners.

Santa Barbara College of Law
20 East Victoria Street, Santa Barbara
(805) 966-0010
www.santabarbaralaw.edu

Conveniently located in the heart of downtown, the Santa Barbara College of Law opened in 1975. The school provides high-quality legal education through an affordable part-time evening program, leading to a juris doctor degree and eligibility to sit for the California State Bar Examination. The faculty are all experienced attorneys or judges, and the campus includes an extensive library and computer facilities. Students usually complete the program in three and a half to four years.

Montecito

Brooks Institute of Photography
801 Alston Road, Montecito
(805) 585-8000, (888) 276-4999
www.brooks.edu

Brooks is a world leader in professional photographic and motion picture education, with state-of-the-art resources, an outstanding faculty, and five beautiful campuses: three in Santa Barbara, one in Montecito, and one in Ventura.

Ernest H. Brooks Sr., a professional photographer, founded the school in 1945 after his return from military service. Today the school has a faculty of more than 32 experts who pass on their knowledge to men and women from around the world. In the photography world, the institute is reputed to have the finest professors and facility in the nation.

Brooks prepares students for careers in the diverse disciplines of professional, commercial, and still photography and filmmaking. It also has programs geared toward the work-

ing photographer who seeks new skills to advance within the industry.

Great emphasis is placed on a well-rounded general education; courses in communications, marketing, and business teach skills essential for success in the competitive marketplace. Students have access to the latest technology and practices in the field.

The institute offers A.A., B.A., and M.S. degrees and a diploma program, short-term courses, and weekend workshops in a variety of photographic disciplines. It also recently added a visual journalism program, which cross-trains students in still cameras, computers, and digital video cameras. Brooks has a rolling admissions policy with six entering dates each year (except motion picture/video majors, who may enter in January, April, and September only). Once every two years, Brooks students travel abroad on an international documentary project (for example, to China, Africa, India, Mexico, or Cuba) and present an exhibit when they return.

Music Academy of the West
1070 Fairway Road, Santa Barbara
(805) 969-4726
www.musicacademy.org

The Music Academy of the West is one of the finest summer music schools in the country. It was established in 1947 by a group of dedicated art patrons and celebrated musicians, including legendary German opera singer Lotte Lehmann.

The academy's eight-week Summer School and Festival provides gifted young musicians with the opportunity for advanced study and performance under the guidance of internationally known faculty artists.

For more than 50 years, the school has attracted a stellar lineup of performing and teaching talent (for example, Metropolitan Opera star Marilyn Horne, director of the academy's voice program, and piano pedagogue Jerome Lowenthal) and thousands of gifted students, many of whom later established critically acclaimed careers. More than 5,000 graduates have passed through the academy's gates, and they fill the ranks of major symphony orchestras and opera houses throughout the world. All those accepted to the academy through its rigorous audition process are awarded full scholarships, covering tuition, lodging, and meals for the entire eight weeks.

The academy's permanent campus is located at Miraflores, a Mediterranean-style estate on a bluff overlooking the Pacific Ocean. It occupies 10 acres of wooded, beautifully landscaped grounds and gardens.

Westmont College
955 La Paz Road, Santa Barbara
(805) 565-6000
www.westmont.edu
Founded in 1937, Westmont College is a residential four-year college committed to the Christian faith. It provides a high-quality undergraduate liberal arts program in a residential campus community. About 1,330 students from the nation and worldwide are currently enrolled at the school. The student/faculty ratio is 13 to 1, with 136 full-time faculty.

Westmont offers bachelor of arts and bachelor of science degrees in 26 liberal arts majors; 10 preprofessional programs; a fifth-year credential program; and numerous internships and practica. The extensive list of majors includes art, psychology, theater arts, religious studies, kinesiology, biology, and chemistry, just to name a few. Forty-three percent go on to graduate school. The average class size is 23. The gorgeous campus occupies 111 wooded acres—a collection of grounds from two former estates and a school for boys—in the Montecito foothills off Cold Spring Road. Westmont organizes numerous creative and performing arts programs, lectures, and sports events.

Carpinteria

Pacifica Graduate Institute
249 Lambert Road, Carpinteria
(805) 969-3626
www.pacifica.edu
Accredited by the Western Association of

Schools and Colleges (WASC), Pacifica Graduate Institute provides graduate degree programs in depth psychology (M.A., Ph.D.), depth psychology with an emphasis in phychotherapy (Ph.D.), clinical psychology (Ph.D.), counseling psychology (M.A.), mythological studies (M.A., Ph.D.), and humanities with an emphasis in mythology and depth psychology. (M.A.). The school occupies a tree-studded, 13-acre campus in the Carpinteria foothills replete with wildlife-friendly plants, organic orchards, and vegetable gardens.

Reflecting the belief that human experience is diverse and multifaceted, Pacifica offers degree programs that are interdisciplinary in nature. Literature, religion, art, and mythology supplement the study of psychology. During the fall, winter, and spring quarters, students attend classes on campus during a three-day learning retreat once a month. Most programs also include a one-week summer session. Between sessions, students continue their coursework through reading, research, and practicum experiences in their homes. This unique educational format is particularly suited to people who wish to pursue graduate education while continuing their current professional and personal commitments.

CHILD CARE

If you're working or just need time to get some "adult" things done, you'll be happy to know that Santa Barbara has many excellent facilities where your children can learn, play, and socialize with their pals under the careful supervision of qualified child care providers. Your options range from licensed homes to large, church-affiliated centers, to on-site child care programs at businesses or institutions.

We must advise you, however, that most child care facilities have long waiting lists, especially those with affordable fees and/or excellent reputations. It's not uncommon for parents to sign up their kids as soon as

A young student pets a newborn goat. NANCY SHOBE

they're born—or even earlier. Many parents find it necessary to arrange for alternative care in their own homes (nannies, babysitters) until a child reaches preschool age.

Santa Barbara has many outstanding preschools, which typically accept children from ages 2 through 5. If you have a baby or toddler, we recommend that you visit the schools and get on the waiting lists as early as possible.

When choosing a preschool, don't immediately write off a school that isn't accredited. Preschool accreditation is a fairly new program. The National Academy of Early Childhood Programs (part of the National Association for the Education of Young Children) administers this voluntary accreditation system, which evaluates whether a program meets nationally recognized criteria for high quality. Accreditation is available to all types of preschools, kindergartens, child care centers, and school-age child care programs. But only a few local centers are currently accredited—it costs money to apply and the process is lengthy.

The best resources for finding out about child care are described below. You can also pick up *Santa Barbara Family Life,* a free monthly magazine that includes listings and ads on child care, preschools, and after-school day care; call (805) 965-4545 or check out www.sbparent.com.

Children's Resource and Referral Program
1124 Castillo Street, Santa Barbara
(805) 962-8988
www.fsacares.org
The Children's Resource and Referral Program is administered through the Santa Barbara Family Care Center. It's one of more than 60 Resource and Referral Programs funded by the California Department of Education. The program provides information about all types of licensed child care centers and private

providers and distributes information on choosing quality child care. It also has a lending library with videos, toys, and resources for caregivers, parents, and community members. Telephone and walk-in referrals are available Monday through Friday from 8:00 a.m. to noon and 1:00 to 3:00 p.m.

ChildTime Professional Nanny Placement Service
536 Brinkerhoff Avenue, Santa Barbara
(805) 962-4433, (805) 564-9428: pager
www.childtimenanny.com
ChildTime is a licensed and bonded nanny placement agency that specializes in matching nannies with families. Established in 1985, ChildTime sets high standards for its nannies. Selection is based on a careful screening and interview process. References, DMV records, and backgrounds are checked. Nannies are required to have CPR certification and to take a Nannies Skills Class.

i Want to meet other moms and dads whose babies are the same age as yours? Call PEP—Postpartum Education for Parents—at (805) 564-3888 or visit www.sbpep.org. This nonprofit volunteer organization will put you in touch with a group of local parents.

Nannies are available for full-time or part-time positions on a live-in or live-out basis. ChildTime also has on-call temporary nannies who will come to your hotel or residence.

After-School Care

All public and most private schools in the area offer after-school care, either on-site or at convenient locations in the vicinity of schools. When you enroll your child at a school, be sure to ask about your options. Some after-school care programs fill quickly, so be sure to do your research well in advance.

MEDIA

It's rare that a news source becomes the news itself, but that is precisely what's happened with Santa Barbara's only daily newspaper, the *Santa Barbara News-Press* (41,000 circulation). In 2000, Santa Barbarans were thrilled when local billionaire and environmentalist Wendy McCaw purchased the paper from the New York Times Co., which had been running it since 1985. Changing ownership from a large conglomerate to an independent bucked the trends in media. But the change in ownership came at a cost, a cost that made national news (*Vanity Fair* wrote an exposé on it), and the story behind the squabble is now being made into a documentary film.

The newspaper hit a snag, shall we say, when editors accused McCaw of meddling in editorial decisions. In less than a year's time, over 35 editors and reporters quit or were fired, leaving a newspaper that is strangely devoid of journalists and news.

For years, Santa Barbarans have been proud of their hometown newspaper. Now locals are hoping the fracas soon will be resolved so they may enjoy their hometown paper once again.

Where this will end, no one seems to know, as the feud between the journalists and their union officials and Wendy McCaw and her company, Ampersand Publishing LLC, and her copublisher/fiancé, Arthur von Wiesenberger, is being dueled out in the courts.

NEWSPAPERS

The much tamer historical origins of the newspaper in Santa Barbara began with the *Santa Barbara Gazette* in 1855. After struggling to survive with a small reader base, the paper eventually sold out to new owners, who moved to San Francisco and thereafter delivered the paper by steamship. This wasn't acceptable to subscribers, who sometimes got the "news" when it was weeks old, and the *Gazette* soon went out of business.

In 1868 the weekly *Santa Barbara Post* began publishing locally, but just over a year later, it was bought out, and the name was changed to the *Santa Barbara Press*. In 1871 it became Santa Barbara's first daily newspaper.

Other newspapers that packed some clout in their day included the *Morning Press,* the *Daily News,* and the *Daily Independent.* Thomas M. Storke, a local boy and Stanford graduate with deep Santa Barbara roots, owned all of these publications at one time or another and in 1938 merged the papers into one, the *Santa Barbara News-Press.*

Santa Barbara

Dailies

Los Angeles Times
1421 State Street, Santa Barbara
(800) 252-9141 subscription
(805) 564-0035
www.latimes.com
For big-city news and investigative reports, as well as world and some local coverage (Santa Barbarans receive the paper's Ventura County regional edition), opt for the Los Angeles Times. This well-respected metropolitan newspaper covering all of Southern California is the largest city paper in the country, with a daily circulation around 900,000 and a Sunday circulation of just over 1.25 million. The *Los Angeles Times* boasts one of the most comprehensive news sites on the Web. Check out its classified ad section for employment opportunities anywhere in the region and Sunday's travel section for the latest in destination deals. Subscriptions cost about $5.30 a

week for Sunday and daily. The newsstand price is 50 cents Monday to Saturday and $1.50 on Sunday.

The New York Times
229 West 43rd Street
New York, NY 10036
(866) 819-5004
www.nytimes.com
The highly educated population of Santa Barbara demands to be in the know, and they are very discerning of their news sources. Perhaps that's why so many major metropolitan newspapers may be found in town, including the *New York Times*. Eavesdrop on a cafe conversation, and you'll undoubtedly find some local folks debating about *"The Times"* latest editorial. Its intellectual cachet is perhaps what has made the paper so successful. Newsstand prices are $1 for Monday to Saturday and $5 for Sunday. Introductory offer subscription costs are daily $6.20 a week, Friday to Sunday $4.35 a week, and Sunday only $3.15 a week.

San Francisco Chronicle
901 Mission Street
San Francisco, CA 94103
(415) 777-1111
www.sfgate.com
Santa Barbara fancies itself as the only major city located between Los Angeles and San Francisco. Although closer to Los Angeles in proximity, Santa Barbara doesn't like to disassociate from its bigger "northern neighbor." Because of this, the *San Francisco Chronicle,* Northern California's largest metropolitan newspaper, with a daily circulation of over half a million, may be found at newsstands around town, but it is not offered for home delivery. Newsstand prices are 50 cents Monday to Saturday and $2 for the Sunday edition.

Santa Barbara News-Press
De la Guerra Plaza, Santa Barbara
(805) 564-5200
www.newspress.com
The *Santa Barbara News-Press* is the city's

main daily paper, with a daily circulation of over 41,000. It's a morning paper covering international, national, state, and local news. The Friday pull-out "Scene" section covers the local music, theater, and arts scenes and runs reviews of movies and local restaurants. Special sections such as the "Life" section of the paper give news about the thriving local nonprofit scene, and the can't-do-without Fiesta edition fills you in on all the events and parties happening in conjunction with the annual August celebration. Subscriptions start at $3.18 a week for daily delivery and $2.37 a week for Friday to Sunday delivery. Newsstand costs are 50 cents Monday to Saturday and $1.50 on Sunday.

Monday–Friday Dailies

Santa Barbara Daily Sound
806 Cliff Drive
Santa Barbara, CA 93109
(805) 564-6001
www.santabarbarafree.com
When the big presses start having difficulty, the little presses have an opportunity to jump in. That's exactly what Jeramy Gordon, president and CEO of NORDROG Publications and editor and publisher of the *Santa Barbara Daily Sound,* did. He launched the first edition of his tiny but mighty newspaper on March 23, 2006, and has successfully printed a paper Monday to Friday ever since. Delivered throughout town, this free paper offers a quick snapshot of the daily news and includes favorite Santa Barbara journalists, including humorous and essayist Leslie Dinaberg, who appears in every Friday's edition. Who knows what tomorrow brings for this tiny paper? For right now, it can be found at local cafes, bookstores, and newsstands.

Weekly

The Santa Barbara Independent
122 West Figueroa Street, Santa Barbara
(805) 965-5205
www.independent.com
The *Independent,* published every Thursday, is a major source of news for the Santa Bar-

bara community. This tabloid-style paper, although irritatingly rough in design, is packed with oodles of information on the theater, nightlife, sports, and dining scenes.

The paper has taken on much of the "other papers'" story (*Santa Barbara News-Press*) and even some of its journalists. (The *Independent* has grown heftier since the *Santa Barbara News-Press*'s upheaval, perhaps the result of advertisers moving their ad dollars?) With a circulation of over 40,000, it's a common sight to see folks sitting at a juice bar or deli reading the *Independent*. The paper is distributed free to readers and may be found at bookstores, cafes, and organic markets around town.

Montecito

Montecito Journal
1122 Coast Village Circle, Montecito
(805) 565-1860
www.montecitojournal.net
Calling itself "The Voice of the Village," the *Montecito Journal* is a weekly tabloid featuring social events, local news, political issues, real estate, and restaurants. "Ernie's World," penned by local writer Ernie Witham, will lighten your day with his funny musings. The *Montecito Journal* prints a calendar of events that will keep you up-to-date with an impressive list of social must-dos. This free publication is distributed throughout the local area.

Carpinteria

Coastal View News
4856 Carpinteria Avenue, Carpinteria
(805) 684-4428
www.coastalview.com
Coastal View News is a small tabloid-type weekly that serves the Carpinteria Valley with news of local business, education, and community events. Its circulation is about 6,000, with free copies available at newsstands and other locations in Carpinteria, Summerland, Montecito, and Santa Barbara. Carpinteria events (except for major happenings like the

annual California Avocado Festival) don't always get good coverage in the Santa Barbara press, so this is a great place to get the scoop on what's going on in Santa Barbara's neighbor to the south.

Goleta

Valley Voice
725 South Kellogg Avenue, Goleta
(805) 681-5905
www.goletavalleyvoice.com
Valley Voice is a free weekly covering all the local news in Goleta. Over the years, several newspapers have failed to succeed in Goleta, but as Goleta residents voted in cityhood, the *Valley Voice* emerged as an important community forum. The *Valley Voice* is a small publication with a circulation of about 16,500, but it gives a nod to the local arts scene, events around town, and Goleta sports teams. You can pick up a copy at local businesses throughout Goleta or downtown in county buildings, post offices, and the public library.

MAGAZINES

Coastal Woman Magazine
Seastar Publications, Inc.
3463 State Street, #208, Santa Barbara
(805) 453-7509
www.coastalwoman.com
The brainchild of this magazine highlighting "real" women around Santa Barbara came from the indomitable Barbara Lanz-Mateo. With an effervescent spirit and journalism background, she launched *Coastal Woman Magazine* as a way to showcase, as her magazine tagline says, "one fabulous woman at a time."

Sitting down with *Coastal Woman Magazine* is like sitting at a cafe with your best friend—you read the local gossip, learn a few things you didn't know, and leave feeling lighter than you did before. *Coastal Woman* is distributed free four times a year throughout town. It boasts a circulation of over 25,000, of which 8,000 copies are mailed to residences.

Montecito Magazine
1144 Edgemound Drive, Santa Barbara
(805) 682-8335
www.montecitomag.com
This handy palm-sized magazine highlights
Montecito's scene with its well-written text
and beautiful, full-color pictures. A quick
thumbing through gives you a glimpse at
Montecito's history, real estate, shops, galleries, restaurants, and entertainment. It's distributed free and is available by subscription.

Santa Barbara Magazine
25 East De la Guerra Street, Santa Barbara
(805) 965-5999
www.sbmag.com
Santa Barbara Magazine is a slick bimonthly
showcasing the well-to-do. In addition to several feature stories and columns about local
people, celebrities, and events, you'll find a
large section of ads for Santa Barbara estates,
private schools, art galleries, expensive automobiles, fine jewelry, and upscale shops.

Its regular features, "Santa Barbara
Scene," "People," "Art," "Getaways," and "Giving Back," highlight people, places, and
events the "average Joe" can only dream
about. With its outstanding photography, it's
an excellent depiction of Santa Barbara's elite.

SPECIAL INTEREST PUBLICATIONS

All of the publications listed below are free
and generally distributed at local bookstores
(Chaucer's is always a good bet) or newsstands. Visitor information publications are
usually available at hotels and tourist stops,
such as Santa Barbara Hot Spots at 1410½
Clifton Street, Santa Barbara (805-564-1637,
www.hotspotusa.com).

Food & Home
209 West Alamar Street, Suite B, Santa
Barbara
(805) 563-6780
www.food-home.com
This well-written quarterly glossy Santa Bar-

bara lifestyle magazine is always a welcome
read. In addition to the buzz on the local dining and bar scene, the magazine presents
entertaining articles on food and wine trends,
family issues, and home improvement. It also
profiles local artists and recipes from restaurants around town. Circulation is 48,000, with
free deliveries to selected homes, bookstores,
premium hotels, and bed-and-breakfasts in
the greater Santa Barbara area and beyond.

Santa Barbara Seasons
2020 Chapala Street, Santa Barbara
(805) 563-0500
www.sbseasons.com
The informative articles in this sophisticated
quarterly spotlight Santa Barbara's history,
architecture, culture, and natural beauty. A
multiple award winner, *Santa Barbara Seasons* has a circulation of 36,000 with an estimated readership of over five times that.
You'll see why for yourself when you pick up a
copy. It's truly beautiful.

INTERNET NEWS SOURCES

Let's face it, we are in a new millennium, and
many people, especially the younger ones,
are no longer turning to print publications for
their news. Instead, they are searching for
news and information online. Besides the online edition of the *Santa Barbara News-Press*
(www.newspress.com), there are a few other
local sources to turn to.

Edhat
www.edhat.com
Log on and you'll get a glimpse of what's happening in Santa Barbara.

Blogabarbara
www.blogabarbara.blogspot.com
Someone out there is blogging about Santa
Barbara, but no one really knows who it is . . .
that is, no one *we* know knows who it is. You'll
catch the latest gossip about Santa Barbara
from this anonymous person's perspective.

Craig Smith's blog
www.west.net/~smith/blog/index.shtml
"Covering Santa Barbara Law and Media like a Wet Blanket" is Craig Smith's tag line. His repartee and keen political conclusions are what has earned Smith, an attorney and professor, accolades in the community. He loves to give his perspective on events around town.

RADIO

The oldest continuously broadcasting station in Santa Barbara is KDB (93.7 FM), which began operations in the Daily News building in 1926 under the call letters KFCR. (When George Barnes purchased the station in 1929, he changed the call letters to KDB, his wife Dorothy's initials.)

After several changes in physical location and formats, KDB began broadcasting classical music exclusively in 1980 and has been doing it 24 hours a day ever since. KDB is one of the only self-supporting classical music stations in the nation and is now owned and operated by the Santa Barbara Foundation.

In January 2007, Rincon Broadcasting LLC announced an agreement to purchase four of Santa Barbara's radio stations—KTYD, KSBL, KIST, and KSPE—and three AM radio stations—KTMS, KIST, and KBKO—from Clear Channel Communications. The format of KIST 107.7 has already been changed from rock to Regional Mexican. Other changes may follow.

Radio listening in Santa Barbara is enhanced by many Ventura, Oxnard, and Los Angeles stations that have enough power to be heard in town, although several may fade in and out, depending on the weather or your reception. Nonetheless, for your listening pleasure, some of these are included on the list.

> **i** Check out KMGQ's Web site at www.kmgq1063.com for information on what's happening around town.

Adult Contemporary

KBBY 95.1 FM, www.b951.com
KRUZ, 97.5 FM, www.kruz.com
KLITE, 101.7 FM, www.klite.com
KFYV, 105.5 FM, www.live1055.fm

Alternative

KJEE, 92.9 FM, www.kjee.com

Christian

KDAR, 98.3 FM, www.kdar.com

Classical

KUSC, 91.5 FM, www.kusc.org
KDB, 93.7 FM, www.kdb.com

College

KCSB, 91.9 FM, www.kcsb.org
University of Santa Barbara

Country

KHAY 100.7 FM, www.khay.com
KRAZ, 105.9 FM, www.krazfm.com

Hip Hop

KCAQ, 104.7 FM, www.q1047.com

News

KFI, 640 AM, www.kfi640am
KABC, 790 AM, www.kabc.com
KTMS, 990 AM, local news, www.990am.com
KNX, 1070 AM, www.knx1070.com
KIST, 1340 AM, www.talkradio1340am.com
KVTA, 1520 AM, www.kvta.com

Oldies

KRTH, 101.1 FM, www.kearth101.com
KVEN 1450 AM, www.kven.com

Public

KSBX, 89.5 FM, www.kcbx.org

Rock

KOCP, 95.9 FM, www.theoctopus959.com
KTYD, 99.9 FM, www.ktyd.com

Smooth Jazz

KMGQ, 106.3 FM, www.kmgq1063.com

Spanish

KXLM, 102.9 FM, www.radiolazer.com
KVYB 103.3 FM, www.1033thevibe.com
KIST, 107.7 FM, and
KBKO, 1490 AM, www.radiobronco.com

TELEVISION

Thomas M. Storke, who was on hand during the infancy of both the newspaper and radio businesses in Santa Barbara, seemed destined to be involved in the development of local television as well. It was not to be, however. Harry Butcher, owner of a local radio station, along with several members of a new media corporation, beat Storke to the punch by going on the air first in the early 1950s.

The new station was KEYT, Channel 3, which is still Santa Barbara's only homegrown commercial television station, and is considered to be an excellent station.

There are two nonprofit public access television stations in Santa Barbara, Channel 17 and Channel 21. Channel 17 offers free airtime to local community members who wish to create a program. Channel 21 is evolving

i Tune in to the *Unity Telethon* at the beginning of every December for a sample of celebrities who are donating their talents to raise money for the Unity Shoppe, a local nonprofit. Started by Kenny Loggins, this telethon has showcased Santa Barbara's celebrities and elite for over two decades.

into airtime for nonprofits by providing educational, arts, and cultural programming.

CABLE TV

Cox Communications (805-683-6651) provides cable and digital cable service to all of Santa Barbara County. If you like to watch TV, you'll need to do business with Cox, which will charge you from about $47.99 a month for limited basic cable (Channels 2–74) to digital cable where the price depends on the package you choose.

SATELLITE COMPANIES

If you want to beam programs from hundreds of stations down to your TV set, you can choose from a variety of full-service satellite companies. DirecTV has several affiliates. Call (800) 280-4388, or visit www.directtv.com. There's also Dish Network (888-300-1926; www.getdishtvspecials.net); and Direct Satellite TV (800-675-8635; www.directsattv.com).

WORSHIP

Santa Barbara is a diverse and tolerant community, and its rich mix of religious and spiritual organizations reflects this fact. From Assemblies of God to Unitarian Universalist and everything in between, you're likely to find a congregation of people here who share your beliefs. Most of the organizations mentioned in this chapter welcome newcomers and offer fellowships, spiritual retreats, and social groups designed to help you bond with other members.

The city's spiritual evolution happened over time, of course. Santa Barbara's early residents, the Chumash Indians, consulted the local shaman for spiritual advice and flourished in harmony with the earth until the arrival of the Spaniards, who made it a top priority to convert them to Christianity. The raising of the cross and the blessing of the Mission Santa Barbara site in December 1786 signaled the beginning of the end of Chumash spiritual and cultural traditions.

As the city evolved through its Spanish, Mexican, and American periods (see the History chapter for a more detailed account), immigrants and new settlers introduced religions other than Roman Catholicism to Santa

i Craving some solitude? Perched high on a mountain ridge above Santa Barbara, Mount Calvary Monastery and Retreat House welcomes people of all religious traditions who want to rest, reflect, and regroup. The guesthouse is run by the Benedictine monks and is available for prayer, study, working, or individual retreats as well as spiritually oriented conferences. For information, visit the monastery Web site at www .mount-calvary.org or call between 9:00 a.m. and 5:00 p.m. Tuesday through Friday at (805) 962-9855, ext. 10.

Barbara and built more churches, creating the cosmopolitan mix of religious and spiritual orientations that exists today.

A large Catholic population still congregates here, and Mission Santa Barbara remains the best-known religious edifice in the city for its historical value as well as its beauty. St. Barbara's Parish still holds masses there on weekday mornings, Saturday afternoons, and Sunday under the direction of the Franciscan fathers, and it's a popular site for weddings and community events. In addition to the Mission, other local Catholic churches include Holy Cross Church, Our Lady of Mount Carmel, St. Mark's in Isla Vista, St. Raphael's in Goleta, and St. Joseph's in Carpinteria.

The first Protestant sermon to be preached in Santa Barbara was reportedly given by the Rev. Adam Bland, a Methodist minister who addressed a small group in the old adobe courthouse in 1854. The Methodists did not formally organize here until 14 years later, however, lagging behind the Congregationalists, Episcopalians, and Presbyterians, who organized in 1866. After these first churches were formed, others followed in rapid succession: The Baptists organized in 1874 with 19 charter members; a Unitarian Society church was founded here in 1885; Seventh-Day Adventists opened a church in 1887; the First Christian Church was organized in 1888; the First Church of Christ, Scientist boasted 16 members when it organized in 1900; Norwegian immigrants founded the Scandinavian Evangelical Lutheran Church in 1902, followed by the Grace Lutheran Church in 1903; and the African Methodist Episcopal Church was founded at Haley and Olive Streets in 1905. The rest, as they say, is history.

If you've just arrived here and are looking to connect with people who share your faith or ideology, you'll find Baptist, Christian Science, Congregationalist, Eastern and Greek

Orthodox, Episcopal, Methodist, Jehovah's Witness, Lutheran, Pentecostal, Presbyterian, Religious Science, Seventh-Day Adventist, and Unitarian congregations within the Santa Barbara area. B'nai B'rith Temple on San Antonio Road serves the largest Jewish congregation in town, and a Jewish Community Center is downtown at 524 Chapala Street. You'll also find Baha'i, New Age, Buddhist, Scientologist, and Vedanta temples, groups, and centers and several nondenominational churches with local memberships.

INFORMATION, PLEASE

One of the best places to look for a particular religious organization is the Yellow Pages of the local phone book—check the listings under "Churches" or "Religious Organizations." Most churches are also listed by name in the white pages.

The *Santa Barbara News-Press* features a comprehensive "Religion" section in its Saturday edition that includes a detailed Religion Calendar, in which local religious organizations list special events and ongoing classes or workshops. Individual places of worship also advertise the schedule of services and sometimes include the subject of the next day's sermon.

The *News-Press*'s Cinema in Focus column, also in the "Religion" section, features a local pastor's evaluation of a current commercial film.

The paper is especially helpful at religious holiday seasons, when special events such as sunrise services or midnight masses are advertised in the Holiday Services pages.

The *Santa Barbara Independent* is a great source for information about less traditional spiritual and religious organizations and events, with small blurbs and ads for New Age workshops, meditation seminars, and the like.

INDEX

ABOUT THE AUTHORS

Nancy A. Shobe

Nancy Shobe is a freelance travel writer and editor, working on such publications as the *Santa Barbara Visitors' Guides and Meeting Planners* and the *Santa Monica Meeting Planner*. She is a columnist for *Coastal Woman* magazine and wrote a weekly column for the *South Coast Beacon*. She has published articles in international and trade publications, and her photography has appeared in regional newspapers and publications.

In addition to her writing, Nancy is an award-winning fund-raiser, having worked for the Los Angeles Music Center, The Webb Schools, Phillips & Associates—Los Angeles, Crane School, and a myriad of nonprofits in Santa Barbara.

Nancy moved to Santa Barbara more than 17 years ago because of the beach, her career, and better schools for her daughter. She spends her weekends swimming at El Capitan Beach or hiking in the mountains, or reading a good book. Visit Nancy's Web site, www.nancy shobe.com.

Karen Hastings

One scorching summer's day in 1990, Karen Hastings left her home in Sydney, Australia, with an overstuffed backpack and a one-way ticket to London. Wanderlust struck at an early age. But now, with a degree in communications and psychology under her belt, Karen felt it was finally time for a little "walkabout."

More than 14 years later, Karen is still living and working overseas, thanks to someone she bumped into on her travels. About three months after leaving Sydney, Karen met her future husband, Brian, in Whistler, Canada. A photographer and proud second-generation Santa Barbaran, Brian shared her passion for travel and adventure. Together they spent the next eight years roaming the globe.

From Canada to Europe to Africa they wandered, supporting their travel addiction with odd jobs along the way. Over the years, they lived and worked in a ski chalet in the French Alps, co-managed a game lodge in Namibia, camped their way around Australia, dived the Cayman Islands, fly-fished in Belize, and crisscrossed Africa in a temperamental old Land Rover. In 1995 Karen worked on assignment as a foreign correspondent for Cahners Travel Group. During this post, she reviewed more than 280 luxury hotels and resorts throughout Africa, Central America, and the Caribbean.

In between hotel-hopping, Karen and Brian frequently returned to Brian's hometown of Santa Barbara. For Karen, the beautiful beaches, eucalyptus groves, sports-loving lifestyle, and laid-back attitude reminded her of Australia. She felt instantly at home. Eventually Karen and Brian decided to abandon their nomadic ways and settle down in sunny Santa Barbara.

In addition to penning two editions of *Insiders' Guide to Santa Barbara,* Karen is the former writer and editor of the *Santa Barbara Visitors' Guide and Meeting Planner.* Her work has also appeared in the *San Diego Union Tribune, Star Service, Santa Barbara Seasons,* and other travel publications. She lives with her husband, Brian, and two children in Australia, and frequently visits Santa Barbara throughout the year.